Fodor's
The Rockies

New 2ND EDITION

"When it comes to information on regional history, what to see and do, and shopping, these guides are exhaustive."
—*USAir Magazine*

"Usable, sophisticated restaurant coverage, with an emphasis on good value."
—Andy Birsh, *Gourmet Magazine* columnist

"Valuable because of their comprehensiveness."
—*Minneapolis Star-Tribune*

"Fodor's always delivers high quality...thoughtfully presented...thorough."
—*Houston Post*

"An excellent choice for those who want everything under one cover."
—*Washington Post*

Fodor's Travel Publications, Inc.
New York • Toronto • London • Sydney • Auckland

Fodor's The Rockies

Editor: Jillian Magalaner Stone

Contributors: Brian Alexander, Steven K. Amsterdam, Rob Andrews, Stacey Clark, Steve Crohn, Susan English, Laura M. Kidder, Michael McClure, Candy Moulton, Geoffry O'Gara, Peter Oliver, Jennifer Paull, Marcy Pritchard, Jim Robbins, Kristine Rodine, Mary Ellen Schultz, M. T. Schwartzman (Gold Guide editor), Jordan Simon, Dinah Spritzer, Scott Warren

Creative Director: Fabrizio La Rocca

Cartographer: David Lindroth

Cover Photograph: Peter Guttman

Text Design: Between the Covers

Copyright © 1995 by Fodor's Travel Publications, Inc.

ISBN 0–679–03064–6

Special Sales

PRINTED IN THE UNITED STATES OF AMERICA

10 9 8 7 6 5 4 3 2 1

CONTENTS

Maps

ON THE ROAD WITH FODOR'S

A GOOD TRAVEL GUIDE is like a wonderful traveling companion. It's charming, it's brimming with sound recommendations and solid ideas, it pulls no punches in describing lodging and dining establishments, and it's consistently full of fascinating facts that make you view what you've traveled to see in a rich new light. In the creation of *The Rockies,* we at Fodor's have gone to great lengths to provide you with the very best of all possible traveling companions—and to make your trip the best of all possible vacations.

About Our Writers

The information in these pages is a collaboration of a number of extraordinary writers.

Jordan Simon defected to the world of journalism in 1987. A former contributing editor of TAXI magazine, he has written for Fodor's *Caribbean* and *Virgin Islands* guides, *Elle, Travel and Leisure, Snow Country, Food Arts, Caribbean Travel & Life, Los Angeles, USAir, Town & Country, Physicians Travel & Meeting Guide, Ski, Modern Bride, International Entertaining, Wine Country International, California* and other publications. He is food and wine editor of *Ski Impact,* author of *Fodor's Branson* and the *Gousha/USA Today Ski Atlas,* co-author of the upcoming *Celestial Seasonings* cookbook, and director of the International Ski Film & Video Festival, held annually in Colorado.

Almost but not quite an Idaho resident, **Susan English** maintains a cabin on the border of Washington State and Idaho. Like a true Idahoan, however, she has her own secret huckleberry patches, and fondly remembers a narrow escape from a horde of furious yellow jackets after having stepped in their nest during an end-of-the-season huckleberry hunt. Formerly a travel editor at the *Spokesman-Review,* she now edits the entertainment section; she has also contributed to several magazines.

Kristin Rodine, a writer and editor based in Missoula, Montana, heads the news service for the University of Montana. Her news and feature stories have appeared in university magazines and newspapers throughout Montana and beyond. A Northwest native, she worked for daily newspapers in Washington, Idaho, and Arizona before moving to Missoula in 1989; within a few weeks she knew she'd found a permanent home in western Montana. Shortly after her arrival in Missoula, the local news carried reports of a mountain lion on the hillside above the university's family housing units, and a young black bear was discovered in a backyard tree near downtown Missoula. She found this reassuring. She loves exploring her new home state with her husband and dog (the cats stay home).

A Utah native, **Stacey Clark** has examined everything from the remotest corners of the national parks to the freshest members of the local artistic community. Her marriage to a non-native enabled her to observe Utah from both sides of the fence. This, combined with her blend of intense scrutiny and gusto for exploring, has led her to write and update for several Fodor's guides, including *The Southwest's Best Bed & Breakfasts.* She is currently working on a guidebook for Utah's centennial.

This July, **Candy Moulton** finally bowed to the demands of technology and sold her horse to buy a computer. Born on a Wyoming ranch, Moulton is the author of three historically-based books on her state: *Legacy of the Tetons: Homesteading in Jackson Hole, Roadside History of Wyoming,* and *Steamboat: Legendary Buckinghorse.* Her fourth work, *Wagon Wheel,* appeared in the spring of 1996. She is also the editor of *Roundup* magazine and has done extensive freelance work. During her research for Fodor's, she discovered two new Wyoming points of interest—the high standards of small-town museums, and the equally exceptional quality of their ice-cream sodas.

What's New

A New Design

If this is not the first Fodor's guide you've purchased, you'll immediately notice our new look. More readable and easier-to-use than ever? We think so—and we hope you do, too.

Our writers have scoured the Rockies to come up with an extensive and well-balanced list of the best B&Bs, inns and hotels, both small and large, new and old. But you don't have to beat the bushes to come up with a reservation. Now we've teamed up with an established hotel-booking service to make it easy for you to secure a room at the property of your choice. It's fast, it's free, and confirmation is guaranteed. If your first choice is booked, the operators can line up your second right away. Just call 1–800/FODORS–1 or 1–800/363–6771 (0800/89–1030 in Great Britain; 0014/800–12–8271 in Australia; 1–800/55–9101 in Ireland).

Travel Updates
In addition, just before your trip, you may want to order a Fodor's Worldview Travel Update. From local publications all over the Rockies, the lively, cosmopolitan editors at Worldview gather information on concerts, plays, opera, dance performances, gallery and museum shows, sports competitions, and other special events that coincide with your visit. See the order blank in the back of this book, call 800/799–9609 or fax 800/799–9619.

And in the Rockies
COLORADO➤ The past few years have been politically turbulent for Colorado, which is still facing social and financial repercussions from the late-1992 passage of **Amendment 2,** a state constitutional amendment eradicating claims of discrimination for special-interest groups. The movement specifically targeted the gay community, barring it from any "special rights" or legal protection, and thereby annulling antidiscrimination ordinances already in place in Denver, Boulder, and Aspen. A two-year boycott of the state was quickly initiated by furious liberal groups hoping to bring economic pressure to bear on the state's conservative factions. Vocal celebs such as Barbara Streisand urged skiers to abandon Colorado's tempting resorts and businesses to take their conventions elsewhere. Nine major cities, including New York and San Francisco, forbade their government employees to travel to Colorado on business. In the end, however, these gaps were

mostly filled by an influx of right-wing conventions and the record snows which many skiers found irresistible.

Legal challenges have landed the amendment before the United States Supreme Court; on October 10, 1995, the justices began hearings on the constitutionality of the Colorado measure. Defense lawyers for Amendment 2 argue that discrimination toward homosexuals, unlike active prejudice based on race, gender, or ethnicity, has not yet been deemed unconstitutional. At press time, gay-rights lawyers were trying an indirect tactic, claiming that the amendment prevented gays and lesbians from participating equally in the political process. However, the idea of a "targeted class" is broad enough to invite attack. The catch phrase that swayed many Colorado voters, "special rights," will be also be hard for gay-rights lawyers to overcome; many voters feel that homosexuals do not require any "special" legal protection. The court has until June 1995 to decide whether to uphold the amendment. But considering the 1986 Supreme Court case in which the judges ruled that the constitutional "right to privacy" did not extend to homosexuals seeking protection from antisodomy ordinances, the prospects look grim for the liberal cause.

Adding to the political hotbed, Colorado's flamboyant senator, **Ben Nighthorse Campbell,** left the Democratic Party on March 3, 1995, and joined the Republicans. Campbell said that his departure was spurred by the Democratic efforts to defeat the proposed constitutional amendment to balance the federal budget. The only Native American member of Congress, Campbell has always been a moderate; now instead of lining up with the right-wing segment of the Democratic Party, he will fall to the left of the conservative GOP.

The controversy-plagued **Denver International Airport** (DIA) has had a bumpy takeoff. Officially opened in February 1995, the airport sports a white-capped roof imitating the surrounding mountains, a computer-controlled baggage and ski handling system, the ability to land three jets simultaneously during snowstorms—and it's fair share of brouhaha. Touted as a fully international facility, currently only 1% of DIA's flights are nondomestic. In addition, airfares rose steeply after United

Airlines monopolized several air routes, and there are needling numbers of noise complaints. Whether or not DIA fulfills its promise as a breakthrough development for the Rockies remains to be seen; in the meantime, the natives are restless.

IDAHO➤ As people continue to search for the elusive last frontier, Idahoans are becoming more and more protective of their state and its abundant natural resources. And why shouldn't they? **Real estate** prices are soaring, especially in Idaho's panhandle, which has been discovered by city dwellers looking for their own piece of peace. Not only are people moving to Idaho, but they're vacationing there in droves. Tourism is now the third-largest industry in the state, and in the past decade, lodging revenues have increased well over 50 percent. One of the most lucrative spots on the Idaho map is Sun Valley Resort, with its famed "Baldy" Mountain. The past couple of years have seen major improvements at this resort, particularly in the **lift system.** New high-speed lifts boosted service, including the Frenchman lift which added 1,502 vertical feet. A series of three log lodges has nearly been completed, of which two, the **Seattle Ridge Lodge** and the **Warm Springs Lodge,** are already open to the public. The "Crown Jewel," **River Run Plaza,** will have a day lodge open by Thanksgiving, followed by skiers services, a children's ski school, and retail spaces open by Christmas.

MONTANA➤ Let's play word association. I say Montana; you say *A River Runs Through It.* Right? Fortunately, or unfortunately—depending on which side of the tourism fence you sit on—the book by Norman Maclean and the recent movie, directed by Robert Redford, have heightened people's awareness of this massive state. As is the case throughout the Rocky Mountain region, tourism and real-estate prices are on the rise. Hollywood types and other bigwigs are flocking to the state, buying up huge ranches, and sending property values sky-high. The fallout from this popularity is that old-timers and locals find it hard to afford their paradise. Even **Big Sky,** the ski resort noted for its pristine isolation, has become a bigger draw since the installation of a **new tram** up to the top of Lone Peak, plus a new lift on the back side of the mountain (both opening in

November 1995). Stealing the distinction from Jackson Hole, Wyoming, Big Sky now offers the most vertical feet of any ski resort in America.

UTAH➤ Salt Lake City's status as a major metropolis has been confirmed with their election as host city for the **2002 Winter Olympic Games.** With many of the athletic venues already in place, Salt Lake presents an extraordinary opportunity to visit or use Olympic facilities. For example, the **Utah Winter Sports Park,** one of the best ski jumping and training sites in the world, will have ski runs available year-round. The **speed skating oval** in the Salt Lake suburb of Kearns will open in the summer of 1996 and be open to inline skaters off-season. Besides the sports facilities, the massive new **Salt Palace Convention Center** is slated for completion by the end of 1995. Finally, just a week after the close of the Olympic Winter Games, Salt Lake will host the **VII Paralympic Winter Games,** the world's top competition for athletes with disabilities.

WYOMING➤ In the aftermath of the 1988 fire in **Yellowstone National Park,** which affected 36% of the land, an interesting phenomenon occurred: tourism increased. Over 3 million families, nature-lovers, and curious environmentalist-wannabes flocked here in 1995 to hike, bike, raft, and climb. Varying degrees of recovery are visible, depending on the intensity of the original fire damage. In other areas of growth, the two-year **Old Faithful Inn** refurbishment project was completed in 1994, and the **Grand Canyon of the Yellowstone** facilities are being improved and "winterized." Next on the list is the replacement of the existing **Snow Lodge at Old Faithful,** scheduled for the fall of 1996.

How To Use This Guide

Organization

Up front is the **Gold Guide,** comprising two sections on gold paper that are chock-full of information about traveling within your destination and traveling in general. Both are in alphabetical order by topic. **Important Contacts A to Z** gives addresses and telephone numbers of organizations and companies that offer destination-related services and detailed information or publications. Here's where you'll find information about how to get to the Rockies from wherever you are. **Smart Travel Tips A to Z** gives specific tips on how to get the most out of your travels, as well as information on how to accomplish what you need to in your destination.

Chapters in Fodor's *The Rockies* are arranged by state, in alphabetical order. Each chapter covers exploring, shopping, sports, dining, lodging, and arts and nightlife and ends with a section called Essentials, which tells you how to get there and get around and gives you important local addresses and telephone numbers.

Stars

Stars in the margin are used to denote highly recommended sights, attractions, hotels, and restaurants.

Restaurant and Hotel Criteria and Price Categories

Restaurants and lodging places are chosen with a view to giving you the cream of the crop in each location and in each price range.

In all restaurant price charts (*see* Dining *in* the Essentials section of each destination chapter), costs are per person, excluding drinks, tip, and tax. In hotel price charts (*see* Lodging *in* the Essentials section of each destination chapter), rates are for standard double rooms, excluding city and state sales taxes.

Hotel Facilities

Note that in general you incur charges when you use many hotel facilities. We wanted to let you know what facilities a hotel has to offer, but we don't always specify whether or not there's a charge, so when planning a vacation that entails a stay of several days, it's wise to ask what's included in the rate.

Hotel Meal Plans

Assume that hotels operate on the **European Plan** (EP, with no meals) unless we note that they use the **American Plan** (AP, with all meals), the **Modified American Plan** (MAP, with breakfast and dinner daily), or the **Continental Plan** (CP, with a Continental breakfast daily).

Dress Code in Restaurants

Look for an overview in the Packing for the Rockies section of Smart Travel Tips A to Z in the Gold Guide pages at the front of this book. In general, we note dress code only when men are required to wear a jacket or a jacket and tie.

Credit Cards

The following abbreviations are used: **AE**, American Express; **D**, Discover; **DC**, Diners Club; **MC**, MasterCard; and **V**, Visa.

Please Write to Us

Everyone who has contributed to Fodor's *The Rockies* has worked hard to make the text accurate. All prices and opening times are based on information supplied to us at press time, and the publisher cannot accept responsibility for any errors that may have occurred. The passage of time will bring changes, so it's always a good idea to call ahead and confirm information when it matters—particularly if you're making a detour to visit specific sights or attractions. When making reservations at a hotel or inn, be sure to mention if you have a disability or are traveling with children, if you prefer a private bath or a certain type of bed, or if you have specific dietary needs or any other concerns.

Were the restaurants we recommended as described? Did our hotel picks exceed your expectations? Did you find a museum we recommended a waste of time? We would love your feedback, positive and negative. If you have complaints, we'll look into them and revise our entries when the facts warrant it. If you've happened upon a special place that we haven't included, we'll pass the information along to the writers so they can check it out. So please send us a letter or postcard (we're at 201 East 50th Street, New York, New York 10022). We'll look forward to hearing from you. And in the meantime, have a wonderful trip!

Karen Cure

Karen Cure
Editorial Director

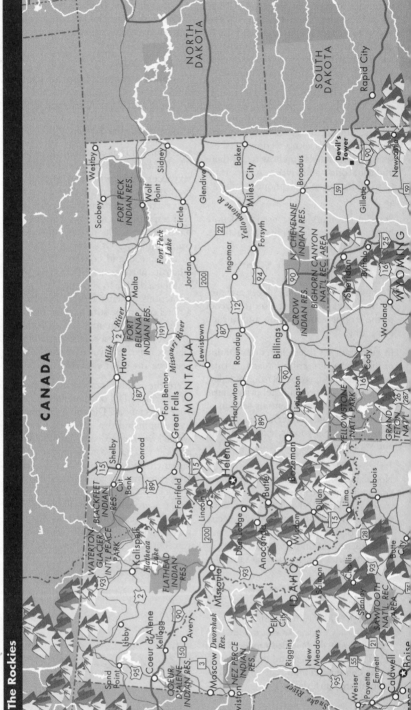

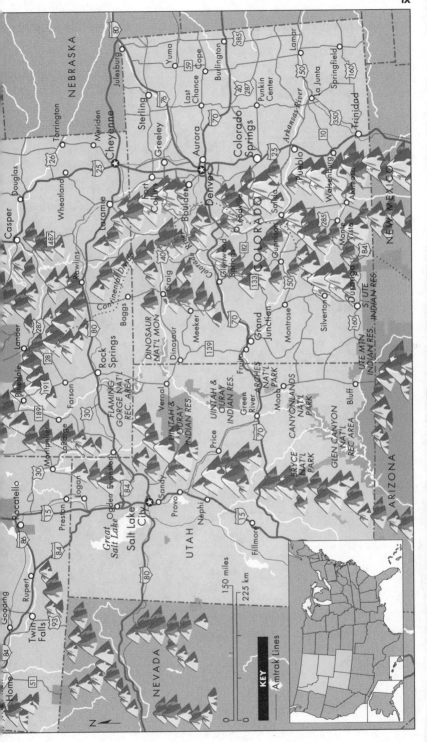

The United States

CANADA

BRITISH COLUMBIA
Vancouver
Victoria
Calgary
ALBERTA
SASKATCHEWAN
MANITO
Regina
Trans-Canada Hwy.
Winnipeg

Seattle
Olympia
WASHINGTON
Columbia R.
Spokane
Great Falls
Missouri R.
MONTANA
Helena
NORTH DAKOTA
Farg
Bismarck

Portland
Salem
OREGON
IDAHO
Boise
Snake R.
Billings
94

SOUTH DAKOTA
Pierre
Missouri R.

WYOMING
Cheyenne
NEBRASKA
Linc

Carson City
Sacramento
San Francisco
NEVADA
Salt Lake City
UTAH
Denver
COLORADO
Colorado Springs
KANSAS

Fresno
CALIFORNIA
Las Vegas
Colorado R.

Santa Barbara
Los Angeles
Flagstaff
ARIZONA
Phoenix
Santa Fe
Albuquerque
NEW MEXICO
Amarillo
OKLAHOMA
Oklahoma City

San Diego
Tucson

PACIFIC OCEAN
BAJA CALIFORNIA
SONORA
El Paso
CHIHUAHUA
Rio Grande

TEXAS
Austin
San Antonio
Dalla

RUSSIA
ARCTIC OCEAN
Bering Strait
Bering Sea
Nome
ALASKA
Fairbanks
CANADA
MEXICO
COAHUILA
NUEVO LEON

ALEUTIAN ISLANDS
Anchorage
Juneau

PACIFIC OCEAN

0   400 miles
0   400 km
N

Honolulu
Oahu
Maui
HAWAII
Hawaii
PACIFIC OCEAN
TAM
AULIP

World Time Zones

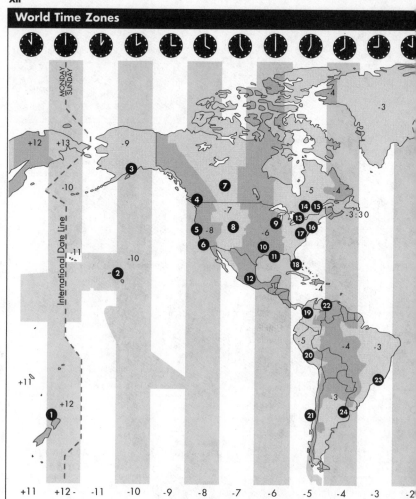

Numbers below vertical bands relate each zone to Greenwich Mean Time (0 hrs.).
Local times frequently differ from these general indications,
as indicated by light-face numbers on map.

Algiers, **29**

Anchorage, **3**

Athens, **41**

Auckland, **1**

Baghdad, **46**

Bangkok, **50**

Beijing, **54**

Berlin, **34**

Bogotá, **19**

Budapest, **37**

Buenos Aires, **24**

Caracas, **22**

Chicago, **9**

Copenhagen, **33**

Dallas, **10**

Delhi, **48**

Denver, **8**

Djakarta, **53**

Dublin, **26**

Edmonton, **7**

Hong Kong, **56**

Honolulu, **2**

Istanbul, **40**

Jerusalem, **42**

Johannesburg, **44**

Lima, **20**

Lisbon, **28**

London
(Greenwich), **27**

Los Angeles, **6**

Madrid, **38**

Manila, **57**

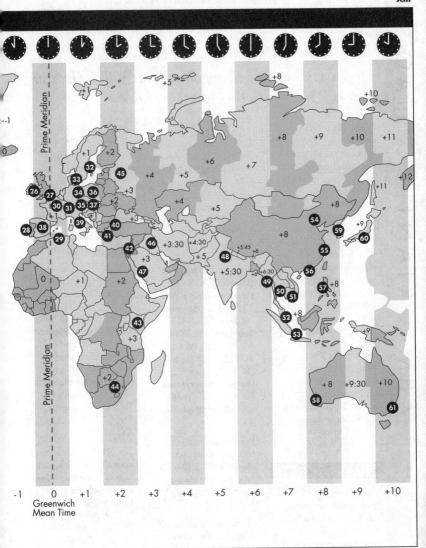

IMPORTANT CONTACTS A TO Z

An Alphabetical Listing of Publications, Organizations, and Companies That Will Help You Before, During, and After Your Trip

No single travel resource can give you every detail about every topic that might interest or concern you at the various stages of your journey—when you're planning your trip, while you're on the road, and after you get back home. The following organizations, books, and brochures will supplement the information in the *Rockies*. For related information, including both basic tips on visiting the Rockies and background information on many of the topics below, study Smart Travel Tips A to Z, the section that follows Important Contacts A to Z.

A

AIR TRAVEL

The major gateways to the Rockies include, in Colorado, the brand-new **Denver International Airport** (☎ 303/270–1300 or 800/247–2336, TTY 800/688–1333); in Idaho, **Boise Air Terminal** (☎ 208/383–3110); in Montana, the **Missoula Airport** (☎ 406/543–7001) and **Glacier Park International Airport** (☎ 406/752–1028) in Kalispell; in Utah, **Salt Lake City International Airport** (☎ 801/575–2400); and in Wyoming, **Jackson Hole Airport** (☎ 307/733–7682).

CARRIERS

Carriers serving the Rockies include **American Airlines** (☎ 800/433–7300), **America West** (☎ 800/235–9292), **Continental** (☎ 800/525–0280), **Delta** (☎ 800/221–1212), **Empire** (☎ 800/392–9233), **Horizon** (☎ 800/547–9308), **Midway** (☎ 800/446–4392), **Northwest** (☎ 800/225–2525), **SkyWest** (☎ 800/453–9417), **Southwest** (☎ 800/435–9792), **TWA** (☎ 800/221–2000), **United** (☎ 800/241–6522), **United Express/Mesa** (☎ 800/662–3736), and **USAir** (☎ 800/428–4322).

For inexpensive, no-frills flights, contact **MarkAir** (☎ 800/627–5247) and **Midwest Express** (☎ 800/452–2022).

From the United Kingdom, carriers serving the Rockies include **American Airlines** (☎ 0345/789–789), **British Airways** (☎ 0181/897–4000 or 0345/222–111), **Continental** (☎ 0800/776-464), **Delta Airlines** (☎ 0800/414–4767), **Northwest** (☎ 01293/561–000), **TWA** (☎ 0800/222–222), **United Airlines** (☎ 0181/990–9900), and **Virgin Atlantic** (☎ 01293/747–747).

COMPLAINTS

To register complaints about charter and scheduled airlines, contact the U.S. Department of Transportation's **Office of Consumer Affairs** (400 7th St. NW, Washington, DC 20590, ☎ 202/366–2220 or 800/322–7873).

PUBLICATIONS

For general information about charter carriers, ask for the Office of Consumer Affairs' brochure **"Plane Talk: Public Charter Flights."** The Department of Transportation also publishes a 58-page booklet, **"Fly Rights"** ($1.75; Consumer Information Center, Dept. 133B, Pueblo, CO 81009).

For other tips and hints, consult the Consumers Union's monthly **"Consumer Reports Travel Letter"** ($39 a year; Box 53629, Boulder, CO 80322, ☎ 800/234–1970) and the newsletter **"Travel Smart"** ($37 a year; 40 Beechdale Rd., Dobbs Ferry, NY 10522, ☎ 800/327–3633); *The Official Frequent Flyer Guidebook,* by Randy Petersen ($14.99 plus $3 shipping; 4715-C Town Center Dr., Colorado Springs, CO 80916, ☎ 719/597–8899 or 800/487–8893); *Airfare Secrets Exposed,* by Sharon Tyler and Matthew Wonder (Universal Information Publishing; $16.95 plus

$3.75 shipping from Sandcastle Publishing, Box 3070-A, South Pasadena, CA 91031, ☎ 213/255-3616 or 800/655-0053); and *202 Tips Even the Best Business Travelers May Not Know,* by Christopher McGinnis ($10 plus $3.00 shipping; Irwin Professional Publishing, 1333 Burr Ridge Parkway, Burr Ridge, IL 60521, ☎ 800/634-3966).

B

BETTER BUSINESS BUREAU

For local contacts, consult the **Council of Better Business Bureaus** (4200 Wilson Blvd., Arlington, VA 22203, ☎ 703/276-0100).

BUS TRAVEL

Greyhound Lines (☎ 800/231-2222) operates bus service to the Rocky Mountain region from many points in the United States.

WITHIN THE ROCKIES

Greyhound Lines has regular intercity routes throughout the region, with connections from Denver to Cheyenne, Boise, Pocatello, and Missoula. Smaller bus companies provide service within local areas. Regional lines include **Springs Transit Management** in Colorado Springs (☎ 719/475-9733); **Boise-Winnemucca Bus Lines** in Idaho (☎ 208/336-3302); **Intermountain Bus Company** (☎ 406/755-4011) and **Rimrock/Trailways** (☎ 800/255-7655), both in Montana; and **Powder River Transportation** (☎ 307/635-1327) in Wyoming.

C

CAR RENTAL

Major car-rental companies represented in the **Rockies** include **Alamo** (☎ 800/327-9633, 0800/272-2000 in the United Kingdom); **Avis** (☎ 800/331-1212, 800/879-2847 in Canada); **Dollar** (known as Eurodollar outside North America, ☎ 800/800-4000, 0181/952-6565 in the United Kingdom); **Hertz** (☎ 800/654-3131, 800/263-0600 in Canada, 0181/679-1799 in the United Kingdom); and **National** (☎ 800/227-7368, 0181/950-5050 in the United Kingdom, where it is known as Europcar).

Rates in **Denver** begin at $29 a day and $147 a week for an economy car with unlimited mileage. In **Boise,** Idaho, rates begin at $34 a day and $197 a week for an economy car with unlimited mileage. In **Salt Lake City,** rates begin at $35 a day and $166 a week. In **Jackson Hole,** Wyoming, rates begin at $26 a day and $139 a week. Prices do not include tax, which ranges from 5% to 10%, or airport fees which may be applicable.

CHILDREN AND TRAVEL

FLYING

Look into **"Flying with Baby"** ($5.95 plus $1 shipping; Third Street Press, Box 261250, Littleton, CO 80126, ☎ 303/595-5959), cowritten by a flight attendant. **"Kids and Teens in Flight,"** free from the U.S. Department of Transportation's Office of Consumer Affairs, offers tips for children flying alone. Every two years the February issue of *Family Travel Times* (*see* Know-How, *below*) details children's services on three dozen airlines.

GAMES

The gamemeister, Milton Bradley, has games to help keep little (and not so little) children from getting fidgety while riding in planes, trains, and automobiles. Try packing the Travel Battleship sea battle game ($7), Travel Connect Four, a vertical strategy game ($8), the Travel Yahtzee dice game ($6), the Travel Trouble dice and board game ($7), and the Travel Guess Who mystery game ($8).

KNOW-HOW

Family Travel Times, published four times a year by Travel with Your Children (TWYCH, 45 W. 18th St., New York, NY 10011, ☎ 212/206-0688; annual subscription $40), covers destinations, types of vacations, and modes of travel.

The *Family Travel Guides* catalogue ($1 postage; ☎ 510/527-5849) lists about 200 books and articles on family travel. *Great Vacations with Your Kids,* by Dorothy Jordon and Marjorie Cohen ($13; Penguin

USA, 120 Woodbine St., Bergenfield, NJ 07621, ☎ 201/387–0600 or 800/253–6476), and *Traveling with Children—And Enjoying It,* by Arlene K. Butler ($11.95 plus $3 shipping; Globe Pequot Press, Box 833, 6 Business Park Rd., Old Saybrook, CT 06475, ☎ 203/395–0440 or 800/243–0495, 800/962–0973 in CT) help plan your trip with children, from toddlers to teens. Also check *Take Your Baby and Go! A Guide for Traveling with Babies, Toddlers and Young Children,* by Sheri Andrews, Judy Bordeaux, and Vivian Vasquez ($5.95 plus $1.50 shipping; Bear Creek Publications, 2507 Minor Ave., Seattle, WA 98102, ☎ 206/322–7604 or 800/326–6566). Also from Globe Pequot are *The 100 Best Family Resorts in North America,* by Jane Wilford with Janet Tice ($12.95), and the two-volume set of *50 Great Family Vacations in North America* ($18.95 each plus $3 shipping). Travel With Your Children (*see above*) also publishes *Skiing with Children* ($29).

TOUR OPERATORS

Contact **Rascals in Paradise** (650 5th St., Suite 505, San Francisco, CA 94107, ☎ 415/978–9800 or 800/872–7225).

If you're outdoorsy, look into **Ecology Tours** (c/o the Audubon Center of the North Woods, Box 530, Sandstone, MN 55072, ☎ 612/245–2648), which

mix travel and nature study; family summer camps and **Ecology Workshops** (613 Riversville Rd., Greenwich, CT 06831, ☎ 203/869–2017) from the Audubon Society; **American Wilderness Experience** (Box 1486, Boulder, CO 80306, ☎ 303/444–2622 or 800/444–0099); and **Wildland Adventures** (3516 N.E 155th St., Seattle, WA 98155, ☎ 206/365–0686 or 800/345–4453).

CUSTOMS

CANADIANS

Contact **Revenue Canada** (2265 St. Laurent Blvd. S, Ottawa, Ontario K1G 4K3, ☎ 613/993–0534) for a copy of the free brochure **"I Declare/Je Déclare"** and for details on duties that exceed the standard duty-free limit.

U.K. CITIZENS

HM Customs and Excise (Dorset House, Stamford St., London SE1 9NG, ☎ 0171/202–4227) can answer questions about U.K. customs regulations and publishes **"A Guide for Travellers,"** detailing standard procedures and import rules.

D
FOR TRAVELERS WITH DISABILITIES

COMPLAINTS

To register complaints under the provisions of the Americans with Disabilities Act, contact the U.S. Department of Justice's **Public Access Section** (Box 66738, Washington, DC 20035, ☎ 202/514–

0301, TTY 202/514–0383, FAX 202/307–1198).

LOCAL INFO

Colorado's **Wilderness on Wheels** (7125 W. Jefferson Ave., Lakewood 80235, ☎ 303/988–2212) can help answer accessibility questions and plan outings. In Montana, contact **DREAM** (Disabled Recreation and Environmental Access Movement, Northwest Montana Human Resources, 1st & Main Bldg., Box 8300, Kalispell 59904, ☎ 406/752–6565). Wyoming's **Access Tours, Inc.** (3900 Smith Park Loop, Box 2985, Jackson 83001, ☎ 307/733–6664) specializes in leisurely tours of several national parks. Contact the **Utah Travel Council** (☎ 801/538–1030) for statewide accessibility information. In Wyoming, call the **Wyoming Tourist Commission** (☎ 307/777–7777) for information on facilities and accommodations for travelers with disabilities.

ORGANIZATIONS

FOR TRAVELERS WITH HEARING IMPAIRMENTS➤ Contact the **American Academy of Otolaryngology** (1 Prince St., Alexandria, VA 22314, ☎ 703/836–4444, FAX 703/683–5100, TTY 703/519–1585).

FOR TRAVELERS WITH MOBILITY PROBLEMS➤ Contact the **Information Center for Individuals with Disabilities** (Fort Point Pl., 27–43 Wormwood St., Boston, MA 02210, ☎ 617/727–

5540, 800/462–5015 in MA, TTY 617/345–9743); **Mobility International USA** (Box 10767, Eugene, OR 97440, ☎ and TTY 503/343–1284, FAX 503/343–6812), the U.S. branch of an international organization based in Belgium (*see below*) that has affiliates in 30 countries; **MossRehab Hospital Travel Information Service** (1200 W. Tabor Rd., Philadelphia, PA 19141, ☎ 215/456–9603, TTY 215/456–9602); the **Society for the Advancement of Travel for the Handicapped** (347 5th Ave., Suite 610, New York, NY 10016, ☎ 212/447–7284, FAX 212/725–8253); the **Travel Industry and Disabled Exchange** (TIDE, 5435 Donna Ave., Tarzana, CA 91356, ☎ 818/344–3640, FAX 818/344–0078); and **Travelin' Talk** (Box 3534, Clarksville, TN 37043, ☎ 615/552–6670, FAX 615/552–1182).

FOR TRAVELERS WITH VISION IMPAIRMENTS➤ Contact the **American Council of the Blind** (1155 15th St. NW, Suite 720, Washington, DC 20005, ☎ 202/467–5081, FAX 202/467–5085) or the **American Foundation for the Blind** (15 W. 16th St., New York, NY 10011, ☎ 212/620–2000, TTY 212/620–2158).

IN THE U.K.

Contact the **Royal Association for Disability and Rehabilitation** (RADAR, 12 City Forum, 250 City Rd., London EC1V 8AF, ☎

0171/250–3222) or **Mobility International** (Rue de Manchester 25, B–1070 Brussels, Belgium, ☎ 00–322–410–6297), an international clearinghouse of travel information for people with disabilities.

PUBLICATIONS

Several publications for travelers with disabilities are available from the **Consumer Information Center** (Box 100, Pueblo, CO 81009, ☎ 719/948–3334). Call or write for a free catalogue of current titles.

Fodor's *Great American Vacations for Travelers with Disabilities* ($18; available in bookstores, or call 800/533–6478) details accessible attractions, restaurants, and hotels at U.S. destinations. The 500-page *Travelin' Talk Directory* ($35; Box 3534, Clarksville, TN 37043, ☎ 615/552–6670) lists people and organizations who help travelers with disabilities. For specialist travel agents worldwide, consult the *Directory of Travel Agencies for the Disabled* ($19.95 plus $2 shipping; Twin Peaks Press, Box 129, Vancouver, WA 98666, ☎ 206/694–2462 or 800/637–2256). The Sierra Club publishes *Easy Access to National Parks* ($16 plus $3 shipping; 730 Polk St., San Francisco, CA 94109, ☎ 415/776–2211 or 800/935–1056).

TRAVEL AGENCIES AND TOUR OPERATORS

The Americans with Disabilities Act requires

that travel firms serve the needs of all travelers. However, some agencies and operators specialize in making group and individual arrangements for travelers with disabilities, among them **Access Adventures** (206 Chestnut Ridge Rd., Rochester, NY 14624, ☎ 716/889–9096), run by a former physical-rehab counselor. In addition, many general-interest operators and agencies (*see* Tour Operators, *below*) can also arrange vacations for travelers with disabilities.

FOR TRAVELERS WITH MOBILITY PROBLEMS➤ A number of operators specialize in working with travelers with mobility impairments: **Access Tours** (Box 2985, Jackson, WY 83001, ☎ 307/733–6664 in summer; 2440 S. Forest, Tucson, AZ 85713, ☎ 602/791–7977 winter–mid-May), which organizes national park tours; **Hinsdale Travel Service** (201 E. Ogden Ave., Suite 100, Hinsdale, IL 60521, ☎ 708/325–1335 or 800/303–5521), a travel agency that will give you access to the services of wheelchair traveler Janice Perkins; and **Wheelchair Journeys** (16979 Redmond Way, Redmond, WA 98052, ☎ 206/885–2210), which can handle arrangements worldwide.

THE GOLD GUIDE / IMPORTANT CONTACTS

FOR TRAVELERS WITH DEVELOPMENTAL DISABILITIES➤ Contact the nonprofit **New Directions** (5276 Hollister Ave., Suite 207, Santa Barbara, CA 93111, ☎ 805/967–2841), as well as the general-interest operators above.

DISCOUNT CLUBS

Options include **Entertainment Travel Editions** (fee $28–$53, depending on destination; Box 1068, Trumbull, CT 06611, ☎ 800/445–4137); **Great American Traveler** ($49.95 annually; Box 27965, Salt Lake City, UT 84127, ☎ 800/548–2812); **Moment's Notice Discount Travel Club** ($25 annually, single or family; 163 Amsterdam Ave., Suite 137, New York, NY 10023, ☎ 212/486–0500); **Privilege Card** ($74.95 annually; 3391 Peachtree Rd. NE, Suite 110, Atlanta, GA 30326, ☎ 404/262–0222 or 800/236–9732); **Travelers Advantage** ($49 annually, single or family; CUC Travel Service, 49 Music Sq. W, Nashville, TN 37203, ☎ 800/548–1116 or 800/648–4037); and **Worldwide Discount Travel Club** ($50 annually for family, $40 single; 1674 Meridian Ave., Miami Beach, FL 33139, ☎ 305/534–2082).

DRIVING

AUTO CLUBS

Look in local phone directories under AAA for the nearest **American Automobile Association,** or contact the national organization (1000 AAA Dr.,

Heathrow, FL 32746–5063, ☎ 407/444–7000 or 800/222–4357 in the U.S.; 800/336–4357 in Canada).

ROAD CONDITIONS

Each state highway department has a number to call for road conditions: **Colorado** (☎ 303/639–1111 within a 2-hour drive of Denver, 303/639–1234 statewide); **Idaho** (☎ 208/336–6600); **Montana** (☎ 406/444–6339 or 800/332–6171); **Utah** (☎ 801/964–6000 in the Salt Lake City area; 800/492–2400 within Utah); and **Wyoming** (☎ 307/635–9966 or 800/442–7850).

G
GAY AND
LESBIAN TRAVEL

ORGANIZATIONS

The **International Gay Travel Association** (Box 4974, Key West, FL 33041, ☎ 800/448–8550), a consortium of 800 businesses, can supply names of travel agents and tour operators.

PUBLICATIONS

The premier international travel magazine for gays and lesbians is **Our World** ($35 for 10 issues; 1104 N. Nova Rd., Suite 251, Daytona Beach, FL 32117, ☎ 904/441–5367). The 16-page monthly **"Out & About"** ($49 for 10 issues; ☎ 212/645–6922 or 800/929–2268) covers gay-friendly resorts, hotels, cruise lines, and airlines.

TOUR OPERATORS

Toto Tours (1326 W. Albion, Suite 3W, Chicago, IL 60626, ☎ 312/274–8686 or 800/565–1241) has group tours worldwide.

TRAVEL AGENCIES

The largest agencies serving gay travelers are **Advance Travel** (10700 Northwest Freeway, Suite 160, Houston, TX 77092, ☎ 713/682–2002 or 800/695–0880); **Islanders/Kennedy Travel** (183 W. 10th St., New York, NY 10014, ☎ 212/242–3222 or 800/988–1181); **Now Voyager** (4406 18th St., San Francisco, CA 94114, ☎ 415/626–1169 or 800/255–6951); and **Yellowbrick Road** (1500 W. Balmoral Ave., Chicago, IL 60640, ☎ 312/561–1800 or 800/642–2488). **Skylink Women's Travel** (746 Ashland Ave., Santa Monica, CA 90405, ☎ 310/452–0506 or 800/225-5759) works with lesbians.

I
INSURANCE

Travel insurance covering baggage, health, and trip cancellation or interruptions available from **Access America** (Box 90315, Richmond, VA 23286, ☎ 804/285–3300 or 800/284–8300); **Carefree Travel Insurance** (Box 9366, 100 Garden City Plaza, Garden City, NY 11530, ☎ 516/294–0220 or 800/323–3149); **Near Services** (Box 1339, Calumet City, IL 60409, ☎ 708/868–6700 or 800/654–6700); **Tele-Trip** (Mutual of Omaha Plaza, Box

31716, Omaha, NE 68131, ☎ 800/228–9792); **Travel Insured International** (Box 280568, East Hartford, CT 06128-0568, ☎ 203/528–7663 or 800/243–3174); **Travel Guard International** (1145 Clark St., Stevens Point, WI 54481, ☎ 715/345–0505 or 800/826–1300); and **Wallach & Company** (107 W. Federal St., Box 480, Middleburg, VA 22117, ☎ 703/687–3166 or 800/237–6615).

IN THE U.K.

The **Association of British Insurers** (51 Gresham St., London EC2V 7HQ, ☎ 0171/600–3333; 30 Gordon St., Glasgow G1 3PU, ☎ 0141/226–3905; Scottish Provident Bldg., Donegall Sq. W, Belfast BT1 6JE, ☎ 01232/249176; and other locations) gives advice by phone and publishes the free **"Holiday Insurance,"** which sets out typical policy provisions and costs.

L
LODGING

For comprehensive statewide accommodation information, contact the following: **Colorado Hotel and Lodging Association** (999 18th St., Suite 1240, Denver, CO 80202, ☎ 303/297–8335); **Idaho Division of Travel Promotion** (Idaho Department of Commerce, 700 W. State St., Boise, ID 83720, ☎ 800/635–7820); **Travel Montana** (Department of Commerce, 1424 9th Ave., Helena, MT 59620, ☎ 406/444–2654 in MT, 800/541–

1447 out of state); **Utah Hotel/Motel Association** (9 Exchange Pl., Suite 715, Salt Lake City, UT 84114, ☎ 801/359–0104); **Wyoming Division of Tourism** (I–25 at College Dr., Cheyenne, WY 82002, ☎ 307/777–7777 or 800/225–5996). For information about hotels near national parks, contact tourism offices and the various parks' superintendents' offices (*see* National Parks *in* the state Essentials sections of each destination chapter).

APARTMENT AND VILLA RENTAL

Among the companies to contact are **Hometours International** (Box 11503, Knoxville, TN 37939, ☎ 615/588–8722 or 800/367–4668) and **Vacation Home Rentals Worldwide** (235 Kensington Ave., Norwood, NJ 07648, ☎ 201/767–9393 or 800/633–3284). Members of the travel club **Hideaways International** ($99 annually; 767 Islington St., Portsmouth, NH 03801, ☎ 603/430–4433 or 800/843–4433) receive two annual guides plus quarterly newsletters, and arrange rentals among themselves.

BED-AND-BREAKFASTS

Sometimes you can book directly through a B&B; arrangements at others must be made through a reservation system such as **Bed & Breakfast Rocky Mountains** (906 S. Pearl, Denver, CO 80209, ☎ 303/744–8415); **Bed & Breakfast Western**

Adventure (Box 4308, Bozeman, MT 59772, ☎ 406/585–0557), covering Montana, Wyoming, and Idaho; the **Montana Bed & Breakfast Association** (5557 Hwy. 93 S, Somers, MT 59932, ☎ 800/453–8870); and **Bed & Breakfast Inns of Utah** (Box 2639, Park City, UT 84060, ☎ 801/595–0332).

GUEST RANCHES

For lists of ranches, contact **Bed & Breakfast Western Adventure** (Box 4308, Bozeman, MT 59772, ☎ 406/585–0557), a reservation system for Idaho, Montana, and Wyoming; the **Colorado Dude/Guest Ranch Association** (Box 300, Tabernash, CO 80478, ☎ 970/887–3128); and the various state tourism offices.

HOME EXCHANGE

Principal clearinghouses include **Intervac International** ($65 annually; Box 590504, San Francisco, CA 94159, ☎ 415/435–3497), which has three annual directories, and **Loan-a-Home** ($35–$45 annually; 2 Park La., Apt. 6E, Mount Vernon, NY 10552-3443, ☎ 914/664–7640), which specializes in long-term exchanges.

HOTELS

All five states covered in this book have seen a boom in hotel construction over the past decade. Among the hotel operators are: **Doubletree** (☎ 800/222–8733), **Four Seasons** (☎ 800/332–3442), **Holiday Inn** (☎ 800/465–4329), **Mar-**

THE GOLD GUIDE / IMPORTANT CONTACTS

riott (☎ 800/228–9290), **Ramada** (☎ 800/228–2828), **Red Lion Inns** (☎ 800/547–8010), **Sheraton** (☎ 800/325–3535), **Stouffer** (☎ 800/468–3751), and **Westin** (☎ 800/228–3000). Locations are in Denver (Colorado); Boise, Coeur d'Alene, and Ketchum (Idaho); Helena, Bozeman, and Billings (Montana); Salt Lake City and Park City (Utah); and Cheyenne, Jackson, and Sundance (Wyoming).

INNS

For complete lists of inns in the Rockies, contact professional associations such as **Distinctive Inns of Colorado** (Box 10472, Colorado Springs, CO 80932, ☎ 800/866–0621); **Montana Innkeepers Association** (Box 1272, Helena, MT 59624, ☎ 406/449–8408); and **Bed and Breakfast Inns of Utah, Inc.** (Box 2639, Park City, UT 84060, ☎ 801/595–0332).

MOTELS

Nationally recognized chains include **Best Western** (☎ 800/528–1234); **Days Inn** (☎ 800/325–2525); **La Quinta Motor Inns** (☎ 800/531–5900); **Motel 6** (☎ 505/891–6161); **Quality Inn** (☎ 800/228–5151); **Rodeway Inns** (☎ 800/228–2000); **Super 8 Motels** (☎ 800/800–8000), and **Travelodge** (☎ 800/578–7878). **Shilo Inn** (☎ 800/222–2244) and **Skyline Motor Inn** (☎ 800/843–8809) are regional chains.

M
MONEY MATTERS

ATMS

For specific **Cirrus** locations in the United States and Canada, call 800/424–7787. For U.S. **Plus** locations, call 800/843–7587 and enter the area code and first three digits of the number you're calling from (or of the calling area where you want to locate an ATM).

WIRING FUNDS

Funds can be wired via **American Express MoneyGram**SM (☎ 800/926–9400 from the U.S. and Canada for locations and information) or **Western Union** (☎ 800/325–6000 for agent locations or to send using MasterCard or Visa, 800/321–2923 in Canada).

P
PASSPORTS AND VISAS

U.K. CITIZENS

For fees, documentation requirements, and to get an emergency passport, call the **London Passport Office** (☎ 0171/271–3000). For visa information, call the **U.S. Embassy Visa Information Line** (☎ 0891/200–290; calls cost 49p per minute or 39p per minute cheap rate) or write the **U.S. Embassy Visa Branch** (5 Upper Grosvenor St., London W1A 2JB). If you live in Northern Ireland, write the **U.S. Consulate General** (Queen's House, Queen St., Belfast BTI 6EQ).

PHOTO HELP

The **Kodak Information Center** (☎ 800/242–2424) answers consumer questions about film and photography. Pick up the **Kodak Guide to Shooting Great Travel Pictures** (Random House, ☎ 800/733–3000; $16.50), which gives you tips on how to take travel pictures like a pro.

R
RAIL TRAVEL

Amtrak (☎ 800/872–7245) connects the Rockies to both coasts and all major American cities, with trains that run through Boise, Salt Lake City, and Denver, and other stops in between. Amtrak trains also run through northern Montana, with stops in Essex and Whitefish, along the southern border of Glacier National Park. Connecting motorcoach services to Yellowstone National Park are provided in the summer from Amtrak's stop in Pocatello, Idaho.

Canada's passenger service, **VIA Rail Canada** (☎ 800/561–3949), stops at Jasper, near the Canadian entrance to Waterton/Glacier International Peace National Park.

SCENIC TRAIN TRIPS

Several Rocky Mountain states have restored unused stretches of track and refurbished turn-of-the-century touring cars. These give you the chance to scout out places beyond the reach of any four-lane freeway.

In Colorado the best-known journeys are to **Pikes Peak** on the highest cog railway in the world (☎ 719/685–5401) and the celebrated **Durango & Silverton** narrow-gauge mining-train trip along the Animas River (☎ 970/247–2733). For more details on these and other rail excursions, contact the **Colorado Railroad Museum** (17155 W. 44th Ave., Box 641, Golden, CO 80402, ☎ 303/279–0111).

In Utah you can catch the famous **Heber Creeper** (☎ 801/654–5601), a turn-of-the-century, steam engine train that rides the rails from Heber City across Heber Valley, alongside Deer Creek Reservoir, down Provo Canyon to Vivian Park.

In Wyoming one of the highest standard-gauge lines in the country, **Wyoming Excursion Trains** (☎ 307/742–9162), chug along through the scenic country from Laramie up into the Snowy Range Mountains and back.

S

SENIOR CITIZENS

EDUCATIONAL TRAVEL

The nonprofit **Elderhostel** (75 Federal St., 3rd Floor, Boston, MA 02110, ☎ 617/426–7788), for people 60 and older, has offered inexpensive study programs since 1975. The nearly 2,000 courses cover everything from marine science to Greek myths

to cowboy poetry. Fees for programs in the United States and Canada, which usually last one week, run about $300, not including transportation.

ORGANIZATIONS

Contact the **American Association of Retired Persons** (AARP, 601 E St. NW, Washington, DC 20049, ☎ 202/434–2277; $8 per person or couple annually). Its Purchase Privilege Program gets members discounts on lodgings, car rentals, and sightseeing tours and entrance fees. The AARP Motoring Plan furnishes domestic trip-routing information and emergency road-service aid for an annual fee of $39.95 per person or couple ($59.95 for a premium version).

For other discounts on lodgings, car rentals, and other travel products, along with magazines and newsletters, contact the **National Council of Senior Citizens** (membership $12 annually; 1331 F St. NW, Washington, DC 20004, ☎ 202/347–8800) and **Mature Outlook** (subscription $9.95 annually; 6001 N. Clark St., Chicago, IL 60660, ☎ 312/465–6466 or 800/336–6330).

PUBLICATIONS

The 50+ Traveler's Guidebook: Where to Go, Where to Stay, What to Do, by Anita Williams and Merrimac Dillon ($12.95; St. Martin's Press, 175 5th Ave., New York, NY 10010, ☎ 212/674–

5151 or 800/288–2131), offers many useful tips. **"The Mature Traveler"** ($29.95; Box 50400, Reno, NV 89513, ☎ 702/786–7419), a monthly newsletter, covers travel deals.

SPORTS

CLIMBING AND MOUNTAINEERING

Among the best climbing schools in the country are the **American Alpine Institute** (1515 12th St., Bellingham, WA 98225, ☎ 206/671–1505) and the **Colorado Mountain School** (Box 2062, Estes Park, CO 80517, ☎ 970/586–5758). Both also lead trips in the Rockies.

CYCLING

Perhaps the best general source of information on biking in the Rockies—including detailed maps and information on trip organizers—is **Adventure Cycling Association** (Box 8308, Missoula, MT 59807, ☎ 406/721–1776).

DUDE RANCHES

For dude-ranch information, see Lodging, *above,* and Packages and Theme Trips under Tour Operators, *below.*

FISHING

For information on fishing licenses and regulations, contact in each respective state: the **Colorado Division of Wildlife** (6060 Broadway, Denver, CO 80216, ☎ 303/297–1192); the **Idaho Department of Fish & Game** (Box 25, 600 S. Walnut St., Boise, ID 83707, ☎ 208/334–3700); the **Montana**

Department of Fish, Wildlife & Parks (1420 E. 6th St., Helena, MT 59620, ☎ 406/444–2535); the **Utah Division of Wildlife Resources** (1596 W. North Temple, Salt Lake City, UT 84116, ☎ 801/538–4700); or **Wyoming Game & Fish** (5400 Bishop Blvd., Cheyenne, WY 82006, ☎ 307/777–4600).

HIKING

The Mountaineers (306 2nd Ave. W, Seattle, WA 98119) and **Sierra Club Books** (930 Polk St., San Francisco, CA 94109) are among the leading publishers of hiking guides for the Rockies. Topographical maps may be available in well-equipped outdoor stores (REI or Eastern Mountain Sports, for example). Maps are also available from the **U.S. Geological Survey** (Distribution Center, Denver, CO 80225). Be specific about the region you're interested in when ordering.

HORSEPACK TRIPS

Good sources of information on horsepack trips in the Rockies are: the **Colorado Outfitters Association** (Box 440021, Aurora, CO 80044, ☎ 303/841–7760); and the **Montana Board of Outfitters** (111 N. Jackson St., Helena, MT 59620, ☎ 406/444–3738).

STUDENTS

GROUPS

Major tour operators include **Contiki Holidays** (300 Plaza Alicante, Suite 900, Garden Grove, CA 92640, ☎

714/740–0808 or 800/466–0610).

HOSTELING

Contact **Hostelling International–American Youth Hostels** (733 15th St. NW, Suite 840, Washington, DC 20005, ☎ 202/783–6161) in the United States, **Hostelling International–Canada** (205 Catherine St., Suite 400, Ottawa, Ontario K2P 1C3, ☎ 613/237–7884) in Canada, and the **Youth Hostel Association of England and Wales** (Trevelyan House, 8 St. Stephen's Hill, St. Albans, Hertfordshire AL1 2DY, ☎ 01727/855215 or 01727/845047) in the United Kingdom. Membership ($25 in the U.S., C$26.75 in Canada, and £9 in the U.K.) gives you access to 5,000 hostels worldwide that charge $7–$20 nightly per person.

ID CARDS

To be eligible for discounts on transportation and admissions, get the **International Student Identity Card** (ISIC) if you're a bona fide student or the **Go 25 Card** if you're under 26. In the United States the ISIC and Go 25 cards cost $18 each and include basic travel accident and illness coverage, plus a toll-free travel hot line. Apply through the Council on International Educational Exchange (*see* Organizations, *below*). Cards are available for $15 each in Canada from **Travel Cuts** (187 College St., Toronto, Ontario M5T 1P7, ☎ 416/979–2406 or 800/667–

2887) and in the United Kingdom for £5 each at student unions and student travel companies.

ORGANIZATIONS

A major contact is the **Council on International Educational Exchange** (CIEE, 205 E. 42nd St., 16th Floor, New York, NY 10017, ☎ 212/661–1450) with locations in Boston (729 Boylston St., 02116, ☎ 617/266–1926); Miami (9100 S. Dadeland Blvd., 33156, ☎ 305/670–9261); Los Angeles (10904 Lindbrook Dr., 90024, ☎ 310/208–3551); 43 other college towns nationwide; and the United Kingdom (28A Poland St., London W1V 3DB, ☎ 0171/437–7767). Twice a year, it publishes *Student Travels* magazine. The CIEE's Council Travel Service offers domestic air passes for bargain travel within the United States and is the exclusive U.S. agent for several student-discount cards.

Campus Connections (325 Chestnut St., Suite 1101, Philadelphia, PA 19106, ☎ 215/625–8585 or 800/428–3235) specializes in discounted accommodations and airfares for students. The **Educational Travel Centre** (438 N. Frances St., Madison, WI 53703, ☎ 608/256–5551) offers rail passes and low-cost airline tickets, mostly for flights departing from Chicago.

In Canada, also contact **Travel Cuts** (*see above*).

T
TOUR OPERATORS

Among the companies selling tours and packages to the Rockies, the following have a proven reputation, are nationally known, and offer plenty of options.

GROUP TOURS

For deluxe escorted tours of the Rockies, contact **Maupintour** (Box 807, Lawrence KS 66044, ☎ 800/255–4266 or 913/843–1211) and **Tauck Tours** (11 Wilton Rd., Westport, CT 06880, ☎ 800/468–2825 or 203/226–6911). Another operator falling between deluxe and first-class is **Globus** (5301 South Federal Circle, Littleton, CO 80123, ☎ 800/221–0090 or 303/797–2800). In the first-class and tourist range, contact **Collette Tours** (162 Middle Street, Pawtucket, RI 02860, ☎ 800/832–4656 or 401/728–3805); and **Mayflower Tours** (1225 Warren Ave., Downers Grove, IL 60515, ☎ 708/960–3430 or 800/323–7604). For budget and tourist class programs, try **Cosmos** (*see* Globus, *above*).

PACKAGES

Independent vacation packages are available from major airlines and tour operators. Contact **American Airlines Fly AAway Vacations** (☎ 800/321–2121); **Globetrotters** (139 Main St., Cambridge, MA 02142, ☎ 800/999–9696 or 617/621–9911); **Continental Airlines' Grand Destinations** (☎ 800/634–5555); **Delta Dream Vacations** (☎ 800/872–7786); **Certified Vacations** (Box 1525, Ft. Lauderdale, FL 33302, ☎ 305/522–1414 or 800/233–7260); **United Vacations** (☎ 800/328–6877); **Kingdom Tours** (300 Market St., Kingston, PA 18704, ☎ 717/283–4241 or 800/872–8857); and **USAir Vacations** (☎ 800/455–0123). **Funjet Vacations,** based in Milwaukee, Wisconsin, and **Gogo Tours,** based in Ramsey, New Jersey, sell packages to the Rockies only through travel agents.

For one-of-a-kind Western itineraries with stays at unique inns and ranches, contact **Off the Beaten Path** (109 E. Main St., Bozeman, MT 59715, ☎ 406/586–1311, FAX 406/587–4147). The company creates detailed trip planners for individual travelers that include little-known attractions and restaurants.

THEME TRIPS

ADVENTURE➤ **All Adventure Travel** (5589 Arapahoe No. 208, Boulder, CO 80303, ☎ 800/537–4025), which represents more than 80 adventure operators, can satisfy virtually any thirst for adventure in the Rockies.

CAMPING➤ For Western U.S. camping trips in the company of travelers from all over the globe, check out the programs of **Trek America** (Box 470, Blairstown, NJ 07825, ☎ 908/362–9198 or 800/221–0596).

CYCLING➤ Bike trips through the Rockies are available from **Backroads** (1516 5th St., Suite A550, Berkeley, CA 94710, ☎ 510/527–1555 or 800/462–2848) and **Cycle America** (Box 485, Cannon Falls, MN 55009, ☎ 800/245–3263).

DUDE RANCHES➤ Contact **All Adventure Travel** (*see* Adventure, *above*) or **Old West Dude Ranch Vacations** (American Wilderness Experience, Box 1486, Boulder, CO 80306, ☎ 800/444–3833 or 303/444–2622).

NATURE➤ For learning vacations in a national park, contact the **National Audubon Society** (National Environmental Education Center, 613 Riversville Rd., Greenwich, CT 06831, ☎ 203/869–2017) and the **National Wildlife Federation** (1400 16th St. NW, Washington, DC 20036, ☎ 703/790–4363 or 800/432–6564). You help maintain trails as a volunteer with the **Sierra Club** (730 Polk St., San Francisco, CA 94109, ☎ 415/776–2211). For something a little cushier, **Questers Worldwide Nature Tours** (275 Park Ave. S, New York, NY 10010, ☎ 212/673–3120 or 800/468–8668) has nature tours with all the comforts of home.

RIVER RAFTING➤ Contact **OARS** (Box 67, Angels Camp, CA 95222, ☎ 209/736–4677) for a complete selection of trips through the Rockies.

FROM THE U.K.

Among those companies you might consider

as you plan your trip to the Rockies are **Cosmosair** (Ground Floor, Dale House, Tiviot Dale, Stockport, Cheshire SK1 1TB, ☎ 0161/480–5799); **Travelpack** (Clarendon House, Clarendon Rd., Eccles, Manchester M30 9AL, ☎ 0161/707–4404, FAX 0161/707–4403); **Kuoni Travel** (Kuoni House, Dorking, Surrey RH5 4AZ, ☎ 01306/742–222, FAX 01306/744-222); **Premier Holidays** (Premier Travel Center, Westbrook, Milton Rd., Cambridge CB4 1YQ, ☎ 01223/516–688, FAX 01223/516–615); **Ramblers Holidays, Ltd.** (Box 43, Welwyn Garden City, Hertfordshire AL8 6PQ, ☎ 01707/331–133, FAX 01707/333–276); and **Trek America, Ltd.** (Trek House, The Bullring, Deddington, Banbury, Oxon OX15 OTT, ☎ 01869/338–777, FAX 01869/338–846).

Travel agencies that offer cheap fares to the Rockies include **Trailfinders** (42–50 Earl's Court Rd., London W8 6FT, ☎ 0171/937–5400); **Travel Cuts** (295a Regent St., London W1R 7YA, ☎ 0171/637–3161); and **Flightfile** (49 Tottenham Court Rd., London W1P 9RE, ☎ 0171/700–2722).

ORGANIZATIONS

The **National Tour Association** (546 E. Main St., Lexington, KY 40508, ☎ 606/226–4444 or 800/755-8687) and **United States Tour Operators Association** (USTOA, 211 E. 51st St., Suite 12B, New York, NY 10022, ☎ 212/750–7371) can provide lists of member operators and information on booking tours.

PUBLICATIONS

Consult the brochure **"On Tour"** and ask for a current list of member operators from the National Tour Association (*see* Organizations, *above*). Also get a copy of the **"Worldwide Tour & Vacation Package Finder"** from the USTOA (*see* Organizations, *above*) and the Better Business Bureau's **"Tips on Travel Packages"** (publication No. 24-195, $2; 4200 Wilson Blvd., Arlington, VA 22203).

TRAVEL AGENCIES

For names of reputable agencies in your area, contact the **American Society of Travel Agents** (1101 King St., Suite 200, Alexandria, VA 22314, ☎ 703/739–2782).

V

VISITOR INFO

Contact the **Colorado Tourism Board** (1625 Broadway, Suite 1700, Denver 80202, ☎ 303/592–5510 or 800/592–1939, FAX 303/592–5406; ski reports 303/831–7669); the **Idaho**

Travel Council (Department of Commerce, 700 W. State St., Boise 83720, ☎ 208/334–2470 or 800/635–7820, FAX 208/334–2631; ski reports 800/635–7820); **Travel Montana** (Department of Commerce, 1424 9th Ave., Helena 59620, ☎ 406/444–2654 or 800/541–1447, FAX 406/444–2808; ski reports 800/847–4868); the **Utah Travel Council** (Council Hall, Capitol Hill, Salt Lake City 84114, ☎ 801/538–1030, FAX 801/538–1399; ski reports 801/521–8102); and the **Wyoming Division of Tourism** (I–25 at College Dr., Cheyenne 82002, ☎ 307/777–7777 or 800/225–5996, FAX 307/777–6904; ski reports 800/225–5996).

In the U.K., also contact the **United States Travel and Tourism Administration** (Box 1EN, London W1A 1EN, ☎ 0171/495–4466). For a free USA pack, write the USTTA at Box 170, Ashford, Kent TN24 0ZX. Enclose stamps worth £1.50.

W

WEATHER

For current conditions and forecasts, plus the local time and helpful travel tips, call the **Weather Channel Connection** (☎ 900/932–8437; 95¢ per minute) from a Touch-Tone phone.

SMART TRAVEL TIPS A TO Z

Basic Information on Traveling in the Rockies and Savvy Tips to Make Your Trip a Breeze

The more you travel, the more you know about how to make trips run like clockwork. To help make your travels hassle-free, Fodor's editors have rounded up dozens of tips from our contributors and travel experts all over the world, as well as basic information on visiting the Rockies. For names of organizations to contact and publications that can give you more information, see Important Contacts A to Z, *above.*

A

AIR TRAVEL

If time is an issue, **always look for nonstop flights,** which require no change of plane. If possible, **avoid connecting flights,** which stop at least once and can involve a change of plane, although the flight number remains the same; if the first leg is late, the second waits.

CUTTING COSTS

The Sunday travel section of most newspapers is a good source of deals.

CONSOLIDATORS➢ Consolidators, who buy tickets at reduced rates from scheduled airlines, sell them at prices below the lowest available from the airlines directly—usually without advance restrictions. Sometimes you can even get your

money back if you need to return the ticket. Carefully read the fine print detailing penalties for changes and cancellations. If you doubt the reliability of a consolidator, **confirm your reservation with the airline.**

MAJOR AIRLINES➢ The least-expensive airfares from the major airlines are priced for round-trip travel and are subject to restrictions. You must usually **book in advance and buy the ticket within 24 hours** to get cheaper fares, and you may have to **stay over a Saturday night.** The lowest fare is subject to availability, and only a small percentage of the plane's total seats are sold at that price. It's good to **call a number of airlines, and when you are quoted a good price, book it on the spot**—the same fare on the same flight may not be available the next day. Airlines generally allow you to change your return date for a $25 to $50 fee, but most low-fare tickets are nonrefundable. However, if you don't use it, you can apply the cost toward the purchase price of a new ticket, again for a small charge.

ALOFT

AIRLINE FOOD➢ If you hate airline food, **ask for special meals when booking.** These can be

vegetarian, low-cholesterol, or kosher, for example; commonly prepared to order in smaller quantities than standard catered fare, they can be tastier.

SMOKING➢ Smoking is banned on all flights within the United States of less than six hours' duration and on all Canadian flights; the ban also applies to domestic segments of international flights aboard U.S. and foreign carriers. Delta has banned smoking system-wide.

B

BUSINESS HOURS

Throughout the Rockies, most retail stores are open from 9 or 9:30 AM until 6 or 7 PM daily in downtown locations and until 9 or 10 in suburban shopping malls. Downtown stores sometimes stay open later Thursday nights. Normal banking hours are weekdays 9–5; some branches are also open on Saturday morning.

C

CAMERAS, CAMCORDERS, AND COMPUTERS

LAPTOPS

Before you depart, **check your portable computer's battery,** because you may be asked at security to turn on the computer to prove that it is what it appears to be. At the airport, you may prefer to **request a manual inspection,** although security X-rays do not harm hard-disk or floppy-disk storage.

PHOTOGRAPHY

If your camera is new or if you haven't used it for a while, **shoot and develop a few rolls of film** before you leave. Always **store film in a cool, dry place**—never in the car's glove compartment or on the shelf under the rear window.

Every pass of film through an X-ray machine increases the chance of clouding. To protect it, carry it in a clear plastic bag and **ask for hand inspection at security.** Such requests are virtually always honored at U.S. airports, and usually are accommodated abroad. Don't depend on a lead-lined bag to protect film in checked luggage—the airline may increase the radiation to see what's inside.

VIDEO

Before your trip, **test your camcorder, invest in a skylight filter to protect the lens, and charge the batteries.** (Airport security personnel may ask you to turn on the camcorder to prove that it's what it appears to be.)

Videotape is not damaged by X-rays, but it may be harmed by the magnetic field of a walk-through metal detector, so **ask that videotapes be hand-checked.**

CHILDREN AND TRAVEL

With dude ranches and many outdoor activities, Colorado is tailor-made for family vacations. But plan ahead, and **involve your youngsters** as you outline your trip. When packing, **bring a supply of things to keep them busy** in the car, on the airplane, on the train, or however you are traveling (*see* Games *under* Children and Travel *in* Important Contacts A to Z, *above*). Driving gives you the option of stopping frequently to let them get out and burn off energy.

On sightseeing days, try to **plan some things that will be of special interest to your children.** They may tolerate a museum and even show interest in a historic building or two, but put a zoo into the itinerary when you can. In addition, **check local newspapers for special events** mounted by public libraries, museums, parks, and YMCA/YWCAs in the area.

BABY-SITTING

For recommended local sitters, **check with your hotel desk.**

DRIVING

If you are renting a car, **arrange for a car seat when you reserve.** Sometimes they're free.

FLYING

On domestic flights, children under 2 not occupying a seat travel free, and older children currently travel on the lowest applicable adult fare.

BAGGAGE➤ In general, the adult baggage allowance applies for children paying half or more of the adult fare.

SAFETY SEATS➤ According to the Federal Aviation Administration (FAA), it's a good idea to **use safety seats aloft.** Airline policy varies. U.S. carriers allow FAA-approved models, but airlines usually require that you buy a ticket, even if your child would otherwise ride free, because the seats must be strapped into regular passenger seats.

FACILITIES➤ When making your reservation, **ask for children's meals or freestanding bassinets** if you need them; the latter are available only to those with seats at the bulkhead, where there's enough legroom. If you don't need a bassinet, **think twice before requesting bulkhead seats**—the only storage for in-flight necessities is in the inconveniently distant overhead bins.

LODGING

Most hotels allow children under a certain age to stay in their parents' room at no extra charge, while others charge them as extra adults; be sure to **ask about the cut-off age.**

CUSTOMS AND DUTIES

ON ARRIVAL

British visitors ages 21 or over may import the following into the United States: 200

cigarettes or 50 cigars or 2 kilograms of tobacco; 1 U.S. liter of alcohol; gifts to the value of $100. Restricted items include meat products, seeds, plants, and fruits. Never carry illegal drugs.

BACK HOME

IN CANADA➤ Once per calendar year, when you've been out of Canada for at least seven days, you may bring in C$300 worth of goods duty-free. If you've been away less than seven days but more than 48 hours, the duty-free exemption drops to C$100 but can be claimed any number of times (as can a C$20 duty-free exemption for absences of 24 hours or more). You cannot combine the yearly and 48-hour exemptions, use the C$300 exemption only partially (to save the balance for a later trip), or pool exemptions with family members. Goods claimed under the C$300 exemption may follow you by mail; those claimed under the lesser exemptions must accompany you.

Alcohol and tobacco products may be included in the yearly and 48-hour exemptions but not in the 24-hour exemption. If you meet the age requirements of the province through which you reenter Canada, you may bring in, duty-free, 1.14 liters (40 imperial ounces) of wine or liquor *or* 24 12-ounce cans or bottles of beer or ale. If you are 16 or older, you may bring in, duty-free, 200 cigarettes, 50 cigars or cigarillos, and 400 tobacco sticks or 400 grams of manufactured tobacco. Alcohol and tobacco must accompany you on your return.

An unlimited number of gifts valued up to C$60 each may be mailed to Canada duty-free. These do not count as part of your exemption. Label the package "Unsolicited Gift— Value under $60." Alcohol and tobacco are excluded.

IN THE U.K.➤ From countries outside the EU, including the United States, you may import duty-free 200 cigarettes, 100 cigarillos, 50 cigars or 250 grams of tobacco; 1 liter of spirits or 2 liters of fortified or sparkling wine; 2 liters of still table wine; 60 milliliters of perfume; 250 milliliters of toilet water; plus £136 worth of other goods, including gifts and souvenirs.

D

FOR TRAVELERS WITH DISABILITIES

When discussing accessibility with an operator or reservationist, **ask hard questions.** Are there any stairs, inside *or* out? Are there grab bars next to the toilet *and* in the shower/tub? How wide is the doorway to the room? To the bathroom? For the most extensive facilities, meeting the latest legal specifications, **opt for newer accommodations,** which more often have been designed with access in mind. Older properties or ships must usually be retrofitted and may offer more limited facilities as a result. Be sure to **discuss your needs before booking.**

DISCOUNT CLUBS

Travel clubs offer members unsold space on airplanes, cruise ships, and package tours at as much as 50% below regular prices. Membership may include a regular bulletin or access to a toll-free hot line giving details of available trips departing from three or four days to several months in the future. Most also offer 50% discounts off hotel rack rates. Before booking with a club, **make sure the hotel or other supplier isn't offering a better deal.**

DRIVING

The Rockies offer some of the most spectacular vistas and challenging driving in the world. Roads range from multilane blacktop to barely graveled backcountry trails; from twisting switchbacks considerably marked with guardrails to primitive campgrounds with a lane so narrow that the driver has to back up to the edge of a steep cliff in order to make a turn. Scenic routes and lookout points are clearly marked, enabling visitors to slow down and pull over to take in the views.

You'll seldom be bored driving through the Rockies. The most mountainous terrain is in Colorado, but this state is also the most populated and accessible of those in the region. Idaho is home to the rockiest and most rugged stretch of the mountains, with an extraordinarily wild beauty that may be too remote and desolate for most travelers. In fact, it is impossible to travel directly through the heart of the state—only two routes go from north to south. Montana's interstate system is more driver-friendly, connecting soaring summits, rivers, glacial valleys, forests, lakes, and vast stretches of prairie, all capped by that endless "Big Sky." It is practically impossible to get around Utah without a car. There are more national parks here than in any other state but Alaska and California, although their interiors are not always accessible by car, as are other national park interior regions. Wyoming's interstate links classic, open-range cowboy country and mountain-range vistas of varying degrees of cragginess with the geothermal wonderland of Yellowstone National Park.

You'll find highways and the national parks to be crowded during the summer months (June, July, and August), and almost deserted (and occasionally impassable) in winter. Follow the posted speed limit, drive defensively, and **make sure your gas tank is full,** since distances between gas stations could make running on empty (or in the reserve zone) a not-so-pleasant memory of your trip.

A word to drivers: One of the more unpleasant sights along the highway are roadkills—animals struck by vehicles. Be aware that deer, elk, and even bears might be attempting to cross the road just as you're driving by. Exercise caution, not only to save an animal's life, but also to avoid possible extensive damage to your car.

Before setting out on any driving trip, it's important to **make sure your vehicle is in top condition.** It is best to have a complete tune-up; at the least, you should make the following checks:

See that all the lights are working, including brake lights, backup lights, and emergency lights; make sure tires are in good shape (including the spare); check the oil; check the engine coolant; fill the windshield-washer bottle; make sure the washer blades are in good condition; and make sure the brakes are in good condition, too. For emergencies, take along flares or reflector triangles, jumper cables, an empty gas can, a fire extinguisher, a flashlight, a plastic tarp, blankets, and coins for phone calls.

AUTO CLUBS

The American Automobile Association (AAA) is a federation of state auto clubs that offers maps, route planning, and emergency road service to its members; members of Britain's Automobile Association (BAA) are granted reciprocal privileges.

BORDER CROSSING

Driving a car across the U.S.–Canadian border is a simple process. Personal vehicles are allowed entry into the neighboring country, provided they are not to be left behind. Drivers in rental cars should **bring along a copy of the rental contract when crossing the border,** bearing an endorsement stating that the vehicle is permitted to cross the border.

SPEED LIMITS

The speed limit on U.S. interstate highways is 65 miles per hour in rural areas and 55 miles per hour in urban zones and on secondary highways.

WINTER DRIVING

Modern highways make mountain driving safe and generally trouble free even in cold weather. Although winter driving can occasionally present some real challenges, road maintenance is good and plowing is prompt. However, in mountain areas, tire chains, studs, or snow tires are essential. If you're planning to drive into high elevations, be sure to **check the weather forecast** beforehand. Even the mountain passes on main highways can be forced to close because of snow conditions. Each state highway department has a number to call for road conditions *see* Driving *in* Important Contacts

A to Z, *above*). Be prepared for stormy weather: **Carry an emergency kit** containing warm clothes, a flashlight, some food, and perhaps a sleeping bag. If you do get stalled by deep snow, do not leave your car. Wait for help, running the engine only if needed, and remember that assistance is never far away.

I
INSURANCE

BAGGAGE

Airline liability for your baggage is limited to $1,250 per person on domestic flights. On international flights, the airlines' liability is $9.07 per pound or $20 per kilogram for checked baggage (roughly $640 per 70-pound bag) and $400 per passenger for unchecked baggage. Insurance for losses exceeding the terms of your airline ticket can be bought directly from the airline at check-in for about $10 per $1,000 of coverage; note that it excludes a rather extensive list of items, shown on your airline ticket.

FLIGHT

You should **think twice before buying flight insurance.** Often purchased as a last-minute impulse at the airport, it pays a lump sum when a plane crashes, either to a beneficiary if the insured dies or sometimes to a surviving passenger who loses eyesight or a limb. Supplementing the airlines' coverage described in the limits-of-liability paragraphs on your ticket, it's expensive and basically unnecessary. Charging an airline ticket to a major credit card often automatically entitles you to coverage and may also embrace travel by bus, train, and ship.

FOR U.K. TRAVELERS

According to the Association of British Insurers, a trade association representing 450 insurance companies, it's wise to **buy extra medical coverage when you visit the United States.** You can buy an annual travel-insurance policy valid for most vacations during the year in which it's purchased. If you go this route, make sure it covers you if you have a preexisting medical condition or are pregnant.

TRIP

Without insurance, you will lose all or most of your money if you must cancel your trip due to illness or any other reason. Especially if your airline ticket, cruise, or package tour is nonrefundable and cannot be changed, it's essential that you **buy trip-cancellation-and-interruption insurance.** When considering how much coverage you need, look for a policy that will cover the cost of your trip plus the nondiscounted price of a one-way airline ticket should you need to return home early. Read the fine print carefully, especially sections defining "family member" and "preexisting

medical conditions." Also **consider default or bankruptcy insurance,** which protects you against a supplier's failure to deliver. However, such policies often do not cover default by a travel agency, tour operator, airline, or cruise line if you bought your tour and the coverage directly from the firm in question.

L
LODGING

APARTMENT AND VILLA RENTALS

If you want a home base that's roomy enough for a family and comes with cooking facilities, **consider a furnished rental.** It's generally cost-wise, too, although not always—some rentals are luxury properties (economical only when your party is large). Home-exchange directories do list rentals—often second homes owned by prospective house swappers—and some services search for a house or apartment for you (even a castle if that's your fancy) and handle the paperwork. Some send an illustrated catalogue and others send photographs of specific properties, sometimes at a charge; up-front registration fees may apply.

BED-AND-BREAKFASTS

Bed-and-breakfasts are private homes whose owners welcome paying guests. They usually have anywhere from two to 10 rooms, some with private baths and some with shared facilities, and always serve breakfast at no extra charge. The decor and hospitality generally reflect the personality and taste of the B&B's owners to a greater degree than you'll find at most inns. Generally, reservations are booked directly, or are made through a reservation system.

CAMPING

Camping is an invigorating and inexpensive way to tour the Rockies. Colorado, Idaho, Montana, Utah, and Wyoming are full of state and national parks and forests with sites that range from rustic, with pit toilets and cold running water, to campgrounds with full hookups, bathhouses with hot showers, and paved trailer pads that can accommodate even jumbo RVs. Fees vary, from $6 to $10 a night for tenters up to $21 for RVs, but are usually waived once the water is turned off for the winter. Sometimes site reservations are accepted, and then only for up to seven days (early birds reserve up to a year in advance); more often, they're not. Campers who prefer a more remote setting may camp in the backcountry; it's free but you'll need a permit, available from park visitor centers and ranger stations. If you're visiting in summer, plan well ahead. *The National Parks: Camping Guide* (Superintendent of Documents, U.S. Government Printing Office, Washington, DC 20402; $3.50) may be helpful.

In addition, you'll find privately operated campgrounds; their facilities and amenities are usually more extensive (swimming pools are common), reservations are more widely accepted, and nightly fees are higher: $7 and up for tents, $23 for RVs.

GUEST RANCHES

If the thought of sitting around a campfire after a hard day on the range makes your heart beat faster, **consider playing dude** on a guest ranch. These range from wilderness-rimmed working ranches that accept guests and encourage them to pitch in with chores and other ranch activities to luxurious resorts, on the fringes of a small city, with an upscale clientele, swimming pools, tennis courts, and a lively roster of horse-related activities such as breakfast rides, moonlight rides, all-day trail rides, and the like. Rafting, fishing, tubing, and other activities in the surrounding wilderness are usually available, and at working ranches, guests may be able to participate in a cattle roundup. In winter, cross-country skiing and snowshoeing keep guests busy. Lodgings can run the gamut from charmingly rustic cabins to the kind of deluxe quarters you expect at a first-class hotel. Meals may be gourmet or plain but hearty. Many ranches offer packages and children's and off-season rates.

HOME EXCHANGE

If you would like to find a house, an apartment, or other vacation property to exchange for your own while on vacation, **become a member of a home-exchange organization,** which will send you its annual directories listing available exchanges and will include your own listing in at least one of them. Arrangements for the actual exchange are made by the two parties to it, not by the organization.

HOTELS

Most big-city hotels cater primarily to business travelers, with such facilities as restaurants, cocktail lounges, swimming pools, exercise equipment, and meeting rooms. Room rates usually reflect the range of amenities offered. Most cities also have less expensive hotels that are clean and comfortable but have fewer facilities. A new accommodations trend is all-suite hotels, which give travelers more room for their money and are gaining popularity with business travelers; examples include Courtyard by Marriott and Embassy Suites.

Many properties offer special weekend rates, sometimes up to 50% off regular prices. However, these deals are usually not extended during peak summer months, when hotels are normally full.

INNS

Charm is the long suit of these establishments,

which generally occupy a restored older building with some historical or architectural significance. They're generally small, with under 20 rooms, and located outside cities. Breakfast may be included in the rates.

MOTELS

The once-familiar roadside motel is fast disappearing from the American landscape. In its place are chain-run motor inns that are strategically located at highway intersections. Some of these establishments offer very basic facilities; others provide restaurants, swimming pools, and other amenities.

RESORTS

Rockies resorts range from fishing lodges to luxury turn-of-the-century showplaces. Ski resort towns throughout the Rockies are home to dozens of resorts in all price ranges; the activities lacking in any individual property can usually be found in the town itself, in summer as well as winter. Off the slopes, there are wonderful rustic-luxurious resorts in the national parks: Jackson Lake Lodge and Jenny Lake Lodge in Grand Teton National Park, and Old Faithful Lodge in Yellowstone. The Broadmoor, in Colorado Springs, is a grand old property dating from the late 19th century. Northwestern Montana is home to Flathead Lake, the largest freshwater lake west of the Mississippi, and Averill's Flathead Lake

Lodge, a deluxe 2,000-acre rustic Western property that spices up its spring season with a rodeo-training school.

M
MONEY
AND EXPENSES

ATMS

Chances are that you can **use your bank card at ATMs** to withdraw money from an account and get cash advances on a credit-card account if your card has been programmed with a personal identification number, or PIN. Before leaving home, **check in on frequency limits** for withdrawals and cash advances.

On cash advances you are charged interest from the day you receive the money, whether from a teller or an ATM. Transaction fees for ATM withdrawals outside your home turf may be higher than for withdrawals at home.

COSTS

Prices for dining and lodging in the Rockies are generally lower than in major North American cities in other areas. First-class hotel rooms in Denver, Salt Lake City, Boise, Missoula, and Cheyenne cost from $75 to $175 a night, although some "value" hotel rooms go for $40 to $60, and, as elsewhere in the United States, rooms in national budget chain motels go for around $30 nightly. Weekend packages, offered by most city hotels, cut prices up to 50% (but

may not be available in peak winter or summer seasons). As a rule, costs outside the major cities are lower, except in some of the deluxe resorts. A cup of coffee costs between 50¢ and $1, the price for a hamburger runs between $3 and $5, and a beer at a bar generally is between $1.50 and $3.

TAXES

The sales tax varies from state to state. It's 3% in Colorado and Wyoming, 5% in Idaho, and 6.125% in Utah. Montana has no sales tax.

If you are crossing the border into Canada, be aware of Canada's goods and services tax (better known as the GST). This is a value-added tax of 7%, applicable on virtually every purchase except basic groceries and a small number of other items. Visitors to Canada, however, may **claim a full rebate of the GST** on any goods taken out of the country as well as on short-term accommodations. Rebates can be claimed either immediately on departure from Canada at participating duty-free shops or by mail. Rebate forms can be obtained by writing to Revenue Canada (*see* Taxes *in* Important Contacts A to Z, *above*) Claims must be for a minimum of $7 worth of tax and can be submitted up to a year from the date of purchase. Purchases made during multiple visits to Canada can be grouped together for rebate purposes.

TRAVELER'S CHECKS

Whether or not to buy traveler's checks depends on where you are headed; **take cash to rural areas and small towns, traveler's checks to cities.** The most widely recognized are American Express, Citicorp, Thomas Cook, and Visa, which are sold by major commercial banks for 1% to 3% of the checks' face value—it pays to **shop around.** Both American Express and Thomas Cook issue checks that can be countersigned and used by you or your traveling companion. Record the numbers of the checks, cross them off as you spend them, and keep this information separate from your checks.

WIRING MONEY

You don't have to be a cardholder to send or receive funds through MoneyGram[SM] from American Express. Just go to a MoneyGram[SM] agent, located in retail and convenience stores and in American Express Travel Offices. Pay up to $1,000 with cash or a credit card, anything over that in cash. The money can be picked up within 10 minutes in cash or check at the nearest MoneyGram agent. There's no limit, and the recipient need only present photo identification. The cost, which includes a free long-distance phone call, runs from 3% to 10%, depending on the

amount sent, the destination, and how you pay.

Money sent from the United States or Canada will be available for pickup at agent locations in 100 countries within 15 minutes. Once the money is in the system, it can be picked up at any one of 25,000 locations. Fees range from 4% to 10%, depending on the amount you send.

P
PACKAGES
AND TOURS

A package or tour to the Rockies can make your vacation less expensive and more convenient. Firms that sell tours and packages purchase airline seats, hotel rooms, and rental cars in bulk and pass some of the savings on to you. In addition, the best operators have local representatives to help you out at your destination.

A GOOD DEAL?

The more your package or tour includes, the better you can predict the ultimate cost of your vacation. Make sure you know exactly what is included, and **beware of hidden costs.** Are taxes, tips, and service charges included? Transfers and baggage handling? Entertainment and excursion fees? These can add up.

Most packages and tours are rated deluxe, first-class superior, first class, tourist, and budget. The key difference is usually accom-

modations. If the package or tour you are considering is priced lower than in your wildest dreams, **be skeptical.** Also, **make sure your travel agent knows the hotels** and other services. Ask about location, room size, beds, and whether it has a pool, room service, or programs for children, if you care about these. Has your agent been there or sent others you can contact?

BUYER BEWARE

Each year consumers are stranded or lose their money when operators go out of business—even very large ones with excellent reputations. If you can't afford a loss, take the time to **check out the operator**—find out how long the company has been in business, and ask several agents about its reputation. Next, **don't book unless the firm has a consumer-protection program.** Members of the United States Tour Operators Association and the National Tour Association are required to set aside funds exclusively to cover your payments and travel arrangements in case of default. Nonmember operators may instead carry insurance; look for the details in the operator's brochure—and the name of an underwriter with a solid reputation. Note: When it comes to tour operators, **don't trust escrow accounts.** Although there are laws governing those of charter-flight operators, no governmental body prevents tour operators from raiding the till.

Next, **contact your local Better Business Bureau and the attorney general's office** in both your own state and the operator's; have any complaints been filed? Last, **pay with a major credit card.** Then you can cancel payment, provided that you can document your complaint. Always **consider trip-cancellation insurance** (*see* Insurance, *above*).

BIG VS. SMALL➤ An operator that handles several hundred thousand travelers annually can use its purchasing power to give you a good price. Its high volume may also indicate financial stability. But some small companies provide more personalized service; because they tend to specialize, they may also be experts on an area.

USING AN AGENT

Travel agents are an excellent resource. In fact, large operators accept bookings only through travel agents. But it's good to **collect brochures from several agencies,** because some agents' suggestions may be skewed by promotional relationships with tour and package firms that reward them for volume sales. If you have a special interest, **find an agent with expertise in that area;** the American Society of Travel Agents can give you leads in the United States. (Don't rely solely on your agent, though; agents may be unaware of small niche opera-

tors, and some special-interest travel companies only sell direct.)

SINGLE TRAVELERS

Prices are usually quoted per person, based on two sharing a room. If traveling solo, you may be required to pay the full double-occupancy rate. Some operators eliminate this surcharge if you agree to be matched up with a roommate of the same sex, even if one is not found by departure time.

PACKING FOR THE ROCKIES

Informality reigns in the Rockies, and casual clothing is acceptable—even expected—in most places. Jeans, sport shirts, and T-shirts fit in almost everywhere, for both men and women. The few restaurants and performing-arts events where dressier outfits are required, largely in resorts and larger cities, are the exception.

If you plan to spend much time outdoors, and certainly if you go in winter, **choose clothing appropriate for cold and wet weather.** Cotton clothing, including denim—although fine on warm, dry days—can be uncomfortable when it gets wet and when the weather's cold. A better choice is clothing made of wool or any of a number of new synthetics that provide warmth without bulk and maintain their insulating properties even when wet.

In summer, you'll want shorts during the day.

But because early morning and night can be cold, and high passes windy, pack a sweater and a light jacket, and perhaps also a wool cap and gloves. Try layering—a T-shirt under another shirt under a jacket—and peel off layers as you go. For walks and hikes, you'll need sturdy footwear. To take you into the wilds, boots should have thick soles and plenty of ankle support; if your shoes are new and you plan to spend much time on the trail, break them in at home. Bring a day pack for short hikes, along with a canteen or water bottle, and don't forget rain gear.

In winter, prepare for below-zero temperatures with good boots, warm socks and liners, long johns, a well-insulated jacket, and a warm hat and mittens.

If you attend dances and other events at Native American reservations, dress conservatively—skirts or long pants for women, long pants for men—or you may be asked to leave.

When traveling to mountain areas, **remember that sunglasses and a sun hat are essential at high altitudes;** the thinner atmosphere requires sunscreen with a greater SPF than you might need at lower elevations. Bring an extra pair of eyeglasses or contact lenses in your carry-on luggage, and if you have a health problem, **pack enough medication** to last the trip. **Don't put prescrip-**

tion drugs or valuables in luggage to be checked, for it could go astray.

LUGGAGE

Free airline baggage allowances depend on the airline, the route, and the class of your ticket; ask in advance. In general, on domestic flights you are entitled to check two bags—neither exceeding 62 inches, or 158 centimeters (length + width + height), or weighing more than 70 pounds (32 kilograms). A third piece may be brought aboard; its total dimensions are generally limited to less than 45 inches (114 centimeters), so it will fit easily under the seat in front of you or in the overhead compartment. In the United States, the FAA gives airlines broad latitude to limit carry-on allowances and tailor them to different aircraft and operational conditions. Charges for excess, oversize, or overweight pieces vary.

SAFEGUARDING YOUR LUGGAGE➤ Before leaving home, **itemize your bags' contents** and their worth, and label them with your name, address, and phone number. (If you use your home address, cover it so that potential thieves can't see it.) Inside your bag, **pack a copy of your itinerary.** At check-in, **make sure that your bag is correctly tagged** with the airport's three-letter destination code. If your bags arrive damaged or not at all, file a written report with the airline before leaving the airport.

PASSPORTS AND VISAS

CANADIANS

No passport is necessary to enter the United States.

U.K. CITIZENS

British citizens need a valid passport. If you are staying fewer than 90 days and traveling on a vacation, with a return or onward ticket, you will probably not need a visa. However, you will need to fill out the Visa Waiver Form, 1-94W, supplied by the airline.

While traveling, **keep one photocopy of the data page** separate from your wallet and leave another copy with someone at home. If you lose your passport, promptly call the nearest embassy or consulate, and the local police; having the data page can speed replacement.

R

RENTING A CAR

CUTTING COSTS

To get the best deal, **book through a travel agent and shop around.** When pricing cars, **ask where the rental lot is located.** Some off-airport locations offer lower rates—even though their lots are only minutes away from the terminal via complimentary shuttle. You may also want to **price local car-rental companies,** whose rates may be lower still, although service and maintenance standards may not be up to those of a national firm. Also **ask your travel agent about a company's customer-service record.** How has it responded to late plane arrivals and vehicle mishaps? Are there often lines at the rental counter, and, if you're traveling during a holiday period, does a confirmed reservation guarantee you a car?

INSURANCE

When you drive a rented car, you are generally responsible for any damage or personal injury that you cause as well as damage to the vehicle. Before you rent, **see what coverage you already have** by means of your personal auto-insurance policy and credit cards. For about $14 a day, rental companies sell insurance, known as a collision damage waiver (CDW), that eliminates your liability for damage to the car; it's always optional and should never be automatically added to your bill.

FOR U.K. CITIZENS

In the United States you must be 21 to rent a car; rates may be higher for those under 25. Extra costs cover child seats, compulsory for children under five (about $3 per day), and additional drivers (about $1.50 per day). To pick up your reserved car you will need the reservation voucher, a passport, a U.K. driver's license, and a travel policy covering each driver.

SURCHARGES

Before picking up the

car in one city and leaving it in another, **ask about drop-off charges or one-way service fees,** which can be substantial. Note, too, that some rental agencies charge extra if you return the car before the time specified on your contract. To avoid a hefty refueling fee, **fill the tank just before you turn in the car.**

S
SAFETY CONCERNS

The Rockies have a lot to offer outdoors and sports enthusiasts—year-round. Regardless of the activity or your level of skill, safety must come first. Remember: **know your limits!**

Many trails are at high altitudes, where oxygen is scarce. They're also frequently desolate. Hikers and bikers should **carry emergency supplies** in their backpacks. Proper equipment includes a flashlight, a compass, waterproof matches, a first-aid kit, a knife, and a light plastic tarp for shelter. Backcountry skiers should add a repair kit, a blanket, an avalanche beacon, and a lightweight shovel to their lists. Always **bring extra food and a canteen of water** as dehydration is a common occurrence at high altitudes. **Never drink from streams or lakes,** unless you boil the water first or purify it with tablets. Giardia, an intestinal parasite, may be present.

Weather can have a tremendous impact on outdoor activities. Always **check the condition of roads and trails, and get the latest weather reports** before setting out. In summer, **take precautions against heat stroke or exhaustion** by resting frequently in shaded areas; in winter, **take precautions against hypothermia** by layering clothing. Ultimately, proper planning, common sense, and good physical conditioning are the strongest guards against the elements.

SENIOR-CITIZEN DISCOUNTS

To qualify for age-related discounts, **mention your senior-citizen status up front** when booking hotel reservations, not when checking out, and before you're seated in restaurants, not when paying your bill. Note that discounts may be limited to certain menus, days, or hours. When renting a car, **ask about promotional car-rental discounts**—they can net lower costs than your senior-citizen discount.

STUDENTS ON THE ROAD

To save money, **look into deals available through student-oriented travel agencies.** To qualify, you'll need to have a bona fide student I.D. card. Members of international student groups also are eligible. *See* Students *in* Important Contacts A to Z, *above.*

T
TELEPHONES

The telephone area codes for the Rocky Mountain region are 303, 970, and 719 for Colorado; 208 for Idaho; 406 for Montana; 801 for Utah; and 307 for Wyoming.

Pay telephones cost 25¢ for local calls (except in Wyoming, where the cost is 35¢). Charge phones, also common, may be used to charge a call to a telephone-company calling card or a credit card, or for collect calls.

Many hotels place a surcharge on local calls made from your room and include a service charge on long-distance calls. It may be cheaper for you to make your calls from a pay phone in the hotel lobby rather than from your room.

LONG-DISTANCE

The long-distance services of AT&T, MCI, and Sprint make calling home relatively convenient and let you avoid hotel surcharges; typically, you dial an 800 number in the United States.

W
WHEN TO GO

Summer is one of the Rockies' two big seasons. Hotels in major tourist destinations book up early, especially in July and August, and hikers crowd the backcountry from June through Labor Day. Temperatures rarely rise above the 80s.

Winter is also prime time. Ski resorts buzz from December to early April, especially during Christmas and President's weeks.

If you don't mind sometimes-capricious weather, spring and fall are opportune seasons to visit; rates drop and crowds are nonexistent, so that you may enjoy a corner of Yellowstone all to yourself. Spring's pleasures are somewhat limited, since snow usually blocks the high country well into June, and mountain-pass roads such as the famous Going-to-the-Sun Highway in Glacier National Park stay closed into June. But spring is a good time for fishing, rafting on rivers swollen with snowmelt, birding, and wildlife-viewing. In fall, aspen splash the mountainsides with gold, and wildlife come down to lower elevations. The fish are spawning, and the angling is excellent.

ALTITUDE

You may feel dizzy and weak and find yourself breathing heavily—signs that the thin mountain air isn't giving you your accustomed dose of oxygen. Take it easy and **rest often for a few days until you're acclimatized**; throughout your stay drink plenty of water and watch your alcohol consumption. If you experience severe headaches and nausea, see a doctor. It is easy, especially in Colorado, where highways climb to 12,000 feet and higher, to go too high too fast. The remedy for altitude-related discomfort is to go down quickly, into heavier air. Other altitude-related problems include dehydration and overexposure to the sun due to the thin air.

CLIMATE

Summer in the Rockies begins in late June or early July. Days are warm, with highs often in the 80s, while nighttime temperatures fall to the 40s and 50s. Afternoon thunderstorms are common over the higher peaks. Fall begins in September, often with a week of unsettled weather around mid-month, followed by four to six gorgeous weeks of Indian summer—frosty nights and warm days. Winter creeps in during November, and deep snows have arrived by December. Temperatures usually hover near freezing by day, thanks to the surprisingly warm mountain sun, dropping considerably overnight, occasionally as low as -60° F. Winter tapers off in March, though snow lingers into April on valley bottoms and into July on mountain passes. The Rockies have a reputation for extreme weather, but that cuts two ways: No condition ever lasts for long. What follows are the average daily maximum and minimum temperatures for the region.

Climate in the Rockies

ASPEN, CO

Jan.	33F	1C	May	64F	18C	Sept.	71F	22C
	6	–14		32	0		35	2
Feb.	37F	3C	June	73F	23C	Oct.	60F	16C
	8	–13		37	3		28	– 2
Mar.	42F	6C	July	80F	27C	Nov.	44F	7C
	15	– 9		44	7		15	– 9
Apr.	53F	12C	Aug.	78F	26C	Dec.	37F	3C
	24	– 4		42	6		8	–13

BOISE, ID

Jan.	37F	3C	May	71F	22C	Sept.	75F	24C
	21	– 6		44	7		46	8
Feb.	42F	6C	June	80F	27C	Oct.	64F	18C
	26	– 3		51	11		39	4
Mar.	53F	12C	July	89F	32C	Nov.	50F	10C
	33	1		57	14		30	– 1
Apr.	62F	17C	Aug.	87F	31C	Dec.	39F	4C
	37	3		55	13		24	– 4

HELENA, MT

Jan.	28F	– 2C	May	62F	17C	Sept.	66F	19C
	12	–11		41	5		44	7
Feb.	32F	0C	June	71F	22C	Oct.	55F	13C
	15	– 9		48	9		35	2
Mar.	42F	6C	July	80F	27C	Nov.	41F	5C
	23	– 5		53	12		24	– 4
Apr.	53F	12C	Aug.	78F	26C	Dec.	32F	0C
	33	1		53	12		17	– 8

SALT LAKE CITY, UT

Jan.	35F	2C	May	73F	23C	Sept.	78F	26C
	17	– 8		44	7		48	9
Feb.	41F	5C	June	82F	28C	Oct.	66F	19C
	24	– 4		51	11		39	4
Mar.	51F	11C	July	91F	33C	Nov.	48F	9C
	30	– 1		60	16		28	– 2
Apr.	62F	17C	Aug.	89F	32C	Dec.	39F	4C
	37	3		60	16		21	– 6

SHERIDAN, WY

Jan.	33F	– 1C	May	66F	19C	Sept.	71F	22C
	6	–14		39	4		41	5
Feb.	35F	2C	June	75F	24C	Oct.	60F	16C
	10	–12		48	9		30	– 1
Mar.	46F	8C	July	86F	30C	Nov.	46F	8C
	21	– 6		53	12		19	– 7
Apr.	55F	13C	Aug.	84F	29C	Dec.	35F	2C
	30	– 1		50	10		10	–12

THE GOLD GUIDE / SMART TRAVEL TIPS

1 Destination: The Rockies

BETWEEN A ROCK AND A HIGH PLACE

I CAUGHT MY FIRST TROUT AS A kid in Colorado in the summer of 1966. It was a fish so small that I doubt it would have cast a shadow large enough to scare a chipmunk. Still, it was, undeniably, a fish, and as such emblematic of a victory of sorts. This, after an excruciating, stomach-churning ride in the back of a jeep, over some old, rutted logging road not far from Aspen and after coughing up dust and passing out briefly from the altitude, somewhere above 10,000 feet. This also after cheating, at least according to real-fisherman standards: I caught the thing with a spoon and a spinning rig. To real fishermen—*fly* fishermen—that's about as honorable as hunting squirrels with a cannon. Nevertheless, there I was holding my first-ever fish, a squirmy glob of quicksilver pinkness, shimmering in the midday sun. A life's first! No fishing purist can rob me of the right and pleasure to remember that occasion fondly.

I can also recall now that once I'd glossed over the puniness of the fish to appreciate it with a sense of grand achievement, I lifted my head to the hills (hackneyed as *that* sounds), smelled what can properly be described as the cleanness of the air, and thought: The Rocky Mountains are a very cool and righteous place. It wasn't just any old thought, mind you; it was a thought so intense that I swear I thought it *physically,* with my whole body, as if buzzed by a mild electrical shock. Once a thought like that gets into your system, it roots itself forever.

If there are three geographical features an American ought to see as a rite of citizenship, they are the Atlantic Ocean, the Pacific Ocean, and the Rocky Mountains. But beyond the dull obligations of democratic duty, the Rockies impress in other simple and profound ways: simple, in that they are, simply, big and beautiful; profound, in that they invoke a primordial spirit of wilderness and timelessness. The Rockies can inspire an appreciation that escapes logic, that comes on when alpenglow is the last light of day or when new snow highlights each feathered ledge in a band of rock cliffs. It occurs when the wold bloom of tundral, high-alpine meadows exceeds any fair description of color, or when you're standing around, above 10,000 feet, with a stupid grin on your face and a dead fish in your hand. The sentiment is something close to faith.

It is also something beyond accurate representation. On relief maps, the two-billion-year-old Rockies are often drawn as a single string of mountains—forming blisters on the page—and defined primarily by the dotted line of the Continental Divide. The plains are over and the mountains begin, and that's that.

But that's *not* that. The Rockies (and here things can get fuzzy, confused by which mountain ranges geologists choose to consider part of the Rockies) cut a swath several hundred miles wide in places and constitute multiple ranges and spurs, each with slightly or markedly differing characteristics. The Colorado Rockies are the highest of the bunch, with the most peaks exceeding 14,000 feet, but ironically they might not seem so because the timberline (the point above which trees won't grow) is unusually high. In short, the Rockies aren't, as the maps might suggest, one big strip of interchangeable rock.

ALL OF THESE RANGES DO, however, share a similar history. Uplift (the pressure inflicted by the movements and swelling of ancient oceans through aeons of time) preyed upon weaknesses in the land mass (weaknesses known appropriately if unsympathetically as "faults"); the land squeezed thusly could go nowhere but *up.* Couple that phenomenon with volcanic activity and mountains were the result.

Thereafter came the sculpting effects of erosion, with water in various forms (ice, snow, rain, fog, and water falls) being the primary chisels. Over the long, long haul, the characteristic formations that we identify as elemental to mountain structure have taken shape: peaks, ridgelines, bowls, cirques, arêtes, scree slopes and so on. On lower slopes, depending on the quality and availability of soil as well as the harshness of weather, trees have grown: mainly cottonwoods and aspens (or "quakies," as the cowboys dubbed them because of the shimmering illusion created by their leaves in the sun and wind); higher up, Douglas fir, lodgepole pine, and Engelmann spruce.

ALTHOUGH THERE ARE THOSE rare events when the Earth shrugs and mountains heave with cataclysmic suddenness, the Rockies are essentially a stationary spectacle, or, as they appeared to settlers from the East in the 1800s, a stationary obstacle. One can only imagine the thoughts of the pioneers and railroaders on seeing the Rockies for the first time: A mix, presumably of awe and annoyance; inspired by the mountains' beauty yet flustered by the impending (and inevitable) difficulties in finding passage to the other side.

It is somewhat easier to tap the mindset of prospectors who, after word spread of the discovery of the Comstock lode in western Nevada in the 1850s, came to the Rockies with visions of vast wealth. I'm not sure whether the mountains imposed a ruggedness on the miners and railroad workers, the vanguard of settlement in the Rockies, or whether it was the other way around. Probably a bit of both. These were rowdy men in a rugged country, and I like their story: Civil War deserters, ex-cons, bushwhackers, and miners whose previous claims had come up empty in California, Nevada, or British Columbia. As Glenn Chesney Quiett put it in *They Built the West*, "It was a rough, dangerous, dirty, sweating, hard-working, hard-drinking, free-spending life."

It was not a life made any more comfortable by Native American tribes residing in the mountains—the Cheyenne, the Crow, the Blackfoot, and others—whose homelands had been invaded by these interlopers pick-axing the countryside. Confrontations were numerous; Quiett relates one story in which the Natives killed a man by lighting a bonfire on his chest, suggesting—quite obviously—that some Natives were going around in very ill humor in regards to the whole idea of the white man's settlement.

Mining, railway construction, lawbreaking, opportunism: The early settlement of the Rockies began taking shape. The route of the railway dictated which Rocky Mountain outposts would become major cities and which wouldn't; that Denver, Colorado, rather than Cheyenne, Wyoming, became the central metropolis of the eastern slope of the Rockies was due largely to politicking by Denver's business elite. It was due also to the paying of a hefty sum to the railroad for the right to have the rail route pass through town. Miners came, established towns, settled in (or some did, anyway), and left their mark and legacy. Indeed, towns that have become popular resorts in the latter half of the 20th century—Aspen, Breckenridge, and Telluride in Colorado and Park City in Utah, for example—have their roots in mining.

UNLIKE GEOLOGY IN ITS incomprehensible slowness, human activity in the Rockies has evolved and changed in a hurry. It has all transpired in little more than 100 years, which isn't even a hiccup's worth of geological time. As precious-metal mining has ebbed (due as much to a swoon in metal prices as a lack of ore) in the last few decades as a mainstay of the Rocky Mountain economy, a boom in tourism has more than filled the gap. Before the 1960s, visitors who spent time in the Rockies were likely to be bohemians, artists, die-hard sportsmen, and national-park visitors in Winnebagos and Airstreams; or passers-by broken down in transit—axle busted en route to California and the American Dream. Today the region hosts families and tourists of all means.

As much as any single event in the region, the creation of Vail (the ski resort 100 miles west of Denver) in 1964 issued an evangelical message to the world that tourism in the Rockies was for Everyman. In 1963, Vail was an empty valley; today it is a tourism machine generating more than $400 million a year in summer and winter business, but not including real-estate turnover, hardly small potatoes. No wonder other

Rockies resorts, following the Vail model in varying degrees, have sprung up since the mid-1960s to tap the mighty tourism dollar.

ANYONE WHO SPENDS ANY time in the Rockies is destined to be touched by the exquisite landscape supporting an intricately entwined network of ecosystems—and is subsequently destined to make judgements and establish values accordingly. I can remember, for example, discovering, on a south-facing slope in April, microscopic buds of wildflowers incubating under shards of warm shale. On north-facing slopes, the snow was still several feet deep. Something about that struck me: The land, severe as it is, takes care of itself. It regenerates all on its own. Things work. Far be it from me to butt in on a miracle like that, or try to improve upon it. Unfortunately, once you accept the premise that you are in the presence of nature efficiently and dispassionately going about its own business—a premise that invariably comes in one form or another to anyone who visits or lives in the Rockies—you tend then to proceed to the next obvious question: What to do about it? Here, things, turn troublesome.

In the last decade or so the Rocky Mountain states have become the political focus of land grabbers, tree huggers, civilization escapees, resort developers, ranchers, sportsmen, seasonal workers, the "Hollywood element." Each group has its own sense of righteous propriety and feelings about how the land should be best managed. For whatever reason—and a sheer, alpine beauty comes immediately to mind—almost everyone who comes to the Rockies for any length of time develops an instinctive (if imagined) sense of aboriginal belonging. It's funny: You hear people who have spent barely a year or two of their lives in the Rockies talk wistfully of "the way things used to be," as if their families had lived there for generations. Such reminiscence, of course, implies an attitude about the way things *ought* to be. The upshot is a messy collision of territorial imperatives: Each group is sure it *knows* what is best for the land, and how to defend it against the greed, shortsightedness, or hare-brained thoughtlessness of others. This can lead to such wacky scenarios as ardent wildlife preservationists stalking hunters, who in turn are stalking animals, the idea being that when the hunter gets lined up for a shot, the preservationists make a holy racket, alerting the animal and averting the kill. It is environmental politics right out of *Caddyshack*.

THE ISSUES ARE IMPOSSIBLY, hopelessly complex. In simplest terms the question is: What's the proper formula in balancing the interest of people, the integrity of the land and its resources, and the needs of wildlife? It is a question inevitably muddled in morality, pragmatism, science, self-interest, and the indisputable fact that nobody really knows for sure. As yet, there is no single, Grand Unifying Theory. The result, in part, has been a balkanized checkerboard: private land, wilderness areas, national parks, national forests, national monuments, state parks, state forests, wildlife preserves, Native American reservations. Tread carefully. The rules change from one land type to the next, and the borders aren't always obvious (except, mysteriously, to wild animals, who seem to know more accurately than surveyors where national-park borders are, within which hunting is prohibited). For example, hunting and campfires are legal in national forests but not in national parks; some private landowners are good sports about rights of way, some charge fees, some will have you arrested for just contemplating trespassing. And so on.

When 323,291 acres of forestland burned in Yellowstone in the summer of '88, fire control was a bitter issue: Would it be better to allow a fire to burn its natural course, even if it might threaten wildlife and human settlements? Fire, the argument goes, is part of a forest's natural way of replenishing itself. Or would it be more correct to fight the fire with every resource at one's disposal, snuffing it out as quickly as possible?

Are mountain resorts scars upon the landscape, as some environmentalists might suggest, or nodes of economic sustenance producing, in most respects, less environmental hazard and impact than mining, ranching, or lumbering? Do visitors to the resorts simply overpopulate an environmentally sensitive region? Or, inspired by the beauty of the land, does their visiting heighten their own environmental sensitivity? And do they then pass that new sensitivity on to others?

The ultimate question is: Who knows?

Fortunately, the Rockies are still big country. There is a lot of room for people to do a lot of shouting, hand-wringing, and placard-waving without upsetting, in any measurable way, the balance of the universe. For all the shouting, for all the resort development that boomed in the '80s; for all the ranchers fencing in land and upsetting animal migratory patterns; for all the Hollywooders moving to Aspen or Livingston, Montana, and wrecking the neighborhood, as some residents imply; for all the environmentalist militating against growth—for all of that, and above and beyond all of that, the Rockies remain relatively uncongested, undeveloped country, where the air above 12,000 feet is still clean.

The population density of Colorado, by far the most populous of the Rocky Mountain states, is about 32 people per square mile. Compare that, for example, with 190 people per square mile in California or more than 1,000 per square mile (gasp!) in New Jersey. There are more people living in the borough of Brooklyn than in the states of Idaho, Montana, and Wyoming combined.

Wandering around in these open spaces, one comes occasionally across the relics of human failure, most likely old mining encampments, now rotting and rusting on their slow way toward vanishing into total decay. They are small reminders that however abusive or misguided people are and have been in their use of this land, the land has the patience to heal itself. Patience that people, with lifespans of infinitesimal shortness in geologic terms, can't fathom. If the mountains had a voice in all the land-management yakkety-yak, they would be saying something like: "We can wait. We don't care."

And in the shorter term, the Rockies have one other ace in the hold in withstanding the incursion of man: their own magisterial presence, their ruggedness. The Rockies were the last part of the country to be "settled" and may be the only part of the country that will never be broadly developed. One doesn't build cities on 40-degree slopes raked by rockslides and avalanches. The land is too severe and the growing seasons too short to sustain viable commercial cultivation (except, to some degree, timber crops). In other words, the high-mountain wilderness is a great place to visit but you wouldn't want to live there. And a great place, too, in the summer sun, when the thin air steals breath and the dust settles on old roads, to catch a fish.

WHAT'S WHERE

Colorado

With the Rocky Mountains as its enormous spine, and deep canyons carved by its three main rivers, Colorado is a state of sharp contrasts. The Colorado Rockies offer every possible skiing experience, from the glitter and gossip of Aspen to the skiing purism of Crested Butte.

Denver, the Mile High City, mixes its cow town aura with a downtown arts district and bustling business centers. To the southwest is the Black Canyon, whose walls narrow so severely that little sunlight can reach the bottom, as well as the mysterious cliff dwellings of the Anasazi people. Near Colorado Springs stands Pikes Peak, the state's most indelible landmark; Katherine Lee Bates wrote "America the Beautiful" while gazing out from its summit.

Idaho

In Idaho, state creed dictates that there is no admittance unless you do something outdoors. Those same outdoors, however, might not seem too hospitable at first. Southern Idaho's flat plains are broken by the Lava Hot Springs and the great gash of the Snake River canyon; in contrast to these stark natural wonders is the plush Sun Valley ski resort. Northern Idaho has its own extremes in Hells Canyon, a cleft even deeper (though narrower) than the Grand Canyon, and the Salmon River, the longest wild river left in the lower 48 states. However, these severe superlatives add up to an outstanding welcome for sports enthusiasts of all stripes. With its impressive terrain, Idaho provides for everything from fly-fishing to white-water river rafting to Alpine skiing.

Montana

The moniker Big Sky Country, as Montana is often called, only tells half the story; as the fourth-largest state, Montana has the land to match. Over 30% of this land is publicly owned, making it a gold mine of national forests and parks. (Literal gold mines exist as well—in the late 1800s, gold strikes led to a flood of settlers, which in turn spurred conflict with the indigenous Native Americans. The famous Battle of Little Bighorn, otherwise known as Custer's Last Stand, was fought here.) The best trout fishing in the country is found at the Yellowstone, Missouri, Madison, Beaverhead, Gallatin, and Bighorn rivers. Montana's mountainous western half bears the "Crown of the Continent," Glacier National Park. The last of the glaciers scraped across the landscape, leaving behind impressive lakes, waterfalls, and knife-edge ridges.

Utah

Few states can match Utah's sheer breadth of topography. The southern end is covered with gargantuan sculpted rock formations, such as those found at Arches, Zion, and Bryce Canyon national parks. The Wasatch Mountains stretch from the Idaho border to central Utah, peppered with excellent ski resorts such as Alta, Park City, and Snowbird. Most of Utah's major cities line the base of these mountains, including Salt Lake City, the capital. Founded by the Church of Jesus Christ of Latter-Day Saints as a Mormon sanctuary, Salt Lake maintains extremely strong religious ties. Moab, situated along the Colorado River, offers another kind of religion: mountain biking. The slick sandstone terrain is a mountain biker's dream, topped by spectacular views of the Canyonlands National Park.

Wyoming

For most people, Wyoming conjures up images of its northwestern area, dominated by Yellowstone National Park and the Grand Teton mountains. Yellowstone is recovering well from the fires of 1988, and visitors can examine first-hand the ecological renewal process. Not to be entirely out-

done by its neighbor, the Teton range harbors one of America's most challenging ski resorts, Jackson Hole. In the southeastern corner of the state, cities once, Laramie and Cheyenne still possess a strong frontier flavor . . . even if they're no longer exactly "hell on wheels."

PLEASURES & PASTIMES

Climbing and Mountaineering

Climbing in its various forms—mountaineering, rock climbing, ice climbing—is a year-round sport in the Rockies. Many high peaks, such as Long's Peak in Colorado, are an easy ascent, but there are also dozens of highly technical climbs, such as the spires of Redrock Park and Garden of the Gods in Colorado, and the jagged Grand Teton in Wyoming. In many areas, especially in the national parks, climbing permits are required, primarily for safety reasons. Rangers want to be sure that you have the experience and skill necessary to undertake the challenge at hand. Thus, it probably goes without saying that no one should attempt technical rock or mountain climbing without proper skills and equipment.

Cycling

Mountain biking, as a sport and cultural phenomenon, has a huge following in the Rockies and is more popular in the region than touring on paved roads. Moab, Utah, has become the mountain biker's mecca, with its fortuitous spreads of asphalt-smooth sandstone, or slickrock, formations. (The Slickrock Trail has both a practice and a main loop.) For an expedition-length ride, the 100-mile White Rim Trail near Moab offers spectacular views of Canyonlands National Park. In Colorado, Crested Butte vies with Moab as the mountain biking center of the Rockies; the trip through the demanding Pearl Pass is supposedly how the biking craze originated. As for road cycling, the San Juan Mountains loop is as beautiful a ride as there is in the country. Keep in mind that elevations in the Rockies are high, and exact their physical toll in an aerobic sport such as cycling. Not only should you be physically fit, but you should be prepared to settle for riding shorter distances than you might be capable of handling at lower elevations. Valley roads tend to be clear of snow by mid- to late-April; roads and trails at higher elevations may not be clear until several months later and may be snow-covered again by early October.

Dining

In 1944, a Denver drive-in owner named Louis Ballast grilled a slice of cheese on top of a hamburger and became famous for patenting his invention, the cheeseburger. It has been suggested that Rocky Mountain cuisine consists of the three Bs: beef, buffalo, and burritos. While these items certainly will appear on menus throughout the region, restaurant chefs rise to the challenge and head to market to round out the offerings with seasonal and local specialties.

In addition to mouthwatering steak and tender lamb, this is prime hunting and fishing territory, so antelope, elk, venison, and grouse are no strangers to the Rockies palate. Rainbow trout, salmon, and bass pulled from someone's favorite (and maybe secret) fishing spot find their way onto almost every menu. Colorado's Rocky Mountain oysters (fried bull testicles) are famous—some would say infamous—for their size and taste.

On the flora side of things, Colorado's sugar-sweet Rocky Ford cantaloupe has passionate admirers. Utah's raspberries and cherries make incredible pies, and huckleberries from Montana or Idaho are used in everything from muffins to ice cream. Apples, peaches, and pears from roadside stands are deliciously tree-ripened. And don't forget about potatoes—natives will tell you that if it's not from Idaho, it's just a spud.

While every state has its share of excellent regional specialties, ethnic foods are finally breaking into the three Bs circle; the posher ski resorts in particular come equipped with a wide range of international cuisine. With such high-end resort towns as Vail and Aspen, Colorado's dining scene is quite sophisticated. Idaho and Wyoming reputedly have the best steaks; no ties are needed as almost all establishments are casual—this holds true for Montana as well. Utah's gourmet restaurants are centered in Salt Lake City and Park City, and the once notoriously strict drinking laws have been significantly altered, so that having a glass of wine with dinner is now common practice.

As for regional beverages, some parts of the Rockies possess excellent vineyards, and local wines are often featured in the best restaurants. Treasure Valley in Idaho is home to the award-winning Ste-Chapelle and Weston wineries, and the industry is one of the fastest-growing in Colorado. Beer is also popular, and microbreweries are enjoying increasing recognition throughout the area. Often located in or connected with a local pub, some of these breweries produce only enough specialty beers (called microbrews) for their own establishments. Colorado has more microbreweries than any other state, and some of their brews, such as Elk, Venison, and Trout, are available from regular beer outlets.

Dude Ranches

Dude ranches fall roughly into two categories: working ranches and guest ranches. Working ranches, in which guests participate in such activities as round-ups and cattle movements, sometimes require horsemanship experience. Guest ranches, with a wide range of activities in addition to horseback riding, rarely do. The slate of possible activities can vary widely from ranch to ranch. At most establishments, guests will be given some taste of the working-ranch experience with demonstrations of rodeo skills and the like. Fishing tends to be given second priority, and after that, almost anything goes. At a typical dude ranch, guests stay in log cabins and are served meals family-style in a lodge or ranch house. Colorado and Wyoming have several ranches on both ends of the spectrum.

Fishing

Trout, whether they be cutthroat, brown, rainbow, Mackinaw, brook, or lake, are the prime game fish in the Rockies. This isn't exactly trophy-fish country, but what they lack in size they make up in volume, especially in stocked waters. Southwestern Montana, the setting of Norman Maclean's fishing-permeated book *A River Runs Through It* and the subsequent film, is teeming with fishing holes along the Madison, Gallatin, and Yellowstone rivers. Provo Canyon in Utah is also an excellent, if overhyped, fishing spot, and the Snake River in Wyoming has its own unique cutthroat trout strain. It is possible to fish year-round in fast-moving streams that don't freeze over; however, summer is by far the most popular fishing season. Fishing licenses, ranging in term from daily to annual, are required in each state, and are available in many convenience stores and sporting-goods shops. Local tackle shops are also a good place to feel out a region's most effective lures.

Hiking

There are literally thousands of miles of hiking trails in the Rockies. The national parks have particularly well-marked and well-maintained trails, and admittance to all trails are free of charge. In fact, hiking is sometimes the only way to get in close proximity to certain highlights on protected land; for example, the famed Mesa Arch rock formation in Canyonlands National Park, Utah can be reached only on foot. Hiking in the south is usually best in spring, when water is plentiful and before the heat of summer sets in. Primarily for safety reasons, overnight hikers are usually expected to register with park or forest rangers. Also keep in mind that run-ins with bears have become increasingly common, especially in northern regions.

Horsepack Trips

Horsepack trips are a great way to visit the Rockies' backcountry, since horses can travel distances and carry supplies that would be impossible for hikers. Montana's Bob Marshall Wilderness is the perfect example; as the largest stretch of roadless wilderness in an already spacious state, a horsepacking trip is almost necessary to absorb the huge expanses. While horsemanship isn't required for most trips, it is helpful, and even an experienced rider can expect to be a little saddlesore for the first few days. June through August is the peak period for horsepacking trips; before signing up with an outfitter, inquire about the skills and experience they expect.

National Parks

Together, the Rockies states have a phenomenal amount of national park land (not to mention the national monuments, national forests, state parks, etc.) National parks are open to the public 365 days a year, and offer a tantalizing range of visitor facilities, including campgrounds, hiking trails, picnic areas, and more. Most national parks charge an entrance fee, which varies according to the kind of entrance vehicle. For more information on any of these, contact the state tourism offices or parks departments (*see* Visitor Info *in* Important Contacts A to Z *in* the Gold Guide.)

COLORADO➤ Rocky Mountain National Park is home to 355 miles of hiking trails and sweeping vistas of high-country lakes, meadows, pine forests, alpine tundra, and snow-dusted peaks dotted with small glaciers. The 265,000-acre park attracts over 2 million visitors annually. Trees grow at right angles, whipped into shape by high winds, and there are minuscule tundra versions of familiar wildflowers. Long's Peak, the highest point in the park, is a surprisingly easy hike.

MONTANA➤ Glacier National Park is predominated by the Continental Divide, where pure mountain streams form the headwaters of the Columbia and Missouri rivers. Glaciers, pine forests, craggy mountaintops, and lush green meadows can all be seen from the curvy Going-to-the-Sun Road, which provides dizzying views of the park's 1,600 square miles. The Crown of the Continent is one of the last grizzly bear territories; the park is also home to mountain goats, bighorn sheep, gray wolves, and over 1,000 species of flowers.

UTAH➤ Arches National Park preserves a 73,378-acre fantasy landscape of red rock arches. Over the centuries, wind and water eroded the rock into 1,500 freestanding arches, the largest collection of such formations in the world. A paved road winds through most of the major sites, but some, such as Devil's Garden and Delicate Arch (depicted on the Utah license plate), are accessible only by hiking trails. The arches are especially striking at sunset, when their color deepens to a fiercely burning red. Another beneficiary of sunset's colorful effects is Bryce Canyon National Park. Actually a series of natural amphitheaters, Bryce is famed for the pink and cream colored spires that reflect the sun's glow. Queen's Garden is eerily peopled with the "chess-men" formations, so called because the spires resemble human profiles. Ebenezer Bryce, the Mormon settler for whom the park is named, is said to have exclaimed that the area was "a hell of a place to lose a cow!" Canyonlands National Park offers views down to the white-water rapids of the Green and Colorado rivers, as well as red rock pinnacles, cliffs, and spires. This park is a particular favorite of adventure-sports enthusiasts, since much of the park can be explored only by foot, mountain bike, or four-wheel drive. In Capitol Reef National Park, a striated reeflike wall juts up a thousand feet over ground level, with domelike features reminiscent of the U.S. Capitol building. Visitors can pick fruit at the park's large orchards, drive along the base of the "reef," or hike down the canyons to see the 1,000-year-old Fremont Petroglyphs. Zion National Park, one of the nation's oldest national parks, is famous for its sheer, 2,500-foot-high sandstone walls and its complex desert ecology. The 147,000-acre park includes Zion Canyon and the Gateway to the Narrows, a squeak-through passageway carved by the Virgin River.

WYOMING➤ In the northwestern part of the state, just below Yellowstone National Park, is the buxom mountain range of Grand Teton National Park. A handful of glacier-scooped lakes, including Jackson and Jenny lakes, offer ample fishing, canoeing, and even windsurfing possibilities. The majority of visitors, however, are pulled toward Yellowstone National Park, which has two entrances in Wyoming. There are 370 miles of public roads within the park, providing (in theory) access to the park's exceptional sights—the tradeoffs are the crawling traffic during tourist season and the fraying road condition. Still, the park cannot fail to impress. The Grand Canyon of the Yellowstone has two towering waterfalls; the mercurial Norris Geyser Basin changes every year, as new steam vents erupt and older ones fizzle out. With over 10,000 geysers, hot springs, fumaroles, and mud pots, the park is the world's largest thermal area. The stunted landscape surrounding a hydrothermal point can seem almost otherworldly, especially in winter when the skeletons of trees scorched by the heat glitter with icicles. The wealth of animal life is equally awesome—spotting trumpeter swans, grazing bison or herds of elk is a wonderfully common occurrence.

Shopping

The Rocky Mountain region combines a frontier reverence for nature and the country's past with a fascination for ski resort glitz and a modern love for megamalls and discount outlet shopping center. Boutiques, galleries, and malls are either right in or nearby the many resort towns and cities throughout all five states covered in this book. Colorado sales tax is 3% on average; Idaho, 5%; Montana, 4% on accommodations only; Utah, 6.25%; and Wyoming, between 5% and 6%.

CRAFTS➤ Remarkable crafts—particularly Native American work—can be bought throughout this part of the country. In Denver, Colorado, the LoDo district is a good place to track down impressive weavings, pottery, jewelry, kachinas, and painting. Southwestern Colorado is generally rumored to be the best place to find both Western and Native American arts and crafts, especially basketry, weaving, and beadwork adapted from Native American methods. In particular, the Toh-Atin Gallery in Durango has a mind-boggling selection in both quantity and quality. As for more esoteric choices, in Coeur d'Alene, Idaho, you can select a custom-made tepee or yurt, while in Missoula, Montana, there is the rare purveyor of indoor trout streams. High-quality Western gear such as cowboy hats and saddles can also be found in Montana. Quite a few worthwhile crafts shops are tucked away in southeastern Utah as well, including Naatsilid Pottery, where customers can watch the artisans create Navajo-influenced pottery. Wyoming is admittedly not known for its shopping options, but King's Ropes and Saddlery in Sheridan is where real cowboys come from all over the world for everything a rancher could wish for.

ANTIQUES➤ In downtown Denver, Colorado, South Broadway is the main drag as far as antiques are concerned; Western and Native American collectibles are also scattered all over the southwestern part of the state. Idaho is an antiquer's dream, as entire towns can fit the bill; most small towns are rife with old-time street signs, utensils, and other Western goods. In Ogden, Utah, 25th Street (the town's version of a red-light district in the 1870s), is now a chichi shopping district with its fair share of antiques stores.

Skiing

Skiing has enormous clout in the Rockies; at last count, there were over 60 ski areas in the region, each with at least a 1,000-foot vertical rise. Downhill skiing is the most popular activity by a large margin, although cross-country skiing and snowboarding have loyal followings. In recent years, resorts have offered an ever-increasing range of special-interest programs, such as classes for women skiers, skiers with disabilities, or recreational racing. Rockies resorts may open their lifts as early as October and close as late as June; however, the ski season usually runs from December until early April. Christmas through New Year's Day and the month of March tend to be the busiest periods for most ski areas. The slower months of January and February often yield good package deals, as do the early and late ends of the season. Cross-country skiing generally has a shorter season due to lack of snow, but as avalanche risks lessen in April, backcountry skiers may take advantage of the sun-baked snow. Overall, ski resorts are each area's best source of information on everything from lodging to snow conditions.

LIFT TICKETS➤ Lift ticket prices are directly linked to each resort's celebrity profile. In other words, the more popular the resort, the higher the lift ticket's price. Single-day, adult, holiday-weekend passes cost the most, but better bargains can be had through off-site purchase locations, multiple-day passes, stretch weekends (a weekend including a Monday or a Friday), season-long tickets, or other options. Occasionally, lift tickets are included in the price of lodging.

LODGING➤ Unless you plan a day trip, lodging is one of the top considerations. While some of the establishments listed in this book are more suitable for overnight stays, most offer several kinds of accommodations—lodges, condominiums, hotels, motels, inns, bed-and-breakfasts—close to or a short distance away from the action. For longer vacations, re-

quest the resort area's accommodations brochure, since a package rate may offer the best deal. Combinations can include rooms, meals, lift tickets, ski lessons, rental equipment, parties, or other features.

EQUIPMENT RENTAL➤ Rental equipment is available at all ski areas and at ski shops around resorts or in other cities. Shop personnel can advise customers on the appropriate equipment according to their size and level of ability; they should also be able to answer questions on how to properly use the gear. Experienced skiers should ask to test the merchandise when choosing premium equipment.

A one-day outing at a nearby ski area is often the best way for first-time skiers to ease their way into the sport. On arrival, go to the base lodge and ask about special beginners' programs. Packages normally include basic equipment (rental skis with bindings, ski boots, ski poles), a lesson lasting at least an hour, and a lift ticket that may be valid only on beginners' slopes.

TRAIL RATING➤ Ski areas have designed fairly accurate standards for rating and marking trails and slopes. Trails are rated Easier (green circle), Intermediate (blue square), Advanced (black diamond), and Expert (double black diamond). Remember that trail difficulty is measured in relation to the other trails *at the same ski area*, not in comparison to trails in other areas; for example, a black-diamond trail in one area may be labeled as a blue square in another area close by. These terrain ratings are most useful in establishing the ratio of trail difficulty at each particular ski area, instead of comparing two or more.

LESSONS➤ In the United States, the Professional Ski Instructors of America (PSIA) has devised a progressive teaching system that is used with relatively little variation at most ski schools. This allows skiers to take lessons at schools at different ski areas and still improve. Classes range in length from 1½ hours to all-day workshops. Many ski areas are now offering specialized programs such as powder skiing courses, mogul clinics, or lessons for women skiers. Of note are the children's ski schools at Vail and Beaver Creek, Colorado; the skiers with disabilities program at Winter Park, Colorado; the "extreme skiing" lessons offered by Doug Coombs (two-time winner of the World Extreme Skiing Championships) at Jackson, Wyoming; and the Mountain Experience Program for challenging, off-trail skiing at Snowbird, Utah.

Most ski schools have adopted the PSIA teaching approach for children, and many also incorporate SKIwee, another standardized teaching technique that includes progress certificates. Classes for children are arranged by ability and age group; often the ski instructor chaperons a meal during the teaching session.

CHILD CARE➤ Day care can be found at almost all ski areas, often accepting children under a year old. Normally, parents must supply formula and diapers for infants, and some young children may want to bring their favorite toys. "Preski" programs (more play than serious instruction) may be offered for children at age 3. Reservations are always a good idea.

Water Sports

Spring, when rivers are flushed with snowmelt, is the best time of year for white-water enthusiasts. April through June is the best time to run rivers in the south; June through August are the principal months on rivers farther north. In general (except on dammed rivers), the flow of water lessens as the season wears on. River runners seeking the maximum whitewater thrills should come early; families and those who want a gentler float should come later.

To prevent overcrowding, almost all major rivers require rafters or kayakers to have permits. For individuals planning their own trips, permits on popular rivers (such as the Middle Fork of the Salmon River or the Selway River in Idaho) can be extremely hard to come by. Permits tend to be awarded first to reputable outfitters, so signing up with an appropriate company is a good way to insure access to the river of your choice.

FODOR'S CHOICE

Views

★ **First glimpse of Vail's sweeping Back Bowls, CO.** The Valhalla of skiers, the Back Bowls seem like an endless expanse of beckoning snow. In summer, the Bowls' enormous cradle works the same magic for mountain-bike fanatics.

★ **The cliff dwellings of the Anasazi people at Mesa Verde, CO.** These haunting ruins were built into the cliff walls over 600 years ago, then mysteriously abandoned.

★ **The black basalt columns in Hells Canyon, ID.** Deeper than the Grand Canyon, and much narrower, Hells Canyon is flanked with rock formations resembling giant black pencils. By floating or rafting through the chasm, you can also see Native American pictographs along the smooth canyon walls.

★ **The shimmering northern lights in MT.** Take your pick of open spaces from which to see this exquisite phenomenon—sometimes delicately tinting the night sky, other times blazing until dawn.

★ **The views from Going-to-the-Sun Highway in Glacier National Park, MT.** This serpentine, 52-mile-long highway has some of the best views in the world. It crests at Logan Pass, where you can take a short hike to the crystalline Hidden Lake.

★ **Snow clinging to the rock formations in Bryce Canyon National Park, UT.** The Martian-like landscape of the ruddy pinnacles and spires of Bryce Canyon is incredibly beautiful when dusted with snow. The bristlecone pines along the amphitheaters' rims heighten the colors' effect.

★ **The view over the Island-in-the-Sky district in Canyonlands National Park from Dead Horse Point State Park, UT.** Where the Green and Colorado rivers come together, towering cliffs stab skyward.

★ **Jackson as seen from the top of Signal Mountain, WY.** A matchless view of the whole of Jackson can be seen from the summit of Signal Mountain.

★ **Erupting geysers and hissing steam vents at the Norris Geyser Basin in Yellowstone National Park, WY.** Norris is the oldest and hottest of Yellowstone's geyser basins; every year its roster of live hydrothermal features changes.

Ski Resorts

★ **Alta, UT for its chance to explore.** Sharing Snowbird's exceptional snowfall, Alta's layout may seem confusing at first. However, Alta is made for exploration, and new discoveries can be made year after year.

★ **Crested Butte, CO, for both its rolling intermediate slopes and its Extreme Limits runs.** The main trail network has easy, maneuverable terrain, while Extreme Limits has several hundred acres of steep bowls, tough chutes, and tight tree skiing.

★ **Jackson Hole, WY for its endless variations.** Jackson has literally thousands of skiable routes from top to bottom—all it takes is a little imagination. In addition, its stunning backcountry terrain is some of the most diverse in the U.S.

★ **Snowbird, UT for its expert runs.** The open bowls are already challenging, but even these pale in comparison to chutes such as Upper Cirque. What makes this bearable is the legendary quantity of powder.

★ **Sun Valley, ID for mogul skiing.** The Hollywood glamour of the 1930s and 40s might have faded somewhat, but Sun Valley still has the cream of the mogul crop.

★ **Vail, CO for its back bowls and resort amenities.** On powder days, the back bowls can offer intermediate and expert skiers a small slice of heaven. The resort village is crafted to anticipate every need (or desire).

Lodging

★ **The Broadmoor, Colorado Springs, CO.** One of America's truly great hotels, the Broadmoor almost seems like a village unto its own. Besides its luxurious accommodations, it commands a private lake, three world-class championship golf courses, eight restaurants, and Colorado's premier indoor ice-skating arena. $$$$

★ **Cliff Lodge, Snowbird, UT.** To some, this distinctive hotel might seem to blend in—and that's precisely part of its attraction. Designed to echo the surrounding scenery, the Cliff Lodge has beautiful views from every angle, and tops it off with the indulgent Cliff Spa. $$$$

★ **Hotel Jerome, Aspen, CO.** Built in 1889, the Hotel Jerome is a deep draft of Victorian grandeur. If you tend toward the lavish, the rose damask curtains of the public rooms alone should satisfy. $$$$

★ **Brown Palace, Denver, CO.** This is the grande dame of Colorado hotels. Scrupulous attention is paid to the details, and the formal restaurant, the Palace Arms, has won several awards. $$$

★ **Clark House on Hayden Lake, Coeur d'Alene, ID.** This hotel was originally a millionaire's eccentric extravagance; after near-demolition, the building was transformed into a giant, sumptuous wedding cake of a place. $$$

★ **Wort Hotel, Jackson, WY.** Locals congregate around the Silver Dollar Bar, named for the 1,921, 1921 silver dollars embedded in the S-shaped bar counter. The hotel seems to have been around as long as the Tetons, but it feels fresh inside. $$$

★ **The Cary House, Hagerman, ID.** Listed on the National Register of Historic Places, this property's turn-of-the-century feel is impeccably blended with modern comforts. $$

★ **Goldsmith's Bed and Breakfast, Missoula, MT.** Just a footbridge away from the University of Montana campus, this B&B was formerly the university president's home. Needless to say, everything is most correct, and right next door is Goldsmith's Premium Ice Cream café. $$

★ **Grist Mill Inn, Monticello, UT.** Housed in a 1933 flour mill, this B&B has six superb suites in the main building, and additional guest rooms in the antique caboose out back. $$

★ **Grand Hotel, Big Timber, MT.** The accommodations here are reminiscent of what you might find over the Longbranch Saloon in *Gunsmoke.* $–$$

★ **Lake Yellowstone Hotel, Yellowstone National Park, WY.** This property is one of the oldest and most elegant park resorts. Old-style luxury tourism in the "wilderness" is recalled by the afternoon chamber music in the lobby. $–$$

★ **Williams House, Breckenridge, CO.** This B&B, a former miner's cottage, is unabashedly romantic. The innkeepers are unfailingly generous with their homemade muffins and secret stashes. $

Places to Eat

★ **Glitretind, Park City, UT.** This restaurant defines elegant ski-resort dining. Offering seafood, beef, and poultry dishes, Glitretind is worth breaking open the piggy bank for. $$$$

★ **Renaissance, Aspen, CO.** The owner-chef of this restaurant calls his cuisine "the alchemy of food," and judging from what comes out of the kitchen, he's probably right. The decor is an abstract imitation of the interior of a sultan's tent. $$$$

★ **Syzygy, Aspen, CO.** Cuisine, service, and an elegant ambience align perfectly, and the chef somehow manages to harmonize French, Oriental, and Southwestern influences to create a fabulous alternative to the standard meat-and-potatoes. $$$$

★ **Aerie, Snowbird, UT.** In what could be Utah's most scenic dining location, Aerie offers a wide range of excellent dishes, an even wider range of wines, and a sushi bar. $$$

★ **Tree Room, Sundance, UT.** For Utah natives, Sundance is as much the home of the Tree Room as it is the home of the film festival. The food changes seasonally, and the presentation, sometimes using fresh flowers, is especially memorable. $$$

★ **Gorky Park, Steamboat Springs, CO.** Haute czarist dishes are served at this opulent establishment, along with a knockout list of 30 homemade vodkas. $$–$$$

★ **Peter Schott's, Boise, ID.** A local celebrity with his own short cooking show, chef-owner Schott runs one of the best restaurants in the state. $$–$$$

★ **The Bunnery, Jackson, WY.** The breakfasts here are irresistible, and their "O.S.M." (oats, sunflower, millet) bread is in demand all over the country. $$

★ **Café Jacques, Laramie, WY.** Although the interior is inspired by French cafés, including a bar counter made of wine corks, creative American cuisine dominates the menu. $$

★ **John Bozeman's Bistro, Bozeman, MT.** Tucked into a National Historic Record building, Bozeman's Bistro has everything from Cajun dishes to creative sandwiches. $–$$

★ **Buffalo Café, Twin Falls, ID.** This tiny café produces an enormous amount of food for breakfast, including the dauntingly sized but delicious Buffalo Chip. $

★ **Windbag Saloon & Grill, Helena, MT.** The cherry wood interior of this family-style restaurant gives it a comfortable atmosphere that goes over well with the burgers and sandwiches. $

FESTIVALS AND SEASONAL EVENTS

DECEMBER➤ Christmas celebrations blanket most Rockies' towns. Denver (CO) hosts the **World's Largest Christmas Lighting Display** with 20,000 floodlights washing the civic buildings in reds, greens, blues, and yellows. In Idaho, Sandpoint becomes "Santapoint" for the **Hometown Christmas.** In Montana, there's an **Old-Time Christmas Exhibit** in Missoula's historic fort, and Bozeman's **Christmas Stroll** features sleigh rides, carolers, hot-chocolate stands, holiday lights, and late shopping hours. Salt Lake City's (UT) show is the **Christmas Lights** ceremony at Temple Square. For the holidays, many ski areas throughout the Rockies mount **torchlight parades,** with large groups of torch-bearing ski instructors tracing patterns down the mountainside.

JANUARY➤ The big events of the month are Denver's two-week **National Western Stock Show and Rodeo,** the world's largest livestock show, and the annual **Sundance Film Festival** in Park City, Utah, which lures film aficionados as well as industry executives to seminars, workshops, and previews of films from around the world. Meanwhile, throughout the Rockies, ski competitions such as the **Steamboat Springs Annual**

Northwest Bank Cowboy Downhill and Breckenridge's **Ullr Fest and World Cup Freestyle,** both in Colorado, keep ski areas lively with races, torchlight skiing, and other events. Other snow towns stage winter carnivals such as the huge one in **McCall, Idaho,** where you'll find world-class ice sculptures along with the usual parades, fireworks, and on-the-snow competitions. Wyoming's **Wild West Winter Carnival** at Boyston State Park has dog races, a demolition derby, softball, and golf, all on ice, as well as snowmobile races, and a "snowdeo."

FEBRUARY➤ In Colorado, the **Ice Fishing Contest** in Walden consists of fishing on four lakes for the nine largest fish. In Idaho, the **Lionel Hampton Jazz Festival** in Moscow attracts some of the world's top jazz musicians. Montana's **Race to the Sky** in Helena is a 500-mile dog-sled race along the Continental Divide; it's the longest such race in the lower 48 states. There is also a 250-mile race for public viewing at check-in sites. The **Western Montana Wine Festival** in Missoula features tastings of regional and West Coast wineries, accompanied by superb food.

MARCH➤ Springfield, Colorado, holds one of its

two annual **Equinox Festivals** as the sun turns nearby Crack Cave into a sort of Stonehedge, highlighting the ancient Ogam calendar and writings of possible Celtic origin, dating from around 471. Pocatello, Idaho, is the site of the **Dodge National Circuit Finals Rodeo,** which draws the top two cowboys from each for 12 national circuits. **St. Patrick's Day** events occur in Butte and Lewiston, Idaho, and in Missoula, Montana; the latter's parade is one of the state's largest. And collectors from around the world attend the **C.M. Russell Auction of Original Art,** held in Great Falls, Montana.

APRIL➤ On Easter, look around for nondenominational **Easter sunrise services;** Park City, Utah, mounts a big annual **Easter Egg Hunt.** Then there are fun events such as **Kit Carson's Annual Mountain Man Rendezvous** in Kit Carson, Colorado, and the city-wide **Dogwood Festival** in Lewiston, Idaho. The annual **International Wildlife Film Festival** in Missoula, Montana, is one of two wildlife film festivals in the world.

MAY➤ Look into the **Fort Vasquez Fur Trappers Rendezvous** in Platteville, Colorado, where fur-trading days return with demonstrations, contests, costumes, games, and Native American crafts and dances. Sandpoint, Idaho, celebrates summer's beginning with a **Waterfest,** including a sand-sculpture contest, a regatta, and waterskiing events. **Buzzard Day** celebrates spring and the return of the turkey vultures to Makoshika State Park in Glendive, Montana. In Montana's cherry-growing country, Polson mounts a **Cherry Blossom Festival** and Big Fork does a laid-back **Cherry-Blossom Week-end**, with a farmers' market, cherry desserts, and various competitions. In Miles City, Montana, rodeo stock for the upcoming season is auctioned off at the **Bucking Horse Sale.** The huge **Flaming Gorge Fishing Derby** in Rock Springs, Wyoming, draws 350 teams of anglers.

SUMMER

JUNE➤ The **Silly Home-built River Raft Race,** held in Las Animas, Colorado, keeps spectators guessing which improbable floating contraptions will reach the finish line and which will explore the bottom of the Arkansas River. Meanwhile, the season of music festivals and cultural events gets into swing in Colorado with Telluride's weekend-long **Bluegrass Festival** and Boulder's **Colorado Shakespeare Festival,** one of the top three in the country; in Idaho, with Wieser's **National Old-Time Fiddlers Contest,** which draws the nation's best to compete; and in Montana with Helena's **Montana Tradi-**

tional Jazz Festival. The **Idaho Women's Fitness Celebration** includes the nation's premier cycling race for women. The **International Barbed Wire Show** in Casper, Montana, features contemporary and antique wire from all over the world. Also in Montana is the **Badlands Indian Celebration** at the Fort Peck Indian Reservation in Brockton and the **Custer's Last Stand Reen-actment** in Hardin, involving more than 200 riders. In Wyoming note the **Woodchoppers Jam-boree & Rodeo** near Saratoga, where competitors make wood chips fly.

JULY➤ The Rockies celebrate an all-American Fourth of July. Among the largest celebrations is the **Fantastic Fourth** in Frisco, Colorado, and the old-fashioned **Cody Stampede** in Buffalo Bill Cody's eponymous Wyoming hometown; also look into the **Fourth of July Parade and Pyrotechnic Extrava-ganza** in West Yellowstone, Montana. In Wyoming, check out the **Grand Teton Music Festival** in Teton Village. For the king of outdoor rodeos, see the world's largest, **Cheyenne Frontier Days** in Cheyenne, Wyoming. Other events commemorate the Rocky Mountains' past: in Utah, the **Railroaders Festival** in Ogden, where the spike-driving and buffalo-chip-throwing contests and the Golden Spike Ceremony commemorate the completion of America's first transcontinental railroad; and in Wyoming, the

Green River Rendezvous near Pinedale, stages a reenactment of mountain life in the 1830s. Thirty to 40 hot-air balloons are a colorful sight over the mountains at the **Teton Valley Hot-Air Balloon Races** in Driggs, Idaho. And don't miss the **Montana State Fair** at the end of the month.

AUGUST➤ Who would ever have guessed that the largest outdoor Middle Eastern dance festival in the nation, featuring some 200 dancers from around the country, would be held in Salt Lake City? But there you have it, the **Belly Dancing Festival.** Rodeos are more typical late-summer fare; witness the **Pikes Peak or Bust Rodeo** in Colorado Springs, Colorado's largest rodeo. Equally common are Native American events showcasing traditional songs, dances, and crafts, such as the **Shoshone-Bannock Indian Festival** in Fort Hall, Idaho and the **Crow Indian Fair and Rodeo** in Crow Agency, Montana—the self-styled tepee capital of the world. Boise's **Western Idaho Fair** is the state's biggest. Also note August's **Cowboy Poetry Gathering** in Lewiston, Montana, where U.S. and Canadian performers share verses about a man and a horse following a cow.

AUTUMN

SEPTEMBER➤ In Colorado, Cripple Creek's **Aspen Leaf Tours,** free trail tours by Jeep through ghost towns and old gold mines, show off the brilliant mountain aspens. In Idaho, you'll find lumberjack competitions at the **Clearwater County Fair and Lumberjack Days** in Orofino; **Idaho Spud Day** in Shelley, with the World Spud-Picking Championship; and the **Nez Percé Cultural Day** in Spalding, celebrating Native American heritage. Montana hosts the **Running of the Sheep** sheep drive in Reedpoint, an event comparable to Pamplona's running of the bulls but with hundreds of sturdy Montana-bred woollies charging down Main Street. There's also the big **Utah State Fair** in Salt Lake City. Wyoming marks the season with the **Jackson Hole Fall Arts Festival**, with concerts, art, poetry, dance, and crafts workshops and lectures throughout the valley.

OCTOBER➤ If the foliage doesn't provide color enough, try the **Flathead Balloon Festival** in Kalispell, Montana. The **Microbrewery Beer Fest** at Grouse Mountain Lodge in Whitefish, Montana, showcases the small-batch beers of local breweries.

NOVEMBER➤ One of the most memorable events is the eagle watch near Helena, Montana, where majestic bald eagles flock to the Missouri River to dive for kokanee salmon. Steelhead are the quarry at Idaho's **Great Snake Lake Steelhead Derby** in Lewiston. In Colorado, look for **Creede's Chocolate Festival,** which puts chocolates of every size, shape, and description imaginable in every corner of the town.

2 Special-Interest Vacations: Winter

THE SPECIAL-INTEREST WINTER ACTIVITY in the Rockies is, of course, downhill skiing, there being (at last count) more than 60 ski areas in the region—each with at least a 1,000-foot vertical drop. The fastest-growing special interest might be snowboarding, which has exploded in popularity over the last 15 years. Despite that growth, however, snowboarders still represent only about 15% of the people on the trails on any given day. They are, after all, still called *ski* areas.

By Peter Oliver

Updated by
Marcy
Pritchard

Because space is limited, only the 20 most prominent ski areas are described in this chapter, meaning that some smaller but very worthy resorts, such as Purgatory, Colorado, didn't make the cut. Also, there are numerous virtual unknowns out there where you can experience fine, crowd-free skiing.

In addition to offering you the rundown on ski areas, we've included information on other activities offered at resorts and surrounding areas. Cross-country skiing (of which there is plenty), dogsledding, snowmobiling, fishing, hot-air ballooning, paragliding, and even golf in some locations late in the season are among the possibilities.

Nevertheless, downhill skiing remains far and away Activity No. 1, and in an effort to keep things that way, resorts in recent years have bent over backward to offer programs for special-interest groups. Almost all of the major resorts now have some form of children's program, women's program, snowboarding program, program for skiers with disabilities, and recreational-racing program. Again for the sake of space, only unique or exemplary programs at each resort are described below. If you're looking for a program to suit your particular interests, call ahead or check at the main ski-school desk; chances are pretty good that you'll find what you're looking for.

The skiing season runs approximately from mid-November to mid-April, depending on the resort and the location. The best package deals usually apply early and late in the season; for packages, check not only with each resort but also with major airlines (American, Continental, Delta, and United) that service the Rockies. Many resorts open late and shut down early not for lack of snow but for lack of business. In fact, some of the best backcountry skiing can be had in late April and May, when avalanche risks subside and the firmer, sun-baked snow is easier to walk and climb on than midwinter powder. Just because the ski resorts give up on skiing doesn't mean you have to.

A few notes: terrain ratings (e.g., beginner, intermediate, advanced) are approximate and may vary considerably from one ski area to the next. In other words, an intermediate trail at one area might be rated as expert elsewhere; rating trails is a matter of judgment rather than science. Thus, the terrain ratings might give you a rough idea of the ratio of beginner versus advanced options at a particular area, but are of much less use in comparing areas with one another. Also, prices were accurate as of spring '95.

COLORADO

Aspen/Snowmass

Aspen is as much a national icon as it is a town—forever in the news as a litmus test of the American public's tolerance of radical-chic politics, conspicuous consumption, and conspicuous love affairs. It's like a scriptless soap opera shot as cinema verité: part resort town, part ski area, part cultural retreat, and part New-Age-politics–thirtysomething-hedonistic-excess comic strip. It is a place where celebrities have affairs and locals have dogs and mountain bikes. It is weird.

In Aspen, high-end clothing boutiques have been known to serve free Campari-and-sodas après-ski, a practice so brazenly elitist that there's a certain charm to it. At the same time, it's a place where people actually live, send their kids to school, and work real jobs that may or may not have to do with skiing. It is, arguably, America's original ski-bum destination, a fact that continues to give the town's character an underlying layer of humor and texture. People can come to Aspen, dress much too expensively, and loudly make fools of themselves, as Donald Trump and Barbara Streisand (among others) have done. But a person can also come to Aspen and have a reasonably straightforward, enjoyable ski vacation, because once you've stripped away the veneer, Aspen is not a bad town or a bad place to ski.

Snowmass was built in 1967 as Aspen's answer to Vail—a ski-specific resort—and although it has never quite matched the panache or popularity of Vail, it has gained a certain stature with age. It used to be that if you stayed at Snowmass, dining meant cooking in your condo and entertainment could only be found 15 miles away in Aspen. In recent years, an effort has been made to breathe a little life and pizzazz into Snowmass Village, and the effect has been noticeable. Better restaurants and a livelier après-ski scene in recent years have lured people into the village after the lifts close. In years past, the tendency was to make quick tracks back to your hotel or condo.

In general, Snowmass is the preferred alternative for families with young children, leaving the town of Aspen to a more hard-partying, up-at-the-crack-of-noon kind of crowd. The selling points of Snowmass as an alternative to Aspen are lots of on-slope, ski-in/ski-out lodging, a slow pace, and quiet.

Visitor Information

Central reservations: ☎ 800/262–7736 for Aspen, 800/332–3245 for Snowmass. General information: **Aspen Skiing Company** (Box 1248, Aspen 81612, ☎ 970/925–1220 or 800/525–6200); **Aspen Visitors Center** (425 Rio Grande Pl., Aspen 81611, ☎ 970/925–1940). Snow reports: ☎ 970/925–1221.

Getting There

United/United Express (☎ 970/925–3400 or 800/241–6522) has frequent flights between Denver and Aspen. United Express also has nonstop flights from Chicago, Dallas, and Los Angeles. Most major airlines (including Continental and United) have numerous flights to and from Denver. Another option is to fly into **Eagle County Airport** (☎ 970/524–9490), 70 miles north of Aspen and served by American, Delta, Northwest, and United. **Aspen Limo** (☎ 800/222–2112) and **High Mountain Taxi** (☎ 800/528–8294) provide service to Aspen from Denver, Eagle County, and Glenwood Springs. **Avis, Budget,** and **Hertz,** among others, rent cars from the Aspen airport; **Hertz** and **Dollar** rent from Eagle County.

Generally speaking, driving to Aspen from Denver in the winter is more trouble than it's worth, unless you are on an extended vacation and plan to stop at other resorts such as Vail. With Independence Pass closed in the winter, the drive takes more than three hours at best, depending on road and weather conditions. On the other hand, the drive from

The Rockies Ski Areas

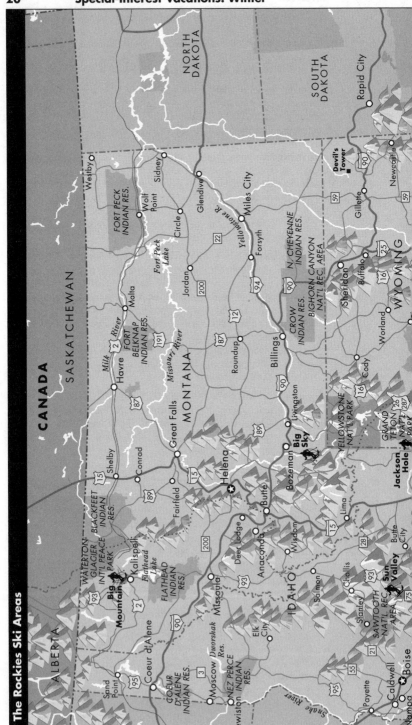

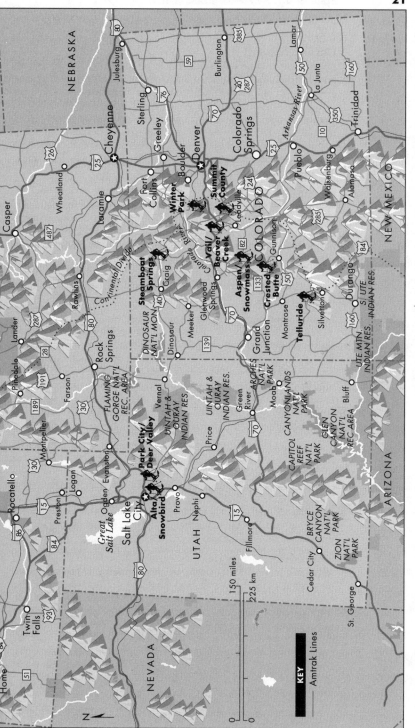

the west is relatively easy, with no high-mountain passes to negotiate. Take the Route 82 exit off I–70 at Glenwood Springs.

Getting Around

A rental car is unnecessary in either Aspen or Snowmass, since both are geared as much for pedestrians as for cars; in many cases it's easier getting around on foot. Furthermore, the Aspen/Snowmass area has perhaps the best free shuttle-bus system (☎ 970/925–8484) in skidom. The free shuttles are backed up by Roaring Fork Transit Agency buses (☎ 970/925–8484; fare: $2–$5, depending on the destination), which run from 4:30 PM into the night. As an alternative, hitchhiking between Aspen and Snowmass is still considered an acceptable form of transportation, but you should use your judgment.

Downhill Skiing

Aspen and Snowmass are really four ski areas rolled into one resort. Three—Aspen (or Ajax) Mountain, Tiehack, and Snowmass—are owned by the Aspen Skiing Company and can be skied on the same ticket. Aspen Highlands, the fourth, has always been the loner with a perplexing character, though it is under the umbrella of Aspen Skiing Company; it has the greatest vertical drop (3,800 feet) of the four Aspen mountains but, in terms of skiable acreage, it may have the least amount of skiing.

Aspen Mountain is considered a mogul skier's dreamland, and from its Bell Mountain chairlift, that's certainly true. However, most Aspen Mountain skiers spend much of their time on intermediate trails off the upper-mountain quad. They also spend their lunchtime on the deck of Bonnie's, the midmountain restaurant, which on a sunny day is one of the great people-watching scenes in the world of skiing. Aspen Mountain's biggest drawback is that too many trails funnel into Spar Gulch, making the end-of-the-day rush to the bottom chaotic and often dangerous.

Tiehack—a place where it is virtually impossible to get into trouble— is terrific for lower intermediates and kids. It's a low-key, lighthearted sort of place, an antidote to the kind of skiing machismo you might encounter at Aspen Mountain. Among its featured attractions is a hangout for kids named Ft. Frog—a name that ought to tell you something about how seriously the area takes itself. If you're looking for an escape from the Aspen bustle, spend a day at Tiehack, with its expert cluster of trails, although "expert" is an extremely relative term.

Snowmass is a huge sprawl of a ski area, best known for Big Burn, itself a great sprawl of wide-open, intermediate skiing. In general, Snowmass is one of the best ski areas in the Rockies for intermediates. The route variations down Big Burn are essentially inexhaustible, but still, there are many, many other places on the mountain for intermediates to find entertainment. Not so for experts: Although there are some truly challenging chutes and glades—such as Hanging Valley—they are too often either closed or virtually unskiable because of snow conditions. On the other side of the coin, the novice and lower-intermediate terrain on the lower part of the mountain makes Snowmass a terrific place for young kids.

Aspen Highlands is essentially a long, long ridge with trails dropping off to either side. Unfortunately the management of Highlands has let the area grow ragged around the edges, especially its antiquated lift system. Highlands does, however, have some superb expert terrain; its Steeplechase cluster of trails and small bowls is one of the best places to be in the Aspen area on a powder day. The payback is the long, slow lift ride back to the summit, but once there, you are treated to one of the best summit views in American skiing.

LESSONS AND PROGRAMS
For all four mountains: Half-day adult group lessons start at $42, but a noteworthy deal is the three-day learn-to-ski or learn-to-snowboard package at Tiehack, which includes lessons and lift tickets for $129. All-day children's programs start at $55 per day.

FACILITIES
Aspen Mountain: 3,267-foot vertical drop; 631 skiable acres; 35% intermediate, 35% advanced, 30% expert; 1 4-passenger gondola, 2 high-speed quad chairs, 5 double chairs, 2 surface lifts. Tiehack: 2,030-foot vertical drop; 410 skiable acres; 35% beginner, 39% intermediate, 26% advanced; 1 high-speed quad chair, 5 double chairs. Snowmass: 4,087-foot vertical drop; 2,500 skiable acres; 10% beginner, 51% intermediate, 18% advanced, 21% expert; 15 lifts. Aspen Highlands: 3,635-foot vertical drop; 597 skiable acres; 20% beginner, 33% intermediate, 17% advanced, 30% expert; 2 high-speed quad chairs, 5 double chairs, 2 surface lifts.

LIFT TICKETS
$49 adults, $27 children 7–12, children under 7 and adults over 70 free. Some savings on multiday tickets. Note: Lift tickets are included in some lodging prices.

RENTALS
Numerous ski shops in Aspen and Snowmass rent equipment. Two of the best and most conveniently located are **Christy Sports** at the Aspen Mountain gondola base (☎ 970/920–1170) and **Aspen Sports** (☎ 970/923–3566) in Snowmass Village. Rentals are also available at the Tiehack base lodge. Rental packages (skis, boots, poles) start at around $16 per day; snowboard packages (boots and boards) run about $25. Bargain shopping at stores around town may turn up lower-priced deals.

Cross-Country Skiing
BACKCOUNTRY SKIING
The **10th Mountain Hut and Trail System,** named in honor of the U.S. Army's skiing 10th Mountain Division, includes 10 huts along the trail connecting Aspen and Vail. The main trail follows a generally avalanche-safe route in altitudes that vary between 8,000 and 12,000 feet. This translates to a fair amount of skiing along tree-lined trails and a good bit of high-alpine up and down. You must be in good shape, and some backcountry skiing experience is extremely helpful. The accommodations along the trail are the Hiltons of backcountry huts, supplied with precut wood for wood-burning stoves, mattresses and pillows, and propane stoves and utensils for cooking. Each hut generally sleeps 16 (more if you're willing to cuddle). *1280 Ute Ave., Aspen 81611, ☎ 970/925–5775. Hut fees: $22 per person per night. Reservations required at least a month in advance, up to a year in advance is recommended for peak ski season.*

The **Alfred A. Braun Hut System** is Aspen's other major backcountry network. The trailhead leads from the Ashcroft Touring Center (*see* Track Skiing, *below*) into the Maroon Bells/Snowmass Wilderness, and generally covers terrain more prone to avalanche possibilities than the 10th Mountain Division Trail. Huts sleep 6–9 people. *Box 7937, Aspen 81612, ☎ 970/925–6618 or 800/643–8621. Hut fees: $14 per person per night. Reservations required at least a day in advance, considerably earlier for weekends and peak-season periods.*

If you're unfamiliar with either hut system or inexperienced in back-country travel, you should hire a guide. One reliable recommendation is **Aspen Alpine Guides** (Box 5122, Aspen 81612, ☎ 970/925–6618 or 800/643–8621). In Aspen, the best stores for renting backcountry gear (including ski equipment, climbing skins, packs, sleeping bags, and mountaineering paraphernalia) are **The Hub** (315 E. Hyman Ave., ☎ 970/925–7970) and **Ute Mountaineer** (308 S. Mill St., ☎ 970/925–2849).

TRACK SKIING

There is something to be said for a wealthy tax base. Subsidized by local taxes (in most towns, public cross-country ski trails would be considered a fiscal extravagance), the Aspen/Snowmass Nordic Council charges no fee for the 80 kilometers (49½ miles) of maintained trails (not all interconnected) in the Roaring Fork Valley. Probably the most varied, in terms of scenery and terrain, is the 30-kilometer (18½-mile) Snowmass Club trail network.

For a longer ski, try the Owl Creek Trail, connecting the Snowmass Club trail system and the Aspen Cross-Country Center trails. More than 16 kilometers (10 miles) long, the trail provides both a good workout and a heavy dosage of woodsy beauty, with many ups and downs across meadows and aspen-gladed hillsides. Lessons and rentals available at the **Aspen Cross-Country Center** (39551 Rte. 82 at the Aspen Golf Course, ☎ 970/925–2145). Diagonal, skating, racing, and light touring setups available. Lessons and rentals are also available at the **Snowmass Lodging Club Cross-Country Center** (Drawer G-2, Snowmass Village, ☎ 970/923–5600) and **The Hub** (*see* Backcountry Skiing, *above*).

Twelve miles from Aspen, the **Ashcroft Touring Center** is sequestered in a high alpine basin up Castle Creek, which runs between Aspen Mountain and Aspen Highlands. The 30 kilometers (18½ miles) of groomed trails are surrounded by the high peaks of the Maroon Bells/Snowmass Wilderness. It is truly one of the most dramatic cross-country sites in the Rockies. *Ashcroft Touring Unlimited, Castle Creek Rd., ☎ 970/925–1044.*

Other Activities

DOGSLEDDING

Krabloonik (1201 Divide Rd., Snowmass, ☎ 970/923–4342), with about 200 dogs at its disposal, can put on a good half-day ride (beginning at 8:30 AM or 12:30 PM). The ride is preceded or followed by lunch at the Krabloonik restaurant, among the best in the Aspen/Snowmass area.

PARAGLIDING

Skiing or running off a mountainside with a parachute attached to your back is the sort of thing you'd expect to be popular in adventure-crazed France, and it is. In the United States, however, paragliding is still a fledgling sport, and Aspen is one of the few places in the country where you can get your ya-yas out this way. The **Aspen Paragliding School** (426 S Spring St., Aspen 81611, ☎ 970/925–7625) offers everything from single rides in tandem with a pilot to weeklong courses ($675) leading up to solo flights.

SNO-CAT SKIING

Aspen Mountain Powder Tours (☎ 970/925–1227) provides access to 1,500 acres on the back side of Aspen Mountain via Sno-Cat tours. Most of the terrain is negotiable by confident intermediates, with about 10,000 vertical feet constituting a typical day's skiing. Reservations are required at least a day in advance, but you should book as far in advance as possible during the season. Tours cost about $200.

Crested Butte

Crested Butte has traditionally presented itself as the promised land of ski towns: After you've sold your soul in the Sodom and Gomorrah of Aspen and Vail, you pass through pearly gates and enter Crested Butte. No pretensions. No resort bluster. No fur, except for that worn by living animals. An honest, down-to-earth Rocky Mountain ski town.

The truth is, Crested Butte is more than *one* ski town, and there *are* similarities to the two big shots: There's Crested Butte, a former mining town (not unlike Aspen), and Mount Crested Butte, a recently built resort town (not unlike Vail). But Crested Butte's relaxed, earthy atmosphere is genuine. Its generally youngish and politically left-leaning populace tends toward being "granola," as they say in the West. In other words, things like natural foods, natural-fiber clothing, and a rugged outdoor spirit are commonplace. For athletic purists, Crested Butte lays claim to sparking the resurgence of telemark skiing about 20 years ago and the emergence, more recently, of mountain biking. You know you're an authentic Crested Butte-ite when you own not one but two mountain bikes: a town bike for hacking around and a performance bike for *serious* hacking around.

Another thing you'll find at Crested Butte that's unlike anything you'll find at either Aspen or Vail—and very un-American too, for that matter—is that they let people ski for nothing. No kidding—free lift tickets up until the week before Christmas. The thinking was that the freebies would drum up business for local lodging and dining establishments during a traditionally slow period for ski areas. In the first year the idea was tried, a lot of skinflint ski bums showed up, and a lot of the local business proprietors were dubious. Since then, the idea has caught on with families and ski clubs; it is one of the few ways for a family of four or more to go on a relatively inexpensive ski vacation these days.

Visitor Information
Crested Butte Central Reservations (☎ 970/349–2411 or 800/607–0050). General information: **Crested Butte Mountain Resort** (12 Snowmass Rd., Box A, Mount Crested Butte, ☎ 970/349–2281); **Crested Butte Chamber of Commerce** (Old Town Hall, Box 1288, Crested Butte, ☎ 970/349–6438 or 800/215–2226). Snow report: ☎ 970/349–2323.

Getting There
American Airlines (☎ 800/433–7300) offers direct flights to Gunnison (28 miles south of Crested Butte) from Chicago through Dallas/Fort Worth. **Delta** (☎ 800/221–1212) has direct flights to Gunnison from Atlanta. **Continental Express** (☎ 800/525–0280) and **United Express** (☎ 800/241–6522) have regular service from Denver. **Alpine Express** (Box 1250, Gunnison 81230, ☎ 970/641–5074) offers van service from Gunnison to Crested Butte.

Crested Butte is 230 miles southwest of Denver.

Getting Around
There is reliable shuttle-bus service between the town of Crested Butte and the resort village, which are about 3 miles apart. However, because most lodging is at the resort village and the better restaurants, shopping, and general atmosphere are in town, you can expect to make many resort-to-town trips, and a car makes the going much easier. **Avis, Budget, Hertz,** and **National** have car rental counters at Gunnison airport.

Downhill Skiing

Crested Butte skiing has a split personality, a judgment that is easily made by checking out the skiers who come here. One side of its personality is the primary trail network, characterized by long intermediate and lower-intermediate runs. This is the sort of skiing that attracts vacationers and families, mostly from the Southwest and Texas. They take advantage of, among other things, a wonderful expanse of easy terrain from the Keystone lift—not just a trail network but instead rolling, tree-dotted meadows with plenty of opportunities to poke around off the beaten track.

The other side of Crested Butte's personality is the so-called Extreme Limits, several hundred acres of steep bowls, gnarly chutes, and tight tree skiing. This is an attraction for extreme skiers (and extreme-skiing wannabes), so it's not surprising that Crested Butte is the site of the national extreme-skiing championships each year.

The best skiing on the main trail network is on the front side of the mountain. The high-speed quad (open for the '92–'93 season) has been a great addition, making 2,000 vertical feet available with just one quick lift ride. Unfortunately this has made the long, slow lift on the Paradise Bowl side seem that much longer and slower, although it accesses some of the mountain's best intermediate terrain.

The Extreme Limits is quirky terrain, capable of being sensational, horrible, or (more often than a lot of experts would like) closed. A few years ago, the only way to get to it was to climb over the ridgeline from the top of the Paradise lift. Although the installation of a poma disc on the lift changed that, it also brought more skiers, some of whom are over their heads on that side of the mountain. This means the fresh snow gets skied up earlier than it used to, especially in those gnarly chutes. Face it: Terrain as steep and rocky as this really requires superb snow conditions to make it truly pleasurable. Otherwise, it can be rough going, and even hazardous.

LESSONS AND PROGRAMS

Two-hour group lessons start at $28; two-hour special workshops begin at $42. One special program of note is Kim Reichhelm's Women's Ski Adventures. Reichhelm, a former world extreme-skiing champion, leads four-day workshops aimed at "breakthrough" experiences for women of all abilities. Call or write Women's Ski Adventures (237 Post Rd. W, Westport, CT 06880, ☎ 800/992–7700) for dates and details. Call the ski school (☎ 970/349–2251) for information on other programs.

FACILITIES

2,775-foot vertical drop; 1,160 skiable acres; 27% beginner, 53% intermediate, 20% advanced for the main trail network; 100% expert for the Extreme Limits; 2 high-speed quad chairs, 3 triple chairs, 4 double chairs, 4 surface lifts.

LIFT TICKETS

$42 adults, children pay their age, children under 12 free when an adult purchases a ticket. Free lift tickets from Thanksgiving week until the week before Christmas.

RENTALS

Full rental packages (including skis, boots, poles) are available through **Crested Butte Ski Rental** (☎ 970/349–2241 or 800/544–8448) and start at $12 per day for adults, $8 children under 11. Substantial discounts available for multiday rentals.

Cross-Country Skiing

BACKCOUNTRY SKIING

Considerable avalanche hazards notwithstanding, Crested Butte abounds with backcountry possibilities, from deep-woods touring to above-tree-line telemarking. Keep in mind that this is high-mountain country (the town itself is around 9,000 feet, and things go up from there) and that skiing in certain areas under certain weather conditions can be nothing short of suicidal. To play it safe, your best bet is to arrange a guided tour with the **Crested Butte Nordic Ski Center** (*see below*).

Another possibility is to spend a few days at **Irwin Lodge,** in a high basin about 12 miles from town. In winter, Sno-Cats carry alpine as well as telemark skiers to a ridge offering terrific views of the 14,000-foot peaks of the Maroon Bells/Snowmass Wilderness. From here, it's more than 2,000 vertical feet of bowl and tree skiing back to the lodge. Equally enjoyable is touring on your own (or with a guide) from the lodge. If there is a drawback, it is that this area is popular with snowmobilers (in fact, the lodge also operates a snowmobile guide service), and you may from time to time find your high-mountain solitude interrupted by the buzzing sounds of machinery. *Box 457, Crested Butte 81224, ☎ 970/349–5308. Prices vary according to activities, time of season, and length of stay.*

At the base of the ski area, **Crested Butte Ski Rental and Repairs** (☎ 970/349–2241) rents touring and telemark equipment. In town, **The Alpineer** (419 6th St., ☎ 970/349–5210) is not only a good backcountry equipment source but can also provide information on backcountry routes and snow conditions.

TRACK SKIING

Three track networks totaling approximately 29 kilometers (18 miles) are maintained by the **Crested Butte Nordic Ski Center.** The largest of the three, the Red Lady Loop, covers mostly flat and rolling terrain across the meadows and through the aspen groves of the valley floor. Views of distant peaks are stunning. The 9 kilometers (5½ miles) of the Bench network include a steep loop through the trees of Gibson Ridge—close to town but seemingly far away in the woods. The 9-kilometer (5½-mile) system set on the Skyland Golf Course, 3 miles out of town, is probably the least interesting of the three, although its worth is enhanced considerably by its on-site restaurant. *2nd St., Box 1269, Crested Butte 81224, ☎ 970/349–1707. Trail fee: $6 adults, $3 children 12 and under. Lessons: 1½-hr group lessons start at $20; 2-hr backcountry tours start at $30. Rental packages (including skis, boots, poles) start at $12 adults, $6 children. The Nordic Ski Center can also arrange backcountry tours for skiers of all abilities.*

Other Activities

HOT-AIR BALLOONING

The conditions must be just right, but on a clear windless morning, this wide-open basin, surrounded on all sides by mountain ranges, must surely be one of the country's best places to be aloft in a balloon. For information, contact **Bighorn Balloons** (☎ 970/349–6335). Flights are $89 per person for a ride of at least 30 minutes; longer rides cost $100.

SNOWMOBILING

See Irwin Lodge *in* Cross-Country Skiing, *above.*

Steamboat Springs

Perhaps more than any other ski resort in the United States, Steamboat has linked its identity to a single person: Billy Kidd, the preeminent U.S. ski racer of the '60s. The everlasting image is of Kidd blasting through the powder with a big grin on his face and a cowboy hat that must be glued to his head since it never blows off. That's how Steamboat projects itself: cowboy living and deep-snow skiing—new resort meets the Old West. In large part, Steamboat pulls it off, even if the cowboy business gets a little hokey at times. It is the sort of hokeyness, though, that works for families, which represent Steamboat's major target market.

This is not to suggest that there is no legitimacy to Steamboat's cowboy image, which dates back to the 1800s when the first ranching communities took root. In fact, these early settlers were also responsible for the advent of skiing in the area, as they strapped wooden boards (vaguely resembling skis) to their feet so they could get around the neighborhood in winter. Later, Steamboat was one of the first ski areas to be developed in the West.

Steamboat carries the banner of "Ski Town, USA," which is simultaneously descriptive and misleading: In reality, this is a modern resort area, sprawling around the base of the ski lifts, and an older town (Steamboat Springs) 2 miles away. The older town indeed has the kind of verve and funkiness you would expect in a real ski town; the resort area, where a good many Steamboat visitors stay, is too spread out—or still too new—to have developed much ski-town character.

Visitor Information

Central reservations: ☎ 970/879–0740 or 800/922–2722. General information: **Steamboat Ski & Resort Corporation** (2305 Mt. Werner Circle, Steamboat Springs 80487, ☎ 970/879–6111). Snow report: ☎ 970/879–7300.

Getting There

Continental (☎ 800/525–0280), **Northwest** (800/225–2525), and **United** (800/241–6522) offer service from several U.S. cities to Yampa Valley Airport, 22 miles from Steamboat. **Continental Express** and **United Express** have connecting service from Denver International Airport to the Steamboat Springs Airport. Rental cars are available at both airports. **Alpine Taxi** (☎ 970/879–2800) and **Steamboat Taxi** (☎ 970/879–3335) provide transportation from the airport to lodging within the resort community. For rental-car and airport-shuttle information, call central reservations (*see* Visitor Information, *above*). **Steamboat Express** offers daily bus service from Denver International Airport to Steamboat. For schedules and information, call central reservations (*see* Visitor Information, *above*).

Steamboat is about a three-hour drive from Denver via I–70 west and U.S. 40 north. The route traverses high-mountain passes, so it's a good idea to check road conditions (☎ 303/639–1234) before you travel.

Getting Around

Steamboat's public bus system is a regular and reliable network that gets you around town and to and from the resort community. Skiers staying in town may find a rental car unnecessary; those staying in the more spread-out resort may appreciate the convenience of having one.

Downhill Skiing

Steamboat is perhaps best known for its tree skiing and "cruising" terrain—the latter term referring to intermediate skiing on wide, groomed runs. The abundance of cruising terrain has made Steamboat immensely popular with intermediates and families who ski only a few times a year and who aren't looking for diabolical challenges to overtax their abilities. Set on a predominantly western exposure—most ski areas are situated on north-facing exposures—the resort benefits from intense sun, which contributes to the cruising quality. Moreover, one of the most extensive lift systems in the West allows skiers to take a lot of fast runs without having to spend much time in line. The Storm Peak and Sundown high-speed quads, for example, each deliver about 2,000 vertical feet in less than seven minutes. Do the math, and you can figure that a day of more than 60,000 vertical feet is entirely within the realm of diehards.

All this is not to suggest, however, that Steamboat lacks challenge entirely. A number of runs, such as Concentration, are not groomed regularly, and although the pitch might not be extraordinarily steep, big moguls can make the going pretty rugged. There are also some real steeps, such as Chute One, but they're few and not especially long. If you're looking for challenging skiing at Steamboat, take on the trees. The ski area has done an admirable job of clearing many gladed areas of such nuisances as saplings, underbrush, and fallen timber, making Steamboat tree skiing a much less hazardous adventure than it can be at some areas. The trees are also where advanced skiers—as well as, in some places, confident intermediates—can find the best of Steamboat's ballyhooed powder. Ironically the resort that is renowned for its "champagne powder" doesn't receive significantly more snow statistically than other major Colorado resorts. At least on the top half of the mountain, however, the snow does tend to retain an unusual lightness and freshness.

LESSONS AND PROGRAMS

Two-hour adult group lessons begin at $34; all-day lessons are $50. Mogul, powder, racing, snowboarding, and telemark clinics are available, and intensive two- and three-day "training camps" are offered in racing and advanced skiing through the Billy Kidd Center for Performance Skiing (☎ 970/879–6111, ext. 543). Children's programs (lessons and/or day care) are offered for kids 6 months to 15 years old through the Kids' Vacation Center (☎ 970/879–6111, ext. 218). Rates begin at $40 per half day, $55 per day. For general ski school information, call 970/879–6111, ext. 531.

FACILITIES

3,668-foot vertical drop; 2,500 skiable acres; 15% beginner, 54% intermediate, 31% advanced; 1 8-passenger gondola, 2 high-speed quad chairs, 1 quad chair, 6 triple chairs, 7 double chairs, 3 surface lifts.

LIFT TICKETS

$44 adults, $25 children, children under 13 free with an adult buying a multiday ticket for 5 days or more (1 child per adult). Savings of 5% or less on multiday tickets.

RENTALS

Equipment packages are available at the gondola base as well as at ski shops in town. Packages (skis, boots, poles) average about $16 a day, less for multiday rentals. Call central reservations (*see* Visitor Information, *above*) for rental information.

Cross-Country Skiing

BACKCOUNTRY SKIING

The most popular area for backcountry skiing is Rabbit Ears Pass southeast of town, the last pass you must cross if you drive from Denver to Steamboat. Much of its appeal is the easy access to high country; trails emanate from the U.S. 40 roadside. There are plenty of touring routes possible, with limited telemarking opportunity. Arrangements for backcountry tours can be made through the **Steamboat Ski Touring Center** (*see* Track Skiing, *below*).

Another popular backcountry spot is Seedhouse Road, north of the town of Clark and about 25 miles north of Steamboat. A marked trail network covers rolling hills, with good views of distant peaks. For maps, trail suggestions, and information on snow conditions and stability, contact the **Hahn's Peak Ranger Office** (57 10th St., Box 771212, Steamboat Springs 80477, ☎ 970/879–1870).

Touring and telemarking rentals are available at various ski shops in the Steamboat area. One of the best is the **Ski Haus** (U.S. 40 and Pine Grove Rd., ☎ 970/879–0385).

TRACK SKIING

The main center for cross-country skiing is the **Steamboat Ski Touring Center,** where most of the 30-kilometer (18½-mile) trail network—laid out on or alongside the Sheraton Steamboat Golf Club—is relatively gentle. The inspiration behind the center is Sven Wiik, a seminal figure in the establishment of cross-country skiing in the United States. A good option for a relaxed afternoon of skiing is to pick up some eats at the Picnic Basket in the touring center building and enjoy lunch alfresco at the picnic area along the Fish Creek Trail, a 5-kilometer (3-mile) loop that winds through pine and aspen groves. *Box 772297, Steamboat Springs 80477, ☎ 970/879–8180. Trail fee: $9 adults per day, $7.50 after 1 PM, $5 children. Rental packages (skis, boots, poles): $10 per day, $8.50 half day.*

Some guest ranches in the area also have groomed track networks. **Home Ranch** (Box 822, Clark 80428, ☎ 970/879–9044), 20 miles north of Steamboat, has 40 kilometers (25 miles) of groomed tracks. **Vista Verde Guest Ranch** (Box 465, Steamboat Springs 80477, ☎ 970/879–3858 or 800/526–7433) also has a groomed trail network, as well as access to adjacent national-forest land for touring.

Other Activities

Outdoor activities—including dogsledding, hot-air ballooning, and snowmobiling—can be arranged by calling the activities department at central reservations (☎ 800/922–2722, ext. 372).

BOBSLEDDING

The term "bobsledding" might be stretching things, since this isn't quite the 80-mile-per-hour rush down a twisting gutter of ice that you've seen at the Olympics. However, when riding a soft-shelled, four-person sled down the course at Howelsen Hill (☎ 970/879–2170), the ski-jumping hill just outside town, it's possible to reach speeds of nearly 50 miles per hour—plenty fast for most people. The cost is $8 per run.

ICE DRIVING

Here's one for anyone who's either been intimidated by snowy roads or gotten teenage thrills from executing doughnuts on icy shopping-mall parking lots. The **Jean-Paul Luc Ice Driving School** (☎ 970/879–6104) offers ½- to 1½-hour clinics that include classroom instruction as well as driving on a snow- and ice-covered track.

SLEIGH RIDES

Several ranches in the area offer horse-drawn sleigh rides, dinner rides being the most popular. Call the central reservations number (*see* Visitor Information, *above*) for details. **Windwalker Tours** (Box 5093, Steamboat Springs 80477, ☎ 970/879–8065) also offers daily afternoon sleigh rides to view elk herds that winter in the area.

SNO-CAT SKIING

Buffalo Pass, northeast of Steamboat, is reputed to be one of the snowiest spots in Colorado, and that's where **Steamboat Powder Cats** (Box 2468, Steamboat Springs 80477, ☎ 970/879–5188 or 800/288–0543) operates. The basics are included: open-meadow skiing, deep powder, and a maximum of only 24 skiers. Sno-Cat skiing is the "poor man's" version of helicopter skiing, although at more than $175 a day, it's not exactly skiing for the lunch-pail crowd. One advantage over helicopters: Sno-Cats don't have to worry about landing and can get to places in bad weather that would be inaccessible by helicopter.

Summit County: Arapahoe Basin, Breckenridge, Copper Mountain, Keystone

Summit County is a hard place to get a fix on: four ski areas, three resorts, three towns in between . . . and Vail just over the pass. Where do you start? This multiplicity is both Summit County's bounty and its curse. It is a curse in that the area seems to have developed without much unified focus or sense of direction. The three major resorts—Breckenridge, Copper Mountain, and Keystone—are caught in that peculiar bind of establishing their own identities while still maintaining an association with the others.

Frisco, Dillon, and Silverthorne—those three towns in between—have accepted that their mandate calls for function over character. They provide moderately priced lodging and dining at approximately equal distances to the ski areas and are close to the highway. The fact is that many Summit County skiers are weekenders from Denver looking for a few days of respite from the city, not a fancy, full-service vacation.

The multimountain, multitown mishmash is not without irony. The one resort with solid historical roots is Breckenridge, built around the Main Street of an old mining town. Yet Breckenridge has become so built up over the years (close to 25,000 beds) that it comes off as the most thoroughly developed resort of the three, rather than the quaintest. The area that *does* have a legitimately unique character is the odd man out here, Arapahoe Basin, which really hasn't made any effort to buff up an image. Arapahoe is pretty much the ski area it was 20 years ago and is popular with a generally younger crowd and especially visited late in the season—April into June. Arapahoe's late-season, on-mountain partying spirit has become legendary.

What does it all add up to? Very briefly: Breckenridge is generally the choice of a young, lively crowd. The skiing focuses mainly on cruising, and so does the nightlife. Copper Mountain is best for skiers committed to skiing. The terrain is the best and most varied in Summit County, but the resort village expresses an angular, antiseptic functionality—a suburban cluster at the mountain base. Keystone is a quiet and, by the often slapdash standards of ski-lodging construction, well-built place. It's popular with families and probably wins the Summit County prize for the most genuine mountain resort.

Visitor Information

Central reservations: ☎ 800/221–1091 for Breckenridge; ☎ 800/458–8386 for Copper Mountain; ☎ 800/222–0188 for Keystone; ☎ 800/365–6365 for Summit County. General information: **Breckenridge Ski Resort** (Box 1058, Breckenridge 80424, ☎ 970/453–5000); **Copper Mountain Resort** (Box 3001, Copper Mountain 80443, ☎ 970/968–2318); **Keystone Resort** (Box 38, Keystone 80435, ☎ 970/468–2316; **Ski the Summit** (Box 267, Dillon 80435, ☎ 970/468–6607 or 800/441–

3533). Snow reports: ☎ 800/789–7669 for Breckenridge; ☎ 970/968–2100 for Copper Mountain; ☎ 970/468–4111 for Keystone/Arapahoe Basin.

Getting There

Summit County is approximately 75 miles west of Denver on I–70. Most major carriers fly into Denver. **Resort Express** (☎ 800/334–7433) provides van service between the airport and the resorts.

Getting Around

Although there is free shuttle-bus service within Summit County, a car is almost essential if you plan to do much traveling between your resort of choice and other points in Summit County. For anyone trying to avoid renting a car, Breckenridge, with the widest array of services and a town shuttle bus, is probably the best place to set up shop.

Downhill Skiing

Let's see . . . close to 5,000 skiable acres, 60-some lifts, more than 300 marked trails. What you need in Summit County isn't a lift ticket but a calculator. Despite their proximity, the four ski areas do have distinctly different characters. A quick summary: For the most part, Breckenridge is the sort of area where you can close your eyes and let your skis run; intermediate cruising is the name of the game. It is ideal for people who like a relaxed day on the slopes without having to worry about overworking the challenge meter. Still, there is some more adventurous, above-tree-line bowl skiing, accessible either by hiking or by a hard-to-ride T-bar. When that high-country skiing is good, it's great, but because of Breck's exposure to stormy weather, conditions can often be less than ideal.

Breckenridge's chief drawback is its horizontal layout, spreading across the flanks of three main peaks, named—with great imagination—Peaks 8, 9, and 10. Want to get from the base of Peak 8 to the summit of Peak 10? A couple of lift rides are necessary, and navigational aids would be helpful.

As mentioned, Copper Mountain has perhaps the best variety of skiing among the Summit County areas. Good, long cruisers, satisfying mogul runs, above-tree-line bowl skiing, tight tree skiing, and a terrific cluster of lower-intermediate terrain. Furthermore, the layout is such that there's minimal contact (literally) between skiers of differing abilities; you don't have fast skiers sharing the same terrain as beginners, as you do at some areas.

One reason for this is that Copper, like Breckenridge, is a horizontal spread, with novice skiers tending toward the right, intermediates in the middle, and experts toward the left. It's a great choice for a family or group of friends with widely varying skills; there's skiing to keep everyone entertained. Copper used to have a cross-mountain navigational problem similar to Breckenridge's, but the well-placed installation of a couple of high-speed quad chairs a few years back improved the situation considerably.

Keystone is hard to get a good read on at first, especially since the slopes you see from the base lodge look quite steep—and they are—but they are not indicative of the rest of the trails. About 90% of Keystone Mountain is geared toward novice and lower-intermediate skiing. Yet Keystone Mountain isn't all there is to Keystone. Slip off the back side, and you've got North Peak and the Outback, with skiing for more skilled intermediates and advanced skiers. None of it, though, is real knock-your-socks-off expert terrain, but Keystone has never tried to market itself as an expert's ski area. It's great for families or for people who ski once or twice a year. Better skiers prefer to toss the boards in the car and head for either Copper or Arapahoe, 6 miles up the road.

They *won't* head for Arapahoe, however, on bad-weather days. What can make Arapahoe delightful is also what damns it in bad weather: its elevation. The *base* elevation is almost 10,800 feet, so that most of Arapahoe's skiing is above tree line. When a storm moves in, you can't tell up from down at Arapahoe, and when the storm passes, skiing can be limited because of avalanche problems.

But if that sounds dreadful, consider the other side of the coin: On sunny spring days, Arapahoe is probably *the* place to be skiing in Colorado. It feels more like skiing in the Alps than Summit County, Colorado, with craggy peaks surrounded by treeless, rolling terrain. Intermediates can have a great time here, although "A-Basin" is best known for its expert challenges: the East Wall, a steep open face with great powder-skiing possibilities; Pallavicini, a wide, steep, tree-lined gutter of a run; and the West Wall cornice, from which young bucks, with varying degrees of bravado and sobriety, like to launch themselves. A typical spring day at Arapahoe: Ski frantically hard in the morning; kick back, catch rays, and swill beers in the afternoon.

LESSONS AND PROGRAMS

All four areas offer a variety of instructional programs, from half-day group lessons to special clinics, notably mogul clinics and women's seminars. Among the better bargains is the $44 all-day class-lesson rate at Breckenridge. One of the better children's programs is at Keystone, with day care and ski groups for kids from two months to 16 years old. A special program of note is the Mahre Training Center at Keystone, intensive three- or five-day clinics held on various dates during the season and hosted by either Phil or Steve Mahre, both Olympic medalists.

FACILITIES

Arapahoe Basin: 2,250-foot vertical drop; 490 skiable acres; 10% beginner, 50% intermediate, 40% advanced; 1 triple chair, 4 double chairs. Breckenridge: 3,398-foot vertical drop; 1,915 skiable acres; 15% beginner, 19% intermediate, 8% advanced intermediate, 23% advanced, 35% expert; 4 high-speed quad chairs, 1 triple chair, 8 double chairs, 3 surface lifts. Copper Mountain: 2,601-foot vertical drop; 1,360 skiable acres; 22% beginner, 27% intermediate, 35% advanced, 16% expert; 3 high-speed quad chairs, 6 triple chairs, 6 double chairs, 4 surface lifts. Keystone: 2,900-foot vertical drop; 1,739 skiable acres; 12% beginner, 36% intermediate, 51% advanced; 2 gondolas, 3 high-speed quad chairs, 1 quad chair, 3 triple chairs, 6 double chairs, 4 surface lifts.

LIFT TICKETS

Tickets cost about $40–$45, depending on the resort; children under 6 and adults over 70 ski free. Tickets purchased at Keystone, Breckenridge, and Arapahoe Basin are valid at any of the three mountains. Multiday ticket savings can exceed 20%.

RENTALS

Rental shops are at the bases of all four ski areas, with rental packages (skis, boots, poles) starting at $12 per day. Considerable savings can be found by bargain shopping at ski stores in Breckenridge, Dillon, Frisco, and Silverthorne.

Cross-Country Skiing

BACKCOUNTRY SKIING

Despite widespread development in Summit County, there are still plenty of opportunities to escape into the backcountry and get away from it all. They don't call it Summit County for nothing; mountain passes above 10,000 feet allow for relatively easy access to high-country terrain and good, high-country snow. This recommendation comes, however, with a word of caution; avalanche-related deaths are all too common in Summit County (more often involving snowmobilers than skiers). Easy access often attracts backcountry travelers whose snow-safety awareness is not what it should be. For information on snow conditions, contact the **Dillon Ranger District Office** (☎ 970/468–5400).

Among the easier, and safer, touring routes is the trip to Boreas Pass, just south of Breckenridge. The trail (about 20 kilometers/12 miles round-trip) follows a former rail route, with good views of distant peaks along the way. Summit County is also developing a system of backcountry huts that will be linked to Aspen's 10th Mountain Hut and Trail System. The first of these huts is Janet's Cabin, about a 10-kilometer (6-mile) ski in from the trailhead off I–70 west of Copper Mountain. For information and reservations, contact the **10th Mountain Hut and Trail System** (1280 Ute Ave., Aspen 81612, ☎ 970/925–5775). (Also *see* Cross-Country Skiing *in* Aspen/Snowmass, *above*.)

TRACK SKIING

The **Breckenridge Nordic Center** (☎ 970/453–6855), with 30 kilometers (18½ miles) of groomed tracks; the **Copper Mountain Cross-Country Center** (☎ 970/968–2882, ext. 6342), with 25 groomed kilometers (15½ miles); the **Frisco Nordic Ski Center** (☎ 970/668–0866), with 35 groomed kilometers (21½ miles); and the **Keystone Cross-Country Center** (☎ 970/468–4130), with 30 groomed kilometers (18½ miles), are Summit County's main areas for track skiing. Of these, the Breckenridge terrain is probably the most gentle, the Copper Mountain terrain the most challenging. All offer lessons and rentals.

Other Activities

A range of nonskiing activities—dogsledding, sleigh rides, snowmobiling—can be arranged through the central reservation services at Breckenridge, Copper, and Keystone (*see* Visitor Information, *above*).

ICE-SKATING

Keystone claims to have the largest outdoor maintained rink in the country. Actually it is not a true rink but a pond regularly resurfaced by maintenance machinery. At the center of Keystone Village, it is great for a leisurely post-ski skate and is open (and lit in the evening) daily 10–10, with skate rentals available.

Telluride

There are at least two Tellurides: Telluride Past and Telluride Future. That leaves the question: Where is Telluride Present? Telluride's distant past—dating to the late 1800s—revolved around mining; more recently, the town had the reputation of being a kind of societal escape hatch. Stuck in a box canyon in Colorado's southwest, Telluride was hard to find and even harder to access. As such, it was a perfect (and perfectly beautiful) hole in the wall of the San Juan Mountains for political and societal recalcitrants (most young and college educated) who'd had it up to here with the status quo. They weren't bothered too much by the few straggling skiers who made their way to Telluride, and from those roots a ski town developed with a distinctively hip, back-to-nature edge.

Telluride Future has to do with the development of a resort village on the other side of the mountain. The concern is how its existence will mesh with Telluride's already established character. The current centerpiece of the resort village is The Peaks at Telluride, which—depending on whom you talk to—is defined as either the luxury hotel Telluride has long needed or an ostentatious sore thumb. As plans for Telluride Future are beginning to be realized, a number of longtime residents say that the writing is on the wall: Telluride as a ski resort has been "discovered." Real estate values are escalating, encouraging many old-time Telluriders to sell out and move elsewhere. Effectively, some purists believe that Telluride can never again be what it was.

A couple of things are certain. First, thanks to very strict zoning ordinances, the old town of Telluride still looks as it always has—a turn-of-the-century mining town against an exquisite backdrop—even if the cost of housing has gone through the roof. However, the village is still a work in progress, and a final judgment on its aesthetic look and character wait for Telluride Future to assert itself fully.

Visitor Information

Central reservations: ☎ 800/525–3455. General information: **Telluride Visitor Services** (666 W. Colorado Ave., Box 653, Telluride 81435, ☎ 970/728–3041); **Telluride Ski & Golf Company** (☎ 970/728–3856); **Telluride Ski Resort** (Box 11155, Telluride 81435, ☎ 970/728–7404). Snow report: ☎ 970/728–3614.

Getting There

Telluride is notorious for being one of the hardest ski resorts in the country to fly into, mainly because its airport elevation is well above 9,000 feet. A little bumpy air, a few clouds, and the next thing you know, you're landing in Montrose, 67 miles away, and taking a van to Telluride. Telluride Regional Airport (☎ 970/728–5313) is just 5 miles from the resort.

Continental Express (☎ 800/525–0280) and **United Express** (☎ 800/241–6522) have frequent connecting flights from Denver into both airports. **America West** (☎ 800/235–9292) flies from Phoenix into Montrose.

Telluride is 330 miles southwest of Denver.

Getting Around

While the separation of the resort village from the town of Telluride has kept the town's historic integrity intact, it has also created a transportation headache: how to get easily from village to town? The completion (by late 1995) of a 2½-mile, over-the-mountain gondola to run day and evenings should solve that problem.

The gondola will make a car unnecessary; both the village and the town are pedestrian-friendly. However, for any out-of-town excursions—and a drive through the spectacular San Juan Mountains is well worthwhile—**Budget, Dollar,** and **Hertz** rent from the Telluride Regional Airport.

Downhill Skiing

Another split image: Telluride is really two ski areas in one. For many years, it had a reputation as being an experts-only ski area. Indeed, the north-facing trails on the town side are impressively steep and long, and by springtime, the moguls are humongous. When the snow is good, this is the site of some of the most outrageous mogul skiing in the world. So reputations are made.

But then there is the other side—literally—of the ski area, the west-facing village, with long, gentle runs. Despite the annoyance of a slow and inefficiently laid out lift system, this is still a terrific place for lower-intermediate skiers and young kids. It's as good as it gets in the West, really.

What Telluride lacks is much in between the super gentle and the super steep. There is the aptly named See Forever, a great, long cruiser, but in order to do it top to bottom, you must also ride lifts forever (or more than 25 minutes, anyway, which on a cold day seems like forever). There are a few good intermediate runs from Lift 5, but they are, unfortunately, short and have nagging flat spots. The ski area's management hopes that a planned expansion will eventually solve the intermediate shortage.

LESSONS AND PROGRAMS

Half-day group lessons begin at $25. First-time beginner lessons are available for alpine and telemark skiers, as well as snowboarders. A five-hour clinic with rentals and restricted beginner lift tickets is available at $60.

FACILITIES

3,522-foot vertical drop (3,165 feet lift serviced); 1,060 skiable acres; 21% beginner, 47% intermediate, 32% advanced/expert; 1 high-speed quad chair, 2 triple chairs, 6 double chairs, 1 surface lift.

LIFT TICKETS

$45 adults, $25 children 6–12, children under 6 free. Adult daily rate as low as $40 on multiday tickets.

RENTALS

Rental packages (skis, boots, poles) are available from **Telluride Sports** (☎ 970/728–4477) with locations at the Mountain Village and Oak Street base areas as well as at 150 West Colorado Street. Rentals are also available from ski shops in town. Packages start at around $12.

Cross-Country Skiing

BACKCOUNTRY SKIING

Among the better backcountry skiing routes in Colorado is the **San Juan Hut System,** leading toward Ridgway along the Sneffels Range. Five huts in the system are each about 11 kilometers (7 miles) apart and are well equipped with beds, blankets, wood-burning stoves, and cooking stoves. Previous backcountry experience is not essential (though highly recommended). *224 E. Colorado Ave. or Box 1663, Telluride 81435, ☎ 970/728–6935. $17 per person per night; rental equipment available. Reservations recommended at least 2 wks in advance.*

About an hour's drive by car from Telluride (though only a few miles as the crow flies) is **St. Paul Lodge** (Box 463, Silverton 81433, ☎ 970/387–5494), a terrific find for anyone enchanted by remote high country. Above 11,000 feet and about a half-hour ski-in from the summit of Red Mountain Pass between Ouray and Silverton, the lodge (a converted mining camp) provides access to a series of above-tree-line bowls and basins. Included in the lodge rates are guide service (essential in this potentially hazardous area), ski equipment, and telemark lessons if necessary, along with meals and lodging.

The San Juan Hut System (*see above*) offers a day-guiding service as an introduction to backcountry skiing. The best place for backcountry equipment rentals in Telluride is **Telluride Mountaineer** (219 E. Colorado Ave., ☎ 970/728–6736).

The **Telluride Nordic Association** is really three Nordic centers under the same aegis, totaling 50 kilometers (31 miles) of groomed track. The three are distinctly different. The 12-kilometer (7½-mile) track along the San Miguel River on the valley floor is relatively flat and good for those who like to develop momentum and rhythm in their skiing. The 5 kilometers (3 miles) of track on the golf course by the Peaks Hotel are more rolling. For distinctly backcountry flavor, try the groomed trails in the Prospect Basin area, reached from the top of Lift 10. In fact, many skiers who go into this area wear sturdy touring or telemarking gear and branch off from the groomed tracks. However, caution is advised here: Parts of the Prospect Basin area are notoriously prone to avalanches. *Box 1784, Telluride 81435, ☎ 970/728–6911 or 970/728–7570. No trail fee, although a 2-ride ticket for Lift 10, to reach Prospect Basin, is $12. Rentals and lessons may be arranged by Telluride Ski & Golf Company (see Visitor Information, above).*

Other Activities

Telluride Outside (Box 685, Telluride 81435, ☎ 970/728-3895 or 800/831-6230) organizes a variety of winter activities in the Telluride area, among them hot-air ballooning, sleigh rides, snowmobile tours, and even winter fly-fishing excursions.

GLIDER RIDES

For an unusual look at the San Juans, **Telluride Soaring** (☎ 970/728–5424) operates out of the Telluride Airport. Rates are about $75 per half hour, $120 per hour, and rides are offered daily, weather permitting.

HELI-SKIING

Among the unusual activities offered by **Telluride Helitrax** (Box 1560, Telluride 81435, ☎ 970/728–4904) are helicopter-assisted Nordic tours and late-season corn-snow skiing in the La Sal Mountains southeast of Telluride. Otherwise, a typical run-of-the-mill day of helicopter skiing includes five runs totaling about 12,000 feet. The cost is $425 per person. Reservations should be made at least two days in advance, and up to two weeks in advance for holiday periods.

ICE CLIMBING

Having your body suspended for any extended length of time on a frigid wall of ice would be considered a form of torture by some. For those who think it can be fun, **Fantasy Ridge Alpinism** (Nugget Bldg., Suite 204, Box 1679, Telluride 81435, ☎ 970/728–3546) offers introductory ice-climbing courses. A five-day course, including four nights of lodging and 3½ days of climbing, costs about $1,100 per person.

Vail/Beaver Creek

Vail is American skiing's big kahuna, the king of the hills. It is either the most, as they used to say in beatnik talk, or too much, depending on your tastes. Vail logs more "skier days" (the ski industry's measure of ticket sales) than any other resort in the country. You don't do that without being big, both as a ski area and as a resort, and Vail—by ski-resort standards—is enormous. It is astounding how much developers have been able to cram into the relatively narrow Vail Valley—and all the more astounding when you consider that a chunk of the valley floor is taken up by a major interstate highway (I–70).

Of course, one valley can only absorb so much, and by the beginning of the '80s, when it became obvious that Vail development had almost maxed out, the satellite resort of Beaver Creek sprang up. "The Beave," as locals call it, has quickly become a substantial resort in its own right— a low-key (relatively speaking) alternative to Vail itself.

Vail and Beaver Creek score high marks on two counts: the total amount of skiing (more than 5,000 skiable acres) and resort amenities. The two combine as the very definition of full-service resort, a well-oiled service machine that must take care of a bed base of roughly 40,000: restaurants, posh lodging, even ski concierges who will help you put on your skis in the morning. Lacking is a sense of soulful character, but what would you expect with an interstate highway running right through town? The original resort village was developed with a neo-Tyrolean theme, which subsequent development practically ignored. Vail today has more of a neosuburban atmosphere. You come to Vail and Beaver Creek to ski, eat, and be pampered, but certainly not to have your soul reclaimed by the splendor of the wilderness.

Visitor Information

Central reservations: ☎ 800/525–2257. General information: **Beaver Creek Resort/Vail Associates Inc.** (PO Box 7, Vail 81658, ☎ 970/949–5750 or 800/525–2257); **Vail Valley Tourism and Convention Bureau** (100 E. Meadow Dr., Vail 81658, ☎ 970/476–1000). Snow and ski report: ☎ 970/476–4888.

Getting There

Eagle County Airport (☎ 970/524–9490), 35 miles west of Vail, is served by American, Delta, Northwest, and United. **America West Airlines** (☎ 800/235–9292) has nonstops from Los Angeles, Phoenix, and San Francisco.

Vail and Beaver Creek are about 100 miles west of Denver International Airport, via I–70.

Getting Around

Vans to Vail (☎ 970/476–4467) and **Vail Valley Taxi** (☎ 970/476–8294) provide transportation between Vail/Beaver Creek and both the Eagle County Airport and Denver. **Budget, Dollar, Hertz, National,** and **Thrifty** rent cars in the Vail valley. A public shuttle-bus service is also available within Vail and between Vail and Beaver Creek.

Downhill Skiing

Vail is perhaps best known for its back bowls, a vast expanse (nearly 3,000 acres) of open-bowl skiing that can be sensational on powder days but generally only so-so at other times, after the fresh snow has been tracked up and worked on by sun and wind. For the most part, the back bowls are not extraordinarily steep, and thus are good places for intermediates to learn how to ski powder.

Skiing on the front side of the mountain is a markedly different experience. There's lots of wide-trail skiing, heavily skewed toward groomed intermediate runs. Vail is an ideal mountain for those in the intermediate- and advanced-skier audience who ski a week or two a season and want to be reminded each year that they do know how to turn a ski. Vail skiing has a way of boosting egos. There are a few steep and long mogul runs for experts, but Vail's true expert terrain represents a relatively small chunk of the huge Vail pie.

Beaver Creek has even less expert terrain. The addition a few years ago of the Grouse Mountain chair did add steep stuff to the Beaver Creek package, but no one really comes to Beaver Creek in search of killer steeps. In fact, it is perhaps one of the best ski areas in America for lower intermediates. The top third of the mountain features a large trail cluster of almost exclusively easygoing stuff, and any skier who doesn't feel up to the slightly steeper lower section of the mountain can ride the lift down to the base. Beaver Creek has a noteworthy advantage over Vail: a single, central base area. It's hard to get lost (not so at Vail), something that families with small, quick-to-wander-off children should consider.

LESSONS AND PROGRAMS

Half-day group lessons start at $49; full-day lessons start at $72. The ski schools at Vail and Beaver Creek are among the best in the country, with several specialty classes and excellent children's programs. For more information, call the Vail and Beaver Creek Ski School (☎ 970/476–3239).

FACILITIES

Beaver Creek: 3,340-foot vertical drop; 1,125 skiable acres; 18% beginner, 39% intermediate, 43% advanced; 3 high-speed quad chairs, 4 triple chairs, 4 double chairs. Vail: 3250-foot vertical drop; 4,014 skiable acres; 32% beginner, 36% intermediate, 32% advanced on the front side; 36% intermediate, 64% advanced in the back bowls; 1 gondola, 8 high-speed quad chairs, 2 regular quads, 3 triple chairs, 6 surface lifts.

LIFT TICKETS

$48 adults, $33 children under 13. Multiday tickets (up to 7 days) available, although per-day savings are minimal. Tickets are good at both Vail and Beaver Creek.

RENTALS

Full rental packages (skis, boots, poles) starting at $16 per day are available at **Beaver Creek Sports** in the Beaver Creek Resort Village. For Beaver Creek rental reservations, call 970/949–2310. In Vail, packages are available at rental shops operated by Vail Associates at the Golden Peak and Lionshead base areas. Performance packages, snowboards, and monoskis are also available for rental. For Vail rental reservations, call 970/479–2050.

Cross-Country Skiing

BACKCOUNTRY SKIING

The 10th Mountain Hut and Trail System reaches far into Vail's backcountry; one route continues to Aspen (*see* Cross-Country Skiing *in* Aspen/Snowmass, *above*). Maps, equipment, and other information are available from the 10th Mountain Hut and Trail System (1280 Ute Ave., Aspen 81612, ☎ 970/925–5775). Hut reservations should be made at least a month in advance.

If you aren't familiar with the trail system, hiring a guide is highly recommended. In Vail, contact **Paragon Guides** (Box 130-O, Vail 81658, ☎ 970/926–5299).

TRACK SKIING

To reach Beaver Creek's cross-country trail network, **McCoy Park,** you must ride the Strawberry Park chairlift. This is a bonus, for it gets you far enough from the resort village that you get a rare sense (around Vail, anyway) that you're in a pristine mountain environment. The 30 kilometers (18½ miles) of groomed tracks have a fair amount of ups and downs—or perhaps because the elevation is above 9,500 feet, it just seems that way. The cross-country skiing at the Vail Nordic Center is less inspiring—a network laid out on what in the summer is a *golf course. McCoy Park, ☎ 970/845–5313. Trail fee: $15 adults, $7 children for full day; $11 adults, $5 children for half day. Lesson and tour packages begin at $32, with snowshoe tours and rentals also available. Daily rental rates range between $15 and $20, depending on equipment.*

Other Activities

The **Activities Desk of Vail** (☎ 970/476–9090) or the **Activities Desk at Beaver Creek** (☎ 970/949–9090) can arrange a variety of nonskiing activities, including dogsledding, hot-air ballooning, and Sno-Cat skiing.

BOBSLEDDING

Vail's on-mountain bobsled run, a 2,900-foot course, begins below Mid-Vail (the large restaurant about halfway up the mountain). Neither the course nor the sleds are quite up to an Olympic standard, but speeds of up to 50 miles per hour are still possible. The sleds hold up to four people, and cost $12 per person.

SNOWMOBILING

Twelve-mile snowmobile tours are conducted at **Piney River Ranch** (Box 7, Vail, CO 81658, ☎ 970/476–3941), just north of Vail. Rates include helmets, snowmobile suits and boots, and sometimes meals, and range from $72 to $135 per person.

Winter Park

There is no more aptly named ski area in America than Winter Park. Technically the area—a public park—is owned by the city of Denver and is frequented primarily by skiers who drive 1½ hours from the city for a winter's day or weekend. Its close proximity to Denver affects Winter Park's character in a variety of ways. For one thing, it is still at heart a day-skier resort, despite efforts by the Winter Park area to spruce up lodging, dining, and other amenities to attract longer-term vacationers.

There's no spiffy resort village, and the après-ski scene, although it can be vibrant, tends to peter out on the early side, since all those day skiers beat their way back to Denver. What this means, too, is that Winter Park tends to be most crowded on weekends, and fairly uncrowded on weekdays: It's often the reverse at resorts such as Aspen or Vail, which usually see a guest turnover on weekends (Saturdays especially).

Winter Park isn't Colorado's most scenic resort; the front-range mountains lack the dramatic rocky structure of, say, the San Juans in Colorado's southwest. In large part, that's because proximity to Denver, rather than scenic drama, was most important in choosing the location of the resort. Not that Winter Park is *ugly* by any means; it's all relative.

Finally, Winter Park can attract an unusually eclectic crowd. On any given day, you might have the U.S. Ski Team in training (the 1993 U.S. National Skiing Championships were held here), a large corps of skiers with disabilities (Winter Park has the best program for skiers with disabilities in the country), and busloads of school kids from the Denver area, most of them throwing snowballs at one another.

Visitor Information

Central reservations: ☎ 800/453–2525. General information: **Winter Park Resort** (Box 36, Winter Park 80482, ☎ 970/726–5514); **Winter Park/Fraser Valley Chamber of Commerce** (Box 3236, Winter Park 80482, ☎ 970/726–4118). Snow report: 900/950–5550.

Getting There

Most major airlines fly into Denver International Airport. **Home James Transportation** provides van service from the airport to the resort; airport-shuttle arrangements can be made by calling central reservations (*see* Visitor Information, *above*).

Winter Park is about 70 miles west of Denver via I–70 west and U.S. 40 north. However, if you drive, be forewarned that Berthoud Pass on U.S. 40 can be treacherous when winter storms blow in.

Winter Park is the only ski resort in the Rockies with train service right to the slopes. In winter, the **Winter Park/Rio Grande Ski Train** (☎ 303/296–4754) provides round-trip weekend service from Denver's Union Station to the ski area. **Amtrak**'s (☎ 800/872–7245 or 800/533–0363) *California Zephyr* also provides daily service to Winter Park from Chicago and the West Coast; some ski packages are available.

Getting Around

A free shuttle-bus service runs between most lodges in the Winter Park area and the ski area, but because things are fairly spread out in the Fraser Valley, having a car is preferable.

Downhill Skiing

Winter Park is really three interconnected ski areas: Winter Park flanked by Mary Jane and Vasquez Ridge. That's both good and bad: It's good in that it spreads skiers out on those busy weekend days; it's bad in that it spreads skiers out. In other words, it's easy to lose your skiing partners at Winter Park, and once that happens, it's hard to find them.

The skiing at Winter Park and Vasquez Ridge leans heavily toward ultrawide, groomed intermediate trails. It's terrific skiing for families, groups, and schussboomers who enjoy testing the ski patrol's resolve by skiing too fast. On busy weekends, Vasquez Ridge is the best place for escaping crowds, partly because it's difficult to figure out how to get there.

Mary Jane is 1,800 vertical feet of unrelenting moguls, with a couple of groomed runs; if you want groomed, though, there are more choices at Winter Park. The Timberline lift behind Mary Jane provides access to the above-tree-line skiing of Parsenn Bowl. The pitch is moderate, making the bowl a terrific place for intermediates to try their luck at powder and crud-snow skiing.

LESSONS AND PROGRAMS

For adults, 1½-hour lessons start at $25; 3-hour workshops start at $45. All-day children's programs, which include lunch, start at $60.

FACILITIES

3,060-foot vertical drop; 1,358 skiable acres; 22% beginner, 58% intermediate, 20% expert; 6 high-speed quad chairs, 5 triple chairs, 9 double chairs.

LIFT TICKETS

$40 adults, $18 children 6–13, children under 6 free. Lower-priced, limited-lift tickets are also available.

RENTALS

Rental equipment is available at the bases of Winter Park and Mary Jane. Slightly lower-priced rental packages (as low as $8 per day) are available at the **Ski Exchange** (☎ 970/726–9240), ⅓ mile from the Winter Park base on Winter Park Drive. Rental equipment is also available from several shops in downtown Winter Park.

Cross-Country Skiing

BACKCOUNTRY SKIING

For backcountry telemarkers, Berthoud Pass, south of Winter Park, is a bonus because you can use the precut ski trails for easy climbing and skiing. Be cautious: The above-tree-line terrain around Berthoud is prone to quick and severe weather changes, as well as avalanches. Locals like to drive to the top of the pass and ski down one of many possible routes on either side; whoever draws the short straw has to drive the car down for pickup.

TRACK SKIING

The closest groomed tracks to Winter Park are the **Idlewood** and **Devil's Thumb** cross-country centers, an interconnected trail system totaling more than 100 kilometers (62 miles). The closer is Idlewood, half a mile from Winter Park on U.S. 40, with skiing mostly along tree-lined trails. Devil's Thumb (7 miles from Winter Park) is the larger of the two, with more ups and downs and more open views. *Box 750, Tabernash 80478, ☎ 970/726–5632. Trail fee: $8 adults, $5 children 6–12. Rentals, lessons, and backcountry tours available. Lodging and restaurant at Devil's Thumb.*

Somewhat farther afield is **Snowy Mountain Ranch,** 12 miles northwest of Winter Park in Tabernash. The 60-kilometer (37-mile) trail system includes 3 kilometers (almost 2 miles) lit for night skiing. The ranch is a YMCA facility (with discounts for YMCA members) that has such added bonuses as a sauna and an indoor pool. *Box 169, Winter Park 80482, ☎ 970/887–2152. Trail fee: $8 adults, $5 children, $3 evening. Lessons, rentals, and on-site lodging available.*

Other Activities

SNOWMOBILING

Rentals and guided tours are available from **Trailblazer Snowmobile Tours** (Box 3437, Winter Park, CO 80482, ☎ 970/726–8452 or 800/669–0134). Rates range from $55 for a two-hour ride to $100 for a four-hour ride.

SNOW TUBING

A lift-serviced snow-tubing hill? Yes, and it's lit at night, no less. The **Fraser Snow Tubing Hill** (☎ 970/726–5954) has two lifts, groomed trails, and a warming hut to make your experience of riding an inner tube down a snowy hill most enjoyable. The rate is $8 per hour before 6 PM, $9 per hour after 6 PM.

IDAHO

Sun Valley

Before there was Aspen, there was Sun Valley. Long before there were such movies as *Aspen Extreme* (1993) to take Hollywood skiing, there was *Sun Valley Serenade* (1941). Sun Valley's celebrity lineup of yesteryear—Gary Cooper, Claudette Colbert, Erroll Flynn, and Ernest Hemingway, among others—makes Aspen's present-day luster seem dull in comparison. A lot of this can be attributed to the power of astute marketing: When W. Averell Harriman, chairman of the Union Pacific Railroad in the 1930s, decided that the railroad company needed some Western attraction to fill train-car seats with tourists, he had visions of the St-Moritz of the Rockies. The location of choice was an old mining town named Ketchum, and imagine how alluring a destination Harriman might have had with a name like that. But his PR team came up with the much sexier name of Sun Valley, flew in a host of Hollywooders for the 1936 opening, and the rest is skiing history.

Sun Valley can still summon up its share of Hollywood glamour; among its regulars are Clint Eastwood, Brooke Shields, and a few folks (e.g., Mariel) named Hemingway. But it would be misleading to suggest that this is what Sun Valley is all about. If anything, it is antiglitter, a place where the stardust settled long ago. Today it is a resort of balanced proportions: Well developed but not (yet) overdeveloped, the town of Ketchum (and its Harriman-inspired satellite, Sun Valley) effectively mixes an air of elegance (and the aura of past glory) with ski-town funkiness.

The ski area is also a well-proportioned mix of trail and open-bowl skiing, easy skiing and tough stuff. The unfortunate rap on Sun Valley has been a lack of snow; not lying in a natural snowbelt and with parts of the mountain exposed to too much of that Sun Valley sun, the ski area has been more likely than most other Western resorts to suffer snow shortages. Recent snow-making improvements have gone a long way toward solving the problem, but Sun Valley is still not the best choice for powder-skiing addicts.

Visitor Information
Central reservations: ☎ 800/786–8259. General information: **Sun Valley Company** (Sun Valley 83353, ☎ 208/622–4111 or 800/786–8259). Snow report: ☎ 800/635–4150.

Getting There
Horizon Air (☎ 800/547–9308) and **Schist** (800/453–9417) offer connecting service primarily from Boise and Salt Lake City, respectively, to Hailey, 12 miles south of Sun Valley. **Sun Valley Bell Service** provides complimentary transportation to the resort (arrangements made through central reservations, *see* Visitor Information, *above*).

By car, Sun Valley is about 160 miles (2½ hours) east of Boise via I–84 and U.S. 93. It is about 80 miles north of Twin Falls via U.S. 93 and Route 75. **Avis, Budget,** and **Hertz** rent from the Boise airport and offer one-way options to Sun Valley, in addition to the regular daily and weekly rates.

Getting Around
A free shuttle-bus system for the Sun Valley-Ketchum area makes a car unnecessary. However, because the resort community sprawls over several square miles, a car may be a welcome convenience, especially for those staying in outlying condos in the Elkhorn or Warm Springs areas.

Downhill Skiing
Dollar Mountain is Sun Valley's original ski hill (although its amenities are not included in facilities for the resort, below) and when you compare it with Bald Mountain—"Baldy" for short—you get a good idea of how far skiing has come in almost 60 years. Dollar alone was enough to lure celebrities in the '30s and '40s, but it's a short beginner's hill by today's standards, utterly dwarfed by Baldy's 3,400 vertical feet.

Two Baldy attributes are the resort's most noteworthy pluses. One is that its vertical is continuous and so are its ski runs (not interrupted by snowmobile tracks, long traverses, or extra lift rides). For example, from the Challenger quad alone, you can cover more than 3,000 vertical feet—a rarity in U.S. skiing. The second plus is Sun Valley's diverse terrain: plenty of good skiing for novices, intermediates, and experts.

Trails reach down three Baldy exposures (east, north, and west), and the art to skiing Sun Valley (at least on sunny days) is to follow the sun around the mountain. The best skiing for novices and lower intermediates is from the Seattle Ridge quad chair, a nice pod of easy skiing set apart from Sun Valley's more challenging terrain. The best skiing for intermediates are long—*very* long—cruisers such as River Run. For experts, Sun Valley's mogul skiing is famous; Exhibition has long been regarded as one of the premier mogul runs in America, although the real mogul action tends to be on the Warm Springs side of the mountain, under the afternoon sun. The quality of Sun Valley bowl skiing can vary dramatically according to snow conditions. After a storm, the skiing—about 1,500 vertical feet of wide-open terrain—can be absolutely exhilarating. Otherwise, depending on the time of day, the snow can be soft, crusty, mushy, or slick.

LESSONS AND PROGRAMS
Three-hour group lessons start at $42, and four-hour children's programs start at $58. A pre-ski children's program, offered weekdays for children under 3, costs $16 per hour. Race, snowboarding, and women's clinics are also offered. For more information, call the ski school (☎ 208/622–2248).

FACILITIES
3,400-foot vertical drop; 2,054 skiable acres; 38% beginner, 45% intermediate, 17% advanced/expert; 3 high-speed quad chairs, 3 quad chairs, 4 triple chairs, 2 double chairs.

LIFT TICKETS
$47 adults, $26 children under 13; up to 15% savings on multiday tickets.

RENTALS
Equipment can be rented at a number of shops in Ketchum or Sun Valley.

Cross-Country Skiing

BACKCOUNTRY SKIING
The nearby **Sawtooth National Recreation Area** offers plenty of backcountry opportunity, with one potential drawback: The term "recreation area"—unlike "park"—means that snowmobiling is permitted. Tours for skiers of all abilities, from first-time tourers to telemarkers, can be arranged through the **Sun Valley Nordic Center** (*see* Track Skiing, *below*).

TRACK SKIING
The **Sun Valley Nordic Center** grooms 40 kilometers (24½ miles) of track on the flatlands and rolling meadows of the valley. Scenic beauty (the trail system doesn't venture far from the resort's developed areas) and challenge (ups and downs are minimal compared with trail systems at many other resorts) are not the strong points here, but the groomers do an excellent job of maintaining the tracks, and instruction is first-rate. One other noteworthy feature: The Nordic center sets some tracks specifically for children—leaving less space between left- and right-ski tracks to account for smaller legs. Because of the open-valley exposure, late-season (late March and onward) trail conditions can be iffy. ☎ *208/622–2250. Trail fee: $11 adults per day, $9 half day (after 1 PM); $6 children 6–12, $5.50 half day. Full-day rental packages start at $14, half day at $12.*

Other Activities

ICE-SKATING

Sure, many resorts have a skating rink or two, but the rink at the Sun Valley Lodge is special. The original rink dates back to 1937 and has been a training and performance spot for skaters from Sonja Heine to Kristi Yamaguchi. Katarina Witt has reportedly named this her favorite place to skate. Shows featuring some of the world's great skaters are still staged here regularly (mainly in the summer); when they aren't being staged, the ice is open to the public. For information, call the **Sun Valley Sports Center** (☎ 208/622–2231).

MONTANA

Big Mountain

Big Mountain (officially named The Big Mountain) has aspirations of bigness beyond the mountain itself. It would like to be *the* big resort, too, and has been trying aggressively to develop its base area and sell real estate to make this happen. But for the moment, Big Mountain is still a little resort, and that's probably something to be thankful for.

Despite ski-area roots that date back to 1936, why hasn't Big Mountain grown much? Perhaps for lack of a sexy name, for starters: Big Mountain, near Whitefish, in Flathead National Forest . . . how enticing does that sound? Also, Whitefish is still a relatively small, remote town, perhaps best reached by train, that forgotten form of travel. (If you want to check out a curious slice of American life, drop by the Whitefish train station at 6 AM, as a sleepy collection of farmers, cowboys, skiers, and dirtballs awaits the arrival of Amtrak's *Empire Builder,* en route from Seattle to Chicago.) Whitefish isn't a bad town, mind you: Folks are quite friendly, but it hasn't stirred up a swankiness or sizzle in the manner of, say, Colorado resort towns. That, too, might be something to be thankful for.

The ski resort is 8 miles from town up a windy mountain and remains comfortably small, popular among train travelers from the Pacific Northwest and the upper Midwest and others simply seeking more of an escape than an event in their ski vacation.

Visitor Information

Central reservations: ☎ 800/858–5439; for nonresort lodging, call the **Flathead Convention and Visitors Association** (☎ 406/756–9091 or 800/543-3105). General information: Box 1400, Whitefish 59937, ☎ 406/862–3511. Snow report: ☎ 406/862–7669.

Getting There

Delta (☎ 800/221–1212), **Horizon Air** (☎ 800/547–9308), and **United Express** (☎ 800/241–6522) offer service to Glacier Park International Airport in Kalispell, 20 miles from the Big Mountain.

Amtrak (☎ 800/872–7245) offers service four times a week to Whitefish from Chicago and Seattle, as well as other points en route.

By car, Big Mountain is 8 miles from Whitefish and 135 miles north of Missoula via U.S. 93.

Getting Around

Having a car is virtually essential at Big Mountain; there is no adequate public transportation between the resort and Whitefish.

Downhill Skiing

At Big Mountain, snowboarders like running into trees. This says more about the nature of Big Mountain's terrain than it does about the sanity of snowboarders (which may or may not be suspect). Its most distinctive features are its widely spaced trees, which—when encased in snow—are known as snow ghosts. Snowboarders seem to think sideswiping snow ghosts is quite a lot of fun.

Big Mountain claims to have 4,000 skiable acres. Although that figure seems inflated, there are, indeed, a lot of terrain to explore and many different lines to discover among those widely spaced trees. The pleasures of exploration and discovery—such as the finding of a fresh cache of powder many days after a snowstorm—are perhaps the main reason to ski Big Mountain.

In general, the pitch is in the intermediate to advanced-intermediate range; there's not a whole lot of supersteep or a whole lot of supereasy skiing. A sameness in pitch, however, doesn't mean a sameness in skiing. With trails falling away on all sides of the mountain, there is a tremendous variation in exposure and hence in snow texture; also take into consideration the number of trees to deal with and the views (the best being northeast toward Glacier National Park).

One of Big Mountain's best features is its bottom-to-top high-speed quad (the "Glacier Chaser"), meaning that runs using the mountain's full 2,200-foot vertical are interrupted by less than 10 minutes of lift-riding time. A negative is weather; foggy days are not uncommon, and that's when you're thankful that those snow ghosts are around as points of visual reference.

LESSONS AND PROGRAMS

Group instruction in downhill is offered for about $23 for a half day ($52 with a lift ticket); cross-country, telemark skiing, and snowboarding lessons are also available. Specialty clinics such as racing and mogul techniques are provided, as well as children's programs. For information call the ski school office (☎ 406/862–3511, ext. 431 or 432).

FACILITIES

2,200-foot vertical drop; 4,000 skiable acres; 25% beginner, 55% intermediate, 20% advanced. 1 high-speed quad chair, 1 quad chair, 4 triple chairs, 1 double chair, 2 surface lifts.

LIFT TICKETS

Day ticket (includes night skiing): $38 adults, $28 juniors (13–18) and senior citizens (over 62), $20 children 7–12. Night skiing (mid-Dec.–Mar., Wed.–Sun. 4:30–10): $12.

RENTALS

Full rental packages (skis, boots, poles) per day: $15 adults, $7.50 children under 7. Snowboard rental: $25 per day.

Cross-Country Skiing

BACKCOUNTRY SKIING

Because of an unusually liberal policy regarding skiing out-of-bounds, backcountry tours are possible from the top of Big Mountain. For the most part, the Big Mountain ski patrol does not prevent skiers from crossing ski-area boundary ropes, although if you do so and get into trouble, you're responsible for paying rescue costs. Although the avalanche danger (*very* relatively speaking) is usually not high around Big Mountain, the chances of getting lost are. It is very easy to ski too far down the wrong drainage, creating the prospect of a tiring and excruciating bushwhack back to the base.

Guide service for backcountry tours (with some telemarking) in Glacier National Park costs $60–$80 per person per day. Excursions are best made on a clear day, since the mountain views are what make the trip. Contact the **Izaak Walton Inn** (*see* Track Skiing, *below*).

TRACK SKIING

There are two track systems in the Whitefish area: 15 groomed kilometers (9 miles) at **The Big Mountain Nordic Center** and another 15 kilometers (9 miles) at the **Glacier Nordic Touring Center** at Grouse Mountain Lodge in Whitefish. Both systems serve their purpose well enough, but don't expect inspiring views or a sense of wilderness seclusion. One advantage that Glacier Nordic Touring Center has is its 5 kilometers (3 miles) of groomed trail for night skiing. Arrangements for cross-country lessons can be made through the ski school office (*see* Lessons and Programs, *above*). *Daily trail fee for The Big Mountain Nordic Center (☎ 406/862–3511): $5 adults, $2 youths 13–18, $1 children 7–12. Rentals (skis, boots, poles): $14 per day. No trail fee for the Glacier Nordic Touring Center (☎ 406/862–4369), but a $2-per-person donation is suggested. Group lessons: $15. Private lessons: $20 per hr. Rentals available at Grouse Mountain Lodge (☎ 406/862–3000, ext. 436).*

Farther afield, the 30 kilometers (18½ miles) of groomed track at **Izaak Walton Inn,** in Essex at the edge of Glacier National Park, *do* combine nicely the pleasures of groomed-trail skiing with the spirit of backcountry skiing. Originally built in 1939 for railroad crews, the inn is now devoted almost exclusively to housing cross-country skiers during the winter. Because it's alongside the railroad tracks, it is also accessible from Whitefish by train. *Box 653, Essex 59916, ☎ 406/888–5700. Track, touring, and telemark rentals available. Multiday packages including skiing, lodging, and meals available.*

Other Activities

DOGSLEDDING

Dog Sled Adventures (Box 34, Olney 59927, ☎ 406/881–2275) leads 12-mile tours in Stillwater State Forest, a few miles northwest of Whitefish.

ICE FISHING

Dangling a line through a sawed hole in the ice isn't the world's most aerobic sport, but because of the many lakes in the Whitefish area, it's a popular pastime. Whitefish Lake is the obvious place to start; the **Tally Lake Ranger District** (☎ 406/862–2508) can recommend other lakes. The best place for ice-fishing gear in Whitefish is **Sportsman & Ski Haus** (105 Baker Ave., ☎ 406/862–3111).

SNOWMOBILING

There are more than 200 groomed snowmobile trails in the Flathead region. **Glacier Motor Sports** (30 9th St., Columbia Falls, ☎ 406/892–2195 or 800/221–5098) rents machines and clothing and also leads guided tours.

Big Sky

Lone Peak, the mountain that looms over Big Sky, is an appropriate metaphor for the resort conceived 25 years ago by the renowned TV newscaster Chet Huntley: Big Sky is a solitary node of civilization in otherwise undeveloped country. Rugged wilderness areas, huge open ranches, and Yellowstone National Park are the main features of this part of Montana. But amid all that wide, empty space, there's Big Sky, which could be considered as much an outpost as a full-service resort.

It is the sort of place where locals are used to driving nearly 50 miles to Bozeman for such simple pleasures as a fresh head of lettuce.

This is not to suggest that Big Sky is uncivilized. Indeed, being just 25 years old and still growing, the resort is quite modern in its design and amenities. It's not as if you can't get a daily newspaper, cable TV, or a substantial, well-prepared meal. Still, the fact remains that Big Sky is one of the most isolated major ski resorts in the country.

This can be both good and bad. It's bad if you're someone who puts a premium on convenient travel arrangements. Getting to Big Sky invariably means at least one plane change en route to Bozeman and about an hour's drive to the resort. It's great, though, if you're someone who appreciates a pervading spirit of the surrounding wilderness and a lack of crowds without having to give up the creature comforts of a warm bed and a good meal.

Recent land transactions around Big Sky have many local people worrying about major real-estate development in the near future that could impinge upon that resort-in-the-wild atmosphere. For the moment, there's a lot more speculation than development activity. It should be some time before hordes of tourists begin descending on Big Sky.

Visitor Information

Central reservations: ☎ 800/548–4486. General information: **Big Sky Ski and Summer Resort** (Box 160001, Big Sky 59716, ☎ 406/995–4211). Snow report: ☎ 406/995–5900.

Getting There

Delta/Schist (☎ 800/221–1212), **Frontier** (☎ 800/432–1359)**Northwest** (☎ 800/225–2525), and **Horizon Air** (☎ 800/547–9308) offer service to Bozeman (Gallatin Field Airport, ☎ 406/388–8321), about 45 miles north of Big Sky. **City Taxi** (☎ 406/586–2341) provides van service to the resort. **Avis, Budget, Hertz,** and **National** rent cars from the airport.

By car, Big Sky is 45 miles south of Bozeman and 50 miles north of West Yellowstone on U.S. 191.

Getting Around

Although there is free shuttle-bus service, it's best to have a car at Big Sky. The resort comprises two developments, the Meadow Village and the Mountain Village, about 6 miles apart. A car is pretty much essential for exploring beyond the resort area (in Yellowstone National Park, for example).

Downhill Skiing

For many years, the attitude of more advanced skiers toward Big Sky was "big deal." There wasn't nearly enough challenging skiing to keep expert skiers interested for long, certainly not for an entire ski week. As a remedy, the Big Sky people strung up the Challenger chairlift, one of the steepest in the country, and figured the problem was solved. Not quite: Big Sky still has the reputation of being a mountain best suited to less skilled skiers, keeping many experts away and keeping the Challenger chair skiing remarkably underpopulated. It's not a huge amount of terrain, but with a nice variety of open-face skiing and tree-and-rock-lined chutes, it *seems* like a lot when you're virtually the only person skiing it. A new aerial tram to the summit gives Big Sky the highest vertical drop in the country, a credit formerly held by Jackson Hole. And if you're looking for more, you can hike up to additional chutes and a very serious couloir.

Now, about that easy-skiing reputation: It wasn't built on thin air. There is, indeed, a good deal of intermediate and lower-intermediate terrain, a combination of wide-open bowl skiing higher up and trail skiing lower down. And as on the Challenger terrain, the skiing on these slopes is pretty unpopulated. To go on any further about the lack of crowds being one of Big Sky's great assets would belabor the point.

The other plus about skiing Big Sky is its wide variety of exposures. Ski areas tend to be built on north-facing slopes where snow usually stays fresher longer, protected from the sun. In addition to these, Big Sky also has plenty of runs facing south and east, and the differing snow textures as a result make for more interesting skiing.

LESSONS AND PROGRAMS
Half-day group-lesson rates are $22; a learn-to-ski package (half-day lesson, equipment rentals, and restricted lift ticket) is $32. Racing, powder, mogul, and snowboarding clinics are also available and start at $22 per person.

FACILITIES
4,180-foot vertical drop; 3,500 skiable acres; 10 beginner, 47% intermediate, 43% advanced; 1 aerial tram, 2 4-passenger gondolas, 2 high-speed quads, 1 quad chair, 3 triple chairs, 3 double chairs, 4 surface lifts.

LIFT TICKETS
$43 adults, $37 children 11–16. Multiday tickets (up to 6 of 7 days) available, with savings of $5 per day.

RENTALS
The resort's **Performance Rentals** (☎ 406/995–5841) at the base of the mountain offers rental packages (skis, boots, poles) at $20 for adults and $14 for children. Moderate rental packages (starting at $13.95 per day for adults, $9 children) are available from **Mad Wolf Ski & Sport** (U.S. 191, 8 mi from ski area, ☎ 406/995-4369).

Cross-Country Skiing

BACKCOUNTRY SKIING
Lone Mountain Ranch (*see* Track Skiing, *below*) offers guided tours in the nearby backcountry as well as in Yellowstone National Park. Tours near Big Sky tend to cover steeper terrain, with opportunities for telemarking, and are best for experienced skiers. Tours in Yellowstone generally cover flat or gently rolling terrain, for which little or no cross-country skiing experience is necessary. In some cases, snow coaches (essentially, snow "buses") take skiers from West Yellowstone to scenic parts of the park for skiing.

TRACK SKIING
Lone Mountain Ranch, a full-service cross-country resort located about 6 miles down the road from the downhill-ski resort, is a rare bird in cross-country circles. Not only are there 75 kilometers (46½ miles) of groomed trails, but there are also lodging and dining facilities for 50 guests. The trail network is superb, with everything from a flat, open golf-course layout to tree-lined trails with as much as 1,600 feet of elevation gain (and loss). Much of the trail network provides a genuine sense of woodsy mountain seclusion. If there is a drawback, it is that moose sometimes wander onto the trails, causing pockmarked tracks and occasional moose-skier confrontations. The things a skier must put up with . . . *Box 160069, Big Sky 59716, ☎ 406/995–4644. Trail fee: $8 per day adults, children under 13 free. Rentals (skis, boots, poles): $10 per day adults, $8 children. Weekly lodging/cross-country skiing packages are available.*

Other Activities

FISHING

On almost any day of the year, no matter how bitter or nasty the weather, there are usually a couple of die-hard anglers laying out lines in the Gallatin River, which runs along U.S. 191. Rivers such as the Madison (one valley west), the Yellowstone (one valley east), and the Gallatin have made southwestern Montana famous among fly fishermen, most of whom visit during the nonwinter months. However, that's not to say the trout stop biting in winter.

Tackle, equipment rentals, and clothing are available at **Gallatin Riverguides** (Box 160212, Big Sky 59716, ☎ 406/995–2290), half a mile south of the Big Sky entrance on U.S. 191. A state fishing license, sold at many local stores, is required. Rental equipment is also offered at **Lone Mountain Ranch** (*see* Cross-Country Skiing, *above*).

SNOWMOBILING

Far and away the most popular nonskiing activity in the region is snowmobiling into Yellowstone National Park. West Yellowstone (50 miles south of Big Sky) prides itself on being the "Snowmobile Capital of the World," and in winter there are at least as many snowmobiles in town as cars.

The most popular excursion is the 60-mile round-trip between West Yellowstone and Old Faithful. Sightings of buffalo and elk are a certainty along the way, and although you'll have to share the track with plenty of other snowmobilers, the scene is nothing like the crowds that descend upon the park in summer.

Several businesses in West Yellowstone rent snowmobiles on a daily basis. One of the best is **Two Top Snowmobile** (645 Gibbon Ave., ☎ 406/646–7802 or 800/522–7802). For longer-term rental packages that include lodging, contact **Yellowstone Tour & Travel** (211 Yellowstone Ave., ☎ 800/221–1151). Guide service is available.

UTAH

Alta/Snowbird

What strange canyon mates Alta and Snowbird make: The two are such close neighbors in Little Cottonwood Canyon that it's possible to ski from one area into the other and back (though not, unfortunately, on the same lift ticket). Yet they are, in almost every way but the quality of their snow, antipodal in character.

Alta is devoutly retro, the sort of place where if the lifts creak (as they often do), the creaks are apt to be revered as part of the Alta legend rather than oiled. Duct tape on ripped nylon overpants is Alta chic, and trail signs are exceedingly rare, since only interloping tourists don't know their way around. Alta is so retro that it is one of the few ski areas left in the country that disallows snowboarding, basically because snowboarding seems to Alta skiers just too faddish and MTV-nouveau. Alta also prides itself in being a preternaturally local ski area, a pride shared by Alta skiers. It's a pride worn so openly on fraying wool sleeves that even those skiers who aren't Alta locals have a peculiar habit of dressing the part and pretending they are.

Snowbird, on the other hand, is Euro-modern, its fast tram quietly whisking skiers in stylish powder suits to the summit. Not only does Snowbird have plenty of trail signs, but most come with Japanese translations. Its concrete-and-steel base facilities express an angular, urban efficiency, the most conspicuous structure being the Cliff Lodge, with a ritzy spa in it, no less. A Cliff Lodge–style complex will be built at the base of Alta sometime after the moon falls out of the night sky.

What the two share is snow—lots of it, with a lightness and quantity that is legendary. In the winter of '93, Snowbird got about three or four more seasons' worth than other resorts. (Alta's figure was approximately the same.) Short of heli-skiing, powder skiing in America gets no better on a consistent basis. It had better be good, because skiing is pretty much all there is to do in the winter in Little Cottonwood Canyon. That's why many Alta and Snowbird visitors lodge 30 minutes away in Salt Lake City, where there are—despite rumors to the contrary—things to do at night.

Visitor Information

Central reservations: ☏ 801/942–0404 for Alta; ☏ 800/453–3000 for Snowbird. General information numbers: **Alta,** ☏ 801/742-3333; **Snowbird,** ☏ 801/742-2222. **Ski Utah** (150 W. 500 South St., Salt Lake City 84101, ☏ 801/534–1779) is an excellent source of information on Utah skiing. Call 800/754–8824 for a free **Utah Winter Vacation Planner.** Snow reports: ☏ 801/521–8102.

Getting There

Salt Lake City International Airport is a major hub for **Delta** (☏ 800/221–1212), with frequent nonstop flights from several U.S. cities. Most other major carriers also fly into Salt Lake.

By car, Alta and Snowbird are about 30 miles from the airport. Take I–215 to the 6200 South Street exit and follow signs for Alta and Snowbird. Keep in mind that all that wonderful snow can make driving in the canyon treacherous. **Canyon Transportation** (☏ 801/255–1841 or 800/255–1841) and **Lewis Bros. Stages** (☏ 801/359–8347 or 800/826-5844) provide individual and group transportation service to the resorts. Also, the **Utah Transit Authority** (☏ 801/287–4636) has regular bus service into Little Cottonwood Canyon.

Getting Around

If you're staying at Alta or Snowbird, there's not much need for a car unless you're planning frequent visits to Salt Lake City or Park City. The **Utah Transit Authority** public bus service (☏ 801/287–4636) between Salt Lake City and the canyon is excellent, the drawback being that buses stop running around 5 PM. Parking at the mouth of the canyon and hitchhiking to the ski areas is a standard mode of transport for many locals. If you do wish to rent a car, most major agencies operate from the Salt Lake airport.

Downhill Skiing

The common denominator is snow, but the differences in the skiing experience at Alta and Snowbird are otherwise significant. While Snowbird presents itself unambiguously with 3,100 vertical feet of in-your-face steepness, Alta is an enigma. Within 15 minutes, by riding the tram and simultaneously scoping out more than 1,000 acres of skiable terrain, you can get a pretty good idea of what Snowbird is all about. On the other hand, you can return to Alta year after year and still discover places to ski you never knew existed before.

Snowbird is an expert's dream and a novice skier's nightmare. Its open bowls, such as Little Cloud and Regulator Johnson, are challenging, while chutes from the Upper Cirque and the Gad Chutes can be positively hair-raising. They're certainly not for skiers in any way doubtful of their skills. On deep-powder days—not uncommon at the

'Bird—those chutes can also be exhilarating for skiers who like that sense of a cushioned free fall with every turn. If you're looking for intermediate cruising runs, however, there's the long, meandering Chips, a few runs from the Gad chairlifts. For lower-intermediate skiers and down, Snowbird is a waste of time. Head for Alta.

Alta devotees (of which there are many) believe in this version of Creation: On the first day, God created Heaven and Earth; on the second, He created Alta. (Some, in fact, even question those priorities.) On your first couple of visits to Alta, you might wonder why people feel this way. You must give Alta time to grow on you; inevitably it will.

Alta is a ski area made to be explored but hard to get around; as mentioned, there are few trail signs. The lift system seems antiquated and poorly laid out, and a lot of trails seem to flatten out quickly or lead nowhere. This is a complex package of terrain, and the more you explore Alta, the richer your rewards.

Alta sprawls across two large basins, Albion and Wildcat, comprising mostly open bowls and meadows but with some trail skiing, too. There is no clear, easily readable fall line as there is at Snowbird; fall lines drop and roll away in many directions and angles. Furthermore, much of the best skiing (for advanced or expert skiers) requires finding obscure traverses or some hiking.

The only solution is simply to stick with it. One day—one run, even—will be your epiphany, and suddenly Alta will explode upon you with possibilities. On the lower slopes of Albion Basin, Alta has a terrific expanse of novice and lower-intermediate terrain. Rolling meadows combine as perhaps the best place in the country for lesser-skilled skiers to learn to ski powder.

LESSONS AND PROGRAMS
At Alta, half-day group lessons for adults and children are available, as are special workshops for teens and adults and children's programs. For information, call the ski school (☎ 801/742–2600). At Snowbird, 2½-hour lessons begin at $45; half-day and full-day children's programs start at $65. Of note is Snowbird's Mountain Experience Program, a combination of guidance and instruction for advanced skiers in challenging, off-slope terrain and variable snow conditions. Full-day workshops start at $65.

FACILITIES
Alta: 2,100-foot vertical drop; 2,200 skiable acres; 25% novice, 40% intermediate, 35% advanced; 6 double chairs, 2 triple chairs. Snowbird: 3,240-foot vertical drop; 2,030 skiable acres; 20% novice, 35% intermediate, 45% advanced. 125-passenger tram, 8 double chairs.

LIFT TICKETS
Alta: $25 per day; Snowbird: $40 for tram and chairs for adults, $26 children under 13, reduced-price chairlift-only tickets available.

RENTALS
Any of several ski shops in the Salt Lake City area offer reasonably priced rental packages, some as low as $5 a day for skis, boots, and poles. Equipment can also be rented at ski shops at Alta and Snowbird; rates range between $8.50 and $25 per day, depending on equipment and store location. Advance rental reservations are available from **Breeze Ski Rentals** (☎ 800/525–0314), with seven stores in the Salt Lake City area, including one at Snowbird's Upper Tram Plaza.

Cross-Country Skiing

There are no groomed tracks in Little Cottonwood Canyon, largely because the canyon configuration is too narrow and steep. Track junkies can go either toward Park City (*see* Cross-Country Skiing *in* Park City/Deer Valley, *below*) or to Solitude ski area (☎ 801/534–1400), with 20 kilometers (12 miles) of groomed trails in Big Cottonwood Canyon. The bottom line for anyone who puts a high premium on logging lots of track mileage is that Alta and Snowbird are poor destinations.

TELEMARKING

Not surprisingly given its retro-ness, Alta has been a center in the resurgence of telemark skiing. The guided **Ski Utah Interconnect** tour (*see* Cross-Country Skiing *in* Park City/Deer Valley, *below*) is a combination of lift-serviced and backcountry skiing that connects Utah's three major skiing canyons: Parley's, Big Cottonwood, and Little Cottonwood. The trip can be negotiated either on telemark skis or regular alpine gear. For the most part, however, avalanche risks make backcountry skiing in this area ill-advised for all but those with the proper safety equipment and considerable backcountry experience.

Other Activities

HELI-SKIING

Because the lift-serviced powder skiing at Alta and Snowbird can be so good, heli-skiing here can often be a real extravagance. On the days when you must go farther afield to find powder, or simply for the blessed solitude of the backcountry, **Wasatch Powderbird Guides** has permits for several thousand acres of skiable terrain, mostly in the basins and drainages on the periphery of Alta and Snowbird. The company guarantees seven runs a day (weather permitting), though it doesn't necessarily guarantee the quality of the snow. In general, heli-skiing is an experience most enjoyable for strong intermediate skiers and better. *Box 920057, Snowbird 84092, ☎ 801/742–2800. Cost: $315–$385 per day, depending on the season. Reservations required at least a day in advance, more during busy periods; a $200 advance deposit guarantees a seat for a specific day. Custom tours available.*

Park City/Deer Valley

Park City and Deer Valley combine as Utah's one true full-service resort, with an old mining town tossed into the package. The skiing might not be as dramatic as elsewhere (e.g., Alta and Snowbird) and the natural snow not quite as plentiful (about 300 inches a winter, compared with about 500 in neighboring Big Cottonwood and Little Cottonwood canyons), but there is a lot of skiing for all levels and much to do besides ski. In large part this has been made possible by the Park City area's geography. While the Cottonwood canyons have a more dramatic beauty, they are too steep and narrow to accommodate much development. Not so in the more rolling and wide-open spaces around Park City, where there are plenty of hotels, restaurants, nightlife, and outdoor activities such as cross-country skiing and snowmobiling.

Park City—sprawling over several square miles—isn't quite a city, as its name implies, but it's no petite resort, either. Main Street, a protected historic district, adds character to an otherwise rather ordinary-looking collection of hotels, condos, restaurants, and businesses. It's not particularly unattractive, but not really inspiring, either.

Deer Valley, 2 miles up the road, was created 15 years ago as the resort that would be skiing's final word in style. The slopes were groomed with a manicurist's attention to detail. Chairlifts had padded seats. Ski "valets" helped you unload your skis. Mountainside lodges actually served something that could be legitimately considered a gourmet lunch. Lots of posh condos and lodges surrounded the resort. The topper was the presence of skiing's master of style and verve, Stein Eriksen.

Some stumbling blocks appeared on the way: A few real estate investors lost their shirts, and many people were turned off by Deer Valley's priciness and the aura of country-club snobbishness. But on the whole, Deer Valley has worked out more or less as planned—perhaps not *the* final word in style and panache, but certainly a notable statement. The buffet at the Silver Lake Lodge may indeed make for the best on-mountain lunch in U.S. skiing.

Visitor Information
Central reservations: ☎ 800/424-3337 for Deer Valley; ☎ 800/222-7275 for Park City; ☎ 801/649–0493 elsewhere in Utah. General information: **Deer Valley** (Box 3149, Park City 84060, ☎ 801/649–1000); **Park City Ski Area** (Box 39, Park City 84060, ☎ 801/649–8111); **Park City Chamber of Commerce** (Box 1630, Park City 84060, ☎ 801/649–6100 or 800/453–1360). **Ski Utah** (150 W. 500 South St., Salt Lake City 84101, ☎ 801/534–1779) is an excellent source of information on Utah skiing. You can get a free **Utah Winter Vacation Planner** from Ski Utah (☎ 800/754–8824). Snow reports: ☎ 801/649–2000 for Deer Valley; ☎ 801/649–9571 for Park City.

Getting There
Salt Lake City International Airport is a major hub for **Delta** (☎ 800/221–1212), with frequent nonstop flights from several U.S. cities. Most other major carriers also fly into Salt Lake.

By car, Park City and Deer Valley are just under 40 miles from Salt Lake City. Take I-80 east to the Park City exit. **Canyon Transportation** (☎ 801/255–1841 or 800/255–1841) and **Lewis Bros. Stages** (☎ 801/359–8347 or 800/826–5844) provide individual and group transportation service to the resorts.

Getting Around
Because of a free shuttle-bus system, a car is not essential when staying at Park City and Deer Valley. But the layout is fairly spread out—it's 6 miles from Deer Valley to Parkwest, another ski area—so a car can be helpful. Most major rental-car companies operate from the Salt Lake City airport.

Downhill Skiing
The rap on Park City has always been that it lacks legitimate expert skiing. Unfair: The east face of Jupiter Peak features some truly hairy, rock-lined chutes, and Portuguese Gap is an elevator shaft lined by trees. The problem is finding these places; the east face requires about a 20-minute traverse and hike from the top of the Jupiter chair.

Park City's main drawback isn't lack of steepness but lack of length; despite a vertical drop of 3,100 feet, it's hard putting together a run of more than about 1,400 vertical feet. The ski area is laid out as a series of segments rather than a single unit. That said, however, Park City probably has the best overall terrain mix of any ski area in Utah, enough to keep skiers of all abilities happy for several days.

Deer Valley, on the other hand, *is* short on legitimate expert terrain: Its forte is wide, meticulously groomed intermediate runs. It is a ski area for those who want to believe that they can ski with the grace of

Stein Eriksen; the moderate pitch of the terrain and the quality of the grooming leads to skiing's version of ballroom dancing. This may change in time for the 1996–97 season: The resort plans to build a new lift in an area called Empire Canyon, which will have additional expert runs and open bowl skiing. You can preview the area during the 1995–96 season by taking a Sno-Cat to the summit and skiing down. For the moment, many a Deer Valley skier's day includes a two- to three-hour midday interlude of feasting on the Silver Lake Lodge buffet and catching major rays on the snow-covered meadow in front of the lodge—an area known appropriately as McHenry's Beach. The skiing experience, in other words, fits right in with the resort's overall image. After a while, however, a certain sense of sameness can set in; that's why it's nice having Park City right next door.

LESSONS AND PROGRAMS
At Park City, a two-hour adult group lesson starts at $37; a four-hour Youth School lesson for children 7–13 starts at $45; an eight-hour ski-school lesson for children three–six costs $68, with lunch included. Call 800/227–2754 for information. Park City also has an excellent instructional program for skiers with disabilities and the Eagle Racing Arena, with three runs and one lift dedicated to racing. At Deer Valley, five-hour adult group lessons start at $57.

FACILITIES
Park City: 3,100-foot vertical drop; 2,200 skiable acres; 17% beginner, 48% intermediate, 35% advanced; 1 4-passenger gondola, 2 high-speed quad chairs, 1 quad chair, 6 triple chairs, 4 double chairs. Deer Valley: 2,200-foot vertical drop; 1,100 skiable acres; 15% beginner, 50% intermediate, 35% advanced; 2 high-speed quad chairs, 9 triple chairs, 2 double chairs.

LIFT TICKETS
Park City: $45 adults, $20 children under 13; night skiing (4–9): $8 adults, $5 children. Deer Valley: $49 adults, $27 children under 13.

RENTALS
Several shops in the Park City and Salt Lake City area rent equipment packages, some for as little as $6 a day. Advance rental reservations are available from **Breeze Ski Rentals** (☎ 800/525–0314), with seven stores in the Salt Lake City area, including one in Park City at the resort center. Rates range between $8.50 and $25 per day, depending on equipment and store. **Jans Mountain Outfitter** (1600 Park Ave., Park City, ☎ 801/649–4949 or 800/745–1020) offers not only equipment packages ($16 per day; $26 for high-performance) but also clothing-rental packages starting at $25 per day.

Cross-Country Skiing
BACKCOUNTRY SKIING
The **Ski Utah Interconnect** is a good trip for alpine skiers who want to get a taste of the backcountry experience. The guided tour covers the three major skiing canyons of the Wasatch Range—Parley's Canyon (in which Park City is located), Big Cottonwood (Brighton and Solitude), and Little Cottonwood (Alta and Snowbird). Ski-area lifts provide uphill transport, and about half of the skiing is within ski-area boundaries. The trip can be negotiated on regular alpine equipment (or on telemark gear) and is recommended only for strong intermediates or better. *Ski Utah Interconnect, c/o Ski Utah, 150 W. 500 South St., Salt Lake City 84101, ☎ 801/534–1907. Daily rates for the 5-area tour from Park City to Snowbird are $95, per person, with return transportation to Park City provided. Reservations required.*

Skiers who want to do some unguided skiing on their own can climb the Guardsman's Pass Road, which is between Deer Valley and Park City and is closed to traffic in winter. Also worth checking out are trails in Iron Canyon near Parkwest.

TRACK SKIING
The only set tracks in the Park City area are at the **White Pine Ski Touring Center,** between Park City and Parkwest. The 20 groomed kilometers (12 miles) are on a flat golf course that's nothing special as far as either scenery or terrain variation is concerned, but adequate for anyone seeking a quick aerobic workout. *Box 680068, Park City 84068,* ☎ *801/649–8710 or 801/649–8701. Trail fee: $8 adults, children under 12 free. Lessons and rentals available.*

Other Activities
HOT-AIR BALLOONING
On a clear day, when the wind is low, it is common to see a hot-air balloon rising above Park City. **Balloon Biz** (Box 17601, Salt Lake City, ☎ 801/278–3051) offers half-hour scenic flights and trips up to two hours. Most flights are just after sunrise, when winds are most predictable.

SNOWMOBILING
The Park City location of **Action Snowmobile Tours** (Guardsman Pass Rd. and Rte. 224, ☎ 801/645–7533) is a mile east of town. Hourly, half-day, and full-day tours are available; proper clothing and gear can be rented here, as well.

WYOMING

Jackson Hole

Jackson Hole is potentially the best ski resort in the United States. The expanse and variety of terrain utterly awe the imagination. There are literally thousands of ways of getting from top to bottom, and not all of them are hellishly steep, which is Jackson's reputation.

There are two reasons why Jackson might not *absolutely* be the country's best ski resort. The first has to do with the base village, a functional but rather ordinary cluster of buildings with limited lodging. Surrounded by protected land (Grand Teton National Park), Teton Village (as it's called) has only limited expansion possibilities. All things considered, this is probably a plus. Still, this is not a good excuse for leaving the existing base layout unimproved; the new management group has pledged to remedy this situation over the next few years. The main alternative to staying in Teton Village is staying in the town of Jackson, about 20 minutes away. All in all, it's not a bad town, but one that has been somewhat hoked up primarily for the sake of the many summer tourists on their way to Grand Teton and Yellowstone national parks.

Jackson's second drawback can be snow, or inconsistency thereof. Because of its location on the eastern flanks of the Tetons, it gets on average about 20 feet less snow in a season than does Grand Targhee, a much smaller resort on the western slope. That predominantly eastern exposure often results in snow conditions (at least on the lower half of the mountain) that are less than ideal, either mushy or crusty.

But when the snow is right, this is truly one of the great skiing experiences in America. Jackson is a place to appreciate both as a skier and a voyeur: Every so often you can witness an extreme skier skiing a line that's positively dazzling in its drama and risk. A glimpse of that alone is worth the price of a lift ticket.

Visitor Information

Central reservations: ☎ 800/443–6931. General information: **Jackson Hole Ski Resort** (Box 290, Teton Village 83025, ☎ 307/733–2292); **Jackson Hole Visitors Council** (532 N. Cache St., Box 982, Jackson 83001, ☎ 307/733–0355 or 800/782–0011). Snow report: ☎ 307/733–2291.

Getting There

American (☎ 800/433–7300) has daily flights from Chicago and Dallas/Fort Worth to Jackson. **Continental** (☎ 800/525–0280) and **Delta** (☎ 800/221–1212) also have flights to Jackson, connecting through Denver or Salt Lake City, respectively. Many lodging facilities offer free airport shuttle-bus service. **Avis, Budget, Hertz,** and **National** rent cars at the airport.

Getting Around

START Public Shuttle Bus (☎ 307/733–4521) offers service between Jackson and Teton Village. Nightly shuttle-bus service is provided by **All Star Transportation** (☎ 307/733–2888). Given the distances between Teton Village, the town of Jackson, and other points of interest in the area, renting a car is a good idea.

Downhill Skiing

Skiing Jackson is a process of imagination as much as the physical process of turning skis. On the trail map, about 60 squiggly lines have been drawn in and designated as named trails, but this does not even begin to suggest the thousands of different skiable routes from top to bottom. The resort claims 2,500 skiable acres, a figure that seems unduly conservative. And while Jackson is best known for its advanced to extreme skiing, it is also a place where imaginative intermediates can go exploring and have the time of their lives.

The tram to the summit of Rendezvous Peak provides access to 4,139 vertical feet of skiing, some of the highest in the United States. If there is a drawback to Jackson skiing, it is that the immediate possibilities from the top are somewhat limited: The choice is either Rendezvous Bowl, wide open and moderately steep; or Corbett's Couloir, perhaps the most famous extreme run in America. You must jump into Corbett's or rappel in by rope. If you don't make that first turn, you don't make any; it can be a long and injurious slide to the bottom. Needless to say, the vast majority of skiers choose Rendezvous Bowl. Thereafter, many, many possibilities unfold. In fact, there is so much skiing (most of it expert and advanced) that one whole side of the mountain (the Hobacks) is generally opened only on fresh powder days.

Most of Jackson's intermediate skiing is from Après Vous Mountain and in Casper Bowl, between Rendezvous and Après Vous. Casper Bowl tends to attract more skiers, but Après Vous is surprisingly underskied (in part because the chair is long and slow). Après Vous is a great place for intermediates to ski groomed runs and to explore off the beaten track. From the chairlifts on Rendezvous Mountain, Gros Ventre (known by locals simply as GV) is flat-out one of the best intermediate runs in the country—about 2,800 vertical feet of big-turn cruising, with a good, consistent pitch most of the way.

Jackson is not a good place for novice skiers. A small cluster of trails near the base is serviceable, but that's about it. The only way novices get to see the summit is to ride the tram to the top, take in the view (which on a clear day is awesome), and ride the tram down.

LESSONS AND PROGRAMS
Half-day group lessons start at $40. A three- to four-hour (depending on group size) Mountain Experience Program for advanced and expert skiers—at $75 per person—is a good introduction to Jackson's challenging terrain. Clinics for teens and people with disabilities are available. The Jackson ski school features extensive children's programs, including day care and lessons for kids six to 13 years old. Of note are extreme-skiing clinics, offered by Doug Coombs, two-time winner of the World Extreme Skiing Championships.

FACILITIES
4,139-foot vertical drop; 2,500 skiable acres; 10% beginner, 40% intermediate, 50% expert; 1 aerial tram, 2 quad chairs, 1 triple chair, 4 double chairs, 1 surface lift.

LIFT TICKETS
$45 adult (all chairlifts), $24 junior (under 15) and senior citizens (65 and older); tram $2 per ride. Savings of about 10% for 5- to 7-day tickets.

RENTALS
Equipment can be rented at **Jackson Hole Ski Shop** (☎ 307/733–2292, ext. 623), with full-package rates starting at around $13 per day for adults, $10 children 6–14, $7 "mini" for children under 6. Equipment can also be rented at **Teton Village Sports** (☎ 307/733–2181) and **Wilderness Sports** (☎ 307/733–4297) in Teton Village and at ski shops in the town of Jackson.

Cross-Country Skiing
BACKCOUNTRY SKIING
Few areas in North America can compete with Jackson Hole when it comes to the breadth, beauty, and variety of backcountry opportunities. For touring skiers, one of the easier areas (because of flatter routes) is along the base of the Tetons toward Jenny and Jackson lakes. In summer, this area can become crowded with national park visitors; solitude is more the order of things in winter. Telemark skiers (or even skiers on alpine gear) can find numerous downhill routes by skiing in from Teton Pass, snow stability permitting. In summer the backcountry excursions along the Teton Crest trail range from easy one-day outings to multiday expeditionary trips (also offered in winter). A guide isn't required for tours to the national park lakes but might be helpful for those unfamiliar with the lay of the land; trails and trail markers set in summer can become obscured by winter snows. When you are touring elsewhere, a guide familiar with the area and avalanche danger is a virtual necessity, for the sake of navigation and safety. The Tetons are big country, and the risks are commensurately big as well.

The **Jackson Hole Nordic Center** (*see* Track Skiing, *below*) leads tours of varying length and difficulty. **Alpine Guides** also leads half-day and full-day backcountry tours into the national parks and other areas near the resort, for more downhill-minded skiers. Arrangements can also be made through the **Jackson Hole Ski School. Jackson Hole Mountain Guides & Climbing School** (Box 7477T, Jackson 83001, ☎ 307/733–4979) leads more strenuous backcountry tours.

TRACK SKIING
The **Jackson Hole Nordic Center** is at the ski-resort base. The 22 kilometers (13½ miles) of groomed track is relatively flat; scenery rather

than heavy aerobic exertion is the main feature. A nice option offered here—because the Nordic Center and the downhill ski area are under the same management—is that downhill skiers with multiday passes can switch over to Nordic skiing in the afternoon for no extra charge. ☎ 307/733–2292. *Trail fee: $8 adult per day, $5 half day; $5 children and senior citizens per day, $3 half day. Rentals (diagonal, skating, touring, and telemark packages available) start at $12 per day adults, $7 children and senior citizens. Lessons (trail fee included) start at $25 adults, $12 children and senior citizens.*

Other Activities

DOGSLEDDING

Dogsledding excursions are available through either **Iditarod Sled Dog Tours** (☎ 307/733–7388) or **Washakie Outfitting** (☎ 307/733–3602).

HELI-SKIING

Daily trips can be arranged through **High Mountain Helicopter Skiing** (☎ 307/733–3274) in Teton Village Sports. In general, a good time to go is when there has been relatively little recent snowfall. For two or three days after a storm, good powder skiing can usually be found within the ski area.

ICE CLIMBING

Among North American climbers, the Tetons are considered a must before hanging up one's ropes and pitons. The mountaineering action continues into winter. Anyone interested in climbing, or learning to climb, can contact **Jackson Hole Mountain Guides & Climbing School** (*see* Cross-Country Skiing, *above*). Offerings range from half-day lessons to multiday trips.

SLEIGH RIDES

The largest herd of elk in North America can be found in winter in the **National Elk Refuge** (☎ 307/733–0277), just north of the town of Jackson. Sleigh rides into the refuge last about 45 minutes and leave the Elk Refuge Visitor Center daily, 10–4, about every 20 minutes. Dinner sleigh rides are also offered at **Spring Creek Resort** (☎ 307/733–8833 or 800/443–6139), with dinner at the resort's Granary restaurant.

SNOWMOBILING

Numerous companies in the Jackson area rent snowmobiles. **Flagg Ranch** (Box 187, Moran 83013, ☎ 307/733–8761 or 800/443–2311), a 1½-hour drive north of Jackson via U.S. 89, is particularly well situated to take advantage of much of the region's most spectacular terrain. Two miles south of Yellowstone and five miles north of Grand Teton National Park, the ranch offers guided and unguided tours of both parks.

3 Special-Interest Vacations: The Outdoors

CHOOSING YOUR VACATION

By Peter Oliver

Updated by
Marcy
Pritchard

IT'S HARD TO IMAGINE VACATIONING OR LIVING in the Rockies without becoming hooked on some kind of outdoor recreation. Any excuse *not* to partake in the outdoors is a lousy excuse, seeing as there is a form of recreation to suit anyone's needs or physical condition. Floating gently down a river on a raft, fishing a fast-flowing stream, riding horseback on a pack trip through the high mountains, climbing 14,000-foot peaks or 1,000-foot rock walls—the opportunities are endless.

Outdoor activities in the Rockies are not only plentiful but also easily accessible. Within an hour of leaving their homes and offices, outdoor jocks can be doing their recreational thing, whatever it might be, in the midst of an exquisitely beautiful backcountry environment. These are people who regard the Rockies as America's greatest open-air playground, and their thinking isn't far off the mark.

Under each heading in this chapter, descriptions of suggested trips are included. These activities are among the best the Rockies have to offer, and they have been chosen to give you ideas for planning an off-the-beaten-path vacation. However, these are *not* complete lists. The Rocky Mountain area is immense, and there is simply not enough space to mention all the recreational opportunities the region holds. If one of the listings doesn't quite fit your specifications, contact the outfitter for other itineraries. Local and regional chambers of commerce are also good sources of information about trip organizers or outfitters operating in a particular area. Another consideration is not to feel limited to a single activity. Many organized trips combine activities: Rafting and fishing is an obvious combination; rafting and mountain biking is a less obvious combo.

Going with a Group

Hiking, pack trips, and river rafting are the recreational activities probably best suited to group travel in the Rockies. Individuals or small groups (four people or fewer), on the other hand, tend to prefer such activities as fishing or mountaineering. Group sizes for organized trips vary considerably, depending on the organizer and the activity. Many trip organizers offer discounts of 10% or more for larger groups, so be sure to inquire. Often, if you are planning a trip with a large group, trip organizers or outfitters are willing to customize. For example, if you're with a group specifically interested in photography or in wildlife, trip organizers have been known to get professional photographers or naturalists to join the group. Recreating as a group gives you leverage with the organizer, and you should use it.

One way to travel with a group is to join before going. Conservation-minded travelers might want to contact the **American Forestry Association** (1516 P St. NW, Washington, DC 20005, ☎ 202/462–3088 or 800/323–1560), a nonprofit organization. An educational alternative is to join a working group; hiking trails tend, for example, to be maintained by volunteers (generally local hiking clubs) that are always recruiting. Park or forest rangers are the best source of information for groups involved in this sort of work. **American Youth Hostels** (Box 37613, Washington, DC 20013, ☎ 202/783–6161) provides service for recreational travelers of all ages (despite the name) and is an especially helpful organization for road cyclists.

Two organizations that teach groups and individuals a variety of wilderness skills—from white-water paddling to mountaineering—are the **Colorado Outward Bound** (945 Pennsylvania St., Denver, CO 80203, ☎ 303/837–0880 or 800/477–2627) and **National Outdoor Leadership School** (Dept. R, 288 Main St., Lander, WY 82520, ☎ 307/332–6973).

Trip Organizers

Many trip organizers specialize in only one type of activity; however, a few companies guide a variety of active trips in the Rockies. (In some cases, these larger companies also act essentially as a clearinghouse or agent for smaller trip outfitters.) At last count, there were something like 5,000 "adventure travel" outfitters operating in North America, a good many of which are here-today, gone-tomorrow operations. Be sure to sign on with a reliable outfitter; getting stuck with a shoddy operator can be disappointing, uncomfortable, and even dangerous. Some sports—white-water rafting and mountaineering, for example—have organizations that license or certify guides, and you should be sure that the guide you're with is properly accredited.

The following are among the most reliable companies that organize active adventures in the Rockies: **American Wilderness Experience** (Box 1486, Boulder, CO 80306, ☎ 800/444–0099); **Mountain Travel/Sobek** (6420 Fairmount Ave., El Cerrito, CA 94530, ☎ 510/527–8100 or 800/227–2384); **The Road Less Traveled** (Box 8187–Q16, Longmont, CO 80501, ☎ 303/678–8750); and **Sierra Club Outings** (730 Polk St., San Francisco, CA 94109, ☎ 415/923–5522).

CANOEING AND KAYAKING

For individual paddlers (as opposed to rafters), the streams and rivers of the Rockies tend to be better suited to kayaking than canoeing. Steep mountains and narrow canyons usually mean fast-flowing water in which the maneuverability of kayaks—especially their ability to roll over and be righted in rough water—is a great asset. A means of transport that has become increasingly popular in recent years for less experienced paddlers is the inflatable kayak.

For true white-water thrill-seekers, June is usually the best month to take on undammed rivers. Before then, high water due to snowmelt runoff can make many rivers dangerous; later in the summer, dwindling flow reduces white-water thrills and exposes rocks. The flow of dammed rivers, of course, can vary at any time of year, according to dam release schedules. Central Idaho and southern Colorado and Utah are where the best rivers for kayaking enthusiasts are found.

It may go without saying that many of the rivers that are good for rafting are also suitable for kayaking and/or canoeing. (For other recommended rivers, *see* Rafting, *below.*)

Before You Go

When planning any vacation on a river, it's important to understand that rivers change, presenting different challenges depending on precipitation and the time of year. To help characterize a river's potential, a class system has been established: A Class I river, for example, is as calm as pond water; a Class V river churns with rapids that can summon all of the mayhem of a washing machine gone haywire. Like any subjective rating system, this one isn't perfect: Conditions can vary dramatically. For example, a river that earns a Class V rating during the spring runoff may be an impassable trickle by late summer. Nevertheless, the rating system gives you an approximate idea of what sort of thrills or hazards to expect. Anything above a Class II river is probably unsuitable for small children.

Expect to get wet; it's part of the fun. Outfitters often provide waterproof containers for cameras, clothing, and sleeping bags, but passengers remain exposed to the elements. If you don't like getting wet, don't go canoeing or kayaking. Also, bring bug repellent as well as a good hat, sunblock, and warm clothing for overnight trips. The sun on the river can be intense, but once it disappears behind canyon walls, the temperature can drop 30° or more. The best footwear is either a pair of water-resistant sandals or old sneakers. Outfitters provide life jackets and, if necessary, paddles and helmets.

To minimize environmental impact as well as ensure a sense of wilderness privacy (riverside campgrounds are often limited to one party per night), a reservation policy is used for many rivers of the West. Often, the reserved times—many of the *prime* times—are prebooked by licensed outfitters, limiting your possibilities if you're planning a self-guided trip. For those rivers with restricted-use policies, you're well advised to write for reservations several months or more in advance. Also, try to be flexible about when and where to go; you might find that the time you want to go is unavailable, or you may find yourself closed out altogether from your first river of choice. If you insist on running a specific river at a specific time, your best bet is to sign on with a guided trip.

The rivers of the Rockies are fed by snowmelt, meaning that the water can be cold, especially early in the summer. Plan accordingly; having warm, dry clothing to change into can mean the difference between a pleasurable and a miserable trip. (Dammed rivers, for which chilled, subsurface water from reservoirs is squeezed through dams, can remain cold throughout the summer.) Figure on spending about $100 a day for a guided trip.

Organizers and Outfitters

Dvorak Kayak & Rafting Expeditions (17921-O U.S. 285, Nathrop, CO 81236, ☎ 800/824–3795) leads trips on the rivers of southwestern Colorado and Utah. **River Travel Center** (Box 6-U, Point Arena, CA 95468, ☎ 800/882–7238) guides trips in Idaho and Utah, among other destinations.

Suggested Trips

Colorado

Black Canyon of the Gunnison River. The 12-mile stretch of the Gunnison River through the Black Canyon (Superintendent, 2233 E. Main St., Box 1648, Montrose 81402, ☎ 970/249–7036) is so narrow and steep that in some sections the distance from rim to rim at the top is less than the distance from the elevation of the rim to the river. In fact, the Black Canyon—a national monument—earned its name because in places very little sunlight reaches the canyon floor. The stretch of the Gunnison through the canyon is one of the premier kayak challenges in North America, with Class IV and V rapids and portages required around bigger drops. It is a section of river that early visitors to the canyon declared unnavigable, and the fact that a few intrepid kayakers are able to make the journey today still stretches belief. This part of the river is only for hardy and experienced paddlers. However, once outside this area designated as a national monument, the canyon opens up, the rapids ease considerably, and the trip becomes more of a quiet float. *Trip organizer:* **Gunnison River Expeditions** *(Box 315, Montrose, CO 81402, ☎ 970/249-4441). Dates: June–Oct. River rating: Class IV–Class V for the upper Gunnison, Class I–Class III for the lower Gunnison.*

Idaho

Salmon River. The Salmon River is not one river but several. As far as kayakers and rafters are concerned, the two Salmons of greatest interest are the Middle Fork (*see* Rafting, *below*) and the Main. The Main is that 80-mile stretch of water with as good a nickname as a river can have: "River of No Return." Although the rapids of the Main are somewhat less fierce or frequent than the rapids on the Middle Fork, the scenery is possibly even more breathtaking. The Main runs through one of the deepest canyons in the country—narrower, certainly, and in places deeper than the Grand Canyon. Running through the heart of the largest wilderness area in the country, the Salmon is a great river for kayakers who appreciate natural beauty and wildlife as much as white-water conquest. *Trip organizer:* **Salmon River Outfitters** *(Box 307, Columbia, CA 95310, ☎ 209/532-2766). Dates: Apr.–Oct. River rating: Class III (possibly Class IV in spring).*

Selway River. Idaho is famous for its white-water rivers, including the Lochsa, the Payette, the Salmon, and the Snake. But perhaps the river that out–white-waters them all—the one that licensed Idaho boaters generally consider the ultimate test of their skill—is the Selway. All the elements that go into making white water come into play here: a steep drop (up to 125 feet per mile), a shallow riverbed, and a narrow passageway. When the snowmelt feeds the river in earnest in June, the Selway can offer true Class V action. By July, it has usually toned down its act to something more like Class IV. Thereafter, the river can become impassably shallow in places. Running through the Selway-Bitterroot Wilderness Area, this is wild country; the two things you can generally count on from the Selway are that you'll get very wet and that you'll see wildlife. Perhaps the biggest challenge of the Selway, though, is simply getting on it. Permits are issued on a lottery basis, and kayaking groups might have to wait a couple of years before landing a prized permit. (Another possibility is that one of the licensed raft companies that runs the river will agree to allow kayakers to accompany a trip, if space is available.) By all accounts, the wait is well worth it. *Trip organizer: Kayakers interested in booking a space on a raft trip should contact the* **River Travel Center** *(see* Organizers and Outfitters, *above). Dates: June–July. River rating: Class III–Class V in early summer.*

Utah

Cataract Canyon. Timing is everything on the section of the Colorado River that runs through Cataract Canyon. Come in spring, and the rapids can rise with Class V force; come in August or September when the river settles back to a Class II or III, and you'll wonder what all the fuss is about. Whatever time of year you come, traveling by kayak (or raft) is one of the best ways to experience Canyonlands National Park (125 W. 200th S, Moab, UT 84532, ☎ 801/259-7164). Not all of the trip, of course, is a battle against white water; gently flowing stretches of the river allow for exploration of Native American ruins and the canyon's dramatic rock formations. *Trip organizer:* **Dvorak Kayak & Rafting Expeditions** *(see* Organizers and Outfitters, *above). Dates: Apr.–Oct. River rating: Class II–Class V in spring.*

Instruction

Cascade Kayak School (Box 60, Garden Valley, ID 83622, ☎ 800/292-7238) features Idaho river trips and instruction by a former U.S. national kayak team coach. **Dvorak Kayak & Rafting Expeditions** (*see* Organizers and Outfitters, *above*) conducts clinics for kayakers of all abilities on the Green River. **Mountain Sports Kayak School** (Box 1986, Steamboat Springs, CO 80488, ☎ 970/879–8794 or 970/879–6910) offers classes primarily for kayakers with previous experience.

For the Family
In general, rafting, which does not necessarily require the paddling skills that kayaking does, is a better way for young children to experience and appreciate river travel (*see* Rafting, *below*).

Resources
American Outdoors (2133 Yarrow St., Lakewood, CO 80227, ☎ 303/377–4811) is a good source of general information on Rocky Mountain Rivers.

CYCLING

The Rockies, not surprisingly, are the land of the mountain bike. In fact, a mountain bike in these parts is as much a cultural statement as it is a recreational vehicle. Not that road bikes are obsolete in the Rockies; several good multiday road tours are possible in the region, although the paved back roads and country inns that make road touring so popular in the Northeast are harder to find in the Rockies.

The mountain bike, on the other hand, has opened up vast stretches of terrain to two-wheelers. A number of ski resorts that run lifts in the summer for sightseers have made arrangements to accommodate mountain bikes, and a popular summer activity for bikers is to launch themselves down ski trails at breakneck speed. The mountain bike has also provided a new means for exploring the backcountry, a fact that doesn't always sit well with hikers. Mountain bikes are prohibited on many trails, especially in national parks, to limit biker-hiker confrontations, but this still leaves thousands of miles of trails and old logging and mining roads to explore.

Before You Go
High, rugged country puts a premium on fitness. Even if you can ride 40 miles at home without breaking a sweat, you might find yourself struggling terribly on steep climbs and in elevations often exceeding 10,000 feet. If you have an extended tour in mind, you might want to come a couple of days early and try some shorter rides, just to acclimatize yourself to the altitude and terrain. Also, it probably goes without saying that engaging in a little pretrip conditioning is likely to make your trip more enjoyable.

On tours where the elevation may vary 4,000 feet or more, the climate can change dramatically. While the valleys may be scorching, high-mountain passes may still be lined with snow in summer. Pack clothing accordingly. (Bicycle racers often stuff newspaper inside their jerseys when descending from high passes to shield themselves from the chill.) Although you shouldn't have much problem renting a bike (trip organizers can usually arrange rentals), it's a good idea to bring your own pair of sturdy, stiff-bottomed cycling shoes to make riding easier, and your own helmet to make riding safer. Summer and early fall are the best times to plan a trip; at other times, snow and ice may still obstruct high-terrain roads and trails.

Guided bike trips generally range in price between $80 and $150 a day, depending on lodging.

Organizers and Outfitters

Kaibab Mountain Bike Tours (Box 339, Moab, UT 84532, ☎ 800/451–1133) specializes mainly in mountain-bike touring in Colorado and Utah. **The Road Less Traveled** (Box 8187–Q16, Longmont, CO 80501, ☎ 303/678–8750) and **Timberline Bicycle Tours** (7975 E. Harvard, No. J, Denver, CO 80231, ☎ 303/759–3804) have extensive lists of bike tours in the Rocky Mountain region.

Suggested Trips

Colorado

Pearl Pass. Mountain-bike historians—if there is such a breed—say that this is the route that got the mountain-biking craze started about 20 years ago. A couple of guys, sitting around in Crested Butte without much to do, decided that a great way to entertain themselves would be to ride the rough old road over Pearl Pass to Aspen. Jeeps did it, so why not bikes? They hopped on board their clunky two-wheelers—a far cry from the sophisticated machinery of today—and with that, a sport was born. Today Crested Butte is probably *the* mountain-biking center of the Rockies (vying with Moab, Utah, for the title), a place where there are more bikes than cars, and probably more bikes than residents, too. It is home each July to **Fat Tire Bike Week** (Box 782, Crested Butte, CO 81224, ☎ 970/349–6817), a week of racing, touring, silly events, and mountain-biker bonding.

The 40-mile trip over Pearl Pass can be done in a day, but you must be in excellent condition to do it. Altitude is the chief enemy of fitness here; the pass itself is close to 13,000 feet. Unless you want to ride back from Aspen, you'll need to make return shuttle arrangements by car or by plane.

San Juan Mountains. The San Juans offer opportunities for both road cyclists and mountain bikers, although in both cases the going can be pretty rugged. For road cyclists, the more-than-200-mile loop linking Durango, Cortez, Ridgway, Ouray, and Silverton is as beautiful a ride as there is in the country, from the mountains to the mesas and back into the mountains. With several high-mountain passes (Red Mountain Pass is above 11,000 feet), however, there is a good deal of high-altitude climbing involved, along with some steep, tricky descents. For mountain bikers, the **San Juan Hut System** (Box 1663, Telluride, CO 81435, ☎ 970/728–6935), used by skiers in winter, creates a 215-mile backcountry link, mostly on old logging and mining roads, between the San Juan Mountains and the canyon country of southeastern Utah. The huts are rustic—without electricity or running water—but with bunk beds and cooking facilities, they're comfortable enough.

Utah

Slickrock Trail. For mountain bikers, this is as much of a shrine as it is a trail. In this regard, the 12-mile trail, originally used by motorcyclists, is a bit like Yankee Stadium: There might be other places like it to strut your stuff, but there is a special aura about strutting your stuff here. The route across polished sandstone demands good balance and bike-handling skills, and erring far from the trail can lead to cliff edges to test one's nerve. Take in the beauty of southern Utah's arid canyon country, and hold on tight. Once you've conquered Slickrock, there are numerous other rides worth checking out in the area, especially in Canyonlands National Park (although before setting out, be sure that bikes are permitted on your trail of choice). If you want company, come in October, when the **Canyonlands Fat Tire Festival** (☎ 801/259–5333) is in session, an event that attracts mountain-bike junkies from around the country. *Trip organizer:* **Rim Tours** *(94 W. 1st N, Moab, UT 84532, ☎ 801/259–5223).*

Instruction

A few ski resorts now have mountain-biking schools in the summer, with the opportunity to ride and learn ski trails. Among the resorts with good instructional programs is **Snowbird** (Snowbird Ski and Summer Resort, Snowbird, UT 84092, ☎ 801/742–2222).

For serious road riders, especially racers, the **Carpenter/Phinney Cycling Camp** (Beaver Creek, CO 81620, ☎ 970/949–5750) at Vail/Beaver Creek is conducted by 1984 Olympic road champion Connie Carpenter and her husband, Davis Phinney, also an Olympic medalist and professional racer. One-week sessions focus on riding technique, training methods, and bicycle maintenance.

For the Family

Multiday tours, as well as the trips listed above, are generally not good recreational choices for families with small children. The riding can be strenuous—made all the more so by the altitude—as well as hazardous, on the road and off. Short half-day or full-day trips with plenty of flat riding are, however, possible at many major Rocky Mountain resorts, where bike rentals in summer are easy to come by. Among the better resorts for this sort of riding are **Aspen** and **Steamboat Springs,** in Colorado; **Sun Valley,** Idaho; and **Park City,** Utah. All are in fairly broad, flat valleys although surrounded—obviously—by mountains. Ask at local bike shops for recommended rides for children. Again, keep in mind that the altitude can be even more taxing on small lungs than on adult lungs, so be conservative in choosing a ride with children.

Resources

American Youth Hostels (Box 37613, Washington, DC 20013, ☎ 202/783–6161) has a strong focus on lodging and tours for cyclists of all ages. **Adventure Cycling Association** (Box 8308, Missoula, MT 59807, ☎ 406/721–1776) is the nation's largest nonprofit recreational cycling organization and is a good source of information on (among other things) bike-tour organizers.

DUDE RANCHES

Wyoming is obviously not the only Rocky Mountain state in which to find dude ranches, but Wyomingites might want you to think so. No state in the Union exalts cowboy life as Wyoming does, and cowboy life is at the heart of what dude ranching is all about. Wyoming has more dude ranches—more than 80 at last count—than any other state.

It was in Wyoming (around Sheridan) that the first dude ranches were opened for business in the early 1900s, which in all likelihood makes dude ranching the earliest form of organized recreational tourism in the Rockies. The dude ranch was originally conceived as a true East-meets-West phenomenon: Wealthy easterners curious about the mythic ruggedness of the West accounted for the "dude" part; ranchers eager to cultivate the money of wealthy tourists as well as their own crops and livestock accounted for the ranch part. Railroad companies, in turn, were happy to have their seats filled, going both west and east. It's no wonder the idea took hold.

The original concept was to give those easterners a taste of real ranch and cowboy life—horseback riding, cattle roping, nights spent in bedrolls by the chuck wagon, and so on. A few dude ranches still promote the working-ranch aspect of the experience, but most have come to realize that there is a larger market in a "softer" ranching experience. In other words, most ranch guests prefer a comfortable bed to sleep in, something more inviting for dinner than jerky and hardtack around the campfire, and recreation other than (or at least in addition to) ranching-related activities. Hence, we get the more modern term "guest ranch." A few old-time dude-ranch owners might insist that there's a difference between a legitimate dude ranch and a guest ranch, but the differences in many cases are more a matter of opinion than definition. In general, though, those ranches that call themselves dude ranches put a heavy emphasis on horseback riding and ranching activities; at guest ranches, such activities share the billing with others, and real ranching is often not part of the mix at all.

The slate of possible activities can vary widely from ranch to ranch. Horseback riding obviously remains Activity No. 1, and at most ranches guests will be given some taste of the working-ranch experience with demonstrations of cowboy (rodeo) skills and the like. Fishing tends to be given second priority, and large ranches usually have access to private waters that otherwise see relatively little fishing activity. After that, almost anything goes: hiking, hunting, mountain biking, tennis, swimming, river rafting (on or off the ranch), and so on. Most ranches try to retain a semblance of ranch life, and at a typical dude ranch, guests stay in log cabins and are served meals family style (everyone eats at the same time, at long tables) in a larger lodge or ranch house. "Family," incidentally, is an important concept here; a dude ranch (or guest ranch) vacation is one of the best ways for a family of widely varying ages and interests to have a shared experience of the Rockies.

Before You Go
Most dude ranches don't require any previous experience with horses, although a few working ranches reserve weeks in spring and fall—when the chore of moving cattle is more intensive than in summer—for experienced riders. No special equipment is necessary, although if you plan to do much fishing, you're best off bringing your own tackle (some ranches have tackle to loan or rent). Be sure to check with the ranch for a list of items you might be expected to bring. If you plan to do much riding, a couple of pairs of sturdy pants, a wide-brimmed hat to shield you from the sun, and outerwear as protection from the possibility of rain or chill should be packed. Casual dress is the norm, for day and evening. Expect to spend at least $110 per day. Depending on the activities you engage in, as well as accommodations, the price can exceed $250 a day.

Organizers and Outfitters
Colorado Dude and Guest Ranch Association (Box 300, Tabernash, CO 80478, ☎ 970/887–3128) and **Old West Dude Ranch Vacations** (c/o American Wilderness Experiences, Box 1486, Boulder, CO 80306, ☎ 800/444–3833).

Suggested Trips

Colorado
Focus Ranch, Slater. This ranch, in the high-mesa country near the Colorado–Wyoming border, is the real thing: a dude ranch that emphasizes ranching and has been steadfast in maintaining its working-ranch character. If you don't like riding, go elsewhere; the predominant activity is working in small groups with professional cowboys to move cattle from one grazing ground to the next. For guests

who need another diversion, there is also good fishing. Although summer activities are skewed toward families, spring and fall are periods reserved for experienced riders and fishermen. *Slater, CO 81653, ☎ 970/583–2410. 5 cabins; accommodations for 30. ⊗ Year-round.*

Wind River Ranch, Estes Park. Any ranch that advertises "modern comfort" and "fine wines" as being among its principal selling points is likely to be more of a guest ranch than a dude ranch, and so it is with Wind River. Not that the ranch lacks historical authenticity: The original homestead dates back more than 100 years. The homesteaders knew what they were doing; this is a spectacular plot of land at the doorstep of Rocky Mountain National Park. The log cabin accommodations are pretty elegant by ranch standards, and the activity roster tends to lean away from horseback riding toward hiking, climbing, and fishing. As for eating, the food here could be called gourmet, a word normally not found in the rancher's lexicon. *Box 3410D, Estes Park, CO 80517, ☎ 970/586–4212 or 800/523–4212. Accommodations for 55. ⊗ June–mid-Sept.*

Wyoming

H F Bar Ranch, Saddlestring. There is something special about being the original, and this ranch can lay claim to being one of the oldest dude ranches in the West. The emphasis is on horseback riding and fishing, accommodations are in cabins, and meals are served family style in the ranch house. In other words, H F Bar follows the dude-ranch book of rules. Another feature here is a remote camp called Willow Park—a destination for horse-pack trips in summer and hunting trips in the fall—15 miles from the ranch in the Big Horn Mountains. *Saddlestring, WY 82840, ☎ 307/684–2487. Ranch open June–mid-Sept; 26 cabins.*

R Lazy S Ranch, Jackson. Jackson Hole, with the spectacle of the Tetons in the background, is true dude-ranch country. Although a number of the "ranches" in the state stretch the ranch concept, the R Lazy S does not—it's one of the largest in the Jackson area. Horseback riding and instruction (for adults and children) is the primary activity, with a secondary emphasis on fishing, either in private waters on the ranch or at other rivers and streams in the area. Accommodations are in the dude-ranch tradition—in log-cabin guest cottages, with meals served in the large main lodge. *Box 308, Teton Village, WY 83025, ☎ 307/733–2655. Accommodations for 45. ⊗ Mid-June–Sept.*

For the Family

Although most dude ranches are ideal for children of all ages, not all feature the same types of activities. Some ranches (more likely to be guest ranches), for example, focus more on fishing and river sports, which are usually of less interest to children than ranching activities. Be sure you know not only the activities a ranch offers but also which are emphasized before booking your vacation.

Resources

Farm, Ranch, and Country Vacations (Farm, Ranch, and Family Vacations, Inc., Box 698, Newfoundland, NJ 07435, ☎ 602/596–0226; $12), by Pat Dickerman, is a good source of information on ranch vacations. State tourism offices can provide lists of dude and guest ranches in the Rocky Mountain region. For other sources of information that can help in selecting a ranch to match your interests, *see* Organizers and Outfitters *above*.

FISHING

Fishing in the Rockies is more than a form of recreation; it is, for many, a secular religion. It breeds the kind of devotion that leads otherwise sane people to stand waist-deep in 35° water in January for hours at a time, or to discuss at length among one another the intricate and intimate details of bug gestation, or to lose their eyesight (as flytiers do) fiddling around with pieces of string and lint. It strains marriages. However, when you consider that the thousands of cold streams and lakes of the Rockies are ideal habitats for trout—cutthroats, browns, rainbows, and lake trout—you can understand why people get so enthusiastic. As Brigham Young said about Salt Lake City, so it could be said about the Rockies by trout fishermen: "This is the right place."

It is hardly an undiscovered place, though; no longer can you toss a line into almost any Rocky Mountain stream and expect a hit within minutes. Nor is this necessarily trophy-fish country. The fish may be plentiful and lively, especially in stocked waters, but considerable fishing activity assures that most of the older, bigger fish are long gone. A partial remedy is that many popular rivers now have catch-and-release stretches, a measure taken to sustain fish populations and to help smaller fish survive to become bigger fish.

Serious fishermen spend a lot of time observing streams to "match the hatch"—that is, to study the insects along a body of water and their state of maturity, then come up with flies from their tackle box that are approximately similar. Less serious anglers can shortcut the process simply by asking tackle-shop proprietors what sort of flies have been working best for a particular area at a particular time and buy flies accordingly. Any angler can make the whole business much, much easier by hiring a knowledgeable guide or signing on with an outfitter.

Before You Go

Fishing licenses, available at tackle shops and a variety of local stores, are required in all Rocky Mountain states. The fishing season may vary from state to state, and from species to species. A few streams are considered "private" streams, in that they are privately stocked by a local club, so be sure you know the rules before making your first cast.

For information on fishing regulations and licenses, contact the following: in Colorado, the **Colorado Division of Wildlife, Central Regional Office** (6060 Broadway, Denver 80216, ☎ 303/297–1192); in Idaho, the **Department of Fish and Game** (600 S. Walnut St., Box 25, Boise 83707, ☎ 208/334–3700); in Montana, the **Montana Department of Fish, Wildlife and Parks** (1420 E. 6th Ave., Helena 59620, ☎ 406/444–2535); in Utah, the **Utah Division of Wildlife Resources** (1596 W. North Temple, Salt Lake City 84116, ☎ 801/538–4700); in Wyoming, **Wyoming Game and Fish** (5400 Bishop Blvd., Cheyenne 82006, ☎ 307/777–4600).

Rocky Mountain water can be cold, especially at higher elevations and especially in spring and fall (and winter, of course). You'd do well to bring waterproof waders or buy them when you arrive in the region. Outfitters and some tackle shops rent equipment, but you're best off bringing your own gear. Lures are another story, though: Whether you plan to fish with flies or other lures, local tackle shops can usually give you a pretty good idea of what works best in a particular region, and you can buy accordingly.

Organizers and Outfitters

Local guide services generally provide the best trip leadership when it comes to fishing. In addition, fishing tends not to be a group activity, although it does tend to be a popular peripheral activity on organized river trips (*see* Canoeing and Kayaking, *above,* and Rafting, *below*) and on pack trips (*see* Pack Trips and Horseback Riding, *below*). Perhaps the most noteworthy organizer of fishing-specific trips is **Orvis** (Rte. 7A, Manchester, VT 05454, ☎ 802/362–1300).

Needless to say, in a region with such a wealth of fishing, there are many guide services and outfitters. For a complete listing of guides or outfitters in a region, probably your best bet is contacting a local or regional chamber of commerce (*see* individual state chapters throughout the book). For state associations of outfitters and guides, also *see* Resources *in* Hiking and Backpacking, *below.*

Suggested Trips

Colorado

Dolores River. The McPhee Dam, constructed in the late 1980s, has changed the character of the Dolores River—changed it for the better, many local anglers would argue. The reservoir formed by the dam has been heavily stocked with rainbow trout by the Colorado Division of Wildlife. The best reservoir fishing, unfortunately, is by boat, which is not the case for the river below the dam. The dam has had a couple of positive influences on fish life in the river: Fish apparently appreciate the nutrients that spill out during regulated dam releases, and the dam also maintains a flow of cool water throughout the summer, something trout enjoy. Here the San Juan Mountains meet mesa country, and it is a pretty place to fish as well as one that is relatively undiscovered (by Colorado standards) when compared with streams and lakes closer to major resorts and population centers. *Trip organizer:* **Outfitter Sporting Goods** (410 Railroad Ave., Dolores, CO 81323, ☎ 970/882–7740) *can provide equipment and information on current fishing conditions.*

Montana

The Southwest. This is the land of *A River Runs Through It,* the acclaimed book (by Norman Maclean) and the movie with trout fishing as a central theme. In fact, several rivers run through the region, notably the Madison, Gallatin, and Yellowstone, which run more or less parallel to one another between Yellowstone National Park and Bozeman, as well as the Big Hole River to the west. All are easily accessible from major roads, which can mean that in summer you might have to drive a ways to find a hole to call your own. However, stream fishing in these parts is a year-round enterprise. Just where the fishing is best along these rivers will vary considerably depending on the source of local knowledge you tap into, but such disagreement no doubt confirms a wealth of opportunity. The Gallatin near Big Sky resort; the Madison south of Ennis as well as at its confluence with the Missouri near Three Forks; the Yellowstone south of Livingstone: These are among the spots that get mentioned most often, though it is hard to go wrong in these parts. And even if you never catch a fish, the mountain ranges that separate these rivers (or vice versa) are among the most beautiful in the Rockies. Just being in this part of the world ought to be enough satisfaction; catching a fish is a bonus. *Trip organizer:* **Blue Ribbon Flies** *(Box 1037, West Yellowstone, MT 59758, ☎ 406/646–7642). The* Montana 1995-1996 Travel Planner *lists more than 150 fishing guides who work in this region.*

Utah

Provo Canyon. Provo Canyon's reputation for having one of the great trout streams in North America is one that many local fisherman regard dubiously. They claim to know better places in Utah to fish, and they complain that the reputation has resulted in overfishing in Provo Canyon. Maybe they're right, but driving through the canyon at any time of year, and in almost any kind of weather, you're assured of seeing believers in the reputation out there in their waders, laying out lines. They are presumably pulling something out of the river to make that immersion in cold water worthwhile. Wilderness seclusion is not the thing here. A heavily used road parallels the river through the canyon, and its location just a few miles from downtown Provo makes this the sort of river where businesspeople can pull on waders over suit trousers and make a few casts after work. But if there is indeed substance to that reputation, this is one of the great places in the Rockies to catch trout.

Wyoming

Wind River Range. For good reason, most visitors to the Jackson Hole area cast their attention westward to the Tetons, as attention-grabbing as any mountain range can be. For that reason, such waters as Jackson and Jenny lakes and the Snake River are heavily fished, especially at the height of the summer tourist season. That's why many local fishermen prefer heading eastward into the Wind River Range of Bridger-Teton National Forest; the scenic grandeur of the Bridger Wilderness area here includes 1,300 lakes and more than 800 miles of streams teeming with fish. This is high country—including Gannett Peak, at 13,804 feet the highest point in Wyoming—meaning that some lakes may remain partially frozen even into July. If the Wind River Range has a drawback, it is lack of easy access: No roads lead through the region, only to it; for the best fishing, you should be prepared to do some hiking. Check at tackle shops in Jackson or Pinedale for recommended fishing spots, but don't necessarily expect to get a straight answer. These are waters Wyomingites would prefer to keep for themselves. *Trip organizer: **Skinner Brothers Guides and Outfitters** (Box 859, Pinedale, WY 82941, ☎ 307/367–2270 or 800/237–9138).*

Instruction

Orvis Fly Fishing Schools (Rte. 7A, Manchester, VT 05255, ☎ 802/362–3622) runs one of the most respected fishing instructional programs in the country and endorses instructional programs around the country. Contact Orvis for a list. Good instruction in the Rocky Mountain region is also offered through **Bud Lilly's Trout Shop** (39 Madison Ave., Box 698 West Yellowstone, MT 59758, ☎ 406/646–7801) and **Telluride Outside** (1982 W. Rte. 145, Box 685, Telluride, CO 81435, ☎ 970/728–3895 or 800/831–6230).

For the Family

Despite the noble effort of *A River Runs Through It* to project an image of fishing as a family sport, the nuances of fishing, especially the patience required, are often lost on children. Perhaps lakes and reservoirs are better choices than streams and rivers as sites for taking the family fishing, because of the possible alternative activities: swimming, boating, or simply exploring the shoreline.

A couple of good choices along the family lines are **Grand Lake,** the largest natural lake in Colorado and not far from Rocky Mountain National Park, and **Jackson Lake** in Grand Teton National Park.

Resources
In Montana, you can contact the **Montana Board of Outfitters** (111 N. Jackson St., Helena 59620, ☎ 406/444–3738); in Idaho, **Idaho Outfitters and Guides Association** (Box 95, Boise 83701, ☎ 800/847–4843). *Field and Stream* magazine is a leading source of information on fishing travel, technique, and equipment.

HIKING AND BACKPACKING

Hiking is the easiest and least expensive way to experience the Rockies; all you need are a sturdy pair of shoes and a desire to explore. (Even a sturdy pair of shoes isn't essential if you stay on well-maintained trails; hikers have been known to travel comfortably for miles in tennis shoes.) There are literally thousands of miles of marked trails in the Rockies, and they are free of any user's fees, as are most backcountry campgrounds (although permits and/or reservations may be required in some places).

It is surprising, then, how few people take advantage of this wealth of recreational opportunity. Each year, visitor surveys in national parks indicate that less than 5% of all visitors venture more than a mile from paved roads. Use of hiking trails outside the national parks is even lighter, and one can only thank the volunteer efforts of local outdoor clubs as well as national organizations for maintaining trails despite such (apparently) little interest among visitors in using them.

There are a couple of things to keep in mind, however. Not all trails are simply hiking trails. On a great many, especially those outside the national parks, don't be surprised to encounter horseback riders, mountain bikers, or even motorized vehicles. Such confrontations can be not only intrusive but also hazardous. Bears, especially in the northern Rockies, present an increasing danger (bear populations have been growing in recent years). Take all bear precautions seriously, and be extra careful traveling in the backcountry in fall, when bears tend to be out foraging in preparation for winter.

Before You Go
In areas (such as national parks) where hiking trails are well marked and well maintained, detailed topographical maps are unnecessary. Rudimentary trail-system maps are usually available at visitor centers or ranger stations for free or for a minimal fee. A good guidebook for the specific region you plan to hike in, however—no matter how well marked the trails—can be extremely helpful. Most guidebooks for hikers provide fairly detailed trail descriptions, including length and elevation gains involved and recommended side trips. Guidebooks to larger areas—a state, for instance—may be helpful in deciding where to go, but they don't serve as well as actual trail guides (*see* Resources, *below*).

If you plan to do much scrambling or bushwhacking, or traveling where trails might not be well marked or maintained, you'll need maps and a compass. Topographical maps are available from the **U.S. Geological Survey** (Distribution Section, Federal Center, Denver, CO 80225). When ordering, be as specific as possible about the area through which you plan to hike; good topographical maps can be expensive. Many local camping, fishing, or hunting stores also carry detailed maps of the surrounding region. One other hiking advantage: It's relatively cheap. Organized-trip costs can be as little as $30 a day. Costs can reach $100 a day for llama trekking.

Organizers and Outfitters

Sierra Club Outings (730 Polk St., San Francisco, CA 94109, ☎ 415/923–5522) and **Wild Horizon Expeditions** (5663 West Fork Rd., Dept. B, Darby, MT 59829, ☎ 406/821–3747) have extensive listings of guided trips in the Rocky Mountain region. One option backpackers might consider is llama trekking, where the beasts bear the burden. A couple of examples: **Teton Llamas** (673N 4200 E, Rigby, ID 83442, ☎ 208/745–6706) leads trips in the Teton area; **High Uinta Llamas** (1010 E. Upper Loop Rd., Kamas, UT 84036, ☎ 801/783–4480) leads trips in the Uintas, Utah's highest mountain range.

Suggested Trips

The following recommended areas for hiking are rated from easy to strenuous. Easier hiking areas involve little climbing—a rarity in the Rockies. Strenuous hiking may involve as much as 5,000 vertical feet in a day's hike, with steep trail sections included.

Idaho

Sawtooth Mountains. At one time, the Sawtooths were in line to become a national park, but it didn't happen: In its zeal to create as much bureaucracy as possible, Congress instead divvied the land up into two parcels—a wilderness area and a national recreation area, each with different regulations. This has not, however, detracted significantly from the beauty of the landscape of rough-edged peaks (hence the name), and perhaps *because* this is not a national park, much of the backcountry here is barely visited, even in the summer. There are 180 lakes, but only the two or three most accessible receive much visitor traffic, mostly locals from the nearby Sun Valley area. Because this is technically national forest, not national park, don't be surprised to encounter mountain bikes and horses on some trails. On many trails, however, don't be surprised if you don't see much of anyone at all. *For information and permits, write to:* **Sawtooth National Forest.** *2647 Kimberly Rd. E, Twin Falls, ID 83301, ☎ 208/737–3200. Trip length: 5–30 mi. Dates: around July–Sept., when trails are generally clear of snow. Difficulty: moderate. Guidebook:* Trails of the Sawtooth and White Cloud Mountains, *by Margaret Fuller.*

Montana

Absaroka-Beartooth Wilderness. While summer visitors swarm into Yellowstone National Park just to the south, relatively few (except for dedicated backcountry travelers) come to the Absaroka-Beartooth Wilderness. One reason is that, unlike Yellowstone, the wilderness area has no paved roads leading into it, although a four-wheel-drive vehicle is not essential for access.

Montana's highest mountains, including 12,799-foot Granite Peak, are encompassed by the wilderness boundaries; because of that, the prime hiking season is relatively short. High-mountain lakes may remain partially frozen even into August. Perhaps the most popular hiking is in the East Fork–Rosebud Creek area, featuring numerous lakes in alpine basins above 9,000 feet. One warning: This is bear country. *For information and permits, write to:* **Custer National Forest** *(2602 1st Ave. N, Box 2556, Billings, MT 59103, ☎ 406/657–6361);* **Gallatin National Forest** *(Federal Bldg., Box 130, Bozeman, MT 59771, ☎ 406/587–6701). Trip length: One-way from East Rosebud Creek to Cooke City is 35 mi. Dates: Aug. is best. Difficulty: moderate–strenuous. Guidebook:* Hiker's Guide to Montana *(Falcon Press).*

Utah

Capitol Reef National Park. While summer visitors crowd the other national parks of southern Utah—Arches, Bryce Canyon, Canyonlands, and Zion—Capitol Reef is the park few people seem to know about. This is, literally, a reef in Utah's desert country—a giant fold in the earth that stretches for more than 100 miles. White rock domes, multicolored cliffs, deep canyons, and natural bridges are the park's physical features, through which the Fremont River has managed to find its course. In summer, hiking on and through all of this rock can be brutally hot (albeit spectacular); a better time to visit is in spring, when days are warm and nights cool, when side-canyon creeks are still full of water, and when wildflowers and cacti are in bloom. Hikes can range from a couple of miles to a couple of days, although in order to get to some of the more remote side canyons or trailheads, a four-wheel-drive vehicle may be helpful. *For information and permits, write to:* **Capitol Reef National Park** *(Superintendent, Torrey, UT 84775, ☎ 801/425–3791). Trip length: 2–15 mi. Dates: Apr.–June is best. Difficulty: moderate. Guidebook: Trail guide and topographical maps available at the visitor center.*

Wyoming

Teton Range. The plus here is that much of the uphill legwork can be dispensed with by aerial tram, the same one that carries Jackson Hole skiers upward in winter. From the top, you can walk through high-mountain basins filled with wildflowers in summer, or along cliff-line ridges, all the while with the stunning facade of the Tetons as a backdrop. A loop of about 30 miles can be made by picking up the Teton Crest Trail, then branching off on the Death Canyon trail. Longer hikes are also possible. Don't necessarily expect solitude; most of the time, you're in Grand Teton National Park, an exceedingly popular tourist destination. However, this route keeps you well away from the visitor crush at the park's main gate, so you aren't likely to encounter hiker traffic jams, either. *For information and permits, write to:* **Grand Teton National Park** *(Drawer 170, Moose, WY 83012, ☎ 307/739–3300). Trip organizer:* **Jackson Hole Mountain Guides** *(Box 7477T, Jackson, WY 83001, ☎ 307/733–4979). Trip length: 30 mi. Dates: July–Aug. are best for weather and wildflowers. Difficulty: moderate. Guidebook:* Hiking the Teton Backcountry, *by Paul Lawrence (Sierra Club Books).*

For the Family

Several ski resorts in the Rockies run lifts in the summer for sightseers, hikers, and mountain bikers. Riding a lift up and hiking down—or taking short hikes along ridgelines—can be a relatively easy way for a family to experience both the beauty of the high country and the joys of hiking. Descents are typically between 2 and 5 miles. National parks tend to be good places to find short, well-marked trails that lead quickly to spectacular scenery, although such routes usually see plenty of traffic in summer. Some trip organizers arrange backpacking outings specifically geared toward families with small children, especially for family groups of eight or more.

Resources

The **American Hiking Society** (Box 20160, Washington, DC 20041, ☎ 703/255–9304) is a general source of hiking information. **The Mountaineers** (306 2nd Ave. W, Seattle, WA 98119) and **Sierra Club Books** (730 Polk St., San Francisco, CA 94109) offer a good selection of Rocky Mountain hiking guides. **Backpacker** magazine (Rodale Press) is the leading national magazine that focuses on hiking and backpacking. Those interested in llama trekking might want to contact the **Colorado Llama Outfitters and Guides Association** (Box 1394, Carbondale, CO 81623).

PACK TRIPS AND HORSEBACK RIDING

As movies and lore will not let us forget, the horse was the animal that enabled settlement of the West. Despite the use of everything from motorcycles to helicopters, ranches continue to rely on horses as a means of transportation. But horses are also an excellent way to get to the Rocky Mountain backcountry, as they can carry loads and travel distances that would be impossible for hikers. (What backpacker, for example, would carry a heavy iron skillet?) In other words, traveling by horseback is a terrific way to experience the big spaces of Rocky Mountain backcountry—the reason there are hundreds of outfitters that guide pack trips throughout the region.

The length, difficulty, and relative luxury of a pack trip can obviously vary considerably, although anyone who expects true luxury is obviously missing the point. Most pack-trip outfitters try to retain the rough edges that are traditionally a part of the pack-trip experience, and that's as it should be. In other words, tents are the usual overnight accommodations (although backcountry lodges or cabins may be used). Morning coffee is traditionally made from grinds dumped in a big pot of hot water and is powerful enough to keep your eardrums ringing for the rest of the day.

Before You Go

Horsemanship is not a prerequisite for most trips, but it is helpful. If you aren't an experienced rider (and even if you are), you can expect to experience some saddle discomfort for the first day or two. If you're unsure of how much of this sort of thing you can put up with, sign up for a shorter trip (one to three days) before taking on an adventure of a week or longer. Another option is to spend a few days at a dude or guest ranch (*see* Dude Ranches, *above*) to get used to life in the saddle, then try a shorter, overnight pack trip organized by the ranch.

Clothing requirements are minimal. A sturdy pair of pants, a wide-brimmed sun hat, and outerwear to protect against rain are about the only necessities. Ask your outfitter for a list of items you'll need. You might be limited in the gear (extra clothing) or luxuries (alcoholic beverages) an outfitter will let you bring along; horses and pack mules are strong but can still carry only so much. Check with your outfitter before showing up at the saddle-up with a trunk full of accessories. Trip costs typically range between $120 and $180 per day.

Organizers and Outfitters

Pack trips tend to be organized by local outfitters or ranches rather than national organizations. Local chambers of commerce can usually provide lists of outfitters who work in a particular area (*see* Resources, *below*).

Suggested Trips

Colorado

Aspen. The T Lazy 7 Ranch outside of Aspen is a good place to find out if pack tripping is for you, before committing yourself to a multiday ride. The ranch rents horses by the hour and by the day (with instruction, if you want). The T Lazy 7's convenient location, on Maroon Creek Road, enables short rides into one of the prettiest, and certainly the most photographed, valleys in Colorado's central Rockies, capped by the twin peaks of the Maroon Bells. If that appeals to you, you can sign up for an overnight pack trip, organized by the ranch, into one of Aspen's surrounding wilderness areas. If you want to find out if you can hack some of the cowboy culture that inevitably comes with pack tripping (both the real thing and show-off stuff put on for tourists), combine a ride with a steak dinner at the ranch, enlivened by country musicians. *Trip organizer:* ***T Lazy 7 Ranch** (3129 Maroon Creek Rd., Aspen, CO 81612, ☎ 970/925–7040 or 970/925–4625; open for horseback riding Memorial Day–mid-Oct.).*

Steamboat Springs. The Yampa and Elk River valleys around Steamboat have a long and continuing ranching history. Indeed, Steamboat has successfully used its cowboy heritage as a way of promoting tourism; the area is full of not only real cowboys but also visitors trying to act the part. Horseback riding is a spectator as well as a participant sport here; every weekend in summer, rodeos are held in the evening at the Steamboat Rodeo Grounds. Riding, instruction, and extended pack trips are offered at a number of ranches in the area, although some may require minimum stays of a week. One ranch that offers the full gamut, from hour-long rides to rides of several days into the surrounding mountains, is Del's Triangle 3 Ranch, about 20 miles north of Steamboat. *Trip organizer:* ***Del's Triangle 3 Ranch** (Box 333, Clark, CO 80428, ☎ 970/879–3495).*

Montana

Bob Marshall Wilderness. Known by locals simply as "the Bob," this wilderness has remained wild enough to have become popular with bears (including a large grizzly population), mountain goats, bighorn sheep, and elk, as well as pack trippers. It is the largest expanse of roadless land in Montana, and while there are trails to be hiked in the Bob, horse-pack trips are a better way to penetrate this huge wilderness. This tends to be big-country riding, best for (though not restricted to) experienced riders, with stretches of more than 20 miles a day common. Among the highlights of the Bob are wildflowers as well as wildlife, mountain scenery (of course), fishing, and the Chinese Wall, a 120-mile-long, reef-like stretch of cliffs, a kind of natural monument to the powers of tectonic forces. *Trip organizer:* ***Snowy Springs Outfitters** (720 Main St., Kalispell, MT 59903, ☎ 406/755–2137). There are dozens of other outfitters who guide horse-pack trips in the Bob. For a list, contact the* ***Montana Board of Outfitters** (111 N. Jackson St., Helena, MT 59620, ☎ 406/444–3738). Dates: July–Aug.*

Wyoming

Pinedale. Pinedale and Jackson are the twin headquarters of the dude-ranch center of the universe. Not surprisingly, this region is also a center for pack tripping. There are mountains to explore in almost every direction (except due south)—the Tetons being the most obvious (and most populated), the Gros Ventres and the Wind Rivers less famous but no less worthy as pack-trip destinations. And, of course, the wonders of Yellowstone lie to the north. Although Pinedale shares a good bit of Jackson's real and faux Western architecture, it isn't nearly as overcome by the inundation of touristy schlock that is Jackson's summertime curse. In other words, Pinedale's authentic cowboy roots tend to be more apparent, making it a good starting point for pack trips into the Wind River Mountains, in particular. There are several ranches and outfitters in the Pinedale area; half-day trail rides, multiday pack trips, spring or fall hunting expeditions—all are possible. *Trip organizer:* ***Bridger Wilderness Outfitters** (Box 561T, Pinedale, WY 82941, ☎ 307/367–2268). Dates: June–Sept. for trail rides and pack trips.*

Instruction

Most ranches and outfitters offer instruction on Western-style riding for those who want it (*also see* Dude Ranches, *above*).

For the Family

Even for adults, an extended pack trip is something best worked up to gradually. That's especially advisable for children. Before launching off on a long trip with younger children (or even teenagers), it's probably a good idea to spend a few days at a dude ranch to find out how well your kids take to horses and riding. The T Lazy 7 Ranch, Bridger Wilderness Outfitters, and Del's Triangle 3 Ranch (*see above* for all) can arrange short rides and instruction for children.

Resources

Local and regional chambers of commerce (*see* individual state chapters throughout the book) are good sources of information on ranches and outfitters. You can get additional information from the **Colorado Outfitters Association** (Box 440021, Aurora, CO 80044, ☎ 303/841–7760), the **Idaho Outfitters and Guides Association** (Box 95, Boise, ID 83701, ☎ 800/847–4843), and the **Montana Board of Outfitters** (111 N. Jackson St., Helena, MT 59620, ☎ 406/444–3738).

RAFTING

River rafting is truly one of the great ways to experience the Rockies. It is a relatively easy way to get into the backcountry, whether on a half-day float or a two-week white-water adventure. For most trips, no special skills or physical conditioning is necessary, although you'll probably want to be in good enough shape to make short hikes to explore side canyons along the way. One bonus of river travel is that, by backcountry standards, you can live—or more accurately, you can *eat*—in relatively high style. Heavy food-and-drink items such as beer, soda, refrigerated meats—items that might be cumbersome on a backpacking or horse-pack trip—are easily stashed and carried along on rafts. But don't expect too much luxury: For extended trips, accommodations in virtually all cases are in tents on riverside beaches.

Note: Raft trips are also run through Cataract Canyon in Utah and on the Selway River in Idaho (*see* Canoeing and Kayaking, *above*).

Before You Go

Rivers are rated according to the ferocity of their water. (For an explanation of class and challenge level, *see* Before You Go *in* Canoeing and Kayaking, *above*.)

"Raft" can mean any of a number of things: an inflated raft in which passengers do the paddling; an inflated raft or wooden dory in which a licensed professional does the work; a motorized raft on which some oar work might be required. Be sure you know what kind of raft you'll be riding—or paddling—before booking a trip. Day trips typically run between $30 and $60 per person. Expect to pay between $80 and $120 for multiday trips.

Organizers and Outfitters

Different companies are licensed to run different rivers, although there may be several companies working the same river. Some organizers combine river rafting with other activities: pack trips, mountain-bike excursions, extended hikes.

The following companies offer a variety of Rocky Mountain river trips: **Adrift Adventures** (Box 577, Moab, UT 84532, ☎ 801/259–8594 or 800/874–4483); **ARTA River Trips** (24000 Casa Loma Rd., Groveland, CA 95321, ☎ 800/323–2782); **Glacier Raft Company** (Box 218D, West Glacier, MT 59936, ☎ 406/888–5454 or 800/332–9995); **Mountain Travel/Sobek** (6420 Fairmount Ave., El Cerrito, CA 94530, ☎ 510/527–8100 or 800/227–2384); **OARS** (Box 67, Angels Camp, CA 95222, ☎ 209/736–4677).

Suggested Trips

Colorado

Dolores River. Beginning in the San Juan Mountains of southwestern Colorado, the Dolores runs north for more than 100 miles before joining the Colorado River near Moab, Utah. This is one of those rivers that tend to flow madly in spring and diminish considerably by midsummer, and for that reason trips are usually run between April and June. Sandstone canyons, Anasazi ruins, and the spring bloom of wildflowers and cacti are trip highlights. For the most part, this is a float, interrupted by rapids that—depending on the flow level—can rate a Class V. *Trip organizer: **OARS** (see Organizers and Outfitters, above). Trip length: 6 or 10 days. Dates: late Apr.–June. River rating: Class II–Class V.*

Idaho

Middle Fork, Salmon River. The Middle Fork is a true rafting legend. Other than running the Colorado River through the Grand Canyon, the Middle Fork offers perhaps the preeminent rafting experience in North America. It is known less, perhaps, for the seriousness of its rapids (mostly rated Class III and IV, although possibly Class V in spring) than for the quantity of rapids. Designated a "wild and scenic river," the 100-mile-plus Middle Fork is not only undammed but also undeveloped; despite the number of river runners who come here each summer, the signs of civilization along the way are exceedingly rare. Steep, tree-studded mountainsides, hot springs, and wildlife are trip highlights—along with all those rapids, of course. *Trip organizers: **Custom River Tours** (Box 7071, Boise, ID 83707, ☎ 208/939–4324); **OARS** or **Sobek** (see Organizers and Outfitters, above). Trip length: 6 days. Dates: June–Sept. River rating: Class III–Class IV (higher in June, lower in Sept.).*

Utah

Green River. The Green River is more of a float than a white-water adventure; although there are plenty of rapids, the most serious rate only a Class III. Floating the Green can be a terrific way to experience Utah's canyon and desert country in midsummer, when the midday heat can brutalize land-bound visitors. The principal geologic features along the way are Desolation and Gray canyons; side trips include visits to Native American ruins and pictographs and a ranch where Butch Cassidy once holed up. Several outfitters run day trips on the Green, but a day trip is hardly worth the effort; the four- or five-day, 80-plus-mile ride is the only way to go. *Trip organizers: **Adrift Adventures** or **OARS** (see Organizers and Outfitters, above). Trip length: 4 or 5 days. Dates: May–Sept. River rating: Class II–Class III.*

Wyoming

Snake River. The Snake has earned a strange footnote in history as the river that Evel Knievel tried (and failed miserably) to jump over on a rocket-powered motorcycle. It deserves better. The Snake is a river for river runners who value scenery over white-water thrills. For the most part, floating rather than taking on rapids is the theme of running the Snake (with trips usually incorporating Jackson Lake); as such, it is a good choice for families with younger children. What makes the trip special is the Teton Range, looming as much as 8,000 feet above the river. *Trip organizers:* **Mad River Float Trips** *(Box 2222, Jackson, WY 83001, ☎ 307/733–6203);* **OARS** *(see Organizers and Outfitters, above). Trip length: 1–5 days. Dates: June–Sept. River rating: Class I–Class II.*

For the Family

Any river can be dangerous, and it is thus not advisable to bring children under seven on any extended river trip. Before taking an extended trip with your children, you might want literally to test the waters with a half-day or one-day excursion. Several outfitters run short trips out of Moab, Utah. For families with younger children, trips aboard larger, motorized rafts are probably safest. Among the trips described here, floating the gentle Snake River is best for young children. The Green is also a fairly gentle river in most places; not so the Dolores or the Middle Fork of the Salmon. Outfitters designate some trips as "adults only," with the cutoff usually being 16 years old.

ROCK CLIMBING AND MOUNTAINEERING

There are two basic things to know about climbing in the Rockies: (1) The Rockies offer almost unlimited climbing opportunities, as you might expect; (2) bad things happen to ill-prepared climbers. The first is stated with great appreciation, and the second is not necessarily stated with great foreboding. It is just a fact. There is one good rule in climbing: If you are unsure of your skills or ability to take on a particular climb, don't do it.

That basic precaution given, the question is: What can you expect when climbing in the Rockies? Not all of the climbing requires great technical skills, if any. Many high peaks, such as Long's Peak in Colorado (*see* Rocky Mountain National Park *in* Suggested Trips, *below*) are walkups. At the same time, of course, there are numerous highly technical climbs, ranging from rock climbing in the mesa and canyon country of southern Colorado and Utah to alpine-style ascents of the mountains of northern Montana. Rare, however, are the sort of big rock faces a climber might encounter in Yosemite or extensive glaciers similar to those found in the Canadian Rockies or in Alaska. Expeditionary climbers, looking for life-on-the-edge challenges or first ascents, go elsewhere.

Before You Go

Climbing in the Rockies is, for some hardcore alpinists, a year-round sport. Certainly rock climbing in the southern region and ice climbing wherever there are stable icefalls are reasonable wintertime sports. Realistically, though, avalanche risks can persist even into May at higher elevations, and winter can begin in earnest by October. The best months, weather-wise, are June and July; the risk of afternoon thunderstorms (also possible earlier in the summer) throw an additional hazard into August climbing.

Generally speaking, the Rockies do not call for great expeditionary preparation. The range is very accessible and the climbs, by alpine standards, relatively short. In other words, long hikes with heavy packs in order to establish a base are rare, and climbs that typically involve less than

6,000 vertical feet are not like dealing with the 10,000 or more vertical feet involved in climbing, say, Mt. Rainier in Washington. There are few major climbs in the Rockies that can't be accomplished in a day or two.

Guide services usually rent technical gear such as helmets, pitons, ropes, and axes. A good guide service can also provide a gear list of necessary items; be sure to ask for one. Some mountaineering stores also rent climbing equipment. As for clothing, temperatures can fluctuate dramatically, even in summer, at higher elevations. Bringing several thin layers of clothing, including a sturdy, waterproof/breathable outer shell, is the best strategy for dealing with weather variations.

Before you sign on with any trip, be sure to clarify to the trip organizer your climbing skills, experience, and physical condition. Climbing tends to be a team sport, and overestimating your capabilities can endanger not only yourself but other team members. A fair self-assessment of your abilities also helps a guide choose an appropriate climbing route; routes (not unlike ski trails) are rated according to their difficulty. The way to a summit may be relatively easy or brutally challenging, depending on the route selected.

Trip costs when going on an organized climb can vary considerably, depending on group size, length of climb, instruction rendered, and equipment supplied. (Outfitters usually rent equipment on a per-item, per-day basis.) Count on spending at least $80 a day. However, the cost of a small-group multiday instructional climb can push $200 a day.

Organizers and Outfitters

The **American Alpine Institute** (1515 12th St., Bellingham, WA 98225, ☎ 360/671–1505) leads trips around the world, ranging from training climbs to expeditionary first ascents. It is one of the most respected climbing organizations in the country.

Suggested Trips

Colorado

Rocky Mountain National Park. There are 78 peaks in the park that rise above 12,000 feet, several of which require no technical skills in order to reach the summit. Via the easiest route, for example, the summit of Long's Peak, the highest point in the park at 14,255 feet, is one of these. This makes the park a good learning and training area for novices.

Climbing in Rocky Mountain National Park has its pros and cons. The pros are variety and ease of access: There are climbs for novices as well as for experienced mountaineers, and most are easily reached from roads leading to and through the park. The cons are (again) ease of access, which can make the park relatively crowded in summer; as many as 800 hikers and climbers have registered to ascend Long's Peak on a single day. Another con is elevation: Not only can the elevation of the park steal one's breath away, but with mountain bases above 9,000 feet, ascents of even the 14,000-footers become relatively short climbs. *For information and permits, write to:* **Rocky Mountain National Park** *(Estes Park, CO 80517, ☎ 970/586–1206 or 970/627–3471). Trip organizer:* **Colorado Mountain School** *(Box 2620S, Estes Park, CO 80517, ☎ 970/586–5758). Guidebook:* Rocky Mountain National Park: Classic Hikes and Climbs, *by Gerry Roach (Fulcrum).*

San Juan Mountains. From the mesas of south central Colorado, the San Juans appear to rise up with startling vertical upthrust, and the trip from Montrose to Ouray, less than 50 miles, is like a trip from one planet to another. Whether the San Juans are Colorado's most dramatic mountains is obviously a matter of debate, but a strong case can certainly be made on their behalf. Not surprisingly, this dramatic verticality lends itself to climbing of various sorts: alpine ascents, rock climbing (notably the Ophir Wall near the small town of Ophir), and ice climbing in winter on waterfalls near Ouray and Telluride. The dominant mountain of the range is Mt. Sneffels, 14,150 feet high, although there are several other peaks that rise above 14,000 feet. Because of the San Juans' southerly location, the climbing season (that is, nonwinter climbing) can last somewhat longer than in the northern Rockies. *For information and permits, write to:* **San Juan National Forest** *(701 Camino del Rio, Room 301, Durango, CO 81301, ☎ 970/247–4874). Trip organizer:* **Fantasy Ridge Alpinism** *(Nugget Bldg., Suite 204, Box 1679, Telluride, CO 81435, ☎ 970/728–3546).*

Wyoming

Grand Teton National Park. In many ways, the 13,770-foot Grand Teton is the most obvious U.S. mountain to climb: 8,000 vertical feet of jagged, exposed rock—more photographed, perhaps, than any other mountain in the nation. It is far from the easiest mountain to climb, however, and requires at least two days of steep rock to deal with on the ascent and rappels of 100 feet (or more) to negotiate on the descent. It is hard to believe that a fellow named Bill Briggs actually skied down the Grand Teton. Fortunately for less experienced climbers, there are other good options in the park, notably 12,325-foot Teewinot Mountain, a more moderate challenge that combines rock, ice, and scrambling. Regardless of the mountain (or route) chosen, the views are as good as they come in the Rockies. *For information and permits, write to:* **Grand Teton National Park** *(Drawer 170, Moose, WY 83012, ☎ 307/739–3300). Trip organizer:* **Jackson Hole Mountain Guides** *(Box 7477T, Jackson, WY 83001, ☎ 307/733–4979). Guidebook:* Climber's Guide to the Tetons *(Grand Teton Natural History Association).*

Wind River Mountains. Much of the appeal of the Wind River Range is the relatively difficult access to major peaks, the most significant of which is Gannett Peak, at 13,804 feet the highest mountain in Wyoming. The trip into the base of the mountain can take two days, with considerable ups and downs and stream crossings that can be dangerous in late spring and early summer. The reward for such effort, however, is seclusion: Climbing Gannett Peak might not be as dramatic as climbing the Grand Teton to the west, but you won't have to face the national park crowds at the beginning or end of the climb. Wind River is a world of granite and glaciers, the latter (though small) being among the last active glaciers in the U.S. Rockies. Other worthy climbs in the Wind River Range are Gannett's neighbors, Mt. Sacajawea and Fremont Peak. *For information and permits, write to:* **Bridger-Teton National Forest** *(Box 1888, Jackson, WY 83001, ☎ 307/739–5500). Trip organizer:* **Jackson Hole Mountain Guides** *(Box 7477T, Jackson, WY 83001, ☎ 307/733–4979).*

Instruction

The **American Alpine Institute** (*see* Organizers and Outfitters, *above*), the **Colorado Mountain School, Fantasy Ridge Alpinism,** and **Jackson Hole Mountain Guides** (*see* Suggested Trips, *above,* for last three references) have instructional programs for novices as well as experienced climbers. One other reputable climbing school in the Jackson area is **Exum School of Mountaineering** (Box 56, Moose 83012, ☎ 307/733-2297). Also, climbing walls (both indoor and outdoor) have opened in many places in the United States, and some offer instructional programs, which are helpful preparation for a trip to the Rockies.

Resources

For technical climbers interested in detailed route descriptions, *The Climber's Guide to North America,* by John Harlin III, is one of the best books on the subject.

4 Colorado

By Jordon
Simon

TEDDY ROOSEVELT SPOKE OF COLORADO as "scenery to bankrupt the English language." Walt Whitman wrote that its beauty "awakens those grandest and subtlest elements in the human soul." For more than 200 years pioneers, poets and presidents alike have rhapsodized over what an increasing number of "out-of-towners" are learning: that Colorado is one of America's prime chunks of real estate.

Colorado is a state of sharp, stunning contrasts. The Rockies create a mountainous spine that's larger than Switzerland, with 52 eternally snow-capped summits towering higher than 14,000 feet. Yet its eastern third is a sea of hypnotically waving grasslands; its southwest, a vibrant multihued desert, carved with pink and mauve canyons, vaulting cinnamon spires, and gnarled red rock monoliths. Its mighty rivers, the Colorado, Arkansas, and Gunnison, etch deep, yawning chasms every bit as impressive as the shimmering blue-tinged glaciers and jagged peaks of the San Juan, Sangre de Cristo, and Front ranges. Add to this glittering sapphire lakes and jade forests, and you have an outdoor paradise second to none.

Much of the state's visual appeal can also be attributed to the legacy of the frontier and mining days, when gold, silver, and railroad barons left an equally rich treasure trove of Victorian architecture in the lavish monuments they built to themselves. The Old West comes alive in Colorado, where you're practically driving through the pages of a history book. The first Europeans to explore were the Spanish, who left their imprint in the lyrical names and distinctive architecture of the southern part of the state. They were followed by trappers, scouts, and explorers, including some of the legendary names in American history—Zebulon Pike, Kit Carson, Stephen Long, and William Bent—intent on exploiting some of the area's rich natural resources, including vast lodes of gold and silver. In so doing they displaced—and often massacred—the original settlers, Pawnee, Comanche, Ute, and Pueblo, whose ancestors, the Anasazi, fashioned the spectacular, haunting cliff dwellings of Mesa Verde National Park.

The controversy and contentiousness live on. In 1992 Colorado made national headlines when it passed Amendment 2, carefully worded (some say deliberately vague) legislation designed to outlaw anti-discrimination bills. In reality, the amendment was aimed directly at homosexuals, and sought to reverse existing local gay-rights ordinances. (Aspen, Boulder, and Denver were among the first communities in the nation to pass such ordinances.)

In response to the legislation, a boycott was called (and has since been canceled) by liberal and gay/lesbian groups nationwide, with mixed results. The state picked up almost as much convention business from conservative organizations as it lost, and a superb 1992-93 snow season brought skiers in droves. Amendment 2 was declared unconstitutional by the state Supreme Court in 1993. Colorado appealed, and the U.S. Supreme Court agreed to hear arguments in the fall of 1995, with a decision to follow in early 1996.

Indeed, despite the Amendment 2 controversy, Colorado has its progressive side: It was the first state to send a Native American to the Senate in 1992: Ben "Nighthorse" Campbell, himself a figure of controversy for his flamboyant style and mannerisms. Senator Camp-

Colorado

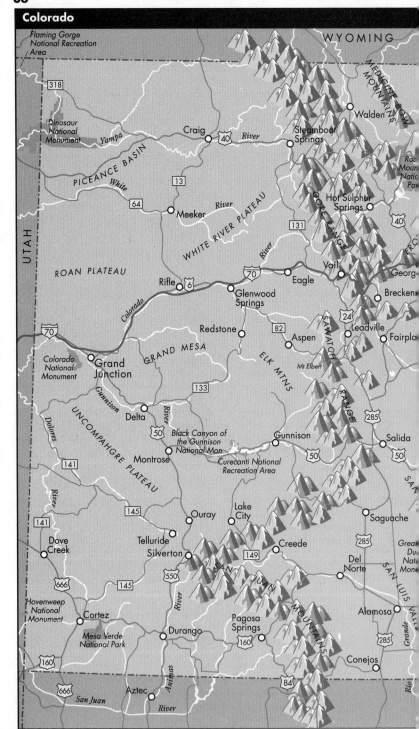

WYOMING

UTAH

Flaming Gorge
National Recreation
Area

318

Dinosaur
National
Monument

Yampa

Craig

40

River

Steamboat
Springs

Walden

MEDICINE BOW MOUNTAINS

Roc
Moun
Natio
Par

PICEANCE BASIN

White

13

64

Meeker

River

WHITE RIVER PLATEAU

River

131

Hot Sulphur
Springs

GORE RANGE

40

ROAN PLATEAU

Colorado

Rifle

6

70

Glenwood
Springs

Eagle

Vail

Georg

70

Redstone

82

Aspen

SAWATCH

24

Leadville

Brecken

Fairpla

Colorado
National
Monument

Grand
Junction

GRAND MESA

Mt Elbert

RANGE

Gunnison

Delta

133

River

285

UNCOMPAHGRE PLATEAU

Dolores

50

Black Canyon of
the Gunnison
National Mon

Gunnison

Salida

141

Montrose

Curecanti National
Recreation Area

50

50

River

145

Ouray

Lake
City

Saguache

SAN

141

Dove
Creek

Telluride

Silverton

550

SAN

149

Creede

285

Del
Norte

Grea
Du
Nati
Mon

SAN LUIS VALL

666

145

JUAN

Alamosa

Hovenweep
National
Monument

Cortez

Durango

MOUNTAINS

285

Mesa Verde
National Park

160

Pagosa
Springs

160

Conejos

Rio

160

666

San Juan

Aztec

River

Anmas

84

bell proved to be a maverick in true Colorado tradition when he switched parties from Democratic to Republican upon reaching Congress.

Along with feisty independence, be it right- or left-wing, Coloradans have always displayed an eccentric, even ostentatious streak. State history is animated by stories of fabulous wealth and equally spectacular ruin in the bountiful precious-metal mines. Discovery of gold in 1859 spurred the first major settlement of Colorado, followed by the inevitable railroad lines for transport. When the lodes petered out, many of the thriving communities became virtual ghost towns, until the discovery of black gold in the oil-shale reserves of northwest Colorado and, especially, white gold on the ski slopes.

Today Colorado is a state of unabashed nature lovers and outdoors enthusiasts. Though most people associate the state with skiing, residents have a saying, "We came for the winters, but we stayed for the summers." In addition to skiing and snowmobiling in winter, they climb, hike, bike, fish, and camp in the summer, making Colorado one of America's premier four-seasons destinations.

DENVER

Denver's buildings jut jaggedly into the skyline, creating an incongruous setting in a state that prides itself on its pristine wilderness. But for all the high-power, high-rise grandeur displayed downtown, Denver is really a cow town at heart. Throughout the 1960s and '70s, when the city mushroomed on a huge surge of oil and energy revenues, Denverites hustled to discard evidence of their Western past to prove their modernity. The last decade, however, has brought an influx of young, well-educated professionals—Denver has the second-largest number of college graduates per capita in the country—lured by Colorado's outdoor mystique and encouraged by the megalopolis's business prospects.

Most Denverites are unabashed nature lovers whose weekends are often spent skiing, camping, hiking, biking, or fishing. For them, preserving the environment and the city's rich mining and ranching heritage are of equally vital importance to the quality of life. Areas like LoDo—the historic lower downtown—now buzz with jazz clubs, restaurants, and art galleries housed in carefully restored century-old buildings. The culturally diverse populace avidly supports the Denver Art Museum, the Museum of Natural History, and the new Museo de las Americas. The expert acting troupe of the Denver Center Theater Company is at home in both traditional mountings of classics and more provocative contemporary works.

Those who don't know Denver may be in for a few big surprises. Although one of its monikers is the "Mile High City," another is "Queen City of the Plains." Denver is flat, with the Rocky Mountains creating a spectacular backdrop; this combination keeps the climate delightfully mild. Denverites do not spend their winters digging out of fierce snowstorms and skiing out their front doors. They take advantage of a comfortable climate, historic city blocks, a cultural center, and sky's-the-limit outdoor adventures just minutes from downtown. All of these factors make this appealing city more than just a layover between home and the Rockies.

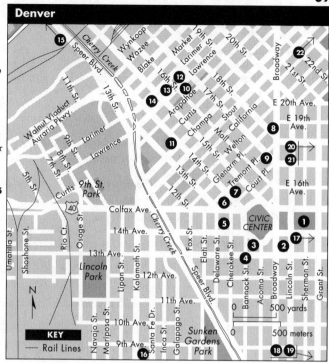

Exploring

Orientation

Most of Denver's top attractions are concentrated downtown, a remarkably compact area that can be toured on foot. However, a car is recommended for exploring outside of downtown proper.

Tour 1: Downtown

Numbers in the margin correspond to points of interest on the Denver map.

★ **Denver** presents its official face to the world at the **Civic Center,** a three-block-long park with lawns, gardens, and a Greek amphitheater

❶ that together form a serene backdrop for the **State Capitol,** which was built in 1894. It was constructed mostly of materials indigenous to Colorado, including marble, granite, and rose onyx. Especially inspiring is the gold-leaf dome, a reminder of the state's mining heritage. Visitors can climb to the balcony for a panoramic view of the Rockies, or merely to the 13th step, which is exactly 1-mile high (above sea level). *1475 Sherman St.,* ☎ *303/866–2604.* ☛ *Free.* ☉ *Mon.–Sat. 9–4; tours available on the half-hour.*

❷ Just off the Civic Center is the **Colorado History Museum,** which contains vibrant depictions of the state's frontier past and how the cultures have collided here. Changing exhibits highlight eras such as the Jazz Age and the Gay '90s; permanent displays include Conestoga wagons, great old touring cars, and an extraordinary time line called "The Colorado Chronicle 1800–1950," which depicts the state's history in amazing detail. The display stretches 112 feet, 6 inches, and dedicates 9 inches to each year. It's crammed with artifacts from rifles to land-grant surveys and old daguerreotypes. *1300 Broadway,* ☎ *303/866–*

3682. ☛ *$3 adults, $1.50 children and senior citizens.* ✆ *Mon.–Sat. 10–4:30, Sun. noon–4:30.*

★ ❸ The **Denver Art Museum,** also off the Civic Center park, was remodeled for its 1993 centennial and has superlative, uniquely displayed holdings in Asian, pre-Columbian, Spanish-Colonial, and contemporary Southwestern art. A model of museum design, with dazzling mountain views as a bonus, the museum is intelligently laid out, highly accessible (providing just enough information while emphasizing the aesthetics), and thoughtfully lit. Children will love the imaginative hands-on exhibits and video corners. If there's a flaw here, it's that space for the fine European collection is limited until renovations are completed in 1997. *100 W. 14th Avenue Pkwy.,* ☎ *303/640–2793.* ☛ *$3 adults, $1.50 students and senior citizens, children under 6 and Sat. free.* ✆ *Tues.–Sat. 10–5, Sun. noon–5.*

❹ Close by is the **Byers-Evans House,** an elaborate redbrick Victorian built in 1883 and restored to its pre–World War I condition. It serves as the **Denver History Museum,** offering exciting interactive video exhibits and history programs about the city. *1310 Bannock St.,* ☎ *303/620–4933.* ☛ *$2.50 adults, $1.25 children and senior citizens.* ✆ *Tues.–Sun. 11–3.*

❺ A few blocks away is Denver's **U.S. Mint,** the source of all those coins stamped with a *D.* Free tours take guests around the facility, where more than 5 billion coins are minted yearly, and where the nation's second-largest hoard of gold is displayed. *W. Colfax Ave. and Cherokee Sts.,* ☎ *303/844–3582.* ☛ *Free. Tours weekdays 8–3 every 20 min, except during inventory (usually last 2 wks in June).*

❻ A fascinating detour is to the **Denver Firefighters Museum,** which occupies the space of Denver's first firehouse. All the original items of the trade are displayed here, including uniforms, nets, fire carts and trucks, bells, and switchboards. *1326 Tremont Pl.,* ☎ *303/892–1100.* ☛ *$2.* ✆ *Weekdays 10–2.*

❼ From here, it's one block up to the tranquil **Trianon Museum and Art Gallery,** and its marvelous collection of 18th- and 19th-century European furnishings and objets d'art. The museum also houses a rare gun collection, with pieces dating from the 16th century onward. Guided tours are offered. *335 14th St.,* ☎ *303/623–0739.* ☛ *$1.* ✆ *Mon.–Sat. 10–4.*

★ Walk up to the **16th Street Mall** to pick up one of the free shuttle buses that run the length of downtown, providing a good, quick tour. These buses are the only vehicles allowed on the otherwise pedestrian-only street, which is lined with shady trees, outdoor cafés, historic buildings, and tempting shops.

★ ❽ Hop off at Tremont Place and walk a block to the **Museum of Western Art,** in a converted frontier-era bordello (on the National Register of Historic Places). It now houses works by those artistic heroes of the Western mythos: Remington, Bierstadt, and Russell, and latter-day masters such as O'Keeffe. The collection is highly distilled; all the vividly composed works are considered by experts to be among the artists' finest and most representative pieces. *1727 Tremont Ave.,* ☎ *303/296–1880.* ☛ *$3 adults, $2 students and senior citizens, children under 7 free.* ✆ *Tues.–Sat. 10–4:30.*

❾ Catercorner from the museum is the majestic **Brown Palace Hotel** (321 17th St.), Denver's hotel empress, built in 1892 and still considered the city's most prestigious address. Reputedly this was the first atrium hotel in the United States: Its ornate lobby and nine stories are crowned by a stunning Tiffany stained-glass window. (*See* Lodging, *below.*)

As you head back down the mall toward lower downtown, you'll see ⑩ the 330-foot-high **Daniels and Fisher Tower** (16th and Arapahoe Sts.), built to emulate the campanile of St. Mark's Cathedral in Venice. ⑪ Head a block east to Curtis, then south about two blocks to the **Denver Performing Arts Complex** (14th and Curtis Sts., ☎ 303/893–4000), a huge, impressively high-tech group of theaters connected by a soaring, glass archway to a futuristic symphony hall. Guided tours are available, but times vary so you must call ahead.

⑫ Return to Arapahoe and go one block to the **Tabor Center,** a festive shopping mall with more than 60 stores and attractions, including fast-food eateries, strolling troubadours, jugglers and fire-eaters, and splash-⑬ ing fountains. Across from Tabor Center is **Writer Square,** whose shops line the entrance to the arched redbrick courtyards of historic ⑭ **Larimer Square** (Larimer and 15th Sts.), Denver's most charming shopping district, where some of the city's oldest retail buildings and classiest specialty shops do business. Larimer Square—actually a street—was saved from the wrecker's ball by a determined preservationist in the 1960s, when the city went demolition-crazy in its eagerness to present a more youthful image.

Larimer runs roughly along a boundary of **LoDo,** an historic lower downtown area now home to art galleries, nightclubs, and restaurants ranging from Denver's most upscale to its most down-home. This part of town was once the city's thriving retail center, then it fell into disuse and slid into slums; in the past few years it has been undergoing a vigorous revival spearheaded not just by avant-garde artists and retailers, but by loft dwellers who have taken over old warehouses here. The handsome new Coors Stadium, home of baseball's Colorado Rockies, has further galvanized the area. Its old-fashioned brick and grillwork facade, ornamented with 41 blue, green, and white terra-cotta columbines (the state flower), was designed to blend in with the surrounding Victorian warehouses.

A little outside the downtown loop (west on 15th St., just past the confluence of the South Platte River and Cherry Creek) is the wonderfully ⑮ odd **Forney Transportation Museum.** Resembling an abandoned auto yard, the property outside is littered with peeling carriages, corroding cabooses, and classic cycles; inside, in the not-quite-thought-out exhibit rooms, are an 1898 Renault coupe, Teddy Roosevelt's tour car, Aly Khan's Rolls, and a Big Boy steam locomotive, among other collectibles. Strangely enough, there's also a room dedicated to 18th-century military uniforms. Anyone who grew up on model cars or Lionel trains will wander this eccentric museum in a happy daze. *1416 Platte St.,* ☎ *303/433–3643.* ☛ *$4 adults, $3.50 senior citizens, $2 children 12–16, $1 children 5–11.* ☉ *Mon.–Sat. 10–5, Sun. 11–5.*

From the Forney, take I–25 south, exit east on Sixth Avenue, and head ⑯ north on Santa Fe Drive. The **Museo de las Americas,** the region's first museum dedicated to the achievements of Latinos in the Americas, has a permanent collection as well as rotating exhibits that cover everything from Hispanics in the state legislature to Latin American women artists in the 20th century. *861 Santa Fe Dr.,* ☎ *303/571–4401.* ☛ *$2 adults, $1 students and senior citizens, children under 13 free.* ☉ *Tues.–Sat. 10–5.*

Tour 2: East of Downtown

A car is recommended on this tour, as it covers an area more spread out than downtown.

⑰ The **Molly Brown House,** on Pennsylvania Street between East 12th and 13th avenues, not far from the capitol, is a Victorian confection that celebrates the life and times of the scandalous, "unsinkable" Molly Brown, heroine of the *Titanic* who courageously saved several lives and continued to provide assistance to survivors back on terra firma. Costumed guides and original furnishings in the museum including flamboyant gilt-edge wallpaper, lace curtains, tile fireplaces, and tapestries) evoke bygone days. A bit of trivia: Margaret Tobin Brown was known as Maggie, not Molly, during her lifetime. Meredith Willson, the composer-lyricist of the musical, *The Unsinkable Molly Brown,* based on Brown's life, thought Molly was easier to sing. *1340 Pennsylvania St.,* ☎ *303/832–4092.* ☛ *$3.* ☺ *Mon.–Sat. 10–4, Sun. noon–4.*

⑱ A few blocks down the street, the Beaux Arts–style **Grant-Humphreys Mansion** is a grandiose, 42-room testament to the proper Denver society that looked down on Molly at the turn of the century. *770 Pennsylvania St.,* ☎ *303/894–2506.* ☛ *$3 adults, $1.50 children 6–17.* ☺ *Tues.–Fri. 10–2.*

⑲ Head east on Eighth Avenue to the **Denver Botanic Gardens,** a flowering respite from the urban hustle and bustle. A conservatory looms above; among its displays is a re-creation of a tropical rain forest; outside are a Japanese garden, a rock garden, gazebos and arboretums, and gorgeous horticultural displays (at their peak during summer). *1005 York St.,* ☎ *303/331–4010.* ☛ *$3 adults, $1.50 senior citizens, $1 children.* ☺ *Daily 9–4:45.*

★ Northeast of downtown, between Colorado Boulevard and York Street, along 17th Avenue, is **City Park,** Denver's largest public space of its kind, with rose gardens, lakes, a golf course, tennis courts, and two of the city's most popular attractions: the Denver Zoo and the Denver Museum of Natural History. A shuttle runs between the two.

⑳ The engaging **Denver Zoo** features a nursery for baby animals; a polar bear exhibit, where visitors can watch the animals swim underwater; seal shows; educational programs on endangered species; and the *Zooliner* train, which snakes through the property as guests are given a safari lecture. The 5-acre, $10 million "Primate Panorama" will open in August 1996 for the zoo's centennial and will house more than 25 species of primates in state-of-the-art environments that simulate the animals' natural habitats. *E. 23rd St., between York St. and Colorado Blvd.,* ☎ *303/331–4110.* ☛ *$4 adults, $2 senior citizens and children.* ☺ *Daily 10–6.*

★ **㉑** The seventh-largest museum in the United States, the **Denver Museum of Natural History,** offers a rich combination of traditional collections—dinosaur remains, a mineralogy display, an Egyptology wing—and intriguing hands-on exhibits such as the "Hall of Life," where you can test your health and fitness on various contraptions. The massive complex includes an IMAX movie theater and the Gates Planetarium. A new permanent exhibit, "Prehistoric Journey," opens in October 1995. Plans call for a walk-through exhibit covering seven stages of the earth's development, with each "envirorama" representing a specific area of North America or Australia at a particular time. *2001 Colorado Blvd.,* ☎ *303/322–7009.* ☛ *To museum: $4 adults, $2 senior citizens and children.* ☛ *To IMAX: $5 adults, $4 senior citizens and children.*

☛ *To planetarium: $3.50 adults, $2.50 senior citizens and children.*
⊙ *Daily 9–5.*

㉒ Return to City Park, and exit north along York Street, then turn west on 30th Avenue to the **Black American West Museum and Heritage Center,** with its revealing collection of documents that depict the vast contributions African Americans made to opening up the West. Nearly a third of the cowboys and many pioneer teachers and doctors were African Americans. *3091 California St.,* ☎ *303/292–2566.* ☛ *$2 adults, $1.50 senior citizens, 75¢ children 12–17, 50¢ children under 12.* ⊙ *Wed.–Fri. 10–2, Sat. noon–5, Sun. 2–5.*

Short Excursion from Denver: Central City/ Black Hawk

Central City, as well as Black Hawk, are easily reached by taking I–70 or Highway 6 west from Denver and turning north on CO 119. Both towns can be explored on foot. When limited-stakes gambling was in-

★ troduced in 1991 to the beautifully preserved old mining towns of **Central City/Black Hawk,** howls of protest were drowned out by cheers from struggling townspeople. Fortunately, strict zoning laws were legislated to protect the towns' architectural integrity, and by and large the laws have been successful. However, the general atmosphere may be more raucous today than it was in its heyday in the 1860s, thanks to the steady stream of tour buses and loudly jingling coffers. Gaming here is restricted to blackjack, poker, and slots, and the maximum bet is $5.

There are nearly 40 casinos in Black Hawk and Central City. All are in historic buildings—from jails to mansions—and their plush interiors have been lavishly decorated to re-create the Old West era—a period when this town was known as the "Richest Square Mile on Earth."

The most notable attraction in Black Hawk is the **Lace House,** a superb example of Carpenter Gothic architecture, with signature lacy gingerbread trim. *161 Main St.,* ☎ *303/582–5382.* ☛ *$1.* ⊙ *Daily 11–6.*

In Central City, make your first stop the intriguing **Gilpin County Historical Society Museum** (228 E. High St., ☎ 303/582–5283; ☛ $3; open daily 9–5), where photos and reproductions, as well as vintage pieces from different periods of Gilpin County history, paint a richly detailed portrait of life in a typical rowdy mining community.

Around the corner, several attractions line Eureka Street. The **Teller House Casino, Restaurant, and Museum** (120 Eureka St., ☎ 303/582–3800) was once one of the West's ritziest hotels. Upstairs is the opulent room that was occupied by President Grant and, later, by Mae West. Downstairs, the floor of the famous Face Bar is adorned with the portrait of a mystery woman named Madeline, painted in 1936 by Herndon Davis. Some say it was created as a lark, others bet it was done for the price of a drink. Down the block is the glorious **Central City Opera House** (621 17th St., ☎ 303/292–6700), which still hosts performances in the summer.

This area is honeycombed with mines, some of which purportedly still contain rich veins of gold. **The Lost Gold Mine** offers tours of two connected shafts filled with original tools and specimens. The requisite souvenir shop outside sells gold-nugget jewelry. *231 Eureka St.,* ☎ *303/642–7533.* ☛ *$3.50 adults, $1.75 children 5–11.* ⊙ *Summer daily 8–8; winter daily 10–6.*

What to See and Do With Children

The Denver Children's Museum is one of the finest of its kind in North America, offering constantly changing hands-on exhibits that lure children into discovery. The biggest attraction is a working television studio, replete with a weather station, a news desk, and a viewing booth where kids can videotape each other and watch the results on "byte"-size monitors. Other interesting aspects of the museum include the "Indians of the Northwest" display, where children can build their own totem poles and the outdoor park with climbing equipment, a year-round ski instruction hill, and a trolley ($2 for adults, $1 for children) that clatters and clangs the 2 miles down the South Platte River to the Forney Transportation Museum. *2121 Crescent Dr.,* ☎ *303/433–7444.* ☛ *$4 children, $3 adults, $1.50 senior citizens over 60.* ☉ *June–Aug., daily 10–5. Sept.–May, Tues.–Sun. 10–5.*

The Denver Zoo (*see* Exploring, *above*).

Elitch Gardens Amusement Park is a Denver family tradition, with three hair-raising roller coasters (one ranked in the nation's top 10); a hand-carved, antique carousel; a 100-foot-high Ferris wheel that provides sensational views of downtown; a high-dive show; summer stock theater; and botanical gardens. Its new downtown location is twice as big as its former site. *I–25 and Speer Blvd.,* ☎ *303/455–4771.* ☛ *$14.95 unlimited ride pass weekdays, $15.95 weekends; chaperon pass (no rides) $8 weekdays, $9 weekends.* ☉ *Weekends mid-Apr.–May; daily June–Labor Day. Hours vary so call ahead.*

Other Points of Interest

★ **Golden,** just 20 minutes west of Denver on I–70 or Highway 6 (W. 6th Ave.), is the destination of thousands of beer lovers who make the pilgrimage to the **Coors Brewery.** One of the world's largest, it was founded in 1873 by Adolph Coors, a 21-year-old German stowaway. The free tour lasts a half hour and explains not only the brewing process, but also how "Rocky Mountain mineral water" (or "Colorado Kool-Aid") is packaged and distributed locally. Informal tastings are held at the end of the tour for those 21 and over; souvenirs are available at the gift shop. *13th and Ford Sts.,* ☎ *303/277–2337.* ☛ *Free.* ☉ *Mon.–Sat. 10–4 (children under 18 must be accompanied by an adult).*

The other favorite Golden attraction is the **Buffalo Bill Grave and Museum.** Contrary to popular belief, Bill Cody never expressed a burning desire to be buried here: The *Denver Post* bought the corpse from Bill's sister, and bribed her to concoct a teary story about his dying wish. Apparently, rival towns were so outraged that the National Guard had to be called in to protect the grave from robbers. The drive up Lookout Mountain to the burial site offers a sensational panoramic view of Denver that alone is worth the price of admission. Adjacent to the grave is a small museum with the usual art and artifacts as well as a run-of-the-mill souvenir shop. *Rte. 5 off I–70 exit 256, or 19th Ave. out of Golden,* ☎ *303/526–0747.* ☛ *$2 adults, $1 children 6–15.* ☉ *May–Oct., daily 9–5; Nov.–Apr., Tues.–Sun., 9–4.*

Just outside of Golden is the **Colorado Railroad Museum,** a must-visit for any choo-choo junkie. More than 50 vintage locomotives and cars are displayed outside. Inside the replica-1880 masonry depot are historical photos and puffing Billy (nickname for steam trains) memorabilia, along with an astounding model train set that steams through a miniature, scaled version of Golden. *17155 W. 44th Ave.,* ☎ *303/279–4591.* ☛ *$3 adults, $1.50 children under 16.* ☉ *Daily 9–5.*

If you have some extra time while in Golden consider walking down 12th Street, a National Historic District with handsome 1860s brick buildings. Among the monuments is the **Astor House** (corner of 12th and Arapahoe Sts.), a museum with period furnishings, and Colorado's first **National Guard Armory,** which was built in 1913 and is the largest cobblestone building in America.

Other attractions in town include the **Colorado School of Mines** (16th and Maple Sts., ☎ 303/273–3823; open daily 9–4:30), the nation's largest and foremost school of mineral engineering. The lovely campus contains an outstanding geology museum displaying minerals, ore, and gemstones from around the world. Also on campus is the prominent **National Earthquake Center** (1711 Illinois St., ☎ 303/236–1500; tours by appointment weekdays 9–11 and 1–3), which is responsible for recording continental drift and seismic activity. Free tours are available weekdays by appointment.

Wrap up your full day with a stop at **Heritage Square** (Hwy. 40 and 6th Ave., ☎ 303/279–2789), a re-creation of an 1880s frontier town, with an opera house, a narrow-gauge railway train ride, a Ferris wheel, a water slide, specialty shops, and a music hall that stages original comedies and musicals as well as traditional melodramas. A vaudeville-style review ends each evening's entertainment.

Shopping

Denver may be the best place in the country for recreational gear and fashions of all stripes. Sporting goods stores hold legendary ski sales around Labor Day.

Shopping Districts and Malls

The posh **Cherry Creek** shopping district is 2 miles from downtown in a pleasant, predominantly residential neighborhood. On one side of First Avenue at Milwaukee Street is the Cherry Creek Shopping Mall, a classy granite-and-glass behemoth that houses some of the nation's top retailers, among them: Abercrombie & Fitch, Bally, Banana Republic, Burberry's, Laura Ashley, Lord & Taylor, Louis Vuitton, Neiman Marcus, Polo/Ralph Lauren, and Saks Fifth Avenue. Across from the Cherry Creek Shopping Mall lies Cherry Creek North, an open-air development of tree-lined streets and shady plazas, with art galleries, specialty shops, and fashionable restaurants.

Historic **Larimer Square** (14th and Larimer Sts.), houses distinctive shops and restaurants. **Writer Square** (1512 Larimer St.) has Tiny Town—a doll-size village inhabited by Michael Garman's inimitable figurines—as well as shops and restaurants. **Tabor Center** (16th St. Mall) is a light-filled atrium whose 60 specialty shops include upscale retailers such as Brooks Brothers and Crabtree & Evelyn, and others that showcase uniquely Coloradan merchandise. It also contains the Bridge Market, which is filled with pushcarts selling everything from Ecuadorian sweaters to endearingly tacky souvenirs. The **Tivoli** (900 Auraria Pkwy., corner of 9th Ave. and Larimer) is a restored historic brewery, with its original pipes and bricks exposed, that houses several moderately priced specialty stores and restaurants.

South of Denver, **Castle Rock Factory Shops** (exit 184 off I–25) offers 25%–75% savings on everything from appliances to apparel at its more than 50 outlets.

Department Stores

Joslins (16th and Curtis Sts., ☎ 303/534–0441) is Denver's oldest department store. The nine **Foley's** department stores throughout metropolitan Denver offer good values; Cherry Creek is their main store in downtown Denver (15 S. Steele St., ☎ 303/333–8555)

Specialty Stores

ANTIQUES

South Broadway between First Avenue and Evans Street, as well as the side streets off this main drag, is chockablock with dusty antiques stores, where patient browsing could net some amazing bargains.

The **Antique Mall of Lakewood** (9635 W. Colfax Ave.) features more than 200 dealer showrooms.

ART AND CRAFTS

LoDo has the trendiest galleries, many in restored Victorian warehouses.

Baobab Tree (1518 Wazee St., ☎ 303/595–0965) sells South African imports, including astonishing masks. **The Art of Craft** (1736 Wazee St., ☎ 303/292–5564) specializes in such wearable art as hand-painted ties and kimonos. **Made in Colorado** (1060 14th St., ☎ 303/298–7812) offers the state's most intriguing products, from Colorado wines to Native American pottery.

Cherry Creek has its share of chic galleries, including **Pismo** (2727 E. 3rd Ave., ☎ 303/333–7724), which showcases exquisite handblown-glass art.

For Native American arts and crafts, head for **Native American Trading Company** (1301 Bannock St., ☎ 303/534–0771), which has an outstanding collection of weavings, pottery, jewelry, and regional painting. The **Mudhead Gallery** (555 17th St., in the Hyatt, ☎ 303/293–0007; and 321 17th St., in the Brown Palace, ☎ 303/293–3377) sells museum-quality Southwestern art, with an especially fine selection of Santa Clara and San Ildefonso pottery, and Hopi kachinas. Old Santa Fe Pottery's (2485 S. Santa Fe Dr., ☎ 303/871–9434) 20 rooms are crammed with Southwestern art, Mexican masks, and hand-painted ceramic tiles.

BEER

Colorado is considered the center of home brewing, and Denver has five brew pubs, each with its own ambience. If you're feeling heady, stop by the **Wine and Hop Shop** (705 E. 6th Ave., ☎ 303/831–7229) for beginner beer- and wine-making kits and a virtual field of fresh hops and grains, or to goggle at the "wall of malt."

BOOKS

The Tattered Cover (1st Ave. at Milwaukee St., ☎ 303/322–7727) is a must for all bibliophiles. It may be the best bookstore in the United States, not only for the near-endless selection of volumes (more than 400,000 on four stories) and helpful, knowledgeable staff, but for the incomparably refined atmosphere: overstuffed armchairs; reading nooks; and afternoon readings, lectures, and musicales.

SPORTING GOODS

Gart Brothers Sports Castle (1000 Broadway, ☎ 303/861–1122) is a huge, multistory shrine to Colorado's love of the outdoors. Entire floors are given over to a single sport at this and the many other branches throughout Denver.

Cry Baby Ranch (1428 Larimer, ☎ 303/623–3979) has a rambunctious assortment of '40s and '50s cowboy kitsch. **Denver Buffalo Company** (1109 Lincoln St., ☎ 303/882–0884) has wonderful Western duds and high-quality souvenirs, not to mention a restaurant that specializes in buffalo—low in fat and cholesterol. There's also a gourmet deli serving BuffDogs (hot dogs made with buffalo meat), corned buffalo, and other such specialties. **Miller Stockman** (16th Ave. and California, ☎ 303/825–5339) is an old-line Denver retailer selling the real McCoy.

Sports and the Outdoors

Participant Sports

CYCLING AND JOGGING

Platte River Greenway is a 20-mile-long path for rollerblading, bicycling, and jogging which runs alongside Cherry Creek and the Platte River; much of it runs through downtown Denver. Paved paths wind through lovely **Matthews-Winters Park,** dotted with plaintive pioneer graves amid the sun-bleached grasses, thistle, and columbine. The **Denver Parks Department** (☎ 303/698–4900) has more suggestions for biking and jogging paths throughout the metropolitan area's 205 parks, including the popular Cherry Creek and Chatfield Lake State Recreation areas.

GOLF

Six courses are operated by the City of Denver and are open to the public: **City Park** (E. 25th Ave. and York St., ☎ 303/295–4420); **Evergreen** (29614 Upper Bear Creek, Evergreen, ☎ 303/674–4128); **Kennedy** (10500 E. Hampden Ave., ☎ 303/751–0311); **Overland Park** (S. Santa Fe Dr. and Jewell Ave., ☎ 303/698–4975); **Wellshire** (3333 S. Colorado Blvd., ☎ 303/692–5636); and **Willis Case** (W. 50th Ave. and Vrain St., ☎ 303/458–4877).

Arrowhead Golf Club (10850 W. Sundown Trail, Littleton, ☎ 303/973–9614), 45 minutes from downtown in Roxborough State Park, was designed by Robert Trent Jones and is set impressively among red sandstone spires. **Plum Creek Golf and Country Club** (331 Players Club, Castle Rock, ☎ 303/688–2611) is an 18-hole Pete Dye–designed championship course.

HEALTH CLUBS

Denver has more fitness clubs per capita than any other American city. The state-of-the-art **International Athletic Club** (1630 Welton St., ☎ 303/623–2100) is a 65,000-square-foot, full-service facility featuring more than 65 aerobics classes weekly. The club has cardiovascular and fitness equipment; weight training; racquetball, squash, and basketball courts; and a running track, among other features. Guest passes are available at many major hotels.

HIKING

Just 15 miles west of Denver, **Red Rocks Park and Amphitheater** (off U.S. 285 or I–70) is a breathtaking, 70-million-year-old wonderland of vaulting oxblood- and cinnamon-color sandstone spires; the outdoor music stage is set in a natural 8,000-seat amphitheater (with perfect acoustics, as only nature could have designed) that has awed even the likes of Leopold Stokowski and the Beatles. Tickets to concerts are stratospheric, but hiking in this metro Denver park is free.

Mt. Falcon Park (off Hwy. 8, Morrison exit, or U.S. 285, Parmalee exit) looks down on Denver and across at Red Rocks. It's amazingly tranquil, laced with meadows and streams and shaded by conifers. The trails are very well marked.

TENNIS
The city has 28 parks with tennis courts. For information call the **Denver Parks Department** (☎ 303/331–4047).

WATER SPORTS
Both **Cherry Creek Marina** (Cherry Creek State Park, Aurora, ☎ 303/779–6144) and **Chatfield Marina** (Chatfield State Park, Littleton, ☎ 303/791–7547) rent sailboats, powerboats, and Windsurfers April–October.

Spectator Sports

AUTO RACING
Bandimere Speedway (3501 S. Rooney Rd., Morrison, ☎ 303/697–6001) features NHRA Championship Drag Racing April–September.

BASEBALL
The **Colorado Rockies,** Denver's National League team, plays April–October in Coors Stadium (off Arapahoe and 21st Sts., ☎ 303/762–543.

BASKETBALL
Denver's NBA franchise team, the **Denver Nuggets,** plays October–April in the McNichols Arena (just west of downtown across I–25, ☎ 303/893–3865).

FOOTBALL
Denver Broncos, the city's NFL team, plays September–December at Mile High Stadium (just west of downtown across I–25, ☎ 303/433–7466).

HORSE RACING
Arapahoe Park (26000 E. Quincy Ave., ☎ 303/690–2400) is the venue for pari-mutuel racing May–September.

Dining

As befits a multiethnic crossroads, Denver offers a dizzying range of eateries: Head for LoDo, 32nd Avenue in the Highland District, or 17th Street for the more inventive kitchens; try Federal Street for cheap ethnic eats—especially Thai and Vietnamese. Throughout Denver, however, you'll find many trendy restaurants offering new American cuisines with an emphasis on indigenous regional ingredients and light, healthful preparations. Denver's hotels also offer some fine restaurants (*see* Lodging, *below*).

Outside Denver, in Central City/Black Hawk, you'll see that virtually every casino has a restaurant with the usual $2.99 daily specials and all-you-can-eat buffets. Nonetheless, there are a few good places to dine.

For price ranges, *see* the Dining chart *in* Colorado Essentials, *below*.

Downtown and Environs

AMERICAN
$$$ **Strings.** This light, airy restaurant with its wide-open kitchen resembles a SoHo loft. It's a preferred hangout for Denver's movers and shakers as well as visiting celebs, whose autographs hang on the walls. The food is billed as casual contemporary; specialties include spaghetti with caviar, asparagus, and champagne cream sauce or monkfish braised in fennel. ✗ *1700 Humboldt St.,* ☎ *303/831–7310. Reservations required. AE, D, DC, MC, V. Closed Sun. lunch.*

$$$ **Zenith American Grill.** This attractive space has a cool high-tech look—
★ track lighting, striking artwork, black-and-white tables—that con-
trasts with the conservative design of most Denver establishments. Chef
Kevin Taylor produces creative variations on the Southwestern theme,
and cleverly lightens the traditional meat-and-potatoes bent of Colorado
cuisine. Standouts include a velvety yet fiery smoked corn soup with
avocado salsa; Texas venison with caramelized apples; sweet potato
custard and spicy sun-dried cherries; and "kick ass" swordfish with
Texas BBQ, chili stir fry, and cilantro lime butter. ✗ *1750 Lawrence
St., ☎ 303/820–2800. Reservations required. AE, MC, V. No lunch
weekends.*

$$–$$$ **Rattlesnake Grill.** Renowned restaurateur Jimmy Schmidt has returned
★ to Denver, where his Rattlesnake Club was bitten by the late '80s re-
cession. His new space is impressive: soft track lighting, picture win-
dows overlooking the action on Cherry Creek Mall, and witty color
photos of food as well as black-and-white landscapes. Keith Josefiak's
food is a sensational fusion of various American regional cuisines with
a soupçon of Provençal flair. You might start with roast garlic and cele-
riac soup or pheasant quesadillas layered with smoked gouda, scallions,
and chili peppers. Among the rotating specials are grilled salmon with
chanterelles, and pork loin chop with dried Michigan cherries, roasted
shallots, and crispy sage. Tempt your sweet tooth with the white choco-
late ravioli served with a hazelnut crème anglaise. ✗ *3000 1st Ave.,
☎ 303/377–8000. Reservations advised. AE, MC, V.*

$ **Wazee Supper Club.** Denverites flock to this hip hole for hot jazz and
the best pizza in town—crisp yet gooey and bursting with flavor. Some
grouse the Wazee has less ambience since it moved down the street,
but the exposed brick walls, jet-black tables, and maroon Naugahyde
chairs still convey its ultracool tone. ✗ *1600 15th St., ☎ 303/623–
9518. No reservations. AE, MC, V.*

$ **The Wynkoop.** This trendy yet unpretentious local institution was
★ Denver's first brew pub, and it's still the best. Try the terrific shepherd's
pie or grilled marlin sandwich; wash it down with wilderness wheat
ale or sagebrush stout; then repair to the gallery, pool hall, and cabaret
for a full night of entertainment. ✗ *1634 18th St., ☎ 303/297–2700.
Reservations for 6 or more weekdays; no reservations on weekends.
AE, DC, MC, V.*

ASIAN

$$ **Imperial Chinese.** Papier-mâché lions greet you at the entrance of this
sleek Szechuan stunner, probably the best Chinese restaurant in a 500-
mile radius. Seafood is the specialty; try the steamed sea bass in ginger or the spicy, fried Dungeness crab. ✗ *1 Broadway, ☎ 303/698–2800.
Reservations advised. AE, DC, MC, V. Closed Sun. lunch.*

$ **Chez Thuy Hoa.** The original chef of T-Wa Inn, Hoa "Wa," left to open
this simple downtown eatery. The decor isn't much to speak of—a few
plants, old-fashioned ceiling fans, and pink napery—but the savory food
keeps it packed during lunchtime (you can usually walk right in at dinner). Try the squid in lemongrass; Dungeness crab salad; or egg rolls
bursting with ground pork or shrimp, mint, sprouts, and cucumber.
✗ *1500 California St., ☎ 303/623–4809. AE, MC, V. Closed Sun. lunch.*

CONTINENTAL

$$$ **Augusta.** With sweeping views of downtown and gleaming brass, glass,
and marble enhanced by pin spotlights showcasing the striking art, this
handsome restaurant is one of the best in the city. Chef Roland Ulber
holds sway in the kitchen, reinvigorating classic Continental fare with
such imaginative preparations as milk-fed veal medallions topped with
foie gras and beautifully set off by a tart lingonberry sauce. At $35,

the five-course tasting menu is one of Denver's greatest bargains ($15 more buys a glass of wine to complement each dish). ✕ *1672 Lawrence St.,* ☎ *303/572–9100. Reservations advised. AE, D, DC, MC, V. Closed lunch.*

$$$ **Cliff Young's.** Although Young no longer oversees operations here,
★ this refined Art Deco restaurant with maroon chairs, dark banquettes, and crisp white napery is still run with meticulous care. Head chef Sean Brasel has introduced Asian and Southwestern touches to the menu, with such specialties as pinwheels of salmon with tangerine ginger compote and wasabi mashed potatoes or seared venison tenderloin with poblano and pumpkin. The new American standbys are still available for devoted regulars, including Colorado rack of lamb and buffalo carpaccio. The dancing to piano and violin music at dinner and the old-school obsequiousness of the wait staff can make the restaurant seem frozen in the 1950s. The ambience is considerably less stuffy (and the prices far lower) at lunch, when the restaurant becomes a haven for harried executives. ✕ *700 E. 17th Ave.,* ☎ *303/831–8900. Reservations advised. AE, D, DC, MC, V. No lunch weekends.*

$$–$$$ **European Café.** Housed with panache in a converted loft that now gleams with polished brass and crystal, the European Café is a favorite for those attending downtown events. Many of chef Radek Cerny's dishes pay homage to such French master chefs as Georges Blanc and Paul Bocuse, and all are beautifully presented. Try the lamb chops with shitake mushrooms in Madeira glaze. ✕ *1515 Market,* ☎ *303/825–6555. Reservations advised. AE, D, DC, MC, V. No lunch weekends.*

FRENCH

$$$ **Cache Cache.** Chef Jack Goldsmith is a practitioner of *cuisine minceur*—no butter or cream is used in his preparations. But the sunny flavors of Provence explode on the palate thanks to the master's savvy use of garlic, tomato, eggplant, fennel, and rosemary. The lamb loin sandwiched between crisp, potato *galettes* (pancakes) on a bed of spinach and ratatouille is sublime; salads are sensational. ✕ *265 Detroit St.,* ☎ *303/394–0044. Reservations advised. AE, MC, V. Closed Sun.*

$$$ **Tante Louise.** This longtime Denver favorite, just 15 minutes from downtown by car, resembles an intimate French country home. Fireplaces, candlelight, and classical music attract a mostly over-fifty crowd. One-third of chef Michael Degenhart's menu is French, one-third is new American, and one-third features low-fat dishes. Try the delicate angel-hair pasta and grilled salmon in beurre blanc, or any of the superlative lamb specials. ✕ *4900 E. Colfax Ave.,* ☎ *303/355–4488. Reservations advised. AE, D, DC, MC, V. Closed Sun.; no lunch except Fri.*

$$ **La Coupole.** This expert French bistro is an oasis in this seedier part of LoDo, where taco joints, abandoned warehouses, and neighborhood bars are the norm. Gleaming brass, black leather banquettes, exposed brick walls, potted plants, lace curtains, and crisp white napery transport happy diners to the Left Bank. Everything is solidly prepared, from monkfish with lobster mayonnaise to chicken breast in morel cream sauce, not to mention a perfect tarte tatin. ✕ *2191 Arapahoe St.,* ☎ *303/297–2288. Reservations advised. AE, D, DC, MC, V. Closed Sun. lunch.*

$$ **Le Central.** This homey bistro calls itself "Denver's affordable French restaurant." The cozy dining rooms are enlivened by brick walls and colorful artwork courtesy of local schoolchildren. While the preparation can be inconsistent, old standbys such as boeuf bourguignon, salmon en croûte, and steak au poivre are dependable. ✕ *112 E. 8th*

Ave., ☎ *303/863–8094. Reservations for 5 or more at dinner. D, MC, V. Closed Mon. lunch.*

ITALIAN

$$ **Barolo Grill.** This restaurant looks like a chichi farmhouse, as if Martha
★ Stewart went gaga over an Italian count: There are dried flowers in
brass urns, hand-painted porcelain, and straw baskets everywhere.
The food isn't precious in the least, however; it's more like Santa Mon-
ica meets San Stefano—bold yet classic, healthful yet flavorful. Choose
from wild boar stewed with apricots, risotto croquettes flavored with
minced shrimp, or smoked-salmon pizza. The wine list is well-considered
and fairly priced. ✗ *3030 E. 6th Ave.,* ☎ *303/393–1040. Reservations
advised. AE, MC, V. Closed lunch and Sun. and Mon.*

MEXICAN

$ **Bluebonnet Café and Lounge.** Its location out of the tourist loop, in
a fairly seedy neighborhood southeast of downtown, doesn't stop the
crowds (mostly tourists) from lining up early for this restaurant. The
early Western, Naugahyde decor and fantastic jukebox set an upbeat
mood for killer margaritas and some of the best burritos and green
chili in town. ✗ *457 S. Broadway,* ☎ *303/778–0147. No reservations.
MC, V.*

STEAKS/WESTERN

$$$ **Buckhorn Exchange.** If hunting makes you queasy, don't enter this Den-
★ ver landmark, a shrine to taxidermy where 500 Bambis stare down at
you from the walls. The handsome men's-club decor—with pressed tin
ceilings, burgundy walls, red-checker tablecloths, rodeo photos, shot-
guns, and those trophies—probably looks the same as it did when the
Buckhorn first opened in 1893. Rumor has it Buffalo Bill was to the
Buckhorn what Norm Peterson was to *Cheers.* The dry-aged, prime-
grade Colorado steaks are huge, juicy, and magnificent, as is the game.
For an appetizer, try the smoked buffalo sausage or black bean soup.
✗ *1000 Osage St.,* ☎ *303/534–9505. Reservations advised. AE, D,
DC, MC, V. Closed weekend lunch.*

Outside Denver

CENTRAL CITY/BLACK HAWK

$$ **Black Forest Inn.** This is an affectionate re-creation of a Bavarian hunt-
ing lodge, replete with antlers, tapestries, and cuckoo clocks. Hearty
specialties range from fine schnitzel to succulent wild game. Afterward,
you can repair to Otto's casino. ✗ *260 Gregory St., Black Hawk,* ☎
303/279–2333. Reservations advised. MC, V.

GOLDEN

$ **The Observatory.** This inimitable upstairs café features a retractable
roof and 8-inch reflecting telescope for stargazing on warm nights. The
menu is simple, with such items as Observa Burgers, Moon Dogs, and
UFOs (unusual food orders), and libations such as Black Holes, Milky
Ways, and Bailey's Comets. ✗ *29259 Hwy. 40, El Rancho, Golden,*
☎ *303/526–1988. No reservations. AE, MC, V.*

Lodging

Denver has lodging choices from the stately Brown Palace to the com-
monplace YMCA, with options such as bed-and-breakfasts and busi-
ness hotels in between. Stapleton properties may very well languish once
hotels open near the new Denver International Airport (DIA) in 1997.
In addition, Adams Mark Hotels purchased the downtown I. M.
Pei–designed Radisson and the old May D&F Department Store across

the street in 1994, with plans to convert them into Denver's largest property (more than 1,000 rooms and a state-of-the-art convention center). Unless you're planning a quick escape to the mountains, consider staying in or around downtown, where most of the city's attractions are within walking distance. For price ranges *see* the Lodging chart *in* Colorado Essentials, *below.*

$$–$$$ **Brown Palace.** This grande dame of Colorado lodging has housed nu-
★ merous public figures from President Eisenhower to the Beatles. The details are exquisite: A dramatic nine-story lobby is topped with a glorious stained-glass ceiling, and rooms are decorated with Victorian flair, using sophisticated wainscoting and art-deco fixtures. A much needed refurbishment in 1995 replaced faded carpets, linens, and upholstery. The Palace Arms, its formal restaurant, has won numerous awards, including one from *Wine Spectator* magazine. Guests have access to a local health club. ⛨ *321 17th St.,* ☎ *303/297–3111 or 800/321–2599;* ⛛ *303/293–9204. 205 rooms, 25 suites. 4 restaurants, 2 bars, concierge. AE, D, DC, MC, V.*

$$ **Burnsley.** Since its face-lift in the 1980s, this 16-story, Bauhaus-style tower has been a haven for executives seeking peace and quiet close to downtown. The tastefully appointed accommodations are all suites and feature balconies and full kitchens. A refurbishment in 1993 brightened up the place, adding floral linens; dusky rose, salmon, and burgundy carpets or upholstery; and old-fashioned riding prints. Many suites have a sofa bed, making this a good bet for families. The swooningly romantic restaurant is a perfect place to pop the question. ⛨ *1000 Grant St.,* ☎ *303/830–1000 or 800/231–3915;* ⛛ *303/830–7676. 82 suites. Restaurant, bar, pool. AE, DC, MC, V.*

$$ **Cambridge Club Hotel.** This 1960s-era luxury suites hotel is on a tree-lined street convenient to downtown, one block from the state capitol building. Each suite is individually decorated with a smart mix of contemporary and traditional furnishings, from Asian to French provincial; all have kitchenettes. Local lobbyists, politicos, and CEOs favor the bar. ⛨ *1560 Sherman St.,* ☎ *303/831–1252 or 800/877–1252;* ⛛ *303/831–4724. 28 suites. Restaurant, bar, kitchenettes. AE, D, DC, MC, V.*

$$ **Loews Giorgio.** The 12-story steel-and-black glass facade conceals the
★ unexpected and delightful Italian Baroque motif within. Rooms are spacious and elegant, with teal colors and blond wood predominating, and such Continental touches as fresh flowers, fruit baskets, and Renaissance-style portraits. The formal Tuscany restaurant serves sumptuous Italian cuisine. Guests may use a nearby health club, and a Continental breakfast is included in the room rate. The only drawback of this property is its location: halfway between downtown and the Denver Tech Center, with little in the immediate vicinity. ⛨ *4150 E. Mississippi Ave.,* ☎ *303/782–9300 or 800/345–9172;* ⛛ *303/758–6542. 200 rooms, 19 suites. Restaurant, bar. AE, D, DC, MC, V.*

$$ **Warwick Hotel.** This stylish business hotel, ideally located on the edge of downtown, offers oversize rooms and suites and features brass and mahogany Thomasville antique reproductions. Most rooms contain wet bars, full refrigerators, and private balconies. A breakfast buffet and access to the health club next door are included in the room rate. ⛨ *1776 Grant St.,* ☎ *303/861–2000 or 800/525–2888;* ⛛ *303/832–0320. 145 rooms, 49 suites. Restaurant, bar, pool, concierge. AE, DC, MC, V.*

$$ **Westin Hotel Tabor Center.** This sleek, luxurious high-rise opens right
★ onto the 16th Street Mall and all the downtown action. Rooms, renovated in 1995, are oversize and done in grays and taupes, with pais-

ley duvets and prints of the Rockies and the Denver skyline on the walls. Each room also has such amenities as an iron and ironing board, a desk pull-out tray for laptop computers, and cable TV and in-room movies. The hotel even buys blocks of tickets for weekend shows at the Denver Performing Arts Complex for guests' exclusive use. ⌖ *1672 Lawrence St., 80202,* ☎ *303/572–9100,* FAX *303/572–7288. 420 rooms. 2 restaurants, bar, pool, health club, racquetball. AE, D, DC, MC, V.*

$–$$ **Castle Marne.** This historic B&B, just east of downtown, sits in a shabbily genteel area. Its balconies, four-story turret, and intricate stone and woodwork present a dramatic facade. On the inside, rooms are richly decorated with antiques and artwork. Birdcages, butterfly cases, and old photos of the house are displayed throughout. Most rooms have brass or mahogany beds, throw rugs, tile fireplaces (nonworking), a profusion of dried and fresh flowers, and clawfoot tubs; a few have hot tubs or whirlpool baths. Rooms don't have TVs, but there's one in the common room. A full gourmet breakfast—served in the dining room—is included in the room rate, as is afternoon tea. ⌖ *1572 Race St.,* ☎ *303/331–0621 or 800/926–2763;* FAX *303/331–0623. 9 rooms. Business services. AE, D, DC, MC, V.*

$–$$ **Oxford Hotel.** During the Victorian era this hotel was an elegant fixture on the Denver landscape. It has been restored to its former turn-of-the-century glory: Rooms are uniquely furnished with French and English period antiques, while the bar re-creates an art-deco ocean liner. Its location is perfect for those seeking a different, artsy environment. Complimentary shoe shines, afternoon sherry, and morning coffee and fruit are among the civilized touches offered here. Although the Oxford is a notch down from the Brown Palace in most respects, it's also less expensive and is home to McCormick's Fish and Oyster House, Denver's premier seafood restaurant. ⌖ *1600 17th St.,* ☎ *303/628–5400 or 800/228–5838;* FAX *303/628–5413. 81 rooms. Restaurant, 2 bars, beauty salon. AE, DC, MC, V.*

$–$$ **Queen Anne Inn.** The Queen Anne occupies two adjacent Victorians north of downtown in the regentrified Clements historic district (some of the neighboring blocks have yet to be reclaimed). This handsome property is a delightful, romantic getaway for B&B mavens. Both houses have handsome oak wainscoting and balustrades, 10-foot vaulted ceilings, numerous bay or stained-glass windows, and such period furnishings as brass and canopy beds, cherry and pine armoires, and oak rocking chairs. The best accommodations are the four gallery suites dedicated to Audubon, Rockwell, Calder, and Remington; each displays reproductions representative of that artist's work. All rooms have phones and private baths. A full breakfast and afternoon wine tastings are offered daily. ⌖ *2147 Tremont Pl.,* ☎ *303/296–6666;* FAX *303/296–2151. 10 rooms, 4 suites. AE, D, MC, V.*

$ **Comfort Inn/Downtown.** The advantages of this well-used hotel are its reasonable rates and its location in the heart of downtown. Rooms are somewhat cramped, but renovations completed in 1995 added new carpeting and draperies throughout. The corner rooms on the upper floors feature wraparound floor-to-ceiling windows with stunning panoramic views. A complimentary Continental breakfast is offered. ⌖ *401 17th St.,* ☎ *303/296–0400 or 800/221–2222;* FAX *303/297–0774. 229 rooms. Laundry service. AE, D, DC, MC, V.*

$ **Holiday Chalet.** Stained-glass windows and homey touches throughout make this Victorian brownstone exceptionally charming. It's also conveniently situated in Capitol Hill, the neighborhood immediately east of downtown. Many of the rooms are furnished with overstuffed Victorian armchairs in light floral fabrics and such cute touches as straw hats; some units have tile fireplaces, others have small sitting rooms. Each room has a kitchenette, which is stocked with breakfast foods. ⌸ *1820 E. Colfax Ave.,* ☎ *303/321–9975 or 800/626–4497. 10 rooms. Kitchenettes. AE, D, DC, MC, V.*

The Arts and Nightlife

The Arts

Friday's *Denver Post* and *Rocky Mountain News* publish calendars of the week's events, as does the slightly alternative *Westword,* which is free and published on Tuesday. **TicketMaster** (☎ 303/830–8497) and **TicketMan** (☎ 303/430–1111 or 800/200–8497) sell tickets by phone to major events, tacking on a slight service charge; the **Ticket Bus** (no phone), on the 16th Street Mall at Curtis Street, sells tickets from 10 until 6 weekdays, and half-price tickets on the day of the performance.

DANCE

The **Colorado Ballet** (☎ 303/237–8888) specializes in the classics; performances are staged at the Denver Performing Arts Complex (14th and Curtis Sts.).

MUSIC

The **Colorado Symphony Orchestra** performs at Boettcher Concert Hall (13th and Curtis Sts., ☎ 303/986–8742); the **Denver Chamber Orchestra** (18th Ave. and Broadway, ☎ 303/825–4911) usually plays at historic Trinity Methodist Church downtown. The **Paramount Theater** (1621 Glenarm Pl., ☎ 303/623–0106) is the site for many large-scale rock concerts. The exquisite **Red Rocks Amphitheater** (☎ 303/572–4704) and **Fiddler's Green** (☎ 303/741–5000) are the primary outdoor concert venues.

OPERA

Opera Colorado (☎ 303/778–6464) offers spring and fall seasons, often with internationally renowned artists, at the Denver Performing Arts Complex. **Central City Opera** (621 17th St., Central City, ☎ 303/292–6700), housed in an exquisite Victorian opera house, has the finest of settings.

THEATER

The **Denver Performing Arts Complex** (14th and Curtis Sts., ☎ 303/893–3272) houses most of the city's large concert and theater venues. The **Denver Center Theater Company** (14th. and Curtis Sts., ☎ 303/893–4100) offers high-caliber repertory theater, including new works by promising playwrights, at the Bonfils Theatre Complex. **Robert Garner Attractions** (☎ 303/893–4100) brings Broadway road companies to Denver. Among the provocative fringe theaters are **Spark Artists Co-operative** (1535 Platte St., ☎ 303/744–3275), which also has a gallery space; **Eulipions, Inc. Cultural Center** (2425 Welton St., ☎ 303/295–6814), which presents plays by and with African Americans; **Changing Scene Theater** (1527½ Champa St., ☎ 303/893–5775); **Industrial Arts Theatre** (120 W. 1st Ave., ☎ 303/744–3245); **Hunger Artists Ensemble Theater** (Margery Reed Hall, Univ. of Denver, S. University Blvd. and Evans Ave., ☎ 303/893–5438); and **El Centro Su Teatro** (4925 High St., ☎ 303/296–0219).

Nightlife

Downtown and **LoDo** are where most Denverites make the scene. Downtown features more mainstream entertainment, whereas LoDo is home to fun, funky rock clubs and small theaters. Remember that Denver's altitude can intensify your reaction to alcohol.

CABARET

The **Wynkoop Cabaret** (1634 18th St., downstairs in The Wynkoop Brewpub, ☎ 303/297–2700) offers everything from top-name jazz acts to up-and-coming stand-up comedians, including cabaret numbers.

COMEDY CLUBS

Comedy Works (1226 15th St., ☎ 303/595–3637) is where Denver comics hone their skills. Well-known performers often drop by. **Chicken Lips Comedy Theater** (1300 17th St., ☎ 303/534–4440) is an improv troupe specializing in topical satire.

COUNTRY AND WESTERN CLUBS

The **Grizzly Rose** (I–25 at Exit 215, ☎ 303/295–1330) has miles of dance floor, national bands, and offers two-step dancing lessons. **Cactus Moon** (10001 Grant St., ☎ 303/451–5200) is larger than most venues and offers "Food, Firewater, and Dancin'." **Stampede Mesquite Grill & Dance Emporium** (2430 S. Havana St., ☎ 303/337–6904) is the latest boot-scooting spot.

DINNER THEATER

The **Country Dinner Playhouse** (6875 S. Clinton St., ☎ 303/799–1410) serves a meal before the performance, which is usually a Broadway-style show. In Golden, the **Heritage Square Music Hall** (☎ 303/279–7800) has a buffet to go along with an evening of old-fashioned melodrama.

DISCOS

Club Infinity (900 Auraria Pkwy., in the Tivoli Mall, ☎ 303/534–7206) nearly lives up to its name, with five bars and an enormous dance floor swept by laser beams. **Industry** (1222 Glenarm Pl., ☎ 303/620–9554) is the latest hip, happening hip-hop spot, with live techno-rave and house music, packing in Denver's youngest and trendiest. **Deadbeat** (404 E. Evans Ave., ☎ 303/758–6853) is where the cool college crowd goes to get carded.

GAY BARS

Charlie's (900 E. Colfax Ave., ☎ 303/839–8890) offers country-western atmosphere and music at the hottest gay bar in town.

JAZZ CLUBS

El Chapultepec (20th and Market Sts., ☎ 303/295–9126) is a depressing, fluorescent-lit, bargain-basement Mexican dive. Still, the limos parked outside hint at its enduring popularity: This is where visiting musicians, from Ol' Blue Eyes to the Marsalis brothers, jam after hours. **Brendan's Pub** (1624 Market St., ☎ 303/595–0609) attracts local jazz and blues talents. The **Burnsley Hotel** (1000 Grant St., ☎ 303/830–1000) hops with live jazz several nights a week.

ROCK-AND-ROLL CLUBS

There are a number of smoky hangouts in this city, the most popular being the down-home **Herman's Hideaway** (1578 S. Broadway, ☎ 303/777–5840), which showcases local and national acts, with a smattering of reggae, blues, and alternative music thrown in to keep things lively. Also popular are the **Bluebird Theater** (3317 E. Colfax Ave., ☎ 303/322–2308); **Cricket on the Hill** (1209 E. 13th Ave., ☎ 303/830–9020); and the **Mercury Café** (2199 California St., ☎ 303/294–9281), which triples as a marvelous health-food restaurant (sublime tofu fettuccine), fringe theater, and rock club specializing in acoustic sets, progressive, and newer wave music.

Rock Island (Wazee and 15th Sts., ☎ 303/572–7625) caters to the young, hip, and restless. Denver's five brew pubs are always hopping: **Rock Bottom Brewery** (1001 16th St., ☎ 303/534–7616) is the flavor-of-the-month, thanks to its rotating special brews and reasonably priced pub grub.

Excursion to the Eastern Plains

One-third of Colorado is prairie land—vast stretches of hypnotically rolling corn and wheat fields, Russian thistle, and tall grasses coppered by the sun. This is middle America, where families have been ranching and farming the same plot of land for generations; where county fairs, livestock shows, and high-school football games are the main forms of entertainment; where the Corn and Bible belts stoically tighten a notch in times of adversity.

If you want to get in touch with America's roots, here is a good place to begin. The small one-horse towns such as Heartstrong and Last Chance—names redolent of the heartland—tell an old story, that of the first pioneers who struggled across the continent in search of a better life. The Pony Express and Overland trails cut right through northeast Colorado (James Michener set his epic historical novel *Centennial* in this territory), where even today you'll find weathered trading posts, lone buttes that guided the weary homesteaders westward, and downhome friendly people who take enormous pride in their land and their heritage.

Tour 1: I–76 and Environs

The first major stop on I–76 is **Fort Morgan,** the seat of Morgan County and a major agricultural center for corn, wheat, and sugar beets, the big cash crops in these parts. But its true claim to fame is as band leader Glenn Miller's birthplace. The **Fort Morgan Museum,** on Main Street, is a repository of local history that describes the town's origins in 1864 as a military fort constructed to protect gold miners and displays Miller memorabilia. Items exhibited include artifacts from the Koehler Site, an excavated landfill nearby that revealed a prehistoric campsite, and classic Americana such as a replica of the soda fountain from an old drugstore. On your way out, pick up a historical downtown walking-tour brochure to tell you about some of the handsome homes lining Main Street. *400 Main St.,* ☎ *970/867–6331.* ☛ *$2 adults, $1 children under 13.* ☺ *Weekdays 10–5, Sat. 11–5; in summer also open Sun. 1–4:30.*

Farther along the interstate is **Sterling,** a peaceful, prosperous town of graceful whitewashed houses with porch swings and shady trees that fringe neighborhood streets. Sterling bills itself as "the City of Living Trees," a tribute to local artist Brad Rhea who has chiseled living trees into fanciful works of art: towering giraffes, festive clowns, golfers (at the country club), and minutemen (at the National Armory). Several downtown buildings, listed on the National Register of Historic Places, are supreme examples of turn-of-the-century pioneer architecture; among them is Logan County Courthouse.

The **Overland Trail Museum,** a replica of a classic old fort carved out of rock, offers displays of homesteading life, with painstaking re-creations of a typical blacksmith shop and schoolhouse, as well as exhibits of Plains Natives and pioneer clothing and utensils. *Jct. of Hwy. 6 and I–76,* ☎ *970/522–3895.* ☛ *Free.* ☺ *Mon.–Sat. 9–5, Sun. 10–5.*

The last stop in Colorado is **Julesburg,** called by Mark Twain "the wickedest city in the west," though today it's hard to picture the sleepy town as Sodom and Gomorrah rolled into one. Julesburg is the proud site of the only Pony Express Station in Colorado, duly celebrated at **Fort Sedgwick Depot Museum,** with assorted paraphernalia from mail patches to saddles. *202 W. 1st St.,* ☎ *970/474–2264.* ☛ *Free.* ☉ *Mon.–Sat. and holidays 9–5, Sun. 11–5.*

Tour 2: I–70

An option to the I–76 tour is to travel on I–70, which cuts a swath through the heart of Colorado and traverses much of the same terrain and small-town life as Tour 1. Since both routes are equally enjoyable, consider which attractions interest you to help you choose. The first major community on this route is **Limon,** which is sadly best known as the locale of a ferocious twister that leveled the town in 1990. Admirably, residents banded together and today there are few apparent signs of the devastation.

Limon's rich past is displayed at the **Limon Heritage Museum,** offering collections of saddles, arrowheads, a restored 1924 Puffing Billy coach, and changing photo and graphics exhibits. *E. Ave. and 1st St.,* ☎ *719/775–2373.* ☛ *Free; donations accepted. Hours vary so call ahead.*

Ten miles east of Limon, along I–70, is the **Genoa Tower Museum,** an intriguing oddity that bills itself as the "highest point between the Rockies and the Mississippi." Aside from providing splendid vistas of the plains, the tower houses an eclectic collection of Native American artifacts, fossils, and Elvis Presley memorabilia. Owner Jerry Chubbock says, "If it ain't here, it don't exist." The Ripleyesque display of animal monstrosities seems to support his boast. *Exit 371, off I–70 (follow signs to museum),* ☎ *719/763–2309.* ☛ *$1 adults, 50¢ children under 13.* ☉ *Daily 8–8.*

The easternmost sizable town along I–70 is **Burlington,** 12 miles from the Kansas border. They take their history seriously here, as evidenced by **Old Town,** a lovingly authentic re-creation of a 1900s Old West village, with more than 20 restored turn-of-the-century buildings complete with antique frontier memorabilia. Daily cancans and weekend gunfights take place in the Longhorn Saloon throughout the summer, as well as rip-roaring melodramas and madam shows (with the occasional cat fight). It's a hoot and a half. *I–70 exit 437,* ☎ *719/346–7382.* ☛ *Free.* ☉ *Memorial Day–Labor Day, daily 8 am–9 pm; Labor Day–Memorial Day, daily 9–6.*

Burlington's other main attraction was designated one of Colorado's 13 National Historic Landmarks. The **Kit Carson County Carousel,** in the Burlington Fairgrounds, Memorial Day–Labor Day, is a fully restored and operational carousel hand-carved by the Philadelphia Toboggan Company in 1905. It's one of fewer than 170 carousels to retain its original paint. Forty-six exquisitely detailed creatures bob and weave to the jaunty accompaniment of a 1909 Wurlitzer Monster Military Band Organ. Among the residents here are richly caparisoned camels, fiercely toothsome tigers, and gamboling goats.

Shopping

Most of the towns have at least one artisan whose work is proudly displayed in general stores, specialty shops, and craft fairs—be it a bronze-cast cowboy sculpture or a quilt. (Poking around the local emporia may net you some interesting finds.) **Lourine's** (101 E. 1st St., Otis, ☎ 970/246–3221) is noted for its hand-painted china. **Nelda's Antiques and Treasure Trove** (215/221 N. Interocean Ave., Holyoke, ☎ 970/854–

3153) advertises "Scale House Antiques and Oddities, from Rags to Riches." For the best (if hokiest) selection of souvenirs, head for the **Old Town Emporium** (I–70 exit 437, ☎ 719/346–7382), in Burlington.

Sports and the Outdoors

The northeast offers prime camping, hiking, fishing, and golf opportunities. The many lakes and reservoirs are havens for water-sports enthusiasts interested in everything from waterskiing to windsurfing. Wildlife- and bird-watchers will enjoy the Pawnee National Grasslands and the Cottonwood, Elliott, and Sandstage state wildlife areas, among others. For more information on the areas recommended below, call the chamber of commerce in each community.

FISHING

For exceptional fishing, try any of the following: Bonny Reservoir, Idalia; Jumbo Reservoir, Sedgwick; Kinney Lake, Hugo; North Sterling Reservoir, Sterling; Prewitt Reservoir, Merino; Stalker Lake and State Fish Hatchery, Wray. Trout and bass are plentiful at all locations.

GOLF

Fort Morgan Municipal Golf Course (Riverside Park, Fort Morgan, ☎ 970/867–5990), **Riverview Golf Course** (Riverview Rd., Sterling, ☎ 970/522–3035), and **Sterling Country Club** (CO 14, Sterling, ☎ 970/522–5523) are all 18-hole championship courses with challenging terrain.

HIKING

Most of the land in the region is so flat that the area is nicknamed "the Great American Desert" and "the Outback." However, the monotonous, dreary stretch of CO 71, just north of Fort Morgan, is improbably broken by the Pawnee Buttes that loom on the horizon. The Plains Natives used these twin, sedimentary upthrusts as lookout posts and today they are prime hiking terrain.

Dining

Livestock are a main source of livelihood on the eastern Plains, where billboards proclaim "Nothing satisfies like beef." However, the calorie- and cholesterol-conscious will appreciate the fresh fish that sometimes appears on menus. If all else fails, there's usually a choice between an Arby's and a Dairy Queen. Reservations are not necessary.

For price ranges *see* the Dining chart *in* Colorado Essentials, *below.*

$–$$ **Country Steak-Out.** Fort Morgan's first steak house—a combination between a diner and a barn—looks as if it hasn't changed since the Dust Bowl era. After a long day of following behind pickup trucks with bumper stickers that admonish you to "Eat beef," you might as well succumb to the succulent steaks served here. ✕ *19592 E. 8th Ave., Fort Morgan, ☎ 970/867–7887. AE, MC, V. Closed Sun. dinner and Mon.*

$ **Fergie's West Inn Pub.** This small, simple restaurant-bar serves up sensational soups and sandwiches, including predictably mouthwatering barbecued beef. ✕ *324 W. Main St., Sterling, ☎ 970/522–4220. No credit cards. Closed weekends.*

$ **Mr. A's Interstate House.** Locals swear by this glorified truck stop, off I–70. The humongous portions and daily specials define economical. Try the chicken fried steak, biscuits and gravy, or green chili. ✕ *415 S. Lincoln St., Burlington, ☎ 719/346–8010. AE, MC, V.*

Lodging

In this part of the state you'll find the usual assortment of chain motor lodges, with a few historic B&Bs in the larger towns. For price ranges *see* the Lodging chart *in* Colorado Essentials, *below.*

$$ **Best Western Sundowner.** This property is a notch above the usual motel, with spacious, tasteful rooms, and several amenities. Continental breakfast is included in the room rate. ⊞ *Overland Trail St., Sterling,* ☎ *970/522–6265. 29 rooms. Restaurant, pool, hot tub, exercise room, coin laundry. AE, MC, V.*

$ **Best Western Park Terrace.** Clean, pleasant rooms with cable TV are what you'll find in this perfectly comfortable, typical motel. ⊞ *725 Main St., Fort Morgan,* ☎ *970/867–8256. 24 rooms. Restaurant, pool. AE, MC, V.*

$ **Chaparral Budget Host.** This serviceable motor lodge is perfectly located right near Old Town, and offers the usual amenities such as cable TV. ⊞ *I–70 exit 437, Burlington,* ☎ *719/346–5361. 39 rooms. Pool, hot tub. AE, MC, V.*

$ **Crest House.** This property has two sections: a small, decently outfitted motel and an exquisite B&B in a lovely old Victorian home, with beveled-glass windows and four-poster beds. Opt for the B&B, though you'll receive the same friendly, thoughtful treatment from the owners wherever you stay. ⊞ *516 Division Ave., Sterling,* ☎ *970/522–3753. 5 rooms in house, 9 in motel. AE, MC, V.*

Getting There

The nearest international airports are in Denver (*see* Arriving and Departing by Plane, *below*) and Cheyenne, Wyoming.

BY CAR

I–70 cuts through the center of Colorado into Kansas, and I–76 angles northeast into Nebraska. If you're driving to Denver from the north or east, follow the itinerary in reverse. If time allows, occasionally get off the main highway and drive the two-lane byways to get a real sense of this region's communities and slower pace of life.

BY BUS

Greyhound Lines (☎ 800/231–2222) offers service to several towns throughout the region, including Fort Morgan, Sterling, Limon, and Burlington.

Important Addresses and Numbers

HOSPITALS

There are medical facilities in Fort Morgan (Colorado Plains Medical Center, 1000 Lincoln St., ☎ 303/867–3391); Sterling (Sterling Regional Medical Center, 615 Fairhurst St., ☎ 970/522–0122); and Burlington (Kit Carson County Memorial Hospital, 286 16th St., ☎ 719/346–5311).

VISITOR INFORMATION

Burlington Chamber of Commerce (480 15th St., Burlington 80807, ☎ 719/346–8070); **Colorado Welcome Center** (48265 I–70, Burlington 80807, ☎ 719/346–5554); **Fort Morgan Area Chamber of Commerce** (300 Main St., Fort Morgan 80701, ☎ 970/867–6702 or 800/354–8660); **Logan County Chamber of Commerce** (Box 1683, Main and Front Sts., Sterling 80751, ☎ 970/522–5070); **Northeast Colorado Travel Region** (420 S. 14th St., Burlington 80807, ☎ 800/777–9075).

Denver Essentials

Arriving and Departing by Plane

AIRPORTS AND AIRLINES

Denver International Airport (☎ 303/270–1900 or 800/247–2336), or DIA, opened its gates in early 1995, replacing Stapleton. It is served by most major domestic carriers and many international ones, including **Alaska Airlines** (☎ 800/426–0333), **American** (☎ 800/433–7300), **America West** (☎ 800/247–5692), **Continental** (☎

800/525–0280), **Delta** (☎ 800/221–1212), **Frontier** (☎ 800/432–1359), **Midway** (☎ 800/446–4392), **SkyWest** (☎ 800/453–9417), **Mesa** (☎ 800/637–2247), **Northwest** (☎ 800/225–2525), **TWA** (☎ 800/221–2000), **United** (☎ 800/241–6522), and **USAir** (☎ 800/425–4322).

Between the Airport and Downtown

BY BUS

The **Airporter** (☎ 303/333–5833) serves downtown and southeast Denver Tech Center hotels, with 15-minute scheduled departures daily between 6 AM and 10:15 PM to downtown, and 30-minute departures to southeast Denver. **Denver Airport Shuttle** (☎ 303/342–5450), or DASH, serves downtown and several nearby ski areas. The region's public bus service, **Regional Transportation District** (RTD, ☎ 303/299–6000 for route and schedule information; 303/299–6700 for other inquiries) runs **SkyRide** to and from DIA; the trip takes 55 minutes, and the fare is $6. There is a transportation center in the airport just outside baggage claim.

BY TAXI

Taxis to downtown cost $25–$30 from DIA. Call **Metro Taxi** (☎ 303/333–3333), **Yellow Cab** (☎ 303/777–7777), or **Zone Cab** (☎ 303/444–8888).

BY LIMOUSINE

Options include **Admiral Limousines** (☎ 303/296–2003 or 800/828–8680), **Celebrity Limousine** (☎ 303/252–1760 or 800/778–1211), **Denver Limousine Services** (☎ 303/766–0400 or 800/766–2090), **Executive Touring Car** (☎ 303/743–8522 or 800/743–8622). Rates average $25 and up, depending on the type of car.

BY CAR

Rental car companies include **Alamo** (☎ 303/321–1176 or 800/327–9633), **Avis** (☎ 303/839–1280 or 800/331–1212), **Budget** (☎ 303/341–2277 or 800/222–6772), **Dollar** (☎ 303/398–2323 or 800/756–3701), **Hertz** (☎ 303/355–2244 or 800/654–3131), and **National** (☎ 303/342–0717) all have airport and downtown representatives.

Arriving and Departing by Car, Train, and Bus

BY CAR

Reaching Denver by car is fairly easy, except during rush hour when the interstates (and downtown) get congested. Interstate highways I–70 and I–25 intersect near downtown; an entrance to I–70 is just outside the airport.

BY TRAIN

Union Station (17th Ave. at Wynkoop, downtown, ☎ 303/524–2812) has Amtrak service.

BY BUS

The **Greyhound Lines** depot is at 1055 19th Street (☎ 303/293–6541 or 800/231–2222).

Getting Around

In downtown Denver, free shuttle-bus service operates about every 10 minutes until 11 PM, running the length of the 16th Street Mall (which bisects downtown) and stopping at two-block intervals. If you plan to spend much time outside downtown, a car is advised, although buses and taxis are available. Even downtown, parking spots are usually easy to find; try to avoid driving in the area during rush hour, when traffic gets heavy.

BY BUS OR TRAIN
The region's public bus service, **RTD** (*see* Between the Airport and Downtown, *above*) is comprehensive, with routes throughout the metropolitan area. The service also links Denver to outlying towns such as Boulder, Longmont, and Nederland. You can buy bus tokens at grocery stores or pay with exact change on the bus. Fares vary according to time and zone. Within the city limits, buses cost $1 during peak hours (6–9 AM, 4–6 PM), 50¢ at other times. You can also buy a **Cultural Connection Trolley** (☎ 303/299–6000) ticket for $1 at several convenient outlets throughout downtown, from the trolley driver, or from most hotel concierges. The trolley operates daily, every half hour 9–6, linking 18 prime attractions from the Denver Performing Arts Complex downtown to the Denver Natural History Museum in City Park. Tickets are good for one stop. RTD's **Light Rail** service (☎ 303/299–6000) began in October 1994. The original 5.3-mile track links southwest and northeast Denver to downtown; routes are continually expanding; the fare is $1.

BY TAXI
Cabs are available by phone and at the airport and can generally be hailed outside major hotels. Companies offering 24-hour service include: **Metro Taxi** (☎ 303/333–3333), $1.40 minimum, $1.40 per mile; and **Yellow Cab** (☎ 303/777–7777), $1.40 minimum, $1.20 per mile.

Guided Tours
ORIENTATION
Gray Line Tour of Denver (☎ 303/289–2841) offers a three-hour city tour, a Denver mountain parks tour, and a mountain casino tour. Tours range from $15 to $40 per person.

WALKING
The preservation group **Historic Denver** (1330 17th St., ☎ 303/534–1858) offers tours of old Denver for a $5 fee. Self-guided walking-tour brochures are available from the Denver Metro Convention and Visitors Bureau (*see* Visitor Information *below*).

Important Addresses and Numbers
POLICE
For nonemergency police assistance, call 303/575–3127.

EMERGENCY ROOMS
Rose Medical Center (4567 E. 9th Ave., ☎ 303/320–2121) and **St. Joseph Hospital** (1835 Franklin St., ☎ 303/837–7240) are both open 24 hours.

DOCTORS
Downtown Health Care (1860 Larimer St., No. 100, ☎ 303/296–2273) is a full medical clinic. **Rose Medical Center** (*see above*) refers patients to doctors, 8–5:30. **Med Search St. Joseph's Hospital** (1835 Franklin St., ☎ 303/866–8000) is a free referral service.

DENTISTS
Metropolitan Denver Dental Society (3690 S. Yosemite St., ☎ 303/488–0243) offers referrals to dentists; **Centre Dental Associates** (1600 Stout St., No. 1370, ☎ 303/592–1133) is open 8–6, with emergency after-hours care available.

LATE-NIGHT PHARMACIES
Walgreens (2000 E. Colfax Ave., ☎ 303/331–0917) is open daily, 24 hours.

The **Denver Metro Convention and Visitors Bureau** (225 W. Colfax Ave., Denver, CO 80202, ☎ 303/892–1112 or 800/888–1990), open weekdays 8–5 and Saturday 9–1, is across from the City and County Building, and provides information and free maps, magazines, and brochures. **Travelers Aid Society** (1245 E. Colfax Ave., ☎ 303/832–8194) offers the same assistance.

I–70 AND THE HIGH ROCKIES

I–70 is the major artery that fearlessly slices the Continental Divide, passing through or near many of Colorado's most fabled resorts and towns: Aspen, Vail, Breckenridge, Steamboat, Keystone, Snowmass, Copper Mountain, Beaver Creek, Winter Park. True powder hounds intone those names like a mantra to appease the snow gods, speaking in hushed tones of the gnarly mogul runs, the wide-open bowls on top of the world. Here is the image that lingers when most people think of Colorado: a Christmas paperweight come to life, with picture-postcard mining towns and quasi-Tyrolean villages framed by cobalt skies and snowcapped peaks. To those in the know, Colorado is as breathtaking the rest of the year, when meadows are woven with larkspur and columbine, the maroon mountains flecked with the jade of juniper and the ghostly white of aspen.

Like most of Colorado, the High Rockies region is a blend of old and new, of tradition and progress. It is historic towns such as Leadville, whose muddy streets still ring with the lusty laughter from saloons, of flamboyant millionaires who built grandiose monuments to themselves before dying penniless. It's also modern resorts such as Vail, whose history began a mere 30 years ago, yet whose founding and expansion involved risk-taking and egos on as monumental a scale. The High Rockies is fur trappers and fur-clad models, rustlers and Rastafarians, heads of cattle and heads of state. One thing links all the players together: a love of the wide-open spaces, and here, those spaces are as vast as the sky.

Exploring I–70 and the High Rockies

Most visitors on their way to the magnificent ski resorts accessed by I–70 whiz through the Eisenhower Tunnel and cross the Continental Divide without paying much attention to the extraordinary engineering achievements that facilitate their journey. Interstate 70 and the tunnel are tributes to human ingenuity and endurance: Before their completion in the 1970s, crossing the High Rockies evoked the long, arduous treks of the pioneers.

Numbers in the margin correspond to points of interest on the I–70 and the High Rockies map.

❶ Idaho Springs, just outside of Denver, is your first stop on I–70, although a more spectacular drive is along U.S. 6, which parallels the interstate and winds through Clear Creek Canyon. In autumn, the quaking aspens ignite the roadside, making this an especially scenic route.

Idaho Springs was the site of Colorado's first major gold strike, which occurred on January 7, 1859. Today, the quaint old town recalls its mining days, especially along downtown's National Historic Landmark District **Miner Street,** the main drag whose pastel Victorians will transport you back a century without too much imagination.

During the Gold Rush days, ore was ferried from Central City via a 22,000-foot tunnel to Idaho Springs. The **Argo Gold Mill** explains the milling process and runs public tours. *2350 Riverside Dr.,* ☎ *970/567–2421.* ☛ *$3.* ⏲ *Mid-May–mid-Oct., daily 9–5.*

Just outside town is the **Phoenix Gold Mine,** still a working site. A seasoned miner leads visitors underground, where they can wield 19th-century excavating tools, and dig or pan for gold. Whatever riches guests find are theirs to keep. *Off Trail Creek Rd.,* ☎ *970/567–0422.* ☛ *$5 adults, $3 children under 12.* ⏲ *Daily 10–6.*

Idaho Springs presently prospers from its **Hot Springs,** at Indian Springs Resort (302 Soda Creek Rd., ☎ 970/567–2191). Around the springs, known to the Ute natives as the "healing waters of the Great Spirit," are geothermal caves that were used by several tribes as a neutral meeting site. Hot baths and a mineral-water swimming pool are the primary draws for the resort, but the scenery from here is equally fantastic. **Bridal Veil Falls,** within sight of the resort, are spun out as delicately as lace on the rocks. Also close by is the imposing **Charlie Tayler Water Wheel**—the largest in the state—constructed by a miner in the 1890s who attributed his strong constitution to that fact that he never shaved, took baths, or kissed women.

Drive 2 miles west up Fall River Road to **St. Mary's Glacier,** a vision of alpine splendor. In summer the sparkling sapphire lake makes a pleasant picnic spot; in winter, intrepid extreme skiers and snowboarders hike up the glacier and bomb down.

For even more glorious surroundings, take the Mt. Evans Scenic and Historic Byway—the highest paved auto road in America—to the summit of the 14,264-foot-high **Mt. Evans.** The pass winds through scenery of incomparable grandeur: past several placid lakes, one after another every few hundred feet; and vegetation galore, from towering Douglas firs to stunted dwarf bristlecone pines.

West on I–70, then north on U.S. 40 (along the glorious Berthoud Pass)
❷ is **Winter Park,** a place that Denverites have come to think of as their own personal ski area. Although it's owned by the City of Denver and makes a favorite day trip—only 67 miles away—it deserves consideration as a destination resort on its own. Winter Park is easily accessible, the skiing and setting are superb, and it offers the best value of any major ski area in the state. It's also equally popular in summer for hiking and biking. Since the glory of the area is its natural setting, and most people come here specifically to enjoy the resources, Winter Park otherwise has few tourist attractions.

The three interconnected mountains—Winter Park, Mary Jane, and Vasquez Ridge—offer a phenomenal variety of terrain. Head to Vasquez Ridge for splendid intermediate cruising; Mary Jane for some of the steepest, most thrilling bumps in Colorado; and Winter Park for a pleasing blend of both. The ski area has worked hard to upgrade its facilities: The elegant **Lodge at Sunspot,** opened in 1993, is one of Colorado's finest on-mountain restaurants.

Just east of the Continental Divide, and just west of the I–70/U.S. 40
❸ junction, is **Georgetown,** also close enough to be a day trip from Denver, but its quiet charms warrant more than a hurried visit. Georgetown rode the crest of the silver boom during the second half of the 19th century. Most of its elegant, impeccably maintained brick buildings, which comprise a National Historic District, date from that period. Fortunately, Georgetown hasn't been tarted up at all, so it provides

I-70 and the High Rockies

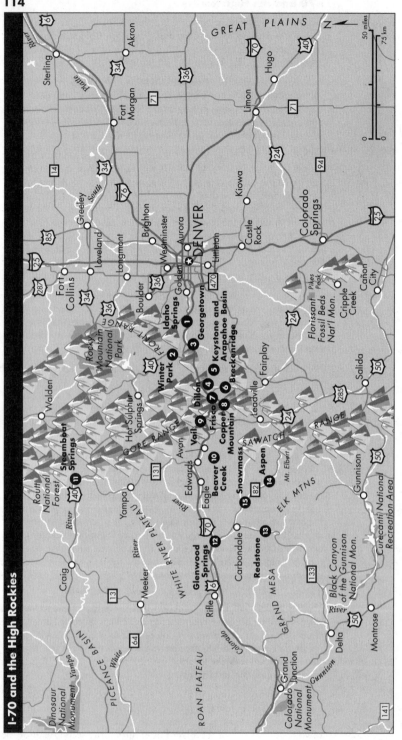

a true sense of what gracious living meant in those rough-and-tumble times. You can wander the five-square-block downtown on your own, or explore it on horse-drawn trolley, courtesy of the **Rutherford Carriage Service** (☎ 303/569–2675), which runs half-hour tours in the summer, daily between 11 and 4.

The **Hamill House,** home of the silver magnate William Arthur Hamill, is a Gothic Revival beauty that displays most of the original wall coverings and furnishings; there's also a unique curved glass conservatory. *3rd and Argentine Sts., ☎ 303/569–2840. ☛ $2.50 adults, $1.50 senior citizens, 50¢ children 12–16. ☉ May–Sept., daily 10–4; Oct.–Apr., weekends noon–4.*

The elaborate **Hotel de Paris,** built almost single-handedly by Frenchman Louis Dupuy in 1875, was one of the Old West's preeminent hosteleries. Now a museum, the hotel depicts how luxuriously the rich were accommodated: Tiffany fixtures, lace curtains, and hand-carved furniture re-create an era of opulence. *6th and Griffith Sts., ☎ 303/569–2311. ☛ $2. ☉ Memorial Day–Oct. 1, daily 9–5; Oct. 2–Memorial Day, weekends noon–4.*

Hop on the **Georgetown Loop Railroad,** a 1920s narrow-gauge steam locomotive that connects the town with the equally historic community of **Silver Plume.** The 6-mile round-trip excursion takes about 70 minutes and winds through vast stands of pine and fir before crossing the 95-foot-high Devil's Gate Bridge, where the track actually loops back over itself as it gains elevation. In Silver Plume, you can tour the **Lebanon Silver Mill and Mine.** *100 Loop Dr., ☎ 303/569–2403. Train operates Memorial Day–Labor Day, daily 10–4; Labor Day–early Oct., weekends 10–4.*

Now get in the car and drive the 20-mile loop of the Guanella Pass Scenic Byway (C.R. 381 and 62) for stunning vistas of the **Mt. Evans Wilderness Area.** Then park yourself at the **Wildlife Viewing Station** by Georgetown Lake, from where you can catch a glimpse of the state's largest herd of rare bighorn sheep.

The western slope of the Rockies (past the Continental Divide) is where the most—and fluffiest—snow falls. As you travel west along I–70, you'll reach one of world's engineering marvels, the 8,941-foot-long **Eisenhower Memorial Tunnel.** Most people who drive through take its presence for granted, but until the first lanes were opened in 1973, the only access route west was the perilous **Loveland Pass,** a twisting, turning roller coaster of a ride. Snow, mud, and a steep grade proved the downfall of many an intrepid motorist. In truly inclement weather, it was impassable, and the east and west slopes were completely cut off from each other.

Authorities first proposed the Eisenhower in 1937 (under a different name, of course). At that time, most geologists warned about unstable rock; for more than three decades their direst predictions came true as rock walls crumbled, steel girders buckled, and gas pockets caused mysterious explosions. When the project was finally completed, more than 500,000 cubic yards of solid granite had been removed from Mt. Trelease. The original cost-estimate in 1937 was $1 million. By the time the second bore was completed in 1979, the tunnel's cost had skyrocketed to $340 million.

A string of superb ski areas now greets you. First is unassuming **Loveland** (*see* Sports and the Outdoors, *below*), a favorite of locals who appreciate the inexpensive lift tickets and short lines. More popular, however, is **Summit County,** a few miles farther on I–70, where four mega-areas—Keystone/Araphoe Basin (A-Basin), Breckenridge, and Copper Mountain—attract skiers from all over the world. There's a saying among Summit County residents: Copper for skiing, Breck for lodging, and Keystone for food. The adage is accurate.

Though the resorts were once marketed together, they are not all owned by the same company. Ralston Purina owns Keystone/A-Basin and purchased Breckenridge in 1993. They plan to link these three areas even more closely. So popular is Summit County, thanks to its incomparable setting, incredible variety of ski terrain, multitude of summer activities, and easy accessibility from Denver, that it welcomes more visitors annually than Aspen and Vail combined. Unfortunately, this creates terrible snarls along I–70, especially on weekends and holidays.

In many respects, Summit County serves as a microcosm of Colorado. It's a combination of grand old mining towns and ultramodern developments, of salty old-timers and yuppies. (Indeed, the county attracts so many young technocrats and professionals it's being touted as the new Silicon Valley.)

❹ **Dillon,** just off I–70 on U.S. 6 East, was founded in the 1870s as a stagecoach stop and trading post for miners, but its location has changed twice since the town's conception. Only a decade after it was founded, Dillon was moved closer to the railroad line. Then, in 1955, plans were drawn up to dam the Blue River, hence forming a reservoir to quench Denver's growing thirst. Dillon would end up submerged under 150 feet of water. Once again the town was moved. Foresighted residents decreed that no building in the new location would be higher than 30 feet, so as not to obstruct the view of the reservoir—now gratefully called Dillon Reservoir, or Lake Dillon. The potential tragedy turned into a boon and a boom for the reborn town, stunningly set on pine-blanketed hills mirrored in the sapphire water. There's no pretension to Dillon, just nature lovers and sports enthusiasts who take advantage of all the recreational opportunities their idyllic home affords.

Continue along U.S. 6 to the first two great ski areas of Summit County, **Keystone** and **Arapahoe Basin.** Arapahoe, the farther of the two areas, was the first to be built in Summit County, in the late '40s. Some say it hasn't changed since; the dig refers, in part, to some of Colorado's notoriously slowest lifts. Still, most of A-Basin's dedicated skiers wouldn't have it any other way. It's also America's highest ski area, with a *base* elevation of 10,780 feet. Most of the runs are above timberline, giving it an almost otherworldly feel. Aficionados love the short lift lines, the literally breathtaking views (and altitudes), the whopping 90% intermediate and expert terrain, and the wide-open bowls that stay open into June. A-Basin came under new management in the late '70s, but, aside from some upgrading of facilities, it has remained true to its resolutely un-chic, gnarly self.

Keystone is another matter. Designed to be cruisers' nirvana, with just enough flash to compete with the glamorous resorts, it compares favorably with the stylish if sterile megadevelopments of the Alps—such as France's Les Arcs. For the most part, its planners were sensitive to the environment, favoring mountain colors and materials that blend inconspicuously with the natural surroundings. Keystone has pursued an aggressive policy of expansion, opening the tougher terrain on North Peak (mogul heaven) and The Outback (glade skiing) in an attempt to change its "easy" reputation and provide a balanced ski experience. Keystone has one drawback: Its sprawling base area. To improve this situation, an ambitious $400 million redevelopment plan will, among other things, overhaul the base lodge and create more accommodations at the mountain itself. Keystone is becoming a magnet in summer, too, with a small lake for water sports, a top-ranked golf course, and the same premium service visitors can expect in winter.

⑥ Double back on U.S. 6 West until it merges with CO 9 South. In a few miles you'll reach **Breckenridge,** a town that many consider the state's prettiest. In 1859 gold was discovered here, and the town sprang to life. For the next several decades Breckenridge's fortunes rose and fell as its lodes of gold and then silver were mined and exhausted. Still, it's the oldest continuously occupied town on the western slope, and fortunately, its architectural legacy from the mining era remains.

The downtown comprises one of Colorado's largest National Historic Districts, with 254 buildings in the National Register of Historic Places. The district is roughly a compact 12 square blocks, bounded by Main and High streets, Washington Avenue, and Wellington Road. The **Breckenridge Activity Center** (201 S. Main St., ☎ 970/453–5579) and **Summit Historical Society** (309 N. Main St., ☎ 970/453–9022) publish guided tours of more than 40 prominent structures, which range from simple log cabins to false-fronts to Victorians with lacy gingerbread trim, all lovingly restored and painted.

TIME OUT   Step back to the '50s, and stop by **Glory Days Café** (311 S. Main St., ☎ 970/453–9495), a tribute to all that is deliriously retro hip from the Eisenhower years, with an authentic 1952 jukebox (and 45s), and cholesterol-laden '50s favorites.

The skiing at Breckenridge, which opened as a resort in 1961, is wonderfully varied over Peaks 7, 8, 9, and 10 of the Tenmile Range. The only downside is the strenuous poling required between Breck's four mountains. There are marvelous bowls and chutes on Peak 8, which is above timberline; gentle sweeping runs on Peak 9; and roller-coaster steeps on Peak 10. Consistent with the town's proud heritage, many runs are named for the old mines, including Bonanza, Cashier, Gold King, and Wellington. Nonetheless, Breck has developed a reputation for embracing the new: One of the first areas to permit snowboarding, it now holds the annual World Snowboarding Championships. Also, for one week each January the town declares itself an independent kingdom during the wild revel called Ullr Fest, which honors the Norse God of snow.

⑦ Back on I–70, just past Route 9, lies the funky, low-key town of **Frisco,** an odd hodgepodge of strip malls near the interstate, with a charming downtown district trimmed with restored bed-and-breakfasts and hell-raising bars. Frisco is a good, moderate (and sane) alternative to the glitzier, pricier resorts in the county, and it's worth exploring even if you're staying elsewhere. The **Frisco Historic Park** (Main and 2nd Sts., ☎ 970/668–3428; ☞ Free; open Tues.–Sat. 11–4) re-creates the boom days with a fully outfitted one-room schoolhouse, jail, and log chapel among the seven authentic 19th-century buildings.

⑧ A few miles further, off I–70, is **Copper Mountain,** another major ski area. Copper is even more self-contained than Keystone, and is dedicated to skiing, although it's picking up as a summer resort. Many skiers think the award-winning design, perfectly contoured to the natural terrain, is one of the world's best. The layout is ideal: Beginner runs are concentrated on the right side (facing the mountain) of the area, intermediate runs in the center, and expert terrain to the left. Weaker skiers can't get into trouble unless they look for it. Accommodations here are uniformly excellent, the nightlife lively for singles and younger couples, and the variety of activities and programs perfect for families.

Just a hop, skip, and a jump west of Summit County on I–70 is one of America's leading destinations, a playground of former presidents (and vice presidents), consistently ranked the finest ski resort in America, if not the world: **Vail.** The four-letter word means Valhalla for skiers and conjures up images of the rich and famous enjoying their privileges. Actually, Vail is one of the least likely success stories in skiing. Seen from the village, the mountain doesn't look all that imposing. There are no glowering glaciers, no couloirs and chutes slashed from the rock, not even an Olympian summit shrouded in clouds. Even local historians admit that the Gore Creek Valley in which Vail regally sits was an impoverished backwater, too isolated to play a prominent or colorful role in Colorado history, until the resort's opening in 1962.

In truth, the men who lent their names to the valley and resort deserved more notoriety than notice. Sir St. George Gore (a regrettably appropriate name) was a swaggering, filthy rich, drunken lout of a baronet who went on a three-year bacchanal in the 1850s and butchered every herd of elk and buffalo in sight. Charles Vail, the otherwise obscure chief engineer of the Colorado Highway Department from 1930 to 1945 was—according to townspeople who dealt with him—an ornery cuss who was rumored to accept kickbacks from contractors.

Then, two visionaries appeared on the scene: Pete Seibert, a veteran of the 10th Mountain Division that prepared for alpine warfare in the surrounding Gore and Sawatch ranges during World War II, and Earl Eaton, a uranium prospector who had grown up in and surveyed these very ranges. In 1957 they ascended the mountain now known as Vail, and upon attaining the summit discovered what skiers now salivate over: the Back Bowls, 4,000 acres of open glades formed when the Ute Indians set "spite fires" to the timberland in retaliation for being driven out by ranchers and miners. After five years of bureaucratic red tape and near-financial suicide, Seibert's dream became reality, and Vail resort was created.

Former owner George Gillett calls Vail "one of God's special works," and in reality it is an almost perfect example of mountain-and-village design. The development is remarkably compact, divided into the residential East Vail, the upscale Vail Village, and the more modest utilitarian Lionshead. Vail resembles a quaint Bavarian hamlet, with homey inns and lodges nestled against cozy A-frame chalets and clock towers. This, along with a heavy European bias among both the population and clientele, gives Vail perhaps the most international flavor and flair of any Colorado resort. It's crafted to anticipate a guest's every need, so you'll find a wealth of dining, shopping, and entertainment options at your fingertips. Everyone here is thoroughly professional: friendly without being familiar, knowing their business but not yours. Despite its tony reputation, the resort has actively courted the family trade in recent years. Children love the kids-only amusement parks at the ski area, with 15 acres of ski-through tepee villages, gold mines, and other rides attractions.

Although the mountain has the sheer exhilarating edge in size over nearly every other North American ski area, it's brilliantly and clearly linked by a well-placed network of lifts and trails. There are 1,220 acres of immensely varied runs on the front side alone, but the Back Bowls are truly skiers' heaven: More than twice the skiable terrain accessed from the front, the back side has eye-popping expanses of fluffy white snow that make both intermediates and experts feel they can ski for days and not run into a single soul. Those same slopes have become a mecca for mountain bike fanatics in summer, and the village now hosts a wide variety of festivals year-round.

TIME OUT The **Hubcap Brewery and Kitchen** (Crossroads Shopping Ctr., ☎ 970/476–5757) is Vail's only microbrewery, offering five regular beers (Vail Pale Ale and Beaver Tail Brown Ale are standouts) and rotating specials. Decor is upscale-diner, with gleaming chrome hubcaps (owner Dean Liotta welcomes additions) adorning the walls. The food is mostly superior pub grub such as calamari, chicken wings, and quesadillas.

At cosmopolitan Vail the emphasis is on luxury, although the pre-fab buildings are beginning to show their age. The best sightseeing is window-shopping, ogling the deluxe merchandise and the consumers—a delightful rather than daunting experience. While you're here, there are two tourist attractions worth visiting. The **Betty Ford Alpine Gardens** (183 Gore Creek Dr., ☎ 970/476–0103; donations accepted; open Memorial Day–Labor Day, daily 9–7) are an oasis of forsythia, heather, wild roses, and shrubs, and have the distinction of being the highest public alpine gardens in the world. The **Colorado Ski Museum/Ski Hall of Fame** (15 Vail Rd., ☎ 970/476–1876; donations accepted; open Tues.–Sat. 9–5) traces the development of the sport throughout the world, with an emphasis on Colorado's contributions. Fascinating displays include century-old skis and tows, early ski fashions, and an entire room devoted to the 10th Mountain Division.

The rest of Vail Valley is composed of solid working-class towns such as **Avon, Eagle, Edwards,** and **Minturn,** which is enjoying a renaissance thanks to the influx of savvy artists and entrepreneurs who have opened several superb galleries and the **Minturn Cellars** winery. There is, however, one exception—**Beaver Creek,** an exclusive four-season development that gives even Utah's ultra-posh Deer Valley a run for its cash flow. It's been open since 1980, and is finally emerging from big sister Vail's shadow. The rap used to be that Beaver Creek was even more immaculately groomed than its soigné clientele. However, when Beaver Creek developed the 110-acre Grouse Mountain in 1991, the resort's reputation changed. With more than 40% of its terrain now rated advanced, skiers flock here on powder days to seek out Grouse and famed runs such as Birds of Prey. Beginners and intermediates can still find the same pampering on the slopes they receive elsewhere in the resort, which is often blissfully uncrowded even on Vail's most congested days. Plans to link Beaver Creek's trail system with that of nearby Arrowhead (*see* Skiing *in* Sports and the Outdoors, *below*) by the 1996–97 season will create one of the state's finest family areas.

Beaver Creek's sublime setting, luxurious accommodations, gourmet restaurants, and world-class golf course designed by Robert Trent Jones make the resort equally popular in summer, especially with families and couples. Elegant without being ostentatious, Vail's quietly glamorous little sister appeals to a select settled crowd, and everything at Beaver Creek lives up to its billing, from the billeting to the bill of fare.

A few miles west, past the town of Edwards, the narrow, winding Route 131 squirrels north from I–70 through the **Yampa Valley.** The lush, wide-open spaces and vistas are both gorgeous and lonely, relieved only by the occasional odd rock formation thrusting up from the ground. This is cattle country, a land of jade forests, jagged outcroppings, and streams silvered by the sun and skirting the **Flat Tops Wilderness Area,** a high, flat mountaintop crowned with a lava dome that glaciers have sculpted into a stunning series of steep cliffs and deep gashes.

TIME OUT **Antlers Café** (Main St., Yampa, no ☎) is owned by Mike Benedict who is, by his own admission, a crusty old codger. Women couldn't sit at the handsome old bar until 1970 ("This ain't no brothel," Mike growled, "and I ain't got no cabaret license."). There's no question where some of his sympathies lie: Amidst the trophies, potbellied stove, antique jukebox, and cash register are such signs as "If you're hungry and out of work, eat an environmentalist." Mike's an equal-opportunity insulter, though, with a delightfully sly grin ("Never mind the dog," reads another sign, "beware of owner."). He'll say you owe him 25 bucks for a photo: He means it!

11 After driving another 30–40 minutes north on Route 131, you'll arrive at **Steamboat Springs,** followed closely by **Steamboat Mountain Village.** Steamboat is aptly nicknamed Ski Town, U.S.A., since the town has "sent" more athletes to the Winter Olympics than any other ski resort in America. Presently, the tally is more than 30, the most famous probably being silver medalist (in the 1972 slalom) Billy Kidd, whose irrepressible grin and 10-gallon hat are instantly recognizable. When he's around, Kidd conducts daily tours of the mountain.

Speaking of the mountain, keep in mind that the part that's visible from the base area is only the tip of the iceberg, and much more terrain lies concealed in back. Steamboat is famed for its eiderdown-soft snow; in fact, the term "champagne powder" was coined here to describe the area's unique feathery dumps, the result of Steamboat's fortuitous position between the arid desert to the west and the moisture-magnet of the Continental Divide to the east, where storm fronts duke it out.

If you're looking for hellacious steeps and menacing couloirs, you won't find them in Steamboat, but you will find perhaps the finest tree skiing in America. Beginners and intermediates rave about the wide-open spaces of Sunshine Bowl and Storm Peak. Steamboat also earns high marks for its comprehensive children's programs, the Kidd Center for Performance Skiing (where you can learn demanding disciplines like powder, mogul, and tree skiing), and two of Colorado's best on-mountain restaurants, Hazie's and Ragnar's.

The modern Steamboat Mountain Village is attractive enough, if lacking in personality: a maze of upscale condos, boutiques, and bars. To its credit, though, this increasingly "hot" destination has retained its down-home, Western friendliness, providing the trappings while avoiding the trap of a premium resort. That may have to do with Steamboat Springs itself, a mere 10-minute drive away, where Stetson hats are sold for use and not for souvenirs. Steamboat's origins are not as a mining town but as a ranching and farming community, setting it apart from a Breckenridge or an Aspen. It has its share of Victorian buildings, most of them fronting Lincoln Avenue, the main drag, but they were built to be functional rather than ornamental.

The **Tread of Pioneers Museum,** in a beautifully restored federal building, is an excellent spot to bone up on local history, and includes ski memorabilia dating back to the turn of the century, when Carl Howelsen opened Howelsen Hill, still the country's preeminent ski-jumping facility. *8th and Oak Sts.,* ☎ *970/879–2214.* ☛ *$2.50 adults, $1 children 6–12.* ⏲ *Daily 11–5.*

The entrance to Steamboat from the mountain is roughly marked by the amusingly garish '50s neon sign from the Rabbit Ears Motel, and the unmistakable stench of sulphur. The town got its name from French trappers who, after hearing the bubbling and churning hot springs, mistakenly thought a steamboat was chugging up the Yampa River.

There are more than 100 hot springs in the immediate vicinity; the **Steamboat Visitor Center** (12th St. and Lincoln Ave., ☎ 970/879–4301) publishes a fun and informative walking tour guide that describes many of the spots. The two most famous are the **Steamboat Springs Health and Recreation Hot Springs** (Lincoln Ave., ☎ 970/879–1828; ☛ $5; open daily 7 AM–8 PM) in town; and the **Strawberry Park Natural Hot Springs** (Strawberry Park Rd., ☎ 970/879–0342; ☛ $5; open daily 8 AM–midnight), 7 miles out of town. The springs may not be as restorative as legend claims, but the inspiring views of the surrounding pristine forest certainly are.

In summer, Steamboat serves as the gateway to magnificent **Routt National Forest,** which offers a wealth of activities from hiking to mountain biking to fishing. Among the nearby attractions are the 283-foot **Fish Creek Falls** and the splendidly rugged **Mt. Zirkel Wilderness Area.** To the north, two sparkling man-made lakes, **Steamboat** and **Pearl,** offer a variety of water sports, including fishing and sailing.

Return the way you came and head west on I–70 to reach the natural and man-made 15-mile-long **Glenwood Canyon.** Nature began the work as the Colorado River carved deep buff-tinted granite, limestone, and quartzite gullies—brilliantly streaked with lavender, rose, and ivory. This process took a half-billion years. Then man stepped in, seeking a more direct route west. In 1992, the work on I–70 through the canyon was completed at a cost of almost $500 million. Much of the expense was attributable to the effort to preserve the natural landscape as much as possible. When contractors blasted cliff faces, for example, they stained the exposed rock to simulate nature's weathering. Biking trails were also created, providing easy access to the hauntingly beautiful **Hanging Lake Recreation Area.** Here Dead Horse Creek sprays ethereal flumes from curling limestone tendrils into a startlingly turquoise pool, as jet-black swifts dart to and fro. It's perhaps the most transcendent of several idyllic spots now reachable on bike or foot. The intrepid can scale the delicate limestone cliffs, pocked with numerous caverns and embroidered with pastel-hued gardens.

I–70 snakes through the canyon on its way to a famed spa that forms the western apex of a triangle with Vail and Aspen. Once upon a time, **12** **Glenwood Springs** was every bit as tony as those chic resorts are today, attracting a faithful legion of the pampered and privileged who came to enjoy the waters (the world's largest natural hot springs), said to cure everything from acne to rheumatism.

Today the entrance to town and its once-splendid prospects of a fertile valley fringed by massive peaks is marred by the proliferation of malls, motels, and fast-food outlets. Remnants of her glory days can still be seen in the grand old **Hotel Colorado** (526 Pine St., ☎ 970/945–6511), regally commanding the vaporous pools from a patrician distance. Modeled after the Villa de Medici in Italy, the property opened its doors in 1893 to become the fashionable retreat of its day. Teddy Roosevelt even made it his unofficial "Little White House" in 1905, and so began the Teddy Bear craze, when a chambermaid stitched together tatters for the President after he returned empty-handed from an exhausting hunt.

The **Yampah Hot Springs,** near the hotel, were discovered by the Ute Indians (Yampah is Ute for "Big Medicine"), and are still popular today.

Even before the heyday of the Hotel Colorado, western notables from Annie Oakley to Doc Holliday came to take the curative waters. In Doc's case, however, the cure didn't work, and six months after his arrival in 1887 he died broke, broken-down, and tubercular. (He lies in Linwood Cemetery, a half-mile east of town.) The smaller pool is 100 feet long and maintained at 104 degrees; the larger is more than two city blocks long (405 feet), and contains in excess of a million gallons of constantly filtered water that is completely refilled every six hours, and maintained at a soothing 90 degrees. *Pine St.,* ☎ *970/945–7131.* ☛ *$6.25 adults, $4 children 3–12.* ☉ *Memorial Day–Labor Day, daily 7:30 am–10 pm; Labor Day–Memorial Day, 9 am–10 pm.*

Two blocks down the street, the **Yampah Spa and Vapor Caves** is a series of three natural underground steam baths. The same 124-degree springs that supply the pool flow under the cave floors. Each chamber is successively hotter than the last; you can scoop mud from the walls for a cleansing facial, as you purify your body (and soul, according to Ute legend). A variety of spa treatments from massages to body wraps is also available. *709 E. 6th St.,* ☎ *970/945–0667.* ☛ *$7.75 for caves alone, more for various treatments.* ☉ *Daily 9–9.*

Twenty minutes south of Glenwood Springs, off Route 82 along Route 117, is another Colorado gem, the small but satisfying **Ski Sunlight,** a favorite of locals who enjoy the varied terrain, sensational views, and lack of pretension. The ratio of shredders (snowboarders) to downhillers here is quite high, as Sunlight has a reputation for "radical air."

At **Carbondale,** Route 82 splits, and Route 133 veers south on its way to **Redstone,** a charming artists' colony whose streets are lined with pretty galleries and boutiques, and whose boundaries are ringed by impressive sandstone cliffs from which the town draws its name. Its history dates back to the late 19th century when J. C. Osgood, director of the Colorado Fuel and Iron Company, built **Cleveholm Manor** (now known as **Redstone Castle**) to entertain the other titans of his day, such as John D. Rockefeller, J. P. Morgan, and Teddy Roosevelt. Among the home's embellishments are gold-leaf ceilings, maroon velvet walls, silk brocade upholstery, marble and mahogany fireplaces, Persian rugs, and Tiffany chandeliers. Today, the hotel is in the National Register of Historic Places, and is open to the public. Stay a night amid baronial splendor in one of the rooms favored by a Roosevelt or a Rockefeller. *58 Redstone Blvd.,* ☎ *970/963–3408.*

Osgood's largesse extended to his employees, for whom he constructed one of the first planned communities, a utopian model in its day. The **Redstone Inn** (82 Redstone Blvd., ☎ 970/963–2526), designated a National Historic Place, is a fine example of the magnate's generosity. Though this structure pales in comparison to the castle, its flourishes include a Tudor bell tower and sumptuous Victorian furnishings. You can also stay overnight at the cozy, relaxing inn.

Meanwhile, Route 82 continues southeast and skirts the Roaring Fork River on its way to **Aspen,** one of the world's fabled resorts and practically a byword for glitz, glamour, and glorious skiing. To the uninitiated, Aspen and Vail are virtually synonymous. To residents, a rivalry exists, despite the current détente that led to the formation of the Aspen/Vail Premier Passport (an interchangeable ski pass that includes a one-way transfer). Comparisons are admittedly odious and at best superficial, though a few instructive generalizations can be made.

The most obvious distinction is the look: Vail is a faux-Bavarian development, Aspen an authentic Victorian mining town. Vail is a lower-key, discreet, relaxed, and relaxing retreat. In see-and-be-seen Aspen, the only bad press is no press (the season doesn't seem to begin without some tabloid scandal). Vail is politicians—where Gerald Ford, Dan Quayle, and John Sununu fled to escape the cares of state. Aspen is recording stars and Hollywood—where Don Johnson and Melanie Griffith remarried (and divorced) and Barbra Streisand took a stand against controversial Amendment 2.

Aspen is a slave to fashion, so much so that the term "Aspen formal" was coined to describe the combination of dressing for the elements (ski hat, wool mittens) and for success (dinner jacket, evening gown). Locals tend to be either violently beautiful or merely wealthy, but fashionable takes on many meanings in Aspen. It's always been a magnet for cultural and countercultural types. After all, bad-boy gonzo journalist Hunter S. Thompson is one of the more visible citizens; and one of Aspen's most beloved figures is unrepentant hippie John Bennett, who tools around in his "Ultimate Taxi" (it's plastered with 3-D glasses, crystal disco balls, and neon necklaces and redolent of dry ice and incense). You'll find everyone from "social x-rays" with Vogue exteriors and vague interiors to long-haired musicians in combat boots and fatigues. To be fair, most Aspenites couldn't care less: Theirs is a freewheeling, tolerant town that welcomes diversity of personal expression. It's all part of the Aspen mystique. Ultimately, it doesn't matter what you wear here, as long as you wear it with conviction.

Before entering Aspen you'll pass through several communities and satellite ski resorts, starting with **Woody Creek,** a determinedly un-chic part of the valley that's most famous as the residence of Hunter S. Thompson. He isn't the only unique contribution to this area, though; if the snow's not too deep you might catch a glimpse of an Aspen landmark, the **Finger House.** Its roof sports an enormous middle finger, painted in Day-Glo colors—the owner's gesture to his wife after a particularly acrimonious divorce.

TIME OUT　A perfect example of this hip anomie is the **Woody Creek Tavern** (0002 Woody Creek Plaza, ☎ 970/923–4585), which has the temerity to sit next to a trailer park. It features pool tables, knotty-pine decor, TVs broadcasting sporting events, great burgers, nachos, and barbecue—and Hunter, who has been known to shoot target practice here every now and then. Don Henley's another habitué, though he usually keeps a low profile.

⑮　Continue southeast along Route 82, and you'll see the turnoffs (Brush Creek or Owl Creek Rds.) to **Snowmass,** one of four ski areas owned by the Aspen Skiing Company. Snowmass Village has its share of chic boutiques and eateries, but is more affordable and down-to-earth than Aspen, and predominantly caters to families. These differences apply equally to the development and to the mountain itself. Aspen Mountain is a rigorous ski experience; Snowmass is Aspen Skiing Company's family resort, with 51% of its 2,500 skiable acres designated intermediate, including the renowned classic cruiser runs off Big Burn lift, the stuff of ego massage. However, don't overlook that Snowmass is four times the size of Aspen Mountain, and has triple the black and double black diamond terrain of its famed sister, including several fearsomely precipitous gullies and Hanging Valley, accessible by a short hike. More and more skiers are discovering Snowmass's other personality, although Aspen Mountain remains the definitive test of skiing ability.

The next area, accessed by West Buttermilk Road, is **Tiehack,** unfortunately known as Aspen's "learning" mountain. It's often dissed and dismissed as a beginner's area, but the Tiehack section on the east contains several wonderfully cut advanced runs (though nothing truly expert), as well as sweeping views of Maroon Creek Valley. It also has superb powder, and deep snow sticks around longer because so few serious skiers realize what they're missing.

Aspen Highlands is the next mountain you'll reach off Maroon Creek Road, and until 1993, it was the only area not owned by the Aspen Skiing Company. This alone made the Highlands a favorite of anti-establishment types; and though it can no longer play on its independence by billing itself as the "maverick ski area," locals ski here for other reasons as well, including the best views among the four mountains, comparatively short lift lines, and some heart-pounding runs. While not quite as hairy as Aspen Mountain, the Highlands offers thrilling descents at Steeplechase and Olympic Bowl, as well as a lovely wide-open bowl called Thunder, where intermediates play. While you're here, enjoy Aspen Highlands' anything-goes spirit, evidenced by special events such as the freestyle contests every Friday, and the now-legendary Ski Patrol Jump, over the deck—and over startled skiers—at the Cloud Nine Picnic Hut. It's held every day at noon, weather permitting.

Continue back on Route 82, and you'll finally reach **Aspen.** Originally called Ute City (after its displaced former residents), it was founded in the late 1870s during a silver rush. The most prominent early citizen was Jerome Wheeler, who in 1889, at the height of Aspen's prosperity, opened two of Aspen's enduring landmarks: the sturdily elegant redbrick **Jerome Hotel** (330 E. Main St., ☎ 970/920–1000), whose ornate lobby, bar, and restaurant today re-create fashionable turn-of-the-century living; and the elegant **Wheeler Opera House** (320 E. Hyman Ave., ☎ 970/925–2750). In 1893, however, silver crashed and Aspen's population dwindled from 15,000 to 250 people by the depression era.

In the late 1930s, the region struck gold when Swiss mountaineer and ski consultant Andre Roche determined that Aspen Mountain would make a prime ski area. By 1941 it had already landed the U.S. Nationals, but Aspen was really put on the world map by Walter Paepcke, who developed the town as a cultural mecca. In 1949, he helped found the Aspen Institute for Humanistic Studies, and organized an international celebration to mark Johann Wolfgang von Goethe's 200th birthday. This event paved the way for such renowned annual festivities as the Aspen Music Festival and the International Design Conference.

Downtown Aspen is easily explored on foot; it's best to wander without a planned itinerary, although the Aspen Historical Society puts out a walking-tour brochure. You can spend an afternoon admiring the sleek window displays and graceful Victorian mansions, many of which now house fine boutiques and restaurants.

You can obtain great insight into Victorian high life at the **Wheeler-Stallard House Museum,** which displays period memorabilia collected by the Aspen Historical Society. *620 W. Bleeker St., ☎ 970/925–3721. ☞ Adults $3.00, children 50¢. ⊙ Jan.–Apr. and mid-June–mid-Sept., Tues.–Fri. 1–4. Closed mid-June–May, mid-Sept.–Dec.*

Your next stop should be the **Aspen Art Museum,** where top local and national artists are exhibited. The complimentary wine-and-cheese-session-cum-gallery tour, held Thursdays at 5:30, is a lot of fun. *590 N. Mill St., ☎ 970/925–8050. ☞ $3 adults, $2 senior citizens and stu-*

dents, children under 12 free. ☉ *Tues., Wed., and Fri.–Sun. noon–6, Thurs. noon–8.*

Between galleries, museums, international conferences, and events, there's so much going on year-round that even in winter many people come to "do the scene," and don't even ski. Still, **Aspen Mountain** (also known as Ajax) is the standard by which many good skiers test themselves. Aspen is not for beginners (there are no green runs); in fact, a black diamond here might rank as a double diamond elsewhere. The narrow mountain is laid out as a series of steep unforgiving ridges with little room for error. Those wanting cruisers ski the ridge tops or valleys: Ruthie's Run, Buckhorn, and International are the classics. Bell Mountain provides some of the best bump skiing anywhere, followed by Walsh's Gulch, Hyrup's, and Kristi's. If you don't like catching air, or don't want your knees to get a workout, go elsewhere!

Aspen is equally popular in summer, with marvelous hiking and biking throughout the **White River National Forest.** One favorite jaunt is to the majestic **Maroon Bells,** twin peaks more than 14,000 feet high, so colorful, thanks to mineral streaking, you'd swear they were blanketed with primrose and Indian paintbrush. It's one of the most photographed spots in the state. Cars are only allowed partway, but Roaring Fork Transit provides shuttle buses that leave regularly in the summer from the Aspen Highlands parking lot.

What to See and Do with Children

Aspen Center for Environmental Studies (Hallam Lake Wildlife Sanctuary, 100 Puppy Smith St., Aspen, ☎ 970/925–5756) is a research center and wildlife sanctuary where children and adults alike can take refuge. The facility sponsors snowshoe walks with naturalist guides in winter, and backyard-wildlife workshops that teach children to create a minisanctuary in their own yard. In summer there are bird-watching hikes and Special Little Naturalist programs for 3–5- and 5–7-year olds, which include nature walks and arts and crafts.

Off the Beaten Path

HUT AND TRAIL SYSTEMS

10th Mountain Hut and Trail System. During World War II a group of hardy soldiers camouflaged in white parkas practiced maneuvers in the stinging cold at Camp Hale, in the Elk Mountain Range between Aspen, Vail, and Leadville. That's where the U.S. Army 10th Mountain Division prepared for alpine fighting on hickory skis. Today, strong intermediates and experts can follow in their tracks on the 300 miles of trails crisscrossing the area. The surprisingly comfortable huts (accommodating up to 16 people in bunks; bring a sleeping bag) are solar-powered and have wood-burning stoves. Huts cost $22 per person per night, and are usually booked well in advance. For details and reservations contact the **10th Mountain Trail Association** (1280 Ute Ave., Aspen 81611, ☎ 970/925–5775).

Alfred A. Braun Hut System. This system explores the backcountry between Aspen and Crested Butte (Box 7937, Aspen 81612, ☎ 970/925–6618), and is run by the U.S. Ski Association. This is an exhilarating but grueling trek—a perfect test of skiing expertise.

LEADVILLE

In the history of Colorado mining, perhaps no town looms larger than **Leadville**—at 10,152 feet, America's highest incorporated town. An easy detour from Copper Mountain and Vail (take U.S. 24 south from I-70, or the breathtaking Route 82 over Independence Pass from

Aspen in summer), this town is a pleasant, nostalgic respite from all the prefab glitz that surrounds it. Two of the state's most fascinating figures are immortalized here: larger-than-life multimillionaire Horace Tabor and his wife Baby Doe (Elizabeth Doe McCourt), the subject of John LaTouche's Pulitzer Prize–winning opera *The Ballad of Baby Doe.*

Tabor amassed a huge fortune (by 1880s standards) of $12 million, much of which he spent building monuments throughout the state to himself and Baby. His power peaked when he purchased a U.S. Senate seat and replaced Senator Teller, who had been appointed Secretary of the Interior, well into his term. Baby Doe was his ambitious mistress and eventual second wife, after he dumped his first, the faithful but frigid Augusta. They made enemies and incurred the scorn of "high society" as only those who throw their money and weight around can. But in 1893 the repeal of the Sherman Act demonetarized silver, and, like so many other mining magnates, Tabor was ruined. He died a pauper in 1899, admonishing Baby to "hang on to the Matchless," his most famous mine, which he was convinced would once again restore her fortunes. It never did. Baby became a recluse, rarely venturing forth from her tiny unheated cabin beside the Matchless. She was discovered frozen to death in 1935.

Their legacy can be found in several attractions in town, including the **Tabor Home** (116 E. 5th St., ☎ 719/486–0551; ☛ $2; open daily 10–4), the modest dwelling where Horace lived with Augusta; the splendiferous **Tabor Opera House** (308 Harrison St., ☎ 719/486–3900; ☛ Free; open Memorial Day–Labor Day, Sun.–Fri. 9–5:30); and the **Matchless Mine** and squalid **Baby Doe's Cabin** (2 mi east of downtown on 7th St., ☎ 719/486–0371; ☛ $2; open Memorial Day–Labor Day 9–5).

Among the many other fascinating museums in Leadville are: The **Mining Hall of Fame and Museum,** which covers virtually every aspect of mining, including displays of various ores, tools, equipment, and dioramas explaining the extraction processes. *120 W. 9th St., ☎ 719/486–1229. ☛ $3 adults, $2 senior citizens, $1.50 children 6–12. ⊙ Daily 9–5.*

Exemplifying how the upper crust such as the Tabors once lived and played are the lavishly decorated rooms of the **Healy House and Dexter Cabin.** *912 Harrison St., ☎ 719/486–0487. ☛ $2.50. ⊙ Memorial Day–Labor Day, daily 10–4:30.*

The **Heritage Museum** also paints a vivid portrait of life in Leadville at its zenith. *120 E. 9th St., ☎ 719/486–1878. ☛ $2.50 adults, $1.50 senior citizens, $1.25 students, children under 6 free. ⊙ Memorial Day–Labor Day, daily 9–5; Labor Day–Memorial Day, Fri. 1–5, weekends 10–5.*

Eccentricity is still a Leadville trait, as witnessed by the annual International Pack Burro Race over Mosquito Pass. The race, held the last weekend of July, ends in Fairplay, another quirky old mining town. The event is immortalized with T-shirts and bumper stickers that read, "Get Your Ass Over the Pass."

Shopping

Needless to say, you can find anything in these glamorous resorts except bargains. Still, window-shopping can be fun, as can a splurge every now and then.

Shopping Districts and Malls

Downtown Aspen is an eye-popping display of conspicuous consumption. Among the malls with ultra-chic stores are **Hyman Street Mall, Cooper Street Mall, Ute City Building,** and **Mill Street Plaza.**

Breckenridge also offers high-end shopping in the **Lincoln West Mall,** the **Main Street Mall,** and **Four Seasons Plaza.**

In Frisco, the **Mining Exchange Building** (313 Main St.) has several shops specializing in Americana, antiques, and collectibles.

Glenwood Springs Mall, in Glenwood, offers everything from Kmart and JCPenney to factory outlets and specialty shops.

Keystone features several top shops in the **Edgewater Mall** and **Argentine Plaza.**

Silverthorne Factory Stores Complex, in Summit County, has developed a reputation for discount shopping for Adolfo, Geoffrey Beene, Liz Claiborne, Evan Picone, Bass Shoe, Royal Doulton, Nike, and many others.

Steamboat's **Old Town Square** is a collection of upscale boutiques and retailers. On the mountain, check out **Ski Time Square, Gondola Square,** and **Torian Plaza.**

To some, Vail is one large upscale mall, but for the best of the best, head for **Gateway Plaza, Crossroads Shopping Center,** and of course, the **Beaver Creek Promenade.**

The top boutiques and galleries in Winter Park are concentrated downtown in **Cooper Creek Square** and **Crestview Place Mall.**

Specialty Stores

ANTIQUES

Fetzer Antiques (305 S. Hunter St., ☎ 970/925–5447) carries Aspen's finest antiques, and specializes in 18th- and 19th-century English and Continental goods. **Uriah Heep's** (303 E. Hopkins Ave., Aspen, ☎ 970/925–7456) purveys an amazing assortment of antique quilts, furnishings, and clothing, as well as exotic textiles, rugs, and folk art. In Frisco, the **Junk-Tique Antique Barn** (313 Main St., ☎ 970/668–3040) is a treasure trove of odds and ends. In Georgetown, the **Georgetown Antique Emporium** (501 Rose St., ☎ 970/569–2727) specializes in oak and brass items.

ART GALLERIES

In the Aspen area, **Anderson Ranch Arts Center** (Snowmass Village, ☎ 970/923–3181) sells the work of resident artists. **Hill Gallery of Photography** (205 S. Mill St., Aspen, ☎ 970/925–1836) captures nature's artistry in works by leading American photographers. **Joel Soroka Gallery** (400 E. Hyman Ave., Aspen, ☎ 970/920–3152) specializes in rare photos. **Rachael Collection** (433 E. Cooper Ave., Aspen, ☎ 970/920–1313) exhibits more than 250 acclaimed American glass artists. **Stars Memorabilia** (521 E. Cooper Ave., Aspen, ☎ 970/920–2920) offers every kind of celebrity memorabilia, from Lincoln's autograph to Pete Townshend's smashed guitar.

In Breckenridge, **Skilled Hands Gallery** (110 S. Main St., ☎ 970/453–7818) is the largest art and crafts gallery in Summit County, offering everything from wood carvings to wind chimes.

Red Men Hall (U.S. 40, Empire, ☎ 970/569–3243), a few miles from Georgetown, showcases Native American art, including jewelry, paintings, and exquisite hand-painted kachina jackets.

In Steamboat, **Amer-Indian Gallery** (747 Lincoln Ave., ☎ 970/879–7116) is owned by North American Native-culture expert Mark St. Pierre (Pulitzer-nominated for his *Madonna Swan: A Lakota Woman's Story*). A wide range of Native art from Alaska to Mexico is featured. **Two Rivers Gallery** (56 9th St., ☎ 970/879–0044) sells cowboy collectibles like antler chandeliers and cow-skull lamps, as well as vintage photographs, prints, sculpture, and paintings. **White Hart Gallery** (843 Lincoln Ave., ☎ 970/879–1015) is a magnificent clutter of Western and Native American paintings and objets d'art.

In the Vail Valley, **Olla Podrida Gallery** (100 E. Meadow Dr., Vail, ☎ 970/476–6919) specializes in contemporary and antique American folk art and craft work. **Windwood Galleries** (151 Main St., Minturn, ☎ 970/827–9232) specializes in Colorado artists, as well as ceramics and artifacts. **Two Elk Gallery** (Main St., Minturn, ☎ 970/827–5307) showcases a dizzying array of items by Colorado artists, from coonskin caps to lodgepole pine furniture.

BOOKS

Off the Beaten Path (56 7th St., Steamboat, ☎ 970/879–9127) is a throwback to the beat generation, with poetry readings, lectures, and concerts. It has an excellent selection of New Age works, in addition to the usual best-sellers and guides.

BOUTIQUES

In Aspen, **Boogie's** (534 E. Cooper Ave., ☎ 970/925–6111) sells kitschy clothes and jewelry; you can grab a bite in their diner, too. **Chepita's** (525 E. Cooper Ave., ☎ 970/925–2871) calls itself a "toy store for adults," and the whimsy continues with kinetic clothing and wood-carved sartorially resplendent pigs, to complement the standard designer watches and jewelry. **Funky Mountain Threads** (520 E. Durant Ave., ☎ 970/925–4665) offers just that: ethnic clothes, festive hats, extravagant beadwork, and imaginative jewelry. **Gracy's** (202 E. Main St., ☎ 970/925–5131) has first-class secondhand clothing. **Scandinavian Designs** (607 E. Cooper Ave., ☎ 970/925–7299) features some of Aspen's finest hand-knit sweaters, as well as everything Scandinavian from Swedish clogs to Norwegian trolls. **Limited Additions** (205 S. Mill St., Aspen, ☎ 970/925–7112) features unique wearable art, handwoven or painted garments, and handcrafted jewelry.

In Steamboat, **Amallama** (Old Town Square, ☎ 970/879–9127) offers folk art, jewelry, and clothing from around the world, including Balinese cradle watchers, carved wooden figures believed to keep evil spirits away from sleeping children. You can make your own earrings at the bead counter. **Avalanche Ranch** (Gondola Square, ☎ 970/879–4392) sells hand-painted T-shirts, hand-knit sweaters, and unusual jewelry and ceramics. **Kirk's Kritters** (806 Lincoln Ave., in the Shirt Stop, ☎ 970/879–1288) offers a zany selection of jewelry and hand-knit sweaters. **Old Town Leather** (929 Lincoln Ave., ☎ 970/879–3558) offers every conceivable leather item, most of them handmade.

Gorsuch (263 Gore Creek Dr., Vail, ☎ 970/476–2294; 70 Promenade, Beaver Creek, ☎ 970/949–7115) is far more than a boutique or a sporting goods store; it offers everything from alpaca sweaters to buffalo coats and pottery to potpourri. **Pepi's Sports** (231 Bridge St., Vail, ☎ 970/476–5202) offers chic ski clothes and accessories, as well as evening wear from Armani to Lauren.

CERAMICS

Aspen Potters (231 E. Main St., ☎ 970/925–8726) offers the latest designs from local artisans. **Geraniums 'n' Sunshine** (520 E. Durant Ave., Aspen, ☎ 970/925–6641) features Susan Eslick's colorful ceramics, as well as unique handcrafted toys and wearable art for kids. **Laughing Monkey** (223 Gore Creek Dr., Vail, ☎ 970/476–8809) has Mexican ceramics.

CRAFTS

Hunter Hogan Tapestries (520 W. Main St., Aspen, ☎ 970/925–8842) is named for the designer of the weavings that are sold here. Most prints have been adapted from African patterns. The aroma of hot wax permeates **Handcarved Candles** (107 N. Main St., Breckenridge, ☎ 970/547–0928), where Al Kinchen fashions extraordinarily intricate tapers. **The Quiet Moose** (110 Lincoln Ave., Breckenridge, ☎ 970/453–6151) specializes in Western and rustic mountain furnishings and home accessories. **Quilts Unlimited** (Silvertree Plaza Mall, 100 Elbert La., Snowmass, ☎ 970/923–5467) sells superb handmade antique and contemporary quilts, as well as various regional handicrafts. **Art Quest** (511 Lincoln Ave., Steamboat, ☎ 970/879–1989) offers a variety of works in silver, glass, paper, ceramics, and alabaster, as well as furniture and jewelry. **Aboriginal Arts** (Crossroads Shopping Center, Vail, ☎ 970/476–7715) offers ethnic jewelry, resin-cast wood carvings, and feather masks from around the South Pacific and the Americas. **Menzel** (12 S. Frontage Rd., Vail, ☎ 970/476–6617) specializes in fanciful, intricate furniture and interiors crafted from 200-year-old pine.

CURIOS AND COLLECTIBLES

The **Ore Rock Cart Shop** (324 S. Main St., Breckenridge, ☎ 970/453–1567) carries unique gifts made from stone, minerals, and precious metals: gold-nugget jewelry, agate bookends, crystals, even fossils and dinosaur bones. **Silver 'n Threads** (509 Rose St., Georgetown, ☎ 970/569–2965) offers a remarkable range of items, from silver ornaments, coins, and jewelry to handcrafted dolls and animals to rare tins and Navajo rock statues. The **Watersweeper and the Dwarf** (717 Grand St., Glenwood Springs, ☎ 970/945–2000) sells handicrafts and Americana fashioned from silver, gold, clay, wood, glass, stone, wool, wax, and patience.

SPORTING GOODS

Aspen Sports (408 E. Cooper Ave., ☎ 970/925–6331; 303 E. Durant Ave., ☎ 970/925–6332; Snowmass Mall, ☎ 970/923–6111; Snowmass Center, ☎ 970/923–3566; Silvertree Hotel, ☎ 970/923–6504) carries a full line of apparel and equipment. **Sport Stalker** (Ski Time Square, Steamboat, ☎ 970/879–2445) offers the latest fashions and gear. **Double Diamond Ski Shop** (520 Lionshead Mall, Vail, ☎ 970/476–5500) is noted not only for its wide selection of merchandise but also for its top-notch service.

WESTERN WEAR AND ACCESSORIES

F. M. Light and Sons (830 Lincoln Ave., Steamboat Springs, ☎ 970/879–1822), owned by the same family for four generations, caters to the Marlboro man in us all. If you're lucky you'll find what you're looking for cheap—how about cowboy hats for $4.98? **Happy Trails** (725 Grand St., Glenwood Springs, ☎ 970/945–6076) has lots of Western-theme goods, much of it on consignment. The **Wild Wild West** (303 Main St., Frisco, ☎ 970/668–2202) has an unbridled selection of everything from bits to boots. **Into the West** (807 Lincoln Ave., Steamboat Springs, ☎ 970/879–8377) is owned by Jace Romick, a former member of the U.S. ski team and a veteran of the rodeo circuit. He crafts splendid, beautifully textured lodgepole furniture, and sells anything tasteful to do with the West: antiques (even ornate potbellied stoves), collectibles, cowhide mirrors, and new handicrafts such as Native American drum tables and fanciful candle holders made from branding irons.

Sports and the Outdoors

Camping

Call the U.S. Forest Service for complete information on camping in the following national forests: **Arapahoe** (☎ 970/444–6001), **Routt** (☎ 970/879–1722), and **White River** (☎ 970/945–2521).

Cycling

Blazing Pedals (Aspen, ☎ 970/925–5651, 970/923–4544 or 800/282–7238) and **Timberline Tours** (Aspen, ☎ 970/920–3217) offer downhill bicycle tours through Aspen and the surrounding countryside.

Steamboat Ski Area (☎ 970/879–6111) has expanded its trail service. **Routt National Forest** has numerous routes in its 1.5-million-acre wilderness. **White River National Forest** has the Rio Grande, Richmond Ridge, and the more strenuous Vail Pass and Independence Pass trails, among many others. **Arapahoe National Forest** offers Boreas Pass, Loveland Pass, Blue River Bikeway, and Tenmile Canyon National Recreation Trail.

Shrine Mountain Adventure (Red Cliff, ☎ 970/827–5363) offers backcountry mountain bike tours, as well as hikes, through the Vail Valley.

Winter Park is one of the leading cycling destinations in the Rockies, thanks to the 660-mile trail system created by the **Winter Park Fat Tire Society** (Box 1337, Winter Park 80482, no ☎). **Mad Adventures** (☎ 970/726–5290 or 800/451–4844) offers instruction and guided bike tours.

Fishing

Among the region's leading destinations are **Dillon Lake** and the **Blue** and **Snake rivers,** in Summit County; **Black Lakes** and the **Eagle River** in Vail Valley; the **Elk** and **Yampa rivers, Dumont Lake,** and **Steamboat Lake** near Steamboat Springs; and the **Frying Pan** and **Roaring Fork rivers** around Aspen. You'll find loads of trout, bass, walleye, pike, and others.

Aspen Outfitting Co. (☎ 970/925–3406) and **Oxbow Outfitting Company** (Aspen, ☎ 970/925–1505) run fly-fishing tours of local waterways. **Steamboat Lake Fishing Company** (Clark, ☎ 970/879–3045) arranges trips on the Elk and Yampa rivers, as well as on local lakes. **Mountain Anglers** (Breckenridge, ☎ 970/453–4665) organizes trips throughout Summit County. **Oxbow Outfitting Co.** (Aspen, ☎ 970/925–1505) runs trips for anglers. **Roaring Fork Anglers** (Glenwood Springs, ☎ 970/945–1800) leads wade and float trips throughout the area. **Summit Guides** (Dillon, ☎ 970/468–8945) offers full- and half-day trips. **Vail Fishing Guides** (☎ 970/476–3296) provides gear as well as guided tours.

The Fraser Valley was a favorite angling spot of President Eisenhower's. For information about fishing in Winter Park and the surrounding region, call the **Arapaho National Forest** (☎ 970/887–3331).

Fitness

Aspen Athletic Club (720 E. Hyman Ave., ☎ 970/925–2531) is fully equipped, and includes a steam room, tanning salon, and massage therapy. The **Aspen Club** (1450 Crystal Lake Rd., ☎ 970/925–8900) has weight-training and cardiovascular equipment, as well as indoor alpine skiing, squash, pools, basketball, and more.

Breckenridge Recreation Center (Kingdom Park, ☎ 970/453–1734) is a state-of-the-art, 62,000-square-foot facility that has a fully equipped health club, two swimming pools, and indoor tennis and racquetball courts.

Cascade Club (Cascade Village, next to Westin, Vail, ☎ 970/476–7400) and **Vail Athletic Club** (352 E. Meadow Dr., ☎ 970/476–7960) are full-service facilities, and include spas.

Copper Mountain Racquet and Athletic Club (209 Ten Mile Circle, Copper Mountain, ☎ 970/968–2882) features full-service fitness rooms, racquetball, tennis, aerobics, saunas, and tanning booths.

Hot Springs Athletic Club (401 N. River Rd., Glenwood Springs, ☎ 970/945–7428) offers Nautilus, saunas, tanning beds, and racquetball.

Golf

Beaver Creek Golf Course (100 Offerson Rd., ☎ 970/949–7123), befitting the resort's reputation, is a 6,400-yard, par-70 stunner designed by Robert Trent Jones.

Breckenridge Golf Club (200 Clubhouse Dr., ☎ 970/453–9104), the only Jack Nicklaus–designed course in America, is a 7,279-yard, par-72 beauty. Dramatically situated, it resembles a nature reserve, with woods and beaver ponds lining the fairways.

Copper Creek Golf Club (Wheeler Circle, Copper Mountain, ☎ 970/968–2339), at 9,650 feet, is America's highest course. Designed by Pete and Perry Dye, the par-70, 6,094-yard course follows the twisting, narrow, natural terrain of Copper's valley.

Eagles Nest Golf Club (305 Golden Eagle Rd., Silverthorne, ☎ 970/468–0681), renowned as the country's most mountainous course, is a par-70 with 6,698 yards, and has several daunting, challenging tee-to-green elevation shifts.

Golf Course at Cordillera (Lodge at Cordillera, Edwards, ☎ 970/926–2200), designed by Hale Irwin, is a par-72, 7,444-yard course with open meadows, ponds, and stands of pine and aspen trees; among the challenges are wandering elk and brown bears.

Keystone Ranch Course (22010 Rte. 6, Dillon, ☎ 970/468–4250) is listed as one of the top 50 resort courses in America by *Golf Digest*. The 7,090-yard, par-72 course, designed by Robert Trent Jones, winds through stunning mountain scenery.

Sheraton Steamboat Golf Club (2000 Clubhouse Dr., ☎ 970/879–1391) is a 6,906-yard, par 72, 18-hole championship course designed by Robert Trent Jones, Jr.

Singletree Golf Course (1265 Berry Creek Rd., Edwards, Vail Valley, ☎ 970/949–4240), a 7,059-yard, par-71 course, is another perennial top-50 resort course, according to *Golf Digest*.

Snowmass Lodge and Golf Club Links (239 Snowmass Village Circle, ☎ 970/923–3148) is an 18-hole, 6,900-yard championship course designed by Arnold Palmer and Ed Seay.

In Winter Park, a 7,000-yard, par-72, 18-hole **Pole Creek Golf Club** (Rte. 40 W, ☎ 970/726–8847), designed by Gary Player and Ron Kirby, is consistently ranked in the top 75 public courses by *Golf Digest.*

Hiking

Near Steamboat Springs, **Routt National Forest** offers miles of trail through aspen and conifer forests, mountain meadows, lakes, and the thunderous 283-foot cascade, Fish Creek Falls. Rabbit Ears Pass is especially beautiful, including the eroded volcanic pinnacles of Rabbit Ears Peaks. The Devil's Causeway is a vertiginous narrow isthmus along the massive ramparts of **Flat Tops Wilderness.** The **Arapahoe** (especially the Wheeler National Recreational Trail and Eagles Nest Wilderness) and **White River national forests** (including the famed Rio Grande Trail, Sunnyside Trail, Hanging Trail, and the Maroon Bells and Collegiate Peaks wilderness areas) offer a similar range of scenic trails. For further information, call the **U.S. Forest Service** (Arapahoe, ☎ 970/444–6001; Routt, ☎ 970/879–1722; White River, ☎ 970/945–2521).

Hiking opportunities in Winter Park include **Byer's Peak** and **Devil's Thumb,** but for more information contact the **Winter Park/Fraser Valley Chamber of Commerce** (☎ 970/726–4118) or **Arapahoe National Forest** (☎ 970/887–3331).

Horseback Riding

Riding trails are generally easy and wind through stunning alpine scenery. Rates begin at $12 an hour. For outfitters try: **A. J. Brink Outfitters** (Sweetwater, north of Vail off exit 133 of I–70, ☎ 970/524–9301); **All Seasons Ranch** (Steamboat, ☎ 970/879–2606); **Aspen Canyon Ranch** (Parshall, Summit County, ☎ 970/725–3518); **Beaver Stables** (Winter Park, ☎ 970/726–9247); **Breckenridge Stables** (☎ 970/453–4438); **Canyon Creek Ranch** (I–70, 7 mi west of Glenwood to exit 109, tel. 970/984–2000); **Eagles Nest Equestrian Center** (Silverthorne, ☎ 970/468–0677); **Piney River Ranch** (Vail, ☎ 970/476–3941); **Sunset Ranch** (Steamboat, ☎ 970/879–0954); and **T Lazy Seven** (Aspen, ☎ 970/925–4614).

Rafting

Adventures Wild (Steamboat Springs, ☎ 970/879–8747) runs excursions to various rivers. Half-day to two-week trips are offered for all levels. Rates start at $30 a person. **Aspen Whitewater/Colorado Riff Raft** (☎ 970/925–1153, 970/925–5405, or 800/759–3939) offers mild to wild excursions on the Shoshone, Upper Roaring Fork, and lower Colorado. **Blazing Paddles/River Rats/Snowmass Whitewater** (☎ 970/923–4544 or 800/282–7238) runs trips to various rivers and canyons in the area and beyond. **Blue Sky Adventures** (Glenwood Springs, ☎ 970/945–6605) offers rafting on the Colorado and Roaring Fork rivers. Also, contact **Performance Tours Rafting** (Breckenridge, ☎ 970/453–0661 or 800/328–7238) and **Mad Adventures** (Winter Park, ☎ 970/726–5290 or 800/451–4844), which let you shoot the rapids of the North Platte, Colorado, and Arkansas rivers. **Rock Garden Rafting** (Glenwood Springs, ☎ 970/945–6737) runs trips down the Colorado and Roaring Fork rivers. **Whitewater Rafting** (Glenwood Springs, ☎ 970/945–8477) and **Timberline Tours** (Vail, ☎ 970/476–1414) also run trips throughout the region.

Skiing

CROSS-COUNTRY

Ashcroft Ski Touring (Aspen, ☎ 970/925–1971) features 40 kilometers (25 miles) of groomed trails in the White River National Forest. **Aspen/Snowmass Nordic Trail System** (☎ 970/923–3148) contains 65 kilometers (40 miles) of trails through the Roaring Fork Valley. **Breck-enridge Nordic Ski Center** (☎ 970/453–6855) maintains 28 kilometers (17 miles) of trails in its system. **Copper Mountain/Trak Cross-Country Center** (☎ 970/968–2882) offers 25 kilometers (15.5 miles) of groomed track and skate lanes. **Devil's Thumb Ranch/Ski Idlewild** (Devil's Thumb is 10 mi north of Winter Park; Ski Idlewild in Winter Park, ☎ 970/726–8231) are full-service resorts with 53 miles of groomed trails between them. **Frisco Nordic Center** (1121 N. Summit Blvd., ☎ 970/668–0866) has 35 kilometers (22 miles) of one-way loops. **Keystone Nordic Center at Ski Tip Lodge** (☎ 970/468–4275) provides 29 kilometers (18 miles) of prepared trails and 56 kilometers (35 miles) of backcountry skiing winding through Arapahoe National Forest. **Steamboat Ski Touring Center** (☎ 970/879–8180) has 30 kilometers (19 miles) on the golf course. **Vail/Beaver Creek Cross-Country Ski Centers** (☎ 970/476–5601, ext. 4390) provide information on the many trails in the Vail Valley.

DOWNHILL

Arrowhead at Vail. West down the Vail Valley lies Arrowhead, a small mountain (1,700-foot vertical drop) with only two lifts accessing gently rolling beginner and intermediate terrain. Currently, this is an ideal place for families who just want to get away from the madding crowds for a day, although Vail Associates plans to link it with Beaver Creek by the 1996–97 season. ☎ 970/476–5601. ⊙ Mid-Dec.–early Apr., 9–3:30.

Aspen Highlands. Nine lifts access 597 acres of terrain with a dizzying 3,635-foot vertical drop. ☎ 970/925–1220. ⊙ Late Nov.–early Apr., 9–4.

Aspen Mountain. Eight lifts, including a high-speed gondola, service the 631 acres of challenging terrain, spanning a vertical of 3,267 feet. ☎ 970/925–1220. ⊙ Late Nov.–mid-Apr., 9–3:30.

Beaver Creek Resort. With 61 trails, 1,125 skiable acres, a 3,340-foot vertical, and 10 lifts (including 2 high-speed quads), uphill capacity is tremendous at this still-uncrowded, upscale winner. ☎ 970/476–5601. ⊙ Late Nov.–mid-Apr., 8:30–3:30.

Breckenridge. Sixteen lifts (including 4 speedy "SuperChair" quads) serve 1,915 skiable acres and a 3,398-foot vertical drop. It offers more than half advanced and expert terrain. ☎ 970/453–5000. ⊙ Mid-Nov.–early May, 8:30-3:45.

Copper Mountain Resort. Copper offers 1,360 acres of skiing on 98 trails and four back bowls, with a 2,601-foot vertical serviced by 19 lifts. The area also provides the "Extreme Experience" on 350 acres of guided adventure skiing. ☎ 970/968–2882. ⊙ Mid-Nov.–late Apr., 8:30–4.

Howelsen Ski Area. This tiny historic area right in Steamboat Springs is Colorado's oldest. Its three lifts, 15 trails, and 440-foot vertical aren't impressive, but it *is* the largest and most complete ski-jumping complex in America, and a major Olympic training ground. Howelsen also offers the "Champagne of Thrills" bobsled course, open daily in season 6 PM–10 PM. ☎ 970/879–8499. ⊙ Dec.–Mar., weekdays noon–10; weekends 9 am–10 pm.

Keystone/Arapahoe Basin. Three mountains—Keystone (which offers an extensive night-skiing system), North Peak, and the new Outback—comprise Keystone Resort, with Arapahoe and Breckenridge available on the same lift ticket. A-Basin offers predominantly intermediate and expert terrain (90% of the 30 trails), with a 2,250-foot vertical drop serviced by five lifts. In all, there are two high-speed gondolas, three high-speed quads, 15 other chairs, and four surface lifts to connect this monstrous area, which just keeps growing. ☎ 970/468–2316. *Keystone open late Oct.–early May, daily 8:30 am–10 pm; A-Basin open early Nov.–early June, 8:30–4.*

Loveland Ski Area. Loveland is considered small-fry, but only because of its proximity to the megaresorts of Summit County. Actually, Loveland—the nearest ski area to Denver (56 mi, just after the Eisenhower Tunnel)—offers a respectable 836 acres serviced by five lifts and spread out over two mountains: Loveland Valley for beginners, and Loveland Basin for everyone else. Basin has some excellent glade and open-bowl skiing, with a 1,680-foot vertical drop. Best of all, it opens early and usually stays open later than any other area except A-Basin. ☎ 970/569–3203. ☉ *Mid-Oct.–May, weekdays 9–4; weekends 8:30–4.*

Ski Cooper. Seventy percent of the 385 skiable acres are rated beginner or intermediate, but the area—with a 1,200-foot vertical drop—also runs Sno-Cat tours into 1,800 acres of pristine backcountry powder. *Off Rte. 24,* ☎ 719/486–3684. ☉ *Late-Nov.–early Apr., 9–4.*

Ski Sunlight. Yet another of Colorado's affordable gems, Ski Sunlight has 50 trails, including the super-steep glades of the East Ridge, serviced by four lifts with 2,010 vertical feet. ☎ 970/945–7491. ☉ *Late-Nov.–early Apr.*

Snowmass. This is a sprawling mountain, with five clearly defined skiing areas totalling 2,500 acres and a 4,087-foot vertical, accessed by 15 lifts. As at Breckenridge, it's a good idea to plan your route carefully, especially if you're meeting someone on the mountain. ☎ 970/925–1220. ☉ *Late-Nov.–mid-Apr., 8:30–3:30.*

Steamboat Ski Area. Twenty-one lifts, including two high-speed quads and a gondola, access 107 trails (2,500 acres), roughly half of them intermediate, with a 3,685-foot vertical drop. ☎ 970/879–6111. ☉ *Late-Nov.–mid-Apr., 9–4.*

Tiehack. This is Aspen's "learning" area, and it offers plenty of wide, gently rolling slopes for beginners and intermediates, more than 410 acres with 45 trails and a vertical of 2,030 feet. *Off Rte. 82,* ☎ 970/925–1220. ☉ *Mid-Dec.–early Apr., 9–4.*

Vail. Vail has an embarrassment of riches: 25 lifts, including a gondola and eight high-speed quads, with an uphill capacity of 41,855 per hour (and they need it—20,000 is the average skier day!); a vertical of 3,250 feet; and more than 4,000 acres of skiing on 121 runs, divided fairly evenly (32% beginner, 36% intermediate, 32% advanced/expert). ☎ 970/476–5601. ☉ *Mid-Nov.–mid-Apr., 8:30–3:30.*

Winter Park/Mary Jane. There are 1,358 skiable acres with a vertical of 3,060 feet. The resort's hub is at the base of Winter Park. Twenty chairlifts (including 4 high-speed quads) and 120 trails connect the three mountains and high alpine bowl. ☎ 970/726–5514. ☉ *Mid-Nov.–mid-Apr. 18, weekdays 9–4; weekends 8:30–4.*

SKI TOURING

Aspen Alpine Guides (☎ 970/925–6618) arranges customized multi-day tours along the 10th Mountain Hut and Trail System connecting Aspen and Vail; and the Alfred A. Braun Hut System connecting Aspen and Crested Butte (*see* Off the Beaten Track, *above*), as do **Elk Mountain Guides** (Aspen, ☎ 970/925–5601) and **Paragon Guides** (Avon,

☎ 970/949–4272). You can also contact the **10th Mountain Hut and Trail System** (☎ 970/925–5775) directly. In Steamboat, **High Country Ski Tours** (☎ 970/879–4857) leads backcountry treks.

Snowboarding

Most ski areas permit at least limited snowboarding; many offer special half pipes for performing tricks, in addition to their skiable terrain. Aspen and Keystone do not allow snowboarding.

Snowmobiling

The following companies run tours throughout the High Rockies region: **Good Times** (Breckenridge, ☎ 970/453–7604 and Frisco, ☎ 970/668–0930); **High Mountain Snowmobile Tours** (Steamboat, ☎ 970/879–9073); **Nova Guides** (Vail/Beaver Creek, ☎ 970/949–4232); **Steamboat Powder Cats** (Steamboat, ☎ 970/879–5188); **Steamboat Snowmobile Tours** (Steamboat, ☎ 970/879–6500); **Piney River Ranch** (Vail, ☎ 970/476–3941); **T Lazy Seven** (Aspen, ☎ 970/925–4614); **Tiger Run Tours** (Breckenridge, ☎ 970/453–2231); **Timberline Snowmobile** (Vail, ☎ 970/476—1414); and **2 Mile Hi Ski-Doo** (Leadville, ☎ 719/486–1183 or 800/933–1183).

Water Sports

Canoeing, kayaking, windsurfing, and sailing are done on many lakes and reservoirs, most notably Dillon (Dillon Yacht Basin, ☎ 970/468–2396; Dillon Marina, ☎ 970/468–5100; Frisco Bay Yacht Club, ☎ 970/668–3022) in Summit County.

Dining

Colorado is a melting pot of cuisines, and nowhere is that diversity and artistry better reflected than at the state's top resorts. Talented young American and European chefs are attracted to resort restaurants because of the diverse clientele and demand for variety on the menus. You can find super sushi in Aspen, terrific tahini in Vail, and blissful blinis in Steamboat Springs. All you have to do is follow your nose.

The downside, however, is that the price for this expertise can be stratospheric. As an indicator, the McDonald's in Aspen and Vail are, respectively, the third and fourth most expensive in the world (Hong Kong and Moscow beat them out). A fun, relatively new trend being offered at several resorts, such as Keystone and Copper Mountain, is a "dine around progressive dinner," which encourages guests to take in a different course at several restaurants. Most areas also have "Popcorn Wagons" that sell high-test espresso, delectable crepes, gourmet sandwiches, and snacks. For price ranges *see* the Dining chart *in* Colorado Essentials, *below.*

Aspen/Snowmass

$$$$ **Piñons.** The food is sublime, the muted ranch decor—with a leather
★ bar, handsome Western art, and enormous brass bowls brimming with tortillas—exquisite. Unfortunately, the wait staff seems oh-so-above-it-all most of the time; maybe they think the attitude is what you're paying for. Still, the cuisine is exotic: pheasant quesadillas or lobster strudel (complemented by morels and chanterelles in phyllo) for appetizers; then segue into elk tournedos sautéed in ginger and pink peppercorn sauce or roasted Colorado striped bass in potato crust swimming on a bed of red onion sauce. ✗ *105 S. Mill St., 2nd floor, Aspen, ☎ 970/920–2021. Reservations advised. AE, MC, V. No lunch.*

$$$$ **Renaissance.** The decor of this stunner is a coolly seductive, abstract
★ rendition of a sultan's tent. Owner-chef Charles Dale apprenticed as

chef saucier to his mentor, Daniel Boulud, at New York's trendiest mineral watering hole, Le Cirque, before opening Renaissance in 1990. He dubs his cuisine "the alchemy of food," and he probably could transform leftovers into culinary gold, thanks to his magical artistry in blending tastes and textures. Opt for his *menu degustation*—six courses matched with the appropriate glass of wine. The menu changes seasonally, as well as the style of preparation for many signature dishes. Among his standouts are *ravioli à la Monegasque* (ravioli with pistachio-nut pesto), freshwater striped bass with fennel-tomato marmalade, and a roast rack of Australian lamb perfectly accompanied by asparagus, morels, and mint salsa. Upstairs, the R Bar offers a taste of the kitchen's splendors at down-to-earth prices, along with live music. ✕ *304 E. Hopkins St., Aspen,* ☎ *970/925–1402. Reservations advised. AE, D, MC, V. No lunch.*

$$$$ **Syzygy.** This posh establishment's name means the alignment of three
★   or more heavenly bodies in the solar system. It reflects personable owner Walt Harris's desire to provide a harmony of expressive cuisine, fine service, and elegant atmosphere. He succeeds, thanks to a sterling, unusually helpful waitstaff and the assured, sublimely seasoned creations of chef Alexander Kim. Kim is clearly impatient with the inevitable meat-and-potatoes bent of the ski crowd, thus assuring that adventurous palates won't be disappointed. His food is crisply flavored and sensuously textured, floating from French to Oriental to Southwestern influences without skipping a beat. Standouts include the pheasant spring roll and lemongrass and lime-crusted prawns to start, followed by such main courses as rack of lamb with juniper glaze over polenta and sweet potato puree, or grilled John Dory with a trio of infused oils of lobster–vanilla bean, arugula, and pinot noir. The patient and knowledgeable will find a few good buys on the extensive wine list. ✕ *520 E. Hyman Ave., Aspen,* ☎ *970/925–3700. Reservations advised. AE, MC, V. No lunch.*

$$$–$$$$ **Krabloonik.** A dogsled whisks you from Snowmass Village to this cozy
★   rustic-elegant cabin (or you can ski there for lunch), where you'll dine sumptuously on some of the best game in Colorado, perhaps carpaccio of smoked moose with lingonberry vinaigrette; elk loin with marsala and sun-dried cherry glaze; pheasant breast with Gorgonzola; or wild boar medallions with morel cream sauce. The Western decor features ski memorabilia and throw rugs. ✕ *4250 Divide Rd., Snowmass,* ☎ *970/923–3953. Reservations required. AE, MC, V. No lunch in summer.*

$$$–$$$$ **Pine Creek Cookhouse.** You cross-country ski or board a horse-drawn sleigh to this homey log cabin—Krabloonik's main competition—where the emphasis is less on game and more on Continental favorites with an Oriental or Southwestern twist. ✕ *11399 Castle Creek, Aspen,* ☎ *970/925–1044. Dinner reservations required. MC, V.*

$$$ **Kenichi.** For some reason, Aspen doesn't have many good Asian restaurants, with the exception of a Thai and two Japanese spots. Kenichi was started by two "defectors" from one of the Japanese favorites. It gets the nod as much for its elegant spacious setting as for the delectable bamboo salmon and Oriental roast duck served Peking style with pancakes, cilantro, scallions, and hoisin sauce, with a side of melting asparagus tempura. ✕ *533 E. Hopkins Ave., Aspen,* ☎ *970/920–2212. Reservations advised. AE, MC, V.*

$$–$$$ **Ajax Tavern.** The brains behind Mustards Grill and Tra Vigne, two of
★   Napa Valley's finest eateries, have created this bright, pleasant restaurant with its mahogany paneling, diamond-patterned floors, leather banquettes, open kitchen, and an eager, unpretentious waitstaff. Nick Morfogen's creative, healthful dishes take advantage of the region's

bountiful produce whenever possible and are reasonably priced. You might begin with house-cured Colorado lamb prosciutto with pecorino and arugula, then opt for cedar-planked rare tuna and sweet potato chips in roasted pepper vinaigrette or chicken breast slow-roasted in its own juices and served on a bed of wild mushrooms and house-smoked bacon. A typical sinful dessert might be poached pear cheesecake with pistachio phyllo crisp. The wine list, showcasing Napa's best, is almost matched by the fine selection of microbrews. ✕ *685 E. Durant Ave.,* ☎ *970/920–9333. Reservations advised. AE, D, MC.*

$$–$$$ **Farfalla.** The food is quite good and the scene spectacular at this north-
★ ern Italian winner. This slick, sleek L.A.-style eatery, well-lit and adorned with fine art, remained all the rage in 1995; go off-peak—at lunch when it's deserted. Specialties include tortellini with asparagus and ham in walnut pesto, and deboned quail in vegetable sauce on a bed of polenta and beans. ✕ *415 E. Main St., Snowmass,* ☎ *970/925– 8222. Reservations accepted for parties of 6 or more; lines form early.* *AE, D, MC, V.*

$$ **Il Poggio.** This spirited trattoria suits all moods, with a light lively café and a quieter, more romantic back room. Chef Chris Blachly is a whiz at the wood-burning oven, turning out delicious grilled items such as rosemary, garlic, and cambozola pizzette; free-range chicken wrapped in pancetta; and duck breast with polenta in honey grappa sauce. ✕ *Elbert La., Snowmass,* ☎ *970/923–4292. Reservations advised for back room. MC, V. No lunch.*

$–$$ **Little Annie's Eating House.** Everything at this charming place is ul-
trasimple, from the wood paneling and red-and-white checked table-cloths to the fresh fish, barbecued ribs and chicken, and Colorado lamb. Annie's is a big favorite with locals who like the relaxed atmosphere, dependable food, and reasonable prices. ✕ *517 E. Hyman Ave., Aspen,* ☎ *970/925–1098. Reservations accepted. MC, V.*

$ **Flying Dog Brew Pub and Grille.** This local hangout, with exposed brick walls and wood beams, has a pleasant ambience. The solid pub grub is a bonus, but mostly customers howl for the wonderful home-brewed beers. Try the sweet and smooth Old Yeller, the gold medal–winning Doggie-Style amber, or the malty Rin Tin Tin. ✕ *424 E. Cooper St. (downstairs), Aspen,* ☎ *970/925–7464. Reservations accepted. MC, V.*

Glenwood Springs

$–$$ **Florinda's.** The russet-and-salmon pink walls of this handsome space are graced by changing exhibits of local artists. Although most items on the menu are Neapolitan—all garlic and attitude—the chef has a deft hand with more creative fare such as veal chops delicately sautéed with shiitake mushrooms in marsala, garlic, sun-dried tomatoes, and topped with romano cheese. ✕ *721 Grand St.,* ☎ *970/945–1245. Reser-vations accepted. AE, MC, V. Closed Sun. No lunch.*

$ **The Bayou.** "Food so good you'll slap yo' mama," trumpets the menu
★ at this casual eatery, whose most distinctive attribute is its frog awning (two bulbous eyes beckon you in). Choose from "pre-stuff, wabbit stuff, udder stuff," such as lip-smacking gumbo that looks like mud (and is supposed to), étouffée and blackened fish, or lethal Cajun martinis and jalapeño beers. On summer weekends live music is played on the patio. ✕ *52103 Rte. 6 at Rte. 24,* ☎ *970/945–1047. Reservations accepted. AE, MC, V.*

$ **The Loft.** The decor here is soothingly Southwestern, with rough-hewn columns and lintels contrasting pleasingly with pastel linens, hanging plants, stained glass, Native American art, and elegant banquettes. The Mexican food is better and cheaper than the Southwestern specialties.

Black-bean burritos are especially tasty and tangy. ✗ *720 Grand St.,* ☎ *970/945–6808. Reservations accepted. AE, MC, V.*

Idaho Springs

$ **Buffalo Bar.** No surprise as to the specialty here: steaks, burgers, fajitas, chili, Philly steak sandwiches—all made with choice buffalo. It's all part of the Western theme, with walls jam-packed with frontier artifacts and memorabilia, and the ornate bar that dates from 1886. There's often great live music that lures people from as far as Summit County. ✗ *1617 Miner St.,* ☎ *970/567–2729. No reservations. AE, MC, V.*

Steamboat Springs

$$$ **Cipriani's.** Chef Joey Bowman, a graduate of the prestigious New En-
★ gland Culinary Institute, has the ability to prepare a classic Caesar salad and then surprise with such inventive dishes as eggplant soup with *tapenade* (caper) croutons swirled with red-pepper rouille; salmon quenelles poached in white wine and served with lobster butter and pinot grigio sauce; or roast duckling with red wine, chili, coriander, garlic, and cumin. Ask to be seated in the more romantic front dining room of this cellar restaurant: Although the low ceilings and subdued lighting give it a somewhat claustrophobic feel, a more raucous atmosphere prevails in the back room, whence families are typically banished. Or go upstairs to the informal Roccioso's, little more than an upscale bar, which shares Cipriani's kitchen and turns out affordable Italian fare. ✗ *Thunderhead Lodge, Ski Time Square,* ☎ *970/879–8824. Reservations advised. AE, MC, V.*

$$$ **L'Apogee.** This expert French restaurant is Steamboat's most intimate, with rose-colored walls, flickering candlelight, and hanging plants. The classic food, with subtle Southwestern and Asian influences, is lovely, especially the rock shrimp soufflé jazzed up with wasabi; roast duckling glazed with red-chili brown sugar, topped with oyster mushroom–green apple demi-glacé, and nestled in crispy rice noodles; and elk chop with kiwis and tamarinds in a roasted garlic-shallot sauce, garnished with pineapple–green peppercorn compote. Still, the menu takes a back seat to the admirable wine list. Oenophile alert: owner Jamie Jenny is a collector whose magnificent wine cellar—cited annually by the *Wine Spectator* as one of America's best—contains more than 750 labels (10,000 bottles). ✗ *911 Lincoln Ave.,* ☎ *970/879–1919. Reservations advised. AE, MC, V.*

$$–$$$ **Antares.** Co-owners Paul LeBrun, Ian Donovan, and Doug Enochs, who
★ cut their culinary teeth at Harwig's and L'Apogee, opened this superlative new eatery in the space formerly occupied by Gorky Park. They retained only the fieldstone walls, frosted windows, pressed tin ceilings, and stained glass, thereby calling attention to the splendid Victorian building itself. LeBrun, the chef, contributes his exciting, eclectic cuisine, which is inspired by America's rich ethnic stew. Hence, you might feast on mussels in a citrus chili chardonnay broth, pompano with a pineapple and Pommery mustard fondue, or Maine lobster over chili pepper linguine. Doug's encyclopedic knowledge of wines is reflected in the comprehensive and fairly priced list. Ian contributes his managerial acumen. Why Antares? Antares was the big red star that guided early explorers, and "we needed a star to guide us," explains Paul. "Besides, we're all Scorpios." Antares the restaurant is certainly a rising star of the first magnitude. ✗ *57½ 8th St.,* ☎ *970/879–9939. Reservations advised. AE, MC, V. No lunch.*

$$–$$$ **Mattie Silk's.** Named after a notorious turn-of-the-century madam, this plush split-level charmer, all velour and lace, looks like a prim wife who has loosened her corset and tarted up in an effort to win back her man.

Chef Dee Conder's sauces, with fresh pungent herbs and very little butter, are assertive and zippy. Try the tender lemon-pepper veal, pounded thin, breaded, then sautéed in a fragrant lemon-cognac sauce. ✕ *Ski Time Square, Steamboat Mountain Village,* ☎ *970/879–2441. Reservations advised. AE, MC, V. No lunch.*

$$ **Riggio's.** This local favorite recently moved to a dramatic new space, whose industrial look (black-and-white tile, exposed pipes) is softened by tapestries, murals, and landscape photos. The menu has changed and now offers tasty pizzas (try the capra, with goat cheese, roasted peppers, garlic or clams, romano, and herbs) and lighter pastas (the sciocca, with rock shrimp, eggplant, tomatoes, and basil sautéed in olive oil, is superb). Standards like manicotti, chicken cacciatore, and saltimbocca are also well prepared. ✕ *1106 Lincoln Ave.,* ☎ *970/879–9010. Reservations advised. AE, D, DC, MC, V. No lunch.*

$$ **Yama Chan's.** Most people think you can't get good sushi in Colorado: Wrong. Somehow, the fish tastes fresher in the crisp mountain air at this simple, superlative Japanese restaurant. The rest of the menu is equally well-presented and prepared. ✕ *Old Town Square, 635 Lincoln Ave.,* ☎ *970/879–8862. Reservations advised. AE, MC, V. Closed Mon. No lunch weekends.*

$–$$ **Harwig's Grill.** This popular eatery is just next door to L'Apogee, and
★ run by the same team. You can order from the neighboring wine list, and the bar offers 40 vintages by the glass, including many lesser-known labels. The menu here reflects owner Jamie Jenny's love of travel, with confidently prepared specialties from around the world: Colorado smoked trout to raclette, jambalaya to shu mei dim sum. The desserts are predictably sinful. ✕ *911 Lincoln Ave.,* ☎ *970/879–1980. Reservations accepted. AE, MC, V. No lunch.*

$–$$ **La Montana.** This Mexican/Southwestern establishment is probably
★ Steamboat's most popular restaurant. The kitchen is wonderfully creative, incorporating indigenous specialties into the traditional menu. Among the standouts are red chili pasta in a shrimp, garlic, and cilantro sauce; mesquite-grilled braided sausage (interwoven strands of elk, lamb, and chorizo sausage); enchiladas layered with Monterey Jack and goat cheese, roasted peppers, and onions; and elk loin crusted with pecan nuts and bourbon cream sauce. ✕ *Après Ski Way and Village Dr.,* ☎ *970/879–5800. Reservations advised. D, MC, V. No lunch.*

$ **Steamboat Smokehouse.** The loud, raucous scene, brick and wood decor, and occasional live music might fool you into thinking this joint is just a bar. Once you try the phenomenal barbecue or hickory-smoked brisket and turkey, however, you'll realize that this is a place where they really know their beans about home cooking. ✕ *912 Lincoln Ave.,* ☎ *970/879–5570. Reservations accepted. MC, V.*

Summit County

$$$$ **Alpenglow Stube.** Without a doubt this is the finest on-mountain din-
★ ing establishment in Colorado (just beating out Hazie's in Steamboat). The decor is warmly elegant, with exposed wood beams, a stone fireplace, antler chandeliers, and floral upholstery. At night, the gondola ride you take to get here is alone worth the cost of the meal. Dinner is a six-course extravaganza, starting with the signature pine cone paté, followed perhaps by scrumptious tuna carpaccio or smoked pheasant ragout with wild mushrooms and red pepper pasta, fresh tangy wild green salad, and such Stube specialties as smoked saddle of rabbit in tricolored peppercorn sauce or rack of boar in Poire William sauce. Lunch is equally delectable, with particularly fine pasta specials. (Removing your ski boots and putting on the plush slippers reserved for diners is a wonderful touch.) ✕ *North Peak, The Outpost, Keystone,*

☎ *970/468–4130. Reservations advised. AE, MC, V. No lunch in summer.*

$$$$ Keystone Ranch. This glorious 1880s log cabin was once part of an
★   actual working cattle ranch, and cowboy memorabilia are strewn
throughout the restaurant, nicely blending with stylish throw rugs and
Western craft work. The gorgeous and massive stone fireplace is a cozy
backdrop for sipping an aperitif or after-dinner coffee. Chef Christo-
pher Wing's rotating, seasonal six-course menu emphasizes indigenous
ingredients, including farm-raised game and fresh fish. You're in luck
if the menu includes rack of lamb infused with pomegranate and car-
damom and encrusted with pine nuts; elk with wild mushrooms in juniper sauce and quince relish; or Gorgonzola flan. Finish your meal
with an unimpeachable Grand Marnier soufflé drizzled with pistachio
cream sauce. ✗ *Keystone Ranch Golf Course,* ☎ *970/468–4130.
Reservations advised. AE, MC, V. No lunch in winter.*

$$$ Jacksan's Sushi House. The knotty-pine walls plastered with money
from around the world contrast intriguingly with the black chairs and
track lighting in this quaint Victorian cabin. The sushi is pricey but
wonderful, as are such scrumptious offerings as tiny enoki mushrooms
steamed in sake and *kani karoage* (soft-shell crab tempura in bonsai
sauce). For a stratospherically priced but hedonistic meal, order the
luscious lobster followed by prized Kobe beef. ✗ *318 N. Main St.,* ☎
970/453–1880. No reservations. AE, MC, V. Closed Mon. No lunch.

$$ Café Alpine. This bright, cheerful place offers terrific soups, salads, and
sandwiches at lunch, and more substantial Continental fare with Asian
flair at dinner (try the roast duck breast Santa Fe with orange mango
and red pepper sauce or saffron and mushroom pheasant ravioli in
roasted tomato garlic sauce). At the tapas bar (served after 4) you can
sample succulent offerings from around the world, including eggplant
crepes, marinated quail breast, blackened tuna sashimi, and lamb
chops Szechuan. The moderately priced wine list, favoring Australian
and Chilean selections, is particularly well thought out. ✗ *106 E.
Adams Ave., Breckenridge,* ☎ *970/453–8218. AE, D, DC, MC, V.*

$$ Gassy Thompson's. Imagine a sports bar crossbred with a hunting lodge,
and you'll get an idea of the ambience and decor of this popular moun-
tain-base hangout. The Continental cuisine is solid if not inspired; grilled
items are best, including honey-mustard chicken breast and pork
medallions. ✗ *Mountain House, Keystone,* ☎ *970/468–4130. No
reservations. AE, MC, V. Closed summer.*

$$ Geronimo Southwest Grill. Red tile floors and boldly colored art set
the stage for robust Southwestern cuisine that draws on Mexican,
Anglo-American, and Native American influences. Try the Zuni squash
soup puréed with roasted pumpkin seeds, oregano, and garlic cream;
beefsteak with chipotle cream sauce; or grilled turkey marinated in orange, red chili, oregano, and cumin. Or opt for solid renditions of old
standbys like chili relleño. The chef uses only fresh ingredients, including
many organic vegetables, which are quickly grilled for crispness and
flavor. ✗ *200 W. Washington Ave., Breckenridge,* ☎ *970/453–9500.
AE, D, MC, V.*

$$ Pesce Fresco. The fish is as fresh as advertised at this engaging spot,
where a jazz pianist plays most nights during ski season. The decor is
upscale coffee shop, but the menu is creative, with salmon dill linguine,
wasabi tuna, and mixed seafood grill the winners. Breakfast is served
here, as well as lunch and dinner. ✗ *Mountain Plaza Bldg., Copper
Mountain,* ☎ *970/968–2882, ext. 6505. Reservations advised. AE, DC,
MC, V.*

$$ **Rackets.** This split-level, high-tech restaurant is Copper's best, and serves predominantly Southwestern cuisine. Start with the calamari breaded with blue cornmeal; smoked duck and piñon sausage over capellini; or Southwestern ravioli (oozing Monterey Jack and green chili); then follow with tender baked cilantro lime scallops or Rocky Mountain trout in bourbon pecan sauce. Rotisserie items are also good bets. ✗ *Racquet & Athletic Club, Copper Mountain,* ☎ *970/968–2882, ext. 6386. Reservations advised. AE, MC, V. No lunch in winter.*

$ **Blue Moose.** Locals flock here for the hearty breakfasts, with menu highlights such as the Mexican Moose—a tortilla crammed with pork, green chili, cheese, sour cream, and scallions. Lunch and dinner are equally satisfying: Chicken vermouth and drunken chicken (marinated with tequila, lime, tomato, green chili, and jalapeño) are particularly noteworthy, as is Mother's fettuccine al pesto. ✗ *540 S. Main St., Breckenridge,* ☎ *970/453–4859. Reservations accepted. No credit cards.*

$ **Frisco Bar & Grill.** You'll find no frills here, just juicy burgers (nine varieties), hellacious nachos, buffalo wings, and a lively crowd in this classic pub with neon signs on the walls and sawdust on the floors. ✗ *720 Granite Boardwalk Blvd., Frisco,* ☎ *970/668–5051. No reservations. AE, MC, V.*

The Vail Valley

$$$$ **Beano's Cabin.** Perhaps the ultimate wilderness dining experience is traveling in a snowmobile-drawn sleigh to this tasteful, assured Beaver Creek hunting lodge. Once there, you'll choose from among seven seasonally rotating entrées and six courses. Ever since chef Chad Scothorn left to start his own restaurant (he's since moved to Utah, Beano's has seen a succession of competent chefs, but they lacked their predecessor's imagination and panache). His tradition of witty pizzas has remained a constant, however, and the convivial setting is unmatched. ✗ *Larkspur Bowl, Beaver Creek,* ☎ *970/949–9090. Reservations required. AE, MC, V.*

$$$$ **Splendido.** Even the people at Vail Associates call this ultraposh eatery
★ the height of decadence, probably because of the marble columns and statuary and custom-made Italian linens that adorn the tables. Chef David Walford, who apprenticed at Northern California's Auberge du Soleil and Masa's, is a master of the new American cuisine borrowing merrily from several different traditions. He is equally adept at turning out grouper baked with Moroccan spices, couscous, and fennel as he is preparing lobster and white bean chili with potato tortillas or elk chop in black pepper–pinot noir sauce with parsnip sweet potato pancakes and chanterelles. Pastry chef Matt Olehy excels at both standards like crème brûlée and such imaginative offerings as caramel-pumpkin *crostata* (puff pastry) with eggnog ice cream. ✗ *17 Chateau La., Beaver Creek,* ☎ *970/845–8808. Reservations advised. AE, MC, V. No lunch.*

$$$–$$$$ **L'Ostello.** The severe minimalist decor contrasts effectively with the richly textured menu at this superlative Italian eatery. The chef creates innovative variations on Italian regional favorites; specialties include blackpepper linguine with duck confit, asparagus, and wild mushrooms in a port reduction; rack of lamb with tomato herb crust, roast eggplant, and goat cheese; and fried potato gnocchi with roasted tomato Parmesan chips. The lodge offers nicely appointed, reasonably priced rooms as well. ✗ *705 W. Lionshead Cir., Vail,* ☎ *970/476–2050. Reservations advised. AE. No lunch.*

$$$–$$$$ **Sweet Basil.** Don't be fooled by the unassuming, teal-and-buff upscale
★ coffee-shop decor, enlivened by towering floral arrangements and abstract art. Chef Thomas Salamunovich, who apprenticed with such mas-

ters as Wolfgang Puck at Postrio and Alain Senderens at Lucas-Carton, has maintained the high standards of his predecessor, David Walford. His Pacific Rim–influenced Mediterranean cuisine is intensely flavored and beautifully presented. Standouts include sesame seared tuna on a bed of crisp Asian vegetables; meaty Portobello and goat cheese tart drizzled with basil-pepper and balsamic vinaigrettes; almond-crusted rack of lamb with shiitake potstickers; and honey-baked pork chop with wild rice pancakes, and ruby grapefruit sauce. The menu changes seasonally, and the daily specials are invariably brilliant. At lunch, dishes are about half the price, and it's deserted on powder days. ✕ *193 E. Gore Creek Dr., Vail,* ☎ *970/476–0125. Reservations advised. AE, MC, V.*

$$$ **Alpen Rose Tea Room.** Claus Fricke's establishment started as a tearoom and bakery in 1976. He's still in the kitchen every evening, cooking feverishly until midnight; and he can still bake truly magnificent pastries. The pink, frilly decor is just as sugar-coated. This is rich, luscious, love-handle cuisine with tons of calories and drowned in butter: so good and so bad for you. The schnitzels, steak tartare, and fresh seafood specials are all home-cooking at its best. ✕ *100 E. Meadows Ave., Vail,* ☎ *970/476–3194. Reservations advised. AE, MC, V. No breakfast or lunch Tues.*

$$$ **Left Bank.** This cozy bistro, with homey touches such as family antiques and paintings, has been a Vail fixture for nearly a quarter century. Liz and Luc Meyer are the gracious hosts who consistently pamper their clientele with fresh, adroitly prepared bistro fare (the kitchen is especially good with game and lamb). How they can make the airy soufflés so fluffy at this altitude is nothing short of miraculous. ✕ *Sitzmark Lodge (not affiliated), 183 Gore Creek Dr., Vail,* ☎ *970/476–3696. Reservations advised. No credit cards. Closed Wed. No lunch.*

$$$ **Michael's American Bistro.** This very sleek, stylish boîte overlooks the atrium of the Gateway Mall, but the space is dramatic: fancifully carved wood columns, lacquered black tables, and striking—almost disturbing—photographs and art on the walls. The hip atmosphere is further accentuated by the cool jazz echoing through the room and the slinky waitstaff garbed entirely in black. They're extremely attentive and will often let you know what the chef thinks is particularly good that day. You could make a meal of the openers alone: grilled smoked quail with orange chutney; gourmet spicy shrimp pizza with roasted onion sauce; vegetable terrine with three pestos. If you can't decide, order the tapas plate, an assortment of three appetizers that changes daily. All courses are superbly presented, with festive colors springing from the plate—giving equal weight to the palette and the palate. The fine, extensive wine list (predominantly American, natch!) has several bargains under $25. ✕ *12 S. Frontage Rd., Vail,* ☎ *970/476–5353. Reservations advised. AE, D, DC, MC, V.*

$$$ **Mirabelle.** From the crackling fireplace to the burgundy and pink
★ linens, this restaurant has achieved the ultimate in romantic, French-country decor. Belgian Daniel Joly is the superb chef who offers as close to classic French haute cuisine as you'll get in Colorado. His preparations are a perfect blend of colors, flavors, and textures. Try the escargots baked in puff pastry with Stilton in Madeira sauce, or shrimp and lobster mousseline accompanied by sautéed shiitakes and chives to start; follow with shrimp nestled in spinach with tapioca caviar and bell pepper coulis, or free-range chicken breast bursting with brie and hazelnuts, in orange hollandaise sauce. Fairly priced wine recommendations are listed beneath each entrée. Desserts are sheer heaven, with caramelized cinnamon pear tart kissed with passion-fruit sorbet and vanilla ice cream the crowning achievement. ✕ *Entrance to Beaver Creek,*

☎ *970/949–7728. Reservations advised. No credit cards. Closed Mon. No lunch.*

$$–$$$ **TraMonti.** This breezy trattoria in the Charter at Beaver Creek showcases the vibrant progressive cuisine of chef Cynde Arnold. She loves experimenting with bold juxtapositions of flavors and is most successful with her gourmet pizzas (such as shrimp, goat cheese, braised scallions, and black olives) and pastas (penne with wild boar and veal bolognese; ravioli stuffed with lobster, mascarpone, sun-dried tomatoes, and basil in saffron cream). ✕ *The Charter at Beaver Creek,* ☎ *970/949–5552. Reservations advised. AE, MC, V. No lunch.*

$$ **Terra Bistro.** In the Vail Athletic Club, this sleek, airy space, with a warm
★ fireplace contrasting with black iron chairs and black-and-white photographs, is a sterling addition to the Vail dining scene. Chef Cyndi Walt's innovative, seasonally changing menu caters to both meat-and-potatoes diners and vegans: The pepper-crusted shell steak with wild mushrooms, garlic-sage mashed potatoes, and Gorgonzola cabernet sauce is delicious; the multigrain risotto with chanterelles, leeks, fontina, and autumn squash purée would convert even the most confirmed carnivore. Tuna and soba rolls with a red-curry-and-lemon-chili dipping sauce, grilled chili relleño with Moroccan spices and crisp vegetables, and feather-light fried calamari are marvelous appetizers. Walt wants diners to feel comfortable after their meals; fortunately, this doesn't mean minute portions at stratospheric prices. Organic state produce and free-range meat and poultry is used whenever possible. ✕ *352 E. Meadow Dr.,* ☎ *970/476–0700. Reservations advised. AE, D, MC, V.*

$–$$ **Blu's.** This fun, casual, constantly hopping place is a Vail institution, with an eclectic affordable menu. The food is always fresh and zippy, from smoked duck, onion, and sage pizza to kick-ass California chicken relleño. Blu's is open for all three meals. ✕ *193 E. Gore Creek, Vail,* ☎ *970/476–3113. No reservations. D, MC, V.*

$ **The Gashouse.** This classic local hangout, in a 50-year-old log cabin with trophy-covered walls, draws up-valley crowds who swear by the steaks, delicious ribs, and sautéed rock shrimp with chili pesto pasta. Stop in for a brew and some heavenly jalapeño chips and watch how the Vail Valley kicks back. ✕ *Rte. 6, Edwards,* ☎ *970/926–2896. AE, MC, V.*

$ **Minturn Country Club.** This rustic, homey joint is a favorite hangout of racers during World Cup ski competitions, when they literally hang from the rafters. Steaks, prime rib, fish, and chicken preparations vary wildly, but you have only yourself to blame if you wanted it medium rare and it comes out well done: you cook everything yourself. ✕ *Main St., Minturn,* ☎ *970/827–4114. No reservations. MC, V. No lunch.*

Winter Park

$$–$$$ **Gasthaus Eichler.** This is Winter Park's most romantic dining spot, with
★ quaint Bavarian decor, antler chandeliers, and stained glass windows, all glowing in the candlelight as Strauss rings softly in the background. Featured are veal and grilled items, in addition to scrumptious versions of German classics such as sauerbraten. The *Rahmschnitzel*—tender veal in a delicate wild mushroom and brandy cream sauce—is extraordinary, as are the feathery light potato pancakes. The Eichler also offers 15 inexpensive, cozy, Old World rooms, with down comforters, lace curtains, armoires, cable TV, and Jacuzzis. ✕ *Winter Park Dr.,* ☎ *970/726–5133 or 800/543–3899. Reservations advised. AE, D, MC, V. No lunch.*

$$–$$$ **Peck House.** This snug, red-and-white, barnlike inn, Colorado's oldest continually operating hostelry, is actually in the quirky town of Empire, on U.S. 40 a few miles north of I–70. It began in 1860 as a boarding house built for wealthy mine investors, and the dining room is crammed with period antiques, including the original etched-glass, gaslight lamp shades from the state capitol, and evocative tinted lithographs. Game is the house specialty: expertly prepared quail and venison (try it with cabernet sauce) are among the standouts. The Peck House also offers 11 charming, inexpensively priced rooms (not all with private bath) awash in Victorian splendor. A Sunday brunch is offered. ✗ *Just off U.S. 40, Empire,* ☎ *970/569–9870. Reservations advised. AE, MC, V.*

$$ **Deno's Mountain Bistro.** In many ways, Deno's is an anomaly: It seems like a casual drinking establishment (there's a sizable selection of beers from around the world), and is by far the liveliest spot in town, yet it also has an impressive international wine list that's comprehensive and fairly priced. The wine is as much a labor of love as a folly in this unpretentious area, thanks to Deno himself, a charismatic, energetic powerhouse. The menu is as eclectic as the wine list, from spicy Szechuan beef egg roll to Cajun barbecued shrimp to veal Marsala, all well prepared and served by a friendly staff, most of whom have been working here for years. ✗ *Winter Park Dr.,* ☎ *970/726–5332. AE, D, MC, V.*

$ **Last Waltz.** This very homey place is festooned with hanging plants and graced with a crackling fireplace and tinkling piano. The huge menu jumps from bagels and lox to burritos, without missing a beat. The south-of-the-border dishes are best: zesty *calientitas* (fried jalapeños filled with cream cheese served with a devilish salsa) and black bean tostadas are especially noteworthy. Breakfast and brunch will power you for those mogul runs. ✗ *Winter Park Dr.,* ☎ *970/726–4877. No reservations. AE, DC, MC, V.*

Lodging

Choices range from rooms at humble motor inns in towns outside the main resorts to rustic luxury villas at Beaver Creek's Saddle Ridge— a series of classic Western-style lodgings complete with fireplaces, Ralph Lauren furnishings, and superb Western art and antiques. (One or two may be available to rent. At $400 per person per night, Trapper's Cabin comes replete with a private chef and activity director.) Winter is high season in Aspen, Vail, Summit County, Winter Park, and Steamboat. Prices often drop by as much as 50% in summer, despite the wealth of activities, events, and festivals. As a spa resort, Glenwood is the lone exception, with higher rates in the summer months.

Winter Park offers affordability, comfort, even luxury—but don't expect the "poshness" that the other top resorts offer. In this area, inns customarily serve both breakfast and dinner family-style, enabling guests to socialize easily. Most of the lodging is more than a mile from the mountain, but a free shuttle service runs throughout the area.

Unless otherwise noted, all accommodations include standard amenities such as phones, cable TV, and full baths in the rooms. For rates *see* the Lodging chart *in* Colorado Essentials, *below.*

Hotels
ASPEN/SNOWMASS

$$$$ **Hotel Jerome.** One of the state's truly grand hotels since 1889, this is
★ a treasure trove of Victoriana and froufrou. The sumptuous public rooms alone have five kinds of wallpaper, antler sconces, and more than $60,000 worth of rose damask curtains. Each luxurious room and suite is individually decorated in soft pastel hues with period furnishings such as carved cherry armoires, with minibar and cable TV; the huge bath-

rooms include oversized marble baths, many with Jacuzzis and separate showers. ✉ *330 E. Main St., Aspen 81611,* ☎ *970/920–1000 or 800/331–7213,* ⓕ *970/925–2784. 44 rooms, 50 suites. 2 restaurants, bar, pool, 2 hot tubs, airport shuttle. AE, MC, V.*

$$$$ **Little Nell.** Built to be the last word in luxury, the Nell is the only truly
★ ski-in/ski-out property in Aspen, and that alone is worth something. The handsomely appointed rooms (all in mountain colors and abounding with wildlife prints) have every conceivable amenity and comfort, including fireplace, patio, marble bath, safe, cable TV, down comforters, and minibar. Equally superior is the waitstaff, who anticipate your every need. The restaurant, under new executive chef George Mahaffey, is one of the best in town. ✉ *675 E. Durant Ave., Aspen 81611,* ☎ *970/920–4600 or 800/525–6200,* ⓕ *970/920–4670. 86 rooms, 11 suites. 2 restaurants, bar, deli, pool, hot tub, health club, ski shop. AE, DC, MC, V.*

$$$$ **Ritz-Carlton.** This redbrick building seems more appropriate to Har-
★ vard than to Aspen. And although it's less formal than some Ritz-Carltons, this one is memorable, even by Aspen's exacting standards. In the august reception area, for example, are elegant burnished hickory walls, crystal chandeliers, Colorado green-granite floors, antique grandfather clocks and secretaries, and a $5 million art collection highlighted by commissioned sculptures and faux-18th-century landscapes and portraiture. The mostly peach-color rooms are more casual than the lobby, with cherry furnishings, luxuriant marble baths, and three phones, among other amenities. The property is ski-out, though not quite ski-in. ✉ *315 E. Dean St., Aspen 81611,* ☎ *970/920–3300 or 800/241–3333,* ⓕ *970/920–7353. 231 rooms, 26 suites. 2 restaurants, 2 bars, pool, beauty salon, indoor and outdoor hot tubs, sauna, steam room, exercise room, meeting rooms, airport shuttle. AE, DC, MC, V.*

$$$–$$$$ **Snowmass Club.** If you like Ralph Lauren's Polo-style, you'll love this
★ elegant property with English hunting-lodge decor: guest rooms have rose-and-jade color schemes, handsome armoires and writing desks, rocking chairs, and four-poster beds. The club is equally popular with sports people: The Ed Seay–designed 18-hole championship golf course doubles as a cross-country ski center in winter, and there's a fully equipped health and racquet club on the premises. This resort is well suited for families: children stay free in their parents' rooms, and there's a fine day-care center. Sage's Bistro is the standout restaurant, featuring executive-chef Scott Phillip's sterling "Contemporary Ranchlands" cuisine. ✉ *Box G-2, Snowmass Village 81615,* ☎ *970/923–5600 or 800/525–0710,* ⓕ *970/923–6944. 76 rooms, 60 villas. Restaurant, bar, 2 pools, hot tub, sauna, spa, steam room, 18-hole golf course, 11 tennis courts, exercise room, racquetball, squash, cross-country skiing, ski shop, airport shuttle. AE, DC, MC, V.*

$$$ **Aspen Club Lodge.** This refined, intimate ski-in hotel has a delightfully
★ European flavor and was extensively remodeled in 1994. The rooms are tastefully outfitted in rich mountain colors and desert pastels, with polished pine woodwork and beams, French doors opening onto the patio or balcony, down comforters, and minifridges. Complimentary buffet breakfast and morning newspapers are just two of the extras. The plush Aspen Club Lodge Restaurant offers stunning views and moderately priced American fare. The management also runs several top-notch condominiums and the sunny, beautifully renovated Independence Square Hotel. Guests may use the nearby Aspen Club International, which has a weight room; pool; Jacuzzi; sauna and steam room; and tennis, squash, and racquetball courts. ✉ *709 E. Durant Ave., Aspen 81611,* ☎ *970/920–6760 or 800/882–2582,* ⓕ *970/920–6778. 84*

rooms, 6 suites. Restaurant, bar, pool, hot tub, ski shop, airport shuttle. AE, MC, V.

$$$ **Hotel Lenado.** This ravishing B&B is Aspen's most romantic property.
★ The smallish but quaint rooms contain either intricate carved applewood or Adirondack ironwood beds (*lenado* is Spanish for wood, and the motif appears throughout the hotel), antique armoires, even woodburning stoves, in addition to modern amenities such as cable TV and tile bath. Gracious and graceful, the Lenado is Aspen at its considerable best. ⊞ *200 S. Aspen St., Aspen 81611, ☎ 970/925–6246 or 800/321–3457, ℻ 970/925–3840. 19 rooms. Breakfast room, lobby lounge, hot tub. AE, DC, MC, V.*

$$$ **Sardy House.** If the Lenado is full, head down the block to this equally sumptuous property under the same management. The tiny reception area opens onto an inviting parlor, with bay windows and dripping with chintz and lace. A narrow winding staircase with a magnificent oak balustrade leads to the precious rooms, decorated in aubergine, mauve, and rose, with Axeminster carpets from Belfast, cherry armoires and beds, wicker furniture, and such welcome touches as Laura Ashley bedclothes and duvets, heated towel racks, and whirlpool tubs. The new wing scrupulously duplicates the authentic Victorian feel of the original house. The restaurant serves exquisite Continental cuisine. The Sardy is straight out of a novel, the kind you read curled up by the fire on a frosty night. ⊞ *128 E. Main St., Aspen 81611, ☎ 970/920–2525 or 800/321–3457, ℻ 970/920–4478. 14 rooms, 6 suites. Restaurant, pool, hot tub, sauna. AE, DC, MC, V.*

$$–$$$ **Silvertree Hotel.** This ski-in/ski-out property is actually built into Snowmass Mountain. It's sprawling, with virtually everything you need on-site. Rooms and suites feature subdued attractive decor, with all the expected amenities of a first-class hotel. Condominium units are also available, with full use of facilities. ⊞ *Box 5009, Snowmass Village 81615, ☎ 970/923–3520 or 800/525–9402, ℻ 970/923–5192. 262 rooms, 15 suites, 200 condo units. 3 restaurants, bar, 2 pools, 2 hot tubs, spa, health club, ski shop, cabaret, meeting rooms. AE, D, DC, MC, V.*

$$ **Boomerang Lodge.** This comfortable, functional property offers a wide range of accommodations, from standard, somewhat drab hotel rooms to smartly appointed studios and deluxe rooms to three-bedroom apartments. There's even a log cabin. The nicest lodgings are the deluxe units, decorated in earth tones and with a Southwestern flair, each with a balcony, an enormous marble bath, a fireplace, and a wet bar. The staff is most hospitable. Continental breakfast is included in the rate. ⊞ *500 W. Hopkins Ave., Aspen 81611, ☎ 970/925–3416 or 800/992–8852, ℻ 970/925–3314. Breakfast room, pool, hot tub, sauna. AE, MC, V.*

$$ **Snowflake Inn.** This is another property with wildly divergent accommodations, all quite comfortable and decorated mostly in tartans or bright colors. The rustic lobby with its stone fireplace and wood beams is a convivial gathering place for the complimentary Continental breakfast and afternoon tea. ⊞ *221 E. Hyman Ave., Aspen 81611, ☎ 970/925–3221 or 800/247–2069, ℻ 970/925–8740. 38 units. Pool, hot tub, sauna. AE, MC, V.*

$ **Skier's Chalet.** This is arguably Aspen's best bargain. The location—100 feet from the ticket office and No. 1A Chairlift—can't be beat. Basic but snug rooms all have cable TV, private bath and phone, and the staff and fellow clientele are unfailingly congenial. A complimentary Continental breakfast is served every morning. ⊞ *233 Gilbert St., Aspen 81611, ☎ 970/920–2037. 20 rooms. Restaurant, pool. MC, V. Closed late-Apr.–late-Nov.*

BRECKENRIDGE

$$ Breckenridge Hilton. This ski-in/ski-out property, the only full-service hotel in Breckenridge, was planned as a condo development, but management ran out of financing. This pays dividends in the enormous bedrooms, which feature pleasing contemporary Southwestern decor in teal, salmon, mauve, and maroon. A half-million dollars was spent on refurbishings in 1993, with one surprising omission: air conditioning (though it's rarely necessary). Swans, on the property, is one of the town's more highly regarded restaurants. ⌕ *550 Village Rd., 80424,* ☎ *970/453–4500,* FAX *970/453–0212. 208 rooms. Restaurant, bar, indoor pool, 2 indoor hot tubs, health club, ski shop, meeting rooms. AE, D, MC, V.*

$$ Lodge at Breckenridge. This special property has the disadvantage of being outside town, though shuttle service is provided to the town and ski area. The compensation is the breathtaking panoramas of the Ten Mile Range from nearly every angle; huge, strategically placed picture windows allow full vantage. The look is mountain chalet, with a rustic-modern decor. The well-lit, spacious rooms all have cable TV and full bath; minisuites also feature fireplace and kitchenette. The complete spa and health club facility is a bonus. ⌕ *112 Overlook Dr., 80424,* ☎ *970/453–9300 or 800/736–1607,* FAX *970/453–0625. 45 units. Restaurant, indoor pool, 2 indoor hot tubs, 2 outdoor hot tubs, spa, health club, racquetball, pro shop. AE, D, MC, V.*

$$ Village at Breckenridge. The word "village" puts it mildly, at this sprawling, self-contained resort, spread-eagled over 14 acres, and offering several varieties of accommodation from lodge-style rooms to three-bedroom condominiums. The decor runs from Southwestern color schemes to gleaming chrome-and-glass units. Studios and efficiencies have fireplaces and kitchenettes. There's even a community theater on the premises. ⌕ *Box 8329, 80424,* ☎ *970/453–2000 or 800/800–7829,* FAX *970/453–1878. 455 units. 9 restaurants, 3 bars, 2 indoor pools, 2 outdoor pools, 12 hot tubs, sauna, 2 health clubs, ski shop, meeting rooms, car rental. AE, D, MC, V.*

$ Williams House. Innkeepers Fred Kinat and Diane Jaynes spent a year
★ restoring this intimate, 1885 miner's cottage, then expanded it with utmost care. From the cozy front parlor with its mantled fireplace and floral spreads, to the exquisite dollhouselike accommodations, the Williams House is a dream bed-and-breakfast. The individually decorated rooms are as romantic as can be, with chintz or lace curtains, Laura Ashley and Ralph Lauren comforters and linens, mahogany beds, walnut wardrobes or cherry armoires, old framed magazine covers, hand-blown globe lamps, fresh flowers and sachets, and footed tubs. In 1994 they opened Willoughby Cottage next door, a perfect romantic retreat complete with scalloped lace curtains, intricately carved Victorian doors and balustrades, an elaborate mantle with hand-painted tiles, a gas-burning fireplace, hot tub, kitchenette, and rustic antique furnishings. Best of all are the affable hosts: Avid skiers ("Cold cereal on powder days," they warn), they take guests to their secret stashes, and on hikes in summer. Diane's muffins, quiches, and *huevos rancheros* (eggs with salsa) are addictive. ⌕ *303 N. Main St., 80424,* ☎ *970/453–2975. 4 rooms, 1 cottage. AE.*

GEORGETOWN

$ Hardy House B&B Inn. This 1877 Victorian has been lovingly restored by owner Sarah Schmidt, whose welcome couldn't be warmer (nor could the potbellied stove that greets you in the parlor). The cozy rooms, all with private bath, are comfortably furnished with antiques and period reproductions, as well as down comforters. ☎ *605 Brownell St., Box 0156, 80444,* ☎ *970/569–3388. 4 rooms. MC, V.*

$ **Hotel Colorado.** The exterior of this building, listed in the National Historic Register, is simply exquisite, with graceful sandstone colonnades and Italianate campaniles. The impression of luxury continues in the imposing, yet gracious, marble lobby and public rooms. Unfortunately, the sunny, individually decorated rooms and suites—most with high ceilings, fireplaces, gorgeous period wainscoting, and balconies affording superlative vistas—are a little threadbare and oddly configured. But everyone, whether notable or notorious, from Doc Holliday to Al Capone, stayed here in its halcyon days. ☎ *526 Pine St., 81601,* ☎ *970/945–6511 or 800/544–3998,* ⒻⒶⓍ *970/045–7030. 96 rooms, 26 suites. 2 restaurants, bar, beauty salon, health club, meeting rooms. AE, DC, MC, V.*

$ **Hotel Denver.** Although this hotel was originally built in 1806, its
★ most striking features are the numerous art-deco touches throughout. Most rooms open onto a view of the springs or a three-story New Orleans–style atrium bedecked with colorful canopies. The accommodations are ultraneat, trim, and comfortable, and are decorated predominantly in maroon and teal. There are plenty of homey touches, such as fresh-baked cookies upon your arrival (the cordial owner also runs the best bakery in town—The Daily Bread). The Daily Bread Too is the excellent hotel restaurant. ☎ *402 7th St., 81601,* ☎ *970/945–6565,* ⒻⒶⓍ *970/945–2204. 60 rooms. Restaurant, bar, beauty salon, exercise room, meeting rooms. AE, D, MC, V.*

$ **Hot Springs Lodge.** This lodge is perfectly located right by the Springs, which are used to heat the property. The attractive rooms, decorated in jade, teal, buff, and rose, stress the Southwestern motif. Deluxe rooms offer a minifridge and tiny balcony, in addition to standard conveniences such as cable TV and full bath. ☎ *401 N. River Rd., 81601,* ☎ *970/945–6571. 107 rooms. Restaurant, bar, hot tub. AE, D, DC, MC, V.*

$ **Sunlight Inn.** This charming traditional ski lodge a few hundred feet from the Ski Sunlight lifts brims with European ambience, from the delightful lounge (with a marvelous carved fireplace and wrought-iron chandeliers) and fine German restaurant to the cozily rustic rooms, all with pine-board walls and rough-hewn armoires. Sunlight is a true getaway-from-it-all place, with no TVs or phones in the rooms. ☎ *10252 C.R. 117, 81601,* ☎ *970/945–5225. 24 rooms (5 share baths). Restaurant, bar, hot tub. MC, V.*

$$–$$$ **Keystone Lodge.** The ugly cinder-block structure gives no hint of the
★ gracious living within. The lodge is a pampering place, and a member of Preferred Hotels. Rooms with king-size beds are on the small side, while rooms with two queen-size beds are enormous, with terraces. All units are beautifully appointed in rich mountain colors, with all the amenities. There are lovely thoughtful touches, like a jar of fresh-baked cookies and a teddy bear with your turndown service. ☎ *Keystone Resort, Box 38, 80435,* ☎ *970/468–4242 or 800/222–0188,* ⒻⒶⓍ *970/468–4343. 152 rooms. 3 restaurants, bar, indoor pool, hot tub, 2 tennis courts, exercise room, children's programs (ages 1-10), convention center. AE, DC, MC, V.*

$$ **Ski Tip Lodge.** This charming, elegant log cabin is an agreeable hostelry
★ whose rooms have quaint names such as Edna's Eyrie, and are uniquely decorated with homespun furnishings, including several four-posters,

and accessories such as quilts and hand-knitted throw rugs. Breakfast and lunch are included in the room rate, and, since the kitchen vies for best in Summit County with the Alpenglow Stube and Keystone Ranch, you won't be sorry if you take advantage of the deal. You might start with pheasant, caribou, and buffalo ravioli in roasted red-pepper sauce, followed with salmon swimming in cilantro pineapple salsa or baked pheasant breast dusted with crushed pecans, hazelnuts, and sage. Be sure to adjourn to the cozy lounge for the decadent desserts and special coffees. Fortunately, nonguests can dine on a limited basis, as well. ☎ *Keystone Resort, Box 38, 80435,* ☎ *970/468–4242 or 800/222–0188,* FAX *970/468–4343. 24 rooms. Restaurant. AE, DC, MC, V.*

LEADVILLE

$ **Hotel Delaware.** This beautifully restored hotel is on the National Register of Historic Places; renovations over the past three years have renewed its original 1888 Victorian condition. The lobby is graced with period antiques, brass fixtures, crystal chandeliers, and oak paneling. The comfortable rooms have lace curtains and antique heirloom quilts, in addition to modern conveniences such as private bath and cable TV. A Continental breakfast is included in the rate. ☎ *700 Harrison Ave., 80461,* ☎ *719/486–1418 or 800/748–2004,* FAX *719/486–2214. 36 rooms. Restaurant, bar, hot tub. AE, DC, MC, V.*

STEAMBOAT SPRINGS

$$$$ **Home Ranch.** You won't be roughing it at this retreat nestled among
★ towering stands of aspen outside Clark (just north of Steamboat): The lodge is a wonderful place to relax and be pampered. The focal point of the cozy living room is a magnificent fieldstone fireplace surrounded by plush leather armchairs and sofas. The dining room, where Clyde Nelson turns out gourmet Southwestern fare, is just as homey, with saddles hanging from the rafters and a whimsical salt-and-pepper-shaker collection displayed on the shelves. Accommodations are either in the main lodge or in individual cabins, each with a hot tub and ter-race. Decor leans toward Native American rugs and prints, lace cur-tains, terra-cotta tile or hardwood floors, stenciled walls, hand-carved beds, quilts, and such delightful touches as old steamer trunks and rock-ing horses. Everything from meals to the full slate of seasonal activi-ties is included in the price; there is a seven-night minimum stay. A member of the prestigious Relais et Châteaux group, which upholds rigorous standards for membership, Home Ranch is the definition of rustic chic and the ultimate in seclusion. ☎ *Box 822, Clark 80428,* ☎ *970/879–1780 or 800/223–7094. 6 rooms, 8 cabins. Dining room, pool, hot tub, horseback riding, fishing, cross-country skiing, ski shop. Closed late-Mar.–early June, early Oct.–late-Dec. AE, D, MC, V.*

$$$$ **Vista Verde Guest Ranch.** Offering similarly deluxe digs and just as many
★ activities as Home Ranch, Vista Verde has lower rates and a more au-thentic Western ambience. The lodge rooms are huge and beautifully appointed, with lace curtains, Western art, and lodgepole furniture. Cab-ins are more rustic, with pine paneling, old-fashioned wood-burning stoves, horseshoe hangers, antique lanterns, and framed old news clip-pings and photos, plus refrigerators, coffeemakers, and porches. Jacques Wilson, a Culinary Institute of America graduate, serves up sumptu-ous country gourmet repasts, which include marvelous wild game, and fresh produce from his herb and vegetable garden. Among the many activities included in the price (along with three meals) are river raft-ing and mountain biking, in addition to the standard trail rides and Nordic skiing. Optional activities (not included) are hot-air balloon-

ing and dogsledding. You can also play *City Slickers* on one of the two genuine cattle drives held every year. ☎ *Box 465, 80477, ☎ 970/879–3858 or 800/526–7433. 3 rooms, 8 cabins. Dining room, 2 hot tubs, sauna, exercise room, horseback riding, fishing, cross-country skiing. Closed mid-Mar.–May and Oct.–mid-Dec. No credit cards (personal checks accepted).*

$$$ **Sheraton Steamboat Resort & Conference Center.** This bustling deluxe hotel is Steamboat's only true ski-in/ski-out property. Rooms are Sheraton standard, fair-sized, with muted decor and most comforts. The hotel also handles Sheraton Plaza (not ski-in/ski-out), economy units with kitchens and cable TV, whose guests enjoy full hotel privileges. ☎ *Box 774808, 80477, ☎ 970/879–2220 or 800/848–8878, FAX 970/879–7686. 270 rooms, 3 suites (26 units in Sheraton Plaza). 2 restaurants, 2 bars, pool, 2 hot tubs, sauna, steam room, ski shop, meeting rooms. AE, D, DC, MC, V.*

$$ **Ptarmigan Inn.** Convenience and comfort are the keynotes of this appealing property situated on the slopes. The modest rooms, decorated in pleasing pastels and earth tones, have cable TV, balcony, and full bath. If the Ptarmigan is full, consider staying at its inexpensive sister property, The Alpiner (424 Lincoln Ave., ☎ 970/879–1430), a basic but comfortable 32-room lodge downtown, whose guests have full use of the Ptarmigan's facilities. ☎ *Box 773240, 80477, ☎ 970/879–1730 or 800/538–7519, FAX 970/879–6044. 78 rooms. Restaurant, bar, pool, hot tub, sauna, ski shop. AE, MC, V.*

$–$$ **Sky Valley Lodge.** This homey property is a few miles from downtown, amid glorious scenery that contributes to the "get-away-from-it-all" feel of the inn. Warm English country-style rooms are decorated in restful mountain colors and feature touches such as fruits and dried flowers. ☎ *31490 E. U.S. 40, 80477, ☎ 970/879–7749 or 800/538–7519, FAX 970/879–7749. 24 rooms. Hot tub. AE, MC, V.*

$ **Harbor Hotel and Condominiums.** This charming, completely refurbished
★ 1930s hotel is smack in the middle of Steamboat's historic district. The inviting brick and wood-paneled lobby sets the tone, further emphasized by the nifty artifacts, such as the old switchboards, that dot the interior of the property. Each room is individually decorated with period furniture, combined with modern amenities for comfort. The property also runs an adjacent motel and condo complex. ☎ *703 Lincoln Ave., 80477, ☎ 970/879–1522 or 800/543–8888, FAX 970/879–1737. 62 units (another 23 rooms, 24 condos in adjacent complex). 2 hot tubs, sauna, steam room. AE, D, DC, MC, V.*

$ **Rabbit Ears Motel.** The playful, pink-neon bunny sign outside this motel has been a local landmark since 1952, making it an unofficial gateway to Steamboat Springs. The location is ideal for those who want the springs (across the street), the ski area (the town bus stops outside), and the downtown shops, bars, and restaurants. All the rooms are kept clean and attractive and are equipped with minifridges and coffeemakers. Most have balconies with views of the Yampa River. A Continental breakfast is included in the rate. ☎ *201 Lincoln Ave., 80477, ☎ 970/879–1150 or 800/828–7702, FAX 970/870–0483. 66 rooms. AE, D, DC, MC, V.*

$ **Steamboat B&B.** This custard and forest-green Victorian was originally a church that owner Gordon Hattersley converted into the area's nicest B&B in 1989, cleverly retaining the arched doorways and stained glass windows. The cozy, comfy rooms have floral wallpaper, lace curtains, landscape photos, potted geraniums, polished hardwood floors, and period antiques and reproductions. If you hear a polite scratching at the door, it's the house cats, Scamper and Joshua. ☎ *442 Pine St., 80477, ☎ 970/879–5724. 7 rooms. Hot tub. AE, D, MC, V.*

THE VAIL VALLEY

$$$$
★ **Hyatt Regency Beaver Creek.** Because this slope-side hotel has been carefully crafted for guests' maximum comfort, it is considered a model accommodation. The lobby, with a magnificent antler chandelier as the centerpiece and huge oriel windows opening onto the mountain, manages to be both cozy and grand. Rooms are sizable and decorated in an appealing French provincial style, and all of them have the usual amenities and such welcome extras as coffeemakers and heated towel racks. Maintaining Beaver Creek's tradition of excellent children's programs, the Camp and Rock Hyatt day-care centers make this resort wildly popular with families. Conventioneers like the full spa and health club, ski-in/ski-out ease, and nearby golf course (with guest tee times). No wonder it's often booked months in advance. ☏ *136 E. Thomas Pl., Avon 81620,* ☎ *970/949–1234 or 800/233–1234,* 𝔽𝔸𝕏 *970/949–4164. 295 rooms, 3 suites, 26 condo units. 3 restaurants, 2 bars, deli, pool, 6 hot tubs, spa, 5 tennis courts, meeting rooms. AE, D, DC, MC, V.*

$$$$ **Lodge at Vail.** The first hotel to open in Vail remains one of the swankier addresses in town. As they say in the hotel business, it has "location, location, location," which translates to ski-in/ski-out status. The medium-size rooms are frilly and floral, a riot of pastels, with mahogany and teak furnishings and marble baths. The 40 suites are individually owned and decorated, but must meet rigorous standards set by management. The Wildflower Inn restaurant, a splendiferous space with vaulting floral arrangements and flowered banquettes, serves "postmodern Hebrew cuisine," jokes chef Jim Cohen, but it's really solidly regional American. Mickey's piano bar is still a favored après-ski spot. ☏ *174 E. Gore Creek Dr., Vail 81657,* ☎ *970/476–5011 or 800/331–5634,* 𝔽𝔸𝕏 *970/476–7425. 60 rooms, 40 suites. 2 restaurants, bar, pool, hot tub, sauna, spa, exercise room, ski shop. AE, D, DC, MC, V.*

$$$–$$$$
★ **Lodge at Cordillera.** This exquisite property is purposely isolated from all the activity in the valley. Surrounded by a pristine wilderness area—nearly half the property's 3,100 acres has been designated as wildlife reserve—the lodge offers privacy and spectacular sweeping vistas. The rooms are decidedly Old World, done up in mountain colors—burgundy, buff, and hunter green—with burled pine furnishings and balconies or transom windows to enjoy the views. An air of quiet luxury prevails throughout this secluded palatial retreat: prints by Picasso and Miró adorn the pine-paneled or exposed-brick walls, and ceilings are of carved recessed wood. You can luxuriate in the spa after a hard day's hiking or cross-country skiing, then sit down to a gourmet repast in the superlative Picasso restaurant. Belgian chef Fabrice Beaudoin weaves subtle magic with the healthful spa cuisine, and glorious views ensure a romantic evening out. An 18-hole Hale Irwin–designed golf course, with breathtaking valley views, opened in 1994. Nordic enthusiasts will appreciate the miles of trails in winter. The lodge operates a shuttle to the lifts. ☏ *Box 1110, Edwards 81632,* ☎ *970/926–2200 or 800/548–2721,* 𝔽𝔸𝕏 *970/926–2486. 28 rooms. Restaurant, bar, indoor-outdoor pool, hot tub, spa, health club, cross-country skiing, meeting rooms. AE, MC, V.*

$$$ **Beaver Creek Lodge.** An atrium centerpiece highlights this all-suite property that's charmingly decorated in European style. The units graciously maintain a sky-blue-and-forest green color scheme, and all feature a kitchenette and gas-burning fireplace as well as the usual amenities. The casually elegant Black Diamond Grill offers an inventive new American menu, which includes a highly touted scallop bisque and a buffalo carpaccio garnished with rattlesnake. ☏ *26 Avondale La.,*

Avon 81620, ☎ *970/845–9800. 70 suites, 16 condo units. Restaurant, bar, indoor-outdoor pool and hot tub, spa, health club, ski shop, meeting rooms. AE, MC, V.*

$$$ **The Pines.** This small, ski-in/ski-out Beaver Creek winner combines posh digs with unpretentious atmosphere—and prices. The rooms are spacious, light, and airy, with blond wood furnishings, pale pink ceilings, and fabrics in dusky rose, mint, and white. Each room has a TV/VCR (tapes are free), minifridge, and coffeemaker; several rooms have balconies overlooking the ski area and mountain range. The air of quiet pampering is furthered by little extras like a ski concierge who arranges complimentary guided mountain tours and a free wax for your skis. The Grouse Mountain Grill serves up superb new American cuisine in an unparalleled setting with huge picture windows and wrought-iron chandeliers. ⊡ *Box 18450, Avon 81620,* ☎ *970/845–7900 or 800/859– 8242,* 𝔽𝔸𝕏 *970/845–7809. 60 rooms, 12 condos. Restaurant, bar, pool, hot tub, spa, exercise room, laundry service. AE, D, MC, V.*

$$$ **Sonnenalp.** This property, in the midst of a pseudo-Bavarian village,
★ impresses as the real thing, and for good reason: The owning Fassler family has been in the hotel business in Germany for generations. Each of the three buildings offers a distinct look and ambience: the Swiss Chalet is quaint, with Bavarian pine armoires and secretaries and down comforters; the Austria Haus is a tad more rustic, with rough-hewn wood walls, stone floors, intricate ironwork, and Bavarian antiques throughout the public rooms; and the large, sunny Bavaria Haus suites have an elegant lodge look, with stuccoed walls, wood beams, and heated marble floors. The superb restaurants include the delightful Stueberl (tiny rooms with wood paneling and sconces), the western saloon Bully Ranch (great barbecue), the enormously popular Swiss Chalet (sensational fondue), and the elegant, Continental Ludwig's. ⊡ *20 Vail Rd., Vail 81657,* ☎ *970/476–5656 or 800/654–8312,* 𝔽𝔸𝕏 *970/476–1639. 36 rooms (Austria Haus), 70 rooms (Swiss Chalet), 80 suites (Bavaria Haus). 4 restaurants, 3 bars, 2 indoor pools, outdoor pool, 2 indoor hot tubs, outdoor hot tub, spa, exercise room. AE, MC, V.*

$$$ **Westin Vail.** Down-to-earth yet glamorous is the best way to describe this ski-in/ski-out hotel that manages—despite its fairly large size—to maintain an intimate feel, thanks to the expert staff. Rooms in the older wing are done in mountain colors; those in the newer Terrace Wing have been beautifully redone in burgundy and mint with rich, deep plaid and floral fabrics, wicker beds, polished wood armoires, and wrought-iron lamps. Alfredo's, the hotel's restaurant, has long been one of the best Italian restaurants in the valley. Guests have access to the adjoining Cascade Athletic Club, whose facilities include indoor and outdoor tennis courts, racquetball and squash courts, and Nautilus and free-weight rooms. ⊡ *1300 Westhaven Dr., Vail 81657,* ☎ *970/476–7111,* 𝔽𝔸𝕏 *970/479–7025. 290 rooms, 28 suites. 2 restaurants, bar, pool, beauty salon, 2 hot tubs, meeting rooms. AE, DC, MC, V.*

$$ **Gasthof Gramshammer.** Pepi Gramshammer, a former Austrian Olympic ski racer, is one of Vail's most beloved, respected citizens, whose labor of love—Wedel Weeks—ranks among the country's best intensive ski programs. His charming rooms are done up in pastels, with original oil paintings and fluffy down comforters. Pepi's and Antlers, the property's two fine restaurants, have a European ambience, with stucco walls, wood-beamed ceilings, and waitresses in dirndls. ⊡ *231 E. Gore Creek Dr., Vail 81657,* ☎ *970/476–5626,* 𝔽𝔸𝕏 *970/476–8816. 28 rooms. 2 restaurants, bar, ski shop. AE, MC, V.*

$$ Sitzmark Lodge. This cozy lodge brims with European ambience, thanks to many repeat international guests (it's often booked months in advance). The good-size rooms look out onto either the mountain or Gore Creek. Decor is a hodgepodge, ranging from dark to blond woods and rose, teal, or floral fabrics. Each unit has a balcony, refrigerator, cable TV, hair dryer, and humidifier; some deluxe rooms have gas-burning fireplaces. The staff is ultrafriendly, encouraging guests to congregate in the sunny, split-level living room for complimentary mulled wine. A Continental breakfast is also gratis in winter. ☎ *183 Gore Creek Dr., Vail 81611,* ☎ *970/476–5001,* FAX *970/476–8702. 35 rooms. Restaurant, pool, indoor and outdoor hot tubs, sauna. AE, MC, V.*

$ Eagle River Inn. The public rooms of this delightful B&B seem straight
★ out of the pages of *Architectural Digest* or *Southwest Interiors:* painted adobe walls, traditional carved-beam ceilings, a glorious kiva, Navajo weavings, bronze coyotes, luminarias, and Zuni baskets. The guest rooms, which have unusual touches like rough-wood furnishings, ceramic lamps, and hand-painted tile baths, overflow with fresh flowers from the enchanting backyard in summer. All rooms have TVs. Scrumptious gourmet breakfasts and evening wine tastings are included in the rate. During the 19th century, the inn actually operated as a hostelry for Rio Grande railroad employees: Imagine 24 rooms with only one toilet and shower! Today, it's one of the most distinctive properties in the Vail Valley, and each room has a small private bath. The only drawback is that you'll need a car to reach the ski slopes—Minturn lacks public transportation. ☎ *145 N. Main St., Box 100, Minturn 81645,* ☎ *970/827–5761 or 800/344–1750,* FAX *970/827–4020. 12 rooms. Hot tub. AE, MC, V.*

$ Roost Lodge. Situated on I–70 and advertising economical rates, com-
★ fortable rooms, and a heated pool, this accommodation is true to its promise—and then some, considering the price. The airy rooms are pleasing, many with four-poster beds, all with basic amenities. The staff is helpful and ingratiating, and complimentary Continental breakfast and afternoon wine and cheese are served daily in ski season. ☎ *1783 N. Frontage Rd. W, Vail 81657,* ☎ *970/476–5451. 72 rooms, 3 suites. Pool, hot tub, sauna. AE, MC, V.*

WINTER PARK

$$–$$$ Iron Horse Resort Retreat. This ski-in/ski-out hotel/condominium complex is the deluxe address in Winter Park. All units except the lodge rooms have a full kitchen, Jacuzzi tub, and sundeck, and are furnished in an attractive, modern rustic style. ☎ *Box 1286, 80482,* ☎ *970/726–8851 or 800/621–8190. 130 1- and 2-bedroom units. Restaurant, bar, pool, health club, ski shop. AE, D, DC, MC, V.*

$–$$ Hidden Mountain Lodge. The only downside of this first-rate property is its location, 20 minutes from the ski area by private shuttle (provided by the lodge). Cross-country skiing is also available in this secluded spot surrounded by the national forest. The pleasing rooms include fireplace, king-size bed, sitting room, microwave, minifridge, balcony, and plush carpeting. What really sets this property apart is the innovative kitchen. Chris Lightfoot's menu changes daily, but might highlight blackened mahimahi, yellowfin tuna in roast-pepper beurre blanc, or Texas baby-back ribs. The restaurant is open on a limited basis to nonguests with 24-hour notice. Room rates include breakfast, dinner, and lift ticket. ☎ *Box 177, 80482,* ☎ *970/726–9266 or 800/221–9125. 18 units. Restaurant, hot tub. AE, MC, V.*

$–$$ Timber House Ski Lodge. This family-run property is as congenial as can be, and the staff makes you feel as though you're staying in someone's sprawling, though slightly disordered, home. The tiny rooms in the old wing have shared baths and rustic decor, with brightly colored curtains and spreads. Smallish rooms in the newer wing have private baths and huge picture windows opening onto the mountains. Dorm rooms and bunk rooms are also available. All-you-can-eat breakfast and dinner are served family-style. ☎ *Box 32, 80482,* ☎ *970/726–8417. 35 rooms. Dining room, hot tub, sauna. AE, MC, V.*

$–$$ **Vintage Hotel.** This well-run hotel/condo complex is Winter Park's other premier resort, offering spacious, comfortable units mostly decorated in soothing earth or mountain tones. Configurations range from standard, inexpensive hotel rooms (with kitchenette and gas fireplace) and studios (with kitchen) to three-bedroom condos. ☎ *Box 1369, 80482,* ☎ *970/726–8801 or 800/472–7017,* FAX *970/726–9250. 118 units. Restaurant, bar, pool, hot tub, sauna. AE, D, DC, MC, V.*

$ **Sundowner Motel.** This is probably the nicest motel on the strip, and a great bargain, considering the free shuttle to the ski area. The rooms, decorated in muted earth tones, are slightly threadbare but have the standard amenities. It's right on the main drag, and convenient to restaurants and shops. ☎ *Box 221, 80482,* ☎ *970/726–9451 or 970/726–5452. 22 rooms. Hot tub. AE, DC, MC, V.*

Condominiums

Condominiums often represent an excellent alternative to the pricier hotels, especially for families and groups. In certain resorts, like Steamboat, Copper Mountain, and Winter Park, they are often the best lodging, period. All the companies listed below represent top-notch properties, usually on or within walking distance of the slopes (or major activities in summer). Most units are individually owned and decorated, and all have full kitchen and cable TV, most with pool and/or hot tub access. **Summit County Central Reservations** (Box 446, Dillon 80435, ☎ 970/468–6222 or 800/365–6365) handles more than 2,000 units in Dillon, Frisco, Breckenridge, Copper Mountain, Keystone, and Silverthorne.

ASPEN/SNOWMASS

Call **Aspen Central Reservations** (☎ 800/262–7736) and **Snowmass Resort Association** (☎ 800/598–2005). Among the recommended management companies are **Coates, Reid & Waldron** (720 E. Hyman Ave., Aspen 81611, ☎ 970/925–1400 or 800/222–7736, FAX 970/920–3765); **Aspen Alps Condominium Association** (700 Ute Ave., Aspen 81611, ☎ 970/925–7820 or 800/228–7820, FAX 970/925–2528); **Aspen Club Properties** (730 E. Durant Ave., Aspen 81611, ☎ 970/925–2000 or 800/633–0336, FAX 970/920–2020); **Destination Resort Management** (610 W. End St., Aspen 81611, ☎ 970/925–5000 or 800/345–1471, FAX 970/925–6891); **McCartney Properties** (421-G Aspen Airport Business Center, Aspen 81611, ☎ 970/925–8717 or 800/433–8465, FAX 970/920–4770). In Snowmass: **Snowmass Lodging Company** (Box 6077, Snowmass Village 81615, ☎ 970/923–5543 or 800/365–0410, FAX 970/923–5740) and **Village Property Management** (Box 5550, Snowmass Village 81615, ☎ 800/525–9402, FAX 970/923–5192).

BRECKENRIDGE

River Mountain Lodge (100 S. Par St., 80424, ☎ 970/453–4711 or 800/325–2342) offers fully equipped units, from studios to two-bedrooms. **Breckenridge Accommodations** (Box 1931, 80424, ☎ 970/453–9140 or 800/872–8789); **AMR Lodging** (400 N. Park Ave., No. 6A, 80424, ☎ 800/334–9162 or ☎ and fax 970/453–4432); **Breckenridge Central Lodging** (Box 709, 80424, ☎ 970/453–2160 or 800/858–5885);

and **Colorado Mountain Lodging** (Drawer 1190, 80424, ☎ 970/453–4121 or 800/627–3766, ℻ 970/453–0533) are a few of the reputable rental agencies. You can also call the **Breckenridge Resort Chamber Central Reservation System** (☎ 800/221–1091 or 970/453–6018).

COPPER MOUNTAIN

Copper Mountain Resort (☎ 970/968–2882 or 800/458–8386) runs all 22 lodging facilities, ranging from hotel-style units to condos. All are either on the slopes or served by shuttles.

KEYSTONE

Keystone Resort Corporation (☎ 800/222–0188) operates all the lodging facilities at the resort, which range from hotel-style accommodations at Keystone Lodge (*see* Lodging, *above*) to various condominium properties.

STEAMBOAT

Steamboat Premier Properties (1855 Ski Time Square, Steamboat Springs 80487, ☎ 970/879–8811 or 800/228–2458, ℻ 970/879–8485) lives up to its name, with the finest condominium units, from studios to three-bedroom units, in three deluxe properties: The Torian Plum, Bronze Tree, and Trappeur's Crossing. **Steamboat Resorts** (Box 2995, Steamboat Springs 80477, ☎ 800/525–5502, ℻ 970/879–8060) and **Mountain Resorts** (2145 Resort Dr., No. 100, Steamboat Springs 80487, ☎ 800/525–2622, ℻ 970/879–3228) also represent top properties.

VAIL/BEAVER CREEK

Vail/Beaver Creek Reservations (☎ 800/525–2257) and the **Vail Valley Tourism & Convention Bureau** (☎ 800/824–5737) can handle all calls, requests, and bookings. Among the recommended Vail properties are Cascade Village, Manor Vail, Vail Village Inn (especially notable for the unusual Menzel-designed woodwork throughout the property),and Simba Resort (all of which have several extras, including restaurants and shops on site). Top Beaver Creek facilities, also with the above extras, include the Poste Montane, St. James Place, and The Charter.

WINTER PARK

The condominiums at Winter Park are an especially good value, particularly those managed by **Winter Park Vacations** (Box 3095, 80482, ☎ 970/726–9421 or 800/228–1025, ℻ 970/726–8004). They are all excellent and feature recreational centers (including pool and hot tub) and laundry facilities, and they run the gamut in price.

The Arts and Nightlife

The Arts

DANCE

Dance Aspen (☎ 970/925–7718) presents a Summer Festival and various internationally acclaimed performers.

FILM

All the towns listed have at least one theater screening first-run films. Aspen hosts a highly regarded film festival in late September.

MUSIC

The various Chambers of Commerce will have information on upcoming events. Aspen's **Wheeler Opera House** (☎ 970/925–2750) is the venue for big-name acts, especially in summer. The **Aspen Music Festival,** featuring chamber music to jazz, runs late-June–September.

THEATER
Snowmass/Aspen Repertory Theatre (Snowmass Village Mall, ☎ 970/923–3773) offers performances.

Nightlife

BARS AND LOUNGES

In Aspen, Thirtysomethings who act like twentysomethings come to **Double Diamond** (450 S. Galena St., ☎ 970/920–6905) for high-energy cruising and dancing with either live entertainment or a DJ.

Whiskey is the claim to fame of **Eric's Bar** (315 E. Hyman Ave., ☎ 970/920–1488), a curious little watering hole, where you can also find a varied lineup of imported beers on tap.

"If you haven't been to the **'J' Bar** (Jerome Hotel, 330 E. Main St., ☎ 970/920–1000), you haven't been to Aspen," is how the saying goes, and though tourists now outnumber locals here, it's still a fun, lively spot, and a necessary Aspen experience.

Legends of Aspen (325 Main St., ☎ 970/925–5860) is a serious jock hangout, with hard-body gods and goddesses doing the scene, and sports memorabilia strewn about as decorative art.

By its own admission, the **Woody Creek Tavern** (Woody Creek Plaza, ☎ 970/923–4585) "has no redeeming features." This may be true, except that Woodies is a great hangout, with a grungy atmosphere, assorted bar games, and notable visitors such as Don Johnson and Hunter S. Thompson.

The Tippler (535 E. Dean St., ☎ 970/925–4977) has been affectionately nicknamed "The Crippler," because happy customers stagger out after such legendary occasions as Tuesday Disco nights, for which fans dress in their best polyester. The Tippler attracts a slightly older crowd looking to party without having the young bloods cut in on their action. Music, mayhem, and mid-life crises are all to be found on one packed deck.

The **Hard Rock Café** (210 S. Galena St., ☎ 970/920–1666) and **Planet Hollywood** (312 S. Galena St., ☎ 970/90–7817), conveniently located a block apart, are perfect for avid star seekers.

In Breckenridge, the two hot après-ski spots in town are the **Breckenridge Brewery** (600 S. Main St., ☎ 970/453–1550), with its six premium homemade beers, and **Hearthstone** (130 S. Ridge St., ☎ 970/453–1148), set in a former bordello, with maroon velour walls and lace curtains. This is a congenial hangout where locals scarf down the addictive happy hour special, jalapeño-wrapped shrimp.

In Copper Mountain, **Double Diamond Bar and Grill** (Base of B-Lift, ☎ 970/968–2882) and **Farley's** (Snowflake Bldg., ☎ 970/968–2577) are hot spots for lunch and happy hour, as is the frequently raucous **Sports Bar at O'Shea's** (base of American Eagle, ☎ 970/968–2882, ext. 6504). The best après-ski scene is at the always-packed **Kokomo's** (Copper Commons, ☎ 970/968–2882, ext. 6591).

Frisco hops during ski season at **Casey's** (Best Western, 1202 Summit Blvd., ☎ 970/668–5094) and **Frisco's** (720 Granite St., ☎ 970/668–5051).

Gassy Thompson's (*see* Dining, *above*) and **Ida Belle's** (both at mountain-base area, ☎ 970/468–4130) are popular Keystone hangouts after hitting the slopes.

Run by former Chicago-area firefighter Tommy Connolly, **Tommy C's** (Rte. 9, behind City Market, ☎ 970/468–2216) is a sports bar in Silverthorne with 18 TVs and four satellite dishes providing whatever athletic fix you crave.

In Steamboat Springs, the **Old Town Pub** (601 Lincoln Ave., ☎ 970/879–2101) has juicy burgers and local flavor, with some great live bands. **Steamboat Brewery** (5th St. and Lincoln Ave., ☎ 970/879–2233) offers an assortment of homemade ales, lagers, porters, and stouts, as well as superior pub grub. On the mountain, **Mattie Silk's** (*see* Dining, *above*) is a favorite après-ski hangout.

The coolest, hottest Vail hangout is **Palmo's** (Gateway Plaza, ☎ 970/476–0646), with eye-catching decor that was designed and carved by Menzel, who utilizes gorgeously textured 200-year-old wormwood (visible throughout the mall; notice the wild stairways) to dazzling effect. The tables alone reputedly cost $3,000 each. There's a wonderful selection of hot drinks, brandies, and single malts.

Garfinkel's (536 W. Lionshead Mall, ☎ 970/476–3789) is a ski-school hangout, predictably popular with the younger set—especially shredders. A young crowd can also be found scarfing down excellent and cheap pizzas until 2 AM at **Vendetta's** (291 Bridge St., ☎ 970/476–5070). The **Red Lion** (top of Bridge St., ☎ 970/476–7676), a Vail tradition, attracts a more sedate crowd, with mellow live acts and a wildly popular deck. **Sarah's** (Christiania at Vail, 356 E. Hanson Ranch Rd., ☎ 970/476–5641) showcases Helmut Fricker, a Vail institution who plays accordion while yodeling up a storm. **Mickey's** (Lodge at Vail, 174 E. Gore Creek Dr., ☎ 970/476–5011) is the place for soothing pop standards on the piano.

After attacking the moguls, the Hyatt's **Crooked Hearth Tavern** (☎ 970/949–1234, ext. 2260) in Beaver Creek is a wonderful place to wind down, usually while listening to the strains of a folk guitarist.

CABARET
The **Crystal Palace** (300 E. Hyman Ave., ☎ 970/925–1455) is an Aspen fixture, offering two seatings nightly with fine food and a fiercely funny up-to-the-minute satirical revue. The **Tower** (Snowmass Mall, ☎ 970/923–4650) features hokey but hilarious magic and juggling acts.

COUNTRY-AND-WESTERN CLUBS
In Aspen/Snowmass, **Cowboys** (Silvertree Hotel, ☎ 970/923–5249) usually has live country-western music and dancing nightly, as does **Shooters Saloon** (Galena and Hopkins Sts., ☎ 970/925–4567).

In Breckenridge, **Breck's** (Hilton, 550 Village Rd., ☎ 970/453–4500) offers free dance lessons each Tuesday night, and live acts Wednesday and Thursday nights.

In Steamboat, **The Saloon** (Sundance Plaza, ☎ 970/879–6303) is in no-man's-land behind a Wendy's, but it's a real cowboy joint that offers two-step lessons early in the evening. The **Loft** section of the **Ore House** restaurant (U.S. 40 and Pine Grove Rd., ☎ 970/879–1190) ropes 'em in for juicy steaks and boot-scooting.

In the Vail Valley, **Cassidy's Hole in the Wall** (82 E. Beaver Creek Blvd., Avon, ☎ 970/949–9449) is a saloon that offers live country-and-western bands nightly, to go with the authentic mouthwatering barbecue.

DISCOS

In Aspen, **Club Soda** (419 E. Hyman Ave., ☎ 970/925–8154) is where the beautiful people and their admirers work up a polite sweat. The **Mustang Club** (517 E. Hopkins Ave., ☎ 970/920–2111) attracts a younger—perhaps even more beautiful—crowd.

In Breckenridge, **Tiffany's** (☎ 970/453–6000, ext. 7914) has a DJ and dancing nightly. **Johsha's** (☎ 970/453–4146) offers live bands, a dance floor, pool tables, and cheap eats.

Club Med (☎ 970/968–2121) at Copper Mountain offers a $25 international dinner buffet that includes bar games, nightly entertainment (at 9 PM), and ☛ to the disco at 10:30 (☛ to the show and disco alone is $10.50).

Vail offers **Sheika's** (☎ 970/476–1515), where the young are restless on the dance floor.

JAZZ CLUBS

Aspen's **Ritz-Carlton Club Room** (315 Dean St., ☎ 970/920–3300) presents live jazz nightly in season. **Cottonwoods** (Snowmass Village Mall, ☎ 970/923–2748) showcases leading artists nightly in season.

Copper Mountain's **Pesce Fresco** (Mountain Plaza Bldg., ☎ 970/968–2882, ext. 6505) offers jazz piano Wednesday–Sunday nights in season.

In Vail, **Babau's Cafe** (L'Ostello Lodge, Lionshead Cir., ☎ 970/476–2050) is a piano jazz club with fine Italian specialties as a plus. **Louie's** (Wall St., ☎ 970/479–9008) is a Cajun restaurant that sizzles even more with zydeco and jazz acts.

ROCK CLUBS

In Breckenridge, **Alligator Lounge** (320 S. Main St., ☎ 970/453–7782) is the hot spot for acoustic, blues, Cajun, and reggae sets.

In Steamboat (on the mountain), **The Tugboat** (Ski Time Square, ☎ 970/879–7070) and **Inferno** (Gondola Square, ☎ 970/879–5111) always feature loud live acts. **Heavenly Daze** (Ski Time Square, ☎ 970/879–8080) has three levels: the ground floor is a brew pub, the second floor a restaurant, and the third floor a combination billiards parlor/rock club/disco.

In Vail, **Nick's** (bottom of Bridge St., ☎ 970/476–3433) has a frat-house feeling, especially on Mondays when shredders attend the "Board Meeting." **Garton's** (Crossroads Shopping Center, ☎ 970/476–0607) offers everything from rock to reggae, Cajun to country, and attracts a slightly older crowd (pushing 30).

The Slope (1161 Winter Park Dr., ☎ 970/726–5727) is Winter Park's most raucous venue, offering everything from rock to retro funk.

I–70 and the High Rockies Essentials

Arriving and Departing by Plane

AIRPORTS AND AIRLINES

Most of the I–70 corridor is served via Denver and its airports (*see* Arriving and Departing by Plane *in* Denver, *above*). There's an extensive list of Denver-based companies that specialize in transportation to the mountain resorts (*see* Between Airports and the Resorts, *below*).

United has flights from Denver (via Aspen Aviation), as well as non-stop service to Los Angeles, Dallas, Phoenix, and Chicago in ski season. Delta flies from Salt Lake City.

Aspen/Snowmass's **Aspen Airport** (☎ 970/920–5385) is served daily by United Express (☎ 800/241–6522).

American (☎ 800/433–7300), America West (☎ 800/247–5692), Northwest (☎ 800/255–2525), and United fly nonstop from various gateways during ski season to **Steamboat Springs Airport** (☎ 970/879–1204).

The Vail Valley is served by **Eagle County Airport** (Gypsum, ☎ 970/524–9490), 35 miles west of Vail. During ski season, Delta, United, and Northwest offer nonstop flights from several gateways. American flies here year-round.

Between Airports and the Resorts
BY BUS OR VAN
To and from Aspen/Snowmass: **Roaring Fork Transit Agency** (☎ 970/925–8484) provides bus service from Aspen Airport to the Ruby Park bus station in Aspen. **Aspen Limousine and Bus Service** (☎ 970/925–9400) runs trips to Denver, Glenwood Springs, and Vail. **Colorado Mountain Express** (☎ 970/949–4227) runs trips to Vail and Aspen.

To and from Summit County (Breckenridge, Copper Mountain, Dillon, Frisco, Keystone): **Resort Express** (☎ 970/468–7600 or 800/334–7433), **Vans to Breckenridge** (☎ 970/668–5466 or 800/222–2212), and **Skier's Connection** (☎ 970/668–0200 or 800/824–1004) have regular service to and from Denver airports.

To and from Steamboat Springs: **Alpine Taxi** (☎ 970/879–8294) offers service from the airport, as well as special rates to Vail, Boulder, and Denver. **Steamboat Express** (☎ 970/879–3400) and **Panorama** (☎ 970/879–3400 or 800/545–6050) also serve DIA and the local airports.

To and from Vail/Beaver Creek: **Airport Transportation Service** (☎ 970/476–7576); **Colorado Mountain Express** (☎ 970/949–4227); and **Vans to Vail** (☎ 970/476–4467 or 800/222–2212).

To and from Winter Park: **Vanex** (☎ 970/726–4047 or 800/521–5401) offers service from Denver. **Greyhound Lines** (☎ 800/231–2222) runs from Denver to Winter Park.

Arriving and Departing by Car, Train, and Bus
BY CAR
If you're entering Colorado from the north or south, take I–25, which intersects with I–70 in Denver. If you're entering from the east or west, I–70 bisects the state. Idaho Springs, Summit Country, the Vail Valley, and Glenwood Springs are all on I–70. Winter Park is north of I–70, on U.S. 40, which has several hairpin turns. Leadville and Ski Cooper are south of I–70 along U.S. 24 or Route 91. Steamboat Springs is most easily reached via Route 131, north from I–70. Aspen/Snowmass can be reached via Route 82, south from I–70.

BY TRAIN
Amtrak (800/872–7245) offers service from Denver's Union Station to the Winter Park Ski Area station in nearby Fraser (where shuttles to the area are available). Glenwood Springs is on the *California Zephyr* route.

The nonstop **Denver Rio Grande Bud Light Ski Train** (☎ 303/296–4754) leaves Denver's Union Station every Sunday morning, chugging through stunning scenery and 29 tunnels before depositing passengers only 50 yards from Winter Park's lifts.

BY BUS
Greyhound Lines (☎ 800/231–2222) offers regular service from Denver to several towns along I–70.

Getting Around

BY BUS OR SHUTTLE
For intercity bus service try **Greyhound Lines** (call local listings). Free shuttles serving the resorts are offered throughout the area.

Aspen/Snowmass: Within Snowmass there is free shuttle service; five colored flags denote the various routes. The **Roaring Fork Transit Agency** (☎ 970/925–8484) provides free shuttle service within Aspen and between Aspen and Snowmass.

Steamboat: **Steamboat Springs Transit** (☎ 970/879–3717) provides transportation between the mountain and the town, and costs 50¢ per trip.

Summit County: **Summit Stage** (☎ 970/453–1339) links Breckenridge, Frisco, Copper Mountain, Dillon, Silverthorne, and Keystone for free. **Breckenridge Free Shuttle and Trolley** (no ☎) runs through town and up to the ski area, **E.A.S.E.** (☎ 970/468–2316, ext. 4200) serves the extended Keystone area, and **KAB Express** (no ☎) serves Keystone/Arapahoe Basin and Breckenridge. The **Frisco Flyer** (☎ 970/668–5276) provides service throughout Frisco.

Vail Valley: **Avon Beaver Creek Transit** (☎ 970/949–6121) runs free shuttles the length of the valley, daily, between 7 AM and 1:30 AM, every 10 minutes.

Winter Park: The **Winter Park Lift** (☎ 970/726–4163) is the area's free shuttle service.

BY CAR
I–70 is a fast, convenient superhighway that is remarkably well maintained. All major sights in this tour are either on I–70 or on clearly marked side routes.

BY TAXI
Aspen/Snowmass: **Aspen Limousine** (☎ 970/925–2400) and **High Mountain Taxi** (☎ 970/925–8294); Glenwood Springs: **Glenwood Taxi** (☎ 970/945–2225); Steamboat Springs: **Alpine Taxi** (☎ 970/879–8294); Summit County: **Around Town Taxi** (☎ 970/453–8294) and in Dillon, **Summit Taxi Service** (☎ 970/468–8294); Vail Valley: **Vail Valley Taxi** (☎ 970/476–8294).

Guided Tours

ORIENTATION
A romantic way to orient yourself to Aspen is by taking the **T Lazy Seven Ranch** (☎ 970/925–4614) stagecoach tour of its downtown area.

In Breckenridge, the **Breckenridge Historical Society** (☎ 970/453–9022; tours run Wed.–Sat. 11 AM) offers lively 1½-hour tours of Colorado's largest National Historic District.

Several tour companies include Idaho Springs on their itineraries, and the **Idaho Springs Visitor Information Center** (2200 Miner St., ☎ 970/567–4382) can supply information.

SPECIAL INTEREST
In summer, narrated bus tours from Aspen to the spectacular **Maroon Bells** are available (☎ 970/925–8484). Steamboat's **Sweet Pea Tours** (☎ 970/879–5820) and **Peak Experience** (☎ 970/879–8125) visit nearby hot springs. Vail's **Nova Guides** (☎ 970/949–4232) offers Jeep

and ATV (all-terrain vehicle) tours, as well as rafting, fishing, snow-mobiling, and hiking expeditions.

Important Addresses and Numbers

HOSPITALS

Aspen/Snowmass: **Aspen Valley Hospital** (0200 Castle Creek Rd., ☎ 970/925–1120); Glenwood Springs: **Valley View Hospital** (6535 Blake St., ☎ 970/945–8566); Summit County: **Summit Medical Center** (Rte. 9 and School Rd., Frisco, ☎ 970/668–3300); Vail Valley: **Vail Mountain Medical** (181 W. Meadow Dr., Vail, ☎ 970/476–5695); **Beaver Creek Village Medical Center** (1280 Village Rd., Beaver Creek, ☎ 970/949–0800).

VISITOR INFORMATION

Aspen Chamber Resort Association (328 E. Hyman Ave., ☎ 970/925–5656; and 425 Rio Grande Pl., ☎ 970/925–1940); **Breckenridge Resort Chamber** (309 N. Main St., ☎ 970/453–6018); **Georgetown Visitor Center** (404 6th St., ☎ 970/569–2555); **Glenwood Springs Chamber Resort Association** (806 Cooper Ave., ☎ 970/945–6589 or 800/221–0098); **Leadville Chamber of Commerce** (809 Harrison St., ☎ 719/486–3900); **Steamboat Springs Chamber Resort Association** (1255 S. Lincoln Ave., ☎ 970/879–0880 or 800/922–2722); **Summit County Chamber of Commerce** (Main St., Frisco, ☎ 970/668–5000 or 800/530–3099); **Vail Valley Tourism and Convention Bureau** (100 E. Meadow Dr., ☎ 970/476–1000 or 800/525–3875); and a Tourist Information Center in the Vail Village and Lionshead parking structures).

SOUTHWEST COLORADO

"Colorado" is a Spanish word meaning ruddy or colorful—adjectives that clearly describe many regions of the state, but particularly the Southwest, with the Four Corners region and the San Juans. The terrain varies widely—from yawning black canyons and desolate monochrome moonscapes to pastel deserts and mesas, shimmering sapphire lakes, and 14,000-foot mountains. It's so rugged in the Southwest that a four-wheel-drive vehicle is necessary to explore the wild and beautiful backcountry.

The region's history and people are as colorful as the landscape, from the mysterious Anasazi (meaning "ancient ones"), who constructed impressive cliff dwellings in Mesa Verde National Park to notorious outlaws such as Butch Cassidy, who embarked on his storied career by robbing the Telluride Bank in 1889. Even today, the more ornery, independent locals, disgusted with the political system, periodically talk of seceding. They're as rough as the country they inhabit.

Southwest Colorado offers such diversity that, depending on where you go, you can have radically different vacations, even during the same season. Visit the world-class resorts of Crested Butte, Purgatory, and Telluride for quality ski and golf holidays; then move on to the Old West railroad town of Durango, followed by a pilgrimage to the Anasazi ruins that dot the area. Even for Colorado, the combination of recreational, historical, and cultural opportunities is diverse.

Exploring

Tour 1: The San Juans, the Four Corners, and the "Million Dollar Highway"

This tour spirals from the towering peaks of the San Juan range to the plunging Black Canyon of the Gunnison, taking in Colorado's most stunning alpine scenery along the way, as well as the eerie remains of old mining camps, before winding through striking desert landscapes, the superlative Anasazi ruins, and the Old West town of Durango.

Numbers in the margin correspond to points of interest on the Southwest Colorado map.

❶ **Crested Butte** is literally just over the mountain from Aspen, but a 15-minute scenic flight or one-hour drive in summer turns into a four-hour trek by car in winter, when Kebler Pass is closed. The town of Crested Butte was declared a National Historic District and, like Aspen, it was once a quaint mining center whose exquisite, pastel, Victorian gingerbread–trimmed houses remain. Unlike Aspen, however, Crested Butte never became chic. A recent controversial ad campaign about its ski area (3 miles from town) touts it as: "Aspen like it used to be, and Vail like it never was."

That boast might make the locals seem crustier than they are; they're just proud and independent, with a puckish sense of humor. In fact, in a state that prides itself on hospitality, Crested Butte just may be the friendliest ski town of them all. Tony, the over-80 proprietor of the Sunoco station, is a font of information (some unprintable) about the place; but you won't have a difficult time finding other sources. A sense of warmth and whimsy pervades the area, most evident in the hot pink, magenta, and chartreuse facades of the buildings along Elk Avenue, the main drag. And for proof that nothing "em-bare-asses" the locals, check out the diehards streaking down the mountain nude on the last day of the season, or join the mavericks (for this event fully clothed) who hike up Snodgrass (slated for development as Crested Butte West) and bomb down every full moon.

Crested Butte Mountain Resort is a trailblazer and renegade in many respects: it initiated a daring—and wildly successful—venture in which everyone skis free the first four weeks of the season, and first timers get free lessons. While many resorts are limiting their "out-of-bounds" terrain due to increasing insurance costs and lawsuits, Crested Butte is thumbing its nose at the establishment by steadily increasing its extreme skiing terrain, which now speaks for 550 ungroomed acres. The Extreme Limits and The North Face should only be attempted by experts but there are plenty of cruisable trails for recreational skiers. In the summer, mountain bikers challenge the same slopes, which are blanketed with columbine and Indian paintbrush.

Crested Butte is considered the quintessential ski bum's town: friendly, reasonably priced, cute as hell, great bars, impressive restaurants, and a gnarly mountain that remains far less crowded than its better-known neighbors.

The Route 135 scenic loop goes west from Crested Butte over Kebler Pass to **Paonia,** and south through banks of cottonwoods (which usu-
❷ ally attract several swooping bald eagles) to **Gunnison.** At the confluence of the Gunnison River and Tomichi Creek, Gunnison has been a fishing and hunting community ever since the Utes adopted it as their summer hunting grounds. It provides economical lodging for those skiing Crested Butte and for backpackers, mountain bikers, and fishermen in summer.

The **Gunnison County Chamber of Commerce** (500 E. Tomichi Ave., ☎ 970/641–1501) issues an informative historical walking-tour brochure of downtown. Those interested in the region's history can also stop by the **Pioneer Museum,** a living history complex that includes

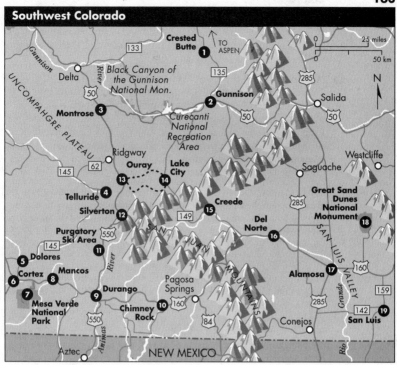

several buildings and relics that date from the late 19th century. *U.S.
50 and S. Adams St.,* ☎ 970/641–4530. ☛ *$3 adults, $1 children 6–
12.* ☉ *Memorial Day–Labor Day, Mon.–Sat. 9–5, Sun. 1–5.*

Aside from its easy access to Crested Butte, Gunnison is recognized for
two other things. Its Western State College, the local seat of higher learning, boasts a 320-foot by 420-foot whitewashed rock shaped like a W
and located on Tenderfoot Mountain, just to the north of the campus.
Ostensibly this is the largest collegiate insignia in the world. Gunnison's other claim to fame is that the town has recorded some of the
coldest temperatures ever reported in the continental United States.

Nine miles west of Gunnison is the **Curecanti National Recreation Area**
(☎ 970/641–2337), set amid a striking eroded volcanic landscape
and stretching for more than 60 miles. The area was created in the '60s
by a series of dams that resulted in three reservoirs, including **Blue Mesa**—
the state's largest body of water. The reservoirs provide a wealth of
aquatic recreational opportunities, as well as fine camping and hiking.
At the western entrance to the recreation area, the **Cimarron Visitor Center** (☎ 970/249–4074; open daily 9–5) displays vintage locomotives,
an 1882 trestle listed on the National Register of Historic Places, and
a reconstruction of a railroad stockyard.

Once liberated from the restrictions of Curecanti, the Gunnison River
slices through one of the West's most awe-inspiring sights, the **Black
Canyon of the Gunnison National Monument,** a vivid testament to the
powers of erosion. This 2,500-foot-deep gash in the earth's crust is 1,300
feet wide at its top and only 40 feet wide at the bottom. The canyon's
name comes from the fact that so little sunlight penetrates its depths,
the eternal shadows permitting scant plant growth on its steep walls.
The Black Canyon lies 60 miles west of Gunnison, on Route 347

North, off U.S. 50. The fine **visitor center** (☎ 970/249–1915 or 970/249–7036; open Apr.–Sept., daily 9–5) includes exhibits on the region's geology, history, and flora and fauna, and schedules nature walks to the canyon's forbidding rim.

❸ Montrose, the self-described "Home of the Black Canyon," is another 7 miles west along U.S. 50. Though it sits amid glorious surroundings, it is an otherwise nondescript town with little more than a collection of truck stops, trailer parks, and strip malls. However, Montrose is perfectly placed for exploring Curecanti and the Black Canyon to the east, the San Juans to the south, the world's largest flattop mountain, Grand Mesa (*see* Exploring *in* Northwest Colorado, *below*) to the north, and the fertile Uncompahgre Plateau to the west.

If you're interested in learning more about the original residents of the area, stop by the excellent **Ute Indian Museum,** a mile south of town on U.S. 550. The museum contains several dioramas and the most comprehensive collection of Ute materials and artifacts in Colorado. *17253 Chipeta Dr.,* ☎ *970/249–3098.* ☛ *$2.* ⊙ *Mid-May–Sept., Mon.–Sat. 10–5 and Sun. 1–5.*

TIME OUT Gum-cracking waitresses serve up huge portions of gravy-laden food at **Sally's Café** (715 S. Townsend Ave., ☎ 970/249–6096). The menu has it all, from Mexi-burgers, patty melts, chicken-fried steak, and grilled PB&J sandwiches to Duncan Hines cakes and dull-as-dirty-dishwater coffee. The decor, too, reflects a quirky, local flavor, with a reindeer made out of an old clock that hangs on the wall, and Sally's own diverse collection of china ("I like my dishes," says Sally with typical understatement).

Head south on U.S. 550 to Ridgway, notable mainly for its strategic location at the junction of U.S. 550 and Route 62. These two routes fan out from the town to form one of the country's most stupendously scenic drives, the **San Juan Skyway,** which weaves through a series of fourteeners (a Rockies term for peaks reaching more than 14,000 feet) and picturesque mining towns. U.S. 550 continues through historic Ouray and Silverton to Durango. Route 62 and Route 145 reach Durango via the extraordinary Anasazi cliff dwellings of Mesa Verde National Park.

Take Route 62 to its juncture with Route 145 East, to one of Colorado's hottest destinations. Tucked like a jewel in a tiny valley caught between
❹ azure sky and gunmetal mountains is **Telluride,** once so inaccessible that it was a favorite hideout for desperadoes such as Butch Cassidy, who robbed his first bank here in 1889. Some locals claim the town is named not after the mineral Tellurium, but the saying "To Hell You Ride."

The savage but beautiful terrain now attracts mountain people of a different sort—alpinists, snowboarders, freestylers, mountain bikers, and freewheeling four-wheelers—who attack any incline, up or down, and do so with abandon. As one local quips, "The Wild Bunch is alive and well."

The ski area, too, is not for the faint of heart. Telluride poses the ultimate test for skiers, with one legendary challenging run after another. In particular, the terrain accessed by Chairlift Nine, including the famed "Spiral Staircase" and "The Plunge," is for experts only (although one side of "The Plunge" is groomed for advanced skiers). Telluride has also expanded its "ultimate skiing" terrain to include more than 400 acres on Gold Hill. Forgotten in the excitement of all the challenge is that Telluride has a superb beginners' and learners' area; it's middle-of-the-road intermediates who may find themselves between a rock and a hard place.

The town's independent spirit is shaped not only by its mining legacy, but also by the social ferment of the '60s and early '70s. Before the ski area opened in 1971, Telluride had been as remote as it was back in Cassidy's day. It was even briefly included on the "Ghost Town Club of Colorado" itinerary, but that was before countercultural types moved in, seeking to lose themselves in the wilderness. By 1974 the town's orientation had changed so radically that the entire council was composed of hippies. Today there is one holdover—Councilman Rasta Stevie (he's white, but his waist-length dreadlocks might have made Bob Marley envious)—who cheerfully admits, "I came to power through the dirtbags." Regardless of future development, Stevie defends an enduring Telluride tradition called the Freebox (Pine St. and Colorado Ave.), where indigent residents can sort through and take whatever used clothing and appliances they need. (One memorable day, just after a fur shop had the temerity to open in town, surprised residents found a wide selection of minks, sables, and chinchillas at the Box. After the mysterious break-in, the furriers got the point and moved on.)

Despite such efforts at keeping such visible signs of wealth away, more and more locals are finding they can no longer afford to live here. Things were fine when the town was isolated, but thanks to the construction of the Telluride Regional Airport in the late 1980s, it's become quite accessible. Today Telluride is positioning itself as an upscale alternative to Vail and Aspen, and celebrities who need only be identified by their first names (Arnold and Oprah, for example) own homes.

Telluride is chic—and not everyone's happy about it. Many townies deplore the mushrooming Telluride Mountain Village development at the base of the ski area, and some bitterly resent The Peaks at Telluride, a glamorous resort/spa. The ambivalence felt about the influx of wealth and new buildings brings into question whether development is inevitable; whether the pristine can be preserved in this fast-paced world. For better or worse, Telluride is gorgeous. Every corner of the town yields stunning prospects of the San Juans, which loom either menacingly or protectively, depending on the lighting.

The 425-foot liquid diamond **Bridal Veil Falls,** Colorado's highest cascade, tumbles lavishly just a short hike from the end of Colorado Avenue, the main street. The town itself offers one pastel Victorian residence or frontier trading post after another, as well as the 1883 **San Miguel County Courthouse** and the 1895 **New Sheridan Hotel and Opera House.** (*Telluride Magazine* prints an excellent historic walking tour in its "Visitors' Guide" section.) Today it's hard to believe that those lovingly restored shops and restaurants once housed gaming parlors and saloons known for the quality of their "waitressing."

That party-hearty spirit lives on, evidenced by the numerous annual events held here. Highly regarded wine and wild mushroom festivals alternate with musical performances celebrating everything from bluegrass to jazz to chamber music. And the Telluride Film Festival is one of the world's leading showcases for the latest releases.

TIME OUT The House (131 N. Fir St., ☎ 970/728–6207) is set in a building once dubbed "The Freak House" for the colorful characters who lived here in the '70s and '80s. These days the atmosphere is more refined—likened to a European pub by owner Tom Wirth—with fine ales on tap, along with cribbage, backgammon, Trivial Pursuit, and chess.

....

Continue southwest along Route 145, which follows the course of the lovely Dolores River. In 1968, construction of an irrigation dam was authorized, forming the **McPhee Reservoir,** a haven for boaters and fishermen. An environmental-impact study was mandated by law, and concluded that hundreds of potentially valuable archaeological sites would be flooded. This led to massive, federally funded excavations and the creation of one of the West's model museums, The Anasazi Heritage Center, 3 miles west of Dolores.

The Anasazi, a mysterious and talented people who thrived until 1300, were probably the ancestors of present-day Pueblo tribes. They left behind a legacy of stunning ruins, both freestanding pueblos and ingenious cliff dwellings. No one knows for sure why they abandoned their homes, although most anthropologists surmise a combination of drought and overfarming sent them off in search of greener pastures.

The first white explorers to stumble upon Anasazi ruins were the Spanish friars Dominguez and Escalante, who set out in 1776 from Santa Fe to find a safe overland route to Monterey, California. The two major ruins at the **Anasazi Heritage Center** (27501 Rte. 184, ☎ 970/882–4811; ☛ Free; open daily 9–5) are named for them. The Dominguez site, right next to the parking lot, is unimpressive, although of great archaeological interest because extremely rare evidence of a "high-status burial" was found here. The Escalante site, a half-mile hike away, is a 20-room masonry pueblo standing eerie guard over McPhee Reservoir.

The state-of-the-art facility houses the finest artifacts culled from more than 1,500 excavations, as well as a theater, a library, a gift shop, and a full-scale replica of an Anasazi pit-house dwelling that illustrates how the Anasazi lived around 850. The complex is particularly notable for its Discovery Center, a series of hands-on, hologramlike interactive displays that enable visitors to weave on a Navajo loom, grind corn, even generate an Anasazi village using a computer.

❺ Continue south along Route 145, passing through **Dolores** to its enchanting **Galloping Goose Museum** (5th St. and Rte. 145, ☎ 970/882–4018), a replica of a Victorian train station that contains an original narrow-gauge locomotive. The gentle rising hump to the southwest is **Sleeping Ute Mountain,** which resembles the reclining silhouette of a Native American replete with headdress. The site is revered by the Ute Mountain tribe as a great warrior god who, mortally wounded in a titanic battle with the evil ones, lapsed into eternal sleep, his flowing blood turning into the life-giving Dolores and Animas rivers.

❻ At the juncture of Route 145 and U.S. 160 is **Cortez,** dominated by the northern escarpment of Mesa Verde and the volcanic blisters of the La Plata mountains to the west. The sprawling town is an unrelieved tedium of Days Inns, Dairy Queens, and Best Westerns, its architecture seemingly determined by neon-sign and aluminum-siding salesmen of the '50s. Hidden among these, however, are fine galleries and a host of pawn shops that can yield surprising finds.

There is a **Colorado Welcome Center** here (160 E. Main St., ☎ 970/565–4048), as well as the excellent **Cortez/Colorado University Center,** its exterior painted to resemble the cliff dwellings of Mesa Verde. Inside the University Center are changing exhibits on regional artists and artisans, as well as permanent displays on the Ute Mountain branch of the Ute tribe, and various periods of Anasazi culture. Summer evenings include Native American dances; sandpainting, rug weaving, and pottery-making demonstrations; and storytelling events. The related **Cultural Park** contains an authentic Navaho hogan and a Ute tepee. *25 N. Market St.,* ☎ *970/565–1151.* ☛ *Free; donations accepted.* ⊙ *Daily 9–5.*

TIME OUT   Earth Song Haven (34 E. Main St., ☎ 970/247–0470) is a fine bookstore, with an espresso bar and tearoom in back. Cortez seems an unlikely spot for this European touch, but the café makes wonderful coffees, sandwiches, and high-calorie desserts such as peanut-butter cream pie.

❼ Cortez is the gateway to **Mesa Verde National Park,** an 80-square-mile area that forms one of America's most riveting attractions. In 1888, two ranchers—Richard Wetherill and Charlie Mason—set off in search of stray cattle and stumbled upon the remarkable and perfectly preserved **Cliff Palace,** apartment-style cliff dwellings built into the canyon walls. By the next day's end they had discovered two more major sites: Spruce Tree House and Square Tower House. Excitement over their find culminated in the 1906 creation of the national park by Congress, making it the first park established to preserve the works of humankind.

Mesa Verde is one of Colorado's highlights, but consider either going off-season (though many of the ruins are closed) or overnighting in the park (after the tour buses have departed) to appreciate its full effect, without the crowds. The entrance, where you can pick up information on the park's attractions and accommodations, is 10 miles east of Cortez on U.S. 160. From here a 15-mile drive corkscrews up the mesa, skirting canyons and plateaus, to the **Far View Visitor Center.** ☎ *970/529–4461 or 970/529–4475.* ☛ *To park: $5 per vehicle.* ⊙ *Visitor center: daily 8–6.*

From the visitor center, you can head in one of two directions within the park. Your first option is to take the scenic route to **Wetherill Mesa** (open Memorial Day–Labor Day), which affords spectacular vistas of the Shiprock Formation in New Mexico and Monument Valley in Arizona and Utah. A minitram departs every half hour between 8:55 AM and 4:55 PM from the Wetherill parking lot, on a 4-mile loop to view the ruins; self-guided and ranger-led tours of Long House, the second-largest dwelling in the park, are also options. The other Far View route, **Ruins Road,** accesses the major sites on Chapin Mesa in two 6-mile loops. If you don't want to hike down into the canyons to view the ruins up close (which requires a free ticket available at the visitor center), this drive offers several strategic overlooks.

The first stop on the Ruins Road is the park's informative archaeological museum, which traces the development of Anasazi/Pueblo culture. It's a short walk from the museum to one of the most extraordinary sites, **Spruce Tree House,** the only ruin open year-round. Here you can climb down into an excavated kiva (Native American ceremonial structure, usually partly underground), symbolic of the womb of Mother Earth, for a better sense of how the Anasazis worshipped.

From the museum trailhead, one loop leads to the most famous ruin, **Cliff Palace,** the largest dwelling of its kind in the world (accessible by a moderately strenuous 15-minute hike), and to the more remote **Balcony House** (an arduous trek into the canyon below). Ranger-guided tours are available. The other loop accesses two major ruins, **Sun Tem-**

ple and **Square Tower House,** both involving a significant amount of walking and climbing.

Cortez is also convenient to two other spectacular Anasazi sites—**Lowry Pueblo** and **Hovenweep National Monument**—the latter of which straddles the Utah-Colorado border (*see* Other Points of Interest, *below*).

Driving east on U.S. 160 from Mesa Verde will take you past an endearing bit of classic American kitsch, the **Mud Creek Hogan** (U.S. 160, ☎ 970/533–7117). More than a dozen enormous arrows stuck in the ground mark the spot of this hokey trading post and museum (where you get the feeling that everything is for sale) adorned with tepees and a giant plastic horse. Beside the shop is a re-creation of a frontier town, replete with saloon, hotel, bank, jail, and livery station. Don't breathe too hard or you'll blow the town over: The "buildings" are only fronts.

8 The highway winds through the lush Mancos Valley, passing through the small and charming town of **Mancos,** which exudes Old West ambience. There are several excellent crafts shops that offer everything from saddles to 10-gallon hats, and a cute **Cowboy Museum** (100 Bauer St., ☎ 970/533–7563) in a restored mansion that also houses a B&B and the Old Mesa Verde Inn restaurant. The **Mancos State Recreation Area** offers a wealth of activities, including **Ski Hesperus** (*see* Sports and the Outdoors, *below*), a small ski area a few miles farther east.

9 U.S. 160 now approaches a classic Western town, **Durango,** of which Will Rogers once observed, "It's out of the way and glad of it." His crack is a bit unfair, considering that as a railroad town Durango has always been a cultural crossroads and melting pot (as well as a place to raise hell). It was founded in 1879 by General William Palmer (president of the all-powerful Denver & Rio Grande Railroad), when nearby Animas City haughtily refused to donate land for a depot; within a decade Durango had absorbed its rival completely. The booming town quickly became the region's main metropolis and a gateway to the Southwest. A walking tour of the historic downtown bears eloquent witness to Durango's prosperity in the late 19th century. The northern end of Main Avenue offers the usual assortment of cheap motels and fast-food outlets, all evidence of Durango's present status as the major hub for tourism in the area.

At 13th Avenue and Main Avenue (also known as Main Street)—the beginning of its National Historic District—the tenor changes dramatically, with old-fashioned gas lamps gracing the streets and a superlative collection of Victorians filled with chic galleries, restaurants, and brand-name outlet stores. The 1882 **Train Depot** (4th St. and Main Ave.), the 1887 **Strater Hotel** (7th St. and Main Ave.), and the three-story sandstone **Newman Building** (8th St. and Main Ave.) are among the elegant edifices restored to their original grandeur. Stop into the **Diamond Belle Saloon** (in the Strater Hotel)—awash in velour and lace, with a player piano, gilt-and-mahogany bar, and scantily clad Gay '90s waitresses—for a wonderfully authentic re-creation of an old-time honky-tonk.

The **Third Avenue National Historic District** (known simply as "The Boulevard"), two blocks east of Main Avenue, offers one of America's most outstanding displays of Victorian residences, ranging from the imposing mansions of railroad and smelting executives to more modest variations erected by well-to-do merchants. The delightful hodgepodge of styles veers from Greek Revival to Gothic Revival to Queen Anne to Spanish Colonial and Mission designs.

In Durango, the most entertaining way to relive those halcyon days is to take a ride on the **Durango & Silverton Narrow Gauge Railroad,** an eight-hour, round-trip journey along the 45-mile railway. You'll travel in comfort in restored 1882 parlor cars, and listen to the train's shrill whistle as the locomotive chugs along the fertile Animas River Valley and, at times, clings precariously to the hillside. *479 Main Ave.,* ☎ *970/247–2733.* ☛ *$42.70 adults, $21.45 children. Operates Apr.–Oct. and late Nov.–Jan. 1 daily; times vary.*

At the junction of U.S. 550 and U.S. 160 you have two options: Pick up U.S. 550 North and continue the tour, or follow U.S. 160 East for a 35-mile excursion to **Chimney Rock,** so-named for the distinctive, twin-rock spires that architecturally are more closely related to the Chaco Canyon Anasazi sites in New Mexico than to those in Mesa Verde. Anthropologists debate whether the rocks served as a trading post or as an astronomical observatory of great religious significance. Whatever the origin, many believe that the mystical ruins retain tremendous power and resonance. Access to the site is only possible with a Forest Service guide; reservations are mandatory for the free tour. For information contact the **Pagosa Springs Forest Ranger District** (☎ 970/264–2268).

If you choose to continue on the tour's direct route, take U.S. 550 North along the section of the San Juan Skyway that's otherwise known as the **Million Dollar Highway.** Depending on whom you ask, the name refers to either the million dollars worth of gold and silver mined each mile along the stretch, the low-grade ore from mining residue that was used to pave the road, the cost of the road's construction, or the million-dollar views it offers.

TIME OUT Seven miles north of Durango lies **Trimble Hot Springs** (U.S. 550, follow signs, ☎ 970/247–0111), a great place to soak your aching bones, especially if you've been doing some hiking.

Fifteen and 25 miles north (respectively) from the U.S. 160 and U.S. 550 junction are two famous recreational playgrounds: the ravishing golf course and development at **Tamarron** (*see* Lodging, *below*) and the **Purgatory Ski Area.** Purgatory is about as down-home as it gets, with clientele that runs toward families, cowboys, and college kids on break. Purgatory's ad campaign proudly tells it like it is: "No movie stars here" and "You don't have to be a celebrity to be treated like a star."

What's unique about Purgatory is its stepped terrain: lots of humps and dips, steep pitches followed by virtual flats. This profile makes it difficult for skiers to lose control. There are some great powder days on the mountain's back side that will convince anyone that Purgatory isn't just "Pleasant Ridge," as it's derisively known in Crested Butte and Telluride. Unfortunately, the resort has had some financial problems recently, and in 1993 it narrowly avoided bankruptcy when Norwest Bank sought a more favorable repayment schedule. However, a deal was worked out that will enable the area to operate as usual at least until the 1996–97 season.

The tortuous northern route begins a dizzying series of switchbacks as it climbs over the Molas Pass, yielding splendid vistas of the Grand Turks, the Needles Range, and Crater Lake. This is prime mountain biking and four-wheeler territory. On the other side of the pass you'll reach **Silverton,** an isolated, unspoiled old mining community ringed by glorious peaks. It reputedly got its name when a miner exclaimed, "We ain't got much gold but we got a ton of silver!" The entire town is a National Historic Landmark District. The Chamber of Commerce (414 Greene St., ☎ 970/387–5654) has issued a fact-filled walking-tour brochure that describes—among other things—the most impressive buildings lining Greene Street: **Miners' Union Hall,** the **Teller House, Town Hall, San Juan County Courthouse** (site of the county historical museum), and the **Grand Imperial Hotel.** These structures hold historical significance, but more history was probably made in the raucous red-light district along Blair Street.

Silverton has always been a rowdy town with a hardy populace, and that spirit remains. Every summer evening at 5:30, gunfights are staged at the corner of Blair and 12th streets. But the lawlessness evoked by such events is only part of the heritage that the town wishes to commemorate. If you look north toward Anvil Mountain, you'll see the community's touching tribute to miners—the **Christ of the Mines Shrine**—built in the '50s out of Carrara marble.

🔞 **Ouray,** 23 miles north, over Red Mountain Pass, is a town trapped in a narrow, steep-walled valley in the bullying shadow cast by rugged peaks of the San Juan Mountains. The ravishing setting amply explains the town's nickname, "The Switzerland of America." It was named for the great Southern Ute chief Ouray, labeled a visionary by the U.S. Army and branded a traitor by his people because he attempted to assimilate the Utes into white society. The mining town is yet another National Historic Landmark District, with a glittering array of lavish old hotels and residences. More than 25 classic edifices are included in the historic walking-tour brochure issued by the Chamber of Commerce (1222 Main St., ☎ 970/325–4746); among the points of interest are the grandiose **Wright's Opera House; the Beaumont, Western,** and **St. Elmo hotels;** and **the Elks Lodge.**

Ouray's architecture is notable, but the town's ultimate glory lies in its surroundings, and it has become an increasingly popular destination for climbers (both mountain and ice varieties), fat-tire fanatics, and hikers. One particularly gorgeous jaunt is to **Box Canyon Falls and Park,** just south of town, off U.S. 550. The turbulent waters of Clear Creek (part of the falls) thunder 285 feet down a narrow gorge. A steel suspension bridge and various well-marked trails afford breathtaking panoramic vistas.

More opportunities to immerse yourself in nature present themselves at the various hot springs in the area. It's hard to tell which is more revivifying: the 104-degree waters or the views of surrounding peaks at the **Ouray Hot Springs Pool.** *U.S. 550 at the north end of town,* ☎ *970/325–4638.* ☛ *$4 adults, $3.50 students 13–17, $2.75 children 5–12 and senior citizens.* ☉ *June–Sept., daily 10–10; Oct.–May, Mon.–Wed. noon–9.*

From Ouray, you can continue north for 13 miles on U.S. 550 on your return to Ridgway, where this tour began; or follow the four-wheel-drive **Alpine Loop Scenic Byway** (*see* Four-Wheel Driving *in* Sports and the Outdoors, *below*), which shimmies through stunning scenery on its way to Lake City, 45 miles south and east.

🔞 **Lake City** is noted for the superb hiking and fishing in Uncompahgre National Forest, especially at Lake San Cristobal. The town—with its collection of lacy gingerbread–trimmed houses and false-front Victorians—also has the largest National Historic Landmark District in Colorado. But Lake City is best known for the lurid history surrounding a notorious gentleman named Alferd Packer. Packer was a member of a party of six prospectors who camped near Lake San Cristobal during the winter of 1874. That spring, only Packer emerged from the mountains, claiming to have been deserted, and to have subsisted on roots and rabbits. Soon after, a Ute came across a grisly scene: strips of human flesh and crushed skulls. Packer protested his innocence and fled, but a manhunt ensued; Packer was finally caught nine years later, tried, and sentenced to life (he was convicted of manslaughter because of a technicality). As one wag noted at the time, "There were but six dimmocrats in Hinsdale County and he et five of 'em." To this day the event is commemorated by an Alferd Packer Barbecue, held annually in June.

Tour 2: The San Luis Valley

At 8,000 square miles, the San Luis Valley is the world's largest alpine valley, stunningly nestled between the San Juan Mountains to the west and the Sangre de Cristo range to the east. Despite its average altitude of 7,500 feet, its sheltering peaks help to create a relatively mild climate. The valley is one of Colorado's major agricultural producers, with huge annual crops of potatoes, carrots, canola, barley, and lettuce. It's so self-sufficient that local businessmen threatened to secede in the '50s to prove that the state couldn't get along without the valley and its valuable produce.

Watered by the mighty Rio Grande and its tributaries, the San Luis Valley also supports a magnificent array of wildlife, including flocks of sandhill and even whooping cranes. The range of terrain is equally impressive, from the soaring fourteener, Mt. Blanca, to the stark moonscape of the Wheeler Geologic Area to the tawny, undulating Great Sand Dunes National Monument.

The area was settled first by the Ute, then by the Spanish who left their indelible imprint in the town names and local architecture. The oldest town (San Luis), the oldest military post (Ft. Garland), and the oldest church (Our Lady of Guadalupe in Conejos) in the state are in this valley. It's no surprise that this is a highly religious, traditional area. The natural beauty is simply awe-inspiring.

⑮ Travel east on Route 149 from Lake City to **Creede,** which once earned a reputation as Colorado's rowdiest mining camp and was immortalized in an evocative poem by the local newspaper editor, Cy Warman: "It's day all day in daytime, and there is no night in Creede." Every other building was a saloon or bordello. Bob Ford, who killed Jesse James, was himself gunned down here; other notorious residents included Calamity Jane and Bat Masterson. As delightful as the town is, its location is even more glorious, with the pristine **Weminuche Wilderness** 30 miles to the south and the **Wheeler Geologic areas** 20 miles to the west, where the unusual rock formations resemble playful abstract sculptures or an M. C. Escher creation.

The **Creede Museum,** occupying the original Denver & Rio Grande Railroad Depot, paints a vivid portrait of those rough-and-tumble days. Highlights include an underground firehouse and mining museum. *6th and San Luis Sts.,* ☎ *719/658–2374.* ☛ *$3.* ☽ *Memorial Day–Labor Day, daily 10–4.*

Continue along Route 149—declared the Silver Thread National Scenic Byway—on its impossibly beautiful journey east through South Fork
⑯ (where Route 149 joins U.S. 160) and the **Rio Grande National Forest** to **Del Norte.** The route flirts with the Rio Grande, passes near the majestic North Clear Creek Falls, and ambles through numerous ghost towns along the way. In and around Del Norte are several historic sites,

one of which is an original 1870s station on the **Barlow-Sanderson Stage-coach Line.**

The **Rio Grande County Museum and Cultural Center,** in town, celebrates the region's multicultural heritage with displays of petroglyphs, mining artifacts, early Spanish relics, and rotating shows of contemporary art. *580 Oak St.,* ☎ *719/657–2847.* ☛ *$2.* ⊙ *Mid-May–Labor Day, Mon.–Sat. 10–5; Labor Day–mid-May, weekdays 10–4.*

Just west of town is the gaping **Penitente Canyon,** which is usually crawling with climbers. Several miles north of town, off Route 112, near La Garita, is another marvel—the towering rock formation **La Ventana Natural Arch.**

About 20 miles farther east at the junction of U.S. 160 and U.S. 285 ⑰ is **Alamosa,** the valley's major city, best known as the Olympic high-altitude training center for long-distance runners. Just outside town is the **Alamosa National Vista Wildlife Refuge;** these natural and man-made wetlands—an anomaly amid the arid surroundings—are an important sanctuary for the nearly extinct whooping crane and its cousin, the sandhill. *9383 El Rancho La.,* ☎ *719/589–4021.* ☛ *Free.* ⊙ *Daily 9–sunset.*

The attractive **Adams State College** complex (in town, along Main Street) contains several superlative examples of 1930s, WPA-commissioned murals in its administrative building. The admirable **Luther Bean Museum and Art Gallery,** on campus, displays European porcelain and furniture collections in a handsome, wood-paneled 19th-century drawing room, and changing exhibits of regional arts and crafts. *Richardson Hall, Main St.,* ☎ *719/589–7151;* ☛ *Free; open weekdays 1–5.*

⑱ Alamosa also serves as the gateway to the **Great Sand Dunes National Monument,** 35 miles northeast and reached via U.S. 160 and Route 150. Created by windswept grains from the Rio Grande floor, the sand dunes—which rise up to 700 feet in height—are an improbable, unforgettable sight silhouetted against the sagebrush plains and looming forested slopes of the San Juans. The dunes, as curvaceous as Rubens' nudes, stretch for 55 square miles and are painted with light and shadow that shift through the day. Their very existence seems tenuous, as if they might blow away before your eyes, yet they're solid enough to withstand the stress of hikers and skiers. The sand is as fine and feathery as you'll find anywhere; it's a place for contemplation and repose, the silence broken only by passing birds and the faint rush of water from the Medano Creek.

If you travel south from Alamosa on U.S. 285, you'll reach the little town of Romeo. From here pick up Route 142 East and travel 15 miles to **Manassa,** the birthplace of Jack Dempsey, one of the greatest heavyweight boxing champions of all time. Dempsey (also known as the Manassa Mauler) is honored in the **Jack Dempsey Museum.** *401 Main St.,* ☎ *719/843–5207.* ☛ *$2 adults, $1 children under 12.* ⊙ *Memorial Day–Labor Day, Mon.–Sat. 9–5.*

Continue east along this scenic byway to the junction of Routes 142 ⑲ and 159 to reach **San Luis,** founded in 1851, the oldest incorporated town in Colorado. Its Hispanic heritage is celebrated in the superb **San Luis Museum and Cultural Center,** with its extensive collection of *santos* (exquisitely decorated figures of saints used for household devotions), *retablos* (paintings on wood), and *bultos* (carved religious figures). Wonderful murals re-telling famous stories and legends of the area adorn the town's gracious tree-lined streets. A latter-day masterpiece is the *Stations of the Cross Shrine*, created by renowned local sculptor Huberto Maestas. Perched above town on a mesa called La Mesa de la Piedad y de la Misericordia (Hill of Piety and Mercy), its 15 figures dramatically depict the last hours of Christ's life. The trail culminates in a tranquil grotto dedicated to the Virgin Mary. *402 Church Pl., ☎ 719/672–3611. ☛ $3. ☉ Memorial Day–Labor Day, weekdays 8–4:30, weekends 10–3.*

Eighteen miles farther north, in the Sangre de Cristos (Blood of Christ, after the ruddy color of the peaks at dawn), is **Ft. Garland,** the site of Colorado's first military post, established in 1856 to protect settlers. The legendary Kit Carson commanded the outfit, and the six original adobe structures are still around, comprising the **Ft. Garland State Museum.** The venue features a re-creation of the commandant's quarters, various period military displays, and a rotating local folk-art exhibit. *Rte. 159, south of U.S. 160, ☎ 719/379–3512. ☛ $3. ☉ Memorial Day–Labor Day, Mon.–Sat. 10–5, Sun. 1–5.*

Consider visiting a portion of the Santa Fe Trail by continuing east on U.S. 160 to the town of Walsenburg. From Walsenburg you can either go south on I–25 to the town of Trinidad; or travel north, passing through Pueblo and winding up in Colorado Springs (*see* South Central Colorado, *below*).

What to See and Do with Children

The **Anasazi Heritage Center** (*see* Tour 1, *above*) features educational, hands-on displays and computer games.

The **Durango & Silverton Narrow Gauge Railroad** (*see* Tour 1, *above*)

Other Points of Interest

Four Corners Monument. A stone slab marks the only spot where four states—Colorado, Arizona, Utah, and New Mexico—meet. Of course, this is photo-op country, so smile and say "cheese"! Snacks and souvenirs are sold by Native Americans. To get here, travel south from Cortez on Route 160 for about 40 miles: You can't miss the signs. *Rte. 160 (follow signs). ☛ $1 per vehicle. ☉ Daily 7 am–8 pm.*

Hovenweep National Monument. This site—whose literal translation from Ute means "deserted valley"—contains several major ruins, including imposing square, oval, and circular man-made towers such as Holly, Cajon, Hackberry, and Horseshoe, all of which are accessible only on foot. The most impressive ruin, called the Castle, underscores the site's uncanny resemblance to a medieval fiefdom. Hovenweep is approached via Route 160 West to County Road G (McElmo Canyon Rd.), which enters the spectacular red-walled McElmo Canyon along the way. *McElmo Canyon Rd., ☎ 970/749–05105 (Mesa Verde National Parks 970/529–4461). ☛ Free; camping entry fee $3. ☉ Daily sunrise–sunset.*

Lowry Pueblo. Small in comparison to Hovenweep, the Lowry site has only eight kivas and 40 rooms, and may have been a "suburb" of larger communities in the area during its occupation from about 800 to 1110. Of particular note are the Great Kiva, one of the largest such structures ever discovered, and a painted kiva, providing a fascinating insight into Anasazi decorative techniques. A brochure, which details the self-guided tour, is available at the entrance to the site. *Rte. 666, 9 mi west of Pleasant View, no ☎. ☛ Free. ☉ Daily 9–5.*

Shopping

Colorado's Southwest is the best place to pick up Western and Native American art and artifacts. Although there are malls and factory outlets in Durango housing the usual retailers, the following list includes only shops and boutiques with unique merchandise.

The San Luis valley offers superb examples of folk crafts, and basketry, embroidery, weaving, and beadwork adapted from Native American traditions.

Specialty Stores

ANTIQUES

Buckskin Trading Co. (636 Main St., Ouray, ☎ 970/325–4044) sports an array of mining, railroading, Native American and cowboy collectibles.

Treasures of Time (Pacific and Davis Sts., Telluride, ☎ 970/728–3383) carries a selection of Western memorabilia, including frontier-style furnishings.

ART GALLERIES

Casa de Madera (680 Grand St., Del Norte, ☎ 719/657–2336) sells marvelous regional wood carvings.

Firedworks Gallery (608 Main St., Alamosa, ☎ 719/589–6064) sells fine art, collectibles, jewelry, weavings and prints.

Gallery West (718 Main St., Alamosa, ☎ 719/589–2275) carries local original paintings, photos, etchings, fiber arts, and designs in clay.

Golden West Indian Arts/Jan Cicero Gallery (101 W. Colorado Ave., Telluride, ☎ 970/728–3664) stocks a superb selection of Southwestern, Native American, and Hispanic art.

Goodman Gallery (3rd St. and Elk Ave., upstairs, Crested Butte, ☎ 970/349–5470) displays and sells Southwestern crafts from regional artisans.

Hellbent Leather and Silver (209 E. Colorado Ave., Telluride, ☎ 970/728–6246; 741 Main Ave., Durango, ☎ 970/247–9088) is a fine source for Native American arts and crafts.

North Moon (133 W. Colorado Ave., Telluride, ☎ 970/728–4145) features exquisite painted lodgepole furnishings, contemporary Native American ceramics that depart from tribal traditions, striking metallic sculptures, and petroglyph-inspired jewelry.

Something Pewter (419 Main St., Manassa, ☎ 719/843–5702) fashions what seems to be everything from bolos to belts, charms to figurines—all in pewter.

Toh-Atin Gallery (149 W. 9th St., Durango, ☎ 970/247–8277) and the related **Toh-Ahtin's Art on Main** (865 Main Ave., ☎ 970/247–4540) around the corner together comprise perhaps the best Western, Native American, and Southwestern art gallery in Colorado, offering a wide-ranging selection of paintings, pottery, prints, records, foodstuffs, clothing, and jewelry.

The Turquoise Shop (423 San Juan Ave., Alamosa, ☎ 719/589–2631) sells sterling silver and turquoise jewelry and various arts and crafts.

BOOKS

Between the Covers Bookstore and Coffee House (224 W. Colorado Ave., Telluride, ☎ 970/728–4504) offers the perfect ambience for browsing through the latest titles while sipping a cappuccino.

Maria's Books (928 Main Ave., Durango, ☎ 970/247–1438) specializes in regional literature and nonfiction.

BOUTIQUES

Appaloosa Trading Co. (501 Main Ave., Durango, ☎ 970/259–1994 is one of the best venues for all things leather, from purses to saddles, hats to boots, as well as jewelry, weaving, and other crafts.

Blair Street Cottage (1342 Blair St., Silverton, ☎ 970/387–5735) specializes in silk batik, with lovely scarves, ties, camisoles, and wall hangings.

Circumstance Leatherworks (306 6th Ave., Ouray, ☎ 970/325–7360) sells belts, purses, and backpacks crafted by Robert Holmes.

Shirt Off My Back (680 Main Ave., Durango, ☎ 970/247–9644) sells lovely silk-screened T-shirts (choose from more than 60 images or create your own).

Wm. Donald (220 E. Colorado Ave., Telluride, ☎ 970/728–3489) offers stylish togs, including hand-tooled leather vests, one-of-a-kind hand-spun angora/mohair jackets, limited edition sweaters with whimsical designs like chili peppers, as well as Coogis from Australia and Pendleton from Oregon.

Unicas Southwest (Ft. Smith Saloon Bldg., Ridgway, ☎ 970/626–5723; 215 E. Colorado Ave., Telluride, ☎ 970/728–4778; 703 Main Ave., Ouray, no ☎) delivers on its advertising promises of "worldly styles" and "fun, fashion, funk, and folk art."

CERAMICS

Beens Pottery (145 E. 6th St., Durango, ☎ 970/247–3220) features pottery by local artist J. Milton Beens, as well as a wide selection of Western watercolors.

Creekside Pottery (126 Elk Ave., Crested Butte, ☎ 970/349–6459) showcases local artist Mary Jursinovic's pottery and landscape lamps.

Mesa Verde Pottery (27601 Rte. 160 E, Cortez, ☎ 970/565–4492) offers a comprehensive sampling of ceramics from most Southwestern tribes.

The Potter's Wheel (221 E. Colorado Ave., Telluride, ☎ 970/728–4912) has a wide selection of both decorative and functional pottery crafted by local artisans.

San Juan Pottery (801 Main St., Ouray, ☎ 970/325–0319) features the work of Coloradan potters, but also carries porcelain jewelry, figurines, Native American baskets, gourds, and weaving.

Ute Mountain Pottery Plant (Jct. Rtes. 160 and 666, Towaoc, ☎ 970/565–8548) invites customers to watch the painstaking processes of molding, trimming, cleaning, painting, and glazing, before adjourning to the showroom to buy pieces straight from the source.

Zappa Pottery (688 Spring Creek Blvd., Montrose, ☎ 970/249–6819) showcases the fine stoneware designs of Nick and Joan Zappa.

CRAFTS AND COLLECTIBLES

Artesanos (115 W. 9th St., Durango, ☎ 970/259–5755) offers a marvelous selection of eclectic furnishings from around the world (the Mexican crafts are remarkably fine).

The **Train Store** (501 Main Ave., Durango, ☎ 970/259–2145) sells unique train and railroad memorabilia, toys, models, books, T-shirts, and videos.

The **Candle Shop** (Blair St., Silverton, ☎ 970/387–5733) sells not only handmade candles, but also wind chimes, hurricane lamps, and local crafts.

Cortez Curiosity Shop (30 E. Main St., Cortez, ☎ 970/565–4856) sells everything from scented candles to tinctures to astrology charts to crystals.

Dietz Market (119 W. 8th St., Durango, ☎ 970/259–6030; 26345 Hwy. 160, Durango, ☎ 970/259–5811 or 800/321–6069) carries pottery, metalwork, candles, weavings, and foodstuffs, all celebrating the region.

Images Gift Shoppe (541 Main St., Ouray, ☎ 970/325–7378) glories in tchotchkes and caters to a broad clientele, with items ranging from pottery to potpourri.

Nazca (218 N. Main St., Gunnison, ☎ 970/641–6438) has a wide selection of crafts, hand-carved candles, and hand-knit sweaters.

FLEA MARKETS

Kellogg's Corner (24 Everett St., Durango, ☎ 970/247–2500) is a daily flea market.

FOOD

Adobe Milling Co. (Main St., Dove Creek, ☎ 970/677–2620) is in the self-styled Pinto Bean Capital of the World, and vends Anasazi beans, Dos Gringos spices, piñon nuts, and other products.

Honeyville Station (33633 U.S. 550 N, Hermosa, ☎ 800/676–7690) sells jams, jellies (try the chokecherry), condiments, and, of course, honey. You can watch how the bees make honey (in glass hives), and may be treated to a lecture by a fully garbed beekeeper.

The San Luis Valley is noted for its produce. Mycophiles should stop by the **Alamosa Mushroom Farm** (1071 South Road 5 South, ☎ 719/589–5882). **Mountain Maid Jelly** (710 2nd St., Saguache, ☎ 719/655–2824) offers a variety of unusual and delicious flavors. **Haefeli's Honey Farms** (0041 South Road 1 East, Monte Vista, ☎ 970/852–2301) sells delectable mountain-bloom honeys.

JEWELRY

The **Enameling Shop** (1249 Greene St., Silverton, ☎ 970/387–5442) features original enamel works by Gary and Robert Richardson, who make buckles, earrings, and bolo ties.

SPORTING GOODS

Olympic Sports (150 W. Colorado Ave., Telluride, ☎ 970/728–4477) has a plethora of equipment and clothing for all seasons.

WESTERN WEAR

In Mancos, **Buck Saddlery** (106 W. Grand Ave., Mancos, ☎ 970/533–7958) is the domain of Buck, Eddie, Mark, and Sheila Proffitt, who custom build some of the sturdiest—and handsomest—saddles you'll ever find, in addition to chaps, holsters, scabbards, elk and buckskin jackets, and glamorous evening purses replete with silver, beads, and fringe. The **Bounty Hunter** (119 W. Grand Ave., Mancos, ☎ 970/533–7215; 226 W. Colorado Ave., Telluride, ☎ 970/728–0256) is the spot for leather, especially boots and vests. It also houses an astonishing selection of hats, among them Panama straw, beaver felt, Australian Outback, and just outrageous.

O'Farrell Hat Company (598 Main Ave., Durango, ☎ 970/259–2517) actually form-fits hats with a "customizer" machine; heads they've fitted include former presidents Bush and Reagan. Also in Durango, **Western Outfitters** (960 Main Ave., Durango, ☎ 970/247–0260) outfits men, women, and children from head to toe in everything from Stetson hats to Tony Lama boots.

Trail Town (U.S. 550 and Rte. 62, Ridgway, no ☎) is an entire mall devoted to the Western lifestyle, with restaurants, a dance hall, and clothing, furniture, and home accessories stores.

Sports and the Outdoors

Camping

The glorious wilderness area of the San Juans and Sangre de Cristos offers a diversity of camping activities. Contact the **Bureau of Land Management** (Durango, ☎ 970/247–4082), the **San Juan National Forest** (Durango, ☎ 970/247–4874), the **Curecanti National Recreation Area** (Montrose, ☎ 970/641–2337), and the **Uncompahgre and Gunnison national forests** (Delta, ☎ 970/874–7691) for more information. Campsites are also available in Mesa Verde and Hovenweep; contact the **National Park Service** at **Mesa Verde National Park** (P.O. Box 8. Mesa Verde, CO 81330, ☎ 970/529–4465).

Boating

Shorty's (Bayfield, ☎ 970/884–2768) and **Mountain Marina** (Bayfield, ☎ 970/884–9450) rent canoes on Vallecito Lake. **Beaver Creek Marina** (Cortez, ☎ 970/882–2258) rents canoes and boats on McPhee Reservoir. **San Juan Skyway Marina** (Ouray, ☎ 970/626–5094) rents canoes and boats at the Ridgway State Recreation Area (U.S. 550, 12 mi north of town). You can also call the **Curecanti National Recreation Area** (Montrose, ☎ 970/641–2337), **Elk Creek Marina** (Montrose, ☎ 970/641–0707), and **Ridgway Reservoir** (Ridgway, ☎ 970/626–5822) for more information about boating.

Climbing

Fantasy Ridge Alpinism (Telluride, ☎ 970/728–3546) and **SouthWest Adventures** (Durango, ☎ 970/259–0370) are two climbing clubs in the region. Ouray is gaining fame in ice-climbing circles, with its abundance of frozen waterfalls. **Mountain Ouray Sports** (☎ 970/325–4284) arranges lessons and guided tours.

World-class climbing can be found outside Del Norte in the **Penitente Canyon,** as well as in the **San Juans,** and in the **Wheeler Geologic Area** outside Creede.

Cycling

Durango/Purgatory has good cycling trails, such as **Hermosa Creek** and **La Plata Canyon Road.** Top Telluride trails include **Ilium Road** and **Sawpit Road.** The entire **San Juan Skyway,** many of whose ascents are quite steep, is a favorite for cyclists.

Crested Butte Mountain offers several miles of scenic trails. **Signal Peak Loop** and **Rage in the Sage Track** outside Gunnison are also popular.

Routes around Silverton run through ghost towns and mining trails, while the Cortez area is popular for the Anasazi ruins.

Mountain Bike Specialists (340 S. Camino del Rio, Durango, ☎ 970/259–6661) arranges tours throughout the Four Corners region.

Fishing

For information on fishing in the region contact: the **Colorado Division of Wildlife** (2300 S. Townsend Ave., Montrose 81401, ☎ 970/249–3431); the **Bureau of Land Management** (701 Camino del Rio, Durango 81301, ☎ 970/247–4082); the **San Juan National Forest** (Durango, ☎ 970/247–4874); and the **Uncompahgre and Gunnison National forests** (2250 Highway 50, Delta 81416, ☎ 970/874–7691).

One of the finest sources of prime trout and bass in Colorado is the **McPhee Reservoir.** The second-largest body of water in the state, it reputedly has the best catch record in Southwest Colorado. Other well-stocked reservoirs in the area include **Jackson, Joe Moore, Taylor,** and **Groundhog.** The **Dolores, Gunnison** and **Mancos rivers,** and **Taylor** and **Bear creeks** are excellent spots as well. North of Durango are Lakes **Haviland, Lemon,** and **Vallecito.** Outside Gunnison, the **Blue Mesa Reservoir** in the Curecanti National Recreation Area (Gunnison, ☎ 970/641–2337) is another top choice, as is Lake San Cristobal.

The **Rio Grande River**—between Del Norte and South Fork—teems with rainbows and lunker browns.

The following operators run trips to various areas within the region: **Alpine Outside** (Crested Butte, ☎ 970/349–5011); **Colorado Fishing Adventures** (Pagosa Springs, ☎ 970/264–4168); **Duranglers** (Durango, ☎ 970/385–4081); **Telluride Angler** (☎ 970/728–0773); and **Telluride Outside** (☎ 970/728–3895).

Four-Wheel Driving

The inspiring **Alpine Loop Scenic Byway** joins Lake City with Ouray and Silverton. This circle is only open in summer, and is paved, except for the dirt roads over Cinnamon and Engineer passes. However, this is four-wheel heaven, dizzily spiraling from 12,800-foot passes to gaping valleys.

Golf

Alamosa Golf Course (6678 River Rd., ☎ 719/589–5330) is an 18-hole championship course.

Cattails Golf Course (State St., Alamosa, ☎ 719/589–9515), also in Alamosa, is an 18-hole course that wraps scenically around the Rio Grande.

Conquistador Golf Course (2018 N. Dolores St., Cortez, ☎ 970/565–9208) is an 18-hole public course with sweeping views of Mesa Verde and Sleeping Ute Mountain.

Dalton Ranch and Golf Club (on U.S. 5507, 7 mi north of Durango, ☎ 970/247–7921) is a Ken Dye–designed 18-hole championship course with inspiring panoramas of red-rock cliffs. The restaurant, which arranges "happy hours" with Trimble Hot Springs across the road, has become a popular hangout for both duffers and skiers, who enjoy watching the resident elk herd on its afternoon stroll.

Dos Rios Golf Club (U.S. 50, 2 mi west of Gunnison, ☎ 970/641–1482) has lovely views; water comes into play on 17 holes.

Fairfield Pagosa Resort (U.S. 160, 3 mi west of Pagosa Springs, ☎ 970/781–4141) offers both an 18-hole and a 9-hole course.

Great Sand Dunes Country Club (5303 Rte. 150, Mosca, ☎ 719/378–2357) is an 18-hole course with the billowing dunes as a backdrop.

Hillcrest Golf Course (2300 Rim Dr., ☎ 970/247–1499) is an 18-hole public course perched on a mesa.

Skyland Country Club (385 Country Club Dr., ☎ 970/349–6127) is a ravishing 18-hole course designed by Robert Trent Jones, Jr. and although it belongs to the country club, it is open to the public.

Tamarron Resort (40292 U.S. 550 N, ☎ 970/259–2000) is an 18-hole, 6,885-yard course, frequently ranked among *Golf Digest's* top 75 resort courses.

Telluride Golf Club (Telluride Mountain Village, ☎ 970/728–3856) boasts breathtaking views of Mt. Wilson and Mt. Sunshine, which dominate this 7,009-yard course.

Hiking

For general information about hiking in Southwest Colorado, contact the **Bureau of Land Management** (701 Camino del Rio, Durango 81301, ☎ 970/247–4082) or the **San Juan National Forest Ranger Districts** (100 N. 6th St., Dolores 81323, ☎ 970/882–7296; 41595 U.S. 160 E, Mancos 81328, ☎ 970/533–7716.

In the Needles Range of the San Juans, picturesque, fairly strenuous hikes include **Molas Pass** to **Crater Lake, Engineer Peak,** and the **Grand Turks.** Trails abound throughout the region, skirting waterfalls and mining ruins. The **Lizard Head Wilderness Area,** dominated by the eerie rock tooth of the same name, showcases the region's alpine scenery at its best.

The **Great Sand Dunes** are a favorite hike. The **Rio Grande National Forest** offers more than a million acres of pristine wilderness.

Horseback Riding

Fantasy Ranch (P.O. Box 236, Crested Butte 81224, ☎ 970/349–5425), **Lazy F Bar Outfitters** (P.O. Box 383, Gunnison 81230, ☎ 970/349–7593), **Rimrock Outfitters** (c/o Echo Basin, 43747 County Road M, Mancos 81328, ☎ 970/533–7000), **Southfork Stables** (28481 Highway 160, Durango 81301, ☎ 970/259–4871), and **Telluride Outside** (P.O. Box 685, Telluride 81435, ☎ 970/728–3895) provide horses for riding tours, which range from one-hour walks to overnight excursions; rates begin at $20. Many outfitters also offer sleigh rides and dinners.

Rafting

River tours can last for an afternoon or for 10 days, depending on the arrangements. Rates begin at $30. **Durango Rivertrippers** (☎ 970/259–0289) runs expeditions down the Animas River. **Gunnison River Expeditions** (Montrose, ☎ 970/249–4441) specializes in Gunnison River tours. **Telluride Whitewater** (☎ 970/728–3895) explores the Gunnison, Dolores, Colorado, and Animas rivers. **Three Rivers Outfitting** (Crested Butte, ☎ 970/349–501, and Almont, ☎ 970/641–1303) runs trips down the Arkansas, Taylor, and Gunnison, and also offers kayaking lessons and raft lure fishing.

Skiing

CROSS-COUNTRY
Crested Butte Nordic Center (☎ 970/349–1707) has a 15 mile groomed track system and also offers guided tours into the backcountry.

Purgatory-Durango Cross-Country Center (☎ 970/247–9000) offers 26 miles of machine-groomed scenic trails just outside the ski area.

Telluride Nordic Center (☎ 970/728–6911) provides almost 80 miles of pristine trails. The areas around Molas Divide and Mesa Verde National Park are also popular.

DOWNHILL
Crested Butte Mountain Resort. 85 trails; 13 lifts; 1,162 acres; 2,775-foot vertical. Good beginner and extreme terrain. *Rte. 135,* ☎ *970/349–2222.* ⊘ *Late-Nov.–early Apr., daily 9–4.*

Purgatory-Durango. 74 trails; 9 chairs; 729 acres; 2,029-foot vertical. A lot of intermediate runs and glade and tree skiing. *U.S. 550,* ☎ *970/247–9000 or 800/525–0892.* ⊘ *Late Nov.–early Apr., daily 9–4.*

Ski Hesperus. 18 trails; 2 lifts. This small, family ski area close to Durango offers 100% night skiing. The Navahos regarded the mountain as a sacred peak, and used it as a directional landmark. *U.S. 160,* ☎ *970/259–3711.* ⊘ *Dec.–early Apr., Sat.–Tues. 9–4 and Wed.–Fri, 4:30–9:30.*

Telluride. 64 trails; 9 chairs and a poma lift; 1,050 acres; 3,165-foot vertical (3,522-foot vertical if you hike to the highest ridge). *Rte. 145,* ☎ *970/728–6900 or 800/525–3455.* ⊘ *Late Nov.–early Apr., daily 9–4.*

Wolf Creek. 50 trails; 5 lifts; 700 acres; 1,425-foot vertical. This is one of Colorado's best-kept secrets and a powder hound's dream: it's uncrowded with no lift lines, and gets phenomenal snow (averaging more than 450 inches a year). The 50 trails run the gamut from wide-open bowls to steep glade skiing. *U.S. 160, at the top of Wolf Creek Pass, Pagosa Springs,* ☎ *970/264–5629.* ⊘ *Early Nov.–mid-Apr., daily 9–4.*

Snowboarding is also permitted at all the above ski areas.

HELI-SKIING
Telluride Helitrax (☎ 970/728–4904) offers thrilling touring through the New Eastern Powder Circuit.

SKI TOURING
San Juan Hut System (Telluride, ☎ 970/728–6935) connects Telluride with Ridgway. There are five huts equipped with beds, blankets, and stoves. Huts are about 7 miles apart.

Snowmobiling
Action Adventures (Crested Butte, ☎ 970/349–5909 or 800/383–1974); **Alpine Expeditions** (Crested Butte, ☎ 970/349–5011 or 800/833–8052); **Snowmobile Adventure Tours** (Purgatory, ☎ 970/247–9000); **Telluride Outside** (☎ 970/728–3895 or 800/831–6230).

Tennis
The following parks offer free public courts. Reservations are advised: **Crested Butte** and **Mt. Crested Butte Town parks** (no ☎s); **Durango City Park** (☎ 970/247–5622); **Ouray Hot Springs Pool** (☎ 970/325–4638); **Telluride Town Park** (☎ 970/728–3071).

Dining

Colorado's Southwest is one of those regions in the good ol' U.S. of A. that has made truck stops and their fare an indelible part of our tradition. What you'll also find here is sensational Southwestern-style cooking, especially around Durango, and superb gourmet dining in

Crested Butte, about which a journalist from the *Denver Post* once opined, "There are more fine restaurants per capita in Crested Butte than anywhere else in America." Telluride isn't far behind, befitting its status as unofficial rival to Vail and Aspen. For rates *see* the Dining chart *in* Colorado Essentials, *below.*

Even if you plan to dine in upscale establishments, Southwest Colorado makes few sartorial demands on the restaurant-goer. In general, the upscale places expect you to look neat and casual; elsewhere, jeans, shorts, or ski pants work well.

Alamosa

$$ True Grits. At this noisy steak house the cuts are predictably good, but that's not the real draw: As the name implies, the restaurant is really a shrine to John Wayne. His portraits hang everywhere: the Duke in action; the Duke in repose; the Duke lost in thought. ✕ *Jct. U.S. 160 and Rte. 17,* ☎ *719/589–9954. Reservations accepted. MC, V.*

$ Ace Inn and Old Town Bar. The decor is rough-hewn: Wood-paneled
★   walls are adorned with dried chilies and assorted kitsch such as antique pepper mills and Eiffel Tower ceramics of uncertain taste. You should definitely bring an empty stomach to this superior Mexican restaurant, for heaping portions of sopaipilla—fried stuffed with beans, rice, and beef smothered in red and green chilies burritos, and chilies rellenos. Save room for the sopaipilla sundae drowned in cinnamon wine sauce. Even the margaritas are daunting: The small one is 28 ounces! ✕ *326 Main St.,* ☎ *719/589–9801. Reservations accepted. MC, V.*

Cortez

$ M&M Family Restaurant and Truck Stop. Semis and RVs jammed into the parking lot attest that M&M is the real McCoy as truck stops go. If chicken-fried steak, enchiladas, and huge breakfasts (served 24 hours a day) are your fancy, you'll be thrilled to eat here. There are posher restaurants in town, but none better—certainly not for these prices. ✕ *7006 U.S. 160 S,* ☎ *970/565–6511. No reservations. AE, MC.*

Crested Butte

$$$–$$$$ Le Bosquet. This charming Western-style Victorian bistro enjoys a sterling reputation and is wonderfully romantic. Unfortunately, it has been woefully uneven of late: some nights brilliant, some not; some dishes extraordinary, others abysmal. For example, you might start with a French onion soup inexplicably made from beef bouillon cubes rather than from stock (and from too many at that), then feast on a sensational rack of venison with pheasant ravioli. Among the always-reliable choices are potato-and-leek pancakes with gravlax and crème fraîche, goat cheese ravioli, and such scrumptious desserts as pear tart and homemade ice cream. ✕ *2nd and Elk Aves.,* ☎ *970/349–5808. Reservations advised. AE, MC, V. No lunch weekends.*

$$$–$$$$ Soupçon. Soupçon ("soup's on," get it?) occupies two intimate rooms
★   in a delightful log cabin—and a cozier place doesn't exist in this town. Mac Bailey, the impish owner-chef (women fall in love nightly: "He's so cute," they gush when he trundles out from the kitchen), brings innovative variations on classic bistro cuisine and changes his menu daily. His roast duckling, usually topped with an impeccably balanced Michigan cherry sauce, may be the best in the state, and the fish dishes are sublime: Try petrale sole lightly breaded in cornmeal, glistening with black bean, ginger, and sake sauce. Desserts, however, are where Mac really shines: Order the Jack Daniel's bread pudding, the hazelnut ice-cream cake, or any souffle. ✕ *Just off 2nd St., behind the Forest Queen,* ☎ *970/349–5448. Reservations advised. AE, MC, V. Dinner only.*

$$$–$$$$ **Timberline.** This handsome, cozy split-level restaurant is set in a restored Victorian home. Among the top starters are fettuccine Alfredo with smoked trout and goat-cheese terrine. Poached salmon au jus or herb-crusted veal chops might make a perfect second course. The weekly prix-fixe menus are a good way to save money. In summer, a pleasant Sunday brunch is offered. ✗ *21 Elk Ave.,* ☎ *970/349–9831. Reservations advised. AE, MC, V. No lunch.*

$$$ **Penelope's.** The Victorian ambience at this local favorite is complemented by a pretty greenhouse. Everything on the menu is solid and dependable, from the Colorado rack of lamb to the roast apricot duck. Sunday brunch here is a Crested Butte institution. ✗ *120 Elk Ave.,* ☎ *970/349–5178. Reservations advised. AE, MC, V. No lunch.*

$$–$$$ **Powerhouse.** This is an enormous barnlike structure, with a delight-
★ ful Gay '90s bar. The cuisine is haute Mexican, with scrumptious standards such as tacos and burritos, and more exotic dishes such as soft-shell crab in cornmeal and delectable mesquite-roasted *cabrito* (kid)—a true delicacy. The margaritas are the best in town, complemented by a knockout list of more than 30 tequilas by the glass. ✗ *130 Elk Ave.,* ☎ *970/349–5494. No reservations. AE, MC, V. No lunch.*

$$ **Swiss Chalet.** The owner duplicates the true Alpine experience, right down to the *bierstube* (pub) with Paulaner on tap. The *Kalbsgeschnetzeltes* (veal loin sautéed with mushrooms and shallots in white-wine cream sauce), raclette, and fondue are luscious, as are such hard-to-find specialties as *buendnerfleisch* (savory air-dried beef soaked in wine). ✗ *621 Gothic Rd., on the mountain,* ☎ *970/349–5917. Reservations advised. AE, MC, V. No lunch in summer.*

$–$$ **The Artichoke.** From the deck of this simple, bustling establishment you can watch the skiers come down the mountain while you nibble on "high-altitude diner cuisine," with a Cajun slant. Artichokes are obviously a specialty, and are prepared in various ways. Among entrée favorites are popcorn shrimp, chicken pot pie, catfish, gumbo, and Philly cheese steak—all of which should satisfy even the heartiest appetites. ✗ *Treasury Center, on the mountain (upstairs),* ☎ *970/349–6688. Reservations accepted. AE, D, MC, V.*

$ **Donita's Cantina.** This down-home Mexican restaurant is hard to miss: It's the one in the hot-pink building. The fare isn't nearly as showy: simply good, solid standards such as fajitas and enchiladas, and a tangy salsa. It may be owing to either the bargain prices or the killer margaritas, but the crowds here are always jovial. ✗ *330 Elk Ave.,* ☎ *970/349–6674. No reservations. AE, D, MC, V. No lunch.*

$ **Slogar.** Set in a lovingly renovated Victorian tavern awash in lace and
★ stained glass, this restaurant—also run by Mac Bailey of Soupçon and Penelope's (*see above*)—is just plain cozy. Slogar's turns out some of the plumpest, juiciest fried chicken west of the Mississippi. The fixings are just as sensational: flaky biscuits, creamy mashed potatoes swimming in hearty chicken gravy, and unique sweet-and-sour coleslaw from a Pennsylvania Dutch recipe that dates back nearly two centuries. You get all that and more, including homemade ice cream, for $10.95! ✗ *2nd and Whiterock Sts.,* ☎ *970/349–5765. Reservations advised. MC, V. No lunch.*

Durango/Purgatory

$$$$ **Café Cascade.** Many locals' choice for the best restaurant on the mountain, if not in the region, this intimate split-level eatery features the Southwestern stylings of chef Tom Hamilton. Sea bass medallions with blue cornbread and red chili sauce and rabbit satay with peanut sauce are his sterling appetizers; grilled caribou with plum and sage sauce, pheasant breast stuffed with roast tomatoes and fresh oregano, and fresh grilled ahi brushed with ginger butter sauce are among the standout entrées. ✕ *50827 U.S. 550 N (1 mi north of Purgatory), Cascade Village,* ☎ *970/259–3500. Reservations advised. AE, D, DC, MC, V. No lunch.*

$$–$$$ **Ariano's.** This popular Italian place occupies a dimly lit room plastered with local art. It offers exceptional pizzas (try the pesto) and pastas, and the best fried calamari in the Four Corners. Next door, under the same ownership, is Pronto, a bright and noisy trattoria where you can get the same pastas for less money. ✕ *150 E. College Dr., Durango,* ☎ *970/247–8146. Reservations advised. AE, MC, V. No lunch.*

$$–$$$ **Ore House.** Durango is a meat-and-potatoes kind of town, and this is Durango's idea of a steak house, where the aroma of beef smacks you in the face as you walk past. This classic eatery offers enormous slabs of aged Angus—cholesterol heaven hand-cut daily. ✕ *147 E. College Dr., Durango,* ☎ *970/245–5707. Reservations advised. AE, D, DC, MC, V.*

$$–$$$ **The Red Snapper.** If you're in the mood for fresh fish, head to this congenial place, decorated with more than 200 gallons of saltwater aquariums. Try the oysters Durango, with jack cheese and salsa; salmon Joaquin with roasted garlic cumin sauce; or snapper Monterey with jack cheese and tarragon. Of course, delicious steaks and prime rib are also available. The salad bar includes more than 40 items. ✕ *144 E. 9th St., Durango,* ☎ *970/259–3417. Reservations advised. AE, MC, V. No lunch.*

$$–$$$ **Sow's Ear.** It's a toss-up between the Ore House and this Purgatory
★ watering hole for the "Best Steak House" award. The Sow's Ear gets the edge, though, for its rustic but elegant decor, with a huge fireplace, hanging plants, and—okay—statues of urinating cowboys. The mouthwatering, fresh-baked seven-grain bread and creative preparations such as blackened fillets and the daunting hodgeebaba—an 18-ounce rib eye smothered with sautéed mushrooms and onions—are a few more reasons Sow's Ear leads the pack. There's a brightly painted climbing wall at the bar for those who need to burn calories (or wait for their table). ✕ *49617 Highway 550, Purgatory,* ☎ *970/247–3527. Reservations advised. AE, D, DC, MC, V. No lunch.*

$–$$ **Lola's Place.** This delightfully whimsical space is filled with hand-
★ painted furnishings and dried flower wreaths. The mango, mint, and mauve walls are bedecked with equally colorful abstract art. The food is just as creative. Chef David Ganley studied his trade under Wolfgang Puck at San Francisco's trendy Postrio. He turns out magnificent regional fare, using organic and indigenous ingredients wherever possible. Standouts include a free-range chicken quesadilla with zesty cilantro in an avocado salsa; vegetable tamales in mole with chipotle, dried cherries, golden raisins, and piñons; and tamales with apple cider. ✕ *725 E. 2nd Ave.,* ☎ *970/385–1920. Reservations advised. AE, MC, V. Closed Sun. No dinner Mon., no lunch Sat.*

$–$$ **Carver's Bakery and Brew Pub.** This microbrewery run by the "Brews Brothers," Bill and Jim Carver, offers about eight beers at any given time, including flavors such as Raspberry Wheat Ale (which brewmaster Patrick Keating nicknames "Seduction Ale"), and Colorado Train Nut Brown Ale. The front room is a well-lit coffeehouse-bakery and the back a more subdued sports bar. There's also a patio out back. From breakfast to the wee hours, the place is always hopping. Try the bratwurst, fajitas—chicken or sirloin strips pan-fried in tequila and salsa, or the homemade bread bowls filled with either soup or salad. ✕ *1022 Main Ave., Durango,* ☎ *970/259–2545. No reservations. AE, D, MC, V.*

$ **Olde Tymer's Café.** Locals flock to this former drugstore, which still drips with atmosphere from days gone by. The balcony, pressed-tin ceiling, and walls plastered with artifacts and locals' photos lend a '20s dance hall look to the place. You can get cheap draft beer, great burgers, and $5 blue-plate specials. ✕ *1000 Main Ave., Durango,* ☎ *970/259–2990. No reservations. AE, MC, V.*

Mancos

$$ **Millwood Junction.** Folks come from four states (no fooling) for the 25-item salad bar and phenomenal Friday-night seafood buffet. Steaks and seafood are featured in this upscale Red Lobster/Sizzler–style eatery. ✕ *Jct. U.S. 160 and Main St.,* ☎ *970/533–7338. No reservations. AE, DC, MC, V. No lunch.*

Montrose

$–$$ **The Whole Enchilada.** You'll get the whole enchilada and then some at this lively place. Portions are gargantuan, and the food goes down easily, especially the tasty chimichangas, blue-corn enchiladas, and homemade pies. The patio is a pleasant place to sit in summer. ✕ *44 S. Grand St.,* ☎ *970/249–1881. Reservations accepted. AE, MC, V.*

Pagosa Springs/Wolf Creek

$–$$ **Elkhorn Café.** Filling and fiery Mexican fare (try the stuffed sopaipillas), as well as robust American standards such as meat loaf and pot roast, draws people from miles around. Fill up on a breakfast burrito before attacking the Wolf Creek bowls. ✕ *438 Main St.,* ☎ *970/264–2146. Reservations accepted. AE, MC, V.*

Telluride

$$$$ **La Marmotte.** This romantic bistro seems transplanted from Provence,
★ with its brick walls, lace curtains, and baskets overflowing with flowers or garlic bulbs. The fish specials, such as delicate flaky salmon in saffron and mussel sauce, are particularly splendid. The only drawback here is a surprisingly skimpy wine list with criminally high prices. ✕ *150 W. San Juan Ave.,* ☎ *970/728–6232. Reservations advised. AE, MC, V. No lunch.*

$$$–$$$$ **Campagna.** Vincent and Joline Esposito transport diners to a Tuscan
★ farmhouse, from the decor (open kitchen, oak and terra-cotta floors, turn-of-the-century photos of the Italian countryside, and Tuscan cookbooks) to the assured, classically simple food. Everything is grilled or roasted with garlic, sage, or rosemary in olive oil, allowing the natural juices and flavors to emerge. Wild mushrooms (porcini or portobello) and wild boar chops are among the enticing possibilities. Finish it off with a letter-perfect tiramisù or hazelnut torte and a fiery homemade grappa. ✕ *435 W. Pacific Ave.,* ☎ *970/728–6190. Reservations advised. AE, MC, V. No lunch.*

$$$$ **Evangeline's.** This intimate boîte has only 30 seats, giving the rather formal dining room dressed in primrose and mint the air of an elegant private soiree. Chef Moore's food is haute Cajun; the nightly changing menu might include oysters Rockefeller, creamed spinach and feta ravioli in roasted red pepper sauce, or a classic shrimp Creole. There is also a $39 prix-fixe meal. ✕ *646 Mountain Village Blvd.,* ☎ *970/728–9717. Reservations advised. AE, MC, V. No lunch.*

$$$–$$$$ **The PowderHouse.** Tony Clinco (a former Golden Gloves winner who
★ found another use for his hands) bills his food as "Rocky Mountain Cuisine." In reality, this is classic Italian married to wild game. Among the winners are pheasant ravioli; smoked buffalo sausage; and the game special—stuffed quail, venison chop, and marinated elk, each in its own sauce. ✕ *226 W. Colorado Ave.,* ☎ *970/728–3622. Reservations advised. AE, MC, V.*

$$$ 221 South Oak Bistro. It had to happen that an ever more trendy Telluride would eventually have a "bistro." This one is very pretty, too, with high-tech Southwestern decor, spot-lit peach walls, and a blond-wood bar. Soft jazz wafts through the casually elegant space. The menu sounds exciting—for example, cured salmon and walnut ravioli—but fails to deliver on its promise. Stick to the simpler dishes such as free-range chicken with herb fettuccine and winter squash, or crispy salmon medallions with yummy roast-garlic potatoes and braised Napa cabbage. ✕ *221 S. Oak St.,* ☎ *970/728–9507. Reservations advised. AE, MC, V.*

$$–$$$ McCrady's. This restaurant has been a Charleston, South Carolina, institution since 1778, and the Telluride branch serves up the same enormous portions of haute Southern comfort food prepared with Southwestern flair. Enjoy a drink at the hunting lodge bar (where you'll find a good selection of reasonably priced wines by the glass), then adjourn downstairs to the handsome dining room. Popcorn shrimp with Cajun mayonnaise and crabcakes with salsa and homemade mayonnaise dipping sauces make first-rate appetizers. You can then segue into monkfish with citrus dressing, grits with shrimp and *tasso* (Cajun cured ham) sauce, or smoked pork chops with apple sage chutney. Here's a bonus: two sizes of nearly every entrée are available (5 and 7 oz. for seafood, 6 and 10 or 12 oz. for meats). ✕ *115 W. Colorado Ave.,* ☎ *970/728–4943. Reservations advised. AE, MC, V. No lunch.*

$–$$ Floradora. This Telluride institution is named for two turn-of-the-century ladies of the evening (although locals call it Howie's, after the owner). The rafters are draped with pennants contributed by patrons over the years. The food is nothing special, but you come here for the ambience. Southwestern and Continental specials include Southwest pizza (with three cheeses, sun-dried tomatoes, roasted red peppers, oregano, garlic, and salsa), blackened catch of the day, and tropical chicken. ✕ *103 W. Colorado Ave.,* ☎ *970/728–3888. Reservations accepted. AE, MC, V.*

$–$$ Roma Bar and Café. In operation since 1897, this restaurant offers tremendous value and an incomparable air of history. The 1860 Brunswick bar, with marvelous 12-foot-high mirrors, has seen everything, including cowboys riding their mounts up to the stools. Flappers even brewed rotgut whiskey in the cellar during Prohibition. The pasta specials are terrific, as are the burgers. ✕ *133 E. Colorado Ave.,* ☎ *970/728–3622. Reservations accepted. AE, MC, V.*

$ Eddie's. This ultracasual spot serves up heaping helpings of pastas, homemade soups and stews, and gourmet pizzas (choose from more than two dozen toppings). The excellent landscape photos that adorn the walls are for sale. ✕ *300 W. Colorado Ave.,* ☎ *970/728–5335. Reservations accepted. AE, MC, V. Closed Mon.*

$ Fat Alley's BBQ. A few family-style tables and benches, along with some old skis and ceiling fans fill this popular spot owned by Tony Clinco of the PowderHouse (*see above*). Messy, mouthwatering ribs are complemented by delectable side dishes like red beans and rice, baked sweet potatoes, snap pea and feta salad, and coleslaw. A few beers and wines are available, in addition to homemade iced tea and pink lemonade. ✕ *122 S. Oak St.,* ☎ *970/728–3985. No reservations. AE, MC, V.*

Lodging

Whatever your lodging preference, you'll be able to find a suitable property in Southwest Colorado: from motor inns in Durango to elegant Telluride bed-and-breakfasts to upscale resort developments such as Tamarron, outside Purgatory/Durango, and The Peaks at Telluride. Winter is high season in Crested Butte, Purgatory, and Telluride (with rates dropping by as much as 50% in summer despite the wealth of festivals and events). Properties in Durango, Ouray, Silverton, and the Mesa Verde area work in the opposite fashion, with many accommodations closing for all or part of the winter. Recently, properties in outlying communities such as Ridgway, Montrose, and Gunnison began offering half-price lift tickets for guests who plan to ski. Unless otherwise noted, rooms have a full bath and include cable TV and phones.

Condominiums throughout Colorado generally provide excellent value, especially for families. All the companies listed in the Lodging section represent top-notch properties, usually within walking distance of the slopes in winter (or major activities in summer). All have full kitchen and cable TV, most with Jacuzzi and/or pool access, among other amenities. For rates *see* the Lodging chart *in* Colorado Essentials, *below.*

Alamosa

$–$$ **Best Western Alamosa Inn.** This sprawling, well-maintained complex, scattered over several blocks, is the best hotel bet in town. Rooms are spacious and offer the standard amenities. ☎ *1919 Main St., 81101,* ☎ *719/589–4943. 121 rooms. Restaurant, bar, indoor pool. AE, D, DC, MC, V.*

$ **Cottonwood Inn B&B.** This pretty cranberry-and-azure house was built
★   in 1908 and lovingly refurbished by an Adams State professor and his wife. Public rooms feature both original and reproduction Stickley woodwork and furnishings; regional photographs and watercolors (most of them for sale) grace the walls. In the four sunny rooms with country-French washed walls, there are hand-painted florettes, framed knits, weavings, dried flowers, lace curtains, and predominantly wicker furnishings. There are also four apartments, two with wonderful oak floors and all with claw-foot tubs. A complimentary breakfast is provided for guests. ☎ *123 San Juan Ave., 81101,* ☎ *719/589–3882 or 800/955– 2623,* 𝔽𝔸𝕏 *719/589–6437. 4 rooms, 2 with private bath; 4 apartments. AE, DC, MC, V.*

Antonito

$ **Conejos River Guest Ranch.** On the Conejos River, this peaceful, family-friendly retreat offers private fishing and wagon rides. The recently remodeled cabins—all fully equipped—and guest rooms are pleasantly outfitted with ranch-style decor, including lodgepole pine furnishings. A complimentary breakfast is provided. ☎ *25390 Rte. 17, 81120,* ☎ *719/376–2464. 6 cabins, 8 rooms. Restaurant, horseback riding, fishing. No credit cards.*

Cortez

$ **Anasazi Motor Inn.** This is definitely the nicest hotel on the strip, mostly because its air-conditioned rooms are spacious and pleasantly decorated in Southwestern colors. Children under 18 stay free in their parents' room. ☎ *666 S. Broadway, 81312,* ☎ *970/565–3773 or 800/972–6232,* 𝔽𝔸𝕏 *970/565–1027. 89 rooms. Restaurant, bar, pool, hot tub, meeting rooms, airport shuttle. AE, D, DC, MC, V.*

Creede

$ **Creede Hotel.** A relic of the silver days, this charming 1890s structure has been fully restored, and the rooms offer the usual Victoriana. The gracious dining room serves excellent meals, in addition to the complimentary gourmet breakfast. ☎ *1892 Main St., 81130,* ☎ *719/658– 2608. 4 rooms. Restaurant. D, MC, V. Closed winter.*

Crested Butte

$$–$$$ **Grande Butte Hotel.** This ski-in/ski-out property offers all the amenities and facilities of other luxury hotels at down-to-earth prices. Huge rooms are decorated in muted earth and pastel tones, and feature a wet bar, whirlpool tubs, and private balcony. The public spaces are dotted with towering plants, regional paintings and sculptures, and oversized overstuffed armchairs and sofas. Giovanni's, the gourmet restaurant, is excellent: Oddly enough, conventional fare such as saltimbocca is far surpassed by such creative, adventurous dishes as ravioli in raspberry sauce and penne with duck breast. Regrettably, while service remains as friendly as ever, the young staff can also be slow and inefficient. ☎ *Box 5006, Mt. Crested Butte 81225,* ☎ *970/349–7561 or 800/642–4422,* FAX *970/349–6332. 210 rooms, 53 suites. 3 restaurants, 2 bars, indoor pool, outdoor hot tub, sauna, laundry service, meeting rooms. AE, D, MC, V.*

$$ **Crested Butte Club.** This quaint, stylish inn is a Victorian dream: Each
★ sumptuous, individually furnished room contains a brass or mahogany bed, Axeminster carpets, and cherry-wood antiques or good-quality reproductions. All have spacious modern bathrooms and little extras such as footed copper and brass tubs or gas fireplaces. The downstairs bar is similarly delightful, but best of all is the full health club on the property, so you don't have to go far to soothe your weary muscles after a hard day's hiking or skiing. The Continental breakfast is complimentary. ☎ *512 2nd St., 81224,* ☎ *970/349–6655,* FAX *970/349–6654. 7 rooms. Bar, indoor lap pool, health club. AE, MC, V.*

$$ **Irwin Lodge.** The Irwin touts itself as "the best-kept secret in the Rock-
★ ies," and it's no idle boast. Talk about seclusion: In winter you must take a thrilling snowmobile ride on several switchbacks to reach this aerie, nearly 1,000 feet above (and 8 miles from) Crested Butte. The lodge sits 10,700 feet above sea level, on a remote ridge overlooking Lake Irwin and the Sangre de Cristo range. Several cozy lounge areas circle a magnificent stone fireplace at the entrance. The smallish, charmingly rustic rooms are tastefully appointed, with pine walls and mahogany furnishings. A hearty breakfast is included in the rate, and a fine Continental lunch and dinner, served family style, are available at a nominal surcharge. The repeat clientele knows that this is the premier place in America to learn powder skiing, as the surrounding area gets an average of 500 inches of fluffy white stuff a year. A Snowcat will take you up to 12,000 feet, with a 2,000-foot vertical. (Nonguests can make arrangements on a limited basis.) Summer activities include fishing, horseback riding, and mountain biking. With no ☎ or TV, just a shortwave radio to civilization, the Irwin represents the ultimate in isolation. ☎ *Box 457, Crested Butte 81224,* ☎ *970/349–5308. 24 rooms, 1 suite. Restaurant, bar, hiking, horseback riding, fishing, mountain bikes, snowmobiling. AE, MC, V.*

CONDOMINIUMS

Crested Butte Vacations (Box A, Mt. Crested Butte 81225, ☎ 800/544–8448, FAX 970/349–2250) can make arrangements for all condominiums on the mountain.

Durango/Purgatory

$$$–$$$$ **Tamarron.** This handsome development, nestled on 750 acres of pro-
★ tected land surrounded by the San Juan National Forest, harmonizes beautifully with the environment; the main lodge seems an extension of the surrounding cliffs. Units are an attractive blend of frontier architecture and Southwestern decor, and nearly all feature a fireplace, a full kitchen, and a terrace. Tamarron is famed for one of the country's most ravishing championship golf courses, and tennis and horse-

back riding are also available. Le Canyon, the gourmet restaurant, is a romantic spot that specializes in table-side pyrotechnics. ☎ *Drawer 3131, Durango 81302 (approx. 10 mi north of Durango),* ☎ *970/259–2000 or 800/678–1000,* FAX *970/259–0745. 411 units. 3 restaurants, 2 bars, indoor-outdoor pool, hot tub, spa, 18-hole golf course, 3 tennis courts, horseback riding, children's programs (ages 4–12). AE, D, DC, MC, V.*

$$–$$$ **Purgatory Village Hotel.** This luxurious ski-in/ski-out property offers
★ both hotel rooms and condos, all decorated with Southwestern flair, including Native American rugs and prints. The condos include full kitchen, private balcony, washer/dryer, whirlpool bath, in-room sauna, and wood-burning fireplace. ☎ *Box 2002, Durango 81302 (located in Purgatory),* ☎ *970/247–9000 or 800/879–7974,* FAX *970/385–2116. 271 units. Restaurant, bar, pool, hot tub, sauna, steam room, exercise room. AE, D, DC, MC, V.*

$$ **Strater Hotel.** This Victorian beauty originally opened in 1887 and has
★ been lovingly restored. Inside, Henry's restaurant and the Diamond Belle Saloon sport crystal chandeliers, beveled windows, original oak beams, flocked wallpaper, and plush velour curtains. The individually decorated rooms are swooningly exquisite: After all, the hotel owns the largest collection of Victorian walnut antiques in the world and even has its own wood-carving shop on site to create exact period reproductions. All rooms feature intricate tracery and wainscoting, hand-carved armoires and beds, brass lamps, and down pillows. Your room might have entertained Butch Cassidy, Gerald Ford, Francis Ford Coppola, Louis L'Amour (he wrote *The Sacketts* here), JFK, or Marilyn Monroe (the latter two at separate times). ☎ *699 Main Ave., Durango 81301,* ☎ *970/247–4431 or 800/247–4431,* FAX *970/259–2208. 93 rooms. Restaurant, bar, hot tub. AE, MC, V.*

$–$$ **New Rochester Hotel/Leland House.** Mother-and-son team Diane
★ and Kirk Komick restored these two Victorian beauties that sit across the street from each other in downtown Durango, both in high Western style. The Rochester had served as a flophouse, and the Komicks rescued some of the original furniture (you can still see water and cigarette stains on the beautifully carved walnut and cherry armoires and tables), creating an atmosphere of funky chic. Steamer trunks, hand-painted settees, wagon-wheel chandeliers, and quilts contribute to the authentic feel. The halls are decorated with photos of stars and original posters of movies shot in the area, including *Butch Cassidy and the Sundance Kid* and *City Slickers;* these films provide the names for the hotel's rooms, as well. Denver and Rio Grande train windows convert the back porch into a parlor car, and gas lamps amidst towering maple trees grace the courtyard. The Leland House utilizes Southwestern pastel fabrics, weathered wood sculpture, old photos of Durango, and antique suitcases to create a similar effect. All rooms and suites here include kitchenette or full kitchen. The Leland House has a gourmet complimentary breakfast, while the Rochester's is Continental. ☎ *New Rochester Hotel: 726 E. 2nd Ave., 81301,* ☎ *970/385–1920 or 800/664–1920,* FAX *970/385–1967. 13 rooms, 2 suites (one with kitchen). Massage. MC, V.* ☎ *Leland House: 721 E. 2nd Ave.,* ☎ *and fax same as above. 4 rooms, 6 suites. Restaurant. MC, V.*

$ **Comfort Inn.** This is one of the nicer properties along Durango's strip because it's clean, comfortable, and has sizable rooms decorated in subdued teals and maroons. ☎ *2930 N. Main St., Durango 81301,* ☎ *970/259–5373. 48 rooms. Pool, hot tub. AE, D, DC, MC, V.*

CONDOMINIUMS
In addition to **Tamarron** and **Purgatory Village Hotel** (*see above* for both), there are fine condo units at **Cascade Village** (50827 U.S. 550 N, Durango 81301, ☎ 970/259–3500 or 800/525–0896; located in Purgatory).

Gunnison

$–$$ **Mary Lawrence Inn.** This restored Victorian is an unexpected and welcome delight in Gunnison. The oversize rooms are furnished with tasteful antiques and Victorian touches such as lace curtains, hand-stencilled walls, handmade quilts, vivid local art, and potpourri. A complimentary gourmet breakfast is offered each morning, along with a smile and advice for the day's adventures from owners Pat and Jim Kennedy. ✆ *601 N. Taylor St., 81230,* ☎ *970/641–3343. 5 rooms (4 with shared bath). MC, V.*

Lake City

$–$$ **Old Carson Inn.** This peaceful log cabin is nestled among stands of towering aspen and spruce. Don and Judy Berry offer five rooms brimming with rustic charm and nicely appointed with down comforters and private bath. The complimentary country breakfast, served family style, should get you off to a good start. ✆ *P.O. Box 144, County Road 30, Hinsdale 81235,* ☎ *970/944–2511. 5 rooms. Hot tub. MC, V.*

Mesa Verde

$ **Far View Lodge.** The rustic rooms at this lodge include private balconies with panoramas of Arizona, Utah, and New Mexico. Soothing Southwestern pastels predominate. Another draw here is the hotel's enthusiastic arrangement of guided tours. There are also nightly talks for guests by either a local Native American or an author before a multimedia show on the Anasazi is shown. ✆ *Box 277, Mancos 81328,* ☎ *970/529–4421. 150 rooms. Restaurant. AE, D, DC, MC, V. Closed mid-Oct.–mid-Apr.*

Montrose

$–$$ **Best Western Red Arrow Motor Inn.** This fully outfitted property is one of the nicest in the area, mainly because of the large, prettily appointed rooms adorned in greens and browns with handsome mahogany furnishings. The full baths include jetted whirlpool tubs. ✆ *1702 E. Main St., 81401,* ☎ *970/249–9641 or 800/468–9323,* FAX *970/249–8380. 60 rooms. Restaurant, bar, hot tub, exercise room, laundry service, meeting rooms. AE, DC, D, MC, V.*

$ **Red Barn Motel.** This friendly property offers pleasing, fair-size rooms with all the usual motel amenities, including a coffeemaker. Apart from the Red Arrow, the Red Barn boasts the most facilities in town, at a considerably lower rate than the competition. Children under 12 stay free in their parents' room. ✆ *1417 E. Main St., 81401,* ☎ *970/249–4507. 71 rooms. 2 restaurants, bar, pool, hot tub, sauna, exercise room. AE, DC, D, MC, V.*

Ouray

$$–$$$ **The Damn Yankee.** The balconies of this charming inn offer views of several soaring peaks surrounding the narrow valley in which Ouray is situated. The gracious parlor holds a baby-grand piano and a woodburning fireplace, and informal musicales by guests are not uncommon. Rooms are a pleasing blend of english country antique and modern comfort, and all include beds draped with down comforters. The third-floor sitting room is always stocked with snacks and soft drinks. In the morning a complimentary gourmet breakfast is provided for guests. ✆ *100*

6th St., 81427, ☎ *970/325–4219 or 800/845–7512. 8 rooms. Hot tub. AE, MC, V.*

$$ Box Canyon Lodge and Hot Springs. The private mineral spring is the attraction here, used first by the Ute, then by the Coger Sanitarium (formerly on site). Soak away your cares in two redwood tubs full of steaming 103–107-degree water, with the stunning mountain views around you. The rooms are nondescript, but modern and comfortable, with all amenities. ☎ *45 3rd St., 81427,* ☎ *970/325–4981. 38 rooms. Hot springs. AE, DC, MC, V.*

$ St. Elmo Hotel. This tiny 1898 hostelry was originally a haven for "min-★ ers down on their luck," so the story goes, thanks to its original owner Kitty Heit, who couldn't resist a sob story. Her son's ghost reputedly hovers about protectively. The rooms are awash with polished wood, stained glass, brass or mahogany beds, marble-top armoires, and other antiques. A complimentary breakfast buffet is served in a sunny parlor. The Bon Ton restaurant, Ouray's best, serves fine Continental cuisine with an Italian flair. ☎ *426 Main St., 81427,* ☎ *970/325–4951. 9 rooms. Restaurant, hot tub, sauna, recreation room. AE,D, MC, V.*

Pagosa Springs

$ Davidson's Country Inn B&B. This three-story log cabin is located on a 32-acre working ranch in the middle of Colorado's stunning San Juan mountains. The location is perfect, just 20 minutes from Wolf Creek Ski Area (which has no lodging of its own). Rooms are comfortable and crammed with family heirlooms and antiques. A complimentary full breakfast is served. ☎ *2763 Highway 160 East, 81147,* ☎ *970/264–5863. 8 rooms, 4 with shared bath. Recreation room. MC, V.*

Silverton

$ Wingate Guest House. The well-traveled Judy Graham (she hails from Wisconsin, has lived in New York, Chicago, and northern California, and has taught at two universities) is the genial hostess of this quaint inn. A prominent landscape artist as well, she adorns the walls of the inn with her own works and those of her friends, along with family photos dating from the Civil War; the entire effect is both sophisticated and homey. The breezy front porch overlooks a majestic thirteener. Large sunny rooms are filled with antiques, and sport down pillows and comforters, as well as an eclectic library culled from Judy's journeys. A complimentary breakfast is served. ☎ *1045 Snowden St.,* ☎ *and fax 970/387–5520. 5 rooms with shared bath. No credit cards.*

$ Wyman Hotel. This wonderful 1902 red-sandstone building has 24-inch-thick walls, cathedral ceilings, and arched windows. The attractive rooms all contain period antiques and pretty wallpapers, brass lamps, and VCR. If the Wyman is full, the owners also run the **Alma House** (220 E. 10th St., ☎ 970/387–5336; open year-round), a charming B&B set in a restored 1902 stone house with neat, tasteful rooms and an excellent restaurant. ☎ *1371 Greene St.,* ☎ *970/387–5372. 18 rooms. AE, MC, V. Closed mid-Oct.–early May.*

Telluride

$$$$ The Peaks at Telluride Resort and Spa. The pastel-color, prisonlike exterior and lapses in service can be excused at this ski-in/ski-out luxury resort, thanks to its invigorating, revitalizing spa facilities. The setting is glorious, dominated by fourteener Mt. Wilson (the peak on the Coors can). Rooms have balconies and are sizable, if somewhat sterile, in Norwegian wood and muted shades of green, with all amenities, including VCR, minibar, and full bath with dual marble vanities and hair dryer. The Peaks spared no expense in the pampering spa (muds and waters for hydrotherapy and facials are imported from Italy's Terme di Saturnia) and fitness center. Extras include a cardiovascular deck and climbing room. In fact, so much money was sunk into the resort, it went into receivership during its first year. The primary effect seems to be the continual turnover of staff (few of them locals) who, though eager, have difficulty answering the simplest questions about the area. ☎ *Country Club Dr.,* ☎ *970/728–6800 or 800/223–6725,* FAX *970/728–6567. 145 rooms, 32 suites. 2 restaurants, bar, indoor-outdoor pool, beauty salon, sauna, spa, 5 tennis courts, exercise room, racquetball, squash, water slide. AE, D, DC, MC, V.*

$$$–$$$$ **Pennington's Mountain Village Inn.** This secluded, exclusive inn fea-
★ tures huge rooms in varying color schemes, with smashing mountain views from private decks, brass beds with cushy down comforters, handcrafted furniture, and stocked minifridges. The pampering includes concierge service, gourmet breakfast, and afternoon hors d'oeuvres. ☎ *100 Pennington Ct., off Mountain Village Blvd.,* ☎ *970/728–5337 or 800/543–1437. 9 rooms, 3 suites. Lobby lounge, hot tub, steam room, recreation room, laundry service. AE, MC, V.*

$$$ **Ice House.** This property offers an appealing blend of Scandinavian and Southwestern decor: blond woods, jade carpets, fabrics in beiges, forest greens, and maroons, Native American tapestries and polished wood ceilings. The spacious rooms feature cable TV, oversized tubs, balconies, and minibars. The hotel provides a free Continental breakfast and a place to store your skis. Best of all, the Oak Street lift is just a little more than a block away. ☎ *310 S. Fir St.,* ☎ *970/728–6300 or 800/544–3436,* FAX *970/728–6358. 42 rooms, 16 2- and 3-bedroom condominiums. Hot tub, sauna. AE, D, DC, MC, V.*

$$$ **San Sophia B&B.** This is a Victorian-style inn, replete with turrets and gingerbread trim, opened in 1989 by Gary and Diane Eschmann, escapees from the corporate life in Iowa City, Iowa. Pristine mountain light streams into every room, warmly accented with whitewashed oak woodwork. Rooms are on the small side, but luxurious, and offer contemporary brass beds with down comforters, tables and nightstands all handcrafted by Colorado artisans, Gary's stylish black-and-white landscape photographs, skylights in the tiled bathrooms, and stained glass windows over the oversized tubs. The color scheme differs from room to room, but favors desert pastels throughout: You might find terra-cotta with teal accents in one room, and mint or grape with blue trim in another. The amiable staff is extremely helpful. The inn is known for its fabulous gourmet breakfasts and après-ski treats. ☎ *330 W. Pacific St.,* ☎ *970/728–3001 or 800/537–4781. 16 rooms. Hot tub. AE, MC, V.*

$–$$ **New Sheridan Hotel.** William Jennings Bryan delivered his rousing "Cross of Gold" speech here in 1896, garnering a presidential nomination in the process. (He was later defeated by McKinley.) Until 1994, when it was purchased by the Four Sisters Inns, the noted California chain, the New Sheridan seemed frozen in time, right down to shared baths and funky furnishings. Now it's new indeed, albeit in tasteful period style. Every room has its own bath, phone, ceiling fan, and cable TV. Decor favors exposed brick walls, old tintypes, marble-top dressing tables, faux Tiffany, crystal, or fringed lamps, and red velour love seats. A complimentary breakfast and afternoon tea complete the picture of fin de siècle gracious living. The lobby has been expanded, and the two historic dining rooms reopened. Other planned additions at press time included a meeting room, a fitness room, and ski lockers. Fortunately, the gorgeous Victorian bar, a local favorite, remains untouched. ⚏ *231 W. Colorado Ave.,* ☎ *970/728–4351. 32 rooms. 2 restaurants, bar. AE, MC, V.*

CONDOMINIUMS
Telluride Central Reservations (☎ 800/525–3455) handles all properties at Telluride Mountain Village, and several in town. **Resort Rentals** (Box 1278, Telluride 81435, ☎ 800/LETS–SKI (800/538–7754) offers several top-notch accommodations in town.

The Arts and Nightlife

The Arts
FILM
The Telluride Film Festival, in September, is considered one of the world's leading showcases of foreign films.

MUSIC
The **Montrose Pavilion** (1800 Pavilion Dr., ☎ 970/249–7015) includes a 602-seat auditorium where well-known musicians, comedians, dance companies, and regional orchestras often perform.

Telluride offers numerous festivals during the summer, including the monstrous jazz and bluegrass festivals.

THEATER
In Durango, the **Diamond Circle Theater** (699 Main Ave., ☎ 970/247–4431) stages rip-roaring melodramas, and the **Durango Lively Arts Co.** (Durango Arts Ctr., 835 Main Ave., ☎ 970/259–2606) presents fine community theater productions. In Silverton, **A Theatre Group** (Miners Union Theatre, Greene St., ☎ 970/387–5337) presents a varied repertory season.

Nightlife
BARS AND LOUNGES
In Durango, the hot spot is the **Diamond Belle Saloon** (Strater Hotel, 699 Main Ave., ☎ 970/247–4431), whose antique, gold-leafed filigree bar, honky-tonk piano player, and waitresses dressed as 1880s saloon girls pack them in.

Leimgruber's Bierstube and Restaurant (573 W. Pacific Ave., ☎ 970/728–4663) is arguably Telluride's most popular après-ski hangout, thanks to gemütlich owner Christel Leimgruber, a wonderful Bavarian ambience enhanced by barmaids in dirndls right out of "The Student Prince," and a clientele that seems on the verge of launching into "The Drinking Song." Leimgruber's offers traditional Alpine food like mixed German and wild-game sausage plates, mouth-puckering sauerbraten, and, of course, apple strudel. If you only want a brew, stop by to down a Paulaner or hoist a glass boot, which holds more than a liter of beer. The elegant turn-of-the-century bar at the **Sheridan Hotel** (231 W. Colorado Ave., ☎ 970/728–4351), the billiards parlor at **Swede-Finn Hall** (472 W. Pacific Ave., ☎ 970/728–2085), and the huge fireplaces at **Club Biota** (112 E. Colorado Ave., ☎ 970/728–6132) are the other popular après-ski nightspots.

In Crested Butte, **Kochevar's** (127 Elk Ave., ☎ 970/349–6756), a hand-hewn 1896 log cabin, is a classic pool hall–saloon. The other popular bar in town is the **Wooden Nickel** (222 Elk Ave., ☎ 970/349–6350), which has two happy hours (daily 3–6 and 10:30–midnight).

CASINOS
Colorado's first tribal gaming facility, offering limited-stakes gambling—slots, poker (video and live), bingo, and 21—is the **Ute Moun-**

tain Casino (3 Weeminuche Drive at Yellow Hat, Towaoc 81334, ☎ 970/565–8800; open daily 8 AM–4 AM). A second facility has opened at the **Sky Ute Lodge and Casino** (Ignacio, ☎ 970/563–4531), 25 miles southeast of Durango.

COUNTRY AND WESTERN

In Durango, **Sundance Saloon** (601 E. 2nd St., ☎ 970/259–2985) is a foot-stomping place to "scoot your boot." In Mancos, the **Mancos Social Club** (Main St., no ☎) can be loads of fun, but can also get wild and sometimes hairy. Ridgway's **The Big Barn** (Trail Town, U.S. 550 and Rte. 62, ☎ 970/626–3600) is just that, offering a 1,000-square-foot dance floor, free video country dance lessons, and live music.

DINNER SHOWS

Bar D Chuckwagon (8080 County Road 250, East Animas Valley, ☎ 970/247–5753) serves barbecued beef, beans, and biscuits, along with a heaping helping of their Bar D Wranglers singing group.

DISCOS

Yesterdays (Holiday Inn, 800 S. Camino del Rio, Durango, ☎ 970/247–5393) has a dance floor and live DJ nightly.

JAZZ CLUBS

In Durango, the **Pelican's Nest** (656 Main Ave., ☎ 970/247–4431) is a cool joint for hot jazz, with a sedate Victorian decor. The funky clientele wears anything from cowboy hats to berets. Telluride's **Café Kokopelli** (16 E. Colorado Ave., ☎ 970/728–6101) is a way-cool coffeehouse that dispenses java by day and jazz at night in an attractive space with brick and stone walls, black-and-white photos, and stained glass windows.

ROCK CLUBS

Farquahrt's (725 Main Ave., Durango, ☎ 970/247–5440) is decorated with antiques, but attracts a lively, youthful crowd that likes to rock and roll to the best local bands. There's also a "ski lodge" version at **Purgatory Mountain Village** (☎ 970/247–9000, ext. 3123).

In Mt. Crested Butte, **Rafters** (☎ 970/349–2298) is packed to the rafters of this big barn with cheap eats, strong drinks, and loud music (often live on weekends).

In Telluride, **One World Café** (114 E. Colorado Ave., ☎ 970/728–5530) is an eclectic club: Japanese fans and lanterns contrast intriguingly with the building's original, corrugated tin roof and stone- and brickwork. Tasty Thai is served in the front restaurant–art gallery. Exquisite stained glass doors lead to the Conga Room disco, where the DJ spins everything from Motown to salsa, and hot funk and ska bands perform regularly. The **Last Dollar Saloon** (100 E. Colorado Ave., ☎ 970/728–4800) couldn't be less chic (and couldn't care less); when it's not a pool hall–saloon, it's the best venue for local rock bands. **Excelsior Café** (200 W. Colorado Ave., ☎ 970/728–4250) is the spot to hear the best in folk rock.

SINGLES CLUBS

Rafters in Crested Butte and **Farquahrt's** in Purgatory/Durango (*see* Rock Clubs, *above*) are the closest things to classic pick-up joints in Southwest Colorado.

Southwest Colorado Essentials

Arriving and Departing by Plane

AIRPORTS AND AIRLINES

Durango: The **Durango-La Plata Airport** (☎ 970/247–8143) receives daily flights from America West (☎ 800/247–5692), Mesa Airlines (☎ 800/637–2247), and United Express (☎ 800/241–6522).

Gunnison: Delta (☎ 800/221–1212), United Express, and American (☎ 800/433–7300; nonstop from Chicago, Dallas, and San Jose) fly into **Gunnison County Airport** (☎ 970/641–0526), which also serves Crested Butte.

Montrose: **Montrose Airport** (☎ 970/249–3203) is served by United and America West.

Telluride: **Telluride Regional Airport** (☎ 970/728–5313) welcomes flights from Delta, Mesa Airlines (☎ 800/MESA–AIR [800/637–2247]), and connecting flights from major airlines. At press time, there was speculation about which airlines those would be.

Between the Airport and the Resort

BY SHUTTLE

Crested Butte: **Alpine Express** (☎ 970/641–5074 or 800/822–4844); Durango: **Durango Transportation** (☎ 970/247–4161 or 800/626–2066); Montrose: **Western Express Taxi** (☎ 970/249–8880); Telluride: **Skip's Taxi** (☎ 970/728–6667) and **Telluride Transit** (☎ 970/728–6000). Shuttles average $15–$20 per person.

Arriving and Departing by Car and Bus

BY CAR

If you're entering Colorado from the south, U.S. 550, U.S. 160, and U.S. 666 access the Four Corners region. From the east or west, I–70 (U.S. 6) intersects U.S. 50 South in Grand Junction, to reach the San Juans and Four Corners area. From the north, I–25 intersects in Denver with I–70, for a long drive to U.S. 50. Alternatively, U.S. 40 enters northwest Colorado from Utah, connecting with Route 64 in Dinosaur, then Route 139 south in Rangely, to I–70 East to Grand Junction.

San Luis Valley can be reached via U.S. 160 from both the west (direct from Durango) and the east (via I–25), or via U.S. 285 from New Mexico.

BY BUS

Greyhound Lines (☎ 800/231–2222) serves most of the major towns in the region via Salt Lake City, Denver, or Albuquerque/Santa Fe.

Getting Around

BY CAR

The main roads are Route 135 between Crested Butte and Gunnison; U.S. 50 linking Poncha Springs, Gunnison, Montrose, and Delta; Route 149 between Gunnison, Lake City, and Creede; U.S. 550 from Montrose to Ridgway; Route 62 and Route 145 linking Ridgway with Telluride, Dolores, and Cortez; Route 110 running from Ridgway through Ouray and Silverton to Durango; and U.S. 160, the closest thing to a major highway in the area, from Cortez to Durango via the Mesa Verde National Park north entrance.

BY BUS OR SHUTTLE

In Crested Butte, the **Crested Butte Shuttle** (no ☎) runs regularly between the town and the ski area.

In Durango, **Durango Lift** (☎ 970/259–5438) has regular bus service up and down Main Street, as well as to Purgatory Ski Area during ski season.

In Telluride, **The Tellu-Ride** (☎ 970/728–5700) offers free shuttle service between the town of Telluride and Mountain Village, as well as down-valley service to Norwood.

BY TAXI

In most cases you'll need to call for a cab; taxis are plentiful and the wait is only about 15 minutes. **Crested Butte Town Taxi** (☎ 970/349–5543); **Durango Transportation** (Durango, ☎ 970/259–4818); **Montrose Taxi** (Montrose, ☎ 970/249–8880); **Skip's Taxi** (Telluride, ☎ 970/728–6667); and **Telluride Transit** (Telluride, ☎ 970/728–6000).

Guided Tours

ORIENTATION

Adventures to the Edge (Crested Butte, ☎ 970/349–5219) creates customized treks, ski tours and alpine ascents in the Crested Butte area. **ARA Mesa Verde Company** (Mancos, ☎ 970/529–4421) runs three- and six-hour tours into Mesa Verde National Park.

Durango Transportation (☎ 970/259–4818) arranges tours of Mesa Verde, Chaco Canyon, and the San Juan Skyway.

Historic Tours of Telluride (☎ 970/728–6639) provides humorous walking tours of this historic town, enlivening them with stories of famed figures like Butch Cassidy and Jack Dempsey. **San Juan Scenic Jeep Tours** (☎ 970/325–4444 or 800/325–4385) explores the high country in open vehicles that allow unobstructed views.

Sierra Vista Tours (☎ 719/379–3277) offers tours of the area, including the Great Sand Dunes.

NATIVE HERITAGE PROGRAMS

Crow Canyon Archaeological Center. The center promotes greater understanding and appreciation of Anasazi culture by guiding visitors through excavations and botanical studies in the region. Also included in the week-long programs are day trips to isolated canyon sites and hands-on lessons in weaving and pottery-making with Native American artisans. Day programs are also available on a reservation-only basis to families and groups. *23390 County Road K, Cortez 81321, ☎ 970/565–8975 or 800/422–8975.*

Ute Mountain Tribal Park. Native American guides lead grueling hikes into this dazzling primitive repository of Anasazi ruins, including the majestic Tree House cliff dwelling and enchanting Eagle's Nest petroglyphs. It's also a wonderful opportunity to learn more about the Ute tribe's culture and customs. Tours usually start at the Ute Mountain Pottery Plant, 15 miles south of Cortez, on U.S. 666. Overnight camping can also be arranged. *Towaoc 81334, ☎ 970/565–3751, ext. 282.*

Important Addresses and Numbers

HOSPITALS

Cortez: **Southwest Memorial Hospital** (1311 N. Mildred St., ☎ 970/565–6666); Durango: **Mercy Medical Center** (375 E. Park Ave., ☎ 970/247–4311); Gunnison: **Gunnison Valley Hospital** (214 E. Denver Ave., ☎ 970/641–1456); Montrose: **Montrose Memorial Hospital** (800 S. 3rd St., ☎ 970/249–2211); San Luis Valley: **San Luis Valley Regional Medical Center** (106 Blanca Ave., Alamosa, ☎ 719/589–2511); Telluride: **Telluride Medical Center** (500 W. Pacific Ave., ☎ 970/728–3848).

VISITOR INFORMATION

Cortez Area Chamber of Commerce (925 S. Broadway 81321, ☎ 970/565–3414 or 800/346–6528); **Crested Butte–Mt. Crested Butte Chamber of Commerce** (7 Emmons Loop 81321, ☎ 970/349–6438 or 800/545–4505); **Durango Chamber Resort Association** (111 S. Camino del Rio 81302, ☎ 970/247–0312 or 800/525–8855); **Gunnison County Chamber of Commerce** (500 E. Tomichi Ave., 81230, ☎ 970/641–1501 or 800/274–7580); **Lake City Chamber of Commerce** (306 N. Silver St., 81235, ☎ 970/944–2527); **Mesa Verde National Park** (Supt. Mesa Verde Park 81330, ☎ 970/529–4465); **Mesa Verde Country** (Box HH, Cortez 81321, ☎ 800/253–1616); **Montrose Chamber of Commerce** (1519 E. Main St., 81401, ☎ 800/873–0244) and **Visitor Information Center** (2490 S. Townsend Ave., 81401, ☎ 970/249–1726); **Ouray County Chamber** (1222 Main St., 81427, ☎ 970/325–4746 or 800/228–1876); **Pagosa Springs Chamber of Commerce** (402 San Juan St., 81147, ☎ 303/264–2360 or 800/252–2204); **San Luis Valley Information Center** (Box 165, 1st St. and Jefferson Ave., Monte Vista 81144, ☎ 719/672–3355); **San Luis Visitor Center** (Box 9, San Luis 81152, ☎ 719/672–3355); **Silverton Chamber of Commerce** (414 Greene St., 81433, ☎ 970/387–5654 or 800/752–4494); **Southwest Colorado Travel Region** (call 800/933–4340 for travel planner and information); **Telluride Chamber Resort Association** (666 W. Colorado Ave., 81435, ☎ 970/728–3041).

SOUTH CENTRAL COLORADO

The contented residents of Colorado's south central region believe they live in an ideal location, and it's hard to argue with them. To the west, the Rockies form a majestic backdrop; to the east, the plains stretch for miles. Taken together, the setting ensures a mild, sunny climate year-round, and makes skiing and golfing on the same day feasible with no more than a two- or three-hour drive. This easy access to diverse outdoor activities attracts tourists seeking a varied vacation: They can climb the Collegiate Peaks one day, and go white-water rafting on the Arkansas River the next.

For those who enjoy culture and history, south central Colorado has plenty to offer, its territory scouted and explored by the likes of Kit Carson and Zebulon Pike. The haunting remains of the Santa Fe Trail, which guided pioneers westward, weave through the southeastern section of the region. Towns such as Cripple Creek and Trinidad are living history. In fact, residents are so proud of their mining heritage that, despite economic hard times, they've earmarked tax revenues to preserve local landmarks. Equally alluring are cities such as Colorado Springs and Pueblo, numbered among the most contemporary in the West, with sleek shining arts and convention centers.

The region also abounds in natural and man-made wonders, such as the yawning Royal Gorge and its astounding suspension bridge; the eerie sandstone formations of the Garden of the Gods; and the space-age architecture of the U.S. Air Force Academy. However, the most indelible landmark is unquestionably Pikes Peak, from whose vantage point Katharine Lee Bates penned "America the Beautiful." The song's lyrics remain an accurate description of south central Colorado's many glories.

Exploring

Numbers in the margin correspond to points of interest on the Colorado Springs and South Central Colorado maps.

Tour 1: Colorado Springs/Manitou Springs and Pikes Peak

❶ **Colorado Springs,** the state's second-largest city, unfortunately made headlines in 1992 when it was identified as the headquarters for several right-wing groups behind the controversial Amendment 2, which outlawed antidiscrimination legislation that gave protection to the gay and lesbian community. With active and retired military personnel and their families comprising nearly a third of the population, it's no surprise that the Springs is staunchly conservative. Although for a brief time a state boycott was called and the Springs continues to be seen as the place where the controversy snowballed, the political situation hasn't affected tourism significantly. The Springs, after all, has a dazzling array of tourist attractions. Pikes Peak, for instance, is the state's most famous landmark, but only one of the city's many natural and man-made wonders. Other tourist draws include the Cave of the Winds, the Garden of the Gods, and historic neighborhoods such as Manitou Springs and Old Colorado City.

Colorado Springs was created by General William Palmer, president of the Denver & Rio Grande Railroad, as a utopian vision of fine living in the 1870s. The original broad, tree-lined boulevards still grace the southwest quadrant of the city. With the discovery of hot springs in the area, the well-to-do descended on the bustling resort town to take the waters and to enjoy the mild climate and fresh air. It soon earned the monikers "Saratoga of the West" and "Little London," the latter for the snob-appeal of its considerable resident and visiting English population. The discovery of gold at nearby Cripple Creek toward the end of the century signaled another boom for the Springs. In the early part of the 1900s, until the mines petered out just before World War I, the residents' per-capita wealth was the highest in the nation.

After World War II, the city fathers invited the military to move in,
❷ and the city's personality changed drastically. Ironically, the **U.S. Air Force Academy,** which set up camp in 1954, has become one of Colorado's largest tourist attractions. A portion of the academy is most notable for its striking futuristic design; but even more extraordinary are the 18,000 beautiful acres of land that have been dedicated as a game reserve and sprinkled with antique and historic aircraft. Most of the campus is off-limits to civilians, but there is a 13½-mile self-guided tour. At the visitors' center you'll find photo exhibits, a model of a cadet's room, a gift shop, a snack bar, and short videos on Air Force history, cadet training, athletics, and academics. Other tour attractions include a B-52 display, sports facilities, a planetarium, a parade ground (the impressive cadet review takes place daily at noon), and the chapel. The Air Force chapel is easily recognized by its unconventional design, which features 17 spires that resemble sharks' teeth or billowing sails. Catholic, Jewish, and Protestant services can be held simultaneously, without the congregations disturbing one another. *Exit 156B, off I–25 N,* ☎ *719/472–2555.* ☛ *Free.* ☺ *Daily 9–5.*

❸ Directly across I–25 from the north gate of the academy is the **Western Museum of Mining and Industry,** preserving the rich history of mining through comprehensive exhibits of equipment and techniques and hands-on demonstrations, including gold panning. This attraction is an oasis during the summer season, thanks to its stunning mountain

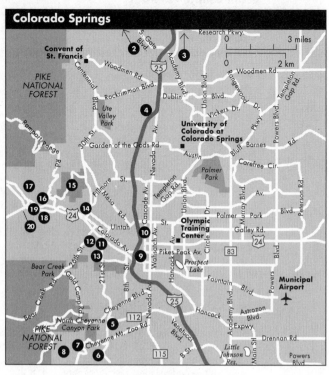

setting. *Exit 156A off I–25 N,* ☎ *719/488–0880.* ☞ *$5 adults, $4 students and senior citizens, $2 children 5–12.* ☉ *Mar.–Nov., Mon.–Sat. 9–4; Sun. noon–4.*

Continue along I–25 South toward downtown and get off at exit 147. A bronze rodeo bull lures visitors to the **Pro Rodeo Hall of Fame and Museum of the American Cowboy.** Even a tenderfoot would get a kick out of this museum, which includes changing displays of Western art; permanent photo exhibits that capture both the excitement of bronco-bustin' and the lonely life of the cowpoke; gorgeous saddles and belt buckles; and multimedia tributes to rodeo's greatest competitors (including the unsung clowns who often save their butts!). *(Exit 147 off 1–25), 101 Pro Rodeo Dr.,* ☎ *719/528–4764.* ☞ *$5 adults, $2 children 5–12.* ☉ *Daily 9–5.*

TIME OUT **Old Chicago** (7115 Commerce Center Dr., ☎ 719/593-7678) is one of many "concept restaurants" popular throughout Colorado. This one features a sports bar in front and a pleasant enclosed atrium and outdoor patio in back. It's a pizza, pasta, and beer (110 varieties) joint, and scores on all counts.

Now take I–25 or Nevada Avenue to the southern end of the city for a glimpse of its posher neighborhoods, of which the pink-stucco, Italianate **Broadmoor,** built in 1918, stands as the most aristocratic symbol. One of the world's great luxury resorts, its 30 buildings and three championship 18-hole golf courses cover 3,500 acres of prime real estate and create a minicity unto itself. It stands as a tribute to the foresight of its original owner, the enterprising Spencer Penrose, one of Colorado Springs' wealthiest (and most conspicuously consuming) philanthropists. Having constructed the zoo, the Cheyenne Mountain

Highway, and Pikes Peak Cog Railway, Penrose is credited with making the town the tourist mecca it is today.

Two superb museums are included in the Broadmoor complex: the **International Skating Hall of Fame and Museum** (20 1st St., ☎ 719/635–5200; ☛ Free; open June–Sept., Mon.–Sat. 10–4 and Oct.–May, weekdays 10–4), which documents the history of the sport and immortalizes its greatest practitioners such as Sonja Henie and the Springs' own Peggy Fleming; and the exquisite **Carriage House** (Lake Circle, no ☎; ☛ Free; open daily 9–noon and 1–5), which displays Penrose's prodigious carriage collection, from broughams (closed carriage with driver outside) to opera buses.

From the Broadmoor, make a left onto Mesa Avenue, and then turn right onto Evans. At the corner of Evans and Pine Grove, a collection of enormous abstract **aluminum sculptures** covers the lawn of Dr. Starr Gideon Kempf. The lampposts, windmills, mythical birds, and other fantastical figures are an ongoing hobby of the doctor's.

Continue along Evans, and then take the Cheyenne Mountain Zoo Road to begin the ascent of Cheyenne Mountain. Aside from stunning panoramic views of the city and Pikes Peak in the distance, the road also offers two major attractions. First up is the **Cheyenne Mountain Zoo,** America's highest zoo, at 7,000 feet, with more than 800 animals amid mossy boulders and ponderosa pines. *Cheyenne Mt. Zoo Rd.,* ☎ 719/475–9555. ☛ *$5.50 adults, $4.50 senior citizens, $3 children 3–11.* ☉ *June–Sept., daily 9–6; Oct.–May, daily 9–5.*

Continue up the spiraling road to the **Will Rogers Shrine of the Sun,** the other big attraction off the zoo road. This "singing" tower guarded by two carved Chinese dogs was dedicated in 1937 after the tragic plane crash that claimed Rogers' life. Its interior is painted with all manner of Western scenes (in which Rogers and Spencer Penrose figure prominently) and is plastered with photos and the homespun sayings of America's favorite cowboy. *Cheyenne Mt. Zoo Rd., no ☎.* ☛ *Free with zoo ticket.* ☉ *Memorial Day–Labor Day, daily 9–5:30; Labor Day–Memorial Day, daily 9–4:30.*

At the base of the mountain, turn west on Cheyenne Road and follow the signs to **Seven Falls.** The road up to this transcendent series of seven cascades is touted as the "grandest mile of scenery in Colorado." Considering the state's splendors, that may be an exaggeration, but the red-rock canyon *is* stunning—though no more so than the falls themselves, plummeting into a tiny emerald pool. A set of 265 steep steps leads to the top, but there is an elevator for those who don't wish to walk. ☎ 719/632–0765. ☛ *$4 adults, $2 children under 13.* ☉ *Daily 9–5.*

Take Cheyenne Mountain Zoo Road back into town and turn north on Nevada Avenue. Colorado Springs' handsome downtown contains many historically significant buildings, including the old El Paso County Courthouse, now the admirable **Pioneers Museum.** This repository of artifacts relating to the entire Pikes Peak area is most notable for the wonderful special exhibits it mounts (or are loaned on tour from institutions such as the Smithsonian), such as a quilt competition commemorating the 100th anniversary of the song "America the Beautiful." *215 S. Tejon St.,* ☎ 719/578–6650. ☛ *Free.* ☉ *Mon.–Sat. 10–5, Sun. 1–5.*

A few blocks north is the **Colorado Springs Fine Arts Center,** an exemplary space that includes a performing-arts theater, an art school, and a room devoted to the work and life of famed Western artist Charles Russell. Also at the center are a handsome sculpture garden, a surprisingly fine permanent collection of modern art, and rotating exhibits that highlight the cultural contributions of the area's diverse ethnic groups. *30 W. Dale St.,* ☎ *719/634–5581.* ☛ *$3 adults, $1.50 senior citizens and students, $1 children 5–12.* ☉ *Tues.–Fri. 9–5, Sat. 10–5, Sun. 1–5.*

Cross under I–25 to Colorado Avenue and take it west, turning left on 21st Street, which you'll follow to the cluster of three wildly different attractions: Ghost Town, the Van Briggle Art Pottery Factory and Showroom, and the Hall of Presidents Living Wax Studio.

⑪ If you can't make it to Buckskin Joe Park and Railway (*see* What to See and Do with Children, *below*), then visit **Ghost Town,** a complete, authentic Western town with a sheriff's office, general store, saloon, and blacksmith. You can play a real player piano and nickelodeon. *400 S. 21st St.,* ☎ *719/634–0696.* ☛ *$3.95 adults, $2 children 6–16.* ☉ *May–Labor Day, Mon.–Sat. 9–6, Sun. noon–6; Sept.–Apr., Mon.–Sat. noon–5, Sun. 10–5.*

⑫ Right across the way is the famous **Van Briggle Art Pottery Factory and Showroom,** in operation since the turn of the century. Van Briggle ceramic work is admired for its graceful lines and pure, vibrant glazes. A free tour of the facility is offered, culminating—naturally—in the mind-boggling showroom. *600 S. 21st St.,* ☎ *719/633–7729.* ☛ *Free.* ☉ *Mon.–Sat. 8:30–5.*

⑬ One block south is the admittedly hokey but enjoyable **Hall of Presidents Living Wax Studio,** with more than 100 wax figures crafted at the famed Madame Tussaud's in London. The exhibits run from Washington at Trenton through Jefferson signing the "Declaration of Independence," right up to the Clintons (though there are surprising omissions, such as Herbert Hoover, for example). There's also an Enchanted Forest, alive with storybook characters from Peter Pan to Pinocchio. *1050 S. 21st St.,* ☎ *719/635–3553.* ☛ *$4 adults, $2 children 5–12.* ☉ *Oct.-May, daily 10–5; June–Sept., daily 9–9.*

⑭ Back on Colorado Avenue you'll find yourself in **Old Colorado City,** once a separate, rowdier town where miners caroused, today it's a National Historic Landmark District whose restored buildings house the city's choicest galleries and boutiques. Continue west along Colorado Avenue to one of the region's most riveting sights: the gnarled jutting ⑮ spires and sensuously abstract monoliths of the **Garden of the Gods.** These magnificent, eroded red-sandstone formations were sculpted more than 300 million years ago. The new (1995) visitor center has several geologic, historic, and hands-on displays.

Follow the road as it loops through the Garden of the Gods, past such oddities as the Three Graces, the Siamese Twins, and the Kissing Camels. High Point, near the south entrance, provides camera hounds with the ultimate photo-op: the jagged formations framing Pikes Peak.

As you exit the park, take U.S. 24 West; on your right are two popular tourist attractions: the Cliff Dwellings Museum and the Cave of ⑯ the Winds. The **Cliff Dwellings Museum,** an obvious tourist trap, is something of an embarrassment to locals. It's replete with Native American flute music piped through the chambers, but this minireplica of Mesa Verde is a decent (and educational) substitute if you haven't seen the real thing. *U.S. 24,* ☎ *719/685–5242.* ☛ *$3 adults, $2 children 12 and under.* ☉ *June–Aug., daily 9–8; May and Sept., daily 9–6; Mar.–Apr. and Oct.–Dec., daily 9–5; Jan.–Feb., weekends 9–5.*

⓱ The **Cave of the Winds** was discovered by two boys in 1880, and has been exploited as a tourist sensation ever since. The entrance is through the requisite "trading post," but once inside the cave you'll forget the hype and commercialism. You'll pass through grand chambers with such names as the Crystal Palace, Oriental Garden, the Old Curiosity Shop, the Temple of Silence, and the Valley of Dreams. The cave contains examples of every major sort of limestone formation, from the traditional stalactites and stalagmites to delicate cave flowers, rare anthracite crystals, flowstone (rather like candle wax), and cave coral. Enthusiastic guides, most of them members of the Grotto Club (a spelunking group), also run more adventurous cave expeditions, called Wild Tours. The entrance to the cave is via **Williams Canyon,** off the highway. Summer evenings, a laser show transforms the canyon into an unsurpassed sound-and-light show of massively corny, yet undeniably effective, proportions. *U.S. 24,* ☏ *719/685–5444.* ☛ *$8.* ☉ *Daily, 9–5; 45-minute tours conducted continuously.*

⓲ On the left of U.S. 24 headed west, is the lovely **Manitou Springs,** home of Manitou Springs mineral water. The **Chamber of Commerce** (354 Manitou Ave., ☏ 719/685–5089) offers free walking tours of the springs, set in this quaint National Historic Landmark District, which exudes a slightly shabby, but genteel charm. The springs are all naturally effervescent; you might stop by Soda Springs for an after-dinner spritz (it tastes and acts just like Alka-Seltzer), or Twin Springs, sweet-tasting and loaded with lithium (which, say residents, is why they're always calm and smiling). Antique trolleys ply the streets in summer. Manitou has a growing artist population; the Manitou Art Project sponsors a year-round public exhibition, and the galleries offer a delightful ArtWalk Thursday evenings in summer.

Among the must-see attractions in town is William Packer's grandiose estate, **Glen Eyrie.** The property is maintained by a nondenominational fundamentalist sect called the Navigators, which publishes various religious literary works. The original gas lamps and sandstone structures remain, many of whose rocks were hewn with the moss still clinging, to give them an aged look. Try to come here for high tea, or during the Christmas season when there's an extravagant drive-through nativity scene. *North of Garden of the Gods, 30th St.,* ☏ *719/598–1212.* ☛ *$5 over 15, $4 senior citizens; tours June–Aug., weekdays twice daily; Sept.–May, Sun.; hours vary so call ahead.*

⓳ Another Manitou Springs attraction, albeit an unusual one, is **Miramont Castle Museum**—a wonderfully Byzantine extravaganza commissioned in 1895 as the private home of French priest Jean-Baptiste Francolon. The museum is a mad medley of exhibits, with 46 rooms offering a wide variety of displays, from original furnishings to antique doll and railroad collections. *9 Capitol Hill Ave.,* ☏ *719/685–1011.* ☛ *$2.* ☉ *June–Aug., daily 10–5; Sept.–May, daily noon–3.*

⓴ The **Pikes Peak Cog Railway,** the world's highest cog railway, departs from Manitou and follows a frolicking stream up a steep canyon, through copses of quaking aspen and towering lodgepole pines, before reaching the timberline and the 14,100-foot summit. *Ruxton Ave. (depot),* ☏ *719/685–5401. Round-trip fare: $21 adults, $9.50 children 5–11. Runs May–Oct., daily 9–6.*

You can also drive the 19-mile **Pikes Peak Highway,** which rises nearly 7,000 feet in its precipitous, dizzying climb to the **Summit House,** a pit-stop café and trading post. This is the same route that leading race-car drivers follow every July in the famed "Race to the Clouds," at 100 miles an hour.

Tour 2: The Collegiate Peaks and the Arkansas River

This tour loops through stunning alpine and desert scenery, passing thrilling natural attractions such as the Florissant Fossil Beds and Royal Gorge.

21 Leave Manitou Springs on U.S. 24 North and West, and travel 15 miles to the town of **Florissant.** Three miles south of town (follow signs) is the little-known **Florissant Fossil Beds National Monument,** a treasure trove for would-be paleontologists, where volcanic ash has perfectly preserved the remains of a 35–40-million-year-old primeval rain forest. The visitor center offers guided walks into the monument, or you can follow the well-marked hiking trails and lose yourself amid the Oligocene period, among 300-foot petrified redwoods. *U.S. 24, follow signs,* ☎ *719/748–3253.* ☛ *$3.* ⏲ *Daily, 10–5.*

22 From Florissant, a dirt road leads to **Cripple Creek,** Colorado's third legalized gambling town. Cripple Creek once had the most lucrative mines in the state—and 10,000 boozing, brawling, bawdy citizens. Today, its old mining structures and the stupendous curtain of the Collegiate Peaks are marred by slag heaps and parking lots. Although the town isn't as picturesque as Central City or Black Hawk (*see* Exploring *in* Denver, *above*), the other gambling hot spots, Cripple Creek—a little rougher and dustier than the others—feels more authentic.

There are a few worthwhile attractions here: The **Cripple Creek District Museum** (east end of Bennett Ave., ☎ 719/689–2634; ☛ $2; open late-May–mid-Oct., daily 10–5; mid-Oct.–late-May, weekends 12–4) provides a fascinating glimpse into mining life at the turn of the century. The **Mollie Kathleen Mine Tour** (Rte. 67, north of town, ☎ 719/689–2466; ☛ $6; open May–Oct., daily 9–5) descends 1,000 feet into the bowels of the earth in a mine that operated continuously from 1892 to 1961. **Imperial Hotel and Casino** (123 N. 3rd St., ☎ 719/689–7777) offers a peek into the era's high life and a chance spin on the wheel of fortune.

A narrow-gauge railroad (depot at Cripple Creek District Museum, ☎ 719/689–2640; fare: $6; runs Memorial Day–Oct., daily 10–5, departs every 45 min) weaves past abandoned mines to Cripple Creek's
23 former rival **Victor.** In bygone days, more than 50 ore-laden trains made this run daily. Today, however, Victor is a sad town, virtually a ghost of its former self; walking the streets—past several abandoned or partially restored buildings—is an eerie experience that does far more to evoke the mining (and post-mining) days than its tarted-up neighbor.

24 Back on U.S. 24 West, continue on to **Buena Vista** (or as locals pronounce it, *byoo*-na *vis*-ta), a town ringed by sky-scraping mountains, the most impressive being the **Collegiate Peaks.** The 14,000-foot giants attract alumni climbers from Yale, Princeton, Harvard, Columbia, and Oxford. A small mining town turned resort community, Buena Vista offers the usual historic buildings alternating with motels.

The most compelling reason to visit this area is for the almost unequaled variety of recreational activities. Hiking, biking, and climbing in the **Collegiate Peaks Wilderness Area** are among the favorite jaunts. Also, Buena Vista bills itself as "The White-water Rafting Capital of the World" and offers numerous excursions down the Arkansas River.

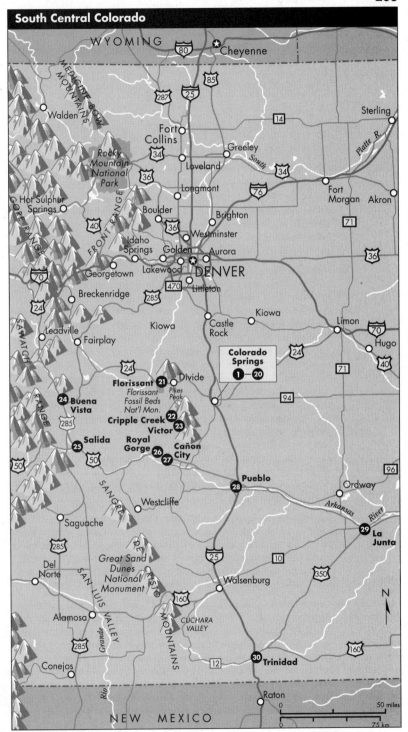

South Central Colorado

TIME OUT   After a full day of activities, check out the **Mt. Princeton Hot Springs** (5 mi west of Nathrop, CR 162, ☎ 719/395–2447), for a restorative soak. The springs has three swimming pools and several private tubs.

Before leaving downtown Buena Vista, meander through the four rooms of the **Buena Vista Heritage Museum.** Each is devoted to a different aspect of regional history: One concentrates on mining equipment and minerals, another is devoted to fashions and household utensils, a third to working models of the three railroads that serviced the area in its heyday, and the last to historical photos. *E. Main St.,* ☎ *719/395–2515.* ☛ *$2 adults, $1 children under 16.* ☉ *Memorial Day–Labor Day, daily 9–5.*

㉕ If Buena Vista has any competition in the beautiful scenery and outdoors activities departments, it comes from **Salida,** approximately 25 miles south along U.S. 24 and CO 291, and situated along the Arkansas River. It, too, is dominated by imposing peaks, with fourteener **Mt. Shavano** its landmark.

㉖ Head east on U.S. 50 to reach one of the Rockies' most powerful sights. The 1,053-foot-deep **Royal Gorge,** often called "The Grand Canyon of Colorado," was carved by the Arkansas River more than 3 million years ago. It's a tribute to the powers of nature, but it's spanned by no less monumental an achievement: the world's highest suspension bridge. Near the bridge, hubristic signs trumpet, "Who says you can't improve on Nature?" Never intended for transport, it was originally constructed in 1929 as a commercial enterprise. It now attracts more than half a million visitors annually, causing a fair amount of exploitation to the area. Families love crossing the bridge, particularly on gusty afternoons when it sways, adding to the thrill. Other activities at the gorge are: riding the astonishing aerial tram (2,200 feet long and 1,178 feet above the canyon floor) and descending the **Scenic Railway** (the world's steepest-incline rail line) to stare at the bridge 1,000 feet above. There is also a theater that presents a 25-minute multimedia show, outdoor musical entertainment in summer, and the usual assortment of food concessions and gift shops. *Royal Gorge Complex,* ☎ *719/275–7507.* ☛ *$8 adults, $6 children 4–11.* ☉ *Oct.–May, daily 9–5; June–Sept., daily 8–8.*

This site has its share of history, too: The famed Royal Gorge War between the Denver & Rio Grande and Santa Fe railroads occurred here in 1877. The battle was over the right-of-way through the canyon, which could only accommodate one rail line. Rival crews would lay tracks during the day and dynamite each other's work at night. The dispute was finally settled in court—the Denver & Rio Grande won.

㉗ **Cañon City,** an undeniably quirky town—and proud of it—is the gateway to the gorge. Where else would you find a shop entitled "Fluff 'em, Buff 'em, Stuff 'em"? Would you have guessed the services it provides: hairstyling, car waxing, and taxidermy? From its aggressive, even tacky, strip-mall veneer (softened, fortunately, by some lovely old buildings) you'd think Cañon City existed solely for tourism. Nothing could be further from the truth. Cañon City's livelihood stems from its lordly position as "Colorado's Prison Capital." There are 10 prisons in the vicinity, all of which the citizens lobbied to get! It might seem a perverse source of income to court, but consider that the prisons have pumped nearly $200 million into the local economy, and, as an affable former-mayor states, "You got these people walking around Denver and the Springs, here at least they're locked up."

Morbid curiosity seekers and sensationalists will revel in the **Colorado Territorial Prison Museum,** which formerly housed the Women's State Correctional Facility. Now, it exhaustively documents prison life in Colorado, through old photos and newspaper accounts, as well as confiscated inmates' weapons, contraband, and one warden's china set. The individual cell exhibits were, of course, funded by local businesses and civic organizations. There's also a video room where you can view titles such as "Prisons Ain't What They Used to Be" and "Drug Avengers." The original gas chamber sits in the courtyard. This museum is grim, grisly, gruesome, and—fascinating. *1st and Macon Sts.,* ☎ *719/269–3015.* ☛ *$3.* ☉ *May–Oct., daily 8:30–8; Nov.–Apr., Wed.–Sun., 10–5.*

To be fair, Cañon City is also called the "Climate Capital of Colorado," for its temperate year-round conditions that attract retirees in droves. Set 12 miles north of town, amid glorious terrain, is the city-owned **Redrock Park,** a magnet for hikers and climbers thanks to its twisted sandstone formations. **Garden Park,** also city-owned, has rich deposits of dinosaur fossils.

A gravel and dirt road (open only in summer) follows the old tracks that were once used to transport ore. Running through both parks and north to Cripple Creek, the route—traversable only with a four-wheel-drive vehicle—winds through red-rock canyons and the **Rampart Range,** over a rickety (but reinforced) wooden trestle bridge. Mountains, canyons, meadows, and sky provide a background of vivid primary colors.

Tour 3: The Santa Fe Trail
This tour winds through the historic towns of Pueblo and Trinidad, in part following the route of the pioneers.

28 Now head east on U.S. 50 to the junction of I–25, at **Pueblo.** This is a city divided: It can't make up its mind whether to promote its historic origins or the active lifestyle it offers, with biking in the mountains and golfing in the desert. A working-class, multiethnic steel town, Pueblo lacks some of the traditional glamour of towns like Aspen, whose growth mushroomed from gold and silver. Though sizable, it remains in the shadow of Colorado Springs to the north. The resulting civic inferiority complex actually led the city council to hire an image consultant to improve its reputation at home and elsewhere.

Civic leaders, as well, have embarked on an ambitious beautification plan, encouraging citizens to volunteer their time and talents. This has especially paid dividends in the extraordinary ongoing **Pueblo Levee Project,** the largest mural in the world. The grass-roots movement began with a lone artist's whimsical "statement," and now includes all manner of witty graffiti and illustrations gracing the levee along the Arkansas River. In addition, Pueblo businesses have banded together to sponsor sculptors whose works now adorn the ramps of I–25.

This civic-mindedness extends to the historical neighborhoods of Pueblo, which have a stunning collection of Victorian homes. The **Union Avenue Historic District,** including the glorious 1889 sandstone-and-brick Union Avenue Depot, is a repository of century-old stores and warehouses, now a fashionable commercial district. Among the landmarks are Mesa Junction, which celebrates Pueblo as a cross-roads, at the point where two trolleys met; and Pitkin Avenue, lined with fabulous gabled and turreted mansions attesting to the town's more prosperous times. Walking-tour brochures of each district are available at the **Chamber of Commerce** (302 N. Santa Fe Ave., ☎ 719/542–

1704). Pueblo's rich history is also on display in several superlative museums.

The **El Pueblo Museum** is ostensibly a repository for the city's history, but extends its scope to chronicle life on the plains from the prehistoric era onward, as well as Pueblo's role as a cultural and geographic crossroads, beginning when it was a trading post in the 1840s. *324 W. 1st St.,* ☎ *719/583–0453.* ☛ *$2.50 adults, $2 senior citizens and children 6–16.* ☼ *Mon.–Sat. 10–4:30, Sun. noon–3.*

At the airport, the **Fred E. Weisbrod Aircraft Museum** traces the development of American military aviation, with its more than two dozen aircraft in mint condition, ranging from a Lockheed F-80 fighter plane to a McDonnell Phantom F-4. *31001 Magnuson, Pueblo Memorial Airport,* ☎ *719/948–9219.* ☛ *Free. Weekdays 10–4, Sat. 10–2, Sun. 1–4.*

Unquestionably, the glory of Pueblo is the **Rosemount Victorian Museum,** one of Colorado's finest historical institutions. This splendiferous 24,000-square-foot, 37-room mansion, showplace of the wealthy Thatcher family, features exquisite maple, oak, and mahogany woodwork throughout, with ivory glaze and gold-leaf trim; Italian marble fireplaces; Tiffany-glass fixtures; and frescoed ceilings. This museum is the height of opulence, and the rooms seem virtually intact. The top floor—originally the servants' quarters—features the odd Andrew McClelland Collection: objects of curiosity this eccentric philanthropist garnered on his worldwide travels, including an Egyptian mummy. *419 W. 14th St.,* ☎ *719/545–5290.* ☛ *$3. Tours offered daily, but times vary so call ahead.*

Pueblo's equally vital concern with the present is documented in the gleaming **Sangre de Cristo Arts Center,** where several rotating exhibits in a well-thought-out space celebrate regional arts and crafts. The center also houses the superb, permanent Western Art collection donated by Francis King; a performing arts theater; and PAWS Children's Museum, which offers fun, interactive audio-visual experiences. *210 N. Santa Fe Trail,* ☎ *719/543–0130.* ☛ *Free.* ☼ *Mon.–Sat. 11–4.*

The more than 110 parks, in addition to hiking and biking trails, help to define Pueblo as a sports and recreation center. The **Greenway and Nature Center** (off 11th St., ☎ 719/545–9114), located on the Arkansas River, offers fine cycling, hiking, and canoeing. A small interpretive center describes the flora and fauna unique to the area, while a **Raptor Rehabilitation Center,** part of the nature center, cares for injured birds of prey.

TIME OUT **Café del Rio** (5200 Nature Center Blvd., ☎ 719/545–1009) boasts a sunny outdoor patio and a festive dining room. The kitchen turns out classic beans-and-burrito fare, as well as super Mexican-themed salads for lunch.

Pueblo also has an uncommonly fine **City Park** (3455 Nuckolls Ave., ☎ 719/561–9664) which has fishing lakes, playgrounds, kiddie rides, tennis courts, a swimming pool, and the excellent Pueblo Zoo—a Biopark that includes an Ecocenter with a tropical rain forest and black-footed penguins. **Lake Pueblo State Recreation Area,** off U.S. 50 West, offers more than 60 miles of shoreline and a full complement of water sports, as well as a beach. If you head east on U.S. 50, leaving the Rockies far behind, you'll be traveling toward the Eastern Plains, where rolling prairies of the northeast give way to hardier desert blooms and the land is stubbled with sage and stunted piñons. One fertile spot—50 miles along the highway—is the town of **Rocky Ford,** dubbed the "Melon Capital of the World" for the famously succulent cantaloupes grown here.

㉙ In another 15 miles, you'll reach **La Junta,** founded as a trading post in the mid-19th century. This wholesome town is notable for its tremendous **Koshare Indian Museum,** which contains extensive holdings of Native American artifacts and crafts (Navaho silver, Zuni pottery, Shoshone buckskin clothing), as well as pieces from Anglo artists such as Remington, known for their depictions of Native Americans. The Koshare Indian Dancers (actually a local Boy Scout troop) perform regularly, keeping their precious traditions alive. *115 W. 18th St.,* ☎ *719/384–4411.* ☛ *$2.* ☉ *Sept.–May, Tues.–Sun. 12:30–4:30; June–Aug., daily 10–5.*

A few miles farther east, parallel to U.S. 50 on Highway 194, is the splendid **Bent's Old Fort National Historic Site,** a perfect example of a living museum, with its painstaking re-creation of the original adobe fort, which burned down. Founded in 1833 by savvy trader William Bent, one of the region's historical giants, the fort anchored the commercially vital **Santa Fe Trail,** providing both protection and a meeting place for the military, trappers, and traders of the era. The museum's interior includes a smithy and soldiers' and trappers' barracks. The guided tours are informative and fascinating. *35110 Hwy. 194 E,* ☎ *719/384– 2596.* ☛ *$2 adults.* ☉ *Memorial Day–Labor Day, daily 8–6; Labor Day–Memorial Day, daily 8–4:30.*

This area of Colorado played a major role in opening up the West, through the Mountain Branch of the Santa Fe Trail. Bent's Fort was the most important stop between the route's origin in Independence, Missouri, and its terminus in Santa Fe, New Mexico. U.S. 50 roughly follows its faded tracks from the Kansas border through the pioneer towns of Lamar and Las Animas to La Junta, where U.S. 350 picks up ㉚ the scent, traveling southwest to **Trinidad.** If you detour onto the quiet county roads, you can still discern its faint outline over the gentle hump of swales and the dip of arroyos. Here, amid the magpies and prairie dogs, it takes little imagination to conjure visions of the pioneers, struggling to travel just 10 miles a day by ox cart over vast stretches of territory. We often take for granted how easily we now travel these same distances.

Initially founded as a rest-and-repair station along the Santa Fe Trail, Trinidad boomed when coal was discovered in the area, followed inevitably by the construction of the railroad. The period from 1880 to 1910 saw major building and expansion. The advent of natural gas, coupled with the Depression, ushered in a gradual decline in population, but not of spirit. Trinidad's citizens willingly contribute 1% of a 4% sales tax to the upkeep of the city's rich architectural heritage. That civic pride is clearly demonstrated in the town's four superb museums, a remarkably large number for a town its size.

Downtown, called the **Corazon de Trinidad,** is a National Historic Landmark District containing splendid Victorian mansions, churches, and the glorious, bright red domes and turrets of the **Aaron House Synagogue.** The Chamber of Commerce (309 Nevada St., ☎ 719/846–9285) publishes an excellent walking tour of the neighborhood, which even retains its original paved brick streets.

Start at the **Baca House/Bloom House/Pioneer Museum Complex.** Visited together, this facility represents the most significant aspects of Trinidad's history. Felipe Baca was a prominent Latin American trader whose 1870 residence—**Baca House**—is replete with original furnishings in the parlor, sitting room, kitchen, dining room, and bedrooms. The displays convey a mix of Anglo (clothes, furniture) and Latin American (santos, rosaries, textiles) influences.

Next door, **Bloom House** provides an effective contrast to the Baca House. Frank Bloom made his money through ranching, banking, and the railroad, and although he was no wealthier than Baca, his mansion (built in the 1880s) reveals a very different lifestyle. The railroad enabled him to fill his ornate Second Empire–style Victorian (with mansard roof and elaborate wrought ironwork) with fine furnishings and fabrics brought from New York and imported from Europe.

The adjacent **Pioneer Museum** is dedicated to the effect of the Santa Fe Trail on the community. Inside the museum are typical ranch hands' quarters, period artifacts, Kit Carson's coat, and an array of antique carriages from surreys to sulkies. *Complex: 300 E. Main St.,* ☎ *719/846–7217.* ☛ *$2.50 adults, $1.25 children and senior citizens.* ☉ *Memorial Day–mid-Sept., Mon.–Sat. 10–4, Sun. 1–4.*

The **A. R. Mitchell Memorial Museum and Gallery** celebrates the life and work of the famous Western illustrator whose distinctive oils, charcoal drawings, and watercolors graced the pages of pulp magazines and ranch romances. The museum also holds his personal collection of other masters of the genre, such as Larry Heller and Harvey Dunn, as well as a re-creation of his atelier. The community holds Mitchell in great esteem: He was responsible for saving the Baca and Bloom houses from demolition, and spearheaded numerous campaigns to restore the historic downtown. For a further glimpse into Trinidad history, be sure to see the **Aultman Collection of Photography** recently installed in the Memorial Museum Gallery. On display are photos by the Aultman family dating back to 1889; they offer a unique visual record of Trinidad. *150 E. Main St.,* ☎ *719/846–4224.* ☛ *Free.* ☉ *Mid-Apr.–Sept., Mon.–Sat. 10–4.*

On the other side of the Purgatoire River, the **Loudon-Henritze Archaeology Museum** takes viewers back millions of years to document the true origins of the region, including early geologic formations, plant and marine animal fossils, and prehistoric artifacts. *Trinidad State Junior College,* ☎ *719/846–5508.* ☛ *Free.* ☉ *June–Sept., weekdays noon–4.*

The **Trinidad Children's Museum** is located in the delightful Old Firehouse No. 1, and displays firefighting memorabilia such as a 1936 American LaFrance fire truck (kids love clanging the loud bell) and the city's original fire alarm system. Upstairs is a fine re-creation of a Victorian schoolroom. *314 N. Commercial St.,* ☎ *719/846–8220.* ☛ *Free.* ☉ *Summer, weekdays 10–2.*

From Trinidad, Route 12—called the Scenic Highway of Legends— curls north through the stunning **Cuchara Valley.** As it starts its climb, you'll pass a series of company towns built to house coal miners. The first, **Cokedale,** is nestled in Reilly Canyon. The entire town is a National Historic Landmark District, and is the most significant example of a turn-of-the-century coal/coke camp in Colorado. As you drive through the area note the telltale streaks of black in the sandstone and granite bluffs fronting the Purgatoire River and its tributaries, the unsightly slag heaps, and the spooky abandoned mining camps dotting the hillsides. The impressive **Stonewall Gap,** a monumental gate of rock, roughly marks the end of the mining district.

Several switchbacks snake through rolling grasslands, and dance in and out of spruce stands whose clearings afford wonderful views of Monument Lake, as you approach **Cuchara Pass.** There is marvelous camping, hiking, and fishing throughout this tranquil part of the **San Isabel National Forest,** emblazoned with a color wheel of wildflowers in spring and summer. Four corkscrewing miles later, you'll reach a dirt road that leads to the twin sapphires of **Bear and Blue lakes,** followed quickly by a small family ski area, **Cuchara Valley,** which is closed indefinitely. Opposite the resort is **Cuchara,** a cute resort town with a rustic look that seems miles from anywhere.

You'll begin to see fantastic rock formations with equally fanciful names, such as Profile Rock, Devil's Staircase, and Giant's Spoon. With a little imagination you can devise your own legends about the names' origins. There are more than 400 of these upthrusts, which radiate like the spokes of a wheel from the valley's dominating landmark, the **Spanish Peaks.** In Spanish they are known as *Dos Hermanos,* or "Two Brothers"; in Ute, their name *Huajatolla* means "breasts of the world." The haunting formations are considered to be a unique geologic phenomenon for their sheer abundance and variety of rock types.

The Highway of Legends passes through the charming, laid-back resort town of **La Veta,** before reaching its junction with I–25 at **Walsenburg,** another city built on coal and the largest town between Pueblo and Trinidad.

What to See and Do with Children

Buckskin Joe Park and Railway. Not only is this the largest Western-style theme park in the region, but it's also actually an authentic ghost town that was literally moved here from its original site 100 miles away. Famous films such as *True Grit* and *Cat Ballou* were shot in this place that vividly evokes the Old West, especially during the re-creation gunfights and hangings that occur daily. Children love the horse-drawn trolley rides, horseback rides, and gold panning, while adults appreciate live entertainment in the Crystal Palace and Saloon. The complex includes its own scenic railway that travels to the rim of Royal Gorge, as well as a Steam Train and Antique Car Museum. *Cañon City, off U.S. 50,* ☎ *719/275–5485. Combination ticket for all attractions: $12 adults, $10 children 5–11.* ☉ *May–Sept., daily 9–9.*

North Pole and Santa's Workshop. Energetic elves bustle about this colorful shrine to the commercialization of Christmas. Kids can feed deer, ride a Ferris wheel and carousel, try their luck in an arcade, visit Santa at the height of summer, and stuff themselves in the Candy Kitchen, Sugar Plum Terrace, or old-fashioned ice-cream parlor. *Cascade, Exit 141 off I–25, then 10 mi on U.S. 24 W,* ☎ *719/684–9432.* ☛ *$8.50 per person.* ☉ *May, Fri.–Wed. 9:30–6; June–Aug., daily 9:30–6; Sept.–Dec. 24, Fri.–Tues. 10–5.*

Pueblo Zoo and City Park (*see* Tour 3 *in* Exploring, *above*)

Royal Gorge and Suspension Bridge (*see* Tour 2 *in* Exploring, *above*)

Off the Beaten Track

Bishop's Castle, an elaborate re-creation of a medieval castle replete with turrets, buttresses, and ornamental iron, is the prodigious (some might say monomaniacal) one-man undertaking of Jim Bishop, who began construction in 1969 and has hauled nearly 50,000 tons of rock used for the construction. Not yet complete, it soars three stories and nearly 75 feet, with plans to build a drawbridge and moat. Bishop finances this enormous endeavor through donations and a gift shop. Anyone can stop by at any time; if you're lucky he'll be there, railing against the establishment (numerous posted signs graphically express his sentiments). *To get there take I–25 south from Pueblo, turn west on Rte. 165 (exit 74) and follow the signs. CR 75,* ☎ *719/564–4366.* ☛ *Free.* ⏲ *Daily, but hours vary.*

Shopping

Shopping Districts and Malls

In Colorado Springs, the areas to shop are **Old Colorado City,** with numerous charming boutiques and galleries; **The Citadel** (S. Academy Blvd., at E. Platte Ave.), which counts **JCPenney** and **Dillard's** among its more than 175 stores; and the very upscale **Broadmoor One Lake Avenue Shopping Arcade.** The streets of **Manitou Springs** and **Cripple Creek** offer one souvenir shop and gallery after another.

Pueblo's **Union Avenue Historic District** and **Mesa Junction** contain several fine antiques shops and boutiques. The **Pueblo Mall** offers the usual assortment of fast-food outlets, video arcades, and franchises, including JCPenney. The **Midtown Center** mall includes chains such as Sears.

Flea Markets

There is a flea market every weekend at the **Pueblo Fairgrounds.**

Specialty Stores

ANTIQUES

Tivoli's Antique Gallery (325 S. Union Ave., Pueblo, ☎ 719/545–1448) sells everything from vintage clothing to furniture.

ART GALLERIES

Art of the Rockies (135 W. 3rd St., Salida, no ☎) is a co-op gallery that showcases the work of 70 regional artists. **Michael Garman Gallery** (2418 W. Colorado Ave., Colorado Springs, ☎ 719/471–1600) carries Western-style paintings and unusual figurines and dioramas. **Commonwheel Artists Co-Op** (102 Cañon Ave., Manitou Springs, ☎ 719/685–1008) celebrates the diversity of art in the region, exhibiting jewelry and fiber, clay, and glass art. **OffBroadway Art Gallery** (221 S. Union Ave., Pueblo, ☎ 719/545–8407) specializes in contemporary art by southern Colorado artists.

BOUTIQUES

Exotic Designs (112 Colorado Ave., Pueblo, ☎ 719/543–4921) sells clothing from around the world. **Heritage House Art** (320 S. Union Ave., Pueblo, ☎ 719/545–2691) has exotic wearable art. **Helstrom Studios** (330 N. Institute St., Colorado Springs, ☎ 719/473–3620) showcases beads, textiles, silks, and batiks. **The Rhinestone Parrot** (725 Manitou Ave., Manitou Springs, ☎ 719/685–5333) sells gorgeous dyed leather; brocaded and appliquéd purses, vests, and jackets; and exquisite ceramic jewelry.

CERAMICS

Pueblo Pottery (229 Midway St., Pueblo, ☎ 719/543–0720) features the lovely designs of Tom and Jean Latka. **Van Briggle Art Pottery and Showroom** (600 S. 21st St., Colorado Springs, ☎ 719/633–7729) offers free tours of its world-famous facility that end with a visit to their showroom. **Pottery by Pankratz** (366 2nd St., Monument, ☎ 719/481–3108) showcases striking raku, porcelain, and stone tableware, teapots, lamps, goblets, vases, and sinks.

CRAFTS

Simpich Character Dolls (2413 W. Colorado Ave., Colorado Springs, ☎ 719/636–3272) fashions wonderfully detailed ceramic figurines and fabric dolls, including extraordinary marionettes. Woodcarver Sophie Cowman's evocative pieces—from spoons to sculpture, made out of scrub oak, fragrant cedar, and cottonwood—are for sale at the **Wood Studio** (725 Manitou Ave., Manitou Springs, no ☎). The **Dulcimer Shop** (740 Manitou Ave., Manitou Springs, ☎ 719/685–9655) sells these instruments. **Victor Trading Co. & Manufacturing Works** (114 S. 3rd St., Victor, ☎ 719/689–2346) has everything from beeswax candles to Bull Hill baskets.

FOOD
Rocky Mountain Chocolates (2431 W. Colorado Ave., Colorado Springs, ☎ 719/635–4131) also has branches in Pueblo, Castle Rock, and Boulder. **Patsy's Candies** (1540 S. 21st St., Colorado Springs, ☎ 719/633–7215) is renowned for its saltwater taffy and chocolate. **Pikes Peak Vineyards** (3901 Janitell Rd., Colorado Springs, ☎ 719/576–0075) offers tastings of its surprisingly fine wines, including merlots and chardonnays. **Seabel's Baskets and Gifts** (105 W. C St., Pueblo, ☎ 719/543–2400) offers gourmet cookware and delicacies.

GLASSWARE
The **Mid 30s Depression Glass Shop** (225 S. Union Ave., Pueblo, ☎ 719/544–1031) has the largest selection of collectible Depression glass in Colorado.

WESTERN PARAPHERNALIA
Bandera Outfitters (2519 W. Colorado Ave., Colorado Springs, ☎ 719/635–6005) has stylish Western wear. **Back at the Ranch** (333 S. Union Ave., Pueblo, ☎ 719/544–7319) provides elegant home accessories for dudes and dudettes.

Sports and the Outdoors

Boating
Two marinas at **Lake Pueblo State Park** (North Shore, ☎ 719/547–3880; South Shore, ☎ 719/564–1043) offer rental boats.

Camping
There are excellent camping facilities at **Pueblo Lake State Recreation Area** (☎ 719/561–9320) and **Trinidad Lake State Recreation Area** (☎ 719/846–6951). Camping is superb in the **San Isabel** and **Pike national forests.** The Forest Service (☎ 719/636–1602) or Bureau of Land Management (☎ 719/275–0631) can provide more information.

Climbing
Garden of the Gods is a popular place to test your skills, thanks to its stark spires and cliffs. Register with the visitor center at the entrance. Also, **Collegiate Peaks** around Buena Vista and Salida offer a variety of ascents from moderate to difficult. The **Royal Gorge, Redrocks Park,** and **Garden Park** outside Cañon City are alive with intrepid clamberers.

Cycling
Pueblo has an extensive **Bike Trail System,** which loops the city, following the Arkansas River part way, then goes out to the reservoir. The **Pueblo Parks and Recreation Department** (☎ 719/566–1745) can provide more information.

Cycling is popular in the **Collegiate Peaks Wilderness Area,** around Buena Vista and Salida. **American Adventure Expeditions** (228 N. F St., Buena Vista, ☎ 719/395–2409) and **Rocky Mountain Tours** (☎ 719/395–4101) provide rentals and tours.

Fishing

Pike, bass, and trout are plentiful in this region. Favorite fishing spots include **Trinidad Lake** (☎ 719/846–6951), **Lake Pueblo** (☎ 719/561–9320), **Spinney Mountain Reservoir** (between Florissant and Buena Vista), and the **Arkansas** and **South Platte rivers.** For more information, call the Colorado Division of Wildlife Southeast Region (☎ 719/473–2945).

Golf

In Colorado Springs, **The Broadmoor** (Broadmoor Complex, ☎ 719/634–7711) offers 54 splendid holes to guests and members. **Colorado Springs Country Club** (3333 Templeton Gap Rd., ☎ 719/473–1782) is another fine 18-hole course, as is the public **Pine Creek Golf Course** (9850 Divot Dr., ☎ 719/594–9999).

Pueblo City Golf Course (City Park, ☎ 719/566–1745) is a handsome, highly rated 18-hole course, and **Pueblo West Golf Course** (Pueblo West Development, 8 mi west of town on U.S. 50, ☎ 719/547–2280) is an 18-hole championship course. **Walking Stick Golf Course** (4301 Walking Stick Blvd., Pueblo, ☎ 719/584–3400) is perennially ranked in the top 50 courses by *Golf Digest.*

Hiking

Cañon City–owned **Redrocks Park,** 12 miles north of town, offers splendid hiking among the sandstone spires. You can hike in relative solitude in **San Isabel National Forest** (☎ 719/545–8737), in the Pueblo area. There are numerous trails in the **Pikes Peak** area, including **Barr Trail** up the mountain and **North Cheyenne Canyon Trail. Garden of the Gods,** outside Colorado Springs, is also popular. Call the El Paso County Parks Department (☎ 719/520–6375) for further information about facilities in the Colorado Springs/Pikes Peak area.

Horseback Riding

Academy Riding Stables (Colorado Springs, ☎ 719/633–5667) offers trail rides through the Garden of the Gods. **Buckskin Joe's** (Cañon City, ☎ 719/275–5149) offers rides in the Cañon City area, from one hour to all day; rates begin at $20. **Cripple Creek Horse Company** (Cripple Creek, ☎ 719/689–3051) offers rides into the Rockies.

In-Line Skating

Popular routes, with good paved trails, are along the **Pueblo Bike Trail** (*see* Cycling, *above*) and in the **Garden of the Gods.**

Skiing

DOWNHILL

Monarch has 4 chairs, 54 trails, 637 acres, and a 1,160-foot vertical drop. The service, which has garnered numerous Tourism Hospitality Achievement Awards, is exceptional. Lift lines and lift ticket prices are nominal by most comparative standards. *U.S. 50 (18 mi from Salida),* ☎ *719/539–3573.* ☉ *Mid-Nov.–mid-Apr., daily 9–4.*

Rafting

Arkansas River Outfitters (Cañon City, ☎ 719/275–3229), **Brown's Royal Gorge Rafting and Helicopter Tours** (Cañon City, ☎ 719/275–5161), **Royal Gorge River Adventures** (Cañon City, ☎ 719/269–3700), and **Sierra Outfitters** (Cañon City, ☎ 719/275–0128) are but a few of the reliable outfits that line U.S. 50, between Cañon City and the Royal Gorge.

Buena Vista and Salida are the other major rafting centers, with **American Adventure Expeditions** (☎ 719/395–2409) and **Rocky Mountain Tours** (☎ 719/395–4101), both in Buena Vista, and **River Runners** (☎

800/525–2081) and **Canyon Marine Expeditions** (☎ 719/539–7476 or 800/643–0707), in Salida, among the many recommended outfitters.

Dining

Steak houses and Mexican cantinas are usually the most dependable restaurants throughout South Central Colorado, though Colorado Springs and Pueblo offer a wide variety of fine eateries. For prices, *see* the Dining chart *in* Colorado Essentials, *below.*

Cañon City

$$–$$$ **Merlino's Belvedere.** This Italian standby has ritzy coffee-shop decor, with floral banquettes, centerpieces, and a "running water rock grotto." Locals swear by the top-notch steaks, seafood, and pasta. It's the usual choice for a big evening out. ✗ *1330 Elm Ave.,* ☎ *719/275–5558. Reservations advised. AE, MC, V.*

$ **Janey's Chile Wagon.** Owner Janey Workman is a former New Yorker
★ who fled the big city. *The National Enquirer* did a feature on her: "Waitress Builds Diner into $350,000 Restaurant!" Her food is haute greasy spoon, with huge portions of delicious burritos and the like, smothered in "green chili that won't stay with you all night, hon." The decor favors neon parrots, velvet paintings, and other tchotchkes, but nothing is as colorful as Janey herself. ✗ *807 Cyanide Ave.,* ☎ *719/275–4885. Reservations accepted. No credit cards. Closed Sun. and Mon.*

Colorado Springs

$$$ **Briarhurst Manor.** The symphony of cherry-wood wainscoting,
★ balustrades and furnishings, Van Briggle wood-and-ceramic fireplaces, tapestries, chinoiserie, and hand-painted glass make this one of the most exquisitely romantic restaurants in Colorado. There are several dining rooms, each with its own look and mood. Among the most charming are the former library and the garden room (a converted private chapel with granite walls). To complete the picture, classical quartets play on the patio in summer. Chef-owner Sigi Krauss is to be commended for literally rescuing this gorgeous old Victorian from the wrecker's ball, and his international clientele appreciates his diversified menu as much as they do the unparalleled ambience. Start with the house-smoked Rocky Mountain trout mousse or alligator pear (avocado stuffed with seafood, topped with both hollandaise and bordelaise sauces), then try the perfectly prepared rack of Colorado lamb or chateaubriand. ✗ *404 Manitou Ave., Manitou Springs,* ☎ *719/685–1864. Reservations advised. AE, D, DC, MC, V. Closed Sun. No lunch.*

$$$ **Corbett's.** Chef Corbett Reed and his father, Findlay, preside over this
★ posh eatery, the new hot spot among Springs elite. The high-tech space—halogen lamps, modern art, black tables and chairs—is matched by an equally contemporary menu (light and health-conscious). Appetizers are particularly sensational: Try house-smoked trout in tangy horseradish sauce set off by sweet pears and sassy chèvre; grilled calamari with crab stuffing and dill aioli; or seared beef roulade with antipasto platter. The wine list is extensive and reasonably priced. ✗ *817 W. Colorado Ave.,* ☎ *719/471–0004. Reservations required. AE, D, DC, MC, V. No lunch weekends. No dinner Mon.*

$$$ **Craftwood Inn.** This intimate, restful spot has been a restaurant for more
★ than 50 years: It once regularly hosted such luminaries as Cary Grant, Bing Crosby, and Liberace. The space has a delightful Old English feel, with wrought-iron chandeliers, stained glass partitions, heavy wood beams, and a majestic stone-and-copper fireplace. To start, try the wild mushroom and hazelnut soup, black-bean ravioli, or warm spinach salad

with wild boar bacon. The mixed game bird and wild grill are particularly memorable entrées, especially when accompanied by a selection from the well-considered and fairly priced wine list. ✗ *404 El Paso Blvd., Manitou Springs,* ☎ *719/685–9000. Reservations suggested. D, MC, V. No lunch.*

$$$ **La Petite Maison.** This pretty Victorian abode has been divided into several romantic dining rooms. Pale pink walls, floral tracery, Parisian gallery posters, and pots overflowing with flowers create the atmosphere of a French country home. The menu offers an expert balance of old-fashioned standards and newfangled Southwestern fare. Recommended appetizers include curried shrimp crepe with banana chutney; and goat cheese–stuffed green chilies with black beans. Top-notch main courses range from pork chops with herbed demi-glacé and roasted-garlic mashed potatoes to sea scallops in a balsamic and garlic cream sauce. ✗ *1015 W. Colorado Ave.,* ☎ *719/632–4887. Reservations required. AE, D, DC, MC, V.*

$$$ **Pepper Tree.** From its hilltop position the Pepper Tree enjoys smashing views of the city that enhance the restaurant's aura of quiet sophistication. Interior decor features a pink-and-maroon color scheme and a mirrored wall. Table-side preparations (including the inevitable and delectable pepper steak) are its stock-in-trade, though the chef will go out on a limb with such daily specials as calamari stuffed with crabmeat and bacon. Still, this is one of those old-fashioned places where flambé is considered the height of both elegance and decadence. ✗ *888 W. Moreno Ave.,* ☎ *719/471–4888. Reservations required. Jacket and tie. AE, MC, V. Closed Sun. No lunch.*

$$ **Margarita.** Plants, adobe walls, terra-cotta tile, and mosaic tables lend an air of refinement to this fine eatery, whose constantly changing menu is an intriguing hybrid of Mexican and Continental influences. ✗ *7350 Pine Creek Rd.,* ☎ *719/598–8667. Reservations advised. AE, MC, V. Closed Mon. No dinner Sun.*

$ **Adam's Mountain Café.** With whirring ceiling fans, hanging plants, floral wallpaper, bucolic country garden prints, and old-fashioned hardwood tables and chairs, this cozy eatery is vaguely reminiscent of someone's great-grandmother's parlor. Come here for smashing breakfasts (wondrous muffins and organic juices); fine pastas (try the orzo Mediterranean, with sun-dried tomatoes, broccoli, onions, walnuts, and peppers sautéed in olive oil with feta, lemon, and tomato); such gourmet sandwiches as red chili–rubbed free-range chicken on grilled polenta with cilantro pesto and lime sour cream; and yummy desserts like apple crisp with dried cherries, almond pound cake, and cappuccino chocolate torte. ✗ *110 Cañon Ave., Manitou Springs,* ☎ *719/685–1430. Reservations accepted. AE, MC, V. No dinner Sun.*

$ **El Tesoro.** At the turn of the century, this lovely historic building served
★ as a brothel, and then for many years it was an atelier for various artists. Today, it's a restaurant that doubles as an art gallery, exhibiting especially noteworthy weavings and prints. The adobe and exposed brick walls and tile work are original; rugs, textiles, and the ubiquitous garlands of chili add still more color. The sterling northern New Mexican food is the real McQueso, a savvy, savory blend of Native American, Spanish, and Anglo-American influences. The staples of this highly evolved cuisine haven't changed in 400 years; corn, beans, squash, heavy meats like pork and goat, and, of course, chili. The *posole* (hominy with pork and red chili) is magical, the green chili heavenly, and innovative originals like mango quesadillas (a brilliant pairing of sweet and spicy elements) simply genius. ✗ *10 N. Sierra Madre St.,* ☎ *719/471–0106. Reservations advised. MC, V. Closed Sun. No lunch Sat. No dinner Mon.–Wed.*

Pueblo

$$ **Irish Pub.** This bustling, consistently jam-packed hot spot is a bar and
★ grill with a difference: It has a good kitchen. The owner *loves* food,
and he has elevated pub grub to an art form. Even the house salad—
field greens studded with pine nuts and feta—is imaginative. Among
the mouthwatering appetizers is a marvelous grilled smoked-duck
sausage with goat cheese, topped with a honey-mustard sauce. Sand-
wiches are equally creative; try the buffalo burger or beaver (yes,
beaver) sandwich. The range of entrées, many of them heart-healthy,
is astonishing: from a dazzling prime rib to a lip-smacking, "border
grill" turkey breast lightly dusted in flour, grilled, and then poached
in chicken broth and raspberry vinaigrette. ✗ *108 W. 3rd St.,* ☎
719/542–9974. Reservations accepted. AE, D, MC, V. Closed Sun.

$$ **La Renaissance.** This converted church and parsonage is the most imposing and elegant space in town, and the impeccably attired, unfail-
ingly courteous wait staff completes the picture. The kitchen is stylish
as well, offering Continental standbys such as filet mignon in mushroom sauce, superb baby-back ribs, and shrimp scampi. Desserts are
sinful enough to be sacrilegious, considering the restaurant's origins.
The dinner price includes appetizer, soup, salad, and dessert. ✗ *217
E. Routt Ave.,* ☎ *719/543–6367. Reservations advised. AE, MC, V.
Closed Sun. No lunch Sat.*

$$ **La Tronica's.** Although it's dressed like a saloon, with mirrored beer
signs and Christmas lights draping the bar, this 50-year-old restaurant
is real "Mamma Mia" Italian. Waitresses, who invariably call you "sweet-
heart," have been here for as long as anyone can remember, and you
may notice them watching approvingly as you take your first bite. Steak,
scrumptious fried chicken (second-best in the Rockies, next to Slogar's
in Crested Butte), and homemade pastas are the lure. ✗ *1143 E.
Abriendo Ave.,* ☎ *719/542–1113. Reservations advised. AE, MC, V.
Closed Sun. and Mon. No lunch.*

$–$$ **Grand Prix.** A neon sign announces the location of this authentic Mexican restaurant run by the Montoya family. Red neon lights and a painted
false ceiling relieve the otherwise spartan decor. The food is classic: pork
and avocado, chorizo, burritos, and Mexican steak, served with heaping helpings of rice and beans, and utilizing the flavorful local Pueblo
chili. ✗ *615 E. Mesa St.,* ☎ *719/542–9825. Reservations accepted.
No credit cards. Closed Sun. and Mon. No lunch Sat.*

Salida

$–$$ **First Street Café.** Occupying a late-19th-century building in the historic
district is this café, with creative heart-healthy and vegetarian specials,
in addition to the expected robust Mexican-American fare. Breakfast
is served here, as well as lunch and dinner. ✗ *137 E. 1st St.,* ☎
719/539–4759. Reservations accepted. AE, D, MC, V.

Trinidad

$–$$ **Nana and Nano's Pasta House.** This homey, classic Neapolitan eatery,
with red-and-white check tablecloths, red curtains, and posters of
Italy, is always saturated with the tempting aroma of garlic and tomato
sauce. Pastas are uniformly excellent, with standards such as fettuccine Alfredo, gnocchi bolognese, and spaghetti al sugo among the
standouts. If you don't have time for a sit-down lunch, stop in their
deli next door for smashing heros and gourmet sandwiches. The Mon-
teleones are your amiable hosts. If you want wine or beer, BYOB. ✗
415 University St., ☎ *719/846–2696. Reservations accepted. AE,
DC, MC, V.* ☉ *Tues.–Fri. lunch in summer. Closed Sun.*

$ La Fiesta. A few Mexican crafts, brick walls, and a fireplace in the back room (one of the nicest seating areas) lend some atmosphere to this hole-in-the-wall restaurant. The faithful clientele comes here for the subtly spicy green chili and burritos. Bring your own wine and beer. La Fiesta is open for all three meals. ✕ *134 W. Main St.,* ☎ *719/846–8221. Reservations accepted. No credit cards. Closed Sun.*

Lodging

Colorado Springs has some of the higher-end chain properties, but, in general, the choice is usually among bed-and-breakfasts, guest houses, and motels on the strip. Unless otherwise noted, all accommodations listed below include phones, cable TV, and private baths. For rates, *see* the Lodging chart *in* Colorado Essentials, *below.*

Buena Vista

$ Adobe Inn. This adobe hacienda has five charming rooms, each named for the predominant decorative motif: antique, Mexican, Native American, Mediterranean, and wicker. Some rooms have a fireplace. The airy solarium is dominated by a magnificent kiva. A complimentary gourmet breakfast is offered to guests. The owners—Marjorie, Paul, and Michael Knox—also run the charming **La Casa del Sol** Mexican restaurant down the street and can make arrangements for guests to dine there. ⌂ *303 U.S. 24 N, 81211,* ☎ *719/395–6340. 5 rooms. Hot tub. MC, V.*

Cañon City

$ Cañon Inn. Some of the famous people who have stayed here—John Belushi, Tom Selleck, Jane Fonda, John Wayne, Glenn Ford, and Goldie Hawn among them—now have their names emblazoned on the door of a hotel room here in their honor. Spacious and ultracomfortable accommodations are offered in two wings. All the rooms are decorated in muted pastels and earth tones. ⌂ *U.S. 50 and Dozier St., 81215,* ☎ *719/275–8676,* ℻ *719/275–8675. 104 rooms. Restaurant, bar, pool, hot tub. AE, D, DC, MC, V.*

Colorado Springs

$$$$ **The Broadmoor.** Here's one of America's truly great hotels. Completely ★ self-contained—more a village than a resort—its 30 buildings sprawl majestically across 3,500 acres. The property celebrated 75 years of deluxe service in 1993, and it maintains its exalted status through continual upgrading and refurbishment. The pink-and-ocher main building, crowned by Mediterranean-style towers, serenely commands a private lake. Rooms here are the loveliest, with period furnishings; accommodations in the other complexes, including 150 new junior suites in the Broadmoor West Tower, are more contemporary in style. The Broadmoor is renowned for its three world-class championship golf courses, former Davis Cup coach Dennis Ralston's tennis camps, and its new pampering spa. There are eight restaurants, of which the Tavern, with its original Toulouse-Lautrec posters; the elegant cranberry-and-silver Penrose Room; and the romantic primrose, mint, and buff Charles Court rank among the state's finest. ⌂ *Box 1439, 80901,* ☎ *719/634–7711 or 800/634–7711,* ℻ *719/577-5779. 483 rooms, 67 suites, 150 junior suites. 8 restaurants, 3 bars, 3 pools, beauty salon, spa, 3 18-hole golf courses, 12 tennis courts, health club, horseback riding, squash, fishing, cinema, meeting rooms, car rental. AE, D, DC, MC, V.*

$$ **Antlers Doubletree Hotel.** Two previous incarnations of this hotel once ★ competed with the Broadmoor for the rich and famous, thanks to its superb, historic location downtown. This third Antlers was completely renovated and expanded in 1991. The large airy lobby strikes an immediate note of class when you enter, and the handsome rooms sport hunting-lodge decor. ⊞ *4 S. Cascade Ave., 80904,* ☎ *719/473–5600 or 800/528–0444,* ℻ *719/389–0259. 274 rooms, 16 suites. 2 restaurants, bar, hot tub, health club, meeting rooms. AE, D, DC, MC, V.*

$$ **Embassy Suites.** This is one of the original properties in this chain, and it's among the best. The airy atrium lobby, crawling with plants, is watched over by the resident, talkative caged birds. Suites are comfortable, favoring teal and dusty rose. To complete the tropical motif, a waterfall tumbles lavishly into the indoor pool. The pool deck offers quite a view of Pikes Peak; jazz groups play here every Thursday night in season. A complimentary breakfast is offered to all guests. ⊞ *7290 Commerce Center Dr., 80919,* ☎ *719/599–9100,* ℻ *719/599–4644. 207 suites. Restaurant, bar, indoor pool, hot tub, exercise room, meeting rooms. AE, D, DC, MC, V.*

$–$$ **The Hearthstone.** Two Victorian houses joined by a carriage house comprise this famed B&B, listed on the National Register of Historic Places. The 25 no-smoking guest rooms (most with private bath) are resplendent with furnishings from the 1880s (cut glass windows, Van Briggle ceramic fireplaces, hand-carved or brass beds, glorious quilts, and rocking chairs); each is individually decorated around a theme, such as the Author's Den, complete with vintage typewriter, and the Solarium, brightened by plants and an expansive skylight. A complimentary breakfast always includes eggs, fresh fruit, and home-baked bread. ⊞ *506 N. Cascade Ave., 80903,* ☎ *719/473–4413 or 800/521–1885. 25 rooms. AE, MC, V.*

$–$$ **Holden House.** Genial innkeepers Sallie and Welling Clark realized their
★ dream when they lovingly restored this 1902 Victorian home and transformed it into a B&B. Three charming rooms in the main house and two in the adjacent carriage house are filled with family heirlooms and antiques. Fireplaces, oversize or claw-foot tubs in the private baths, and down pillows and quilts make guest rooms even more cozy. The complimentary breakfast is a gourmet's delight. ⊞ *1102 W. Pikes Peak Ave., 80904,* ☎ *719/471–3980. 5 rooms. AE, D, MC, V.*

$–$$ **Victoria's Keep.** Proud owners Marvin and Vicki Keith renovated this turreted 1891 Queen Anne in 1993 to create this unique B&B. The parlor verges on the Dickensian, with its slightly fussy, Victorian clutter. There are carved tile ceilings and intricate tracery, as well as the Keiths' impressive collections of china and Depression glass throughout the house. Each room has its own fireplace and some distinguishing feature, whether it be a Jacuzzi or a claw-foot tub, stained glass windows, or thrilling views of Miramont Castle. The decor is similarly eclectic, from ultramodern wicker furnishings to Victorian antiques. Marvin is an accomplished chef; his gourmet breakfasts might include poached eggs with brandy cream sauce or stuffed French toast. Every evening he puts out another complimentary spread, including wine, cheese, and delectable appetizers. Guests also have free use of mountain bikes. ⊞ *202 Ruxton Ave., Manitou Springs 80829,* ☎ *800/905–5337. 5 rooms. Hot tub. AE, D, MC, V.*

Pueblo

$$ **Abriendo Inn.** This exquisite 1906 home, listed on the National Reg-
★ ister of Historic Places, overflows with character. Gracious owners Kerrelyn and Chuck Trent did most of the painting, papering, and refurbishing themselves. The house now gleams with its original, lovingly restored parquet floors, stained glass, and Minnequa oak wainscoting. The seven no-smoking rooms are richly appointed with antiques, oak armoires, quilts, crocheted bedspreads, and either brass

or four-poster beds. Fresh fruit and cookies are left out for guests, and gourmet breakfast and evening cheese and crackers are included in the rate. ⚏ *300 W. Abriendo Ave., 81004,* ☎ *719/544–2703. 7 rooms. AE, MC, V.*

$$ **Inn at Pueblo West Best Western.** This handsome sprawling resort is a notch above most Best Westerns. Although it's out of the way for those who want to be close to town (about 15 minutes away by car), the golf course and activities on nearby Lake Pueblo keep guests busy. Large rooms in dark mountain colors and with terraces have an elegant woodsy feel. ⚏ *201 S. McCulloch Blvd., 81007,* ☎ *719/547–2111 or 800/448–1972. 80 rooms. Restaurant, bar, pool, 4 tennis courts. AE, D, DC, MC, V.*

Salida

$ **The Poor Country Farm Inn.** On the Arkansas River, this cozy Victorian home has breathtaking mountain prospects. Rooms are filled with antiques and family memorabilia. A complimentary gourmet breakfast is provided to guests. *8495 CR 60, 81201,* ☎ *719/539–3818. 5 rooms, 4 with shared bath; co-ed dorm sleeps 8. MC, V.*

Trinidad

$ **Best Western Country Club Inn.** To apply the term "country club" is exaggerating this lodging's amenities. Still, rooms are clean and comfortable and are decorated in warm earth tones. ⚏ *(Exit 13A off I–25) 900 W. Adams, 81082,* ☎ *719/846–2215. 55 rooms. Restaurant, bar, hot tub, exercise room, coin laundry. AE, D, DC, MC, V.*

Victor

$–$$ **Victor Hotel.** In 1991, more than $1 million was dedicated to renovating this hotel, listed on the National Register of Historic Places. Public spaces have been restored to their Victorian splendor, adding to the list of reasons why Victor Hotel is the nicest place to stay in the Cripple Creek area. Other attributes include tastefully decorated rooms with stunning mountain views. Unfortunately, aside from the original open brickwork and a few old-fashioned tubs and radiators, the decor and furnishings are prosaically modern, and bathrooms are tiny. ⚏ *4th and Victor Sts., 80860,* ☎ *719/689–3553. 30 rooms. Restaurant. AE, D, MC, V.*

The Arts and Nightlife

The Arts

Pueblo's **Sangre de Cristo Arts and Conference Center** (210 N. Santa Fe Trail, ☎ 719/542–1211) presents the **Southern Colorado Repertory Theatre, Pueblo Ballet,** and **Dancespectra.**

Colorado Springs' **Pikes Peak Center** (190 S. Cascade Ave., ☎ 719/520–7469) presents the **Colorado Springs Symphony,** as well as touring theater and dance companies.

MUSIC

The **Pueblo Symphony** (503 N. Main St., Suite 414, ☎ 719/546–0333) offers cowboy to classical music throughout the year.

Salida draws some of the musicians from the Aspen Music Festival during the summer, becoming the **Aspen-Salida Music Festival,** July–August.

THEATER

Air Force Academy, Arnold Hall (Colorado Springs, ☎ 719/472–4497) presents touring and local companies.

Broadway Theatre League (Memorial Hall, Pueblo, ☎ 719/545–4721) presents touring shows and specialty acts.

Powerhouse Players (200 W. Sackett St., Salida, ☎ 719/539–2455), a community theater based in Dallas, presents a variety of musical revues and straight plays throughout the summer in the town's historic steam plant.

Nightlife

BARS AND LOUNGES

In Buena Vista, head to the **Green Parrot** (304 Main St., ☎ 719/395–8985), which has live music weekends.

In Colorado Springs, the **Golden Bee** (International Center, The Broadmoor, ☎ 719/634–7711) is an institution. The gloriously old-fashioned bar, with pressed-tin ceilings and magnificent woodwork, features a piano player leading sing-alongs. **Judge Baldwin's** (4 S. Cascade Ave., Antlers Hotel, ☎ 719/473–5600) is a lively brew pub. **Phantom Canyon Brewing Co.** (2 E. Pikes Peak Ave., ☎ 719/635–2800), in a turn-of-the-century warehouse, has colorful rotating art exhibits and great pub grub (try the sensational gourmet pizzas, barbecued shrimp braised in India Pale Ale, or the sinful black-and-tan cheesecake brownie).

In Pueblo, **Gus' Place** (Elm and Mesa Sts., ☎ 719/542–0756) is a big Yuppie hangout that once held the record for the most kegs emptied in an evening. **Peppers** (4109 Club Manor Dr., ☎ 719/542–8629) has something going on every evening, from oldies nights to stand-up comedy. The **Irish Pub** (108 W. 3rd St., ☎ 719/542–9974) is always hopping after work hours.

CASINOS

Cripple Creek has several casinos that offer limited-stakes gambling (*see* Tour 2, *in* Exploring, *above*).

COMEDY CLUBS

Laffs Comedy Corner (1305 N. Academy Blvd., Colorado Springs, ☎ 719/591–0707) showcases live stand-up comedy; some of the performers here are nationally known.

COUNTRY AND WESTERN

Colorado Springs has several C&W spots. **Cowboys** (Rustic Hills North Shopping Ctr., ☎ 719/596–1212) is for hard-core two-steppers. **Gambler's Dance Hall and Saloon** (3958 N. Academy Blvd., ☎ 719/574–3369) attracts a younger, family-oriented clientele. **Rodeo** (3506 N. Academy Blvd., ☎ 719/597–6121) tends to have a Yuppie crowd.

Pueblo's **The Chief** (611 N. Main St., ☎ 719/546–1246) is a classic honky-tonk that has live bands most evenings.

In Trinidad, the **El Rancho Bar** (Santa Fe Ave., ☎ 719/846–9049) is a wildly popular hangout in a barn setting.

DINNER SHOWS

Cripple Creek's **Imperial Hotel Theater** (123 N. 3rd. St., ☎ 719/689–2922) is renowned for its Victorian melodramas. In Colorado Springs, the **Flying W Ranch** (3300 Chuckwagon Rd., ☎ 719/598–4000), open mid-May–October, ropes them in for the its sensational Western stage show and chuck-wagon dinner. The **Iron Springs Chateau** (Manitou Springs, across from Pikes Peak Cog Railway, ☎ 719/685–5104) offers stagings of comedy melodramas.

DISCOS
In Colorado Springs, you can dance part of the night away at **Stars** (the Broadmoor, 1 Lake Ave., ☎ 719/634–7711), a sleek, intimate boîte with a striking black granite bar, a black marble floor inlaid with gold stars, and walls covered with photos of celebrities who have stayed at the Broadmoor over the years, and **The Heat** (3506 N. Academy St., ☎ 719/591–2100), which attracts a younger, less sedate crowd.

In Pueblo, try **Images** (4001 N. Elizabeth St., ☎ 719/543–8050).

JAZZ CLUBS
There is usually live jazz at the **Charles Court** (the Broadmoor, Colorado Springs, ☎ 719/634–7711) several nights weekly.

ROCK CLUBS
In Trinidad, **The Other Place** (466 W. Main St., ☎ 719/846–9012) hires top local bands on weekends to play its intimate classy space.

SINGLES
In Colorado Springs, try **Old Chicago** (118 N. Tejon Ave., ☎ 719/634–8812).

South Central Colorado Essentials

Arriving and Departing by Plane
AIRPORTS AND AIRLINES
Colorado Springs: **Colorado Springs Municipal Airport** (☎ 719/596–0188) is served by American Airlines (☎ 800/433–4700), America West (☎ 800/247–5692), Continental (☎ 800/525–0280), Delta (☎ 800/221–1212), TWA (☎ 800/221–2000), and United (☎ 800/241–6522).

Pueblo: **Pueblo Memorial Airport** (☎ 719/948–3355) welcomes flights from United Express.

Between the Airport and the Hotels/Downtown
BY BUS OR SHUTTLE
Airport Transportation Service (☎ 719/635–3518) offers regular shuttles from the Colorado Springs airport to hotels. **Colorado Springs/Pueblo Airporter** (☎ 719/578–5232) services the stretch of I–25 between the two cities.

BY TAXI
In Colorado Springs: **Yellow Cab** (☎ 719/634–5000). In Pueblo: **City Cab** (☎ 719/543–2525).

Arriving and Departing by Car, Train, and Bus
BY CAR
I–25, which bisects Colorado and runs north–south from New Mexico to Wyoming, is the major artery accessing the area.

BY TRAIN
Amtrak (☎ 800/872–7245) stops in Trinidad and La Junta.

BY BUS
Greyhound Lines (☎ 800/231–2222) and **TNM&O Coaches** (☎ 719/544–6295) serve most of the major towns in the region.

Getting Around
BY BUS
Colorado Springs Transit (☎ 719/475–9733) serves most of the Colorado Springs metropolitan area, including Manitou Springs.

Pueblo Transit (☎ 719/542–4306) services Pueblo and outlying areas.

The **Trinidad Trolley** stops at parks and historical sites, departing from the parking lot next to City Hall (for information, call the Chamber of Commerce, ☎ 719/846–9285).

In Colorado Springs: **Yellow Cab** (☎ 719/634–5000); in Pueblo: **City Cab** (☎ 719/543–2525); in Trinidad: **City Cab** (☎ 719/846–2237).

Pueblo and Colorado Springs are both on I–25. Florissant and Buena Vista are reached via U.S. 24 off I–25; Cañon City and the Royal Gorge via U.S. 50. Salida can be reached via CO 291 from either U.S. 24 or U.S. 50. La Junta can be reached via U.S. 50 from Pueblo or U.S. 350 from Trinidad.

Guided Tours
ORIENTATION
Gray Line (☎ 719/633–1181) offers tours of the Colorado Springs area, including Pikes Peak and Manitou Springs, as well as jaunts to Cripple Creek.

Important Addresses and Numbers
HOSPITALS
Arkansas Valley Regional Medical Center (1100 Carson Ave., La Junta, ☎ 719/384–5412); **Colorado Springs Memorial Hospital** (1400 E. Boulder Ave., Colorado Springs, ☎ 719/475–5000); **Heart of the Rockies Regional Medical Center** (448 E. 1st St., Salida, ☎ 719/539–6661); **Mt. San Rafael Hospital** (410 Benedicta St., Trinidad, ☎ 719/846–9213); **Parkview Episcopal Medical Center** (400 W. 16th St., Pueblo, ☎ 719/584–4000); **St. Thomas More Hospital** (1019 Sheridan St., Canon City, ☎ 719/275–3381).

VISITOR INFORMATION
Buena Vista Chamber of Commerce (U.S. 24, Buena Vista 81211, ☎ 719/395–6612); **Cañon City Chamber of Commerce** (Bin 749, Cañon City 81215, ☎ 719/275–2331); **Colorado Springs Convention and Visitors Bureau** (104 S. Cascade Ave., Suite 104, Colorado Springs 80903, ☎ 719/635–7506 or 800/368–4748); **Cripple Creek Chamber of Commerce** (Box 650, Cripple Creek 80813, ☎ 719/689–2169 or 800/526–8777); **Florissant/Lake George Chamber of Commerce** (Box 507, Florissant 80816, ☎ 719/748–3395); **Heart of the Rockies Chamber of Commerce** (406 W. Rainbow Blvd., Salida 81201, ☎ 719/539–2068); **Huerfano County Chamber of Commerce** (Box 493, Walsenburg 81089, ☎ 719/738–1065); **La Junta Chamber of Commerce** (110 Santa Fe Ave., La Junta 81050, ☎ 719/384–7411); **La Veta/Cuchara Chamber of Commerce** (Box 32, La Veta 81055, ☎ 719/742–3676); **Lamar Chamber of Commerce** (Box 860, Lamar 81052, ☎ 719/336–4379); **Manitou Springs Chamber of Commerce** (354 Manitou Ave., Manitou Springs 80829, ☎ 719/685–5089 or 800/642–2567); **Pueblo Chamber of Commerce and Convention & Visitors Bureau** (302 N. Santa Fe Ave., Pueblo 81003, ☎ 719/542–1704 or 800/233–3446); **Trinidad/Las Animas Chamber of Commerce** (309 Nevada St., Trinidad 81082, ☎ 719/846–9285).

NORTH CENTRAL COLORADO

North central Colorado is an appealing blend of Old West and New Age. More a ranching than a mining area, it's strewn with rich evocations of pioneer life, as well as turn-of-the-century resort towns such as Estes Park and Grand Lake. Yet the region is anchored by Boulder, one of the country's most progressive cities and a town virtually synonymous (some might say obsessed) with environmental concern and physical fitness. As the local joke goes, even the dogs jog.

Boulderites take full advantage of the town's glorious natural setting, nestled amid the peaks of the Front Range, indulging in everything from rock climbing to mountain biking. A short drive south brings them to the ski areas along I–70. To the west and north, the Roosevelt and Arapahoe national forests and the Great Lakes of Colorado provide a host of recreational opportunities from hiking to fishing to cross-country skiing and snowmobiling. To the northeast, Estes Park stands as the gateway to America's alpine wonderland—Rocky Mountain National Park, which spans three ecosystems that 900 species of plants, 250 species of birds, and 25 species of mammals, including elk, muletail deer, moose, bobcats, and even black bears, call home.

Exploring

Numbers in the margin correspond to points of interest on the North Central Colorado map.

❶ No place in Colorado better epitomizes the state's outdoor mania than **Boulder.** There are more bikes than cars in this uncommonly beautiful and beautifully uncommon city, embroidered with 25,000 acres of parks and greenbelts laced with jogging tracks and bike trails. You're also more likely to see ponytails than crew cuts: Boulder is a college town with an arty, liberal reputation. Physically fit and environmentally hip, it's a city of cyclists and recyclers who, when they're not out enjoying their natural surroundings, enjoy nothing more than sitting at a sidewalk café, watching the rest of the world jog by.

Boulder's heartbeat is the **Pearl Street Mall,** a mind-boggling, eye-catching array of chic shops and trendy restaurants where all of Boulder hangs out. As a bonus, the mall slices through Mapleton Hill, a historic district of great charm.

On the outskirts of the city there are three free attractions worth visiting. The first is the **Celestial Seasonings Plant** (4600 Sleepytime Dr., ☎ 303/581–1202; tours Mon.–Sat. 10–3), offering free tours of this well-known herbal tea company's processing and manufacturing facility. An unmistakable aroma permeates the parking lot; inside you can see the product ingredients in their raw form (the Mint Room is isolated due to its potent scent) and how they're blended. The tour ends up in the gift shop for a tea-tasting. Also aromatic are the free tours of the **Boulder Beer Company** (2880 Wilderness Pl., ☎ 303/444–8448). These run Monday–Saturday, at 2 PM, and culminate in a tasting. The last free attraction is the **Leanin' Tree Museum of Western Art** (6055 Longbow Dr., ☎ 303/530–1442; open weekdays 8–4:30)—brought to you by the folks who make wildly popular and humorous Western-themed greeting cards—whose superlative collection ranges from traditionalists in the Remington and Bierstadt manner to stylistic innovators of the Western genre. One room is devoted to the paintings of the original greeting-card genius, Lloyd Mitchell.

Take Broadway north to the **University of Colorado** (☎ 303/492–6301) campus, where spacious lawns separate a handsome collection of stone buildings with red tile roofs. Tours are available weekday afternoons. A favorite nearby student hangout is the bohemian neighborhood called The Hill (around 13th and College streets, west of the campus), home to lots of coffeehouses and hip boutiques, and always happening day or night.

North Central Colorado

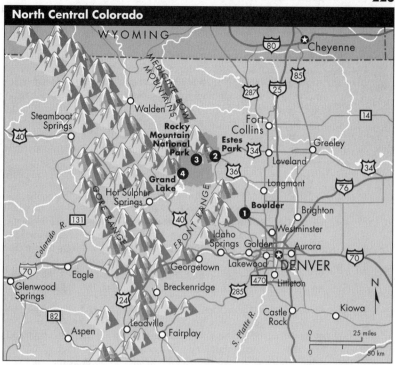

TIME OUT **Alfalfa's** (Broadway and Arapahoe St., ☎ 303/442–0082) is a New Age organic supermarket, where one-stop shopping will net you everything from "cruelty-free" cosmetics to herbal and homeopathic remedies. The deli offers predictably healthful fare, with a crisp, fresh salad bar, homemade muffins and soups (usually something like tofu miso), and custom-blended vegetable and fruit juices.

The prettiest views of town can be had by following Baseline Drive (off Broadway) up to **Chatauqua Park,** site of the Colorado Music Festival, and a favorite oasis of locals on weekends. Continue farther up Flagstaff Mountain to Panorama Point and Boulder Mountain Park, where people jog, bike, climb, and rarely remain still. The admirable parks system also includes the trademark red sandstone **Flatirons.** These massive structures, so named for their flat rock faces, are popular among rock climbers and hikers; they can be seen from almost every vantage point in town.

The most direct route to Rocky Mountain National Park is along U.S. 36 North, via the quaint town of **Lyons.** The scenery gives little hint of the grandeur to come when you reach **Estes Park.** If ever there was a classic picture-postcard Rockies view, Estes Park has it. Even the McDonald's has glorious views and a facade that complements its surroundings, thanks to strict zoning laws that require all businesses to present a rustic exterior. The town itself is very family-oriented: Many of the small hotels lining the country roads are mom-and-pop outfits that have been passed down through several generations.

TIME OUT At **Ed's Cantina** (362 E. Elkhorn Ave., ☎ 970/586–2919) the walls are festooned with pennants and neon signs advertising beer and ball clubs.

Huge, filling breakfast burritos and tasty burgers are the more reliable choices at this popular locals' hangout.

If you would rather explore Estes' environs than the park, you have a number of options. As a resort town, Estes attracted the attention of genius entrepreneur F. O. Stanley, inventor of the Stanley Steamer automobile and several photographic processes. In 1905, having been told by his doctors he would soon die of tuberculosis, he constructed the regal **Stanley Hotel** on a promontory overlooking the town. Stanley went on to live another 30-odd years, an extension that he attributed to the fresh air. The hotel soon became one of the most glamorous resorts in the Rockies, a position it holds to this day. Incidentally, the hotel was the inspiration for Stephen King's spooky book, *The Shining,* later made into a movie by Stanley Kubrick starring Jack Nicholson.

From the Stanley, turn left to return to U.S. 36. In two blocks you'll see the **Estes Park Area Historical Museum.** The archeological evidence displayed here makes an eloquent case that Native Americans used the area as a summer resort. The museum also offers the usual assortment of pioneer artifacts and mounts interesting changing exhibits. *200 4th St.,* ☎ *970/586–6256.* ☛ *$2 adults, $1 children.* ☉ *May–Oct., Mon.–Sat. 10–5, Sun. 1–5; Mar.–Apr., Fri.–Sat. 10–5, Sun. 1–5.*

Double back on U.S. 36 where it intersects with U.S. 34; follow U.S. 34 to MacGregor Avenue and take it for a mile. The **MacGregor Ranch Museum,** in the National Register of Historic Places, offers spectacular views of the Twin Owls and Longs Peak (towering more than 14,000 feet). Although the original ranch was homesteaded in 1873, the present house was built in 1896, and provides a well-preserved record of typical ranch life, thanks to a wealth of material discovered in the attic. *MacGregor Ave.,* ☎ *970/586–3749.* ☛ *Free.* ☉ *June–Sept., Tues.–Sat. 10–5.*

③ These sights give you a good education about the history of the area, but the real attraction in the neighborhood is **Rocky Mountain National Park** (☎ 970/586–1206; ☛ $5 weekly per vehicle), sculpted by violent volcanic uplifts and receding glaciers that savagely clawed the earth in their wake. There are three distinct ecosystems in the park, including verdant subalpine, a cathedral of towering proud ponderosa pines; alpine; and harsh, unforgiving tundra, with wind-whipped trees that grow at right angles and dollhouse-size versions of familiar plants and wildflowers. The park also teems with wildlife, from beaver to bighorn sheep, with the largest concentrations of sheep and majestic elk in Horseshoe Meadow.

The fine visitor centers at the east and west ends of the park, on, respectively, U.S. 36 and U.S. 34 (also called Trail Ridge Rd., the world's highest continuous paved highway; open only in summer), offer maps, brochures, newsletters, and comprehensive information on the park's statistics and facilities. The park is a splendid place to wander. The scenery, accessed by various trails, can be similar, but still inspiring. Trail Ridge Road accesses several lovely hikes along its meandering way, through terrain filigreed with silvery streams and turquoise lakes. The views around each bend—of moraines and glaciers, and craggy hills framing emerald meadows carpeted with columbine and Indian paintbrush—are truly awesome: nature's workshop on an epic scale.

Take U.S. 36 South for about 4 miles to Bear Lake Road and the **Moraine Park Museum** (open May–Sept., daily 10–6), which offers lectures, slide

Rocky Mountain National Park

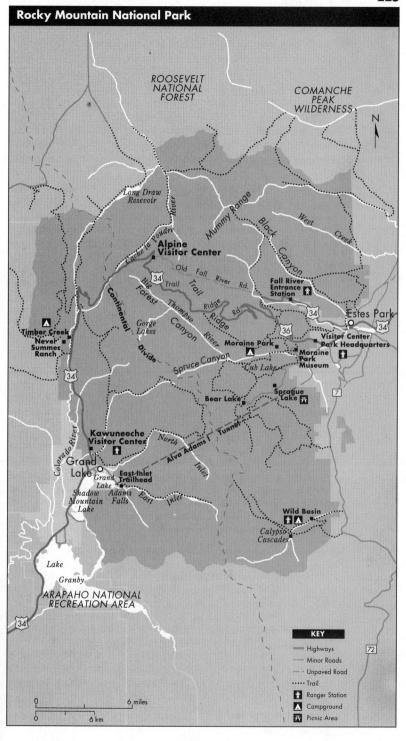

ROOSEVELT
NATIONAL
FOREST

COMANCHE
PEAK
WILDERNESS

N

Long Draw
Resevoir

Mummy Range

Black Canyon

West Creek

Cache la Poudre River

**Alpine
Visitor Center**

34

Old Fall River Rd.

Trail

Trail

**Fall River
Entrance
Station**

34

Estes Park

Big Thompson River

Forest Canyon

Ridge

Ridge Rd.

36

**Visitor Center
Park Headquarters**

Continental

Gorge
Lakes

Moraine Park

**Moraine
Park
Museum**

Divide

Spruce Canyon

Cub Lake

**Timber Creek
Never
Summer
Ranch**

34

Bear Lake

**Sprague
Lake**

7

**Kawuneeche
Visitor Center**

North

Alva Adams | Tunnel

Inlet

Colorado River

**Grand
Lake**

Grand
Lake

**East Inlet
Trailhead**

Adams
Falls

East Inlet

Wild Basin

Shadow
Mountain
Lake

Calypso
Cascades

Lake
Granby

**ARAPAHO NATIONAL
RECREATION
AREA**

34

72

KEY

Highways
Minor Roads
Unpaved Road
Trail
Ranger Station
Campground
Picnic Area

0   6 miles

0   6 km

shows, and displays on the park's geology and botany. From the museum you can take the twisting, 9-mile-long Bear Lake Road as it winds past shimmering waterfalls perpetually shrouded with rainbows. The drive offers superlative views of Longs Peak (Colorado's highest) and the glaciers surrounding Bear Lake.

If you choose not to follow Bear Lake Road, head west from the museum on Trail Ridge Road. Many Peaks Curve affords breathtaking views of the crest of the Continental Divide and of the Alluvial Fan, a huge gash created in 1982 by a vicious flood after an earthen dam broke. Erosion occurred immediately, rather than over the millions of years that nature usually requires, and today it resembles a lonely lunar landscape.

❹ **Grand Lake** is the western gateway to the park, and it, too, enjoys an idyllic setting, on the shores of the state's largest natural lake, of the same name; this is the highest-altitude yacht anchorage in America. According to Ute legend, the fine mists that shroud the lake punctually at dawn are the risen spirits of women and children whose raft capsized as they were fleeing a marauding party of Cheyennes and Arapahoes. Grand Lake feeds into two much larger man-made reservoirs, **Lake Granby** and **Shadow Mountain Lake,** forming the "Great Lakes of Colorado." The entire area is a paradise for hikers and fishermen, and for snowmobilers in winter. Even the town, while it has the usual assortment of souvenir shops and motels, seems less spoiled than many other resort communities.

Off the Beaten Track

Fort Collins was originally established to protect traders from the natives, while the former negotiated the treacherous Overland Trail. Unexpectedly, however, the town grew on two industries: education (Colorado State University was founded here in 1879) and agriculture (rich crops of alfalfa and sugar beets). The Visitors and Convention Bureau has designated a historic walking tour of more than 20 buildings, including the stately sandstone **Avery House** and the original university structures. **Old Town Square** is an urban renewal project that re-creates a pioneer town, whose buildings house upscale stores and cafés set around playing fountains. The **Fort Collins Museum** (200 Matthews St., ☎ 970/221–6738; ☛ $2 adults, $1 children under 12; open Tues.–Sat. 10–5, Sun. noon–5) includes an 1860s stone cabin and an 1884 schoolhouse on the grounds.

Shopping

Shopping Districts and Malls

Boulder's **Pearl Street Mall** is a shopping extravaganza, with numerous upscale boutiques and galleries. **The Hill,** by the University of Colorado, is a great place for hip duds and CDs. Main Street in the tiny town of **Niwot** (northeast of Boulder on CO 119) is one long strip of antiques stores. Main Street in **Lyons** (north of Boulder on U.S. 36) also has several fine antiques shops. In Estes Park, the **Park Theatre Mall** and **Old Church Shops Mall** feature a wide variety of upscale stores that hawk primarily indigenous crafts. Fort Collins's **Old Town Square** is a pleasant collection of cafés and intriguing shops.

Specialty Stores

ART GALLERIES

Pearl Street Mall, in Boulder, features a number of art galleries and boutiques that carry crafts. **Art Source International** (1237 Pearl St., ☎ 303/444–4080) is Colorado's largest antique print and map dealer. **Hand-**

made in Colorado (1426 Pearl St., ☏ 303/938–8394) sells only the best Colorado-made goods. **Boulder Arts & Crafts Cooperative** (1421 Pearl St., ☏ 303/443–3683) offers exquisite hand-painted silk scarves, hand-woven garments, glass art, and pottery. **McLaren & Markowitz Gallery** (1011 Pearl St., ☏ 303/449–6807) features fine jewelry, sculpture, paintings, and pottery—primarily with a Southwestern feel. **White Horse Gallery** (1218 Pearl St., ☏ 303/443–6116) offers top-of-the-line Native American and Southwestern art and artifacts.

In Estes Park, **Michael Ricker Pewter** (U.S. 34 East, base of Lake Estes Dam, ☏ 970/586–2030) offers free tours of its casting studio and gallery, where you can see the world's largest pewter sculpture. **Glassworks** (340 Elkhorn Ave., ☏ 970/586–8619) offers glassblowing demonstrations and sells a rainbow of glass creations. **Gallery of the Winds** (222 Moraine Ave., ☏ 970/586–5514) is dedicated to promoting top regional artists in various media.

In Grand Lake, **Grand Lake Art Gallery** (1117 Grand Ave., ☏ 970/627–3104) purveys superlative weavings, pottery, stained glass, gourds, and landscapes, primarily by regional artists.

CHILDREN

The Christmas Shoppe (Park Theatre Mall, Estes Park, ☏ 970/586–2882) delights kids of all ages with every conceivable Noël-related ornament, doll, curio, and knickknack from around the world. **Jilly Beans** (1136 Spruce St., Boulder, ☏ 303/443–1757) sells enchanting hand-crafted toys and furnishings. **The Printed Page** (1219 Pearl St., Boulder, ☏ 970/443–8450) presents unique and exquisite old-fashioned toys.

CLOTHING

In Boulder, **Alpaca Connection** (1326 Pearl St., ☏ 303/447–2047) offers Indian silks, Bolivian alpaca, and Ecuadorian merino wool garments. **Chico's** (1200 Pearl St., Boulder, ☏ 303/449–3381) traffics in funky jewelry and natural fibers and fabrics from around the globe. **Pura Vida Imports** (2012 10th St., Boulder, ☏ 303/440–5601) specializes in women's clothing and accessories with an international accent. In Estes Park, **JB Sweaters** (140 E. Elkhorn Ave., ☏ 970/586–6101) features hand-knit sweaters, shirts, and ties for men and women. In Greeley, **Ephemera Artistic Garments** (☏ 970/330–9508) sells Rachael Pitkin's wonderfully colorful and humorous hats by appointment only.

OUTDOOR GEAR

In Boulder, visit **Hangouts** (1328 Pearl St., ☏ 303/442–2533) for their splendid handmade hammocks. **McGuckin's Hardware** (Village Shopping Ctr., ☏ 303/443–1822) is a Boulder institution that features a mind-boggling array of equipment and tools.

WESTERN PARAPHERNALIA

Artesanias (1420 Pearl St., Boulder, ☏ 303/442–3777) sells Zapotec rugs, Mexican santos, decorative iron, and handcrafted furniture. **Rocky Mountain Comfort** (116 E. Elkhorn Ave., Estes Park, ☏ 970/586–0512) has home accessories with the lodge look, including furniture, quilts, baskets, and throws, and even local foodstuffs. **Stage Western Family Clothing** (104 Moraine Ave., Estes Park, ☏ 970/586–3430), permeated by the pungent aroma of leather, offers imaginative cowboy hats, boots, and belts. **Aspen Kickin'** (Main St., Nederland, ☏ 303/642–7397) offers marvelous handcrafted log furniture.

Sports and the Outdoors

Cycling

The **Boulder Creek path** winds for 16 miles from Eben G. Fine Park, at the base of Boulder Canyon, to 55th Street, passing gardens and a fish observatory along the way. There is excellent cycling throughout the **Roosevelt National Forest** (☎ 970/498–1100).

Camping

Camping facilities abound in the 800,000 acres of **Roosevelt National Forest** (☎ 970/498–1100). There are five top-notch sites in **Rocky Mountain National Park** (☎ 970/586–1206).

Fishing

The best fishing can be found on **Grand Lake, Lake Granby,** and the **Big Thompson River** near Estes Park, and the **Horsetooth Reservoir, Red Feather Lakes,** and **Cache la Poudre River** west of Fort Collins. For more information, call the Colorado Division of Wildlife Northeast Region (☎ 970/484–2836). **Rocky Mountain Adventures** (Estes Park, ☎ 970/586–6191) offers guided fly- and float-fishing.

Golf

Collindale Golf Course (1441 E. Horsetooth St., Ft. Collins, ☎ 970/221–6651) is an 18-hole public course.

Estes Park Golf Club (1080 S. St. Vrain St., ☎ 970/586–8146) is one of the oldest and prettiest 18-hole courses in the state.

In Boulder, **Flatirons Golf Course** (5706 Arapahoe Ave., ☎ 303/442–7851) is an 18-hole public course at the foot of the eponymous mountains; and **Lake Valley Golf Club** (Neva Rd., 5 mi north of Boulder, ☎ 303/444–2144) is another 18-hole course with fine views.

Grand Lake Golf Course (CR 48, Grand Lake, ☎ 970/627–8008) is an 18-hole course 8,240 feet above sea level.

Hiking

The premier hiking, of course, is within **Rocky Mountain National Park.** The **Colorado Mountain Club** (Estes Park, ☎ 970/586–6623) sponsors day and overnight trips into the park. Other splendid hiking is within the superb **Boulder Mountain Parks** system, including Chatauqua Park and Sunshine Canyon. **Roosevelt National Forest** (☎ 970/498–1100) offers fine backcountry hiking in the Estes Park area. For information, call the **Boulder Parks and Recreation Department** (☎ 303/441–3000).

In Grand County, near Lake Granby, **Indian Peaks Wilderness Area** (☎ 970/887–3331) is another prime location.

West of Fort Collins, in truly unspoiled surroundings, the **Colorado State Forest** (☎ 970/723–8366) offers superb hiking.

Horseback Riding

National Park Village Stables (☎ 970/586–5269) and **Sombrero Stables** (☎ 970/586–4577) offer trail rides through the Estes Park region, including Rocky Mountain National Park. **Sundance Adventure Center** (Ward, ☎ 303/459–0225) offers trail rides as well as pack trips, rock-climbing trips, and mountain biking and Jeep tours in less-traveled parts of the Rockies.

Rafting

A-1 Wildwater (☎ 970/586–6548 or 800/369–4165), **Rapid Transit Rafting** (☎ 970/586–8852 or 800/367–8523), and **Whitewater Raft-**

ing (☏ 970/586–6191 or 800/858–6808) run trips out of Estes Park up the Poudre River.

Skiing

CROSS-COUNTRY

The lower valleys of **Rocky Mountain National Park** (☏ 970/586–1206) are accessible year-round and provide miles of trails. The **Grand Lake Touring Center** (☏ 970/627–8008) offers 32 miles of trails with breathtaking vistas of the Never Summer Range and the Continental Divide. The **Never Summer Yurt System** (Box 1254, Ft. Collins 80522, ☏ 970/484–3903) is a hut-to-hut system. **Snow Mountain Ranch** (U.S. 40, 15 miles west of Winter Park, ☏ 970/887–2152) has 62 miles of groomed trails.

DOWNHILL

Eldora Mountain Resort. 43 trails; 9 lifts; 386 acres; 1,400-foot vertical. There is night skiing Wednesday–Saturday. *Rte. 119, Nederland,* ☏ *303/440–8700.* ⊙ *Mid-Nov.–mid-Apr. 9–4.*

SilverCreek Ski Area. 26 trails; 3 chairs, 1 T-bar; 248 acres; 1,000-foot vertical. Here's an excellent family area with many bargains. *U.S. 40, SilverCreek,* ☏ *970/887–3384.* ⊙ *Early Dec.–early Apr. 9–4.*

Snowmobiling

Grand Lake is considered by many to be Colorado's snowmobiling capital, with more than 130 miles of trails, many winding through virgin forest. Recommended outfitters, most of which can arrange guided tours, include **Catride** (☏ 970/627–8866), **Grand Lake Motor Sports** (☏ 970/627–3806), **Grand Lake Snowmobiles** (☏ 970/627–8304), **Lone Eagle Rentals** (☏ 970/627–3310), **Mustang Sports** (☏ 970/627–8177), and **Spirit Lake Rentals** (☏ 970/627–9288).

Water Sports

Grand Lake and **Lake Granby** are the premier boating centers. Call the **Spirit Lake Marina** (Grand Lake, ☏ 970/627–8158), **Trail Ridge Marina** (Shadow Mountain Lake, ☏ 970/627–3586), and **Beacon Landing** (Grand Lake, ☏ 970/627–3671) for information on renting pontoon boats and Windsurfers.

Dining

Boulder has almost as impressive a range of ethnic eateries as the much-larger Denver. Most prices are quite reasonable, thanks to a large student population that can't afford very expensive meals. There is far less diversity elsewhere in the region, although you can count on finding solid American or Continental restaurants throughout. For price ranges *see* the Dining chart *in* Colorado Essentials, *below.*

Boulder

$$$$ **Flagstaff House.** This refined restaurant atop Flagstaff Mountain is one
★ of Colorado's finest. Sit on the enclosed patio and drink in the sublime views of Boulder to go with a selection from the remarkably comprehensive wine list. Chef Mark Monet is noted for his exquisite combinations of ingredients and fanciful, playful presentations. The menu changes daily, but sample inspirations might include lobster ravioli and shrimp in shiitake broth; potato roll of smoked rabbit and duck with sautéed foie gras; mesquite-smoked alligator and rattlesnake; and elk dumplings with ginger and sweet onion. Those are just appetizers. Opt for the daily tasting menu. ✗ *Baseline Rd.,* ☏ *303/442–4640. Reservations required. AE, DC, MC, V.*

$$$ **Red Lion Inn.** Up in Boulder Canyon sits this beautiful inn, a local institution for natives and travelers alike. Ask to be seated in the original dining room—with its fireplace, antlers, Austrian murals, red tablecloths, and white napery—for the feeling of being in the Alps. The stone walls and potbellied stove in the bar make it a cozy place to wait for a table. The Red Lion is revered for its excellent game: Start with rattlesnake cakes or wild game sausage, then try the elk or caribou steak. Or order a satisfying old-fashioned specialty such as steak Diane or veal Oscar. ✗ *Rte. 119,* ☎ *303/442–9368. Reservations required. AE, MC, V. No lunch.*

$$ **Antica Roma.** By far the most romantic restaurant in Boulder, this trattoria is a virtual stage set for *Marriage of Figaro,* replete with a spotlit balcony, tinkling fountain, exposed brick, painted beams, and ironwork lamps. Breads and appetizers such as *brescaola* (smoked meats) and *bruschetta* (thick slabs of coarse bread slathered with tomatoes, garlic, olive oil, and cheese) are sensational. Unfortunately, pastas are heavy and undistinguished, just a cut above frozen entrées; stick to such simple dishes as grilled swordfish or salmon, and drink in the wonderful ambience. ✗ *1308 Pearl St.,* ☎ *303/442–0378. Reservations advised. AE, MC, V.*

$$ **Gold Hill Inn.** This humble log cabin 10 miles west of Boulder hardly
★   looks like a bastion of haute cuisine, but the six-course, $19.50 prix fixe dinner is to rave about. Sample entrées may be paella or lamb venison marinated for four days in buttermilk, juniper berries, and cloves. ✗ *Sunshine Canyon, 10 mi from Boulder,* ☎ *303/443–6461. Reservations advised. No credit cards. Closed Tues. No lunch.*

$$ **Imperial Mataam Fez.** You eat with your hands at this lavish Moroccan restaurant that looks like it came straight from *The Arabian Nights.* The prix-fixe dinner includes five courses, with such fragrant dishes as lamb with honey and almonds and hare paprika couscous. There are branches in Denver, Colorado Springs, and Vail, but this is the original. ✗ *2226 Pearl St.,* ☎ *303/440–4167. Reservations advised. AE, MC, V. No lunch.*

$$ **Mediterranean Café.** After work, when all of Boulder shows up to enjoy tapas, "The Med" becomes a real scene (you may feel quite closed in, despite the restaurant's light and airy design). The decor of this yuppieteria can be described as Portofino meets Santa Fe, with abstract art, terra-cotta floors, rough-hewn painted ceilings (glittering Christmas lights twinkling against a teal "sky"), and brightly colored tile. The open kitchen turns out satisfactory food—an Italian/Spanish/Provençal hybrid—which is complemented by an extensive, well-priced wine list. Come here for a dose of local attitude or stop by just to gaze at all the pretty people. ✗ *1002 Walnut St.,* ☎ *303/444–5335. Reservations advised. AE, MC, V. No lunch weekends.*

$$ **Sushi Zanmai.** The restaurant section is a cool, sleek place to enjoy
★   delectable seafood and very good hibachi items, but the action's really at the zany sushi bar, where the chefs periodically burst into song: "If you knew Sushi" is a popular request. There's always karaoke here, although the official night is Saturday. ✗ *1221 Spruce St.,* ☎ *303/440–0733. Reservations advised. AE, MC, V. No lunch weekends.*

$–$$ **Bangkok Cuisine.** This very pretty restaurant looks more like a French bistro than a typical Thai place, with cut glass lamps, brass fixtures, and mauve tablecloths. In addition to expertly prepared staples such as satay, lemon grass soup, pad Thai (Thai noodles), and the inimitable curries, try less familiar items such as Gung Pao—juicy shrimp charbroiled with red chili paste. ✗ *2017 13th St.,* ☎ *303/440–4830. Reservations accepted. AE, D, MC, V.*

$–$$ ★ **Zolo Grill.** David Query, who was once a personal chef to Malcolm Forbes, left Q's at the Boulderado to open this superlative Southwestern restaurant. Its huge picture windows overlook one of Boulder's most active strip malls (and the Flatirons beyond); blond wood furnishings, striking abstract art, and a high-tech open kitchen complete the urbane decor. The wonderfully inventive menu offers everything from oysters with red chili to blackened shrimp cakes to barbecued red chili duck tacos. The margaritas are sassy, and there's a short but fairly priced wine list (about half the wines are available by the glass). And the way-cool T-shirts are for sale. ✕ *2525 Arapahoe Blvd.,* ☎ *303/449–0444. Reservations advised. AE, D, MC, V.*

$ **L.A. Diner.** This temple of chrome and formica calls itself the Last American Diner, and is open for all three meals. Good ol' rock and roll blasts from the speakers, waiters zip by on roller skates, and the menu runs to classic diner food, from meat loaf to malts. ✕ *1955 28th St.,* ☎ *303/447–1997. Reservations accepted. MC, V.*

Estes Park

$$ **Nicky's Cattleman Restaurant.** Elegant wood beams, oak paneling, maroon carpeting and upholstery, and a huge picture window fronting the mountain and river, make this one of the most sophisticated dining spots in town. They age and cut their own meat here, and specialties include sensational sirloin prepared Greek style with onions, peppers, and feta, and prime rib broiled in rock salt. Nicky's also offers motorlodge rooms with shag carpeting. ✕ *1350 U.S. 34,* ☎ *970/586–5376. Reservations accepted. AE, D, MC, V. No lunch.*

$–$$ **Friar's.** The name refers to the fact that the restaurant occupies a former church. The back room is woodsier and more elegant; the front room sunnier, with blackboard tables (chalk is supplied). The food ranges from dependable salads and sandwiches to fine daily fish and chicken specials. ✕ *157 W. Elkhorn Ave.,* ☎ *970/586–2806. Reservations accepted. AE, D, DC, MC, V.*

Fort Collins

$ **Rio Grande Mexican Restaurant.** One of the best Mexican restaurants in the area, the Rio Grande always satisfies with old favorites like sopaipillas, burritos, and Mexican steak, as well as more fiery Tex-Mex fare. Minimargaritas are 99¢, and strong enough to impart a pleasant buzz. ✕ *150 W. College Ave.,* ☎ *970/224–5428. Reservations accepted. D, MC, V.*

Fraser

$–$$ **Crooked Creek Saloon.** This barnlike valley hot spot is festooned with pennants and trophies, along with old roundup photos, branding irons, and Native American art. "Eat 'til it hurts, drink 'til it feels better" is the Crooked Creek motto, and you might as well succumb. Sandwiches, from blackened chicken to turkey Oscar (smoked turkey, crabmeat, broccoli, and hollandaise), are terrific, as are the burgers, pastas, salads, and Mexican specialties. There's occasional live music and nonstop conviviality from the pool-and-pinball crowd. ✕ *U.S. 40,* ☎ *970/726–9250. Reservations accepted. AE, MC, V.*

Granby

$–$$ **Longbranch Restaurant.** *The* restaurant in Granby, this stylish Western coffee shop with warming fireplace, wood paneling, and wagonwheel chandeliers offers German, Mexican, Continental, and American fare. Not surprisingly, the quality is uneven; stick to what the German owners do best—goulash, schnitzel, and sauerbraten, with heavenly homemade spaetzle. The strudel is disappointing, but you'll probably be too full to eat dessert anyway! ✗ *185 E. Agate Ave. (U.S. 40),* ☎ *970/887–2209. Reservations advised. AE, MC, V.*

Grand Lake

$$ **Candee's Lakefront Restaurant.** The plain interior of this attractive old wooden building is redeemed by vaulted picture windows looking out over the lake. Or better yet, in summer sit out on the patio for open-air lakeside views. The no-frills menu runs to filet mignon, teriyaki, or honey-dipped fried chicken; the trout here is so fresh it seems to have jumped from the lake right onto your plate. ✗ *1007 Lake Ave.,* ☎ *970/627–9484. Reservations advised. AE, MC, V. Closed Mon. No dinner Sun.*

$–$$ **Mountain Inn.** The log cabin interior, decorated with old Singer sewing machines and Rotary Club banners, imparts a pleasant, woodsy feel. The fare ranges from fine Rocky Mountain oysters and veggie tempura to flavorful prime rib, beer-batter shrimp, and trout amandine. The Mexican food is also superior, if mild. The real standouts are the bread bowl stews and chicken pot pies. ✗ *612 Grand Ave.,* ☎ *970/627–3385. Reservations accepted. AE, MC, V.*

Lodging

There is a wide selection of accommodations, from charming Victorian B&Bs and guest houses to family-run motels and lodges to dude ranches. Unless otherwise noted, all accommodations include phones, cable TV, and private bath. For rates *see* the Lodging chart *in* Colorado Essentials, *below.*

Boulder

$$–$$$ **Hotel Boulderado.** It's hard to believe that this elegant 1909 beauty had
★ deteriorated into a flophouse by the late 1970s; fortunately, though, new ownership restored it in 1980. The public spaces are wonderful places to idle: Spend some time in the gracious lobby, which resembles a private men's club; or on the second floor, with romantic nooks galore—especially suitable for enjoying a quiet drink (or you can head to the always-hopping Catacomb Blues Bar). When choosing your accommodations, opt for the old building, with spacious rooms filled with period antiques and reproductions, over the new wing, which is plush and comfortable but has less character. The gourmet restaurant, Q's, features the stylish new American cuisine of John Platt. Guests have access to a nearby health club. ☎ *2115 13th St., 80302,* ☎ *303/442–4344 or 800/433–4344,* ☏ *303/442–4378. 103 rooms. 3 restaurants, 2 bars. AE, DC, MC, V.*

$$–$$$ **Victoria B&B.** This ideally situated, restored 1870s Victorian offers the
★ most exquisite accommodations in the area. Large rooms, each named after a present or former owner and all with private bath, run toward the Laura Ashley English country-home look. Brass beds, down comforters, terry-cloth robes, lace curtains, rocking chairs, dried flowers, and period antiques complete the picture. In addition to the complimentary Continental breakfast, baked goods (try the scones or gingersnaps), and tea are served every afternoon in a sunny parlor scented with potpourri. ☎ *1305 Pine St., 80302,* ☎ *303/938–1300. 7 rooms. AE, MC, V.*

$$ **Briar Rose B&B.** Innkeeper Margaret Weisenbach makes guests feel completely at home at this appealing bed-and-breakfast. Perhaps the fact that she and her husband also live here accounts for the comfortable, lived-in feel of the place. There are five rooms in the sturdy, 1890s brick main house and four in the adjacent carriage house. The individually decorated rooms abound in froufrou, like floral carpeting and flowers stenciled above the headboards. All rooms have down comforters and private baths; the most expensive have wood-burning fireplaces. ⌂ *2151 Arapahoe Ave., 80302,* ☎ *303/442–3007. 9 rooms. AE, DC, MC, V.*

$$ **Clarion Harvest House.** This relatively large property has an unusual
★   semicircular design, set amid immaculate gardens dotted with splashing fountains. Spacious rooms are done up in light woods and pastel colors, and some have full baths with a mountain view. In keeping with Boulder's environmental concerns, 32 rooms have been designated as ecologically sound, with all trash recycled and water recirculated and treated. ⌂ *1345 28th St., 80302,* ☎ *303/443–3850,* FAX *303/443–1480. 259 rooms. Restaurant, 2 bars, indoor/outdoor pool and hot tub, 15 tennis courts, basketball, exercise room, volleyball, playground, laundry service, meeting rooms, car rental. AE, D, DC, MC, V.*

$$ **Coburn Hotel.** Designer and architect Scott Coburn wanted to create a tasteful lodging that would offer the services of a hotel and the intimacy of a B&B, and he has succeeded. The grand foyer, with pine floors, a fieldstone fireplace, stained glass windows, wicker armchairs, a rotating gallery of modern art, and enormous cacti, leads into a coffee bar with saddle stools. Rooms vary slightly in amenities, views, and details: half have fireplaces and a third have Jacuzzis; phone and cable TV are standard throughout. Decor, mostly in beige and forest green, is Scandinavia meets the Old West: hand-carved wood and iron beds, down comforters, duck decoys, petrified-wood wreaths, cowboy prints, pine armoires, and lamps fashioned from old candy tins. A "green" hotel, the Coburn uses low-flush toilets, reduced-flow showerheads, and 100% cotton linens, and it does not use chemicals for cleaning. The location catercorner from a Salvation Army shelter might prove discomforting for some. ⌂ *2040 16th St., 80302,* ☎ *303/545–5200,* FAX *303/440–6740. 12 rooms. AE, MC, V.*

$$ **Pearl Street Inn.** The decor is reserved and refined at this striking B&B, favoring subtle shades of purple, plush carpeting, wildlife prints and antiques, and brass or mahogany four-poster beds. The dining alcove and outdoor patio are lovely places to enjoy the complimentary gourmet breakfasts. For dinner the restaurant serves lovely meals and is open to the public. ⌂ *1820 Pearl St., 80302,* ☎ *303/444–5584 or 800/232–5949. 7 rooms. Restaurant. AE, MC, V.*

$–$$ **Magpie Inn.** Cottonwoods shade the sidewalk of this impressive red-brick Victorian with jade trim. The sunny, individually decorated guest rooms are just as elegant, with polished hardwood or brass beds, rocking chairs or armoires, throw rugs, lace curtains, hand-stenciled walls, and a profusion of dried flowers; two also have marble gas-burning fireplaces. Attracting a high percentage of business travelers, the Magpie has a somewhat impersonal feel for a B&B. Here's an example: Breakfast is served family-style, but guests are left to introduce themselves (and they usually don't). Still, the location is ideal, and the inn itself is unimpeachable. ⌂ *1001 Spruce St., 80302,* ☎ *303/449–6528. 7 rooms. AE, MC, V.*

$ **Foot of the Mountain Motel.** The motel is a series of connecting wood
★   cabins, and is conveniently located across from the city park where the bike path originates. It seems far from Boulder's bustle, yet it's only a few minutes' walk from downtown. Each cozy cabin has either a mountain or stream view, and is outfitted with TV, heater, minifridge, hot plate, and large bath. ⌂ *200 Arapahoe Ave., 80302,* ☎ *303/442–5688. 18 units. AE, D, MC, V.*

Estes Park

$$$$ **Aspen Lodge Ranch Resort and Conference Center.** The main building
★ is the largest log structure in Colorado, a majestic edifice of lodgepole
pine. The imposing reception area has cathedral ceilings, antler chandeliers, and a vaulted stone fireplace. Balconies jut from the rustic lodge
rooms and open onto thrilling views of Long's Peak or the Twin Sisters. While the decor is similar throughout, each has distinctive touches
such as Native American weavings and original art by the owners' friends.
There are also 20 nicely appointed maroon-, jade-, and smoke-colored
cabins with gingerbread trim. Rides are offered to a 2,000-acre working ranch and to Roosevelt National Forest. Children will love the elab-
orately themed programs, including a national park tour and Native
American lore and crafts. You can two-step or square dance in the homey
lounge after sampling the excellent Colorado cuisine of chef Ross Ka-
mens. The resort is named for the unusually high number of aspens
on the property, which according to Ute and Arapahoe lore signifies
a sacred, special place. It certainly is. ☎ *6120 Rte. 7, 80517, ☎*
970/586–8133 or 800/332–6867. 32 rooms, 20 cabins. Restaurant,
bar, pool, hot tub, sauna, 4 tennis courts, basketball, exercise room,
horseback riding, racquetball, fishing, cross-country skiing, snowmo-
biling, laundry services, convention center. AP in summer. AE, D, DC,
MC, V.

$$–$$$ **Boulder Brook.** Units at this secluded retreat are on the river, and in-
dividually decorated in either contemporary rustic or country provincial style. All feature full kitchen or kitchenette, private deck, gas
fireplace, double-headed showers, cable TV, and VCR. Half the units
have whirlpool tubs, for which you'll pay a great deal more. ☎ *1900*
Fall River Rd., 80517, ☎ 970/586–0910. 16 units. Hot tub. AE, D,
MC, V.

$$ **Best Western Lake Estes Resort.** All the well-maintained rooms are good-
sized and outfitted with a hodgepodge of furniture; some extremely
nice mahogany pieces are mixed with others that would have been bet-
ter left in someone's attic. All rooms include minifridges and hair dry-
ers, as well as the usual amenities. The newer chalet suites have gas-
or wood-burning fireplaces. Ask for a unit with a lake view. ☎ *1650*
Big Thompson Hwy., 80517, ☎ 970/586–3386. 58 rooms. Restau-
rant, pool, hot tub, sauna, video games, playground, coin laundry. AE,
D, DC, MC, V.

$$ **Stanley Hotel.** Perched regally on a hill commanding the town, the
Stanley is one of Colorado's great old hotels (*see* Tour 1 *in* Explor-
ing, *above*). As is often the case, the sunny rooms, decorated with antiques and period reproductions, are not as sumptuous as they once
were. Still, there is an incomparable air of history to this 1905 hotel,
along with all the modern conveniences. The McGregor Room is the
classiest restaurant in town. ☎ *333 Wonderview Ave., 80517, ☎*
970/586–3371 or 800/976–1377, ⊠ 970/586–3673. 92 rooms.
Restaurant, bar, pool, 2 tennis courts, croquet, laundry service, meet-
ing rooms. AE, MC, V.

$ **YMCA Estes Park Center of the Rockies.** This self-contained property
is so huge it's easy to get lost. In fact, it even has its own zip code! Both
lodge rooms and cabins are simple, clean, and attractive, and all are
constructed of sturdy oak. Cabins also have a fully stocked kitchen.
☎ *2515 Tunnel Rd., 80511, ☎ 970/586–3341. 565 rooms, 230 cab-*
ins. 4 restaurants, indoor pool, basketball, exercise room, roller-skat-
ing rink, playground. No credit cards.

Fort Collins

$ **Ramada Inn.** For a city its size, Fort Collins offers no truly distinctive lodging. This typical chain establishment is unspectacular, but it's a better buy than the nearby competitors, Marriott and Holiday Inn. ⌨ *3709 E. Mulberry St., 80524, ☎ 970/493–7800. 150 rooms. Restaurant, bar, indoor pool, hot tub, sauna. AE, D, DC, MC, V.*

Granby

$$$$ **C Lazy U Guest Ranch.** If you can envision a deluxe dude ranch, this
★ one is a formal affair for Colorado, attracting an international clientele, including both Hollywood royalty and the real thing. You enjoy your own personal horse, gourmet meals accompanied by vintage wines, luxurious Western-theme accommodations, loads of live entertainment, and any outdoor activity you can dream up. All units have extras that are unheard of in most ranches, like hair dryers and humidifiers; many also have a fireplace and refrigerator. The instructors are invariably top-notch, and the children's programs are unbeatable. The ratio of guests to staff is nearly one to one, which gives you an idea of the personal attention you can expect. The C Lazy U seeks to provide the ultimate in hedonism without ostentation, and it succeeds admirably. ⌨ *Box 379-D, 80446, ☎ 970/887–3344. 20 cabins, 19 rooms. Restaurant, bar, pool, hot tub, sauna, 2 tennis courts, exercise room, horseback riding, racquetball, fishing, cross-country skiing. AP. Closed Apr.–June, Oct.–Dec. 21. AE, MC, V.*

$$ **Inn at SilverCreek.** This large, bustling hotel is an excellent value for families, who comprise the bulk of the clientele. The various accommodations—from standard hotel rooms to suites—are attractively decorated in earth tones and have whirlpool baths and steam cabinets, cable TVs, and balconies; all but standard rooms have moss-rock fireplaces and kitchenettes with microwaves. Studios have Murphy and sofa beds, and top-floor loft units sleep six comfortably. Views—especially from rooms in the rear overlooking the parking lot—are uninspiring; and the kid population can get a bit noisy at times, but since most people are just here to sleep and perhaps to eat, these are minor drawbacks in return for bargain prices. ⌨ *U.S. 40, 80446, ☎ 970/887–2131 or 800/926–4386, FAX 970/887–2350. 342 units. Bar, deli, pool, 2 hot tubs, 2 outdoor hot tubs, massage, sauna, 2 tennis courts, exercise room, racquetball, video games, coin laundry, convention center. AE, D, DC, MC, V.*

Grand Lake

$–$$ **Grand Lake Lodge.** This rustic retreat, built of lodgepole pine in 1921, calls itself "Colorado's favorite front porch," thanks to its stupendous views of Grand and Shadow Mountain lakes. The restaurant offers the same gorgeous vistas, in addition to fine mesquite-grilled fish. Cabins are comfortably but simply furnished—no TVs or phones—for those who truly want to get away from it all. ⌨ *Off U.S. 34, north of Grand Lake, ☎ 970/627–3967. 66 cabins. Restaurant, bar, pool. AE, D, MC, V.* ☺ *June–Sept.*

$ **Bighorn Lodge.** This downtown motel has a rustic look, which helps it to blend in well with its surroundings. Mr. and Mrs. Schnittker, the owners, built the place themselves, and they set great store by the property. Their pride is reflected in the spotless rooms, all with cable TV, phones, and ceiling fans; soundproof walls; maroon carpeting; sailing prints; and pastel fabrics and wallpaper. The Schnittkers will gladly give you the lowdown on the area. ⌨ *613 Grand Ave., 80447, ☎ 970/627–8101 or 800/621–5923. 20 rooms. Hot tub. AE, D, DC, MC, V.*

$ **Rapids Lodge.** This handsome lodgepole-pine structure is one of the
★ oldest hotels in the area. Lodge rooms—each with cable TV and ceiling fan—are frilly, with dust ruffle quilts, floral wallpaper and fabrics,
and mismatched furnishings like old plush chartreuse armchairs, claw-
foot tubs, and carved hardwood beds. Cabins, all with kitchenettes,
are more rustic. The delightful restaurant is Grand Lake's most romantic,
with stained glass, timber beams, and views of the roaring Tonahatu
River; the kitchen turns out sumptuous Continental cuisine. ☎ Han-
cock Ave., 80447, ☎ 970/627–3707. 9 rooms, 3 cabins. Restaurant,
bar. AE, DC, MC, V. Closed Nov.–mid-Dec., Mon. and Tues. mid-
Dec.–May.

$ **Western Riviera.** This friendly motel books up far in advance, thanks
to the low prices, affable owners, and comfortable accommodations.
Even the cheapest units—while small—are pleasant, done in mauve and
earth tones, with lake views and cable TV; for $13 more a night you
can get a sizable, stylish room with pine furniture. Cabins, with a kitchenette (including a microwave), a bedroom, and a living room with a
sleeper sofa, are a tremendous bargain for families. ☎ 419 Garfield
Ave., 80447, ☎ 970/627–3580. 25 units. Hot tub. DC, MC, V. Closed
mid-Mar.–mid-May, mid-Oct.–mid-Dec.

Hot Sulphur Springs

$ **Riverside Hotel.** Colorado is full of fun and funky finds like this his-
toric 1903 hotel. You enter the lobby through a jungle of plants (cul-
tivated by owner Abe Rodriguez) and find yourself in a room dominated
by a magnificent fieldstone fireplace, its mantel covered with trophies,
pottery, and other tchotchkes. The lobby leads into a grand old mirrored bar and a cozy dining room with a huge potbellied stove, a piano,
and landscape paintings of the kind charitably called folk art. Offering views of the Colorado River, the restaurant serves up simple but
well-prepared steaks and fresh-as-can-be fish; it's worth having a meal
here even if you don't stay at the hotel. Abe describes the decor of the
upstairs rooms as "middle-to-late Salvation Army"; you'll find iron or
oak beds, floral quilts, and heavy oak dressers or armoires. All rooms
have a washbasin or a sink; corner rooms are the sunniest and most
spacious. ☎ 509 Grand Ave., 80451, ☎ 970/725–3589. 21 rooms with
shared bath. Restaurant, bar, fishing. No credit cards.

Kremmling

$$$$ **Latigo Ranch.** Considerably more down-to-earth than many other Colorado guest ranches, Latigo has a caring staff that does everything it
can to give you an authentic ranch experience (short of making you
muck the stables). Accommodations are in comfortable but rather
dowdy cabins fitted out with wood-burning stoves and full baths.
While providing fewer amenities than comparable properties, the ranch
offers absolutely stunning views of the Indian Peaks range, complete
seclusion (10 miles—and 30 minutes on heart-stopping roads—to the
nearest town), and superb cross-country trails. The owners are not your
average ranchers: Jim Yost was an anthropologist, and he'll regale you
with stories of Ecuadorian hill tribes; his partner, Randy George, was
a chemical engineer who now engineers the "nouvelle ranch cuisine"
that is served in the dining room (BYOB). Guests quickly become ac-
quainted in the cozy dining room or the recreation center, where they
play pool, watch videos, or peruse the huge library for the perfect bed-
time reading. Jim and Randy also offer cattle roundups and photography workshops during the year. All activities and meals are included
in the price; there's a one-week minimum stay in summer. ☎ CR 161,
Box 237, 80459, ☎ 970/724–9008 or 800/227–9655. 10 1- to 3-bed-
room cabins. Dining room, pool, hot tub, horseback riding, fishing,

cross-country skiing, tobogganing, coin laundry. AE, MC, V. Closed Apr.–May, mid-Oct.–mid-Dec.

Nederland

$$ **Lodge at Nederland.** Although relatively new (1993), and ultramodern within, the lodge is made of rough-hewn timber, giving it a rustic feel. All rooms are spacious and have refrigerators, coffeemakers, hair dryers, cable TV, and balconies; rooms upstairs have marvelous cathedral ceilings; and those downstairs have gas fireplaces. The enthusiastic staff will help to arrange any outdoor activity you desire—and the possibilities are just about endless. Although there's no restaurant at the lodge, the small, arty town of Nederland—with more than its share of hippie throwbacks—has several good eateries (try Bob's Bakery for breakfast and the Pioneer Inn for dinner). An excellent choice for those who want to be centrally located, the property is within a half-hour drive of Boulder, Eldora ski area, and Central City. ⬚ *55 Lakeview Dr., 80466,* ☎ *303/258–9463 or 800/279–9463,* ₣ₐₓ *303/258–0413. 23 rooms, 1 suite. Hot tub. AE, D, DC, MC, V.*

The Arts and Nightlife

The Arts

MUSIC

There are concerts throughout the summer in Boulder's peaceful **Chatauqua Community Hall** (900 Baseline Rd., 303/442–3282) including the superb **Colorado Music Festival** (303/449–1397). **The Boulder Theater** (2032 14th St., ☎ 303/444–3600) is a venue for top touring bands. **The Boulder Philharmonic** (CU Macky Auditorium and Old Main Theatre, ☎ 303/449–1343) presents its own concert season, as well as chamber music concerts, the Boulder Ballet Ensemble, and special performances by visiting divas such as Kathleen Battle.

THEATER

The **Mary Rippon Theater** on the University of Colorado campus (☎ 303/442–8181) offers excellent student productions throughout the year, as well as the Colorado Shakespeare Festival each summer. **Chucho's Coffee Shop** (1336 Pearl St., no ☎) has poetry readings and an experimental theater series.

In Estes Park, concerts and top-notch semiprofessional theatrical productions are staged periodically at the **Stanley Hotel** (☎ 970/586–3371 or 800/976–1377). Concerts and performances are also staged by *Creative Ensemble Productions* (☎ 970/586–6864); call for current listings.

Nightlife

BARS AND LOUNGES

In Boulder, the **West End Tavern** (926 Pearl St., ☎ 303/444–3535) and **Potter's** (1207 Pearl St., ☎ 303/444–3100) are popular after-work hangouts, both with fine pub grub. Potter's also offers live bands and dancing periodically. **Mediterranean Café** (*see* Dining, *above*) is Boulder's current hot spot. The microbreweries, **Boulder Brewing** (2880 Wilderness Pl., ☎ 303/444–8448), **Walnut Brewery** (1123 Walnut St., ☎ 303/447–1345), and **Oasis Brewery** (1095 Canyon St., ☎ 303/449–0363) are also popular. The **Mezzanine Lounge** (☎ 303/442–4344) in the Boulderado has Victorian-style love seats, and is a romantic place for an after-dinner drink.

In Estes Park, the watering holes of choice are the venerable **Wheel Bar** (132 E. Elkhorn Ave., ☎ 970/586–9381); the **Gaslight Pub** (246 Moraine Ave., ☎ 970/586–0994), which has occasional live music; and the locals' favorite, **J.R. Chapins Lounge** (Holiday Inn, 101 S. St. Vrain St., ☎ 970/586–2332).

In Fort Collins, the places to hang (usually with the college crowd) are **Coopersmith's Brew Pub** (Old Town Square, ☎ 970/498–0483), **Old Town Ale House** (Old Town Square, ☎ 970/493–2213), and the sports bar **Chesterfield, Bottomsley, and Potts** (1415 W. Elizabeth St., ☎ 970/221–1139), famed for its burgers and international selection of beers.

In Grand Lake, the hands-down local favorite is the **Stagecoach Inn** (Boardwalk, ☎ 970/627–8079), as much for its cheap booze and good eats as for the live entertainment on weekends.

COMEDY CLUBS

Comedy Works (Old Town Square, Fort Collins, ☎ 970/221–5481) is a good place to check out the local talent.

COUNTRY-AND-WESTERN CLUBS

Boulder City Limits (47th St. and Diagonal Hwy., ☎ 303/444–6666) has dancing nightly. **Lonigans** (110 W. Elkhorn Ave., Estes Park, ☎ 970/586–4346) offers live blues and country-and-western bands several nights weekly.

DINNER SHOWS

Boulder Dinner Theater (5501 Arapahoe Ave., ☎ 303/449–6000) presents Broadway-style productions.

DISCOS

The Broker (301 Baseline Ave., Boulder, ☎ 303/449–1752) is the closest thing to a disco in these parts. In Fort Collins, try the collegiate **Fort Ram** (450 N. Linden St., ☎ 970/482–5026).

JAZZ CLUBS

In Boulder, the **Catacombs Blues Bar** (Hotel Boulderado, 2115 13th St., ☎ 303/443–0486) offers the best in local and national talent.

In Fort Collins, **The Page** (181 N. College Ave., ☎ 970/482–1714) offers an eclectic roundup of live rock, jazz, and blues.

ROCK CLUBS

In Boulder, the **Marquee Club** (1109 Walnut St., ☎ 303/447–1803) favors house music, '50s pop, and alternative bands. **Tulagi** (1129 13th St., ☎ 303/442–1369), **Club 156** (CU campus, ☎ 303/492–8888), and **The Sink** (1165 13th St., ☎ 303/444–7465) are where the college set hangs out, listening to bands like Small Dog Frenzy, Foreskin 500, the Psychedelic Zombies, and Julius Seizure. The **Fox Theater** (1135 13th St., ☎ 303/443–3399 or 303/447–0095) is an Art Deco movie palace that now hosts top touring bands as well as the wildly popular Tuesday night Disco Inferno, a sea of leisure suits—the wider the lapel the better.

In Fort Collins, **Lindens** (214 Linden St., ☎ 970/482–9291), **Sunset Night Club** (242 Linden St., ☎ 970/416–5499), and **The Mountain Tap** (167 N. College Ave., ☎ 970/484–4974) jam with the hottest rock, folk, and blues in the area. **Mishawaka Inn** (Poudre Canyon, 15 mi north of Ft. Collins, ☎ 970/482–4420) usually corrals some name bands.

SINGLES CLUBS

Fort Ram in Fort Collins (*see above*) and **Potter's** in Boulder (*see above*) are generally the best places to meet people.

North Central Colorado Essentials

Arriving and Departing by Plane

AIRPORTS AND AIRLINES

Boulder and Estes Park are served by **Denver International Airport** (*see* Denver Essentials *above*); regular shuttles are available from Denver (*see* By Bus or Shuttle, *below*). **Fort Collins-Loveland Municipal Airport** (☎ 970/221–1300) welcomes flights from **America West** and **Delta.**

Between the Airport and the Hotels/Downtown

BY BUS OR SHUTTLE

Airport Express (Fort Collins, ☎ 970/482–0505) runs shuttles from Denver and the Fort Collins airport. **Boulder Airporter** (☎ 303/321–3222) and **Boulder Ground Transportation** (☎ 303/444–4410) provide transportation from Denver. **Charles Tour & Travel Services** (☎ 970/586–5151) offers rides to Estes Park from Denver and Boulder. Costs run from $10 to $30 depending on pick-up location.

BY TAXI

Boulder Yellow Cab (☎ 303/442–2277) costs $1.50 for the first ⅛ mile and 20¢ for each subsequent mile.

Arriving and Departing by Car and Bus

BY CAR

The region is easily accessed via I–25, which runs north–south.

BY BUS

Greyhound Lines (☎ 800/231–2222) serves most of the major towns in the region.

Getting Around

BY CAR

U.S. 36 North accesses Boulder and Estes Park from Denver. Fort Collins and Longmont can be reached from Denver, via I–25 North. The main thoroughfare through Rocky Mountain National Park, connecting Grand Lake with Estes Park, is U.S. 34, which is partially closed October–May. Grand Lake can also be reached by U.S. 40 into U.S. 34, from Georgetown on I–70.

BY TAXI

Boulder Yellow Cab (☎ 303/442–2277) costs $1.50 for the first ⅛ mile and 20¢ for each subsequent mile; **Charles Taxi** (Estes Park, ☎ 970/586–8440) quotes individual rates; and **Shamrock Taxi** (Fort Collins, ☎ 970/224–2222) costs $2.30 for the first mile, $1.40 for each mile thereafter.

BY BUS

In Fort Collins: **Transfort** (☎ 970/221–6620) runs along major thoroughfares, charging 75¢.

Guided Tours

ORIENTATION

Doo-Dah Tours (☎ 303/449–0433) and **Explore Tours** (☎ 303/530–5116) offer tours of the Boulder area and other nearby attractions, including Rocky Mountain National Park and the Peak to Peak Highway.

SPECIAL INTEREST

Boulder Historical Tours (☎ 303/444–5192) sponsors tours of various Boulder neighborhoods during the summer.

Charles Tour & Travel Services (☎ 970/586–5151) runs trips to Rocky Mountain National Park.

Important Addresses and Numbers

HOSPITALS

Boulder Community Hospital (1100 Balsam Ave., Boulder, ☎ 303/440–2037); **Estes Park Medical Center** (555 Prospect Ave., Estes Park, ☎ 970/586–2317); **Poudre Valley Hospital** (1024 S. Lemay Ave., Fort Collins, ☎ 970/482–4111).

VISITOR INFORMATION

Boulder Convention & Visitors Bureau (2440 Pearl St., Boulder 80302, ☎ 303/442–2911 or 800/444–0447); **Estes Park Area Chamber of Commerce** (Box 3050, Estes Park 80517, ☎ 970/586–4431 or 800/443–); **Fort Collins Area Convention & Visitors Bureau** (420 S. Howes, Suite 101, Fort Collins 80522, ☎ 970/482–5821 or 800/274–3678); **Grand Lake Area Chamber of Commerce** (Box 57, Grand Lake 80447, ☎ 970/627–3402).

NORTHWEST COLORADO

As you drive through northwest Colorado, its largely barren terrain sculpted by eons of erosion, it may be difficult to imagine the region as a primeval rain forest. Yet millions of years ago much of Colorado was submerged under a roiling sea.

That period left a vivid legacy in three equally precious resources: vast oil reserves, abundant uranium deposits, and one of the world's largest collections of dinosaur remains. Throughout the area the evidence of these buried treasures is made obvious by unsightly uranium tailings and abandoned oil derricks, and the huge mounds of dirt left from unearthing valuable fossils. Some of the important paleontological finds made here have radically changed the fossil record and the way we look at our reptilian ancestors. These discoveries even fueled the imagination of *Jurassic Park* author Michael Crichton: the book's fierce and ferocious predator, velociraptor, was first uncovered here.

Dinomaniacs will have a field day in both Dinosaur National Monument in the extreme northwest corner of the state, and Grand Junction, the region's main settlement. Grand Junction also makes an excellent base for exploring the starkly beautiful rock formations of the Colorado National Monument; the important petroglyphs of Canyon Pintado; the forest and lakes of Grand Mesa, the world's largest flattop mountain; and the surprising orchards and vineyards of Palisade and Delta to the south and east.

Exploring

Our tour begins and ends in Steamboat Springs (*see* Exploring *in* I–70 and the High Rockies, *above*), which serves as one gateway to the area's many attractions on a loop tour. If you plan to explore the area on a series of day trips, Grand Junction (*see below*) makes the ideal hub: Most of the sights covered in this section are less than a two-hour drive in various directions.

U.S. 40 winds through the lush grasslands of the Yampa Valley, the blue ribbon of the river rimmed with the color of flame-bright willows. Farther on, billowing white plumes belch from Colorado's largest coal-processing plant, the Colorado-Ute Power Station. Welcome to Craig.

Numbers in the margin correspond to points of interest on the Northwest Colorado map.

❶ **Craig** is a growing cow town, made newly prosperous by coal and oil, but it's also set in pristine wilderness, teeming with wildlife. The **Sandstone Hiking Trail** along Alta Vista Drive is a splendid vantage point for viewing the local elk and deer herds, as well as ancient Native American petroglyphs carved into the side of the cliff.

In town is the **Museum of Northwest Colorado,** with its eclectic collection of everything from arrowheads to a fire truck. The upstairs of this restored county courthouse is devoted to one man's obsession: Bill Mackin, one of the leading traders in cowboy collectibles, has spent a lifetime gathering guns, bits, saddles, bootjacks, holsters, and spurs of all descriptions. *590 Yampa Ave.,* ☎ *970/824–6360.* ☛ *Free (donations accepted).* ☉ *Jan.–Apr., weekdays 10–5; May–Dec., weekdays 10–5 and Sat. 10–4.*

Outside Craig, U.S. 40 gradually shifts into hillier sagebrush country. This is ideal land for raising cattle, which are about all you'll see for miles on this desolate stretch of highway. The route winds through increasingly minuscule towns every 15 miles or so, including Maybell, Elk Springs, Massadona, Blue Mountain—some not even on the map.

At Maybell, the road forks. If you follow Route 318 northwest for about 30 miles you'll reach **Browns Park Wildlife Refuge** (1318 Rte. 318, ☎ 970/365–3613; ☛ Free; open 9 AM–sunset), and pass lacy waterfalls and canyons carved by the Green River straddled by swinging bridges. The area was a notorious hideaway for the likes of Butch Cassidy and the Sundance Kid, Tom Horn, and John Bennett. This is an unspoiled, almost primitive spot, ideal for watching antelope and bighorn sheep, as well as nesting waterfowl such as mallards, redheads, and teal.

If you continue along U.S. 40, you'll note that the earth becomes increasingly creased and furrowed, divided by arroyos and broken by
❷ the mauve- and rose-streaked cliffs of **Dinosaur National Monument** (☎ 970/374–2216). The Dinosaur Quarry is actually located on the Utah side of the monument, but the Colorado section offers some of the most spectacular hiking in the West, along the **Harpers Corner/Echo Park Drive** and the ominous-sounding **Canyon of Lodore** (where rafting is available along the rapids of the Green River). The drive is only accessible in summer—even then, four-wheel drive is preferable—and some of the most breathtaking overlooks are well off the beaten track. Still, the 62-mile round-trip paved Harpers Corner Drive will take you past looming buttes and yawning sunbaked gorges etched by the Green and Yampa rivers. The dirt Echo Park Road is dotted with angular rock formations stippled with petroglyphs; the route skirts the rim of narrow 3,000-foot-deep crevasses that ripple from beige to black depending on the angle of the sun. Wherever you go, remember this austerely beautiful park is fragile: Avoid the rich black soil, which contains actual cryptoyams—one-celled creatures that are the building blocks of life in the desert; and don't touch the petroglyphs.

Dinosaur, a few miles west of the monument's visitor center, is a sad little town whose streets are named for the giant reptiles. It offers little more than pit stops and dinky motels. If you've traveled this far, though, you're almost better off camping in the park, which is first-come, first-served.

TIME OUT **B&B Family Restaurant** (Ceratosaurus St. and U.S. 40, ☎ 970/374–2744) capitalizes on its location; a dino emblazons the side of the building. The decor is simple: one wall papered with potato sacks and another adorned with cheesy wildlife art; there are also still surprisingly beautiful remnants of an old bar with intricate carving and mirrors. How-

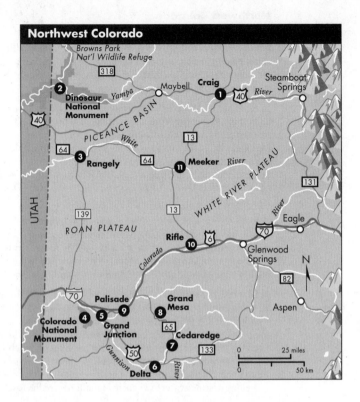

Northwest Colorado

ever, the menu is cute and unusual. Where else can you get Brontoburgers, Stegosaurus rib-eyes, and Plateosaurus rib-eyes.

3 Drive south on Route 64 to the next sizable town, **Rangely,** which proudly touts itself as "The Oil Capital of Colorado." It's also nicknamed Strangely: As the town's primary attractions attest, a perverse sense of humor is required to live in this desolate neck of the woods. The life of oil riggers and uranium miners is a hard one, after all.

Rangely, along with Chevron Oil, cosponsors the Raven A1 Memorial Exhibit, 4 miles west on Route 64, which recounts the history of oil-field development. Back in town, the **Rangely Museum,** located in the trim 1913 green-and-white schoolhouse, offers the obligatory educational display on oil shale and a rotating display of "petroleum products that serve you every day." The museum seems to be a little desperate for related artifacts, exemplified by the exhibit of a kitchen table, with a Log Cabin syrup tin and a cherry pitter sitting upon it. Also at this venue is an explanation of the Slush Pit Country Club, a golf course created by the oil workers ("play at your own risk, not responsible for tick bites, no holds barred, a golfing nightmare, nine holes of hell"). Regrettably, their course—whose hazards included junk pits, pumps, and pipelines; and whose greens were oil and sand—no longer exists. *434 W. Main St.,* ☎ *970/675–2612.* ☛ *Free; donations requested.* ☉ *Daily 9–5, but hours vary so call ahead.*

Among Rangely's most compelling sights, however, are the superb Fremont petroglyphs—dating from between 600 and 1300—in Douglas Creek Canyon, south of town along Route 139. This stretch is known as the **Canyon Pintado Historic District,** and the examples of rock art are among the best-preserved in the West. A brochure listing the sites is available; half the fun is clambering up the rocks to find them.

Route 139 meets up with I–70 a few miles east of the Utah border. Turn east onto the highway and you'll shortly reach the western entrance of the **Colorado National Monument** (☎ 970/858–3617). The 23-mile Rim Rock Drive climbs this colorful plateau that's been nearly 1 billion years in the making, yielding sterling views of the gaping canyons and gnarled knobby monoliths below. This is dramatic, rugged country, stubbled with stunted piñon trees and junipers; populated by mule deer, gray foxes, and bobcats; and perpetually swept by ravens, swifts, and golden eagles. The starkly beautiful sandstone and shale formations include Balanced Rock, Independence Monument, and the slender, willowy sculptures of the Kissing Couple and Praying Hands.

An eccentric visionary named John Otto was instrumental in having the park declared a national monument in 1911. To get his way, the headstrong Otto frequently threatened members of Congress with everything from blackmail to beatings, acts that caused him to be institutionalized on three occasions. But as locals observed, ". . . He's the sanest man in town 'cause he's got the papers to prove it."

West of the monument, it's a treacherous 7-mile hike into **Rattlesnake Canyon;** the intrepid will be rewarded with thrilling natural arches and spires. The canyon can be accessed in summer via four-wheel drive from the upper end of Rim Rock Drive. Just opposite the western entrance to the monument is **Devil's Canyon Science and Learning Center.** This sparkling new dinosaur facility was created by the Dinamation International Society, the folks who fabricate robotic dinos. Their techno-wizardry is on vivid display in this playground for children of all ages. In addition to the amazingly lifelike robotics (including a hatching egg), there are more than 20 interactive displays. Children can stand in an earthquake simulator, dig up "fossils" in a mock quarry, or make dino prints in dirt (along with reptile and bird tracks for comparison). Kids get a special passport that's stamped as they visit each dinosaur exhibit, and they have the chance to watch local volunteers at work cleaning and preparing fossils for study.

The center does an admirable job of sustaining a sense of fun while making its exhibits relevant to a child's contemporary world. As Dr. Robert Bakker, expedition leader for the Dinamation International Society advises, "Don't think of T. rex as a 'tyrant lizard,' but as a 10,000-pound roadrunner that could eat a school bus." *Exit 19 off I–70, 550 Crossroads Ct. , Fruita,* ☎ *970/858–7282 or 800/344–3466.* ☛ *$5 adults, $3.50 children 3–12 and senior citizens.* ☉ *Memorial Day–Labor Day, daily 8:30–7; Labor Day–Memorial Day, daily 9– 5.*

The geographic hub for exploring this area—whose many other enticing attractions include dinosaur quarries, vineyards, and a host of recreational activities—is **Grand Junction,** caught between the gunmetal Grand Mesa to the south and the multihued Bookcliffs to the north. As the largest city between Denver and Salt Lake City, it provides a variety of services and facilities to the surrounding populace, and offers a fair amount of cosmopolitan sophistication for a comparatively small town.

TIME OUT **Mountain Roasted** (620 Main St., ☎ 970/242–5282) is the brainchild of John Price, who speculated that gourmet coffees and an arty atmosphere would go over big in Grand Junction. In addition to the rotating aromatic coffees, he sells biscotti, homemade muffins, and pastries, not

to mention mugs, sweatshirts, and assorted coffee- and tea-related paraphernalia. The local art gracing the walls is also for sale, and live music
is offered several evenings a week: jazz Tuesdays, acoustic guitar
Wednesdays, a grab bag Fridays.

Grand Junction's cultural sophistication is readily apparent in the **Art on the Corner** exhibit, a year-round event showcasing leading regional sculptors whose latest works are installed on the Main Street Mall. Each year the community selects and purchases its favorites for permanent display. Art on the Corner is organized by the **Western Colorado Center for the Arts** (1803 N. 7th St., ☎ 970/243–7337; ☛ Free; open daily 9–5), which rotates its fine permanent collection of Native American tapestries and Western contemporary art, including the only complete series of lithographs by noted printmaker Paul Pletka. The fantastically carved doors, done by a WPA artist in the '30s, are alone worth the visit. Take time to enjoy the elegant historic homes along North 7th Street afterward.

The **Museum of Western Colorado** runs three facilities—this museum, the Cross Orchards Living History Farm, and the Dinosaur Valley Museum—as well as oversees paleontological excavations (*see* Dinosaur Valley Museum, *below*). The museum itself relates the history of the area dating from the 1880s, with an 11-decade time line, a firearms display, and two gorgeous parlor organs, among other items. *248 S. 4th St., ☎ 970/242–0971. ☛ $2 adults, $1 children 2–12. ☉ Mon.–Sat. 10–4:45.*

The **Cross Orchards Living History Farm** re-creates a historic agricultural community of the early 20th century on its 24½-acre site, listed on the National Register of Historic Places. A workers' bunkhouse, blacksmith shop, country store, and an extensive collection of vintage farming and roadbuilding equipment are among the exhibits to be seen on the 1½-2 hour tours. *3073 Patterson (F) Rd., ☎ 970/434–9814. ☛ $4 adults, $3.50 senior citizens, $2.50 children 2–12. ☉ Tues.–Sat. 9–5. Tours run May 1–Nov. 1. Group tours by arrangement throughout the year.*

The most fascinating facility in town is the **Dinosaur Valley Museum,** with half-size, moving, roaring replicas of the dinos found in the region. This instructive museum is designed for children and adults alike with numerous hands-on exhibits that emphasize understanding the wealth of the local fossil record. Aside from being able to handle real fossils in the open storage displays, you can also enjoy looking into a working laboratory and talking with the volunteers preparing and cataloguing the latest excavated specimens. Three working sites run by the museum are open to the public: **Riggs Hill, Dinosaur Hill,** and the **Rabbit Valley Trail Through Time.** Each is a self-guided tour that will increase your knowledge and appreciation of paleontology. You can pick up information and trail maps at Dinosaur Valley. *4th and Main Sts., ☎ 970/241–9210. ☛ $4 adults, $3.50 senior citizens, $2.50 children 2–12. ☉ Memorial Day–Labor Day, daily 9–5:30; Labor Day–Memorial Day, Tues.–Sat. 10–4:30.*

❻ Head south on U.S. 50 to **Delta,** the headquarters of the **Grand Mesa, Gunnison,** and **Uncompahgre national forests.** The town is ideally located for exploring the region's natural wonders and also has an interesting attraction that has earned Delta the accolade, "The City of Murals." Seven murals, most of them lining Main Street, were painted by local artists in the late 1980s and celebrate various aspects of life in the area, from wildlife in "Delta County Ark" and ranching in

"High Country Roundup," to agriculture in both "A Tribute to Agriculture" and "Labels of Delta County."

There are also museums of interest in Delta: **Ft. Uncompahgre** (Confluence Park, ☎ 970/874–8349; ☛ $3.50 adults, $2.50 children and senior citizens; open Memorial Day–Labor Day, Wed.–Sun. 10–5; Sept.–Oct. and Mar.–May, Tues.–Sat. 10–5; Nov.–Dec., Thurs.–Sat. 10–5; closed Jan.–Feb.), where docents in period attire guide visitors through this 1826 fur-trading post; and the **Delta County Historical Society** (251 Meeker St., no ☎; ☛ $1; open Tues.–Fri. 10–4, Sat. 10–1), with an eclectic display that includes local dinosaur finds, an 1886 jail, and a butterfly collection.

❼ Now loop north onto Route 65 to **Cedaredge,** where the **Grand Mesa Scenic Byway** begins. This exceptionally pretty town sits in the shadow of the Grand Mesa and is complemented by the silvery San Juans shimmering to the south. Among Cedaredge's attractions is its **Pioneer Town** (Rte. 65, ☎ 970/856–7554; ☛ Free; open June–Sept., daily 10–4), a cluster of 23 authentic buildings that re-create turn-of-the-century life.

❽ From here, Route 65 begins its ascent of **Grand Mesa,** the world's largest flattop mountain, which towers 10,000 feet above the surrounding terrain and sprawls an astounding 50 square miles. The mesa landscape is dotted with more than 200 sparkling lakes— a fisherman's paradise in summer. According to Ute legend, a great eagle carried off a Native American child, and in retaliation the father hurled its eaglets to the base of the mesa, where they were devoured by a serpent. The enraged eagle seized the serpent and tore it into hundreds of pieces, which formed deep pits upon hitting the earth. The eagle's ire caused the mesa to rattle with thunder, and torrents of rain filled the pits, creating lakes.

The stands of golden quakies (aspens) blanketing the mesa are glorious in autumn. Even on brilliantly sunny days, wispy clouds seem to catch and reflect the sun's rays, draping the summit in prismatic light. The views of the Grand Valley and the Bookcliffs (escarpments) are absolutely ravishing here, and an excellent little ski area, **Powderhorn**, takes full advantage of them. The slopes intriguingly follow the fall line of the mesa, carving out natural bowls, those on the western side being steeper than they first appear.

❾ Return to I–70 (the other side of Grand Mesa), and head to **Palisade,** a hamlet nestled between the wintry Grand Mesa and the semiarid terrain. The surprisingly temperate microclimate produces delectable Elberta peaches, apples, plums, pears, and cherries, making Palisade the center of Colorado's orchard and vineyard territory. Plucky wine makers have been experimenting with several varietals since the early '80s, and the results have been encouraging. There are 14 vineyards all told in the state; the best are located right here in the Grand Valley.

You can find all the great European grapes here: Riesling, chardonnay, pinot noir, cabernet, merlot; so far, the top results have been obtained with merlot and chardonnay. Wine lovers will appreciate the heady, uncomplicated varietal bouquet and surprising depth and complexity of some of the vintages. Four vineyards are open to the public, offering regular tours and tastings (call for hours). When you tour you'll be able to meet wine makers and discuss their craft, an opportunity you generally don't have in the larger facilities in California or Oregon. The oldest, largest, and most successful commercially (to date) is **Colorado Cellars** (3553 E Rd., ☎ 970/464–7921). **Carlson Vineyards** (461 35 Rd., ☎ 970/464–5554) produces wines with fey labels—

tyrannosaurus red, prairie dog—that belie their seriousness; probably the best wines to buy here are those made from other fruit (try the peach or the pearadactyl). The two most promising in quality are undoubtedly **Plum Creek Cellars** (3708 G Rd., ☎ 970/464–7586) and **Grande River Vineyards** (787 37.3 Rd., ☎ 970/464–5867), whose owner Steve Smith is experimenting with Rhone varietals (Syrah and Viognier), with tremendous returns.

TIME OUT   **Slice-O-Life Bakery** (105 W. 3rd St., Palisade, ☎ 970/464–0577) is run by two of the zaniest bakers in Colorado, Mary and Tim Lincoln. All the savory, aromatic goodies are baked with whole grains and fresh local fruits. Grab a bottle of wine at one of the nearby wineries, couple it with some fresh fruit from an orchard, and you have the makings of a wonderful picnic.

🔟 Head east on I–70 to **Rifle.** This unassuming community (which lives up to its name with gun racks outnumbering ski racks on cars) is developing quite a reputation among mountain bikers for the series of high-quality trails along the **Roan Cliffs,** and with ice climbers for the frozen waterfalls and ice caves in the **Rifle Gap State Recreation Area.** Rifle boasts a tremendous variety of terrain that veers from semiarid to subalpine and invites both hikers, bikers, and climbers.

Take Route 325 north out of town to the **recreation area** ($3 admission), passing Rifle Gap on the way. As you gaze at the huge rock window, try to imagine a huge, orange nylon curtain billowing between the steep walls. Famed installation artist Christo did; two of his efforts were foiled due to wind, save for one amazing day when his *Valley Curtain* piece was gloriously unfolded for a brief few hours. The road wraps around a tiny reservoir before reaching the actual designated area, which officially starts with **Rifle Falls,** a triple flume cascading down moss-covered cliffs. The caves here are ideal for amateur spelunking.

Continue along Route 325, past the **Rifle Fish Hatchery** (pausing to admire the huge schools of trout being raised, including an intriguing new iridescent blue hybrid) to Little Box Canyon Road. Here is **Rifle Mountain Park,** whose sheer cliffs are stippled with holds and pocked with caves that make it a favorite among rock and ice climbers. The dirt road eventually ends up in the **White River National Forest,** a popular camping area.

⓫ Back on I–70, turn north on scenic Route 13 to **Meeker,** named for Nathan Meeker, who attempted to "civilize" the Utes with little success. When Meeker began to fear that the Utes resented his arrogant disregard for their land rights, he sent for the cavalry. The Utes became further enraged and ambushed the troops in the 1879 Meeker Massacre, which ushered in yet another period of intransigence on the part of the U.S. government. Meeker is predominantly known as an outdoorsy town, but its handsome historical buildings include the still-operating **Meeker Hotel** on Main Street and the worthy **White River Museum** (565 Park St., ☎ 970/878–9982; ☛ Free; open May–Nov., Mon.–Sat. 9–5), which features pioneer artifacts and historical photos.

East of Meeker is the **Flattops Scenic Byway,** a terrain shaped by molten lava flows and glaciers that gouged tiny jewel-like lakes in the folds of the mountains.

What to See and Do with Children

Children will adore the dino exhibits at **Dinosaur Valley** and **Devil's Canyon** (*see* Exploring, *above*).

Rim Rock Deer Park and Trading Post offers a variety of rafting and horseback-riding expeditions, as well as a petting zoo, a deer park, and a somewhat hoary wildlife museum. *Hwy. 340, Exit 19, Fruita,* ☏ *970/858–9555.* ☛ *$1.* ☽ *May–Sept., daily 8–5.*

Other Points of Interest

Tabeguache/Unaweep Scenic Byway. This 150-mile stretch of savage scenery (Rte. 141) sweeps south from Grand Junction, arcing almost to the Utah border before curling over to Naturita, where you can pick up Rte. 145 to Telluride. It slices through the Uncompahgre Plateau, an area of great geologic interest. Unaweep means "Canyon with Two Mouths," and indeed the piddling streams seem insufficient to carve these harsh gashes. Along the way you'll see an engineering marvel: The 7-mile long **Hanging Flume,** used to transport water, virtually defies gravity by clinging to the sheer cliff.

One of Colorado's oddest communities, **Nucla,** also lies along this route (3 miles north of Naturita on Rte. 97). Founded as an early experiment in communal living (though the current conservative residents could hardly be called hippies), Nucla today is famous for one thing: *The Top Dog World Prairie Dog Shootout,* held every June. Residents justify the carnage by insisting that prairie dogs are only pests and that they run roughshod over the grazing lands. The event, which is shamelessly promoted as a tourist attraction, does tend to bring out the best in Nucla humor. As one resident was quoted in the *Denver Post:* "It's a lot like sex and the Catholic Church. Everyone agrees the job has to be done; the controversy is whether we get to enjoy it."

Shopping

Specialty Stores

ANTIQUES

A Haggle of Vendors Emporium (510 Main St., Grand Junction, no ☏) is just what it says; it's as if every attic you'd ever seen had emptied its contents here.

ART GALLERIES

Southwest Imagery (236 Main St., Grand Junction, ☏ 970/243–9906) carries Native American and Southwestern art and jewelry. **Frameworks** (309 Main St., Grand Junction, ☏ 970/243–7074) focuses on contemporary interpretations of Native American traditions and carries serigraphs, sculpture, oils, pottery, prints, and photos. **Thunderock** (128 N. 5th St., Grand Junction, ☏ 970/242–4890) offers Navajo rugs and sand paintings, Hopi jewelry, and Zuni basketry and woodcarvings. **The Apple Shed** (250 S. Grand Mesa Dr., Cedaredge, ☏ 970/856–7007) is a group of galleries that sell an impressive array of Colorado crafts.

CERAMICS

Terry Shepherd (825 N. 7th St., Grand Junction, ☏ 970/243–4282) sells his own stoneware and salt-vapor designs, where the salt forms trails on the pottery.

FOOD

Enstrom's (200 S. 7th St., Grand Junction, ☏ 970/242–1655) makes scrumptious candy, and is world renowned for their toffee. **Harold and Nola Voorhees** (3702 G 7/10 Rd., Palisade, ☏ 970/464–7220) sell an intriguing range of dried fruits, including cherries, pears, apricots, and peaches. Also stop by the **wineries** (*see* Exploring, *above*) to sample Colorado's excellent home-grown product.

HOME FURNISHINGS

In Grand Junction, **Sunspinner** (409 Main St., ☎ 970/245–5529) specializes in stained glass; **Quilt Junction** (412 Main St., ☎ 970/245–6700) stocks a wide variety of quilts and also offers workshops; **Linen Shelf** (316 Main St., ☎ 970/242–3234) has a nice selection of bedclothes and the like. **Windfeather Designs** (1204 Bluff St., Delta, no ☎) offers Jean Madole's extraordinary weaving, a reinterpretation of designs from extinct cultures such as the Mimbre. **Mama Macumba** (Cedaredge, ☎ 970/856–7792) creates wildly imaginative furnishings in explosive colors.

WESTERN WEAR

Champion Boots and Saddlery (545 Main St., ☎ 970/242–2465), in business since 1936, is the best place in the area for the likes of Tony Lama boots or Minnetonka moccasins.

Sports and the Outdoors

Camping

In **Dinosaur National Monument** (☎ 970/374–3000) pristine campsites are available at **Gates of Lodore** (970/365–3693), **Deerlodge Park** (no ☎), and **Echo Park** (no ☎). Most sites are free and on a first-come, first-served basis. **Colorado National Monument** (☎ 970/858–3617) allows backcountry camping. **Grand Mesa National Forest** (☎ 970/874–7691) and the **White River National Forest** (☎ 970/625–2085), around Rifle, have several campsites available.

Climbing

Rifle Gap Falls and **Lake State Recreation Area** (☎ 970/625–1607) are magnets for rock and ice climbers, depending on the season. **Vertical Horizon Rock Guides** (Grand Junction, ☎ 970/245–8513) and **Tower Guides** (Grand Junction, ☎ 970/245–6992) both offer guided climbs and lessons in the area.

Cycling

Rim Rock Drive is the gorgeous, if strenuous 23-mile route through Colorado National Monument. **Kokopelli's Trail** links Grand Junction with the famed **Slickrock Trail** outside Moab, Utah. The 128-mile stretch winds through high desert and the Colorado River valley before climbing the La Sal Mountains. Those interested in bike tours should get in touch with **Scenic Byways** (Grand Junction, ☎ 970/242–4645) or call the **Colorado Plateau Mountain Bike Trail Association** (☎ 970/241–9561).

The biking around Rifle is gaining momentum among aficionados for the variety of trails and views around the Roan Cliffs. Call the Rifle Chamber of Commerce (☎ 970/625–2085) for details.

Fishing

The **Grand Mesa Lakes** provide some of the best angling opportunities in Colorado. For information, contact the **Grand Mesa National Forest** (☎ 970/874–7691) or the **U.S. Forest Service** (☎ 970/242–8211). The **Rifle Gap Reservoir** (☎ 970/625–1607) is plentifully stocked with rainbow trout and walleye pike. Around Craig and Meeker, the **Yampa** and **Green rivers, Trappers Lake, Lake Avery,** and **Elkhead Reservoir** are known for pike and trout; contact the Craig **Sportsman's Center** (☎ 970/824–3046) for information.

Golf

Battlement Mesa Golf Course (3930 N. Battlement Mesa Parkway, Battlement Mesa, ☎ 970/285–7274) is an 18-hole championship course with ravishing views of the Grand Valley and Grand Mesa in the distance.

Tiara Rado Golf Course (2063 S. Broadway, Grand Junction, ☎ 970/245–8085) is an 18-hole championship course set stunningly at the foot of the Colorado National Monument.

Yampa Valley Golf Course (CR 394, Craig, ☎ 970/824–3673) is an 18-hole course dotted with copses of willow and cottonwood by the Yampa River.

Hiking

The **Colorado National Monument** (☎ 970/858–3617) and adjacent **Rattlesnake Canyon** (call the Bureau of Land Management, ☎ 970/243–6561) offer superb and challenging hiking. The **Crag Crest Trail** on top of Grand Mesa (☎ 970/874–7691) affords breathtaking views of the canyons and cliffs below. **Battlement Mesa** outside Rifle, also offers rugged trails. There are numerous panoramic nature trails in **Dinosaur National Monument** (☎ 970/374–2216).

Horseback Riding

Rim Rock Deer Park (Grand Junction, ☎ 970/858–9555) offers everything from one-hour rides into Colorado National Monument to overnight pack rides.

Rafting

Adventure Bound River Expeditions (Grand Junction, ☎ 970/245–5428) runs trips on the Colorado and Green rivers (the latter through the spectacular canyons of Dinosaur National Monument).

Skiing

CROSS-COUNTRY

The acres of untracked powder amid stands of aspen and spruce on Grand Mesa are a Nordic nirvana. For information, contact the **Grand Mesa National Forest** (☎ 970/874–7691) or the **Grand Mesa Nordic Council** (☎ 970/434–9753). **Skyway Ski Touring** (Grand Mesa, ☎ 970/248–0454) offers lessons and tours.

DOWNHILL

Powderhorn. 20 trails; 4 lifts; 240 acres; 1,650-foot-vertical drop. *Rte. 65, Grand Mesa,* ☎ *970/242–5637.* ☉ *Nov.–mid-Apr., 9–4.*

Dining

The Grand Junction dining scene is fairly sophisticated, compared to other towns in the region, though it's hardly fancy or exotic. On the other hand, there's a lot of standard beef and burritos. For price ranges, *see* the Dining chart *in* Colorado Essentials, *below.*

Craig

$–$$ Golden Cavvy. A "cavvy" is the pick of a team of horses, and this restaurant is certainly the selection in town, for the price. It's a standard coffee shop enlivened by mirrors, hanging plants, faux-antique chandeliers, and the incredible masonry of the original 1900s fireplace of the Baker Hotel (which burned down on this spot). Hearty breakfasts, homemade pies and ice cream, pork chops, and anything deep-fried (try the mesquite-fried chicken) are your best bets. ✗ *538 Yampa Ave.,* ☎ *970/824–6038. Reservations accepted. AE, DC, MC, V.*

Grand Junction

$$ G. B. Gladstone's. This local hangout sports its own style of turn-of-the-century decor: stained glass windows, faux-Victorian gas lamps, and antique skis and kayaks on the walls. It's particularly lively on Friday nights, but whatever the day, you can enjoy such savory starters as jumpin' jacks (fried jack cheese and cheddar rolls stuffed with jalapeños) and Frankie's hot steak strips, as well as the freshest fish in town (try the blackened sea bass if it's a daily special). The meat and poultry specials are good too, especially the fine prime rib; teriyaki steak; and Thai pesto linguine with broiled chicken strips, basil, garlic, and chilies. ✗ *2531 N. 12th St.,* ☎ *970/241–6000. Reservations accepted. AE, D, DC, MC, V.*

$$ **River City Bar & Restaurant.** Exposed brick and whitewashed walls sur-
★ round you at this casual spot, where a little toy train chugs along tracks winding above the tables. The menu is eclectic and Grand Junction's most creative, with standouts such as Greek-style leg of lamb; but the pastas, salads, and appetizers (you could make a meal out of the sampler alone) are really exceptional. Try the linguine Venice Beach (with tomato, feta cheese, and basil), or pasta topped with mouthwatering shrimp jambalaya or chicken tandoori. Salads celebrate the area's produce: Palisade peach salad (field greens, walnuts, peaches, and jicama) and lime chicken salad (lime-marinated chicken strips, spinach, avocado, artichoke, olives, and homemade croutons in peanut dressing) are delicious. Marvelous appetizers include bean bites (black and pinto beans grilled in minipatties), focaccia, and artichoke hearts with sheep dip (sheep's milk, cheese, and herbs). There's an excellent selection of beers and wines (including many Colorado vineyards) by the glass, and entertainment several nights a week. ✗ *748 North Ave.,* ☎ *970/245–8040. Reservations accepted. AE, D, MC, V. No lunch Sun.*

$$ **The Winery.** This is *the* place for the big night out and special occasions. It's very pretty, awash in stained glass, wood beams, exposed brick, and hanging plants. The menu isn't terribly adventuresome, but it does turn out top-notch steak, chicken, prime rib, and shrimp in simple, flavorful sauces. ✗ *642 Main St.,* ☎ *970/242–4100. Reservations recommended. AE, D, DC, MC, V. No lunch.*

$ **Grits.** This gussied-up coffee shop (hanging plants, faux gas lamp chandeliers, leatherette banquettes, walls cleverly stenciled with petroglyphs) attempts to transform diner food into a gourmet's delight by cannily incorporating a host of international influences, from Thai to Italian. Sometimes the menu is overly ambitious, but superior choices include chunky crab cakes with red pepper mayonnaise, spaghetti with shrimp and dill cream sauce, onion rings with fiery *chipotle* (hot pepper) ketchup, and luscious baked acorn squash with multigrain stuffing. There's always Dorothy's meat loaf or mustard-fried catfish for the less adventuresome. Portions are huge and served with heaping helpings of starch and veggies (the cornbread and fried cheddar herb grits are sublime). An extensive selection of Colorado wines complements the offerings. ✗ *2704 Rte. 50,* ☎ *970/243–8871. Reservations accepted. MC, V.*

Meeker

$–$$ **Sleepy Cat Lodge and Restaurant.** The original lodge burned down in
★ 1991, but the new Sleepy Cat (owned by the same family since 1946) rose like a phoenix, and is even better than before. The huge log structure is filled with gorgeous beveled glass and the requisite trophies and bearskins mounted on the walls. Soup and salad bar accompany full and filling dinners, and you get your choice of sautéed mushrooms, corn on the cob, wild rice, fried or baked potato, and sundae or sherbet. Wonderful ribs, huge cuts of steak, teriyaki chicken, and pan-fried trout are among the top choices. There are several cozy cabins for rent as well. ✗ *CR 8, 16 mi east of Meeker,* ☎ *970/878–4413. Reservations accepted. D, MC, V. No lunch.*

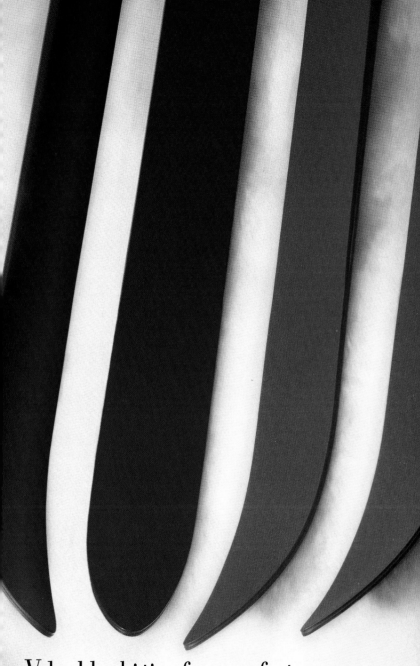

Valuable ski tips for a perfect season.

Fly United Airlines there and back.
There are very few runs we don't cover. We've added more flights, with more
weekend nonstops, straight to the slopes too. And on many flights you can have
all your equipment pre-delivered to and from your destination with our exclusive
Up the Hill, Down the Hill® service. No wonder we're the skier's airline.
For information, call 1-800-241-6522. Come fly our friendly skies.

 **UNITED AIRLINES**

No matter where you go, travel is easier when you know the code.[SM]

dial 1 8 0 0 CALL ATT®

Dial 1 800 CALL ATT and you'll always get through from any phone with any card* and you'll always get AT&T's best deal.** It's the one number to remember when calling away from home.

*Other long distance company calling cards excluded.
**Additional discounts available.

AT&T
Your True Choice

Rifle

$$ Fireside Inn. This is a charming dining spot, with an enormous stone fireplace as its centerpiece. The owner is German, and along with Continental favorites such as veal marsala and prime rib au jus, he offers tasty Wiener schnitzel and other German favorites. The Fireside Inn serves breakfast, as well as lunch and dinner. ✕ *100 E. 4th St.,* ☎ *970/625–2233. Reservations advised. AE, D, MC, V.*

Lodging

Grand Junction offers the widest selection of accommodations; outside the town, expect motels and fairly rustic guest ranches. You'll find limited accommodations at Dinosaur National Monument; camping is probably your best bet. Unless otherwise noted, rooms include a phone, cable TV, and a private bath. For rates, *see* the Lodging chart *in* Colorado Essentials, *below.*

Cedaredge

$ Cedars' Edge Llamas B&B. The pretty cedar house and guest cottage offer four neatly appointed rooms. Breakfast is on a private deck or in the sunroom, which affords astonishing 100-mile views. The best part about staying at Ray and Gail Record's retreat, however, is the llama herd (yes, they accompany guests on picnics). Complimentary breakfast is provided. 🏚 *2169 Rte. 65, 81413,* ☎ *970/856–6836. 4 rooms. MC, V.*

Craig

$ Holiday Inn. This property, thoroughly remodeled in 1992, is pleasant enough for a remote Holiday Inn. It boasts the usual "holidome" with pool, and rooms are a good size; they're decorated in teal and floral fabrics. 🏚 *300 Rte. 13 S, 81625,* ☎ *970/824–4000,* 📠 *970/824–3950. 169 rooms. Restaurant, bar, indoor pool, hot tub, exercise room, nightclub, recreation room. AE, D, DC, MC, V.*

Grand Junction

$$ Grand Junction Hilton. By far the premier property in the area, the Hilton
★ offers quiet pampering at affordable rates, although some of the units could use refurbishing. Rooms are large and have welcome extras such as a phone *and* TV in the bathroom. The bar and nightclub are longtime local favorites. 🏚 *743 Horizon Dr., 81506,* ☎ *970/241–8888,* 📠 *970/242–7266. 262 rooms, 2 suites. 2 restaurants, 2 bars, pool, hot tub, 3 tennis courts, exercise room, recreation room, travel services, airport shuttle. AE, D, DC, MC, V.*

$–$$ Ramada Inn. Management does its utmost to create a warm, inviting
★ ambience, and succeeds with plush high-back chairs in the welcoming lobby and a private library/club look in the main restaurant, Oliver's. More than $1 million was invested in refurbishment in the last five years, and it shows. Old-fashioned charm and dark mountain colors characterize the rooms. Kings and parlor quarters, with period decor, are the most appealing. 🏚 *2790 Crossroads Ave., 81506,* ☎ *970/241–8411,* 📠 *970/241–1077. 157 units. Restaurant, bar, patisserie, indoor pool, hot tub, health club privileges, nightclub, meeting rooms, airport shuttle. AE, D, DC, MC, V.*

$ Budget Host. The owner continually refurbishes this property (you can occasionally catch him scrubbing the floors), whose teal-and-white exterior seems more country inn than motor lodge. Care is also lavished on the smart, fresh rooms, which sport an early-American look with Stanley cherry furniture, burgundy carpets, and floral spreads. 🏚 *721 Horizon Dr., 81506,* ☎ *970/243–6050 or 800/888–5736. 54 rooms. Outdoor pool. AE, D, DC, MC, V.*

$ **Junction Country Inn.** Built in 1907 as the showplace mansion for a contractor, this gracious inn boasts lovely hardwood floors and wainscoting throughout. The cozy rooms all have floral wallpaper and historical prints, and three accommodations (only one has a private bath) are particularly good for families. One unit has a sunporch, one has two daybeds, another has an extra room. Complimentary breakfast is served in a sunny dining room that's dominated by a map covered with pushpins, each representing a guest's hometown. ⌧ *861 Grand St., 81506,* ☎ *970/241–2817. 4 rooms. AE, MC, V.*

$ **Melrose Hotel.** This funky 85-year-old, brick-red-and-forest-green building functions as both a full-service hotel and a hostel. Most of the reasonably priced hotel rooms feature TV, air-conditioning, sink (some have a private shower), and the original woodwork. Most are bright and airy, with a smattering of antiques. This is a great place to connect with students from around the world. Marcus and Sabrina Bebb-Jones couldn't be more friendly and helpful, full of tips on how to save money in the area. Hostelers enjoy a pleasant common room with library, TV/VCR, and kitchen facilities. Breakfast is complimentary. ⌧ *337 Colorado St., 81501,* ☎ *970/242–9636. 21 hotel rooms, 10 with private bath, 5 dorms. Laundry services. MC, V.*

$ **Peachtree Inn.** This pleasant property—with pool and restaurant—offers more amenities and facilities than most "strip" motels. The appealing room decor includes grey carpeting and a mauve and light-blue color scheme. ⌧ *1600 North St., 81501,* ☎ *970/245–5770 or 800/525–0030. 70 rooms. Restaurant, bar, pool. AE, D, MC, V.*

Rifle

$ **Rusty Cannon Motel.** This motor lodge offers spacious accommodations, and is plain but clean and comfortable. ⌧ *701 Taughenbaugh Blvd., 81650,* ☎ *970/625–4004. 89 rooms. Pool, exercise room. AE, D, DC, MC, V.*

The Arts and Nightlife

The Arts

MUSIC

Grand Junction's **Country Jam** (Grand Junction Chamber of Commerce, ☎ 970/244–1480), held annually in June, attracts the biggest name acts, such as Garth Brooks and Willie Nelson. The 65-piece **Grand Junction Symphony** (☎ 970/243–6787) is highly regarded.

Nightlife

BARS AND LOUNGES

In Grand Junction, **River City** (748 North Ave., ☎ 970/245–8040), the Hilton's **Observatory Lounge** (☎ 970/241–8888), **G. B. Gladstone's** (2531 N. 12th St., ☎ 970/241–6000), and the **Rockslide Brewery** (401 Main St., ☎ 970/245–2111), which has won awards for its ales, porters and stouts, are the preferred local hangouts.

COUNTRY-AND-WESTERN CLUBS

Grand Junction kicks up its heels at the **Branding Iron Lounge** (2701 U.S. 50, ☎ 970/242–9897) and **The Rose** (2993 North Ave., ☎ 970/245–0606).

DISCOS

Bailey's (Ramada Inn, 2790 Crossroads Ave., Grand Junction, ☎ 970/241–8411) has a rather elegant ambience, much like a cozy club. **Cinnamon's** (Holiday Inn, 755 Horizon Dr., Grand Junction, ☎ 970/243–6790) is the closest thing to a disco: It has a dance floor and a DJ. For a more Western atmosphere, try **Charades** (Grand Junction Hilton, 743 Horizon Dr., Grand Junction, ☎ 970/241–8888).

JAZZ CLUBS
The Station (Main & 7th Sts., ☎ 970/241–4613) attracts a bohemian crowd as much for its smoking jazz and blues sets as for the righteous lattes and rotating art exhibits.

ROCK CLUBS
Cahoots Crossing (490 28¼ Rd., Grand Junction, ☎ 970/241–2282) features live bands several nights weekly. **Club Zephyr** (715 Horizon Dr., ☎ 970/242–4782) attracts an even younger crowd that slams to alternative bands with names like Jesus Monkey Fish and Weird Lizard Disease.

Northwest Colorado Essentials

Arriving and Departing by Plane
AIRPORTS AND AIRLINES
Walker Field Airport (☎ 970/244–9100) in Grand Junction is the only major airport in the region, and is served by **American, America West, Continental, Delta, TWA, United,** and **USAir.**

Arriving and Departing by Car, Train, and Bus
BY CAR
I–70 bisects Colorado running east–west; it's the easiest way to approach the region.

BY TRAIN
Amtrak (☎ 800/USA–7245) stops in Grand Junction.

BY BUS
Greyhound Lines (☎ 800/231–2222) serves most of the major towns in the region.

Getting Around
BY TAXI
In Grand Junction, call **Sunshine Taxi** (☎ 970/245–8294); **A Touch of Class** (☎ 970/245–5466) has regular service into Grand Junction and outlying communities from Walker Field.

BY CAR
I–70 (U.S. 6) is the major thoroughfare, accessing Grand Junction, Rifle, and Grand Mesa (via Rte. 65, which runs to Delta). Meeker is reached from Rifle via Route 13 and Rangely/Dinosaur via Route 64. U.S. 40 East from Utah is the best way to reach Dinosaur National Monument and Craig.

Guided Tours
ORIENTATION
Coopertours (Grand Junction, ☎ 970/245–4993) specializes in tours for artists and photographers. **Eagle Tree Tours** (Grand Junction, ☎ 970/241–4792), **Western Scenic Lines** (Grand Junction, ☎ 970/242–0558), and **West of the Rockies** (Grand Junction, ☎ 970/245–4865) offer tours of Colorado National Monument and the Grand Junction area, including some with four-wheel drive, hiking, or biking.

SPECIAL INTEREST
Cabra d'Oro Pack Goats (1459 Grove Creek Rd., Collbran 81624, ☎ 970/487–3388) offers unique tours of Grand and Battlement mesas and the Colorado National Monument. **Dinamation International Society** (Devil's Canyon Science and Learning Center, 550 Crossroads Ct., Fruita 81521, ☎ 970/858–7282 or 800/344–3466) runs five-to six-

day paleontological treks that include work in a dinosaur quarry. **Meander Tours** (Box 354, Rte. 1, Collbran 81624, ☏ 970/487–3402) offers Native American and other specially themed tours.

Important Addresses and Numbers

HOSPITALS

Craig Memorial Hospital (785 Russell Ave., Craig, ☏ 970/824–9411); **Grand Junction Community Hospital** (2021 N. 12th St., Grand Junction, ☏ 970/242–0920); **Pioneers Hospital** (785 Cleveland St., Meeker, ☏ 970/878–5700); **St. Mary's Hospital** (2635 N. 7th St., Grand Junction, ☏ 970/244–2273).

VISITOR INFORMATION

Battlement Mesa, Inc. (Box 6000, Battlement Mesa 81636, ☏ 970/285–9700 or 800/545–6372); **Cedaredge Chamber of Commerce** (Box 278, Cedaredge 81413, ☏ 970/856–6961); **Delta Chamber of Commerce and Visitors Center** (3rd and Main Sts., Delta 81646, ☏ 970/874–8616 or 800/436–3041); **Dinosaur Chamber of Commerce** (Box 102, Dinosaur 81610, no ☏); **Greater Craig Chamber of Commerce** (360 E. Victory Way, Craig 81625, ☏ 970/824–5689); **Grand Junction Area Chamber of Commerce** (740 Horizon Dr., Grand Junction 81501, ☏ 970/244–1480 or 800/962–2547); **Meeker Chamber of Commerce** (Box 869, Meeker 81641, ☏ 970/878–5510); **Nucla/Naturita Area Chamber of Commerce** (Box 104, Nucla 81424, ☏ 970/864–7233); **Palisade Chamber of Commerce** (Box 729, Palisade 81526, ☏ 970/464–5616); **Plateau Valley Chamber of Commerce** (120 Main St., Collbran 81624, ☏ 970/487–3457); **Rangely Chamber of Commerce** (209 E. Main St., Rangely 81646, ☏ 970/675–5290); **Rifle Area Chamber of Commerce** (200 Lions Park Circle, Rifle 81650, ☏ 970/625–2085).

COLORADO ESSENTIALS

Getting Around

By Bus

Greyhound Lines operates regular intercity routes with connections from Denver. Smaller bus companies provide service within local areas. One such line is **Springs Transit Management** in Colorado Springs (☏ 719/475–9733).

By Car

The U.S. Interstate highway network provides quick, easy access to Colorado despite imposing mountain barriers. Denver is served by I–25, running north–south through Colorado Springs and Pueblo; I–70, running east–west via Vail, Glenwood Springs, and Grand Junction; and I–76 running northeast from Denver via Fort Morgan into Wyoming. U.S. 666 flirts with the southwest corner of the state. U.S. 160 traverses southern Colorado, while U.S. 40 accesses the northwest section.

By Plane

Regional carriers include **Mesa** (☏ 800/637–2247), **Midwest Express** (☏ 800/452–2022), **Delta/SkyWest** (☏ 800/221–1212), which flies out of Salt Lake City, and **United Express** (☏ 800/241–6522 or 800/662–3736).

By Train

Amtrak (☏ 800/872–7245), the U.S. passenger rail system has daily service to Denver's Union Station. The railroad, of course, helped to shape and develop the American West, and it's still a marvelous way to see the state at leisure. The westbound route to California cuts through the spectacular Glenwood Canyon.

Guided Tours

Gray Line of Denver (Box 17527, Denver 80217, ☎ 303/289–2841) offers two- to five-day tours of the surrounding areas. **Maupintour** (Box 807, Lawrence, KS 66044, ☎ 913/843–1211 or 800/255–4266) runs an 8-day tour that takes in Denver, Estes Park, Vail, Grand Junction, Durango, and Colorado Springs. This company also offers an 11-day rail tour that includes parts of New Mexico. **Tauck Tours** (276 Post Rd. W, Westport, CT 06880, ☎ 203/226–6911) offers an 8-day tour of the state. If your time is limited or the entire itinerary doesn't appeal to you, you can take only part of the tour (at least 50%) for a slight surcharge.

Dining

The dining scene in Colorado is quite sophisticated, especially in Denver and the resort towns. Still, restaurants in smaller areas such as Crested Butte rank among the country's most vibrant and creative. Of course beef, buffalo, and burritos appear in many of the restaurants throughout the state, but a dazzling range of international cuisine from Southwestern to classic French, Italian, and Thai can be found just as easily.

CATEGORY	RESORTS AND CITIES	TOWNS AND COUNTRY
$$$$	over $40	over $35
$$$	$30–$40	$25–$35
$$	$20–$30	$15–$25
$	under $20	under $15

All prices are for a three-course meal, excluding drinks, service, and tip.

Lodging

Take your pick from the numerous selections across the state: resorts, chain hotels, dude ranches, bed-and-breakfasts, guest houses. Colorado has all sorts of accommodations to match any budget.

CATEGORY	RESORTS AND CITIES	TOWNS AND COUNTRY
$$$$	over $350	over $225
$$$	$250–$350	$150–$225
$$	$125–$250	$90–$150
$	under $125	under $90

All prices are for a standard double room in high season, excluding tax and service.

Parks and Forests

National Parks

Colorado boasts two glorious national parks: Just north of Denver is **Rocky Mountain** (Estes Park 80517, ☎ 970/586–1206), and in the southwest corner is **Mesa Verde** (Mesa Verde 81330, ☎ 970/529–4461). The former celebrates Colorado's sublime wilderness scenery, full of glowering glaciers, glittering alpine lakes, meadows woven with wildflowers and majestic stands of aspen and evergreens. The latter contains an awe-inspiring collection of hauntingly beautiful ancient cliff dwellings, abandoned by the Anasazi centuries ago and set amid exquisite sandstone and red-rock formations.

National Forests

Colorado's 11 national forests (though not all included in this chapter), comprising over two-thirds of the state—**Arapaho, Roosevelt, Grand Mesa, Gunnison, Pike, Rio Grande, Routt, San Isabel, San Juan, Uncompahgre,** and **White River**—offer an abundance of recreational and sightseeing activities.

Shopping

You'll find outlets of many top designers in Denver's malls and department stores, as well as in chic resorts such as Aspen and Vail. But the real buys in Colorado are indigenous artifacts, crafts, and specialties. Western and Native American art galleries, ceramics and jewelry shops, and stores specializing in Western memorabilia and cowboy clothing dot the landscape, especially in the southwest. Beware of the numerous "authentic trading posts" that line the roads: Although they're fun and kitschy, they're usually tourist traps with second-rate merchandise.

Sports

Beaches

Believe it or not, Colorado *has* beaches: sandy stretches adorn such large lakes as Grand Lake, which abuts Rocky Mountain National Park, and Lake San Cristobal in the south-central part of the state. Even in summer, however, the water is far too cold for swimming without a wetsuit; still, the beaches are nice for sunning on a pleasant afternoon.

Fishing

Fishing is legal year-round (though several restrictions apply in Rocky Mountain National Park), but you must obtain a license. Fees for nonresidents are $40.25 annually, $18.25 for a five-day period, and $5.25 for a single day. For more information, including the "Fishing Hotspots" and "Watchable Wildlife" booklets, contact the **Colorado Division of Wildlife** (6060 Broadway, Denver 80216, ☎ 303/297–1192).

Golf

Golfers love Colorado's championship courses—for the combination of the stunning mountain scenery and the additional loft on their drives. For more information, see the regional sports listings, or contact the **Colorado Golf Association** (5655 S. Yosemite, Suite 101, Englewood 80111, ☎ 303/779–4653); **Colorado Golf Country USA** (559 E. 2nd Ave., Castle Rock 80104, ☎ 303/688–8262; or the **Colorado Golf Resort Association** (2110 S. Ash, Denver 80222, ☎ 303/699–4653).

Hiking and Backpacking

Contact the **U.S. Bureau of Land Management** and the **U.S. Forest Service** (Box 25127, Lakewood 80225, ☎ 303/275–5350) for information on Colorado's sterling trekking opportunities. The Colorado Trail is an incredibly scenic 465-mile route that winds its way from Durango to Denver and is popular with both bikers and hikers. For more information, contact **The Colorado Trail** (548 Pine Song Trail, Golden 80401, ☎ 303/526–0809).

Mountain Biking

In summer, more and more ski areas are opening their chairlifts to mountain bikers. There are numerous trails winding through the mountain passes, with arduous ascents and exhilarating descents. For a free trail map, send a SASE to **Colorado Plateau Mountain Bike Trail Associa-**

tion (Box 4602, Grand Junction 81502, no ☎) You can also obtain brochures and maps from the **Colorado State Office of the U.S. Bureau of Land Management** (Dept. of the Interior, 2850 Youngfield St., Lakewood 80215, ☎ 303/239–3600).

Rafting

Rivers such as the Colorado, Arkansas, and Animas abound in Level IV and V rapids, as well as gentler stretches for beginners. For more information, contact the **Colorado River Outfitters Association** (Box 1662, Buena Vista 81211, ☎ 303/369–4632).

Skiing

Residents and travelers alike claim that the state's snow—champagne powder—is the lightest and fluffiest anywhere. For complete information on Colorado's more than 30 ski areas—from the large, world-famous resorts to the "Gems of Colorado" (smaller resorts that would be considered quite large elsewhere)—contact **Colorado Ski Country USA** (1560 Broadway, Suite 1440, Denver 80202, ☎ 303/837–0793). More adventuresome types may want to contact **Heli-Ski USA** (Box 1560, Telluride 81435, ☎ 303/728–6990).

If Nordic skiing is more your speed, contact the **Colorado Cross-Country Ski Association** (Box 1336, Winter Park 80482, ☎ 800/869–4560), which can recommend one of the dozens of great ski-touring centers in Colorado.

Snowmobiling

Snowmobiling is a wonderful way to explore virgin terrain. For information, contact the **Colorado Snowmobile Association** (Box 1260, Grand Lake 80447, ☎ 800/235–4480).

Festivals and Seasonal Events

Winter

Christmas is the focus. Denver hosts the **World's Largest Christmas Lighting Display,** with 20,000 floodlights washing civic buildings in reds, greens, blues, and yellows (☎ 303/892–1112), while Silverton searches for a yule log at its **Yule Log Celebration** (☎ 303/387–5654 or 800/752–4494). The **Vail Festival of Lights** promotes a whole range of attractions including World Cup ski races, Dickensian carolers, brilliant lighting displays, and Christmas ice-skating spectaculars.

The big events of January are Denver's two-week **National Western Stock Show and Rodeo,** the world's largest livestock show, and ski competitions such as the **Steamboat Springs Annual Northwest Bank Cowboy Downhill, the Aspen/Snowmass Winterskol, and Breckenridge's Ullr Fest and World Cup Freestyle.**

In February, Steamboat Springs hosts the oldest continuous **Winter Carnival** west of the Mississippi.

Spring

In March, Springfield holds one of its two annual **Equinox Festivals** as the sun turns nearby Crack Cave into a sort of Stonehenge, highlighting the ancient Ogam calendar and writings of possible Celtic origin, around AD 471. Over 70 tribes convene for the Denver Pow Wow, with Native American dancers, artisans, and musicians. Charity and celebrity events rope them in at many ski areas, including the **Crested Butte American Airlines Celebrity Ski to Benefit the Cystic Fibrosis Foundation, the Colorado Special Olympics** (at Copper Mountain), **Jimmy Heuga's Mazda Ski Express** (raising money to fight MS) at various areas, and the **Beaver Creek American Ski Classic** (hosted by former president Gerald Ford).

In April, **Kit Carson's Annual Mountain Man Rendezvous** relives the time of the mountain men in a colorful festival in Kit Carson. **A Taste of Vail** showcases that area's superlative restaurants.

In May, look into the **Fort Vasquez Fur Trappers Rendezvous,** in Platteville, where fur-trading days return with demonstrations, contests, costumes, games, and Native American crafts and dances.

Summer

June sees the **Silly Homebuilt River Raft Race,** held in Las Animas. It keeps spectators guessing which improbable floating contraptions will reach the finish line and which will explore the bottom of the Arkansas River, along which the event takes place. Meanwhile, the season of music festivals and cultural events gets into swing with Telluride's weekend-long **Bluegrass Festival** (☎ 303/728–3041), the **Aspen Music Festival, Steamboat's Western Weekend** (with rodeo events, a country-music festival, chili cook-off, Cowboy Poetry gathering, and more), and **Springs in the Mountains Chamber Music Festival,** Vail's **Bravo! Colorado Music Festival,** Glenwood Springs' **Strawberry Days,** and Grand Junction's **Country Jam.** Also popular in summer is Boulder's **Colorado Shakespeare Festival** (☎ 303/492–1527), one of the top three in the country.

Colorado celebrates an all-American Fourth of July. Among the largest celebrations is the **Fantastic Fourth in Frisco** (☎ 303/668–5800). Arts events galore continue throughout July, including **Dance Aspen, Aspen International Design Conference,** Denver's **Black Arts and Asian Arts Festivals,** Winter Park's **Jazz and American Music Festivals,** and the **Breckenridge Music Institute Concert Series.**

Rodeos are typical late-summer fare; in August, you can witness the **Pikes Peak or Bust Rodeo** in Colorado Springs (☎ 719/635–7506, 800/368–4748 outside the state), the state's largest. Country fairs are also big business, especially Pueblo's star-studded state fair. Other top events include the **Estes Park Folk Festival, Music in Ouray Chamber Concert Series,** Telluride's **Jazz Celebration** and **Wild Mushroom Festival,** and the **Bolshoi Academy**'s annual residency in Vail.

Autumn

In September, Cripple Creek's **Aspen Leaf Tours,** free trail tours by Jeep through ghost towns and old gold mines, show off the brilliant mountain aspens (Cripple Creek Chamber of Commerce, ☎ 719/689–2169). The **Denver International Air Show** (☎ 303/892–1112), the country's largest such event, draws jet teams from around the world, antique aircraft, parachutists, high-tech military planes, and aerial acrobats. Other daredevils take to the skies in Colorado Springs' **Hot Air Balloon Classic** and the **Telluride Hang Gliding Festival.** Major **film festivals** take place in Aspen, Breckenridge, and Telluride (one of the world's leading showcases for foreign and independent cinema).

Oktoberfests and Harvest Celebrations dominate October, most notably Carbondale's **Potato Days,** Haxtun's **Corn Festival,** and the Cedaredge and Penrose **Applefests.**

In November, Creede's **Chocolate Festival** puts chocolates of every size, shape, and description in every corner of town (☎ 719/658–2374 or 800/327–2102). The Yuletide season is rung in with spectacular **Christmas tree lightings** and parades in Denver, Cañon City, Estes Park, and other locales.

Important Addresses and Phone Numbers

Emergencies

Dialing 911 will summon police, fire, and ambulance services throughout the state of Colorado.

Visitor Information

Contact the **Colorado State Tourist Office** (☎ 800/433–2656) to receive a vacation planner and **TravelBank Colorado** (Box 200594, Denver, CO 80220, ☎ and fax 303/320–8550) for information via modem. In Canada, call the **U.S. Travel and Tourism Office** (480 University Ave., Suite 602, Toronto, Ontario M5G IV2, ☎ 416/595–0335, FAX 416/595–5211).

5 Idaho

By Brian
Alexander

Updated by
Susan English

SURE, NOW EVERYBODY IS TALKING ABOUT IDAHO.
They talk about escaping cities for the simple life.
They talk about mountain biking in summer on
mountains they ski on during winter. They talk about fishing the
Salmon and Snake rivers and about rafting the white water through
tremendous chunks of wilderness. They talk about Cecil Andrus, longtime governor of Idaho (he's now retired), and how he never seems to
be without a fly-fishing vest.

They won't let you into this state unless you do something outdoors.
That's the official state religion, and it has been embraced by thousands
of new immigrants from California, Washington, New York, and elsewhere. It's why they say that if God doesn't live here, He at least has
a vacation home.

The popularity was a long time coming, however. Until the 1980s, Idaho
may well have qualified as the most ignored state in the Union. Native American tribes like the Nez Percé, the Coeur d'Alene, and the
Shoshone-Bannock settled here because they found the rivers full of
fish, the land fertile, and the game abundant, but, despite Lewis and
Clark's trip through the state in 1805, white folks didn't show up in
numbers until the 1840s, when pioneers on the Oregon Trail came, saw,
and kept heading west. It wasn't until 1860, when a few Mormons came
up from Utah at the direction of Brigham Young and settled in Franklin,
that a true settlement was established.

No wonder. At first glance Idaho is an inhospitable place. The Snake
River plain in southern Idaho is high-plateau desert, largely made up
of a thin layer of soil over the ancient lava flows. It's hot in summer
and cold in winter. The Sawtooth Mountains, with peaks as high as
11,800 feet, loom to the north. Northern Idaho is covered in alpine
forest and glacier-carved lakes, a pleasant sight when the heavy winter snow melts.

These days, though, we have Gore-Tex and down and waterproofing,
and what looked like misery to pioneers looks like fun to us. So, despite the cries of native Idahoans about all the newcomers arriving in
their Volvos and bringing their espresso shops with them, people keep
coming. Still, Idaho has just over 1 million people spread over its
82,413 square miles. That's 12 people per square mile. Considering
that 350,000 Idahoans live in just 10 towns—125,000 in Boise alone—
there's a lot of land out there with nobody on it. Only .4% of the state
(215,000 acres) is considered urban or built-up, and virtually the entire eastern two-thirds is wilderness or national forest. Point all this
out to Idahoans, and they'll shoot back that the population increased
by 62,000 from 1980 to 1990 and that you're not from around here,
or else you'd feel how crowded it's gotten.

The fact is, Idahoans do feel some pressure. They lived a certain way
for nearly 150 years: They fished, hunted, did a little skiing, trapped
furbearing animals and cut down trees. Now people, including many
newcomers, are telling them that way of life is all wrong. There is a
palpable cultural rift between new arrivals and old-timers, and one can't
help feeling that the new arrivals will eventually carry the day.

For now, though—aside from celebrity-filled Sun Valley, which some
Idahoans look upon as a completely different planet—this is a meat-
and-potatoes, cowboys and fishermen, back-to-basics kind of place.
It is a conservative agricultural state despite the growth of manufac-

turing. There are the famous potatoes, of course, but also barley, sugar beets, hops, and beans. Idaho raises 70% of the nation's trout, and the dollar value of cattle outstrips even that of potatoes. Lumber, too, is still a tremendous industry in Idaho. That's why small boxes of "Spotted Owl Helper" decorate more than one small-town bar.

Things still operate very informally here. Unless you are conducting business, it is possible to go into any restaurant sans coat and tie and feel completely at home. This is a state where the lieutenant governor could enter a local tight jeans contest, win it, travel out of town to the national finals, and hear little more from his constituents than a chuckle.

PIONEER COUNTRY

During the 1840s, westbound pioneers on the Oregon Trail seemed to lose their way in southeastern Idaho. They tried several routes, the remnants of which now crisscross the region, attempting to find the best way out. Now if you tell people in Boise, for example, that you plan to spend time in this area, they'll look at you cross-eyed and ask why. What's here is a kind of time capsule. Those living in larger towns may have forgotten what it's like in hamlets of 230 or 407 or even 103, but they still exist in the southeast. Here women drive pickups with bumper stickers declaring WRANGLER BUTTS DRIVE ME NUTS. One village is locally renowned for its automatic car wash. The towns, collectively known as pioneer towns, were usually founded by hardy souls from Utah who trapped or hunted or farmed. Today they are almost unchanged since the days when folks like Pegleg Smith opened trading posts; often the only modern building is the local Mormon church.

Exploring

Numbers in the margin correspond to points of interest on the Idaho map.

If you're coming from Wyoming or you just want to drive in some beautiful countryside, a good place to start a tour of Pioneer Country is along a stretch of the **Teton Scenic Byway,** Route 33 to Route 31 through **Tetonia, Driggs,** and **Victor.** Strictly farming and ranching towns until the Grand Targhee ski resort (just across the Wyoming border) was built in 1969, they're now part Western ski town, part ranching community.

Continue south on Route 31 through the Snake River valley, one of the state's most beautiful drives in any season. In winter, hoofprints of elk, deer, and smaller animals zigzag across the hills, and in spring and summer, wildflowers coat the mountains. At **Swan Valley,** you'll meet up with U.S. 26, which crosses the Snake River, the artery that gives life to all of southern Idaho, and continues into Idaho Falls.

❶ **Idaho Falls** sits at the edge of the Snake River plain, which arcs across southern Idaho. This town of 50,000 people sprouted when an industrious stagecoach worker figured a bridge across a narrow section of the Snake would be much faster for overland stages than the ferry used upstream. He completed the bridge in 1866, and a community, called Eagle Rock, developed at the site. Later the name was changed to Idaho Falls, despite the lack of natural falls. In 1911 a weir was built in the river to generate power, lending some legitimacy to the name.

The town's history is illustrated at the **Bonneville Museum,** which is small but more impressive than most small-town museums. Somehow

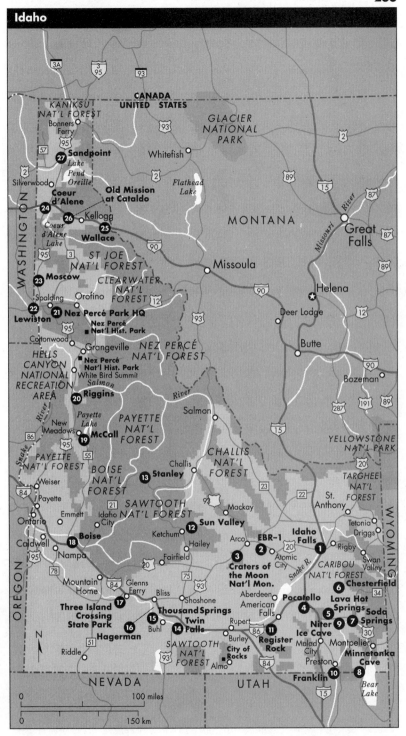

the volunteer historical society that operates it has managed to re-create early Eagle Rock in the basement. The faux street is complete with a dentist's office, dry-goods store, and other facades. Upstairs, displays include objects and photos from the early days of Bonneville County, including an extensive selection of Shoshone-Bannock artifacts. *Eastern and Elm Sts.,* ☎ *208/522–1400.* ☛ *$1 adults, 25¢ children 5–18.* ☉ *Weekdays 10–5, Sat. 1–5. Closed holidays. (In winter, hours are slightly irregular.)*

TIME OUT If the weather is warm and the skies blue, take a break on the **greenbelt,** which runs along the Snake River from Market Street north to U.S. 20. Locals take lunch breaks and bike, walk, or rollerblade along the paved paths. Picnic tables are set up at intervals.

Today Idaho Falls is almost completely dependent on income generated by Idaho National Engineering Laboratory (INEL). Here, back ❷ in 1951 when the atom was our friend, **EBR-1** became the nation's first nuclear reactor to generate usable amounts of electricity. When you're driving on U.S. 20 to the site, near the aptly named Atomic City, it's easy to see why makers of B movies thought odd things might crawl out of the desert around nuclear facilities. EBR-1 is now a National Historic Landmark. *35 mi west of Idaho Falls on U.S. 20,* ☎ *208/526–0050.* ☛ *Free.* ☉ *Memorial Day–Labor Day, daily 8–4.*

In case movie directors need more inspiration about what the world might look like post–nuclear war, they could travel still farther west ❸ to **Craters of the Moon National Monument.** Just 15,000 years ago, the earth opened up north of here and poured molten rock over the landscape. The flows pushed the Snake River south and left this part of the Snake River valley a ghostly plain punctuated by lava tubes and mysterious-looking formations. The visitor center, just off the highway, provides an introduction to the area, but those who want to learn and see more can drive the 7-mile loop road on a self-guided tour. *20 mi west of INEL on U.S. 93,* ☎ *208/527–3257. Loop* ☛ *$4 per vehicle. Visitor center open June 15–Labor Day, daily 8–6; Labor Day–June 14, daily 8–4:30. Loop road closed to cars Nov. 1–Apr. 15 (approximately).*

A smaller version of Craters of the Moon, the **Hell's Half Acre Lava Flows,** is about 25 miles south of Idaho Falls on I–15. They include a rest stop and interpretive sign.

To see more of what Idaho was like a long, long time ago, continue ❹ on I–15 to the other good-size town in the southeast, **Pocatello.** Here, on the campus of Idaho State University, is the **Idaho Museum of Natural History.** The museum has a fine collection of Ice Age animal skeletons and the Fujii Western Rock Collection. Take U.S. 91 to Yellowstone Avenue and follow the signs to the campus. *S. 5th Ave. and E. Dillon St.,* ☎ *208/236–3168.* ☛ *$3 adults, $2.50 senior citizens, $2 children 2–12.* ☉ *Mon.–Sat. 9–5, Sun. noon–5. Closed Jan. 1, Thanksgiving, Dec. 25.*

Head south on 4th Avenue about 2 miles until you reach Avenue of the Chiefs. Turn right and head up the hill. There you'll find Ross Park and the **Old Fort Hall Replica;** Fort Hall was a major pioneer outpost northeast of Pocatello on what is now the Fort Hall Indian Reservation. *In front of Bannock County Historical Museum,* ☎ *208/233–0434.* ☛ *$1 adults, 50¢ youths 13–18, 25¢ children 6–12; free winters.* ☉ *Year-round; hours vary.*

❺ Take I–15 south and then U.S. 30 east to **Lava Hot Springs,** one of the funkiest little towns in Idaho. Lava, with a population of about 400, has one main street, turn-of-the-century brick buildings, and some of the most desirable **hot springs** in the United States. The springs passed from Native American hands to the U.S. Army to the state of Idaho and are now operated by a state foundation, which has turned the pools into a garden spot. The springs have almost no sulfur but are rich in other minerals. This brings people who, for a variety of reasons, believe in the powers of mineral springs. You can soak here in the water that comes out of the ground at 110°F or swim in the pool at the other end of town (*see* What to See and Do with Children, *below*). *430 E. Main St.,* ☎ *208/776–5221 or 800/423–8597.* ☛ *$4 adults, $3.50 children under 12.* ✆ *Apr.–Sept., daily 8 AM–11 PM; Oct.–Mar., daily 9 AM–10 PM.*

❻ About 7 miles east of Lava Hot Springs is the 16-mile paved road to **Chesterfield.** Virtually a ghost town now, it was founded in 1880 by Mormons, complete with the Mormon grid system for blocks. Many of the original buildings still stand as if waiting for the inhabitants to return. Chesterfield is listed on the National Register of Historic Places.

❼ **Soda Springs,** about 18 miles farther east on U.S. 30, is home to another regional landmark. No, not the Monsanto slag pour, which the town lists as a tourist attraction, but the only **man-made geyser** on earth, a sight that's more reputation than reality. It seems the town fathers were drilling for a swimming pool when they hit carbon dioxide, a gas that permeates this region. The carbon dioxide mixed with groundwater under pressure and started shooting out of the ground. Local boosters capped the geyser with a valve. Now, every hour during daylight, they turn the geyser on, unless, that is, the wind is coming from the west, which would douse the parking lot. From U.S. 30, turn left onto Main Street. The geyser is right behind the Statesman's Lounge and Enders Café on the left side of the street.

❽ At this point in the tour, adventurous travelers may want to take a side trip on U.S. 30 east to Montpelier, another interesting pioneer town, and then U.S. 89 south to St. Charles. Just west of St. Charles, first on a county highway and then on a U.S. Forest Service road (both numbered 30012), lies the **Minnetonka Cave,** a classic nine-room limestone cavern dotted with stalactites and stalagmites. The forest service gives 90-minute tours throughout the summer. Take a jacket. The cavern is naturally a constant 40°F. *1.2 mi west of St. Charles,* ☎ *208/523–3278.* ☛ *$2.50 adults, $1.50 children 6–15.* ✆ *For tours mid-June–Labor Day (approximately, depending on weather), daily 10:30–5, leaving every half hr.*

❾ Nearby Bear Lake, famous for its odd turquoise color, is a local favorite with anglers and campers. From here, backtrack north on U.S. 89 and west on U.S. 30 past Soda Springs, and pick up Route 34 south. Drive through Grace, population 970, toward the village of Niter, population under 100 (and probably not listed on any map you have). About 3 miles beyond Grace, you'll see a small sign directing you left onto Ice Cave Road, to the **Niter Ice Cave.** It may look like a small hole in the ground, but the cave, used by pioneers to keep food cold, is nearly half a mile long. You can climb in if you want, but be sure to have a flashlight and be prepared to get dirty.

Continue south on Route 34 through rolling ranch lands that were the object of range wars between farmers, who wanted to put up fences, and shepherds and cattlemen, who wanted an open range. The land around here has been owned by some of the local families for more than 100 years.

⑩ At Preston, take U.S. 91 south to **Franklin,** the oldest town in Idaho. It was established on April 14, 1860, by order of Brigham Young, who sent settlers north from Utah. At first the pioneers struggled, but eventually a sawmill was installed and more cash flowed in. Today the town, population 478, contains the Franklin Historic District along Main Street. Turn left off U.S. 91; the **village hall,** built in 1904, is on the right. Across the street, the **Lorenzo Hatch house** (1870) is a fine example of Greek Revival architecture, popular in many Western pioneer towns. The exterior masonry is a marvel, considering how primitive the town was in 1870. Nearby stands the **Franklin Cooperative Mercantile Institution,** a great stone structure; it was built to house the local cooperative store and now contains a museum.

Continue south out of town on U.S. 91, and just before the Utah border you'll see the town **cemetery.** Many grave sites are more than 100 years old.

Cross into Utah, take Route 61 to Cornish, and drive north on Route 23 toward Weston, where you pick up Route 36 to Malad City. From here, you can either take I–15 north back to Pocatello, or, if the weather is good and all roads are open, head south on I–15 to Route 38 west, follow it to Holbrook, and turn north on Route 37. This road winds through the Curlew National Grasslands and past abandoned homestead cabins sitting lonely on the rolling hills.

⑪ This is the most scenic way to the final stop in Pioneer Country. When Route 37 meets I–86, drive west. After about 8 miles, signs for **Register Rock** lead you into a canyon where wagons on their way west often stopped to camp. During the night, pioneers, like the cave painters of Lascaux, left proof of their passage by painting or carving their names into the stone. The rock is now protected by a roofed and fenced enclosure. ☛ *Free.* ☺ *Daylight hours.*

What to See and Do with Children
At one end of **Lava Hot Springs** is a giant **swimming and diving complex.** Here the water is kept at 86°F. Suits, towels, and lockers are available. *U.S. 30 exit at Center St.,* ☎ *208/776–5221.* ☛ *$4 adults, $3.50 children under 12.* ☺ *Memorial Day–Labor Day, Sun.–Fri. 11–8, Sat. 10–8.*

Shopping

Shopping Malls
Grand Teton Mall (17th St., 3 mi east of central Idaho Falls) has helped to pull small shops out of downtown Idaho Falls, creating empty storefronts along its main street. The mall has a variety of specialty and department stores, including **The Bon Marché** and **Made in Idaho,** which, as its name suggests, sells a variety of Idaho-based products.

Sports and the Outdoors

Cycling
The **greenbelt** in Idaho Falls is an excellent place to pedal. For information on bike rentals, call **Idaho Falls City Parks** (☎ 208/529–1480).

Fishing
Bear Lake and **Henry's Lake** (the latter near the Montana border) are known for cutthroat trout.

Golf

Area courses include **Pinecrest** (701 E. Elva St., Idaho Falls, ☎ 208/529–1485), **Sage Lakes** (100 E. 65 N., Idaho Falls, ☎ 208/528–5535), **Sandcreek** (5230 Hackman Rd., Idaho Falls, ☎ 208/529–1115), **Teton Lakes** (N. Hibbared Hwy., Rexburg, ☎ 208/359–3036), and **Thunder Canyon** (9898 E. Merrick Rd., Lava Hot Springs, ☎ 208/776–5048).

Skiing

CROSS-COUNTRY

An especially interesting spot for Nordic skiing is **Craters of the Moon National Monument,** near Arco. In this eerie landscape, the National Park Service makes a trail on the loop road.

Dining and Lodging

Idaho Falls

DINING

$$ Dolores Casella's Downtowner. This tiny, sparsely decorated restaurant on the street level of an office building is operated by a local food aficionado who also writes for the local paper on matters gastronomical. Meals are themed, but the accent is usually Continental. ✗ 447 Shoup St., ☎ 208/524–2524. Reservations accepted. MC, V. Closed Sun. and Mon. No lunch Sat.

$$ Sandpiper. Although the nautical theme may have gone a little overboard (pun intended), this seafood and steak establishment is one of the better dining spots in town. Since it sits on the bank of the Snake River, there are lovely views from the back windows. ✗ 750 Lindsay Blvd., ☎ 208/524–3344. Reservations accepted. AE, D, DC, MC, V. No lunch.

$ Mama Inez. The Idaho Falls outpost of this popular Mexican restaurant chain is regarded as the best ethnic food in town. ✗ 338 Park Ave., ☎ 208/525–8968. MC, V.

$ Smitty's. The waitresses still call you "honey" in this cross between a Big Boy and a roadhouse. The pancakes are meals in themselves, and if you don't want it fancy, the burgers, steaks, and chicken are reliable. Local businesspeople come in for breakfast, which is served all day. According to waitresses, this place is packed in summer with families heading for Yellowstone National Park. ✗ 645 W. Broadway, ☎ 208/523–6450. No credit cards.

LODGING

$–$$ Best Western AmeriTel. The newest motel in town, this immediately became a top choice business destination. There is fitness equipment and such business amenities as fax and copy facilities and in-room modem lines. A Continental breakfast, served in the lobby, is included in the room charges. ⊞ 900 Lindsay Blvd., 83402, ☎ 208/523–6000 or 800/528–1234, ℻ 208/523–0000. 94 rooms. In-room modem lines, indoor pool, hot tub, exercise room, business services, meeting rooms. AE, D, MC, V.

$ Best Western Driftwood. Although a little tattered around the edges, this motel on the bank of the Snake just behind the Lindsay motel strip has a nice lawn area in summer. Rooms have coffeemakers, and some have refrigerators. ⊞ 575 Riverview Pkwy., 83402, ☎ 208/523–2242 or 800/528–1234, ℻ 208/523–0316. 74 rooms. Coin laundry. AE, D, MC, V.

Lava Hot Springs

DINING

$ Blue Moon. This place has the most impressive sign in town, and the sandwiches and burgers are solid. At night, the smoke gets heavy, the pool tables see a lot of use, and the beer flows pretty freely. Some of the miners and cowboys have even been known to mix it up. ✕ *89 1st St.,* ☎ *208/776–5806. MC, V.*

$ **Silver Grill Café.** If you want nouvelle cuisine, head for Sun Valley. This is strictly "food that won the West." The seats are covered in vinyl, the tabletops are Formica (and just what are you gonna do about it?), but the sandwiches, burgers, and steaks are pretty good. ✕ *78 E. Main St.,* ☎ *208/776–5562. D, MC, V.*

DINING AND LODGING

$–$$ **Royal Hotel.** Lisa Toly fell into innkeeping by accident but has since managed to take an old miners' rooming house and turn it into a cozy bed-and-breakfast. Renovated in 1993, the interior is decorated in turn-of-the-century colors and furnishings. Rooms are small, but the second floor has one especially for guests to make snacks, and the honeymoon suite has a Jacuzzi. The full breakfast, including Toly's home-baked apple turnovers and frittata, is the best in town, or, if you're in time for lunch—and especially if you've got a hungry brood—stop in for a pizza. As improbable as it sounds, Toly makes pizza that would make any New Yorker smile. ▥ *11 E. Main St., 83246,* ☎ *208/776–5216. 3 rooms, 1 suite; all with private bath. Dining room. AE, D, MC, V.*

LODGING

$$–$$$ **Lava Hot Springs Inn.** This grand old building was a hospital, a retirement/nursing-home facility, and now, after a complete renovation in the late 1980s, a European-style bed-and-breakfast inn. (A buffet breakfast is included.) The interior is done in pink-and-black art deco, and the rooms are neat and well appointed. Five suites have private baths with Jacuzzis, and a hot mineral pool, just steps away from the back door, overlooks the Portneuf River. ▥ *94 E. Portneuf Ave., 83246,* ☎ *208/776–5830. 18 rooms, 2 with baths; 5 suites with baths. Dining room, hot springs, library. AE, D, MC, V.*

$$ **Riverside Inn and Hot Springs.** Also by the Portneuf River, this 1914 inn, which has mineral hot tubs, was once quite the romantic getaway. Over time, it fell into disrepair but was restored in the 1980s and now has an immaculate interior. Some of its neighbors have not yet caught the renovation bug sweeping this tiny town, however. A Continental breakfast is included. ▥ *255 Portneuf Ave., 83246,* ☎ *208/776–5504. 16 rooms, 12 with bath. 5 Hot springs, library. D, MC, V.*

Pocatello
LODGING

$$–$$$ **Best Western Cotton Tree Inn.** This motel is conveniently located off I–15 at Exit 71. Some rooms have kitchenettes. ▥ *1415 Bench Rd., 83201,* ☎ *208/237–7650 or 800/528–1234,* ▧ *208/238–1355. 149 rooms. Restaurant, bar, hot tub, racquetball, coin laundry. AE, D, DC, MC, V.*

The Arts

The **Idaho Falls Symphony** (☎ 208/529–1080) presents a five-concert series each year, often with renowned special guests. Each August the **Shoshone-Bannock Indian Festival** celebrates the culture of the region's original inhabitants; for information, contact the Pioneer Country Travel Council (*see* Important Addresses and Numbers *in* Pioneer County Essentials, *below*).

Pioneer Country Essentials

Arriving and Departing

BY BUS

Greyhound Lines (☎ 800/231–2222) has regular service along the Boise–Idaho Falls corridor. To the east, buses run to Rexburg and West Yellowstone, Montana.

BY CAR

From the south, I–15 connects Salt Lake and other Utah cities to southeastern Idaho; from the north, it comes from western Montana. In Idaho, I–15 runs through Idaho Falls and Pocatello, where it intersects I–86 (the main route west), and along the edge of the pioneer towns in the southeast corner. From the east, the most scenic route into the region descends from Wyoming's Teton Pass and connects with Idaho's Routes 33 and 31 at Victor in the Targhee National Forest. Route 31 runs to Swan Valley and U.S. 26, which goes to Idaho Falls.

BY PLANE

The commuter carriers **Horizon** (☎ 800/426–0333), the Alaska Airlines partner, and **SkyWest** (☎ 800/453–9417), the Delta Air Lines partner, have service to **Idaho Falls** and **Pocatello.** In addition, **American** (☎ 800/433–7300) and **Delta** (☎ 800/221–1212) have flights to Idaho Falls.

BY TRAIN

Amtrak (☎ 800/872–7245) connects Pocatello's **Union Pacific Station** (300 S. Harrison Ave., ☎ 208/236–5555) to points east and west.

Getting Around

BY BUS

Pocatello has an urban bus service. Schedules can be obtained from the chamber of commerce (☎ 208/233–1525).

BY CAR

A car is the only way to see most of the region. The major rental companies have booths at both the Pocatello and Idaho Falls airports. Be aware, however, that rentals in Idaho, especially during ski season, can be pricey.

Guided Tours

SPECIAL INTEREST

The **Idaho National Engineering Laboratory (INEL),** on 890 square miles of sage desert northwest of Idaho Falls and site of more nuclear reactors (52) than anywhere else on earth, conducts research on subjects ranging from nuclear-powered naval vessels to radioactive-waste management. Tours of the facility, including EBR-1 (*see* Exploring Pioneer Country, *above*) can be arranged through **INEL Public Affairs** (785 DOE Pl., MS 3516, Idaho Falls 83401, ☎ 208/526–0050).

Important Addresses and Numbers

EMERGENCIES

In an emergency, dial 911 except in Franklin County, where you should call 208/852–1234.

HOSPITAL EMERGENCY ROOMS

In Idaho Falls, there is the **Eastern Idaho Medical Center** (3100 Channing Way, ☎ 208/529–6111) and in Pocatello, **Pocatello Regional Medical Center** (777 Hospital Way, ☎ 208/234–0777).

VISITOR INFORMATION
Pioneer Country Travel Council (Box 668, Lava Hot Springs 83246, ☎ 208/776–5273 or 800/423–8597), **Yellowstone/Teton Territory** (Box 50498, Idaho Falls 83402, ☎ 208/523–1010 or 800/634–3246).

SOUTH CENTRAL IDAHO

South central Idaho was a sleepy backwater, home to a few ranchers and Basque shepherds until 1935, when W. Averell Harriman, head of the Union Pacific Railroad, realized he needed more riders for his trains. He hired a European count, who presumably understood what makes for a good ski area, to scout the West and come up with a site for a resort. The site turned out to be Ketchum, Idaho, and the result was Sun Valley. Although Twin Falls and the Magic Valley around it are still largely agricultural, growing beans and hops, there is considerable tourism, spurred by Sun Valley's presence 80 miles north. Still, the Oregon Trail and the scenic Thousand Springs area in the Snake River valley are interesting stops in their own right.

Exploring

Numbers in the margin correspond to points of interest on the Idaho map.

⑫ Since the late 1930s and especially after World War II, **Sun Valley** has been one of the premier ski destinations in the country (*see* Sports and the Outdoors, *below*). The precursor of later resorts, it helped to create the idea that the slopes used for skiing in the winter could also draw visitors for summer activities. Today Sun Valley and its neighbor, **Ketchum,** are gold-plated resort towns with a gentrified Western feel. "Lifestyles of the Rich and Famous" could do a whole season just on people who have homes in the area. The nearby Wood River is also a haven for outdoor activities, which residents pursue with manic energy.

Sightseeing in the area is largely limited to Hemingway's grave site in the Ketchum cemetery (off Rte. 75 near 10th St.), a small memorial to him just north of the Sun Valley resort up Sun Valley Road, and Arnold Schwarzenegger's Humvee.

⑬ A brief side trip, about an hour's drive north on Route 75, lands you in the very genuine town of **Stanley.** In the middle of the Sawtooth National Recreation Area, it's about as old-time Idaho as you can get. Trappers, guides, boatmen, and dropouts from the world live here, and on weekend nights, especially in summer, the music starts up in the saloons and the "Stanley Stomp" takes over. Beer and two-stepping in the shadow of the jagged Sawtooths can make you feel as though you've stepped into a John Ford western.

⑭ Return south on Route 75 and U.S. 93 to **Twin Falls,** flanked by the Snake River and the bridges that cross it. Taking U.S. 93 leads across the Perrine Bridge and into the heart of Twin Falls. A few miles east of town, off I–84, Route 50 runs across the Hansen Memorial Bridge. Either way, unsuspecting drivers may feel a sudden sense of vertigo. Both bridges cross the massive Snake River canyon, justly known for its drama. The flat plain to the north simply falls away into the chasm below, as if the hand of nature took a stick and gouged the earth.

That's basically what happened. About 15,000 years ago, a massive inland sea, Lake Bonneville (the remnant of which is the Great Salt Lake), crashed through its natural dikes in southeast Idaho and poured into the Snake. For about six weeks, a volume of water many times greater than the flow of the Amazon acted like a giant plow as it thundered down the Snake and carved the canyon.

Driving into Twin Falls feels like putting on a comfortable sweater. It is perhaps as all-American a city as you'll find anywhere. After a shopping mall was built just on the town side of the Perrine Bridge, downtown merchants banded together to take on the new competition. The result is a downtown straight out of the 1950s, with neon signs, a score of small shops, and some new eateries and bars. The massive Greek Revival courthouse (Shoshone St.) faces a band shell in the park across the street, home to summertime concerts. The downtown's only drawback is its maddening adherence to the classic Mormon street grid. There are, for example, four 3rd avenues, one for each point on the compass.

TIME OUT Locals who eat downtown often stop in for a pastry dessert and espresso or other specialty coffee at **Metropolis** (125 Main Ave., ☎ 208/734–4457). Pastry chefs Eric and Susan Ettesvold are formally trained chefs from Los Angeles, and, for her prowess with dough, Susan once represented the United States at a culinary competition. The café carries a complete line of baked goods, from baguettes to blintzes, and serves a light lunch. (There is also a monthly dinner, for which there is a long waiting list.)

Twin Falls used to be famous as the site of Shoshone Falls, a waterfall higher than Niagara, and for the Twin Falls, just to the east. Snake River dams have greatly reduced the flow over these once-majestic attractions, but, for a short period in the spring, during the height of the snowmelt in the Snake River watershed in the Tetons, the falls sometimes return to their former glory. In any case, follow signs off Route 30 east of town for the **canyonside park by Shoshone Falls.** The drive gives you a good look at the canyon's geology, a bonus especially if the falls are tame. The park is open in daylight hours.

From Twin Falls, take U.S. 30 west; past Buhl, the road gradually tumbles into the Snake River canyon until it is nearly level with the river ⑮ at the **Thousand Springs** area. Here, dozens of springs literally pour out of the north canyon wall. Geologists think the water comes from mountains to the north and that it may take up to 100 years for it to make the underground journey to the Snake. It's possible to tour the area by boat (*see* Guided Tours *in* South Central Idaho Essentials, *below*).

⑯ U.S. 30 crosses the Snake and continues into **Hagerman,** a favorite getaway spot for Boiseites and home of the "world-famous" Idaho state fossil, a complete skeleton of a small Ice Age horse. On the way, look for large, round boulders scattered over the landscape. These "melon rocks" were eroded into that shape and dumped here by the Bonneville flood.

Stop in at the **Idaho State Bank building** (State and Hagerman Sts.), which dates from 1887, when it served as a general store. The teller area has been restored to a wooden and brass showplace, just the way a bank would have looked in the 1880s.

Farther down State Street is the tiny **Hagerman Valley Historical Museum,** known locally as the fossil museum. It's home to the fossil horse as well as artifacts from the area's past. *State and Main Sts.,* ☎ *208/837–6288.* ☛ *Free.* ⊙ *Wed.–Sun. 1–4.*

Across the street, the **Fossil Beds National Monument headquarters** provides detailed information on the fossils in the area. The Pliocene fossil beds along the river were declared a national monument in 1988, and plans are in the works for a new visitor center and a visitor program, so tourists will be able to see these incredibly rich fossil fields. To date, over 100 species have been identified. *221 N. State St.,* ☎ *208/837–4793.* ☞ *Free.* ☉ *Weekdays 8–5.*

Frank Lloyd Wright, perhaps the greatest architect of the 20th century, believed that buildings should harmonize with their sites. An excellent example of this philosophy, Idaho's only **Frank Lloyd Wright house** is about 2 miles west of Hagerman off U.S. 30. At the Snake River Pottery sign, turn left and go 1.1 miles. It's to the left, overlooking the Snake River and its magnificent canyon. For the best view, go as far as the driveway of Snake River Pottery (the oldest producer of pottery in Idaho) and head back up the road. (The house can also be seen from an overlook a mile farther uphill on U.S. 30.) Since it's a private home, please don't disturb the occupants.

The bad news is that U.S. 30 melds into I–84 at Bliss. The good news is that the town of Glenns Ferry is only a 30-minute drive. Here you'll find **Three Island Crossing State Park,** site of one of the most dangerous Snake River crossings on the Oregon Trail. The pioneers were forced to cross channels separated by the three islands, often losing stock and belongings in each one. It's doubtful they would have made it without their Shoshone guides. The trail itself, winding down the hills on the opposite bank, stands out like a dark vein on the landscape.

What to See and Do with Children

Bill Mason Outfitters (Sun Valley Village, Box 127, Sun Valley 83353, ☎ 208/622–9305) boasts that its classes can teach even a novice to fly-fish in just 15 minutes, and it's true. You may not be a champion, but you'll be able to cast and even catch fish. Classes for kids (morning and afternoon sessions daily) include equipment, instruction, transportation, and fishing on a private, stocked pond. Reservations are required.

Shopping

Shopping Districts/Malls

Central **Ketchum** is made up almost completely of small shops, art galleries, and cafés. Everything from Ralph Lauren designs to Indian beadwork beckons from shop windows.

Sun Valley Village, in the Sun Valley Resort's pedestrian mall, offers 13 mostly upscale specialty shops ranging from **Bill Mason Outfitters,** for anglers, to **Towne and Park Jewelers.**

Downtown **Twin Falls** has a variety of small stores. Shopping along **Main Avenue** around the intersection with **Shoshone Street** is much the way shopping in small American towns used to be before malls arrived. If you're hankering for a mall, however, the **Magic Valley Mall** (1485 Pole Line Rd.) is near the Perrine Bridge.

Specialty Stores

GALLERIES

There are no fewer than 19 art galleries in central **Ketchum,** offering a range of art from the wildly esoteric to traditional Western. For more information on gallery tours or a map, contact **Sun Valley Gallery Association** (Box 1241, Sun Valley 83353, ☎ 208/726–2602).

Sports and the Outdoors

Cycling

A public biking/in-line skating/walking trail runs most of the length of the Wood River valley in the **Sun Valley** area. It's possible to ride all the way from Hailey to a point about 2 miles north of the Sun Valley Resort, a distance of about 18 miles. Maps are available from the **Blaine County Recreation District** (Box 297, Hailey 83333, ☎ 208/788–2117). **Pete Lane's Sports** (Sun Valley Mall, ☎ 208/622–2276) has rentals by the hour or the day.

Fishing

The Sun Valley area on the **Wood River** (also known as the Big Wood but not to be confused with the Little Wood) and **Silver Creek** are known worldwide for dry fly-fishing. For tackle and classes, try **Bill Mason Outfitters** (*see* What to See and Do with Children, *above*).

Golf

Without question, two of Idaho's three premier golf courses are at the **Radisson Elkhorn** (Sun Valley, ☎ 208/622–4511) and **Sun Valley Resort** (Sun Valley, ☎ 208/622–2251). They are both expensive (more than $80), but a number of golf packages can lower the cost. Another area course is **Canyon Springs** (Canyon Springs Rd., Twin Falls, ☎ 208/734–7609).

Rock Climbing

The **City of Rocks,** southeast of Twin Falls, draws European and American rock climbers to its sheer faces. The rock formations towering out of the desert are considered some of the most challenging in the American West.

Skiing

CROSS-COUNTRY

The **Sun Valley Resort** has trails evenly divided among beginner, intermediate, and advanced. Most trails run along the golf course, and classical and skating lanes are groomed into the tracks. For information on the condition of other trails throughout the valley, call 208/762–6662; for cross-country and downhill skiing and racing information, contact the **Sun Valley Ski Association** (Box 2420, Sun Valley 83353, ☎ 208/622–3003). You can rent cross-country skis at **Sun Valley Nordic Center** (Sun Valley Resort golf course, ☎ 208/622–2251); **The Elephant's Perch** (280 N. East Ave., ☎ 208/726–3497), and **Backwoods Sports** (711 N. Main St., ☎ 208/726–8818).

DOWNHILL

There's no doubt that **Sun Valley** (☎ 800/635–8261), when it has snow—which it now always does, thanks to a multimillion-dollar investment in snowmaking equipment—is one of the best ski resorts in the country. Bald Mountain, primarily an intermediate and advanced hill, has one small area, Seattle Ridge, essentially for beginners. However, because of the mountain's steep 3,400-foot vertical drop, an intermediate run here might earn a black diamond elsewhere. Dollar, a much smaller teaching hill near the Radisson Elkhorn, is almost completely beginner terrain. Together they have 75 runs serviced by three quads, five double chairs, and seven T-bars. On-hill facilities include four restaurants, and the children's program is among the most complete of any ski resort. Some purists might find Baldy a little crowded with glittery lodge sitters, but they add color and lend a festive atmosphere to the day.

Dining and Lodging

Hagerman

DINING

$ The Riverbank. People drive all the way from Twin Falls for this small restaurant's fried catfish. Near the Snake River and formerly the branch of a bank, this cement-block building has an interior that is about as soothing as, well, a bank's, but locals swear by the food. ✕ *191 State St.,* ☎ *208/837–6462. MC, V. Closed Mon. No lunch Tues.–Sat.*

LODGING

$$ The Cary House. Just outside town on a site that extends to the cliffs
★ overlooking the Snake is this restored and updated farmhouse. Built in 1908, it is listed on the National Register of Historic Places. Owners Linda and Darrell Heinemann have re-created a 1900s feel without sacrificing today's comforts. Horses graze outside the windows. Rooms are decorated with antiques from the region but are fully carpeted. Linda's complete gourmet breakfast varies but emphasizes local ingredients. ▣ *17985 U.S. 30, 83332,* ☎ *208/837–4848. 4 rooms. Dining room, horseback riding. No credit cards.*

Sun Valley

DINING

$$$ Peter's. This local favorite is a casual, bright bistro offering northern Italian and Austrian dishes. Veal, pork, fresh fish, and other seafood get some exotic treatments. ✕ *6th St. and 2nd Ave., Ketchum,* ☎ *208/726–9515. Reservations accepted. AE, D, MC, V. No lunch weekends.*

$$$ A Winter's Feast. No doubt about it, this is different. The owner calls it gourmet yurt dining. Okay, well, this is Sun Valley. The idea here is to cross-country ski along an easy trail for about half a mile, take the skis off, enter a Mongolian yurt, and indulge in a five-course gourmet meal. You're supposed to feel as if you're eating in the wilds, but the lights shining from million-dollar homes on the hill detract from the intended ruggedness. The food is expertly created by Colleen Crain. Entrées include home-smoked salmon, beef tenderloin, and rack of lamb. ✕ *Near Warm Springs condo/resort complex, Ketchum,* ☎ *208/726–5775. Reservations required. MC, V.*

$$–$$$ The Christiana. This is as old-line as Sun Valley gets. Hemingway had cocktails here during his final months. The menu reflects that heritage with beef fillets in béarnaise sauce, salmon in hollandaise, and other traditional favorites. ✕ *Sun Valley Rd. and Walnut St., Ketchum,* ☎ *208/726–3388. Reservations advised. AE, D, MC, V.*

$–$$ Gretchen's. This rustic, cozy restaurant offers breakfast, lunch, and dinner. The salmon and trout are fresh and especially well prepared, and the hamburgers are enormous. The young staff is very enthusiastic. ✕ *Sun Valley Village,* ☎ *208/622–2097. AE, MC, V.*

$ Perry's. The Belgian waffles in this café are favorites of local skiers who want a carbohydrate and sugar rush. Hot oatmeal, cereals, fresh fruits, yogurts, and muffins round out the breakfast menu; hot and cold sandwiches and a selection of salads are offered for lunch. Eat-in and take-out service are available. ✕ *131 W. 4th St., Ketchum,* ☎ *208/726–7703. MC, V. No dinner.*

DINING AND LODGING

$$$ Sun Valley Resort. This is, of course, what started it all, and it's still the most complete year-round vacation option in Idaho. Lodge, inn, condominium, and cottage accommodations are available, and the list of facilities is almost endless (there's even an indoor hockey rink). The lodge's poured-concrete exterior is almost indistinguishable from wood (from a slight distance), while the interior decor has a traditional European feel. Lodge apartments, primarily for families, are more modern. **The Lodge Dining Room,** a dramatic, circular, two-level room, is Sun Valley's signature restaurant. A large chandelier hangs above the dance floor, booths are tucked along the wall, and a soft jazz trio plays nightly. The Continental menu features old standards and fresh fish, and there is an extensive wine list. Sunday brunch is a mammoth affair. ☎ *Sun Valley Co., 83353,* ☎ *800/786–8259. Restaurant:* ☎ *208/622–2097; reservations required; no lunch Mon.–Sat. 560 units. 13 restaurants, 3 pools, 18 tennis courts, bowling, horseback riding, ice-skating, Nordic school downhill skiing, cinema. AE, D, DC, MC, V.*

LODGING

$$$ Idaho Country Inn. This quiet inn in a residential neighborhood looks like a tremendous log home with a river-rock foundation. Inside, the wood accents continue. Four-poster beds made of local wood, such as pine or willow, furnish the spacious, rustic rooms. The building is new, however, so the works are modern. The river-rock fireplace in the sitting room is tempting, as is the plate of cookies kept at fireside. Breakfast is included. ☎ *134 Latigo La., Sun Valley 83353,* ☎ *208/726–1019. 10 rooms. Dining room. AE, MC, V.*

$$$ Knob Hill Inn. With lots of wood and log furnishings, the interior of this exclusive inn suits Ketchum's Western character, but, since this is a brand-new building, everything that should be modern is. All rooms have large tubs, wet bars, and balconies with mountain views. Intermediate rooms, suites, and penthouse suites have fireplaces. A full breakfast, afternoon refreshments, and fresh baked goods are included. ☎ *960 N. Main St., Box 800, Ketchum 83340,* ☎ *208/726–8010 or 800/526–8010,* ℻ *208/726–2712. 20 rooms, 4 suites. Restaurant, indoor-outdoor pool, sauna, exercise room. AE, MC, V.*

$$–$$$ Radisson Elkhorn Resort. This is Sun Valley's "other" resort, a large hotel and affiliated condominiums just over the hill from the Sun Valley Resort. The Elkhorn's lodge has fully appointed hotel rooms with modern decor and refrigerators. Upgraded rooms have fireplaces, kitchens, and Jacuzzis. The resort offers a variety of year-round activities but is best known for its massive 7,100-yard, Robert Trent Jones–designed golf course. ☎ *Box 6009, Sun Valley 83354,* ☎ *208/622–4511 or 800/333–3333. 3 restaurants, bar, pool, golf course, 18 tennis courts, nightclub. AE, D, MC, V.*

$$ Lift Tower Lodge. Don't let the rusting lift tower outside the front door put you off. Here's a casual, homey place about three minutes by car from the River Run lift of Baldy. Upgrading over the past two years has spruced up this old establishment and added new decor to some of the simple and utilitarian rooms, which have single, double, or queen beds; remote cable-TVs; and small refrigerators. There is a free Continental breakfast but no restaurant. ☎ *Box 185, Ketchum 83340,* ☎ *208/726–5163 or 800/462–8646,* ℻ *208/726–2614. 14 rooms. Outdoor hot tub. AE, D, DC, MC, V.*

Twin Falls

DINING

$$–$$$ Rock Creek. This steak, prime rib, and seafood house west of downtown is a throwback to the days before cholesterol and red meat became taboo. With a dark red interior, thick booths, and a massive salad bar, it's known for its wide selection of single-malt whiskeys and vintage ports and probably the most complete wine list in town. ✕ *200 Addison Ave. W,* ☎ *208/734–4154. AE, MC, V.*

$$ **Aroma.** Opened by Mark and Dawn Makin in 1985, when downtown Twin Falls was struggling, this small Italian restaurant has become a local favorite by serving such standards as lasagna, ravioli, and pizza. Tablecloths are plastic and the decor simple in what amounts to a storefront operation, but service is friendly and the food reliable. ✕ *147 Shoshone St. N, ☎ 208/733–0167. Reservations accepted. MC, V. Closed Sun. and Mon.*

$ **Buffalo Café.** Ask anybody in town where to go for breakfast, and you'll
★ get the same answer. This tiny café, with a twin in Sun Valley, is a shack squeezed next to a tire store, across from a truck lot surrounded by barbed wire. You can sit at the counter or at one of 10 tables, but if you go on Sunday, expect to wait. The house specialty is the Buffalo Chip, a concoction of eggs, fried potatoes, cheese, bacon, peppers, and onion. (The brave can ask for a Mexi-chip, made with spicy chorizo sausage.) A half order should fill most stomachs. ✕ *218 4th Ave. W, ☎ 208/734–0271. No credit cards. No dinner.*

LODGING

$$ **AmeriTel Inn.** This new motel was recently remodeled and expanded. Kitchenettes are available, and a Continental breakfast is served. 🏨 *1377 Blue Lakes Blvd. N, 83301, ☎ 208/736–8000 or 800/822–8946. 118 rooms. Indoor pool, hot tub, exercise room, meeting room. AE, D, DC, MC, V.*

$$ **Best Western Canyon Springs Inn.** This property is slightly less expensive than the AmeriTel next door. The rooms, which are very well kept, are larger than those at most other motels. 🏨 *1357 Blue Lakes Blvd. N, 83301, ☎ 208/734–5000 or 800/727–5003. 112 rooms. Restaurant, bar, pool. AE, D, DC, MC, V.*

$ **Best Western Apollo.** This smaller motel offers clean, reliable rooms but no restaurant or lounge. A Continental breakfast is served in the lobby, and restaurants are a short walk away. 🏨 *296 Addison Ave. W, 83301, ☎ 208/733–2010 or 800/528–1234. 50 rooms. Hot tub. AE, D, DC, MC, V.*

The Arts

Sun Valley

In addition to the Sun Valley Music Festival and Swing and Dixie Jazz Jamboree (*see* Festivals and Seasonal Events *in* Idaho Essentials, *below*), Sun Valley plays host to a number of arts programs. From January through May, the **Sun Valley Center for the Arts and Humanities** (Box 656, Sun Valley 83353, ☎ 208/726–9491) puts on concerts, a film festival, readings by such luminaries as Allen Ginsberg, and art exhibits.

Nightlife

Sun Valley

The nightspot for a decade has been **Whiskey Jacques** (Main St. and Sun Valley Rd., Ketchum, ☎ 208/726–5297). It's a cross between a nightclub and a cowboy bar. Live music, Western dancing, and lots of drinking help to create a rowdy crowd and a few red eyes on ski slopes the next day. The Sun Valley Resort's **Duchin Room** (☎ 208/622–2097) is more subdued and features live jazz trios.

Twin Falls

Dunken's (102 Main Ave., ☎ 208/733–8114), Tim Jones's homage to microbreweries, has become a regular stop for downtown workers. There are 19 taps, covering most of the better Northwest brews. Many regulars come for a beer, some good conversation, and a few games of cribbage, dominoes, or chess. If you bring an out-of-town newspaper, Jones will be your friend for life.

South Central Idaho Essentials

Arriving and Departing by Plane

AIRPORTS AND AIRLINES

Twin Falls and **Sun Valley** are served by **Horizon** (☎ 800/426–0333) and **SkyWest** (☎ 800/453–9417). Because the Sun Valley airport—actually in Hailey, south of Ketchum—is at a high elevation, be prepared for delays or diversions. In winter, the same snow that attracts skiers can also close the airport. The alternate route is to land in Twin Falls (or Boise) and rent a car. Sun Valley hotels often offer guests free shuttle service from Hailey; ask when making reservations.

Arriving and Departing by Car, Train, and Bus

BY CAR

The region's main highway, I–84, stretches from Boise in the west, through Twin Falls, and then east and south into Utah. However, a much more scenic route from Boise to Twin Falls is U.S. 30, which turns off at Bliss and follows the Snake River canyon. From Boise to Sun Valley, there are several options. In summer, Routes 21 and 75 through the Sawtooth National Recreation Area make for a long but very beautiful drive. In winter, the road is often closed, so be sure to check road conditions. The shortest route is to head east on I–84 to Mountain Home and then take U.S. 20 east to Route 75 north.

BY TRAIN

Shoshone's **Union Pacific Station** (N. Rail St., no ☎), north of Twin Falls, receives **Amtrak** service from Boise and Pocatello.

BY BUS

Greyhound Lines offers service into Twin Falls from Boise or Idaho Falls.

Getting Around

BY CAR

From Twin Falls, take U.S. 93 north to Route 75 north to reach Sun Valley. For a scenic route west, take U.S. 30.

BY BUS

Sun Valley and Ketchum offer free service on **KART** (Ketchum Area Rapid Transit) to most major lodgings, downtown Ketchum, and the River Run and Warm Springs ski lifts. Buses run about every 20 minutes from Sun Valley and Elkhorn resorts and about every hour from central Ketchum. Call KART (☎ 208/726–7140) for schedules and routes.

Guided Tours

ORIENTATION TOURS

Sun Valley Stages (119 S. Park Ave. W, Twin Falls 83303, ☎ 208/622–4200) can arrange tours or charters of the Sun Valley area. **Town and Country Scenic Tours and Transportation** (319 4th Ave., Hailey 83333, ☎ 208/788–2012 or 800/234–1569) arranges tours throughout south central Idaho.

SPECIAL INTEREST

About 10 miles west of Buhl, where several swimming-pool operators have set up hot-springs pools and river-swimming areas, **Thousand Springs Tours** runs a 2½-hour excursion. Tour boats leave from Sligar's and motor about 5 miles up the Snake; they stop at various points, including eddies in which the water is a clear green, a favorite spot for scuba divers. The tour is by reservation only. *State and Hagerman Sts.,*

Box 117, Hagerman 83332, ☎ 208/837–9006. Cost: $16 adults, $11 children under 7. Runs mid-Apr.–Sept., daily; first tour at 10.

Important Addresses and Numbers

HOSPITAL EMERGENCY ROOMS

In Sun Valley, there is **Wood River Medical Center** (past Sun Valley Mall, near resort golf course, ☎ 208/622–3333), and in Twin Falls, **Magic Valley Regional Medical Center** (650 Addison Ave. W, ☎ 208/737–2000, TTY 208/737–2114).

VISITOR INFORMATION

South Central Idaho Travel Committee (858 Blue Lakes Blvd. N, Twin Falls 83301, ☎ 800/255–8946), **Twin Falls Chamber of Commerce** (same address, ☎ 208/733–3974).

BOISE

"It's tough to be the object of so much swooning, so much rosy wooing . . . ," wrote *Idaho Statesman* reporter Marianne Flagg in 1992. "Now please stop writing about us." With a river running through it, a ski hill towering over it, and hundreds of square miles of nature all around it, including a desert to the south and alpine forests to the north, Boise is worried that its "discovery" will bring an end to its old (and pretty good) quality of life. A number of major corporate headquarters, including Boise Cascade and Ore-Ida, are here, and things have been moving along swimmingly for a number of years.

Make no mistake, though: Even with 125,000 people and a university, Boise is still a small town. People know one another and exchange waves as they whiz by on their in-line skates or mountain bikes. A murder, a very rare event, is shattering news. And while it doesn't have the nightlife or great restaurants of other cities, there are a few notables.

Exploring

Numbers in the margin correspond to points of interest on the Idaho map.

⑱ The best place for you to start your exploration of **Boise** is at the **state capitol** (Capitol Blvd.), which is a scale replica of the Capitol in Washington, D.C. You can walk in the main rotunda during business hours. The rest of the city fans out from the capitol steps. From here, walk northwest to 8th Street, the heart of downtown. Streets on both sides of 8th are lined with cafés, businesses, and shops (*see* Shopping, *below*).

TIME OUT Bar Guernica (Grove St. and Capitol Blvd.), a popular bar and café, is a convenient downtown window to Idaho's long history of Basque culture. Many people come for the exotic Basque food, which features spicy meats, but burgers are also served, as are specialty coffees. You may have to squeeze yourself into this narrow, redbrick, corner café if you go on a weekend night.

After exploring the capitol area, head east on Warm Springs Avenue through the **Warm Springs** neighborhood, where the houses are heated by underground hot springs.

Turn left on Old Penitentiary Road for a visit to the **Old Idaho Penitentiary,** one of only three territorial pens still standing. The jail, built in 1870, was used until 1974 without much improvement in conditions. Things became so intolerable that prisoners staged a series of rebellions starting in the 1960s. The final revolt, in 1973, prompted the move to a more modern facility. The cell blocks have been left exactly as they were after the riot. Scorched stone walls, tiny cells with calendars still in place, and metal bunks evoke the ghosts of prisoners. A self-guided tour takes at least 90 minutes. *2445 Old Penitentiary Rd., ☎ 208/334–2844. ☛ $3 adults, $2 senior citizens and children 6–12. ☉ Daily noon–5. Closed state holidays.*

Returning to Warm Springs Avenue, head back toward downtown, but turn left onto Walnut Avenue. Behind the state's Department of Fish and Game, the **Morrison-Knudsen Nature Center** features a man-made Idaho stream—a kind of outdoor natural museum in a park. The stream has been constructed so that viewers can look from above and below the water's surface to see fish swimming, laying eggs, and doing what fish do. The exhibit is completely self-maintaining. Whatever happens, happens. *600 S. Walnut Ave., no ☎. ☛ Free. ☉ Daily sunrise–sunset.*

From Walnut Avenue, follow Park Boulevard into **Julia Davis Park,** home of the **Idaho Historical Museum.** The museum surveys Idaho's past and includes very detailed reconstructions of building interiors that make accompanying text about the pioneer days come to life; a working wood shop is open Sat. 11–3. *610 Julia Davis Dr., ☎ 208/334–2120. ☛ Free. ☉ Mon.–Sat. 9–5, Sun. 1–5. Closed Jan. 1, Thanksgiving, and Dec. 25.*

Julia Davis Park is also the spot to pick up the Boise Tour Train (*see* Guided Tours *in* Boise Essentials, *below*), but perhaps it's most notable as a key gateway to the city's renowned **greenbelt,** which runs along both banks of the Boise River and stretches 4 miles in either direction from downtown. In all, there are about 19 miles of paved pathways linking parks and attractions, and it's not unusual to see deer and other browsing wildlife along the way. The trails are also favorites of in-line skaters, bicyclists, walkers, and joggers.

Continue west and cross the river at Americana Boulevard. In the 1000 block is **Kathryn Albertson Park** (local magnates named the parks for their wives), a tiny wilderness in the middle of Boise. A walking trail nearly a mile long leads visitors through lagoons and a grassland. An urban wildlife area, the park is home to many varieties of birds and the occasional large game animal.

Short Excursions from Boise

It wasn't easy, but after a fight, the federal government set aside the 482,640-acre **Birds of Prey Natural Area,** 30 miles south of Boise along the Snake River's northern shore. Although not easily accessible, it has become a key stop for those fascinated by North American raptors. A good place to start is the **World Center for Birds of Prey.** Species like the harpy eagle and peregrine falcon are on view here. Tours are by appointment only. Take Exit 50 off I–84, head south for 6 miles on South Cole Road, and follow the signs. *5666 W. Flying Hawk La., ☎ 208/362–8687. ☛ $4 adults, $3 senior citizens, $2 children 4–16. ☉ Mar.–Oct., Tues.–Sun. 9–4:30; Nov.–Feb., Tues.–Sun. 10–4. Closed holidays.*

The natural area itself is another 24 miles south. Take I–84 west to Route 69 south, but past Kuna the road is unimproved. You can get a closer look from the river. Day trips, and three-day trips April–June and September–October, through **Whitewater Shop River Tours** (252 N. Meridian Rd., Kuna 83634, ☎ 208/922–5285) run from $50 to $99 per person.

What to See and Do with Children

The **Discovery Center of Idaho** has joined the list of hands-on science museums for children (and adults who act like children). Almost every exhibit moves, talks, or otherwise acts up in response to a child's interaction with it. *131 Myrtle St.,* ☎ *208/343–9895.* ✏ *$3 adults, $2 senior citizens and children 5–18.* ☾ *Memorial Day–Labor Day, Wed.–Fri. 10–5, weekends noon–5; Labor Day–Memorial Day, Wed.–Fri. 9–5, Sat. 10–5, Sun. noon–5.*

Off the Beaten Track

Idaho has its own small wine industry, which, say proud locals, is catching up to Oregon's and Washington state's, especially in the white varietals. You can see for yourself how successful the wineries have become by visiting them; five of the 12 are located west of Boise in Nampa and Caldwell, and one is in Hagerman (*see* Exploring South Central Idaho, *above*). Entry to all wineries is free. For a map, contact **Idaho Grape Growers and Wine Producers Commission** (Box 790, Boise 83701, ☎ 208/334–2227).

Shopping

Shopping Districts/Streets

A rich selection of stores lines 8th Street downtown. **The 8th Street Shops** (8th St., between Grove and Broad Sts.) make up a restored turn-of-the-century block with specialty shops and small restaurants. **The 8th Street Marketplace** (Capitol Blvd. and Front St.), a brick warehouse converted into stores, sits on the east side of 8th Street. **Boise Center** (Front St., between 8th and 9th Sts.), the city's new convention center, also houses a **St. Chapelle Winery** tasting room and a shop called **Taters,** stuffed with all manner of things spud.

In **Hyde Park,** around the intersection of 13th and Eastman streets, just northwest of the state capitol, antiques shops line the streets, and several cafés and specialty stores with classic awnings and decorated windows vie for your attention.

Specialty Stores

BOOKS AND MAGAZINES

The Book Shop (908 Main St., ☎ 208/342–2659) has a huge selection of books, including the best array of books about Idaho in the state. **Hannifin's** (1024 Main St., ☎ 208/342–7473) is a block away but about 90 years in the past. The men who work in this cigar and magazine shop are as old and grizzled as the building, which opened in 1907. You can buy just about any magazine published, including a rather colorful selection of pornography discreetly placed behind glass windows in the back of the store.

FISHING GEAR

Wherever more than 10 people live in Idaho, there is a store that sells fishing gear and permits, but **Moon's Kitchen and Criner's Tackle and Cutlery** (815 Bannock St., ☎ 208/385–0472) is one of a kind. It may be the only store in the country to combine hamburgers and milk shakes with fishing tackle.

Sports and the Outdoors

Cycling

The **greenbelt** is a great place to cycle. Mountain biking is popular on the hills just outside central Boise. Trails include the **8th Street Extension** (north on 8th St. to where the pavement ends) and **Cartwright Road** (Harrison Blvd. north to Hill Rd., to Bogus Basin Rd., then left on

Cartwright). **Willow Lane Athletic Complex** (end of Willow La., off W. State St.) and **Wheels R Fun** (831 S. 13th St., at Shoreline Park) have bicycle rentals.

Golf

Courses include **Quail Hollow** (4520 N. 36th St., ☎ 208/344–7807), **Shadow Valley** (15711 Rte. 55, ☎ 208/939–6699), and **Warm Springs** (2495 Warm Springs Ave., ☎ 208/343–5661).

Skiing

DOWNHILL

Only 16 miles north of town, **Bogus Basin** (2405 Bogus Basin Rd., 83702, ☎ 208/336–4500) is Boise's winter backyard playground. It's known for night skiing, which leads suit-clad executives to climb in their 4×4s and change into ski gear on the way. There are some serious black diamond runs as well as a healthy proportion of tame beginner trails. The vertical drop is 1,800 feet; six double chairs and four rope tows serve 45 runs.

Tubing

In summer, thousands of people go tubing—sitting in an inner tube and floating down the river. A special bus service from **Ann Morrison Memorial Park** (Americana Blvd.) carries tubers to **Barber Park,** about 6 miles to the east across the Ada County line. From there, floaters drift back to Ann Morrison Park. Across from the park, **Wheels R Fun** (see Cycling, above), open April–October, carries inner tubes for floating the river.

Dining

$$–$$$ **Peter Schott's.** The dining room in the Sun Valley Resort might argue
★ the point, but this small restaurant on the first floor of the Idanha Hotel is generally regarded as the best restaurant in Idaho. Its light walls, fireplace, and bookshelves create an intimate feel. Schott used to run the restaurants at Sun Valley Resort after immigrating from Austria. Now a local celebrity with his own two-minute cooking show, Schott calls his food new American cuisine, but he also throws in a little northern Italian. Fresh fish dominates the menu, and the wine list is complete (155 selections) but not extravagant. It's possible for two people to have dinner and a bottle of wine for $50 (not including tip). ✕ *928 Main St., ☎ 208/336–9100. Reservations advised. AE, D, DC, MC, V. Closed Sun. No lunch.*

$–$$ **Manly's Café.** Your instinct will tell you not to try this white clapboard roadhouse about a mile south of Boise State University, but it didn't become a local legend for its looks. Rather, this classic greasy spoon with an attitude is known for great slabs of prime rib stretched over a platter and served with french fries. Many patrons eat at the small counter, others wait for tables, but they all eat. ✕ *1225 Federal Way, 208/336–7885. No credit cards. Closed Sun. and Mon.*

$–$$ **Table Rock Brew Pub and Grill.** This microbrewery makes the second-best beer in Idaho, and it has managed to turn that skill into a happening restaurant, especially on weekend nights. Neon lights; long, high tables; an energetic staff; and loud pop music create a kinetic atmosphere. Food is basic—onion rings, chili, salads, and burgers—but it is served in great heaps. ✕ *705 Fulton St., ☎ 208/342–0944. AE, D, DC, MC, V.*

$ **Harrison Hollow Brewhouse.** This brew pub is a favorite stop for skiers heading to or returning from Bogus Basin. It's decorated like a cross between a sports bar and a Western cabin. TVs keep patrons up-to-date on scores and games. Speakers pour forth blues and R&B because an owner loves them, and photos of great blues guitarists adorn a wall in the bar area. The menu offers sandwiches, bar food, and ribs. ✕ *24555 Harrison Hollow Rd.,* ☎ *208/343–6820. AE, MC, V.*

Lodging

$$–$$$ **Owyhee Plaza.** Several Hawaiians got lost in the Idaho wilderness in the 1800s and became local legend. Idahoans, not knowing how to spell Hawaii, settled on Owyhee, now the name of a county and this hotel, built in 1910. Refurbished during the '50s, the building lost a little of its charm, but its old glory can still be seen in the style of its giant light fixtures and the dark wood paneling. An adjacent motel offers moderately priced rooms. ⌧ *1109 Main St., 83702,* ☎ *208/343–4611 or 800/233–4611. 100 rooms. 2 restaurants, bar, beauty salon, meeting rooms. AE, MC, V.*

$$ **Idaho Heritage Inn.** Tom and Phyllis Lupher operate this B&B in a for-
★ mer governor's mansion about a mile east of downtown. Each room is very different, but all have names with political themes. Antiques, wallpaper, and old-style bed frames retain an early 1900s feel. The top-floor room, carved out of the attic, is very private. A full breakfast is included. ⌧ *109 W. Idaho St., 83702,* ☎ *208/342–8066. 6 rooms. Dining room. AE, D, MC, V.*

$–$$ **The Idanha.** Built in 1901 and once Boise's showplace, this hotel is rec-
★ ommended with a very large grain of salt. Today the brown shag carpeting is a little ratty. TV reception depends on a set of rabbit ears and luck. The steam heat is piped in from three blocks away through old-style radiators, accompanied by a symphony of clangs and hisses, if, that is, the night clerk remembers to turn the heat on. On the second floor, a sign with a large red arrow reads ROOM 206/FIRE ESCAPE. It's to be hoped that the person in 206 will be willing to unlock the door. On the other hand, in what other hotel would a kitchenette feature appliances from 1939? There is even a cast of odd hotel residents. Movies have been made based on less. This is a true classic that deserves to be brought back to life. ⌧ *928 Main St., 83702,* ☎ *208/342–3611. 45 rooms. Restaurant, bar. AE, D, DC, MC, V.*

The Arts

The **Morrison Center for the Performing Arts** (2101 Campus La., ☎ 208/385–1609) offers one of the most extensive arts programs in any city this size. The **Boise Opera Company, Ballet Idaho** (a collaboration with Ballet Oregon), the **Boise Philharmonic,** and the **Boise Master Chorale** all have full season programs. In summer, an outdoor theater is home to the **Idaho Shakespeare Festival** (412 S. 9th St., ☎ 208/336–9221).

Nightlife

Bars and Lounges

In addition to the lively brew pubs **Harrison Hollow** and **Table Rock** (*see* Dining, *above*), there are several bars that offer live jazz and pop on weekends in the neighborhood around 6th and West Idaho streets, downtown.

Boise Essentials

Arriving and Departing

BY BUS

Boise-Winnemucca Stages (☎ 208/336–3300) serves the U.S. 95 corridor from Nevada to Boise, with stops in towns around Boise. **Grey-**

hound Lines has service to the **Boise Bus Depot** (1212 W. Bannock St., ☎ 208/343–3681).

BY CAR
I–84 is the primary east–west route into Boise. From the north, take Route 55. From the south, you may find it easier to take U.S. 93 through Jackpot, Nevada, which joins U.S. 30 near Twin Falls, rather than taking the smaller and twisting Routes 225 (Nevada) and 51 (Idaho).

BY PLANE
Jet service into **Boise Municipal Airport** (☎ 208/383–3110) is provided by **American** (☎ 800/433–7300), **Delta** (☎ 800/221–1212), and **United** (☎ 800/241–6522). Most flights originate in Salt Lake City, although United flies direct from Chicago. The commuter carriers **Horizon** (☎ 800/426–0333) and **SkyWest** (☎ 800/453–9417) also serve Boise.

Between the Airport and Downtown
BY BUS
The city's bus service, **Boise Urban Stages** (☎ 208/336–1010), called simply "the Bus," runs frequently from the airport to major points around the city. The cost is approximately 75¢ to downtown.

BY TAXI
Boise has several cab companies. A taxi stand is just outside the terminal building. The cost is $6–$7 to downtown, depending on the destination.

BY TRAIN
Morrison-Knudsen Depot (1701 Eastover Terr., ☎ 208/336–5992) is a stop for the **Amtrak** *Pioneer,* which connects Boise to Oregon in the west and to Pocatello and Wyoming in the east.

Getting Around
BY BUS
Boise Urban Stages (☎ 208/336–1010), referred to as "the Bus" (*see above*), is cheap, runs frequently, and provides good service throughout the city.

BY TAXI
Local cab companies include **Blue Line** (☎ 208/384–1111), **Boise City Taxi** (☎ 208/377–3333), and **Metro Cab** (☎ 208/866–0633).

Guided Tours
ORIENTATION
The **Boise Tour Train** is a re-created motorized locomotive that takes sightseers on a tour of Boise. *Julia Davis Park, ☎ 208/342–4796 or 800/999–5993. Fare: $5.50 adults, $5 senior citizens, $3 children 3–12. Hours of operation vary by day and season. Closed Nov.–Apr.*

Important Addresses and Numbers
HOSPITAL EMERGENCY ROOMS
Boise has two full-service hospitals: **St. Alphonsus Regional Medical Center** (1055 N. Curtis Rd., ☎ 208/378–2121, emergency room 208/378–3221) and **St. Luke's Regional Medical Center** (190 Bannock St., ☎ 208/386–2222, emergency room 208/386–2344).

VISITOR INFORMATION
Boise Convention and Visitors Bureau (168 N. 9th St., Suite 200, 83702, ☎ 208/344–7777 or 800/635–5240), **Southwest Idaho Travel Association** (Box 2106, 83701, ☎ 800/635–5240).

NORTHERN IDAHO

Most Idahoans consider the Salmon River the unofficial boundary between north and south, since it bisects the state almost perfectly and separates the Pacific and Mountain time zones. The Salmon is also one of the state's great scenic attractions. It is the longest wild river left in the United States, outside of Alaska, and the Middle Fork, which begins as runoff from the Sawtooths and flows through the River of No Return Wilderness Area, is recognized around the world for one of the wildest, most gorgeous river raft trips on earth. The river system is a magnet for anglers, too. Riggins, near its western end; Stanley, high in the Sawtooths near the Middle Fork; and Salmon, to the east near Montana, are the gateways to the Salmon and its wilderness.

Another informal dividing line crosses the White Bird Summit, north of Riggins. Over the summit, Idaho begins to feel more like the Northwest, as opposed to the West. Lewiston, for example, is an inland port whose traffic comes from the Columbia River; it's also the portal to Hells Canyon, a natural wonder that forms the border between Oregon and Idaho.

The panhandle of Idaho is a logging region that has been "discovered" by refugees from larger cities in California, Washington State, and elsewhere. The resort towns of Coeur d'Alene and Sandpoint are just the sort of places that drive visitors to look up the words "Real Estate" in the Yellow Pages.

Exploring

Numbers in the margin correspond to points of interest on the Idaho map.

19 Although the town of **McCall** is close to Boise and falls within the capital's sphere of influence, it has the alpine feel of the northern half of the state. The 108-mile drive north from Boise on Route 55 is one of the most beautiful in Idaho, if not the country. The road runs along the shore of the Payette River as it jumps down the mountains, over boulders, and through alpine forests. The arid plains of the Snake River give way to higher and higher mountains covered by tremendous stands of pines.

Long a timber town, McCall was known as a hunting and fishing spot in summer and, thanks to a nearby mountain and prodigious winter snows, a ski destination in winter. The film *Northwest Passage* was shot here in 1938. In 1948, a lodge was built on the shore of Payette Lake as a sort of manly hideaway, but during the 1980s, the area was discovered by Californians. Now espresso shops dot the main street, and the lodge, bought by a San Diego developer, has been remodeled and gone upscale. Locals are a little ambivalent about all this, but there's no doubt the changes have made McCall one of the most popular resort destinations in the state.

Route 55 reaches its peak a few miles outside McCall and then gradually snakes its way down hillsides. It joins U.S. 95 and the Little Salmon River at New Meadows and heads into mining territory, where gold and silver, and rumors of both, brought hundreds of mostly disappointed men to the region. About 50 miles north of the junction, where the **20** Little Salmon flows into the main Salmon River, the tiny town of **Riggins** is a wide spot in the road. It's also the last stop in the Mountain Time Zone; across the river, it's an hour earlier. Hunters and anglers flock here for chukar, elk, and steelhead.

Immediately outside Riggins, U.S. 95 crosses the Salmon and begins the 40-mile climb toward **White Bird Summit,** which rises 4,245 feet above sea level. There were no roads from north to south Idaho until 1915, when the White Bird Grade was finished. It climbed nearly 3,000 feet in 14 miles of agonizing hairpins and switchbacks. The new road was finished in 1975.

A little over halfway up the new grade, a small scenic overlook sits above the valley where the Nez Percé War started. In 1877, Chief Joseph and his band of Nez Percé, who had not signed a treaty with the whites as had other bands, were nevertheless on their way to resettle at the nearby reservation when trouble broke out. About 80 Native Americans, using guerrilla tactics and surprise, decimated a much larger white force without losing a person. The army retreated, but the legendary pursuit of Joseph's band across 1,500 miles of Idaho and Montana began. An interpretive shelter tells the story of the battle.

From White Bird Summit, U.S. 95 plunges rapidly into the Camas Prairie and into Grangeville, a farming town. Here, the Nez Percé dug the roots of the camas plant, a dietary staple. About 20 miles past Grangeville, the road enters the modern **Nez Percé Indian Reservation,** home to treaty and nontreaty Nez Percé. (There is still some minor antagonism between the groups.) The road heads through Lapwai and enters Spalding.

Though the park itself is really a series of sites spread over three states, ❹ the **Nez Percé National Historic Park headquarters** is in Spalding. The headquarters building gives a detailed look at the Nez Percé, or Ne-Mee-Poo, as they called themselves, and their history, including a 30-minute film about the tribe, their contacts with Lewis and Clark, and their lives today. A small museum exhibits artifacts from Chiefs Joseph and White Bird, including textiles, pipes, and, poignantly, a ribbon and a coin given to the tribe by Meriwether Lewis as thanks for help. *Follow signs on U.S. 95,* ☎ *208/843–2261.* ☛ *Free.* ☉ *Daily 8–4:30.*

Just 10 miles farther up U.S. 95, which joins U.S. 12, the hardwork-❷ ing mill town of **Lewiston** is tucked into the hills at the junction of the Snake and Clearwater rivers. It was once the capital of the Idaho Territory but is now known regionally for its relatively mild temperatures and early golf season. Its blue-collar economy is based on its inland seaport and the giant paper mill just on its eastern edge.

Lewiston and Clarkston (its twin city in Washington), named for you know whom, are also known as the gateways to **Hells Canyon,** a geologic wonder deeper than the Grand Canyon. Canyon tours have become big business in Lewiston (*see* Guided Tours, *below*). The hills in the canyon resemble ancient Mayan temples as they rise high above the waterway. Columnar basalts, rock formations that look like giant black pencils standing next to one another, frame the river. In some spots, ancient Native American pictographs can be seen on smooth rock faces. Bald eagles swoop down from cliffs to hunt for food, and deer scatter along the hillsides.

Miners tried to exploit the area, but they gave up. Today a few hardy sheep and cattle ranchers are all that's left of the pioneers who first settled here. The **Kirkwood Historic Ranch,** a 6-mile walk from Pittsburgh Landing or a four-hour jet-boat ride from Lewiston, has been preserved to show how the pioneers lived. Aside from making homes from cut lumber instead of logs, ranchers today live in nearly the same style. ☛ *Free. Ranch house open daily during daylight.*

(23) From Lewiston, U.S. 95 climbs 2,000 feet virtually straight up out of the valley and into rolling farmland. About 40 miles later, it cuts through the middle of **Moscow,** home of the University of Idaho. Students often joke that the university was placed in Moscow because there is absolutely nothing to do here except study. The city does feature a fine set of late-19th-century buildings, however, and one of the best jazz festivals in the country (*see* Festivals and Seasonal Events *in* Idaho Essentials, *below*).

From Moscow, U.S. 95 winds its way through tiny farm towns to the **Coeur d'Alene Indian Reservation.** French-Canadian trappers mingled with the local Native Americans in the early 1800s and found them to be astute traders. Because of their tough bargaining skills, the trappers called them Coeur d'Alenes (Pointed Hearts). Today the tribe has found another way to get money: a bingo gaming hall.

(24) **Coeur d'Alene** itself is just 10 miles farther north. Idaho's second-most famous resort town sits on the shores of Coeur d'Alene Lake, surrounded by evergreen-covered hills. Although the town was originally a Native American settlement, then a U.S. Army fort, and, in the 1880s, an entrepôt for mining and timber in this part of Idaho, it has always attracted visitors. Now it does so with a vengeance, but the town, especially along Sherman Avenue, the main drag, still has a pleasant village atmosphere. Although primarily known as a summer destination and as Spokane's Playground, Coeur d'Alene has boosted the number of winter visitors by promoting Silver Mountain, a ski area about 50 miles to the east (*see* Sports and the Outdoors, *below*). The city also makes a good base from which to explore the historic mining towns of Wallace and Kellogg, both east on I-90.

(25) **Wallace,** the quainter of the two, is one of the few towns to be included in its entirety on the National Register of Historic Places. About 50 miles east of Coeur d'Alene, it was first settled in the 1880s mining rush, and today much of the town center looks exactly as it did at the turn of the century.

(26) One of the best historical attractions in the area is the **Old Mission at Cataldo,** 24 miles east of Coeur d'Alene on I-90. Influenced by trappers and visited by missionaries, a group of Coeur d'Alenes took up Roman Catholicism. In 1850, together with Father Anthony Ravalli, they began construction of the mission, now the oldest building in Idaho. The mission church is massive, considering that it was built almost totally by hand with an ax and a few other old hand tools. Behind the altar you can see the mud-and-stick construction used on the walls. The giant beams overhead were dragged from the forest, and rock for the foundation was quarried from a hill half a mile away. The adjacent mission house, home to generations of priests, is furnished the way it would have been at the turn of the century. An interpretive center provides more details about the Coeur d'Alenes and the site, which is accessible to travelers with mobility impairments. *Old Mission State Park, Cataldo,* ☎ *208/682–3814.* ☛ *$2 per vehicle.* ☉ *Memorial Day–Labor Day, daily 8–6; Labor Day–Memorial Day, daily 9–5.*

TIME OUT On the way back from Wallace and Kellogg, Silver Mountain, or the mission, take Exit 43 off I-90 and head north along the river. After about 1½ miles you'll see **The Snakepit.** Its proper name is Enaville Resort, but nobody calls it that. Now a restaurant, the 1880s-era log building was once a notorious bordello for loggers and miners. The bartender will be happy to show you the small dumbwaiter behind the bar, used to send drinks up to the rooms, or the bullet holes in the ceil-

ing made by a disgruntled customer. The menu offers burgers, fish,
Rocky Mountain oysters (bull testicles), and steak, including a 40-ounce
number that, believe it or not, sells big around here.

27 Northern Idaho's other resort town, **Sandpoint,** lies just 40 miles north
of Coeur d'Alene on the shores of Lake Pend Oreille, the second-deep-
est lake in the United States. Nestled between the lake and the Selkirk
and Cabinet mountain ranges, Sandpoint has been a railroad depot and
a mining town, but now it survives on tourism and lumber. The town
is small—five blocks of shops and restaurants form its core—and the
brick and stone buildings are almost unchanged since the early 1900s.
Locals say the town is 20 years behind Coeur d'Alene. They mean it
as a compliment. Like Coeur d'Alene, this is a summer destination with
fine lake beaches, extensive woodlands, and nearby mountains. However, now the local ski hill, Schweitzer (*see* Sports and the Outdoors,
below), is transforming itself into a first-class ski area, and Sandpoint,
it has been said, is what places like Vail and Jackson, Wyoming were
just before they expanded.

What to See and Do with Children

In between shopping, swimming, sailing, and fishing in Coeur d'Alene,
visit **Tubbs Hill,** adjacent to the parking lot just east of the resort's tower.
A 2-mile loop trail winds around the hill. Small wooden signs describe
plant and rock types found in the area as well as the remnants of historical buildings. An interpretive guide is available from the city's
parks department (221 S. 5th St., ☎ 208/769–2250).

Shopping

Shopping Malls

The Shops at Coeur d'Alene (2nd St. and Sherman Ave.) is an enclosed
mini-mall with small shops and resort-wear retailers, including United
Colors of Benetton and Worn Out West, which specializes in shirts with
wildlife designs.

Specialty Stores

BOOKS

Wilson's Variety (401 Sherman Ave., ☎ 208/664–8346), in Coeur d'A-
lene, carries a wide selection of books about Idaho, including guides
on geology and history, and topographical maps.

CANDY

The Original Penny Candy Store (325 Sherman Ave., ☎ 208/667–0992),
in Coeur d'Alene, is a re-created turn-of-the-century dry-goods and candy
store with an array of exotic candies from around the world, from sour-
green-apple balls to strawberry bonbons.

CRAFTS

The next time you need a custom Mongolian yurt, try **Little Bear Trading Company** (324 1st St., Sandpoint, ☎ 208/263–1116). The shop
owner, Bear (that's it, just Bear), makes tepees and yurts for clients around
the country. The small store also carries Native American crafts, beads,
and feathers, as well as materials from Africa and Central and South
America.

FURNITURE

Cabin Fever (113 Cedar St., Sandpoint, ☎ 208/263–7179) has one of
the best assortments of garden adornments and curios for cabins in North
Idaho. Lodge decor reigns at **Partners** (404 Sherman Ave., Coeur d'A-
lene, ☎ 208/664–4438), where you can find everything from beds to
love seats to tables, all made from peeled-pine tree trunks and limbs;

decorative birdhouses and Navajo-print pillows are also for sale. Antique lodge furnishings are available at **Sherman Arms Antiques** (412 Sherman Ave., Coeur D'Alene, ☎ 208/667–0527).

GIFTS

The only retail outlet for the mail-order **Coldwater Creek** (foot of Cedar St., Sandpoint, ☎ 208/263–2265) took over the Cedar Street Bridge Public Market, which used to house a variety of specialty shops and a restaurant in addition to a smaller version of the Coldwater Creek store. Merchandise includes wildlife-inspired jewelry, posters, and books; bird feeders; and other nature-oriented gifts. **Journeys American Indian Arts** (117 S. 4th St., Coeur d'Alene, ☎ 208/664–5227) carries beads and other jewelry supplies, as well as a wealth of Native American drums, moccasins, baskets, and books.

Sports and the Outdoors

Cycling

The premier cycling journey is the **Centennial Trail,** a new paved path leading from east of Coeur d'Alene all the way to Spokane. **Silver** and **Schweitzer ski areas** (*see* Skiing, *below*) are especially renowned for mountain biking. In Coeur d'Alene, bikes can be rented at the **Coeur d'Alene Resort's activities desk** (*see* Dining and Lodging, *below*) or from **Coeur d'Alene Surrey Cycles** (Box 14, Hayden Lake, ☎ 208/664–6324); in Sandpoint, rent cycles at **Sandpoint Recreational Rentals** (209 E. Superior St., ☎ 208/265–4557).

Fishing

Despite the river's name, don't look for too many salmon. Most runs have been dammed away, and a total of two sockeye made it back up the Salmon to Red Fish Lake near Stanley in 1991. **Coeur d'Alene Lake** was successfully stocked with chinook a number of years ago, and people have been pulling out some large fish there.

Lake Pend Oreille is renowned for kamloops, a large variety of rainbow trout, and the **Middle Fork of the Salmon** is known for cutthroat trout. Significant populations of steelhead, one of the state's trophy fish, are found in the **Clearwater** and northern sections of the **Snake.** The Snake and **Kootenai** rivers are famous for sturgeon, an ancient species that can grow to well over 6 feet; however, sturgeon may not be removed from the water, even for weighing.

Golf

Northern Idaho courses include **Avondale Golf Club** (10745 Avondale Loop, Hayden Lake, ☎ 208/662–5963); **Bryden Canyon Golf Course** (445 O'Connor Rd., Lewiston, ☎ 208/746–0863); **Coeur d'Alene Golf Club** (2201 Fairway Dr., Coeur d'Alene, ☎ 208/765–0218); **Coeur d'Alene Resort** (900 Floating Green Dr., Coeur d'Alene, ☎ 208/667–4653 or 800/688–5253), among the nation's loveliest but very expensive (greens fees: $150 per person, but packages can lower cost); **Hidden Lakes Country Club** (8838 Lower Pack River Rd., Sandpoint, ☎ 208/263–1642); **the Highlands Golf and Country Club** (701 N. Inverness Dr., Post Falls, ☎ 208/773–3673); **Kimberland Meadows** (New Meadows, ☎ 208/347–2164); **McCall Golf Course** (Davis St., McCall, ☎ 208/634–7200); and **Stoneridge Golf Course** (Blanchard Rd., Blanchard, ☎ 208/437–4682).

Rafting

The three premier raft trips in Idaho are on the **Selway, Lochsa,** and the **Middle Fork of the Salmon.** Rafting these rivers should not be undertaken casually. Although the Lochsa parallels U.S. 12, the Selway and the Middle Fork run ferociously through true wilderness. Unless you are an expert, it's a good idea to pick a recognized outfitter. Even then, you should be a good swimmer and in solid general health. Permits from the U.S. Forest Service are usually required to run these rivers, but they're often hard to get and may require waiting periods (another good reason to use an outfitter). Call 800/635–7820 for permit information.

Skiing

CROSS-COUNTRY

In addition to a commercial cross-country trail at **Schweitzer Mountain,** there are several Nordic trails in and around **McCall, Coeur d'Alene,** and **Priest Lake,** north of Sandpoint. Contact the **Idaho Department of Parks and Recreation** (*see* National and State Parks *in* Idaho Essentials, *below*) for information and maps.

DOWNHILL

Brundage Mountain (Box 1062, McCall 83638, ☎ 208/634–4151), a small hill outside McCall, is in the snowiest area in Idaho. Although the runs are a little short and black diamond speed freaks may want to test their sanity elsewhere, Brundage does have enough to keep intermediates and beginners interested. Advanced skiers find solace in the powder glades. On top of the hill are spectacular views of the Seven Devils peaks and Payette Lake. With a vertical drop of 1,800 feet, Brundage has a triple and two double chairs and a platter tow.

For years, only people in Spokane and Sandpoint knew much about **Schweitzer** (Box 815, Sandpoint 83864, ☎ 800/831–8810), but it's on the way to becoming a top Western ski destination. It offers on-hill accommodations, children's programs, and a full-service ski school, in addition to two mountain bowls with spine-tingling black diamond runs so steep your elbows scrape the snow on turns. Open-bowl skiing is available for the intermediate and advanced, and beginners can choose from among half a dozen tree-lined runs. There is a vertical drop of 2,400 feet. A quad and five double chairs access 48 runs.

Silver Mountain (610 Bunker Ave., Kellogg 83837, ☎ 208/783–1111) solved an accessibility problem by installing the world's longest single-stage gondola. Adjacent to Kellogg, the hill offers a complete family learning program. Locals think the advanced terrain at Schweitzer is better, but Silver offers some excellent wooded powder skiing and some steep runs. Fifty-two trails cover a vertical drop of 2,200 feet and are reached by a quad, two triple chairs, two double chairs, and a surface lift in addition to the gondola.

Water Sports

Boating on the lakes of northern Idaho is one reason many people go there. **Coeur d'Alene** and **Pend Oreille lakes** have miles and miles of shoreline with small coves, bays, and stream inflow points. Though each has popular beaches, you can find your own secluded spot within minutes of leaving the boat dock.

Dining and Lodging

Coeur d'Alene

DINING

$$ Jimmy D's. This comfortable downtown spot is a favorite of locals, including several inn owners who have their food catered. Redbrick walls decorated with art, candlelit tables, and a small bar forge a bistrolike atmosphere. The menu is uncomplicated but well done: pastas, steaks, chicken, and fish. There is also a strong selection of wines, perhaps because the former owner of Jimmy D's runs a wine store and nightclub across the street. ✗ *320 Sherman Ave.,* ☎ *208/664–9774. Reservations accepted. AE, D, MC, V.*

$ **Hudson's Hamburgers.** When they say hamburgers, they mean it. It's burgers, ham and cheese, or egg sandwiches, and that's it. These folks have been in business since 1907, and even local rivals have been forced to admit that Hudson's basic burgers are the town favorites. Sit at the counter and watch how burgers used to be made. The most expensive item on the six-item menu is a double cheeseburger for $3.50. ✗ *207 Sherman Ave.,* ☎ *208/664–5444. No credit cards. Closed Sun. and Mon. No dinner.*

$ **Toro Viejo.** Yes, you can get the real enchilada in northern Idaho. This family-run restaurant offers authentic Mexican food prepared hot and spicy. Mama Briseno cooks all the food, and the kids wait tables. It can get crowded in this new eatery, so consider a reservation. ✗ *117 N. 2nd St.,* ☎ *208/667–7676. Reservations accepted. MC, V.*

$ **T. W. Fisher's Brewpub.** Fisher's microbrewery offers some of the best beer made in Idaho, along with a solid menu of burgers, chicken, salads, and other bar food. The pub is a lively place, with sports on TV, a wood and brass U-shaped bar, and a mainly young crowd. Brewery tours are given at 1:30 and 5:30 daily. ✗ *204 N. 2nd St.,* ☎ *208/664– 2739. AE, D, MC, V.*

DINING AND LODGING

$$$ **Coeur d'Alene Resort.** Since its re-creation in 1986, the resort has become a favorite getaway for people in the Pacific Northwest. Construction of the tall modern tower was controversial, but its effect has been mitigated somewhat by the long floating boardwalk around the marina. Inside, the lobby area is stuffed with small eateries and shops. The restaurant, **Beverly's,** sits atop the tower and serves up commanding views of the lake as well as primarily Continental cuisine and a broad wine selection. Standard rooms, especially in the former motel section, are small, with very basic amenities dating from the 1960s; more expensive tower rooms are more spacious. A concierge service can arrange a wide range of activities, from horseback riding to mountain-bike rentals. In winter, buses to Silver Mountain cost $15, and ski packages are available. ⌂ *2nd and Front Sts., 83814,* ☎ *208/765– 4000 or 800/688–5253. 338 rooms. 3 restaurants (reservations advised), 3 bars, lobby lounge, indoor pool, sauna, 18-hole golf course, exercise room, bowling, beach, recreation room, children's programs (ages 4–14), shops. AE, D, DC, MC, V.*

LODGING

$$$ **Clark House on Hayden Lake.** This giant house, half hidden in the trees ★ across the street from Hayden Lake, is a B&B on steroids. The structure was built in 1910 by F. Lewis Clark, an eccentric millionaire, as a copy of one of Kaiser Wilhelm's palaces. By the late 1980s, the local fire department was ready to torch it for practice. Two local B&B operators wanted to buy it but were scared off by the massive restoration required. In stepped Monty Danner, his partners, and nearly $1 million in restoration funds. The result is a giant wedding cake of a place with wide-open rooms, an art deco feel, hardwood floors in public areas, and an expansive walled garden. The luxurious guest suites all have queen or king beds, three have fireplaces, and three overlook the garden or a small cedar forest. A formal, four-course breakfast is served, and an on-site chef has begun full dinner service. ⌂ *E. 4550 S. Hayden Lake Rd., Hayden Lake 83835,* ☎ *208/772–3470. 5 suites. Dining room. AE, D, DC, MC, V.*

$$–$$$ **Warwick Inn.** This wood frame house, on a quiet street near the Ft. Sherman grounds, a block from the lakefront and a quarter mile from town center, was built about 1900. Rooms are stuffed with lace, floral fabrics, and country French antiques, and all are immaculate. Bonnie Warwick's breakfasts are enormous affairs, usually featuring local fare such as huckleberry waffles. Wine and snacks are served in the afternoon, and each room has sherry. ⌂ *303 Military Dr., 83814,* ☎ *208/765–6565. 3 rooms, 1 with bath. Breakfast room. AE, MC, V.*

$$ **Berry Patch Inn.** On two acres of landscaped grounds (complete with gardens and a waterfall), atop a mountain just west of Coeur D'Alene Lake, this 4,500-square-foot cedar chalet has wonderful views of Mt. Spokane and the Cabinet Mountains to the north. Paths through an adjacent forest are perfect for summer strolls. Inside, the spacious living room has a large stone fireplace, a TV, VCR, and stereo. Decor throughout is country elegant. The guest room on the main floor is large, with a private entrance through French doors and a large private bath with twin marble sinks. A cream, white, and natural color scheme makes this a preferable retreat for honeymooning couples. Upstairs, one room faces south and, on clear evenings, is flooded with moonlight; birch furntiture and a rustic blue, green, and hunter-plaid color scheme make this a handsome choice for guests. The other guest room has white wicker furniture and pastel decor; it overlooks the Mt. Spokane ski area. Breakfasts include an abundance of fresh fruit with poppy-seed dressing and such entrées as griddle cakes stuffed with oats and green apple and topped with huckleberries in sour cream. ⌂ *1150 N. Four Winds Rd., 83814,* ☎ *208/765–4994,* FAX *800/644-2668. 3 rooms; 1 with private bath, 2 share 1½ baths. Breakfast room. MC, V.*

Lewiston

DINING

$$ **Bojack's.** Frankly, the pickings are slim for good dining spots in Lewiston, but Bojack's, downtown, is renowned locally for good steaks, spaghetti, and salads. From the outside it doesn't look like much more than a dark lounge, but inside, it's, umm, a dark lounge with a restaurant added on. ✗ *311 Main St.,* ☎ *208/746–9532. AE, MC, V. No lunch.*

DINING AND LODGING

$ **Sacajawea Motor Inn.** The basic motel-type rooms are clean, quiet, and a good bargain. Also, lots of locals eat at the attached restaurant, **The Helm,** because they know exactly what to expect: good, reliable, simple food for breakfast, lunch, or dinner. It is much like a Denny's with its counter and vinyl booths. The menu carries steaks, burgers, chops, chicken, pancakes, and a variety of sandwiches. ⌂ *1824 Main St., 83501,* ☎ *208/746–1393 or 800/333–1393. 90 rooms. Restaurant, pool, hot tub, exercise room. AE, D, DC, MC, V.*

LODGING

$$–$$$ **Ramada Inn.** On the east side of town, this is as dependable as most other links in the national chain. It's often used for local meetings. The sports bar, with its own microbrewery serving up five specially brewed beers, stocks 100 brands, including local microbrews and imports. ⌂ *621 21st St., 83501,* ☎ *208/799–1000 or 800/232–6730. 136 rooms. Restaurant, bar, sports bar, pool, hot tub. AE, D, DC, MC, V.*

McCall

DINING

$ **The Pancake House.** At the south edge of town, this breakfast spot has become a skiers' favorite thanks to its massive pancakes. It offers counter or table service, but you may have a short wait since everybody in McCall seems to eat here. ✗ *201 N. 3rd St., ☎ 208/634–5849. MC, V. No dinner.*

DINING AND LODGING

$$–$$$ **The Shore Lodge.** Thanks to its lakefront location, the lodge has become almost synonymous with McCall. The interior is decorated with lots of hunter green, dark wood, and plaid upholstery—an English hunting lodge moved to Idaho. In the public areas, the theme works well, but some guest rooms painted with dark green ceilings can feel almost cavelike. Lakefront suites are large, with high ceilings and excellent views, whereas street-side units are like small motel rooms. In keeping with the lodge's mood, **The Narrows,** its restaurant, has chandeliers made of intertwined antlers, burled-wood furniture, and a dramatic view of the lake. Game selections include elk, venison, and duck, and the sharp-cheddar and beer soup with red pepper and potato is warming and smooth. Service is friendly, but some diners may feel the restaurant is overreaching its grasp. In summer, there is outdoor lakefront dining. ▣ *501 W. Lake St., 83638, ☎ 208/634–2244 or 800/657–6464. 117 rooms. Restaurant (reservations advised; no lunch; $$$), bar, café, hot tub, sauna, exercise room. AE, D, MC, V.*

LODGING

$$–$$$ **Hotel McCall.** This hybrid between a hotel and a B&B is in the center of town. The building, constructed in 1939, is more attractive outside than in. Rooms (and prices) vary widely; six are small, dark, and share a bath, while others are almost grand and have lots of light and antique furnishings. A Continental breakfast is included. ▣ *3rd and Lake Sts., Box 1778, 83638, ☎ 208/634–8105. 22 rooms, 16 with bath. Dining room. AE, MC, V.*

Riggins
LODGING

$$$ **The Lodge at Riggins Hot Springs.** This lodge, named for hot springs
★ that have been harnessed into pools on the bank of the Salmon River, is just over 10 miles upriver from Riggins along a narrow, winding road. Inside, Western antiques and Native American crafts abound, and a sitting room is dominated by a large rock fireplace. Rooms have pine paneling and wooden bed frames. Full country breakfasts, snack lunches, and gourmet dinners, such as lamb in raspberry sauce, are included. Kate Bradbury, a novice innkeeper, already knows how to do it right. The lodge works with Exodus outfitters, owned by Bradbury's brother, to create package excursions for hunters, anglers, and rafters. ▣ *Box 1247, 83549, ☎ 208/628–3785. 10 rooms. Dining room, pool, hot tub, mineral baths, sauna, billiards. MC, V.*

$ **Salmon River Motel.** The rooms are clean, comfortable, and spare, but they offer TVs and sounds of the river. One of Riggins's four restaurants is on site. ▣ *1203 U.S. 95, 83549, ☎ 208/628–3231. 16 rooms. Restaurant. MC, V.*

Sandpoint
DINING

$$ **The Garden Restaurant.** This restaurant overlooking Lake Pend Or-
★ eille has been the Sandpoint standard since 1971, thanks to its wandering menu and greenhouse feel. Fare ranges from sandwiches, pastas, and steaks to sophisticated items like owner (and expert mushroom hunter) Richard Hollars's exotic mushroom soups. The wine list features West Coast and European varietals. Sunday brunch is very pop-

ular. ✕ *115 E. Lake St.,* ☎ *208/263–5187. AE, D, MC, V. Closed Tues. in winter.*

DINING AND LODGING

$$ **Connie's Best Western.** This may be the best-maintained motel in
★ Idaho. Rooms are spotless and tastefully decorated for a motel, with special touches like marbleized wallpaper. Most rooms come with a small refrigerator and two sinks. Family suites offer microwaves. A two-room suite with a Jacuzzi and a wet bar feels downright decadent. At **Connie's Café,** locals gather for breakfast at the counter, but the basic fare—pancakes, eggs, cereal, sandwiches (often big enough for two), steaks, and chicken—is also served in the café, cocktail lounge, or dining room with fireplace. ⌂ *323 Cedar St., 83864,* ☎ *208/263–9581 or 800/528–1234. 53 rooms. Restaurant ($), pool, hot tub, meeting rooms. AE, D, MC, V.*

LODGING

$$$ **Green Gables Lodge.** At ski resorts you pay for location, and that's what this lodge 50 yards from Schweitzer's ski lift offers. There is a cozy, European-chalet feel in the public areas. Standard rooms are basic, motel-type units, while more deluxe rooms, like Jacuzzi suites, are bigger and offer microwave/wet-bar facilities. ⌂ *Box 815, 83864,* ☎ *208/265–0257 or 800/831–8810,* FAX *208/263–7961. 82 rooms. 2 restaurants, pool, 2 hot tubs. AE, MC, V.*

$–$$ **Quality Inn.** The rooms are clean and pleasant, and units on the second floor have water views. ⌂ *807 N. 5th Ave., 83864,* ☎ *208/263–2111 or 800/635–2534. 57 rooms. Restaurant, bar, indoor pool, hot tub. AE, D, MC, V.*

$ **Super 8 Motel.** There's nothing fancy here except a hot tub and free in-room coffee, but ski freaks who want to schuss their brains out and collapse at night without breaking a budget can stay at this reliable motel a mile north of town. ⌂ *3245 U.S. 95 N, 83864,* ☎ *208/263–2210 or 800/843–1991. 60 rooms. Hot tub. AE, D, MC, V.*

The Arts

A number of art and music festivals take place around northern Idaho (*see* Festivals and Seasonal Events *in* Idaho Essentials, *below*).

Nightlife

Bars and Lounges
RIGGINS
Locals hang out at the **Shortbranch Bar** (U.S. 95), that rare establishment that gives drinks on credit to folks it knows (but please pay off the tab when you hit $100). Yes, it's a small-town dive, but a dive of the best kind.

SANDPOINT
The **Kamloops** (302 N. 1st St., ☎ 208/263–6715) often leaves its mike open for blues and R&B musicians during the week, so you never know what you'll hear. On weekends, it has live rock and blues acts.

Northern Idaho Essentials
Arriving and Departing
BY BUS
Greyhound Lines stops at the **Coeur d'Alene Bus Depot** (1527 Northwest Blvd., ☎ 208/667–3343).

From Boise, Route 55 heads north to McCall. From Spokane take U.S. 2 north to Sandpoint. From western Montana, you can take I–90 to Coeur d'Alene and then U.S. 95 north to Sandpoint.

BY PLANE
Horizon (☎ 800/426–0333) serves **Lewiston/Clarkston,** the only commercial airport north of Boise. Air travelers heading for Moscow fly to Pullman, Washington, and those going to the Idaho panhandle fly to Spokane, a 35-minute drive from Coeur d'Alene.

BY TRAIN
Amtrak serves **Sandpoint Depot** (Railroad Ave., ☎ 800/872–7245) from Montana to the east and Spokane and Seattle to the west.

Getting Around
BY CAR
A car is essential here. The primary north–south highway is U.S. 95; I–90 and U.S. 2 run east–west.

Guided Tours
SPECIAL INTEREST
Hells Canyon tours are a thriving business. Most tour operators give historical and geological information on one- or two-day trips on the Snake. Some outfitters run jet boats upriver from Lewiston into the Hells Canyon National Recreation Area, while others put rafts in near Oxbow Dam and float downstream. Some offer lodging inside the canyon in cabins or lodges. One, **Beamer's Landing Hells Canyon Tours** (Box 1223, Lewiston 83501, ☎ 800/522–6966), has the contract to deliver the U.S. mail to remote ranches in the canyon and offers a two-day mail-run trip that includes a stop at a sheep ranch. Other outfitters are **Northwest Voyagers** (Box 373G, Lucile 83542, ☎ 800/727–9977) and **Snake Dancer Excursions** (614 Lapwai Rd., Lewiston 83501, ☎ 800/234–1941).

Important Addresses and Numbers
HOSPITAL EMERGENCY ROOMS
In Coeur d'Alene, there is the **Kootenai Medical Center** (2003 Lincoln Way, ☎ 208/666–2000); in Lewiston, **St. Joseph Hospital** (5th Ave. and 6th St., ☎ 208/743–2511); and in Sandpoint, **Bonner General Hospital** (3rd and Fir Sts., ☎ 208/265–1007).

VISITOR INFORMATION
For regional information: **North Idaho Travel Committee** (Box 928, Sandpoint 83864, ☎ 208/263–2161). For towns: **Greater Coeur d'Alene Convention and Visitors Bureau** (Box 1088, Coeur d'Alene 83816, ☎ 208/664–0587), **McCall Area Chamber of Commerce** (116 N. 3rd St., McCall 83638, ☎ 208/634–7631).

IDAHO ESSENTIALS

Getting Around

By Bus
Major Idaho towns are served by Greyhound Lines (☎ 800/231–2222) and by Boise-Winnemucca Stages (☎ 208/336–3300).

By Car
A car is really the best way to see the state. This is the West, after all, and interesting sights are sometimes spread out over the landscape. Remember that Westerners often have an expanded view

of distance. So when an Idahoan says "right around the corner," translate that as under an hour's drive. The good news is that the words "traffic jam" have not yet entered the state's vocabulary. Interstates and the much more interesting two-lane state and U.S. routes are uncrowded, with rare exceptions (like Boise to McCall on Friday at 5:30). Best of all, a car allows you to travel the state's back roads, where some of Idaho's truly unique sights are waiting. There are two caveats, however. First, be sure to keep an eye on your gas gauge; in some parts of the state, the next gas station may be no closer than "right around the corner." Second, many Idaho roads, usually roads leading into the wilderness, simply shut down for the winter. Others experience periodic snow closures. Major newspapers carry road condition reports on their weather pages, or you can call the state's road report hot line (☎ 208/336–6600) or those for specific regions: Boise (☎ 208/334–3731), Coeur d'Alene (☎ 208/772–0531), Idaho Falls (☎ 208/522–5141), Lewiston (☎ 208/743–9546), Pocatello (☎ 208/232–1426), and Twin Falls (☎ 208/733–7210).

By Plane
Commuter airlines serve airports in Boise, Idaho Falls, Lewiston, Pocatello, Sun Valley, and Twin Falls (*see* Arriving and Departing sections *in* individual regions, *above*). In addition, there are many airstrips scattered around Idaho, especially in wilderness areas. These strips, open only in summer and early fall, are used by private planes and those chartered by outfitters.

By Train
Amtrak's *Pioneer* (☎ 800/872–7245) roughly parallels I–84 and stops in Boise, Shoshone, and Pocatello.

Guided Tours

Most tourism in Idaho is related to the outdoors. Packagers can combine dif-ferent sites, such as the Salmon and Snake rivers, or activities, such as fishing and rafting, on their trips. It is against the law for anyone who is not a member of the **Idaho Outfitters and Guides Association** (Box 95, Boise 83701, ☎ 208/342–1919) to provide guiding or outfitting services; contact it for a free directory of members.

Dining

It is virtually impossible to go hungry in Idaho, especially if you like basic American cooking. What restaurants lack in Continental flair, they make up for in volume. Meals are often served on platters big enough to be mistaken for UFOs. But what Idaho does, it does well: A bad steak is a sin here. There are a few standouts in places like Boise, Coeur d'Alene, Sandpoint, and, of course, Sun Valley, where it's possible to find food prepared with as much sophistication as you'd find in any U.S. city. Dress is predominantly casual, although at the more expensive establishments men might feel more comfortable wearing a jacket and tie. Unless otherwise noted in the reviews, reservations aren't taken.

CATEGORY	COST*
$$$	over $20
$$	$10–$20
$	under $10

per person, excluding drinks, service, and 5% state sales tax

Lodging

Although there are a few bed-and-breakfasts, including one or two very good ones, most of the lodging in southern Idaho is in Best Westerns, AmeriTels, and other national and regional motel chains on the I–84 corridor. Boise itself has 2,500 motel rooms, but from Boise north, lodging becomes more diverse: B&Bs, guest ranches, grand old hotels, and resort lodges. Long-term condominium, apartment, and home rentals are available in the Ketchum/Sun Valley area. Guest ranches near wilderness areas offer complete vacation packages, including horseback riding, rodeos, and even cattle herding; a list is available from the Idaho Outfitters and Guides Association (*see* Guided Tours, *above*). Unless otherwise noted in the reviews, rooms have private baths.

CATEGORY	COST*
$$$	over $95
$$	$50–$95
$	under $50

All prices are for a standard double room.

Parks and Forests

National Parks

Surprisingly, there is only one national park in Idaho, the **Nez Percé National Historic Park** (*see* Exploring Northern Idaho, *above*). The park is really a scattered group of individual sites where events of the Nez Percé War took place. However, the state is virtually covered in federal lands, including the largest contiguous wilderness in the lower 48 states.

State Parks

Idaho has 21 state parks spread throughout the state. Though they contain everything from a mission to an RV campground, most are on a river or lake. Primitive campsites cost $5 per day, basic sites $7, and developed sites $8. Electric and sewer hookups cost an additional $4. There is an entrance fee of $2 for motorized vehicles at most parks, but it is incorporated into camping fees. An annual passport for $25 provides unlimited entrance to all state parks for one calendar year. Group facilities are available at some parks. For a complete guide, contact the **Idaho Department of Parks and Recreation** (Box 65, Boise 83720, ☎ 208/334–4199 or 800/635–7820).

Shopping

Every city in Idaho has the generic mall, but luckily most also have unique districts with flavors not found elsewhere. The state is an excellent place for antiques hunters. Although towns like Coeur d'Alene and Boise have antiques shops, often Idaho's antiques are still being used as store signs or restaurant condiment containers. In some parts of Idaho, whole towns are antiques.

Sports

There's a reason Hemingway liked Idaho so much. It has some of the best fly-fishing in the world and is known for its steelhead and sturgeon. (Unfortunately, sockeye salmon have been dammed out of existence, and chinook are barely hanging on.) Locals will tell you the fishing is always good in Idaho. Maybe, but some spots are better than others. An excellent publication, *The Official Guide to Fishing in Idaho,* which details boat ramp locations, regulations, the best spots for various species, and even filleting instructions, is available from the Department of Fish and Game (*see below*).

There are certain rules and codes about fishing that Idahoans take very seriously. Taking undersize fish or not releasing in a catch-and-release area isn't just frowned upon, it's against the law. Also, always be sure to obtain the proper licenses. For details on fishing and to obtain a license, contact the **Idaho Department of Fish and Game** (600 S. Walnut St., Box 25, Boise 83707, ☎ 800/635–7820) or the Idaho Outfitters and Guides Association (*see* Tour Groups, *above*).

Because the state falls in the Northwest's weather pattern, it receives plenty of winter precipitation, but as elsewhere in the West, the snow is often dry and powdery. For skiers, it's the best of both worlds. Idaho, especially Sun Valley, is known for alpine skiing. The popularity of Nordic skiing has soared, however, and many alpine resorts now offer groomed cross-country tracks at their hill's base or near the principal lodge. Idaho's Department of Parks and Recreation (*see* National and State Parks, *above*) makes trails in many of the state parks.

In addition, since ski resorts are trying to make themselves attractive year-round, mountain biking is now available on Idaho's major ski hills. Most resorts run their lifts in summer to carry bikers to the top of the hills.

Aficionados will tell you there is no better state for canoeing and rafting, with the possible exception of Alaska. Canoe and raft trips range from placid to suicidal, and because the state is so outdoor-conscious, the public has access to virtually every body of water.

The golf courses listed have 18 holes and require reservations for tee times. Fees vary but are in the $20–$50 range unless otherwise stated.

Festivals and Seasonal Events

Winter
Sandpoint Winter Carnival, Sandpoint, mid-January: a 10-day festival of winter activities. **Winter Olympics Week,** Sun Valley, mid-January: a winter carnival complete with celebrity ski racing, food fair, and dances. **McCall Winter Carnival,** McCall, last weekend in January/first week in February: winter sports with a little snowman and ice-sculpture making thrown in. **Lionel Hampton/Chevron Jazz Festival,** Moscow, last weekend in February: some of the best jazz musicians in the world.

Spring
Riggins Rodeo, Riggins, first weekend in May: the rodeo that starts the season and makes this tiny town burst with visitors.

Summer
Idaho Shakespeare Festival, Boise, all summer: Shakespeare under the stars. **National Old-Time Fiddlers Contest,** Weiser, last week in June: the nation's most prestigious fiddlers' summit. **Sun Valley Music Festival,** Sun Valley, July–mid-August: classical and jazz performers. **Festival at Sandpoint,** Sandpoint, the last two weeks of July and the first two weeks in August: a celebration of music that includes classical, pop, and jazz, under the direction of famed maestro Gunther Schuller. **Art on the Green,** Coeur d'Alene, first weekend in August: arts, crafts, and dance in one of Idaho's largest festivals. **Three Island Crossing,** Glenns Ferry, first weekend in August: a re-creation of the pioneers' treacherous Snake River crossing. **Shoshone-Bannock Indian Festival,** Fort Hall, mid-Au-

gust: includes an all-Indian old-timers' rodeo, one of the best in the state.

Fall
Pocatello Dixieland Jamboree, Pocatello, September: Dixieland bands from across the country. **Swing and Dixie Jazz Jamboree,** Sun Valley, mid-October: big-band and Dixieland music.

Important Addresses and Numbers

Emergencies
In emergency situations, **call 911** (almost everywhere in the state) or visit a hospital emergency room (*see* Emergencies sections in individual regions, *above*). For nonemergencies, check in telephone directories, with chambers of commerce, or at your lodging for names of doctors, dentists, or late-night pharmacies.

Visitor Information
Idaho Travel Council (PO Box 83720, Boise 83720, ☎ 208/334–2470 or 800/635–7820).

In addition, almost every town of any size in Idaho has a small visitor information booth set up on the main road at the edge of town. Many rest stops along major arteries and the visitor centers at prime attractions offer a new system with touch-screen computer terminals for planning where to stay and what to see.

6 Montana

THEY CALL IT BIG SKY COUNTRY, but that's only part of the story; the land is big, too: The fourth-largest state stretches from North Dakota on the eastern side to Idaho on the west, 600-and-some-odd miles. From north to south, meanwhile, is a distance of about 400 miles. Not only is this a massive chunk of land, but it's also barely peopled. There are roughly 800,000 Montanans on all this ground, most of them in the major cities of Billings, Great Falls, Missoula, and Helena.

By Jim Robbins

Updated by Kristin Rodine

Montana is divided into two regions: the Rocky Mountain cordillera, which enters Montana in the northwest corner, taking up most of the western half of the state with timbered mountains and broad, grassy river valleys; and the plains and rolling hills to the east.

When night comes down, the skies are so dark and clear, the stars look like shiny glass beads suspended in a midnight sky. Northern lights shimmer like red and green curtains against velvet black skies and at other times scream across the full scope of the sky, ending only when the light of dawn erases them. If there is a factor that makes Montana so unusual, it is the light. Sometimes it shoots down from behind the clouds in long, radiant spotlight shafts, outlining the clouds in gold. There is a pink and orange light that falls gently like dust on Western slopes. A brilliant crimson takes over clouds at sunset. The fiery red and orange light of sunset in the desert Rockies illuminates the mountains so intensely, they appear to be lit from within like glowing coal.

The land here is teeming with wildlife. Bald eagles soar by the thousands and zero in on streams that teem with fish: rainbow, brown, cutthroat, and brook trout among them. Cougars scream in the night. With manes flapping, wild horses gallop over red hillsides; thousands of elk move from the high country to the lowlands in the fall, and back to the high country come summer.

Long gone, but not forgotten, are some of Montana's most famous wildlife, whose skeletons remain as evidence of their greatness. Some of the richest dinosaur fossil beds in the world are found in the Rocky Mountain Front Range, where the mountains meet the plains. Recently, discoveries of fossils and dinosaur eggs have challenged the notion that dinosaurs were cold-blooded; it's possible they were warm-blooded animals who cared for their young, closer to mammals than reptiles.

Evidence of early human occupation dates back 12,000 years. For generations before the Europeans arrived here, Native Americans inhabited what is now Montana. In 1805–06, the Lewis and Clark Expedition came through, seeking a transcontinental route to the Pacific, and expanded trade relations with the natives.

Montana remained a remote place, however, through much of the 19th century and was valued for its rich trade in buffalo hides and beaver pelts. It was the discovery of gold at Gold Creek, Montana (between Missoula and Helena), in 1858 that began to change the region dramatically. After large gold strikes at Grasshopper Creek and Alder Gulch, miners came to the southwest mountains of Montana by the thousands. In 1862, the Territory of Montana was created. Pressure by miners and settlers for native lands in the area was unrelenting; inhabitants were forced from their homelands and restricted to reservations. Major events in the West's Indian wars—the Battle of the Little Bighorn and the Flight of the Nez Percé—were played out in Montana, indelibly shaping the history of this region and the nation.

The state of Montana entered the Union in 1889, and its motto "Oro y Plata" (gold and silver) stands. With the landscape relatively untouched, history remains alive here. Ranching and farming, mining and logging are still the ways of life, and a small-town atmosphere and friendly outlook greet travelers even in the state's larger towns and cities. The natural splendor, the state's free-running rivers, vast mountain ranges, and large populations of wildlife make this what Montanans call "The Last Best Place."

BILLINGS TO HELENA

I–90, near Billings, travels through much of the heart of Montana, including the grasslands, foothills, and full-blown mountain ranges. U.S. 287, which loops through Helena, affords a tour of Montana's historic capital.

Exploring

Numbers in the margin correspond to points of interest on the Montana map.

This 460-mile tour runs from the high plains of eastern Montana along the meandering Yellowstone River and finally into the timber-draped mountains of the west and the state capital, Helena. As you drive west along the interstate, the landscape will seem to get wider and larger. Give the trip at least three or four days.

❶ This tour begins in **Billings,** the regional capital of the coal and oil industry, whose population of 100,000 makes it not only the largest city in Montana but also the largest city for 500 miles in any direction. The "Magic City" was developed with the coming of the railroad in 1882, and named after one of its board of directors, Frederick Billings. Billings is in the middle of the rolling plains of eastern Montana, at the foot of the rimrocks—buckskin-colored cliffs. The Bighorn Mountains are about an hour's drive south and offer hiking, fishing, camping, and all kinds of recreation.

The inspiring **Moss Mansion,** at 3rd and Division Streets, was built in 1903 for businessman P. B. Moss by Dutch architect Henry Hardenbergh (designer of the original Waldorf-Astoria Hotel in New York City). It still contains many of the elaborate original furnishings, ranging in style from Moorish to Art Nouveau Empire. *914 Division St.,* ☎ *406/256–5100.* ☛ *$5 adults, $4 senior citizens, $3 children.* ☽ *Labor Day–mid-Nov., daily 1–3; mid-Nov.–early Jan., weekdays 1–3, Sat. 10–5, Sun. 1–5; early Jan.–Apr., daily 1–3; May–mid-June, Sun.–Fri. 1–3, Sat. 10–3. Group tours by appointment.*

A worthwhile attraction that offers insight into the history and culture of the Yellowstone River region is the **Western Heritage Center,** on the corner of 29th and Montana avenues. Its permanent exhibit includes oral histories, artifacts, and interactive displays tracing the lives of Native Americans, ranchers, homesteaders, immigrants, and railroad workers during the period 1880–1940. *2822 Montana Ave.,* ☎ *406/256–6809.* ☛ *Free.* ☽ *Tues.–Sat. 10–5, Sun. 1–5.*

The **Yellowstone Art Center,** in the original county jail (401 N. 27th Ave., ☎ 406/256–6804), will be closed during 1996 for major expansion

Montana

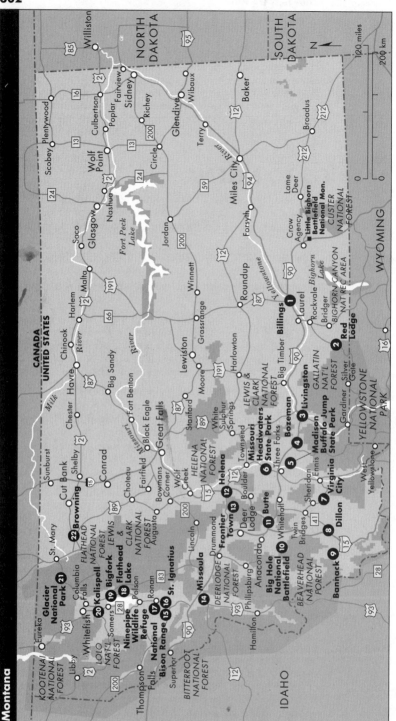

and renovation, but its contemporary art collections will be displayed at other sites. Call for more information.

TIME OUT Have a slice of homemade quiche at **Café Jones** (2712 2nd Ave. N, ☎ 406/259-7676), a small downtown bistro. The chrome tables and un-usual lamps are reminiscent of the 1950s. Try the special coffee drinks.

Just a few miles east of town, off I-90, is **Pictograph Cave,** a state mon-ument with ocher and black-and-white early drawings of figures, te-pees, and wildlife. *Follow signs from Lockwood exit of I-90,* ☎ *406/245-0227.* ☛ *50¢ per person or $3 per car.* ☉ *May–Oct., daily 8–7:30.*

❷ Take U.S. 212 from Billings and travel 60 miles southwest to **Red Lodge.** Nestled against the foot of the pine-draped Pryor Mountains, Red Lodge was named for a band of Cheyenne who marked their set-tlement with paintings of red earth. It became a town in the late 1880s when the Northern Pacific Railroad laid tracks here to take coal back to Billings. At one time, "Liver Eatin' " Jeremiah Johnson was sheriff here. Now the historic little burg is listed on the National Register of Historic Places and is in the process of becoming a full-blown resort town, complete with a ski area, trout fishing, horseback riding, and a golf course. Each August, the town holds a nine-day **Festival of Na-tions** to celebrate the numerous ethnic heritages of people who worked in the mines nearby.

From Red Lodge, you can continue south on U.S. 212 over the pre-cipitous **Beartooth Pass,** which winds its way through lush alpine country to the "back door" of Yellowstone National Park in Wyoming. The highway is usually open from May to September, but bad weather can close it at any time.

To continue the original tour, take Route 78 back to I-90, and follow **❸** the interstate west to the town of **Livingston.** The stunning mountain backdrop to this town was once Crow territory, and a chief called Ara-pooish said about it: "The Crow country is good country. The Great Spirit has put it in exactly the right place. When you are in it, you fare well; when you go out of it, you fare worse."

The railroads brought white people to settle, and Livingston, along the banks of the beautiful Yellowstone River, was built to serve the rail-road. The railroad has been replaced by small businesses that cater to tourists, but the town of 12,000 has retained much of its turn-of-the-century flavor. Perhaps you'll recognize it from Robert Redford's movie *A River Runs Through It* (adapted from the book of the same title by Norman Maclean), which was filmed here.

From the interstate take the second exit, turn right, and come through town on Park Street to the old **Northern Pacific Depot,** an Italian villa-style structure with mosaic trim, a terrazzo floor, and wrought-iron ticket windows. The depot is now a museum that houses displays on West-ern and railroad history and art by artists from the region and around the country. *200 W. Park St.,* ☎ *406/222-2300.* ☛ *$3 adults, $2 se-nior citizens and children, $8 families.* ☉ *Mid-May–mid-Oct., Mon.–Sat. 9–5, Sun. 1–5.*

Two blocks away, on the north side of town and housed in a historic schoolhouse, is the **Park County Museum,** which features an old ca-boose, a sheep wagon, a stagecoach, and other pioneer memorabilia. *118 W. Chinook St.,* ☎ *406/222-3506.* ☛ *$2 adults, $1 senior citi-zens and children 6–17.* ☉ *June–Labor Day, daily noon–5 and 7–9.*

Just south of town, the **Yellowstone River** comes roaring down the Yellowstone Plateau, just north of Yellowstone Park, and flows through Paradise Valley. Primitive public campsites (available on a first-come, first-served basis) and fishing access sites can be found at various places along the river, which is especially popular for trout fishing, rafting, and canoeing.

❹ Get back on I–90 and drive about 25 miles west of Livingston to **Bozeman,** a college town of 25,000. In 1864, a trader named John Bozeman led his wagon train through this valley en route to the booming gold fields at Virginia City and throughout southwest Montana. For several years it was the site of Ft. Ellis, established to protect settlers making their way west along the Bozeman Trail, which extended into Montana Territory. Recently the city has become a recreation capital for everything from trout fishing to white-water river rafting to backcountry mountain biking. Arts and culture have also flowered here in the home of the state's second-largest university. Each April, for example, members of New York's Metropolitan Opera stage a performance. The town has a strong Western heritage, and each June the **College National Rodeo Finals** (☎ 406/587–2637) are held at the Montana State University (MSU) field house.

At the southeast corner of the campus is the inspirational **Museum of the Rockies,** which celebrates the history of the Rockies region, including southern Montana. Eclectic exhibits include everything from prehistory to pioneers and a planetarium. There are dinosaur displays, complete with bones and eggs dug up in Montana, and a room where visitors can watch workers clean dinosaur fossils. Children love the hands-on science activities in the Martin Discovery Room and the Tensley Homestead, with home-crafts demonstrations including butter churning, weaving, and blacksmithing. *600 W. Kagy Blvd.,* ☎ *406/994–3466.* ☛ *$5 adults, $3 youths 13–18, $2 children 5–12.* ☺ *Memorial Day–Labor Day, daily 9–9; Labor Day–Memorial Day, Mon.–Sat. 9–5, Sun. 12:30–5.*

Continue west on I–90 for about 20 miles to the Logan exit; from that exit you'll turn onto a gravel road. Follow signs south for about 7 miles
❺ to the **Madison Buffalo Jump State Park.** Within the park is the cliff where Plains natives stampeded bison to their deaths more than 2,000 years ago. An interpretive center explains how the technique enabled Native Americans to gather food and hides. ☎ *406/285–3198.* ☛ *50¢ per person or $3 per vehicle (includes entrance to Missouri Headwaters State Park).* ☺ *Year-round, daily dawn–dusk.*

Travel a few more miles along I–90, exit at Three Forks, and drive north
❻ about 3 miles to the **Missouri Headwaters State Park,** a National Historic Landmark. This is where the Madison, Jefferson, and Gallatin rivers come together to form the mighty Missouri River. Lewis and Clark named the three forks after Secretary of the Treasury Albert Gallatin, Secretary of State James Madison, and President Thomas Jefferson. There are historical exhibits, interpretive signs, picnic sites, hiking trails, and camping. ☎ *406/285–3198.* ☛ *$3 per vehicle (included in Madison Buffalo Jump State Park admission, see above).* ☺ *Year-round, daily dawn–dusk.*

Take U.S. 287 south from the state park and at Ennis turn onto Montana Route 287 (a state road) heading west to **Virginia City** and its smaller
❼ neighbor, Nevada City. These remnants of Montana's frontier days are two of the most unusual attractions the state has to offer. When miners stampeded into the state in the 1860s, one of the places where the

diggings were rich was in Virginia City's Alder Gulch; the city prospered and eventually became the capital of Montana Territory. The success of the city enticed criminals, who held up miners; in turn, vigilance committees—eager to maintain order—grew, held lightning-fast trials, and strung up the bad guys. Some of the graves of those hung by vigilantes remain atop a hill overlooking town. Today Virginia City is a real tourist attraction where you can tour town on an old-time fire truck, walk along a boardwalk, wander through stores stocked with 19th-century goods, and ride a narrow-gauge railroad.

Nevada City has a smaller collection of historic buildings, a music hall with fascinating coin-operated instruments, and all sorts of restaurants and shops.

8 From Nevada City, take Route 287 north to Route 41 south to **Dillon.** (More direct routes involve unpaved and unmarked roads.) Dillon is a capital of southwestern Montana's ranch country and was a shipping point for cattle and sheep on the Union Pacific Railroad. There is hiking and mountain biking in the nearby Ruby and Tendoy mountains, and the fishing on the Beaverhead River is very good. The **Beaverhead County Museum** exhibits Native American artifacts, ranching and mining memorabilia, a homesteader's cabin, mining equipment and agricultural artifacts, and a boardwalk imprinted with the area's ranch brands. *15 S. Montana St.,* ☎ *406/683–5027.* ☞ *Free.* ☉ *Memorial Day–Labor Day, weekdays 10–8, weekends 1–5; Labor Day–Memorial Day, weekdays 10–noon, weekends 1–5.*

9 Follow Route 278 out of Dillon and watch for a sign just before Badger Pass. Take the well-maintained gravel road for 3 miles to **Bannack,** Montana's first territorial capital. Today the town, which is protected as a state park, is a good example of a frontier boom town, and is fortunately off the beaten tourist path. Montana's vigilantes were active here, and one of the most notorious was Henry Plummer, the sheriff himself. The gallows on which he was hanged still stands in Bannack. Rumors persist that Plummer's stash of stolen gold was hidden somewhere in the mountains near here and never found.

10 Return to Route 278 and take it about 40 miles northwest to Route 43. Go west on Route 43 to **Big Hole National Battlefield** (☎ 406/689–3155), where part of one of the West's greatest and most tragic stories played out. In 1877, Nez Percé warriors in central Idaho killed some white settlers as retribution for earlier killings by whites. The Nez Percé, knowing the army would make no distinction between the guilty and innocent, fled—the beginning of a 1,700-mile odyssey. They engaged 10 separate U.S. commands in 13 battles and skirmishes. One of the fiercest of those was here at Big Hole Battlefield, where both sides suffered serious losses. From here, the Nez Percé headed toward Yellowstone.

A visitor center overlooks the meadows of the Big Hole, which remain as they were at the time of the battle. Tepee poles erected by the park service mark the site of the Nez Percé village and serve as haunting reminders of what transpired here.

11 Double back along Route 43 and pick up I–15 north to its junction with I–90. The two roads run together into the city of **Butte.** Coined the "Richest Hill on Earth," Butte was once a wealthy and rollicking copper-, gold-, and silver-mining town. The underground copper mines were dug up in the 1950s, creating the **Berkeley Open Pit Mine,** which extends more than a mile across and reaches 1,800 feet deep. A viewing platform allows you to look into the now-abandoned, mammoth pit. *Continental Dr.,* ☎ *406/494–5595.* ☛ *Free.* ⊙ *Daily 8–dusk, weather permitting.*

Adjacent to the pit is downtown Butte, a National Historic Landmark area with numerous ornate buildings reminiscent of the Old West days. While meandering through the streets, consider this: Butte has the dubious distinction of containing the largest toxic waste site in the country—thanks to the old mining wastes.

Keeping watch over the city—as seen from the east ridge of the Rocky Mountains—is **Our Lady of the Rockies,** a 90-foot-tall, 80-ton statue of the Virgin Mary on the Continental Divide; it's lit at night. For tours, stop by the visitor center. *434 N. Main St.,* ☎ *406/782–1221 or 800/800–5239.* ☛ *$10 adults, $9 senior citizens and youths 13–17, $5 children 5–12.* ⊙ *Sept.–Apr., daily 10–4, May–Aug., daily 9–5.*

⑫ From Butte, continue north on I–15 for about 65 miles to **Helena,** Montana's capital. This jewel of a town where the prairie meets the mountains started as a rowdy mining camp in 1864 and became a banking and commerce center in the nascent Montana Territory. With statehood came a fight between the towns of Anaconda and Helena over which would be the capital. In a notoriously corrupt campaign in which both sides bought votes, Helena won. The iron ball of urban renewal robbed the town of much of its history, but Helena still has ornate brick and granite historic buildings along the Last Chance Gulch, of early mining fame. Some gambling is still legal in Montana—a legacy of frontier days.

Across from the state capitol, the **Montana Historical Society Museum** displays one of the most important collections of Western artist Charles M. Russell's work in its MacKay Gallery. Early black-and-white photos of Yellowstone National Park taken by F. Jay Haynes are on display in the Haynes Gallery. The expansive Montana Homeland exhibit, which features nearly 2,000 historical artifacts, documents, and photographs, gives visitors a thorough look at Montana from the time of the first native settlers to the present. The venue also hosts special events and "family days" during the summer, including programs on folk music, Native American culture, and cowboys. Call ahead for information on upcoming events. *225 N. Roberts St.,* ☎ *406/444–2694.* ☛ *Free.* ⊙ *Memorial Day–Labor Day, weekdays 8–6, weekends and holidays 9–5; Labor Day–Memorial Day, weekdays 8–5, Sat. 9–5, closed Sun. and holidays.*

Out in front of the Historical Society Museum catch the *Last Chancer,* an hour-long tour train that threads through Helena's historic neighborhoods, from the stately miners' mansions on the west side to the site where four miners made their first discovery on the gulch. It runs from May until September on the hour. ☎ *406/442–1023.* ☛ *$4.50 adults, $4 senior citizens, $3 children 2–12.*

Walk a few blocks down 6th Avenue to the center of historic downtown Helena. Ask at the Downtown Helena Office (121 N. Last Chance Gulch, ☎ 406/442–9869) for **"The Heart of Helena,"** a self-guided walking tour of historic downtown. On the corner of Last Chance Gulch and Lawrence Street, the lobby of the **Norwest Bank** displays a collection of gold nuggets taken from area diggings. *350 N. Last Chance Gulch,* ☎ *406/447–2000.* ☛ *Free.* ⊙ *Weekdays 9:30–4.*

The **Holter Museum of Art,** a block off Last Chance Gulch, houses both permanent and changing exhibits of visual arts. The emphasis is on Montana artists, folk art, crafts, photography, painting, and sculpture. *12*

E. Lawrence Ave., ☎ *406/442–6400.* ☛ *Free.* ☉ *Memorial Day–Labor Day, Tues.–Sat. 10–5, Sun. noon–5; Labor Day–Memorial Day, Tues.–Sun. noon–5.*

If you're tired of looking at attractions and want to stretch your legs, consider taking an hour-long hike to the top of **Mt. Helena,** the centerpiece of the **Mt. Helena City Park,** on the edge of town. From the summit, you'll have panoramic views of Helena, the Helena Valley, and the Rocky Mountains to the west. To reach the park, drive to the Adams Street parking lot on the city's west side or ask at the chamber of commerce (*see* Visitor Information *in* Billings to Helena Essentials, *below*) for directions.

TIME OUT For an old-fashioned sweet treat, pull up a stool at the **Parrot,** a soda fountain and candy store built in the 1920s that sells everything from chocolate malts with homemade ice cream to hand-dipped chocolates. 42 N. Last Chance Gulch, ☎ 406/442–1470. ☉ Mon.–Sat. 9–5:30.

⑬ Fifteen miles west of town, atop the Continental Divide at McDonald Pass, is **Frontier Town,** a kitschy, eccentric tourist attraction built in the 1950s. Frontier-style buildings handmade from huge trees and mammoth boulders are filled with reproduction and antique furnishings. Swagger into the saloon and order a beer at the long bar cut from a single huge tree. There is also a good restaurant. *U.S. 12,* ☎ *406/442–4560.* ☛ *Free.* ☉ *Apr.–Oct., daily 9* AM*–10* PM.

What to See and Do with Children
Frontier Town (*see* Exploring Billings to Helena, *above*).

Montana Historical Society Museum (*see* Exploring Billings to Helena, *above*).

Museum of the Rockies (*see* Exploring Billings to Helena, *above*).

Off the Beaten Track
History buffs may want to travel on I–94 east from Billings for 145 miles to see some more of Montana's Old West. There you'll find the ranch town of **Miles City** (population 10,000) at the confluence of the cottonwood-lined Tongue and the Yellowstone rivers. The federal Treaty of 1868 said this would be Native country "as long as the grass is green and the sky is blue." That promise changed, however, when gold was found in the Black Hills of South Dakota to the east, and white settlers streamed into this part of the world. Ranchers eventually took over, and in 1884, the last of the great herds of buffalo was slaughtered near here to make room for cattle. Ranching has been a way of life ever since.

In May, locals hold the **Bucking Horse Sale** (☎ 406/232–2890) a three-day event downtown, with a rodeo and a giant block party. The **Range Rider's Museum** is jammed to the rafters with saddles, chaps, spurs, guns, and other cowboy paraphernalia, some of it dating from days of the wide-open range when cattlemen from Texas drove beeves here. *Exit 135 off I–94 to Old Hwy. 10 W,* ☎ *406/232–6146.* ☛ *$3.50 adults, 50¢ children.* ☉ *Apr.–Oct., daily 8–8.*

Sixty miles southeast of Billings, off I–90, is the **Little Bighorn Battlefield Monument,** on the Crow Indian Reservation. When the smoke cleared on June 25, 1876, neither Lieutenant Colonel George Armstrong Custer nor his 200 or so blue-shirted troopers were alive to tell the story of their meeting with several thousand Northern Plains natives on this rolling, windswept prairie along the Little Bighorn River. It was a

Pyrrhic victory for the tribes; the loss would force the U.S government to redouble its efforts to clear them off the plains. Now a national monument, the site has a new interpretive display that includes material from recent archaeological excavations. The display explains what led to the momentous clash of two cultures and speculates on what might have happened during the battle. ☎ *406/638–2621.* ☛ *Free.* ☺ *Memorial Day–Labor Day, daily 8–7:45; Labor Day–Oct., daily 8–5; Nov.–Memorial Day, daily 8–4:30.*

Shopping

Specialty Stores

ART GALLERIES

Livingston's beauty has inspired artists, as evidenced by the many fine art galleries in town. Paintings, sculptures and works in other mediums can be found at the **Wishing Tree Gallery** (113 W. Callender St., ☎ 406/222–7528). The **Danforth Gallery** (106 N. Main St., ☎ 406/222–6510) is a community art center that displays and sells contemporary works by local and regional artists. **Visions West Gallery** (108 S. Main St., ☎ 406/222–0337) specializes in Western and wildlife art, including a wide range of works on a fly-fishing theme, from paintings and bronzes to hand-carved flies.

BOOKS

The floorboards creak as you walk through **Sax and Fryer's** (109 W. Callender St., Livingston, ☎ 406/222–1421), an old-time bookstore specializing in Western literature. It also sells gifts.

CERAMICS

Many of the nation's best ceramic artists come to work in residency at the **Archie Bray Foundation** (2915 Country Club Ave., Helena, ☎ 406/443–3502). Wander near the five antiquated, 8-foot high, dome-shaped brick kilns on a self-guided walking tour and visit the gift shop, which sells work produced by foundation artists. ☺ Weekdays 10–5, Saturdays 10–5, Sundays 1–5.

HOME FURNISHINGS

Kibler and Kirch (22 N. Broadway, Red Lodge, ☎ 406/446–2802) sells lodgepole pine beds, cowboy pillows, antiques, and original art.

WESTERN PARAPHERNALIA

Rand's Custom Hats (2205 1st Ave. N, Billings, ☎ 406/259–4886 or 800/346–9815) creates cowboy hats for working cowboys as well as the celluloid variety and will make a felt fur hat exactly the size and shape of your head. Prices range from $200 to $2,000. They also produce custom leather carrying cases.

A charming little store in downtown Billings, **Stillwater Traders** (2821 2nd Ave. N, ☎ 406/252–6211) corrals unique items such as night-lights shaped like trout, cowboy dishes, Western-style clothing, and toys and T-shirts with a Western theme.

Sports and the Outdoors

Canoeing/Rafting

Glacier Wilderness Guides and its affiliate **Montana Raft Company** (☎ 800/521–7238) lead trips through stomach-churning white water, and often combine the adventure with horseback riding or hiking.

Cycling

Backcountry Bicycle Tours of Bozeman (Box 4209, Bozeman, 59772, ☎ 406/586–3556) offers touring all over the state. Old logging roads running through the mountains of western Montana and on national forest lands offer some of the best mountain-biking in the state. Trail biking is not allowed in the national parks. For route information, call the **Helena National Forest** (☎ 406/449–5201).

Fishing
High Plains Outfitters of Helena (31 Division St., ☎ 406/442–9671) offers guided trips on various rivers in Montana, including the Missouri, the Big Hole, and the Blackfoot, and wading on smaller rivers and streams.

Golf
The **Red Lodge Golf Course** (828 Upper Continental St., ☎ 406/446–3344) offers a beautiful view of the mountains. In Billings, try **Lake Hills** (1930 Clubhouse Way, ☎ 406/252–9244).

Hiking and Backpacking
Wild Horizon Expeditions (West Fork Rd., Darby 59829, ☎ 406/821–3747) is a wilderness guide service that specializes in six- to eight-day backpack trips into some of Montana's remotest wild places, where you're not likely to see other people. Expert guides discuss the plants, wildlife, and geology.

Skiing
CROSS-COUNTRY
This region of the state has a lot of opportunities for cross-country skiers, and the sport's popularity has grown immensely. One of the best Nordic ski places is the Big Sky resort's **Lone Mountain Guest Ranch** (U.S. 191, between Bozeman and West Yellowstone, ☎ 406/995–4644).

DOWNHILL
One of the nicest things about skiing in Montana is short lift lines. There are 25 miles of trails at **Red Lodge Mountain** (101 Ski Run Rd., Red Lodge, ☎ 406/446–2610), an hour south of Billings. Near Bozeman, **Bridger Bowl** (15795 Bridger Canyon Rd., Bozeman, ☎ 406/587–2111) is a top-ranked ski area. There's a variety of terrain, from steep, rocky chutes to gentle slopes and meadows. **Big Sky Resort** (1 Lone Mountain Trail, Big Sky, ☎ 406/995–5000 or 800/548–4486), 45 miles from Bozeman, is a good, family resort with 55 miles of groomed trails.

Dining

Billings
$–$$ **CJ's Restaurant.** The kitchen at this popular spot turns out juicy mesquite-grilled ribs, steaks, chicken, and seafood, with a choice of three barbecue sauces—from mild to three-alarm. The wine list is well chosen. High-backed chairs and intimate dining areas create a comfortable, casual atmosphere. ✕ *2456 Central Ave., ☎ 406/656–1400. Reservations advised. AE, D, DC, MC, V.*

$ **Jake's.** This pleasant downtown fern bar features steaks, seafood, and an inspired salad bar. The dimly lit restaurant, decorated with brass and wood, can seat 130 guests. ✕ *2701 1st Ave. N, ☎ 406/259–9375. Reservations advised. AE, MC, V. Closed Sun.*

Bozeman
$–$$ **John Bozeman's Bistro.** It may be small, but the menu—from hot
★ seafood stir-fry and Cajun cookery to creative sandwiches and soups— is one of the best in the state. Bozeman's Bistro is also known for its setting in a National Historic Register building, with a brick interior and well-preserved wood floors. In bustling downtown Bozeman, the

bistro isn't far from some good antiques and furniture shops. ✕ 242 E. Main St., ☎ 406/587–4100. Reservations advised. AE, D, MC, V. Closed Mon.

$ **Mackenzie River Pizza.** Zesty gourmet pizzas featuring tomato or pesto sauces, sun-dried tomatoes, artichoke hearts, and more are baked in a brick oven before your eyes. Eat here in this bustling joint, or take it to go. ✕ 232 E. Main St., ☎ 406/587–0055. No reservations. AE, MC, V.

Helena

$ **On Broadway.** Wooden booths, discreet lighting, and brick walls contribute to the comfortable ambience at this Italian restaurant. Popular dishes include New York strip steak, scampi *fra diavolo* (shrimp with mushrooms, peppers, spicy wine and tomato sauce), and chicken prosciutto. On Broadway is a nice place to chat, with a leisurely dining pace. ✕ 106 Broadway, ☎ 406/443–1929. No reservations. AE, DC, MC, V. Closed Sun.

$ **Windbag Saloon & Grill.** This historic restaurant in the heart of downtown was a sporting house called Big Dorothy's until 1973, when a crusading county attorney forced Dorothy to close up shop. Now it's a family restaurant that serves burgers, quiche, salads, and sandwiches for lunch and dinner. Inside the historic building is a bounty of cherry wood that give this place a warm, comfortable feel. It also has a large selection of imported beers, on tap and in bottles. ✕ 19 S. Last Chance Gulch, ☎ 406/443–9669. Reservations accepted. AE, DC, MC, V. No lunch Sun.
★

Livingston

$ **Livingston Bar and Grill.** Just across the main thoroughfare from this quiet, homey restaurant is the town's railway depot, where the trains once rolled in. The pleasant ambience inside, with lots of art and rustic details, matches the historic setting. Among the menu items are buffalo burgers, chicken sandwiches and seafood dishes including deep-sea trout and bass. ✕ 130 N. Main St., ☎ 406/222–7909. Reservations advised. MC, V. No dinner except Sun.

Red Lodge

$–$$ **17 Broadway.** This cozy, unpretentious little restaurant on Red Lodge's main street has an award-winning chef who offers casual gourmet cuisine. Try the campfire trout (pan-fried trout with rosemary-and-pecan breading) or shrimp *akumal* (shrimp sautéed in tequila). ✕ 17 S. Broadway, ☎ 406/446–1717. Reservations accepted. AE, MC, V. Closed Mon. Memorial Day–Labor Day.

Townsend

$–$$ **Rosario's.** If this place looks like a converted gas station, that's because it is. Don't let the decor fool you, though, as it's been turned into one of Montana's finest Italian restaurants. On the edge of the little Missouri River town of Townsend, between Bozeman and Helena, this is home to some of the tastiest veal and pasta dishes, pizza, and calzones on the east side of the Continental Divide. ✕ 316 N. Front St., 406/266–3603. Reservations advised. No credit cards. Closed Mon. and Tues.
★

Lodging

Big Timber

$–$$ **Grand Hotel.** This is a renovated classic Western hotel in the middle of downtown Big Timber—on I–90 between Billings and Livingston. The rooms are small, clean, and comfortable and furnished in antiques—
★

the kind of accommodations you might find over the Longbranch Saloon in "Gunsmoke." A full breakfast is included in the daily room rate. ☎ *139 McLeod St., 59011, ☎ 406/932–4459. 10 rooms, 2 with bath. Bar, dining room, meeting room. DC, MC, V.*

Billings

$ **Olive Hotel.** This turn-of-the-century accommodation has been well restored and now features a vintage Gus McRae Room, named after the character in *Lonesome Dove,* the television miniseries based on Larry McMurtry's popular novel about an 1880s cattle drive that ended in Miles City. In the large standard room is a brass bed and private bath with a pull-chain toilet. The hotel is in historic downtown, next to a city park. ☎ *501 Main St., 59301, ☎ 406/232–2450 or 800/424–4777, FAX 406/232–5866. 59 rooms. Restaurant. AE, D, DC, MC, V.*

$ **Ponderosa.** Just down the street from the Radisson (*see below*) is this comfortable, more modern motel. All the rooms have carpets and are painted in pastel colors. There's a heated pool in the courtyard, surrounded by plenty of greenery. ☎ *2511 1st Ave. N, 59101, ☎ 406/259–5511 or 800/628–9081, FAX 406/245–8004. 130 rooms. Bar, café, pool, sauna, spa, exercise room. AE, D, DC, MC, V.*

$$ **Radisson Northern Hotel.** This historic 1905 building in downtown Billings was destroyed by fire in 1940, then rebuilt. Although remodeled in 1990, it still provides a sense of the city's past. Rooms follow an American West theme, with woven rugs, bedspreads, and a gaming table. Views are glorious. The massive fireplace is the centerpiece of a comfortable lobby—a common gathering place for guests and locals. ☎ *Broadway at 1st Ave. N, Box 1296, 59101, ☎ 406/245–5121 or 800/333–3333, FAX 406/259–9862. 160 rooms. Restaurant, bar. AE, D, DC, MC, V.*

Bozeman

$$ **Voss Inn.** This bed-and-breakfast occupies an elegant 1883 Victorian
★ house and is lavishly furnished with antiques. Stop by the parlor for afternoon tea or to catch up on the news with other guests who drop in to watch TV or to chat. The knowledgeable owners run day and overnight fishing trips to Yellowstone for interested guests. ☎ *319 S. Willson Ave., 59715, ☎ 406/587–0982. 6 rooms. MC, V.*

$–$$ **Gallatin Gateway Inn.** Built by the Milwaukee Railroad as a stopping-off point for visitors to Yellowstone National Park, this sumptuous inn is conveniently situated, just 10 miles from town on U.S. 191, and 30 minutes from Big Sky Ski Resort. It did have its dog days, however, when it fell into disrepair and became a seedy bar that featured female Jell-O wrestling (honest). After a renovation in 1987, the inn recaptured its reputation, with a wonderful restaurant and an outdoor swimming pool. The uniquely furnished rooms have contemporary, modern Western decor and are painted in soothing pastels. The bathrooms, with original tile work and brass fixtures, exude simple elegance. ☎ *U.S. 191, Box 376, Gallatin Gateway 59730, ☎ and FAX 406/763–4672. 29 rooms with private bath, 3 2-room combos with shared bath. Restaurant, pool, tennis court. AE, DC, MC, V.*

Butte

$–$$ **Fairmont Hot Springs.** If you have children, you should bring them to
★ this resort near Anaconda and not far from Butte. Although not much as far as architecture goes, it has naturally heated indoor and outdoor swimming pools; a water slide; and a petting zoo in a beautiful setting. For golfing enthusiasts, there's an 18-hole course on the grounds. ☎ *1500 Fairmont Rd., Gregson 59711, ☎ 406/797–3241 or 800/443–2381, FAX 406/797–3337. 152 rooms. Restaurant, bar, coffee shop, mas-*

sage, 18-hole golf course, 2 tennis courts, volleyball. AE, D, DC, MC, V.

Helena

$$ **Sanders Bed and Breakfast.** This three-story Victorian mansion was
★ built by Colonel Wilbur Sanders, the prosecuting attorney at some of
the summary trials hosted by the Montana vigilantes. The colonel's rock
collection is still in the front hall, and the B&B has retained his fur-
nishings. Most of the rooms have beautiful views overlooking moun-
tain-ringed downtown Helena, and the breakfasts are something to
behold. ☎ *328 N. Ewing St., 59601,* ☎ *406/442–3309,* FAX *406/443–
2361. 6 rooms with private bath; 1 room with bath down the hall. AE,
MC, V.*

Livingston

$$$$ **Mountain Sky Guest Ranch.** Not only is this accommodation 30 miles
north of lovely Yellowstone National Park, but it also rests in the mid-
dle of scenic Paradise Valley. This full-service guest ranch has riding,
tennis, fishing, a heated pool, and a sauna. Seven-night bookings are
arranged mid-June–Labor Day; there's a three-night minimum during
the low season. ☎ *Box 1128, Bozeman 59715,* ☎ *406/587–1244 or
800/548–3392,* FAX *406/333-4911. 27 units. Dining room, pool, sauna,
2 tennis courts, horseback riding, fishing. MC, V.*

$$ **63 Ranch.** This dude ranch, 12 miles southeast of Livingston, is one
of Montana's oldest, and rests on 2,000 acres of land. It has been owned
by the same family since 1929. A full range of activities is offered, from
horseback riding to fishing to pack trips, but only seven-night (Sunday–Sunday) packages are offered for stays in their commodious cabins. ☎ *Box 979A, 59047,* ☎ *406/222–0570,* FAX *222–9446. 8 cabins.
Dining room, horseback riding, fishing, coin laundry. No credit cards.*

$–$$ **Murray Hotel.** In the old days, this hotel in downtown Livingston catered
★ to early visitors to Yellowstone who came by train. It has been remodeled,
and the simple, elegant dining room, now called the Winchester Café,
is second to none. Recently renovated rooms retain the charm of earlier era. Public spaces re-create the hotel's 1904 beginnings. Each an-
tiques-filled guest room reflects a different theme, and the staff tries
to match guests with a room to fit their needs and interests. One room
boasts furnishings used in the film "A River Runs Through It." Another commemorates the five years director Sam Peckinpah lived at the
Murray; it's decorated with movie posters and memorabilia along
with furnishings from the director's room. ☎ *201 W. Park St., 59047,*
☎ *406/222–1350. 32 rooms, 30 with bath. Restaurant, bar, grill. AE,
MC, V.*

Red Lodge

$–$$ **Pollard Hotel.** This 1893 landmark in the heart of Red Lodge's his-
toric district has been lovingly restored to the charms of an earlier era.
Public rooms have handsome oak paneling and green, brown, and gold
flocked wallpapers. Enjoy a drink in the History Room surrounded by
photos recalling the hotel's past. Reproduction Victorian furniture
throughout revivifies a fin-de-siècle feeling. ☎ *2 N. Broadway, Box
1217, 59068,* ☎ *406/446–0001 or 800/765–5273,* FAX *406/446–
3733. 36 rooms. Dining room, no-smoking rooms, hot tub, sauna, exercise room. AE, DC, MC, V.*

$–$$ **Rock Creek Resort.** This resort, which just added a handsome rustic
lodge facility in 1995, is just 4½ miles south of town on U.S. 212; it's
built along a babbling, rock-strewn creek and decorated in a Southwestern motif. It has a wonderful restaurant—the Old Piney Dell—in
a historic old cabin. The menu features simple American, Mexican, and

regional fare. ☎ *Rte. 2, Box 3500, 59068,* ☎ *406/446–1111,* FAX
*406/446–3688. 90 rooms. 2 restaurants, 2 bar, indoor pool, sauna, 4
tennis courts, basketball, soccer, volleyball, fishing, cross-country skiing, playground. AE, D, DC, MC, V.*

Three Forks

$–$$ **Sacajawea Inn.** This carefully restored, 33-room historic hotel—built
in 1910—is named after the Native American woman who guided Lewis
and Clark on their journey to map the West. Rooms are decorated with
arts and crafts reminiscent of the early 1900s. On summer evenings,
the owners serve iced tea to guests who sit in a line of wooden rock-
ers on the expansive front porch. The headwaters of the Missouri
River—where the Madison, Gallatin, and Jefferson rivers flow together—is just a few miles away. The restaurant serves a sumptuous
Sunday brunch as well as other fine meals. ☎ *5 N. Main St., Box 648,
59752,* ☎ *406/285–6515 or 800/821–7326,* FAX *406/285–6515. 33
rooms. Restaurant, no-smoking rooms, meeting room. AE, D, MC, V.*

The Arts and Nightlife

The Arts

The largest theater for performing arts between Minneapolis and
Spokane is the **Alberta Bair Theater for the Performing Arts** (Broadway and 3rd Ave. N, Billings 59105, ☎ 406/255–6052). Presentations
are by orchestras, chorale groups, and theater and dance troupes,
among others.

In Helena, an oasis for the arts is the **Myrna Loy Center for the Performing Arts** (15 N. Ewing, ☎ 406/443–0287). In a remodeled historic jail, the center—named after the Montana-born actress—offers
live performances by nationally and internationally recognized musicians and dancers. There are also two theaters here that show foreign
and independent films.

Nightlife

On summer nights you can watch cowboys coming out of the chute
at the **Billings Night Rodeo,** at the Four Cross Arena. There's everything from professional rodeo to Native American rodeo to rodeo
schools. ☛ *$6. Rodeo runs June–Aug., daily 7 PM–10 PM.*

Billings to Helena Essentials

Arriving and Departing

BY BUS

Intermountain Transportation Co. has buses that stop in Helena (☎
406/442–5860) and Butte (☎ 406/723–3287). **Greyhound Lines** (☎
800/231–2222) and **Rimrock Stages** (☎ 406/442–5860) serve Billings
and Bozeman. In summer, **Karst Stage** (☎ 406/586–8567 or 800/332–
0504) runs between Bozeman, Livingston, Billings, and Yellowstone.

BY CAR

Use I–90 for Billings, Livingston, Bozeman, and Butte. U.S. 89 and U.S.
212 link this region with Yellowstone. I–15 passes through Helena.

BY PLANE

Logan Field International Airport in Billings is the largest in the state
and is served by **Continental** (☎ 800/525–0280), **Delta** (☎ 800/221–
1212), **Northwest** (☎ 800/225–2525), and **United** (☎ 800/241–6522).
Farther west, in Bozeman, **Gallatin Field Airport** is also served by **Delta,
Continental,** and **Northwest,** as well as **SkyWest** (☎ 800/453–9417).
Butte is served by the **Bert Mooney Airport.**

Amtrak's (☎ 800/872–7245) *Empire Builder* stops daily in Havre, Malta, and Whitefish.

Getting Around
Public transportation in Montana is basically limited to the options previously listed (*see* Arriving and Departing, *above*). Renting a car is the only effective way to follow the Exploring tours.

Guided Tours
ORIENTATION
Karst Stage (*see* Arriving and Departing by Bus, *above*), in Bozeman, does group tours of the state and one-day tours of Yellowstone National Park for individuals.

Important Addresses and Numbers
EMERGENCIES
For police, fire, ambulance, or other emergencies, dial **911.** The **Montana Highway Patrol** can be reached at 800/525–5555.

EMERGENCY ROOMS
Area hospitals with emergency rooms include **Billings Deaconess Medical Center** (Box 31000, Billings 59107, ☎ 406/657–4000); **Bozeman Deaconess Medical Center** (915 Highland Blvd., Bozeman 59715, ☎ 406/585–5000); and **St. Peter's Community Hospital** (2475 Broadway, Helena 59601, ☎ 406/442–2480).

VISITOR INFORMATION
Local tourism information is available from the **Billings Chamber of Commerce** (Box 31177, Billings 59107, ☎ 406/245–4111); **Bozeman Convention and Visitors Bureau** (Box B, Bozeman 59715, ☎ 406/587–2111 or 800/228–4224); **Helena Chamber of Commerce** (201 E. Lyndale, Helena 59601, ☎ 406/442–4120 or 800/743–5362); **Livingston Chamber of Commerce** (212 W. Park St., Livingston 59047, ☎ 406/222–0850); **Miles City Chamber of Commerce** (901 Main St., Miles City 59301, ☎ 406/232–2890); **Red Lodge Chamber of Commerce** (Box 998, Red Lodge 59068, ☎ 406/446–1718); and **Virginia City Chamber of Commerce** (Box 218, Virginia City 59755, ☎ 406/843–5345).

MISSOULA TO GLACIER NATIONAL PARK

Exploring

Numbers in the margin correspond to points of interest on the Montana map.

🔴 This trip starts in **Missoula** and makes its way through the heart of Montana's mountainous western half, with its long, finger-shaped lakes and towering pines framing the snow-mottled peaks of mountain range after mountain range. Some 30% of Montana is publicly owned land, and the national forests, national parks, and state parks on this drive have plenty of campgrounds and hiking and biking trails.

If you are continuing from Helena, take U.S. 12 west and follow it about 40 miles to I–90; stay on I–90 all the way to Missoula. The aptly nicknamed "Garden City" is one of the most beautiful in Big Sky Country, and its population of 80,000 makes it the largest city in western Montana. Maple trees line the residential streets, the Clark Fork River slices through the center of town, and the University of Montana is set against the slopes of Mt. Sentinel. A gravel trail along the river passes the university's campus and is ideal for walking and cycling.

North of town, a short way on U.S. 93 and not far from the airport, is the **Smokejumper Visitors Center,** which has exhibits, motion pictures, and murals that detail and explain various fire-fighting techniques. *5765 Hwy. 10 W, ☎ 406/329–4934. ☛ Free. ☉ Memorial Day–Labor Day, daily 8:30–5; Labor Day–Memorial Day, weekdays 8:30–5.*

Where West Broadway intersects with Pattee Street, go a block to the **Missoula Museum of the Arts** with its changing exhibits of contemporary work and a small permanent collection. *335 N. Pattee St., ☎ 406/728–0447. ☛ Free. ☉ Mon.–Sat. noon–5.*

TIME OUT   Take a break while touring downtown Missoula and have a cappuccino or a glass of fresh-squeezed juice at **Butterfly Herbs** (232 N. Higgins Ave., ☎ 406/728–8780). If you can't decide what you fancy, try the "Over the Rainbow"—a drink with flavors including strawberry, hot pepper, orange, ginger, and mint. The shop also sells baked goods, gourmet candies, soaps, candles, china, and other odds and ends.

Travel north on U.S. 93 to its junction with Route 200 in Ravalli, and
⑮ follow signs to the **National Bison Range** at Moiese. This 20,000-acre refuge at the foot of the Mission Mountains was established in 1908 by President Theodore Roosevelt. Today the U.S. Fish and Wildlife Service ranches a herd of several hundred bison. A self-guided auto tour allows close-up views of bison, elk, antelope, deer, and mountain sheep, and a visitor center explains the life, habitat, and history of the buffalo. *☎ 406/644–2211. ☛ $4 per vehicle. ☉ Mid-May–Sept., daily 8–8; Oct.–mid-May, weekdays 8–4:30.*

⑯ Return to U.S. 93 and continue north to the town of **St. Ignatius.** The **St. Ignatius Mission**—a church, cabin, and collection of other buildings—was built in the 1890s with bricks made with local clay by missionaries and Native Americans. The 58 murals on the walls and ceilings of the church were used to teach Bible stories to the natives. In the St. Ignatius Mission Museum—an old log cabin—is an exhibit of early artifacts and arts and crafts. *☎ 406/745–2768. ☛ Free. ☉ May–mid-Oct., daily 9–5.*

⑰ Farther north on U.S. 93 is the **Ninepipe Wildlife Refuge,** *the* place for bird-watchers. This sprawling wetland complex in the shadow of the Mission Mountains is home to everything from marsh hawks to kestrels to red-winged blackbirds. Different parts of the refuge are open during various seasons; call ahead. *☎ 406/644–2211.*

About 20 minutes from the wildlife refuge, where U.S. 93 meets Route
⑱ 35, are the glassy waters of **Flathead Lake.** The largest natural freshwater lake west of the Continental Divide, this body of water is a wonderful place for sailing, fishing, or swimming. Toward the end of July, on the east side of the lake, farmers harvest cherries and sell them at roadside stands.

The Swan River empties into Flathead Lake at the small, idyllic resort
⑲ community of **Bigfork.** The town is filled with shops and restaurants, and there is a host of activities in the area: boating, hiking, horseback riding, golf, and cross-country skiing.

Follow Route 82 west from Bigfork back to U.S. 93 and go north to
⑳ **Kalispell,** a lumber town and burgeoning tourist destination of about 12,000. Local farmers harvest such produce as Christmas trees, peppermint, and sweet cherries. The mild climate of the Flathead Valley

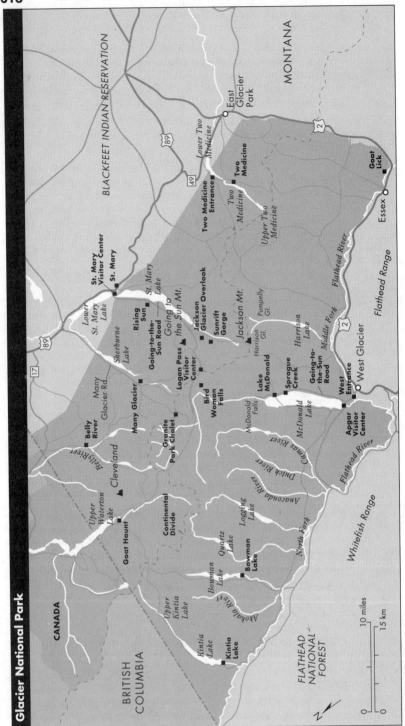

Glacier National Park

CANADA

BRITISH COLUMBIA

MONTANA

BLACKFEET INDIAN RESERVATION

FLATHEAD NATIONAL FOREST

Whitefish Range

Flathead Range

East Glacier Park

Essex

Goat Lick

Two Medicine Entrance

Two Medicine

Lower Two Medicine

Two Medicine

Upper Two Medicine

St. Mary Visitor Center

St. Mary

Lower St. Mary Lake

St. Mary Lake

Rising Sun

Going to the Sun Road

Going to the Sun Mt.

Logan Pass Visitor Center

Jackson Glacier Overlook

Sunrift Gorge

Jackson Mt.

Pumpelly Gl.

Harrison Gl.

Harrison Lake

Bird Woman Falls

Lake McDonald

Sprague Creek

Going-to-the-Sun Road

West Entrance

West Glacier

Apgar Visitor Center

McDonald Falls

McDonald Lake

Sherburne Lake

Many Glacier Rd.

Many Glacier

Granite Park Chalet

Belly River

Belly River

Cleveland

Continental Divide

Goat Haunt

Upper Waterton Lake

Camas River

Dutch River

Anaconda River

Flathead River

North Fork

Middle Fork

Logging Lake

Quartz Lake

Bowman Lake

Bowman Lake

Upper Kintla Lake

Kintla Lake

Kintla Lake

Akokala River

Flathead River

10 miles

15 km

N

makes this area the recreation capital of northwest Montana, with opportunities for rafting, hiking, mountain biking, downhill skiing, and fishing, among other sports.

One of Kalispell's highlights is the **Conrad Mansion National Historic Site Museum,** a 26-room Norman-style mansion that was the home of C. E. Conrad, the manager of a freighter on the Missouri River and the founder of the town of Kalispell. Come Christmas, the mansion is lavishly decorated and filled with the wares of local artisans. *4th St. (6 blocks east of Main St.),* ☎ *406/755–2166.* ☛ *$4 adults, $1 children.* ☉ *Daily mid-May–mid-June, 10–5:30; mid-June–mid-Sept., 9–8; mid-Sept.–mid-Oct., 10–5:30.*

Also in Kalispell is the **Hockaday Center for the Arts,** housed in the renovated Carnegie Library. National and international contemporary art exhibits are featured here on a rotating basis. *2nd Ave. E and 3rd St.,* ☎ *406/755–5268.* ☛ *Free.* ☉ *Tues.–Fri. 10–5, Sat. 10–3.*

㉑ Return to U.S. 93 where it meets Route 40, then follow Route 40 to the small village of Apgar, where you'll begin a loop through **Glacier National Park.** The view into the park's interior from Apgar has few equals: Its majestic, snowcapped peaks look like an illusion rising in the distance at the end of Lake McDonald.

Glacier is known as the "Crown of the Continent," for good reason. About a 100 million years ago, continents collided and this part of the world was thrust skyward. The last of the massive Ice Age glaciers swept through here 10,000 years ago, acting like a giant rasp on the landscape, moving huge amounts of soil and rock and etching details such as waterfalls, some 200 lakes, knife-edge ridges, and spires into the mountains. Rivers, gravity, and the yearly cycle of freezing and thawing put the finishing touches on the landscape. The only glaciers that remain here now are relatively tiny year-round patches of ice and snow hidden, like refugees, in the dark, cool, high-altitude recesses of the northern mountains.

Triple Divide Peak in the backcountry north of the park is a real curiosity. When the snow from most mountains melts, the water drains to either the Pacific or Atlantic. This peak provides water to the Atlantic, Pacific, and Arctic oceans.

In spring and summer, the alpine wildflowers make up for their short season with an unmatched intensity of color. As the sun warms Glacier in the spring, lilies grow up next to the lip of receding snowbanks. Then the mountain meadows explode in the pinks and reds of devil's paintbrush, white phlox, lavender shooting stars, pale blue wild irises, moss campion, and mountain heather—all blooming together in a high-mountain Expressionist painting. Later in the summer, the fragrant white balls of bear grass bloom, looking like lightbulbs on the end of a stick.

Glacier is one of the last enclaves of the grizzly bear, and the wild country in and around the park is home to the largest population of grizzlies in the lower 48 states. Snow-white mountain goats with their wispy white beards and curious stares are often seen in alpine areas, and sure-footed bighorn sheep graze the high meadows during the short summers.

A haven for outdoor enthusiasts, Glacier National Park offers whitewater river rafting, horseback riding, bird-watching, and scenery gazing, to name a few activities. Glacier is also a backpacker's heaven, and more than 700 miles of maintained trails twist and switchback through towering pines, steel gray mountains, and valleys, past turquoise high-alpine lakes, and over wind-whipped ridges that command vast expanses of wilderness.

Head east along the shore of finger-shaped Lake McDonald on the serpentine, 52-mile, Going-to-the-Sun Highway, one of the most scenic drives in the world. If you want a little exercise, stop near **Avalanche Creek,** where you can pick up a 3-mile trail leading to **Avalanche Lake,** one of many mountain-ringed lakes in the park. The walk is relatively easy, making this one of the most accessible backcountry lakes in the park.

At **Logan Pass,** at the top of Going-to-the-Sun Highway, there's a visitor center, with crystalline Hidden Lake a short hike from its parking lot. Mountain goats climb rocky cliffs at the lake, wildflowers bloom, and ribbons of water pour off the rocks. Before you set out on any hike in the park, however, remember to grab a jacket: Locals say there are only two seasons here, winter and the Fourth of July, and the only one you can really count on is winter.

22 When you drive over the highway to the east side of the Continental Divide, you might want to stop in **Browning,** the center of the Blackfoot Nation. Until the late 19th century, the Blackfeet hunted the great northern buffalo herd, moving with them across the vast northern plains of Canada and the United States. At one time, the Blackfoot homeland stretched all the way from the Missouri River north to the Bow and Red Deer rivers in Canada, and from the Rocky Mountains to 300 miles east. Rugged terrain and remoteness left Blackfoot territory some of the last Native American country in the contiguous United States to be opened to whites.

The **Museum of the Plains Indian,** on the north end of town, has been in operation since the 1930s. Now run by the Blackfeet, the museum houses a stunning collection of ancient artifacts from the Blackfeet and other Plains peoples. *Near jct. of U.S. 2 and U.S. 89,* ☎ *406/338– 2230.* ☛ *Free.* ☉ *June–Sept., daily 9–5; Oct.–May, weekdays 10–4:30.*

During the second week of July, the Blackfeet host **North American Indian Days** (☎ 406/338–7276) in Browning. This gathering of tribes is a pageant of drumming, chanting, and tepees as far as the eye can see.

Leave Browning and head west on U.S. 2. On this route you'll travel over Marias Pass. At 5,216 feet, this is the lowest major pass over the Rocky Mountains, and the spot where the Great Northern Railroad crossed the Great Divide in 1891. Near Essex is a goat lick—a natural salt formation along the highway that attracts mountain goats. It's a good place to watch these animals.

U.S. 2 brings you around to West Glacier, near the start of the loop in Apgar (*see above*).

Shopping

Specialty Stores

GIFTS

Rockin' Rudy's (237 Blaine, ☎ 406/542–0077; Univ. Ctr., Univ. of Mont., ☎ 406/721–9250) in Missoula could be called the store that has everything, including new and used records, CDs, and tapes; T-shirts; imported dresses, hats, and accessories; postcards; greeting cards; and other gifts.

Want to bring an unusual gift home? How about an indoor trout stream? Steve Fisher of **Indoor Trout Streams** (6640 Hwy. 10 E, Missoula, ☎ 406/258–6800) builds custom-made streams from 5 to 30 feet long, complete with insects and trout to match the new drapes. You can make an appointment to see his creations.

Sports and the Outdoors

Boating
Glacier National Park has an abundance of places to enjoy boat-ing, sailing, and canoeing. The **Glacier Boat Co.** (☎ 406/732–4480), located in the town of Many Glacier on the east side of the park, has a wide range of boat rentals to help you explore the options.

Cycling
The folks at **Adventure Cycling** (☎ 406/721–1776 or 406/721–8719), in downtown Missoula, have good suggestions for nearby bike routes.

Fishing
Within Glacier National Park is an unlimited range of fishing possibilities. A fishing license is free, but it is expected that you familiarize yourself with all park fishing regulations before you use any facilities. Stop by a park office (☎ 406/888–5441) to pick up a copy of the regulations and speak with a guide.

Golf
The 36-hole golf course near **Whitefish Lake** (Box 666, U.S. 93 N, ☎ 406/862–4000) is among the most beautiful in the state. On the east side of Glacier, there is the **Glacier Golf Course** (Box 147, E. Glacier, ☎ 406/226–9311) with nine holes. Near Missoula, the **Highlands Golf Club** (102 Ben Hogan Dr., ☎ 406/728–7360), with nine holes, and the **Larchmont Golf Course** (☎ 406/721–4416) with 18 holes, are fine courses.

Hiking and Backpacking
Maps for hiking are available at the Apgar Visitor Center, (☎ 406/888–5441) near the western entrance of Glacier. If you want to backpack, you must pick up a backcountry permit at the same location. Trails of various lengths and levels are well marked within the park. Novices and those who want the help of an experienced guide can sign up with **Glacier Wilderness Guides** (1 Highline Dr., ☎ 406/888–5466 or 800/521–7238), just outside the park in West Glacier. This service runs daylong to weeklong trips and also combines hiking and rafting expeditions (*see* Rafting, *below*).

Rafting
Montana Raft Company (U.S. 2, across from the Amtrak station in West Glacier, ☎ 800/521–7238) will take you on a raft trip through the stomach-churning white water of the Middle Fork of the Flathead and combine it with a hike or horseback ride.

Skiing
DOWNHILL
Big Mountain (Box 1400, Whitefish 59937, ☎ 406/862–3511 or 800/858–4439), 28 miles from Glacier National Park, has 61 marked runs; a 2,300-foot vertical drop; 3,000 skiable acres—plus out-of-bounds for Sno-Cat skiing—and nine lifts, including a high-speed quad. During summer, the gondola continues to operate high above the mountains, exposing the resort's beauty.

Dining

Missoula

$–$$ **Alley Cat.** As the name suggests, this quaint little eatery in downtown
★ Missoula is in an alley and has a subtle feline motif. The wooden booths
provide privacy and coziness while you dine on imaginative Continental
fare, including seafood, steaks, and chicken dishes. ✗ *125½ Main St.,*
☎ *406/728–3535. Reservations advised. MC, V. Closed Sun. No
lunch.*

$–$$ **Guy's Lolo Creek Steakhouse.** For a real taste of Montana, head for
★ this steakhouse in a massive log structure eight miles south of Missoula,
in Lolo. The dining room has a hunting-lodge atmosphere, replete with
stuffed wildlife on the walls. While most diners opt for one of Guy's
signature sirloins—cooked over a crackling open-pit barbecue and
available in three sizes—there are other well-prepared, grilled meat,
chicken, and seafood dishes to choose from; nongrilled selections are
available as well. ✗ *6600 U.S. 12 W, Lolo,* ☎ *406/273–2622. AE, D,
MC, V. Closed Mon. No lunch.*

$ **Zimorino's Red Pies over Montana.** Some of the best pizza that has ever
been tossed anywhere is tossed here. Eat in, take out, or call for a de-
livery. Beer and wine are served. ✗ *424 N. Higgins Ave.,* ☎ *406/549–
7434. Reservations advised. MC. V. No lunch.*

Lodging

Bigfork

$$ **O'Duach'ain Country Inn Bed and Breakfast.** In a quiet lodgepole-pine
forest near Flathead Lake and the Swan River, this lovely property con-
sists of two log-cabin structures: a main house with three guest rooms
and a smaller building with two suites. Rooms and common spaces
are furnished with Old West antiques and Navajo rugs on the walls;
two stone fireplaces warm the main house. A full gourmet breakfast,
featuring stuffed Irish toast and other house specialties, is included in
the room rate. ⌨ *675 Ferndale Dr., 59911,* ☎ *406/837–6851,* FAX
*406/837–4390. 3 rooms with shared bath, 2 suites with private bath.
Dining room, hot tub, hiking, travel services. AE, MC, V.*

Glacier National Park and Environs

$ **Izaak Walton Inn.** This small, out-of-the-way inn is set along the
Marias Pass, between East and West Glacier. Originally built as a dor-
mitory for railroad workers, the inn has a historic presence and is a
convenient lodging for cross-country skiers mountain bikers, and hik-
ers. Just outside the front door are more than 18 miles of groomed trails
for such activities. Also, for those who don't have a car, Amtrak trains
stop right outside the inn, whose front overlooks the train yard. Ask
for a room in the back where it's quieter. For train buffs, four cabooses
have been renovated and are available for cabin-style lodging. ⌨ *123
Izaak Walton Rd., Essex 59916,* ☎ *406/888–5700,* FAX *406/888–
5200. 31 rooms, 11 with bath. Restaurant, sauna, recreation room,
coin laundry. MC, V.*

GLACIER NATIONAL PARK–OWNED PROPERTIES

The three massive stone and timber structures described below were
built in the early part of this century by the Great Northern Railroad,
and today are owned by Glacier Park, Inc. They are available
June–September and must be reserved far in advance because they book
up early. *For all hotels contact: Glacier Park, Inc., Dial Corporate Cen-
ter, Phoenix, AZ 85077,* ☎ *602/207–6000. D, MC, V.*

$$–$$$ **Glacier Park Lodge.** On the east side of the park and across from the Amtrak station is this beautiful hotel made of giant timbers. ⌷ ☎ *406/226–9311. 154 rooms. Restaurant, bar, snack bar, pool, golf course, playground.*

$$–$$$ **Many Glacier Hotel.** Also on the east side of the park is this hotel on Swiftcurrent Lake with commanding views of the surrounding mountains. ⌷ ☎ *406/732–4411. 208 rooms. Restaurant, bar, ice cream parlor, hiking.*

$–$$ **Lake McDonald Lodge.** This resort is on the shore of Lake McDonald and offers cabins, which sleep up to four and don't have kitchens; motel rooms, which are the largest; and units in the lodge itself. ⌷ ☎ *406/888–5431. 100 rooms. Restaurant, bar, coffee shop, hiking, boating, fishing.*

Missoula

$$ **Goldsmith's Bed and Breakfast.** Built in 1911 for the first president of
★ the University of Montana, this lodging is on the shore of the Clark Fork River, at the end of a footbridge that leads to the campus. Within the prairie-style building, with big white eaves and a huge porch, are period furnishings, wool carpets, and fresh flowers. Each private room is unique, and public rooms include a library and TV sitting area. A bonus to staying at this B&B is that it's right next to Goldsmith's Premium Ice Cream, a café that features homemade ice cream and gourmet coffee, in addition to breakfast, lunch, and dinner. ⌷ *809 E. Front St., 59801,* ☎ *406/721–6732. 3 rooms, 4 suites. AE, D, MC, V.*

$$ **Village Red Lion Motor Inn.** Stretching along the Clark Fork River, this reliable chain offers inviting rooms, some of which face the mountains; others overlook the pool. Also on the grounds, which are close to the campus, is a lovely garden. ⌷ *100 Madison Ave., 59802,* ☎ *406/728–3100 or 800/237–7445,* ℻ *406/728–2530. 172 rooms. Restaurant, bar, coffee shop, pool, hot tub. AE, D, DC, MC, V.*

$ **Holiday Inn Missoula–Parkside.** The Missoula member of this chain is a large, comfortable hotel with a lush atrium in the center, and comfortable, modern rooms. However, the property's most valued asset is its location in Missoula's riverfront park, a stone's throw from the Clark Fork. ⌷ *200 S. Pattee St., 59802,* ☎ *406/721–8550 or 800/465–4329,* ℻ *406/721–7427. 200 rooms. Restaurant, bar, pool. AE, D, DC, MC, V.*

Polson

$$ **Best Western Kwa-Taq-Nuk.** On the shore of crystalline Flathead Lake
★ is this resort owned by the Confederated Salish and Kootenai Tribes. In addition to the deluxe accommodations, guests enjoy sweeping views of the lake and the majestic Mission Mountains from their rooms. The hotel is well situated to provide visitors with golfing, rafting, and lake cruise adventures. ⌷ *303 U.S. 93 E, 59860,* ☎ *406/883–3636 or 800/882–6363,* ℻ *406/883–5392. 112 rooms. Restaurant, bar, lobby lounge, indoor and outdoor pools, hot tub, boating. AE, D, DC, MC, V.*

Missoula to Glacier National Park Essentials

Arriving and Departing

BY BUS

Greyhound Lines (☎ 800/231–2222) serves Missoula. **Intermountain Bus Company** (☎ 406/755–4011) stops in Kalispell.

BY CAR

I–90 and U.S. 93 pass through Missoula. U.S. 93 and Route 35 lead off I–90 to Kalispell in the Flathead Valley; from there, U.S. 2 leads to Glacier Park .

Johnson Bell Airport (☎ 406/728–4381), on U.S. 93 just north of Missoula, is served by **Delta** (☎ 800/221–1212), **Northwest** (☎ 800/225–2525), and **United** (☎ 800/241–6522). **Glacier International Airport** (☎ 406/752–1028), 8 miles northeast of Kalispell on U.S. 2, is serviced by **Delta, Northwest,** and **United.**

BY TRAIN
Amtrak (☎ 800/872–7245) stops in East Glacier Park.

Getting Around
A car is the only effective way to follow the Exploring tour.

Guided Tours
ORIENTATION
Glacier Park, Inc. (☎ 406/226–5551 or 800/332–9351) operates a fleet of vintage-1930s red-and-black buses that navigate along Going-to-the-Sun Highway.

SPECIAL INTEREST
Sun Tours (☎ 406/226–9220) offers tours of Glacier from a Native American perspective.

Important Addresses and Numbers
EMERGENCIES
For police, fire, ambulance, or other emergencies, dial **911.** The **Montana Highway Patrol** can be reached at ☎ 800/525–5555.

EMERGENCY ROOMS
Area hospitals with emergency rooms include Missoula's **St. Patrick Hospital** (500 W. Broadway, ☎ 406/543–7271) and **Kalispell Regional Hospital** (310 Sunnyview La., ☎ 406/752–5111).

VISITOR INFORMATION
Local information is available from the following sources: **Blackfoot Nation** (Box 850, Browning 59417, ☎ 406/338–7276), **Glacier National Park** (West Glacier 59936, ☎ 406/888–5441), and **Missoula Chamber of Commerce** (Box 7577, Missoula 59807), ☎ 406/543–6623 or 800/526–3465).

MONTANA ESSENTIALS

Getting Around

By Bus
Greyhound Lines (☎ 800/231–2222) services the southern part of the state. **Rimrock Stages** (☎ 406/549–2339 or 800/255–7655) runs regular bus service between Missoula, Bozeman, and Billings.

By Car
Going east to west, I–94 runs from the North Dakota border and into I–90 near Billings, where it becomes I–90 all the way to the Idaho border. Interstate 90, meanwhile, comes up from Wyoming to join I–94. From north to south, I–15 comes into southern Montana from Idaho, and runs through Dillon, Butte, Helena, and Great Falls on its way to the Canadian border.

By Plane
Billings's **Logan Field International Airport** is the largest in the state and is serviced by Continental (☎ 800/525–0280), Delta/SkyWest (☎ 800/221–1212), Northwest (☎ 800/225–2525), and United (☎ 800/241–6522). **Gallatin Field Airport,** just outside Bozeman, **Glacier**

International Airport in Kalispell, and **Johnson Bell Airport** in Missoula are other major facilities in the state.

By Train
Amtrak's *Empire Builder* (☎ 800/USA–RAIL) runs east–west across Montana's Highline, the most northern part of the state. Major stops along the route, which parallels U.S. 2, include Havre, Shelby, Glacier National Park, and Whitefish.

Dining

No matter where you eat in Montana, dress is casual. Leave your ties at home. Good ethnic cuisine is a rarity, but beef and seafood are available at most restaurants.

CATEGORY	RESORTS AND CITIES	TOWNS AND COUNTRY*
$$$$	over $40	over $30
$$$	$30-$40	$25-$30
$$	$20-$30	$15-$25
$	under $20	under $15

Prices are per person for a three-course dinner, not including drinks, tax, and tip.

Lodging

Montana's lodging falls generally into two categories: historic hotels and bed-and-breakfasts, and newer motels along commercial strips. Unless otherwise noted, hotel rooms have private baths.

CATEGORY	RESORTS AND CITIES	TOWNS AND COUNTRY*
$$$$	over $325	over $200
$$$	$225-$325	$140-$200
$$	$125-$225	$80-$140
$	under $125	under $80

Prices are for a standard double room in high season, not including tax and service.

Parks

Montana has more than its share of parks. All of **Glacier** and a little of **Yellowstone National Park** (*see* Chapter 8, Wyoming) are in Montana. The **Little Bighorn Battlefield National Monument,** where George Armstrong Custer met his fate, and the **Big Hole National Battlefield,** where the Nez Percé fought one of their most ferocious battles with the U.S. cavalry, are also found here.

Shopping

Montana is the place to stop for everything from fine cowboy boots to Western hats to handmade saddles. There are also some unique finds here, such as "turd bird" figures made from horse manure; or a Frisbee shaped like a cowpat.

Sports

Montana is very fitness-oriented, as are most of the Rockies states. Cycling, hiking, fishing, and skiing opportunities abound, and outfitters are available for almost every sport.

This state is home to almost 1,000 species of animals, from deer to dippers, mountain lions to moose. The **Montana Department of Fish, Wildlife and Parks** (1420 E. 6th Ave., Helena 59620, ☎ 406/444–2535) publishes the *Montana Wildlife Viewing Guide* ($5), keyed to sites throughout the state marked with an icon that represents a pair of binoculars. These signs along the highway indicate 100 of the best places to see some of the state's wildlife.

Camping

Some 30% of Montana's land is publicly owned, and there is camping on much of it—in national forests and parks. The Montana state highway map, which is free from gas stations, hotels, and Travel Montana (*see* Visitor Information, *below*), lists many of the campgrounds. Any of the national forest offices around the state can provide information on camping in Montana's forests.

Cycling

For information on cycling in the state, contact **Adventure Cycling** (☎ 406/721–1776 or 406/721–8719).

Fishing

Montana has the best rainbow, brown, and brook trout fishing in the country. The Yellowstone, Missouri, Madison, Beaverhead, Gallatin, and Bighorn rivers are the cream of the crop, and there are numerous lakes and small streams. State law says that all land along rivers to the high-water mark is publicly owned and access is guaranteed. Montana has numerous outfitters who can take you fishing for a day or a week.

Licenses are required for fishing. An annual, nonresident season license costs $45 and is good through February of the season it was purchased. A two-day license is $15 for the first two days and $10 for every two days after that. For more information, contact the **Montana Department of Fish, Wildlife, and Parks** (1420 E. 6th Ave., Helena 59601, ☎ 406/444–2535).

Golf

There are more than 70 public and private golf courses all over the state of Montana. The season is short, running from mid-May to October. Chambers of commerce in most cities can give you information on nearby courses.

Hiking and Backpacking

Hiking opportunities abound in Montana, almost anywhere you travel. Many of the trails involve arduous climbing, changeable weather, and wild animals: It's best to know what you are getting into before you go. *The Hiker's Guide to Montana*, by Bill Schneider, offers a lot of useful, basic information, and is available from most bookstores.

Spectator Sports

Baseball

The **Billings Mustangs**, the **Butte Copper Kings**, the **Great Fall Dodgers**, and the **Helena Brewers** are major-league farm teams that play in June and July. Call the chamber of commerce in each city for information.

Rodeo

All cities and most towns in Montana have a summer rodeo. Check with the chamber of commerce in each city.

Festivals and Seasonal Events

In mid-January, Great Falls hosts the **Montana Pro Rodeo Circuit Finals** (☎ 406/727–8115), which has a barbecue, rodeo dance, and auction in addition to the competition. The **"Race to the Sky" Dogsled Race** (☎ 406/442–2335), the longest event of its kind in the lower 48 (500 miles), goes along the Continental Divide and takes 4 to 5 days. There is viewing at check-in points.

The three-day **Whitefish Winter Carnival** (☎ 406/862–3501) with sidewalk sales, parades, dinners, and other activities, is held annually early in February.

In June, Helena has the **Montana Traditional Jazz Festival** (☎ 406/449–7969), five days in which Dixieland jazz bands from around the country play at various locations in downtown Helena.

The first full weekend of August is Bozeman's **Sweet Pea Festival** (☎ 406/586–4003), a four-day festival of music, children's art activities, Shakespeare in the park, dance workshops, and evening concerts. Also in August, the Crow Nation holds its annual **Crow Fair Powwow** (☎ 406/638–2228) in Crow Agency, featuring parades, crafts displays, and a nightly rodeo.

In early October, Flathead Valley hosts the **Flathead International Balloon Festival** (☎ 800/543–3105 or 406/755–6100), which consists of activities throughout the valley, including a competition, games, and, of course, hot-air balloons.

In late October, Billings hosts the **Northern International Livestock Exposition** (☎ 406/256–2495), featuring a rodeo, horse and cattle shows and sales, art shows and a cowboy revue.

From mid-November through mid-December more than 400 eagles feed on spawning salmon below the Canyon Ferry Dam. The visitor center is staffed by volunteers who answer questions seven days a week during this time, and there are spotting scopes set up on weekends for the **Eagle Watch** (☎ 406/444–4720).

Towns throughout the state hold **Christmas strolls** and other holiday activities during December. Contact Travel Montana for details.

Important Addresses and Numbers

Emergencies

In emergency situations call **911** or visit a hospital emergency room (*see* Emergencies sections in individual regions, *above*). The **Montana Highway Patrol** can be reached at 800/525–5555. For nonemergencies, check in telephone directories, with chambers of commerce, or at your lodging for names of doctors, dentists, and late-night pharmacies.

Visitor Information

Travel Montana (Dept. of Commerce, 1424 9th Ave., Helena 59620, ☎ 406/444–2654 or 800/847–4868) provides information and free publications, including a comprehensive directory of lodgings, guest ranches, campgrounds, outfitters, and special events.

7 Utah

By Scott
Warren

Updated by
Stacey Clark

ALTHOUGH 10 OTHER STATES EXCEED UTAH'S 84,990-square-mile area, few, if any, can match the breadth and diversity of its topography. Around virtually every bend, mountains pierce the skyline. Oceans of sagebrush roll out to the horizon. Improbable canyons score the earth. Snow-white salt flats shimmer, lush evergreen forests rim alpine meadows, and azure lakes glisten in the sun.

Given that spectacular scenery pervades virtually every corner of Utah, visitors can be thankful that much of the state falls under public domain. Federally owned lands include five national parks, six national monuments, a national historic site, two national recreation areas, seven national forests, and more than 22 million acres held by the Bureau of Land Management (BLM). Add to this nearly four dozen state parks, and it's easy to see why there are unlimited opportunities to enjoy the great outdoors. Whether your interest is hiking a trail, touring a scenic byway, skiing a powdery slope, fishing a lake, setting sails to the wind, watching wildlife, shooting the rapids, or capturing a scenic panorama on film, you can find it in Utah.

Its natural beauty notwithstanding, Utah is unique in other respects. Prior to 1847, Utah was like many other western areas. It was home to the Ute, Navajo, Paiute, Gosiute, and Shoshone Indians. It had witnessed the birth and eventual disappearance of the Fremont and Anasazi peoples. Spanish expeditions had come and gone, and streams and river valleys were stalked by rough-and-ready mountain men.

But on July 24, 1847, an event took place that would set Utah on a unique course. On that day, a small band of Mormons led by Brigham Young got its first look at the Great Salt Lake valley. Casting his gaze over the arid land, Young declared to his followers: "This is the right place." Within hours the pioneers began planting crops and diverting water for irrigation, and within days Brigham Young drew up plans for what would become one of the most successful social experiments ever.

As members of the relatively new Church of Jesus Christ of Latter-Day Saints (LDS), these pioneers had migrated west to escape religious intolerance. Establishing a new promised land adjacent to the Great Salt Lake, they were joined by tens of thousands of other Mormons in the two decades that followed. Many settled in Salt Lake City, while others were directed by Young to establish smaller towns in distant corners of the territory. To populate this particularly harsh land took an effort that was no less than heroic, but the reward was to be a society free from outside influence and control. Or so the pioneers had hoped.

Although the Mormons were determined to keep to themselves, their land of Zion was not to be. In 1862, U.S. troops were dispatched to Salt Lake City to keep an eye on them. In 1868, the discovery of silver in the nearby Wasatch Mountains led to a flood of prospectors and miners and, as a result, to the growth of riotous mining camps. In the year following, the completion of the first transcontinental railroad ushered in additional waves of non-Mormon ("gentile" in LDS terminology) settlers. By the turn of the century, Utah's religious and social homogeneity had been effectively destroyed.

Today, because 70% of all Utahns count themselves as members of the Mormon church, Utah is decidedly conservative. Utah was, for instance, the only state in the nation that placed Bill Clinton third behind George

Bush and Ross Perot in the 1992 presidential election. Politics aside, Utah is not nearly as provincial as many nonresidents have come to believe. When it comes to hotels, restaurants, the arts, and other worldly pleasures, places like Salt Lake City, Park City, and Ogden are as contemporary as any town in the nation. A legislative overhaul of Utah's infamous drinking laws has rendered those beasts essentially harmless. However, many nightspots require that you purchase temporary "membership" for about $5 (which entitles you to order liquor). Combine this with the state's natural splendor, wealth of recreational opportunities, and growing list of guest services and facilities, and it can safely be said that having fun is not prohibited in Utah.

SALT LAKE CITY

Nestled at the foot of the rugged Wasatch Mountains and extending to the south shore of the body of water for which it's named, Salt Lake City features one of the most scenic backdrops in the country. As the capital of progress-minded Utah, it is emerging as a prominent population and economic center of the Rocky Mountains. Within the last decade, the number of people living in the Salt Lake valley has climbed to over three-quarters of a million. As a reflection of this growth, a small but dynamic skyline has sprouted, along with ever-widening rings of suburbia. Smog occasionally bedevils the town, and crime is on the upswing, but for all intents and purposes, Salt Lake maintains the charm of a small, personable city. It is still an easy place to get around, and its residents are as down-to-earth as you will find anywhere.

Just as Salt Lake has grown considerably in recent years, so too has it come of age. The downtown now features several high-rise hotels, Salt Lake restaurants serve up a whole world of tastes, and there is finally a nightlife worthy of discussion. The Salt Lake arts scene is as prodigious as you'd expect to find in a city twice its size. All over town, fashionable retail enclaves are springing up. The community takes great pride in its NBA team, the Utah Jazz, and is eagerly planning for its role as host of the Winter Olympics in 2002.

Exploring

Numbers in the margin correspond to points of interest on the Utah and Salt Lake City and Salt Lake City Vicinity maps.

❶ As with most Utah municipalities, **Salt Lake City** is based on a grid plan that was devised by Brigham Young in the 19th century. Most street names have a directional and a numerical designation, which describes their location in relation to one of two axes. Streets with "East" or "West" in their names are east or west of (and parallel to) Main Street, which runs north–south, while "North" and "South" streets run parallel to South Temple Street. The numbers tell how far the streets are from the axes. (For example, 200 East Street is two blocks east of Main Street.) To confuse the matter further, addresses typically include two directional references and two numerical references; 320 East 200 South Street, for instance, is in the east 300 block of 200 South Street. As an added complication, three of Salt Lake's most prominent streets are named after the Mormon Temple: North Temple, South Temple, and West Temple.

❷ If for no other reason than to orient yourself to Salt Lake's street system, **Temple Square** is a good place to begin a walking tour of the city. Brigham Young chose this spot for a temple upon arriving in the Salt Lake valley, but work on the building did not begin for another six years. Constructed with blocks of granite hauled by oxen and then by train from Little Cottonwood Canyon, the Mormon Temple took 40 years to the day to complete. Its walls measure 16 feet thick at the base, and perched 210 feet above ground level is a golden statue of the trumpeting angel Moroni. Off-limits to all but faithful followers of the Mormon religion, the temple is used for marriages, baptisms, and other religious functions. Non-Mormons can learn more about the activities within the temple at the North and South visitor centers. Dioramas, photos of the temple interior, a baptismal font, and other displays offer considerable insight into the Mormon religion. *50 W. North Temple St.,* ☎ *801/240–2534.* ☛ *Free.* ☉ *Memorial Day–Labor Day, daily 8–10; Labor Day–Memorial Day, daily 9–9.*

Other buildings of interest at Temple Square include the **Assembly Hall,** which was completed in 1882 with leftover granite from the temple, and the **Tabernacle,** home of the world-renowned Mormon Tabernacle Choir (*see* The Arts, *below*). This unusual dome-shape structure was built in the 1860s as a meeting place. Void of interior supports, the 8,000-seat building is known for its exquisite acoustics.

As impressive as the architectural trappings of Temple Square are, don't forget to enjoy the quiet environs of the grounds themselves. But don't be surprised if a member of the church politely inquires about any interest you might have in learning more about Mormonism.

❸ Across West Temple Street from Temple Square are two Mormon-owned and -operated institutions. The first of these, the **Museum of Church History and Art,** houses a variety of artifacts and works of art related to the history of the Mormon faith. *45 N. West Temple St.,* ☎ *801/240–3310.* ☛ *Free.* ☉ *Weekdays 9–9, weekends 10–7.*

❹ Next door, the **Family History Library** is home to the largest collection of genealogical data in the world. Genealogy is important to Mormons because they believe in baptizing their ancestors, even after death. Anyone can use the facility, however. *35 N. West Temple St.,* ☎ *801/240–2331.* ☛ *Free.* ☉ *Mon. 7:30–6, Tues.–Fri. 7:30–10, Sat. 7:30–5.*

❺ East of Temple Square across Main Street, the **Joseph Smith Memorial Building** is a Mormon community center where visitors can use a computer program to learn how to do genealogical research or watch an hour-long film on early Mormon history and the emigration of Mormons to the Salt Lake Valley in the mid-19th century. The center also has two restaurants. *South Temple and Main Sts.,* ☎ *801/240–1266.* ☛ *Free.* ☉ *Weekdays 9–9, weekends 10–7.*

❻ Dominating the block east of Temple Square is the **LDS Church Office Building.** Standing 28 stories high, this is Salt Lake's tallest structure. Although there is not a lot to see here, tours do include a visit to an observation deck on the 26th floor. Indicative of the breadth of the church's business dealings, this building has its own zip code just to deal with the volume of mail it receives. *50 E. North Temple St.,* ☎ *801/240–2452.* ☛ *Free.* ☉ *Weekdays 9–4:30.*

❼ Around the corner from the Church Office Building is the **Beehive House,** Brigham Young's official residence. Now a national historic landmark, the home was constructed in 1854 and is topped with a replica of a beehive, symbolizing industry. To house his 27 wives and 56 children, Young built the **Lion House** next door (it's not open for tours). *67 E. South Temple St.,* ☎ *801/240–2671.* ☛ *Free.* ☉ *Mon.–Sat. 9:30–4:30, Sun. 10–1.*

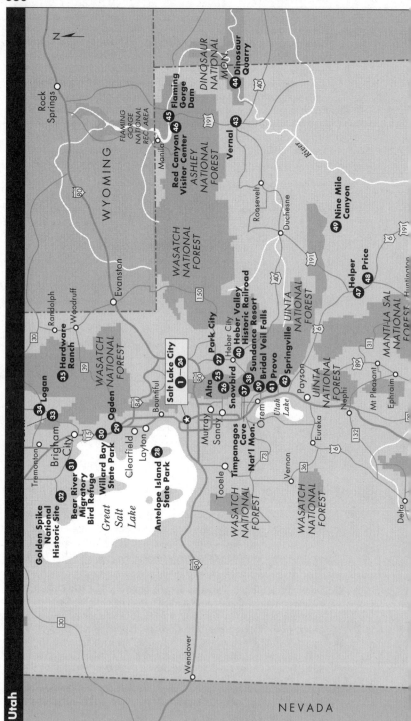

Utah

N

Rock Springs

WYOMING

FLAMING GORGE NATIONAL REC. AREA

DINOSAUR NATIONAL MON.

44 Dinosaur Quarry

45 Flaming Gorge Dam

46 Red Canyon Visitor Center

Manila

ASHLEY NATIONAL FOREST

43 Vernal

Roosevelt

Duchesne

49 Nine Mile Canyon

Evanston

WASATCH NATIONAL FOREST

Randolph

Woodruff

35 Hardware Ranch

Logan

WASATCH NATIONAL FOREST

Ogden

34 **33**

Brigham City

Tremonton

31 Bear River Migratory Bird Refuge

32 Golden Spike National Historic Site

Great Salt Lake

30 Willard Bay State Park

29

Clearfield

Layton

Bountiful

28 Antelope Island State Park

Murray

Sandy

Tooele

WASATCH NATIONAL FOREST

Wendover

Salt Lake City
1 — 24

Park City

27

25

26

Alta

Snowbird

Timpanogos Cave Nat'l Mon.

Heber City

40 Heber Valley Historic Railroad

Sundance Resort

37 **38**

39

41 Provo

Orem

Utah Lake

Bridal Veil Falls

42 Springville

Payson

Nephi

UINTA NATIONAL FOREST

Helper **47**

48 Price

MANTI-LA SAL FOREST

Huntington

Mt Pleasant

Ephraim

Eureka

Vernon

36

WASATCH NATIONAL FOREST

Delta

NEVADA

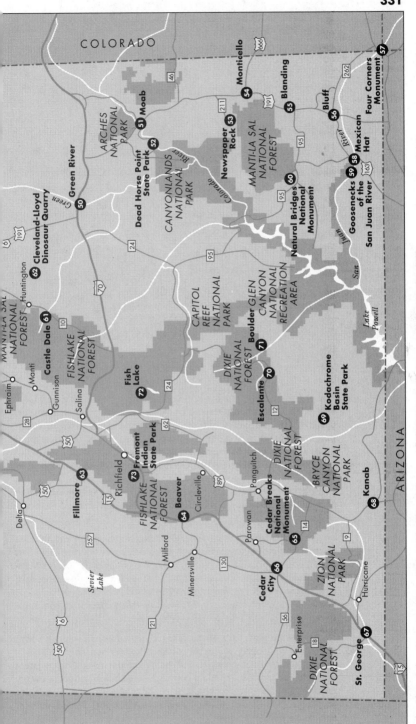

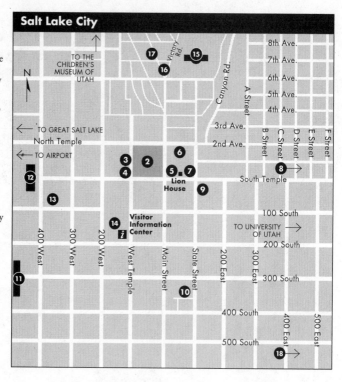

The pervasiveness of the Mormon religion notwithstanding, Salt Lake City is not and was not devoid of representation by other faiths, especially in its early years. In the blocks east of downtown are three impressive houses of worship. Dating back to 1871, the Episcopal **Cathedral Church of St. Mark** (231 E. 100 South St.) is Salt Lake's oldest non-Mormon church. The Gothic-inspired **Catholic Cathedral of Madeleine** (331 E. South Temple St.) features twin spires, gargoyles, and plenty of stained glass windows. Nearby, the **First Presbyterian Church** (371 E. South Temple St.) features beautifully crafted red sandstone construction.

In addition to being home to the Mormon church's competition, East South Temple Street was also a favored neighborhood for early Salt ⑧ Lake's well-to-do. Among its many splendid homes is the **Kearns Mansion.** Built by silver-mining tycoon Thomas Kearns, the impressive structure is now the governor's mansion. *603 E. South Temple St., ☎ 801/538–1005. ☛ Free. ⊗ For tours June–Nov., Tues. and Thurs. 1– 4.*

Another impressive turn-of-the-century structure, half a block south ⑨ of the Beehive House, houses the **Hansen Planetarium.** This stargazer's delight features various exhibits, including a moon rock display. There is a great book/gift shop and, of course, a domed theater. Special events include laser shows set to music and live stage performances. *15 S. State St., ☎ 801/538–2098. ☛ Free; shows are $2–$5. ⊗ Weekdays 9–8, Sat. 10 am–midnight, Sun. 1–5.*

Continue south on State Street to the middle of the 300 South block, ⑩ and turn right to see the **Exchange Place Historic District.** Reminiscent of early Chicago, this cluster of buildings reaching 11 stories includes Salt Lake's first skyscrapers. As the city's center for non-Mormon

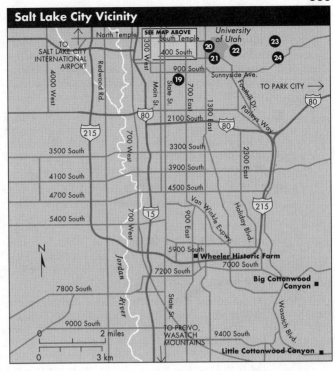

Salt Lake City Vicinity

commerce, it was one of the West's leading business centers early in this century.

TIME OUT If you're ready for a break, stop for a picnic on the beautiful grounds of the impressive **City and County Building** (State St., between 400 and 500 South Sts.). Construction of this large structure, once the state capitol, began in 1892 and took two years to complete, at a cost of $900,000. The building was renovated in 1989 at a cost of nearly $35 million.

A few blocks west of downtown are additional relics of Salt Lake's colorful past. Two train stations, enormous edifices built a year apart, underscore the two railroads' fierce competition for dominance in the region. At the west end of 300 South Street, the 1910 **Rio Grande Depot** (300 S. Rio Grande St.) is still in operation, handling Salt Lake's Amtrak service and also housing the Utah State Historical Society Museum.

The 1909 **Union Pacific Railroad Depot** at South Temple and 4th West, on the other hand, stands vacant. Adorned with western murals and stained glass, it's a vivid monument to the importance that the railroad played in the settling of Utah and the West.

Heading back toward Temple Square, you'll see two buildings in sharp contrast to the turn-of-the-century train depots. The enormous glass cube known as the **Delta Center** (301 W. South Temple St., ☎ 801/325–2000) is home court for the Utah Jazz (*see* Spectator Sports, *below*).

Previously, the Jazz played at the **Salt Palace** (100 S. West Temple St.), now a convention center.

North of downtown Salt Lake, but still within walking distance, is the **Utah State Capitol.** Topping Capitol Hill, this marvelous structure was begun in 1912, after the state happened upon $800,000 in inheritance taxes from the estate of Union Pacific Railroad president Edward Harriman. Taking less than three years to complete, the structure is considered one of the finest examples of Renaissance Revival architecture in the nation. Beneath the 165-foot-high rotunda is a series of murals, commissioned during the Depression, that depict the state's history. From the steps outside, you get a marvelous view of the entire Salt Lake valley. *Capitol Hill,* ☎ *801/538–3000.* ☛ *Free.*

16 Also on Capitol Hill is the **Pioneer Memorial Museum.** Featuring four floors of exhibits, many of which relate to the area's settlement by Mormon pioneers, the museum has one of the most extensive collections of settlement-era relics in the West. *300 N. Main St.,* ☎ *801/538–1050.* ☛ *Free but donations accepted.* ☉ *Mon.–Sat. 9–5.*

17 Northwest of Capitol Hill are the small Victorian homes of the **Marmalade Historic District.** So called because its streets were named after fruit trees, this small but interesting neighborhood has been restored thanks to the efforts of the Utah Heritage Foundation. In contrast to most of Salt Lake City's streets, these avenues are steep and narrow. The Utah Heritage Foundation (*see* Guided Tours *in* Salt Lake City Essentials, *below*) sells a brochure about the district, including a self-guided tour, for $2.

18 At this point, you'll probably want to switch to a car to visit sights outside central Salt Lake City. A few blocks southeast of downtown is another of Salt Lake's unique historical treasures, **Trolley Square** (600 S. 700 East St., ☎ 801/521–9877). From 1908 to 1945, this sprawling redbrick structure housed nearly 150 trolleys and electric trains for the Utah Light and Railway Company. In the face of more contemporary modes of transport, however, the facility was closed. After a complete overhaul, the mission-style edifice reopened in 1972 and today is home to a collection of more than 100 boutiques, shops, movie theaters, and restaurants, making it one of the more intriguing retail centers in the West.

19 A few blocks south of Trolley Square is the expansive Liberty Park, home to the **Tracy Aviary.** Set on 11 acres, this facility features some 250 species of birds from around the globe: ostriches, bald eagles, flamingos, parrots, several types of waterfowl, and many more. *700 E. 900 South St.,* ☎ *801/322–2473.* ☛ *$3 adults, $1.50 senior citizens and children over 3.* ☉ *Daily 9–6.*

A short distance east of downtown is the **University of Utah** campus. Dating from 1850, this large institution was relocated to its present site in 1900 and now has an enrollment of nearly 27,000. Among the school's accomplishments are headline-grabbing advancements in artificial-organ research and cold fusion.

20 For the public, there's a pair of museums worth a visit. The **Utah Museum of Natural History** contains a number of exhibits about the state's pre-pioneer past. In addition to collections of rocks, minerals, dinosaurs, and other fossils, there are displays about the prehistoric human inhabitants of the West. Utah wildlife is well represented, and you can even learn why Utah is so enamored of seagulls. *President's Circle at 200 South St. entrance to campus,* ☎ *801/581–4303.* ☛ *$3 adults, $1.50 senior citizens and children over 3.* ☉ *Mon.–Sat. 9:30–5:30, Sun. and holidays noon–5.*

21 The **Utah Museum of Fine Arts** features both venerable and contemporary art from around the world. Included in the permanent collection are ancient Egyptian relics, Italian Renaissance paintings, Chinese ceramics, traditional Japanese screens, Navajo rugs, and American art from the 17th century to the present. Special exhibits are regularly mounted. *South Campus Dr. (continuation of 400 South St.), just south of Marriott Library,* ☎ *801/581–7332. ☛ Free. ☉ Weekdays 10–5, weekends 2–5.*

㉒ Just east of the U of U campus is **Ft. Douglas.** Established in 1862, this former military post resulted from strained relations between the U.S. government and the Mormon settlers. Under the premise that Brigham Young might side with the Confederates during the Civil War, a brigade of California and Nevada volunteers set up shop on this site to keep an eye on things. During their free time, the soldiers took to prospecting in the nearby mountains, which in turn led to the establishment of mining camps like Park City (*see* The Wasatch Mountains, *below*). Today Ft. Douglas showcases several examples of military architecture spread out across manicured grounds. There's also a small museum highlighting the fort's military history. *Off Wasatch Blvd.,* ☎ *801/588–5188. Grounds open daily till dusk. Museum: ☉ 10–noon, 1–4 Tues.–Sat.*

㉓ Just beyond Ft. Douglas, the **Red Butte Garden and Arboretum** not only features a fascinating collection of flora from various corners of the earth but also is a great respite from the bustle of the city. With 16 acres of gardens and 150 acres of natural areas, the grounds can provide many pleasurable hours of strolling. Trails access the nearby mountain terrain. *University of Utah at mouth of Red Butte Canyon,* ☎ *801/581–5322. ☛ $3 adults, $2 senior citizens and children over 4. ☉ Daily 9–sunset.*

㉔ Farther east, at the mouth of Emigration Canyon, is **This Is The Place State Park.** As the site where Brigham Young first looked out upon the Great Salt Lake valley, this park features the This Is the Place Monument, a 12-foot bronze statue of Young and two cohorts, as well as Old Deseret, a collection of original pioneer homes. Inside the visitor center, displays relate the toils of those who followed the 1,300-mile Mormon Trail (now a national historic trail) from Nauvoo, Illinois, to Salt Lake City. *2601 Sunnyside Ave.,* ☎ *801/584–8391. ☛ $1.50 adults, $1 children. ☉ May–Sept., daily 8 am–10 pm; Sept.–May, daily 8–5.*

What to See and Do with Children

The **Children's Museum of Utah** opened in 1983 with the mission to "create the love of learning through hands-on experience," and that's exactly what it does. Kids can operate a TV station, pilot a jetliner, draw with computers, perform heart surgery, or unearth a saber-toothed tiger as part of the many interactive exhibits. *840 N. 300 West St.,* ☎ *801/328–3383. ☛ $3 adults, $2.75 senior citizens and children. ☉ Mon. 9:30–9, Tues.–Sat. 9:30–5, Sun. noon–5.*

Hogle Zoo features 1,200 animals, big and small, from all over the world. There is a children's zoo in the summer months, plus a miniature train that conducts young visitors on make-believe journeys. *2600 Sunnyside Ave.,* ☎ *801/582–1631. ☛ $5 adults, $3 senior citizens and children over 3. ☉ Daily 9–dusk.*

With nearly a dozen pools, 20 water slides, and the world's first water roller coaster, **Raging Waters** will delight kids of all ages. *1200 W. 1700 South St.,* ☎ *801/973–9900. ☛ $12.95 ages 12 and over, $9.95 children 4–11. ☉ Memorial Day–Labor Day, daily 11–8.*

At **Wheeler Historic Farm,** visitors can experience early farm life. They can take an "afternoon chores tour," try their hand at milking a cow, or ride a draft horse–drawn wagon. *6351 S. 900 East St.,* ☎ *801/264–2212.* ☛ *$1 adults, 50¢ senior citizens and children.* ⊘ *Daily 8–dusk.*

Off the Beaten Track

Depending on your point of view, the **Bingham Canyon Copper Mine** is either a marvel of human engineering or simply a great big eyesore. At any rate, this enormous open-pit mine is touted as the world's largest excavation. Measuring nearly 2½ miles across and ½ mile deep, it is the result of the removal of 5 billion tons of rock. Since operations began more than 80 years ago by the Kennecott Utah Copper company, over 12 million tons of copper have been produced. Visitors may view the mine from an overlook, but be sure to check on hours before making the 22-mile trip out there. The site also has a visitor center. *Rte. 48 west from I–15 past Copperton,* ☎ *801/322–7300.* ☛ *$2 per vehicle.* ⊘ *Apr.–Oct., daily 8–dusk.*

As one of the West's most unusual natural features, the **Great Salt Lake** is second only to the Dead Sea in saltiness. (It is up to eight times saltier than the ocean.) Ready access to this natural wonder is possible at the **Great Salt Lake State Park,** 16 miles west of Salt Lake City, on the lake's south shore. Here a marina and beach allow you to set sail—either by boat or by floating on your back—across the buoyant water. What makes the lake so salty? Because there is no outlet to the ocean, salts and other minerals carried down by rivers and streams become concentrated in this enormous evaporation pond. *From Exit 104 on I–80, follow the north Frontage Rd. east to park entrance.* ☛ *$3 per vehicle.* ⊘ *Daily, 7 am–10 pm.*

Head west from town on I–80, past the Great Salt Lake, and you'll eventually reach the **Bonneville Salt Flats,** an area nearly as devoid of life as the surface of the moon. Left behind by the receding waters of ancient Lake Bonneville, these extremely level salt flats support precious little in the way of plants and animals. One thing you will find here, however, is the Bonneville Speedway. First used in 1896, vehicles of varying designs have topped 600 miles per hour on the 80-foot-wide, 9-mile-long track. The BLM, managing agency of the salt flats, has seen an alarming 30% reduction in salt volume in the last 30 years.

Jordan River State Park (1084 N. Redwood Rd., ☎ 801/533–4496) is an 8½-mile riverside complex offering jogging paths, canoeing, picnic facilities, a golf course, and bicycling. Like the river for which it's named, the Jordan River runs from fresh water (Utah Lake) to salt (Great Salt Lake).

Shopping

Shopping Districts

Crossroads Plaza (50 S. Main St., ☎ 801/531–1799) offers an all-inclusive downtown shopping experience. Among its 140 stores and restaurants are Nordstrom and Mervyn's.

Under the commission of Brigham Young, Archibald Gardner built a flour mill in 1877. Today you can visit the mill and stroll among a number of stores in the adjacent **Gardner Historic Village** (1095 W. 7800 South St., ☎ 801/566–8903). Items for sale include furniture, collectibles, and knickknacks.

Founded by Brigham Young in 1868, the Zions Cooperative Mercantile Institution was America's first department store. The cast-iron facade on the Main Street entrance of the **ZCMI Center Uptown** (36 S. State St., ☎ 801/321–8743) dates to 1902. History notwithstanding, this thoroughly modern shopping center features not only a ZCMI store but also Eddie Bauer and Gart Brothers outlets. The center is closed Sundays.

Specialty Stores

ANTIQUES
Honest Jon's Hills House Antiques (126 S. 200 West St., ☎ 801/359–4852) carries a nice collection of Early American furniture. **Salt Lake Antiques** (279 E. 300 South St., ☎ 801/322–1273) is a 17,000-square-foot jumble of art, furniture, jewelry, and knickknacks.

BOOKS
In a rambling house, with room after room filled with books, **The King's English** (1511 S. 1500 East St., ☎ 801/484–9100) is a fun place to browse. **Sam Weller's Zion Book Store** (254 S. Main St., ☎ 801/328–2586) stocks over half a million new and used books.

CRAFTS
Mormon Handicraft (105 N. Main St., ☎ 801/355–2141) sells exquisite quilts, crafts, and children's clothing made by valley residents.

Sports and the Outdoors

Participant Sports

CYCLING
Salt Lake City is a comparatively easy city to tour by bicycle, thanks to extra-wide streets and not-so-frenetic traffic. An especially good route is **City Creek Canyon,** east of the state capitol. On odd-numbered days from mid-May through September the road is closed to motor vehicles.

GOLF
Salt Lake is home to numerous golf courses, and the city itself operates seven facilities throughout the valley. Some good 18-hole courses include **Bonneville** (954 Connor Rd., ☎ 801/596–5041), **Meadow Brook** (4197 S. 1300 West St., Murray, ☎ 801/266–0971), **Rose Park** (1386 N. Redwood Rd., ☎ 801/596–5030), **University** (100 S. 1900 East St., ☎ 801/581–6511), and **Wingpointe** (Salt Lake International Airport, ☎ 801/575–2345).

JOGGING
Salt Lake has a number of areas ideal for jogging. **City Creek Canyon** is always popular, as are **Liberty Park, Sugarhouse Park,** and **Jordan River State Park.**

Spectator Sports

BASEBALL
The Pacific Coast League, Triple A **Salt Lake Buzz** (77 W. 1300 South St., ☎ 801/485–3800) play at Franklin Quest Field, which has the Wasatch Mountains for a backdrop.

BASKETBALL
The **Utah Jazz** (301 W. South Temple St., ☎ 801/355–3865) is Salt Lake City's NBA team and a real crowd pleaser, having enjoyed a string of winning seasons in recent years. Home games are played at the Delta Center.

Dining

American/Continental

$$ Lamb's Restaurant. Having opened its doors in 1919, Lamb's claims to be Utah's oldest restaurant. The decor is reminiscent of a turn-of-the-century diner, and the menu has beef, chicken, and seafood dishes, plus a selection of sandwiches. ✗ *169 S. Main St.,* ☏ *801/364–7166. Reservations advised. AE, D, DC, MC, V. Closed Sun.*

$ **Squatter's Pub Brewery.** It might seem delightfully sinister to enjoy home-
★ brewed beer in a conservative state like Utah, but that's exactly what you'll find in this pub on the first floor of the old Boston Hotel. Combining a lively atmosphere with great food and drink, Squatter's comes highly recommended by locals and visitors alike. In addition to the popular Squatterburger, the Sicilian-style pizza, and the generous plate of fish-and-chips, it also serves killer bread pudding, plus six different ales. Because it bases production on demand, the pub promises the freshest brew in town. From pale ale to cream stout, no preservatives are used. ✗ *147 W. Broadway,* ☏ *801/363–2739. No reservations. AE, D, DC, MC, V.*

French

$$$$ **La Caille at Quail Run.** It's hard to imagine a dining experience as in-
★ teresting and tasty as the one here. Start with the escargots à la Bourguignonne, followed by the best wilted-spinach salad anywhere. Then choose from such treats as sautéed swordfish, Chateaubriand, and rack of New Zealand lamb. Add personable servers dressed in period costume, the stately surroundings of an 18th-century French château replica, and a 22-acre nature preserve. The result is a dinner worth every penny. ✗ *9565 Wasatch Blvd.,* ☏ *801/942–1751. Reservations required. AE, DC, MC, V.*

Italian

$$$ **Nino's.** In one of downtown Salt Lake's most spectacular settings, atop the University Club Building, the restaurant offers stunning nighttime views. A variety of wonderful chicken, veal, seafood, and pasta dishes highlight the northern Italian cuisine. ✗ *136 E. South Temple St.,* ☏ *801/359–0506. Reservations advised. AE, DC, MC, V. Closed Sun.*

$ **Spaghetti Factory.** In historic Trolley Square, this animated restaurant serves a lot of spaghetti for very little money. It's a good place to take a hungry family. ✗ *600 S. 700 East St., Trolley Sq.,* ☏ *801/521–0424. No reservations. D, MC, V.*

Seafood

$$ **Market Street Grill.** Known for its fresh and well-prepared seafood, this
★ restaurant has a lively atmosphere. It is owned by Gastronomy, Inc., a Salt Lake chain that transforms historic buildings into tasteful dining spots. Although you can count on every entrée being a winner, be sure to check the daily fish specials before ordering. ✗ *48 Market St.,* ☏ *801/322–4668. No reservations. AE, MC, V.*

Southwestern

$$ **Santa Fe Restaurant.** This restaurant, in scenic Emigration Canyon, has earned acclaim for its cuisine. The extensive menu offers a variety of appetizers, salads, American selections, and specialties of the Southwest. Also available are regional dishes: buffalo steak and rainbow trout, to name just two. A brunch is served on Sunday. ✗ *2100 Emigration Canyon,* ☏ *801/582–5888. Reservations advised. MC, V. No lunch Sat. No dinner Sun.*

$ **Café Pierpont.** Tasty Southwestern cuisine is served in a fun, family-
★ oriented setting. Kids small enough to walk through the wrought-iron cactus at the door eat for free. The menu includes four fajita, nine combination, and several enchilada plates; in addition to beef and chicken, there's a liberal scattering of seafood dishes. ✗ *122 W.*

Pierpont Ave., ☏ 801/364–1222. No reservations. AE, MC, V. No lunch weekends.

Thai

$ **Bangkok Thai.** With a wide selection of authentic Thai dishes, this is a good place to find something different. Categories include curry, wok-fried, seafood, rice and noodle, and vegetarian dishes. ✕ *1400 S. Foothill Dr., ☏ 801/583–7840. Reservations advised. AE, MC, V. No lunch weekends.*

Lodging

Downtown

$$$$ **Brigham Street Inn.** If you love historic bed-and-breakfasts, this is the
★ place to stay. On East South Temple (formerly Brigham Street), this turn-of-the-century mansion was carefully restored by Salt Lake architect John Pace. Each of the nine guest rooms was decorated by a different interior designer. The end result: a collection of superbly appointed rooms, each with its own personality. The original woodwork has been preserved throughout, one example of the special attention paid to preserving the home's character. The breakfast is Continental. ☎ *1135 E. South Temple St., 84102, ☏ 801/364–4461, FAX 801/521–3201. 9 rooms. Dining room. AE, D, DC, MC, V.*

$$–$$$ **Red Lion Hotel.** Like most links in the Red Lion chain, this hotel is surprisingly glitzy. Within walking distance of many downtown attractions, it is also within a block of several great restaurants, though a complimentary Continental breakfast is offered. The hotel caters to skiers, making available such things as lift tickets and complimentary ski storage. ☎ *255 S. West Temple St., 84101, ☏ 801/328–2000 or 800/547–8010, FAX 801/532–1953. 503 rooms. 2 restaurants, 2 bars, pool, hot tub, sauna, exercise room, coin laundry, airport shuttle. AE, D, DC, MC, V.*

$$ **Little America Hotel & Towers.** Inside Salt Lake's largest hotel are such
★ niceties as brass railings, chandeliers, and marble tubs. Perhaps because Little America is a small regional chain (six properties in all), it can afford to pay close attention to details. ☎ *500 S. Main St., 84101, ☏ 801/363–6781 or 800/453–9450, FAX 801/596–5911. 850 rooms. 2 restaurants, bar, indoor pool, hot tub, exercise room, coin laundry, airport shuttle. AE, D, DC, MC, V.*

$$ **Peery Hotel.** Constructed in 1910, the Peery is a salute to a bygone era, though the entire structure has been carefully renovated. Rooms are nicely appointed, service is personal, and, what's more, the front door is within two blocks of 25 restaurants and nightclubs. A free Continental breakfast is served. ☎ *110 W. 300 South St., 84101, ☏ 801/521–4300 or 800/331–0073, FAX 801/575–5014. 77 rooms. 2 restaurants, bar, hot tub, exercise room, coin laundry, airport shuttle. AE, D, DC, MC, V.*

$$ **Shilo Inn.** A couple of blocks from Temple Square, this hotel combines the convenience of being right downtown with good rates. Service is reasonable, and the amenities are better than what you'd expect for the price. For example, there is a complimentary Continental breakfast. ☎ *206 S. West Temple St., 84101, ☏ 801/521–9500 or 800/222–2244, FAX 801/359–6527. 200 rooms. 2 restaurants, bar, pool, hot tub, saunas, coin laundry, airport shuttle. AE, D, DC, MC, V.*

$ **The Avenues.** In a historic neighborhood, this is the best bet for hostel-style accommodations. Bed areas are clean and comfortable. ☎ *107*

F St., 84103, ☎ 801/359–3855. *14 multibed rooms share bath. Coin laundry. No credit cards.*

$ Deseret Inn. This '60s-style motor inn offers a basic room at a good price but little else. Rooms are somewhat plain, and the exterior trim could use some paint. Nevertheless, it would be hard to beat the price unless you look outside downtown. ⌂ *50 W. 500 South St., 84101,* ☎ *801/532–2900 or 800/359–2170,* ℻ *801/532–2900. 88 rooms. Restaurant, hot tub. AE, D, DC, MC, V.*

Airport and Greater Salt Lake Valley

$$–$$$ Radisson Hotel Airport. This hotel is elegant and very comfortable.
★ Rooms include a wet bar and refrigerator. Try the free Continental breakfast and the Club Room for fun dining possibilities. This is the best bet near the airport. ⌂ *2177 W. North Temple St., 84116,* ☎ *801/364–5800 or 800/333–3333,* ℻ *801/364–5823. 127 rooms. Restaurant, bar, pool, hot tub, exercise room, airport shuttle. AE, D, DC, MC, V.*

$$ Hampton Inn. Because this facility is relatively new, and because Hampton Inns generally offer pleasant rooms with nice furnishings for a moderate price, this is a worthwhile place to stay if you're just passing through. It's by I–15, so there are no attractions nearby. ⌂ *10690 S. Holiday Park Dr., Sandy 84070,* ☎ *801/571–0800 or 800/426–7806,* ℻ *801/571–0800. 131 rooms. Indoor pool, hot tub, coin laundry. AE, D, DC, MC, V.*

The Arts

Dance

Salt Lake's three main dance companies also perform at the historic **Capitol Theatre** (50 W. 200 South St.). **Ballet West** (☎ 801/355–2787) is considered one of the nation's top ballet companies, performing both classical and original works. **Repertory Dance Theatre** (☎ 801/534–6345) presents modern-dance performances. **Ririe-Woodbury Dance Company** (☎ 801/328–1062) is Salt Lake's premier modern-dance troupe. It's recognized for its innovation and commitment to community education.

Music

The **Mormon Tabernacle Choir** (Temple Sq., ☎ 801/240–2534) may be heard in performance in the Tabernacle on Sunday mornings at 9:30 (be seated by 9:15) or during rehearsals on Thursdays at 8 PM. The **Utah Symphony** (123 W. South Temple St., ☎ 801/533–5626) performs 260 concerts annually, both at home in the acoustically acclaimed Maurice Abravanel Concert Hall (part of the Salt Palace Convention Center) and in cities across the nation and abroad.

Opera

Utah Opera Company (Capitol Theatre, 50 W. 200 South St., ☎ 801/355–2787) produces four operas a year, which often feature nationally recognized stars. If you don't care for opera, check out the ornate facade of the Capitol Theatre anyway.

Theater

Desert Star Playhouse (4861 S. State St., ☎ 801/266–7600) specializes in musical-comedy melodrama. You are encouraged to hiss at the bad guy and cheer for the hero. **Pioneer Theatre Company** (300 S. 1340 East St., ☎ 801/581–6961) features several different classic and contemporary musicals during its season, which runs from September through May. **Salt Lake Acting Company** (168 W. 500 North St., ☎ 801/363–0525) is nationally recognized for its development of new plays. Performances run year-round.

Nightlife

Bars and Lounges

The **Green Parrot Café** (155 W. 200 South St., ☎ 801/363–3201) has been a favorite local hangout for years. Lunch and dinner are served, and the small stage occasionally hosts bands. In the downtown Marriott, **Solitude Lounge** (75 S. West Temple St., ☎ 801/531–0800) offers a relaxed and intimate respite from the city.

Comedy Clubs

South of town, **The Comedy Circuit** (10 N. Main St., Midvale, ☎ 801/561–7777) is Utah's best choice for stand-up comedy. Some of the nation's top acts stop here while on tour.

Nightclubs

Club Max (255 S. West Temple St., ☎ 801/328–7047) is a high-energy dance club in the Red Lion Hotel. The **Dead Goat Saloon** (165 S. West Temple St., ☎ 801/328–4628) features live music nightly. The tempo is upbeat, and the grill is fired up every day for lunch and dinner. **The Zephyr Club** (301 S. West Temple St., ☎ 801/355–5646) showcases both local and nationally recognized bands in a lively atmosphere. The decor is art deco.

Salt Lake City Essentials

Arriving and Departing

BY BUS

Greyhound Lines (☎ 801/355–9579) runs several buses each day to the terminal at 160 West South Temple.

BY CAR

From I–80, take I–15 north to 600 South Street to reach the city center. Salt Lake City's streets are extra wide and typically not congested. Most are two-way.

BY PLANE

Salt Lake International Airport (☎ 801/575–2400) is 7 miles northwest of downtown Salt Lake City. It is served by **American** (☎ 800/433–1790); **America West** (☎ 800/235–9292); **Continental** (☎ 801/359–9800 or 800/525–0280); **Delta** (☎ 801/532–7123 or 800/221–1212), which maintains a hub here; **Northwest** (☎ 800/225–2525); **Southwest** (☎ 801/466–7747); **TWA** (☎ 801/539–1111 or 800/892–2746); and **United** (☎ 800/241–6522).

Between the Airport and Center City. All major car rental agencies have desks at Salt Lake International. From the airport, drive 7 miles east on I–80 to 600 South Street and follow signs for city center. The **Utah Transit Authority** (☎ 801/287–4636) runs bus service between the airport and downtown. Buses run regularly and are less expensive than cabs. In addition, most downtown hotels offer free airport pickup for guests. **Yellow Cab** (☎ 801/521–2100) provides 24-hour service to all of the Salt Lake valley. The cost of a ride into town is about $11.

BY TRAIN

The **Rio Grande Depot** (300 S. Rio Grande St., ☎ 801/531–0189) has daily **Amtrak** service.

Getting Around

BY BUS

Salt Lake has a very workable public transportation system in the **Utah Transit Authority** (☎ 801/287–4636). A Free Fare Zone covers a 15-block area downtown and on Capitol Hill. Service to the ski resorts costs $1.50–$4; most other routes cost 75¢ per ride.

Guided Tours

ORIENTATION

Lewis Brothers Tours (Box 51027, 84151, ☎ 801/359–8677 or 800/826–5844) conducts tours of Salt Lake City sights in *Old Salty,* an open-air, rubber-tired train. Tours depart from Temple and Trolley squares.

SPECIAL INTEREST

Utah Heritage Foundation (485 Canyon Rd., 84110, ☎ 801/533–0858) offers the most authoritative tours of Salt Lake's historic sights. Two-week advance notice is required.

Important Addresses and Numbers

EMERGENCIES

Salt Lake hospitals include **HCA St. Mark's Hospital** (1200 E. 3900 South St., ☎ 801/268–7111), **Holy Cross Hospital** (1050 E. South Temple St., ☎ 801/350–4111), **LDS Hospital** (8th Ave. and C St., ☎ 801/321–1100), **Primary Children's Medical Center** (100 N. Medical Dr., ☎ 801/588–2000), and **University Hospital and Clinics** (50 N. Medical Dr., ☎ 801/581–2121).

LATE-NIGHT PHARMACIES

The pharmacy at **Smith's Supermarket** (876 E. 800 South St., ☎ 801/355–5257) is open 24 hours a day; the one at **Harmon's Supermarket** (3200 S. 1300 East St., ☎ 801/487–5461) is open until midnight. **Crossroads Drug** (Crossroads Plaza, 50 S. Main St., ☎ 801/355–5823) is open until 9 on weekdays.

VISITOR INFORMATION

The **Salt Lake Convention and Visitors Bureau** (180 S. West Temple St., 84101, ☎ 801/521–2822) is open weekdays 8–5 and Saturdays 9–4.

THE WASATCH MOUNTAINS

Rising to elevations of more than 11,000 feet and stretching some 160 miles from the Idaho border to central Utah, the Wasatch Range is an imposing and important geographic feature in the western United States. From a geologic perspective, the mountains are a complex assemblage of igneous, sedimentary, and metamorphic formations. From a demographic one, these mountains or, more precisely, their western base—a corridor known as the Wasatch Front—is home to three-quarters of all Utahns. Not only Salt Lake City residents but also those in Ogden, Logan, and Provo are greeted each morning with a spectacular view of the Wasatch.

Scientific and social implications aside, the Wasatch Range is one of the nation's premier mountain playgrounds. Uppermost in many visitors' minds is the legendary skiing found at resorts like Snowbird, Alta, and Park City. What many don't realize, however, is that these same ski towns double as wonderful summer destinations. Picturesque mountain communities, miles of hiking and bicycling trails, bright blue lakes, and truly spectacular alpine scenery add up to a vacation that's hard to beat.

Exploring the Ski Resorts

Numbers in the margin correspond to points of interest on the Utah map.

From Salt Lake City, follow I–15 south and I–215 east to the turnoff for Little Cottonwood Canyon. Nine miles up the canyon is Utah's oldest—and the nation's second-oldest—ski area: **Alta.** Alta actually began as a silver-mining camp in the 1800s. So frenzied was the pace back then that the year-round population topped 1,000. The eventual crash of the silver market, however, left the canyon virtually empty until it was recognized for its potential as a winter sports area. A lift was pieced together from an old mine tram, and in January of 1939 the Alta Lifts Company was in business. Today Alta is widely acclaimed for both what it has and what it doesn't have. The ski area (*see* Sports and the Outdoors, *below*) promises a generous helping of Wasatch powder—up to 500 inches a year. What you won't find is the glitz and pomp that other resorts exude.

A mile down Little Cottonwood Canyon is a study in contrasts. Since the early '70s, **Snowbird,** or more simply "the Bird," has taken skiing to new heights. The Snowbird Ski and Summer Resort (*see* Sports and the Outdoors, *below*) is one of the nation's most modern ski facilities, and at the base area, a cluster of modern structures house elegant guest rooms, exquisite restaurants, and pleasurable nightclubs. The largest of these buildings, the Cliff Lodge (*see* Dining and Lodging, *below*), is like an entire ski town under one roof.

During the summer, Little Cottonwood Canyon is still the place to be for outdoor fun. From Memorial Day weekend to October, Snowbird fires up its tram to ferry sightseers and hikers to the top. From here you get one of the most spectacular views in the West.

Up range (i.e., north) from Little Cottonwood Canyon is Big Cottonwood Canyon—home to two smaller ski areas, **Brighton** and **Solitude** (*see* Sports and the Outdoors, *below*).

Although not far from Big and Little Cottonwood canyons as the crow flies, **Park City** is best accessed by following I–80 east from Salt Lake City through Parley's Canyon. On the back side of the Wasatch Mountains, it is Utah's only real ski town, and because it is a mere 40-minute drive from Salt Lake International Airport, it is the most accessible ski town in the country.

Historically, Park City was a rip-roaring mining town like no other. Silver was discovered here in 1868, and in the years immediately following, the town's population grew by leaps and bounds. In the process it earned the nickname "Sin City." Certainly, it was uncommon for any municipality within spitting distance of Salt Lake to have more than two dozen saloons and a thriving red-light district. Despite the generosity of the mountains, Park City eventually fell victim to depressed silver prices. It was not until 1946 that its current livelihood began to take shape in the form of the small Snow Park ski hill, which opened a few miles north. In 1963, Treasure Mountains Resort began operations with its skier's subway—an underground train and hoist system that ferried skiers to the mountain's top. In the years since, facilities were upgraded, and Treasure Mountains became the Park City Ski Area (*see* Sports and the Outdoors, *below*).

Today, because Park City includes a mind-numbing collection of condominiums, it could be considered just another ill-conceived resort town.

At its heart, however, is a historic downtown district that rings with authenticity. "Charming" is a word that comes to mind when describing the buildings that line Main Street, but, what's more important, this collection of turn-of-the-century edifices reminds visitors that Park City is a real town with real roots.

Although it's the skiing that attracts most visitors to Park City, the town also serves as an excellent base camp for summer activities. Hiking trails are plentiful. A scenic drive over Guardsman Pass (via a gravel road that is passable for most vehicles) reveals incredible mountain vistas and a plethora of alpine wildflowers. There are some acclaimed golf greens, hot-air ballooning is taking off (pun intended), and an increasing number of mountain bikers are finding that the ski slopes make for truly exceptional pedaling. Wolf Mountain, a smaller ski area in town (*see* Sports and the Outdoors, *below*), hosts an impressive concert series, which has brought such acts as Bob Dylan, the Grateful Dead, and Muddy Waters to its outdoor stage.

Exploring the Northern Wasatch Mountains

In the 35 miles along I–15 from Salt Lake to Ogden (the next large city north) are a string of municipalities that serve as bedroom communities for the larger towns. Although there are not many sights to take in along this stretch of road, a side trip west at Exit 335 takes you to **Antelope Island State Park.** The largest island in the Great Salt Lake, this water-bound mountain appears deserted and desolate from shore, but it is home to a variety of wildlife, including a herd of 600 bison. In 1983, the lake level rose dramatically and flooded the causeway that leads to the island. The water has since receded, and the island's beaches, campground, and hiking areas are again accessible. *Rtes. 108 and 127 to causeway,* ☏ *801/773–2941.* ☞ *$5 per vehicle including fee for causeway.* ⊘ *Daily 7 am–10 pm.*

With a population of nearly 65,000, **Ogden** combines a small-town feel with the infrastructure of a larger city. Upon the site of a stockade and trading post built by mountain man Miles Goodyear, Brigham Young directed the settlement of Ogden in 1850. Despite its Mormon roots, however, Ogden was to change radically with the arrival of the transcontinental railroad in the area in 1869. The town quickly became a major Western crossroads, and it received a great influx of non-Mormons. With the advent of World War II, the military began to have a considerable presence in town, which, with Hill Air Force Base nearby, it still has today. Ogden is also a college town; Weber State University is within the city limits.

On your way into town from the south, at Exit 341 off I–15, are Hill Air Force Base and the **Hill Aerospace Museum.** Among the many interesting planes housed in this large hangar are the SR-71 Blackbird (a reconnaissance aircraft that made a transatlantic flight in under two hours) and a B-17 Flying Fortress. *Hill Air Force Base,* ☏ *801/777–6818.* ☞ *Free.* ⊘ *Tues.–Fri. 9–4:30, weekends 9–5:30.*

Given Ogden's history, it's safe to assume that it has a number of vintage buildings and museums. The best of the latter are found in the **Ogden Union Station.** Built in 1924, this impressive Spanish Revival structure demonstrates the considerable esteem railroad travel once enjoyed and houses some interesting museums: the Utah State Railroad Museum, the Browning-Kimball Car Museum, and the Browning Firearms Museum. (Browning is a renowned gun manufacturer.) *25th*

St. and Wall Ave., ☎ *801/629–8444.* ☛ *$3.50 adults, $1.50 children 3–17.* ⊘ *Weekdays 10–6, Sat. noon–6.*

Highlighting a chapter in history that unfolded decades prior to the railroad era, **Ft. Buenaventura State Park** is an 84-acre tract with exact replicas of the stockade and cabins that Miles Goodyear built in 1846. Guides in period costume interpret the ways of the early trappers, and hundreds of mountain-man enthusiasts rendezvous at the fort in September, at Thanksgiving, and over Easter weekend. Camping and picnicking facilities are available. *2450 A Ave.,* ☎ *801/621–4808.* ☛ *$3 per vehicle.* ⊘ *Daily 8–sunset.*

Back in downtown Ogden, the **Ogden River Parkway** follows the banks of the Ogden River for 3 miles to the mouth of Ogden Canyon. A real people place, this urban greenway hosts a number of outdoor activities, including bicycling, walking, jogging, tennis, baseball, and fishing. What really distinguishes it, however, are the two parks found along the way: the MTC Learning Park, which has botanical gardens and pavilion facilities, and the **George S. Eccles Dinosaur Park,** which features 26 life-size dinosaur replicas, one of the largest collections of its kind in the nation. *1544 E. Park Blvd.,* ☎ *801/393–3466.* ☛ *$2.50 adults, $1 youths 6–17, 50¢ children 2–5.* ⊘ *Apr.–Nov., daily 10–dusk.*

With the Ogden River Parkway pointing the way, follow Route 39 (a designated scenic byway) into **Ogden Canyon.** A few miles beyond the canyon mouth, the mountains open up to make room for **Pineview Reservoir.** During the summer, this 2,000-acre lake is festooned with colorful sailboards and the graceful arcs of water-skiers. The fishing is good, and some nice beaches, campgrounds, and marinas dot the shore. Anderson Cove, along the southern end of the lake, is quite popular, as is Middle Inlet, along the eastern shore. During the winter, Ogden Canyon reveals some great (and inexpensive) alternatives to the Salt Lake City ski scene, including Snowbasin and Powder Mountain (*see* Sports and the Outdoors, *below*).

TIME OUT For what some consider to be the best burger in the country, as well as the most down-home barroom atmosphere in Utah, visit the **Shooting Star Saloon** (7350 E. 200 South St., ☎ 801/745–2002) in Huntsville. From the dollar bills pinned to the ceiling to the stuffed head of a 300-pound St. Bernard on the wall to the graffiti in the bathrooms, there is something to look at in every corner.

㉚ After you return to I–15 north, the next point of interest is **Willard Bay State Park.** About 10,000 acres in size, the bay is actually a freshwater arm of the Great Salt Lake. Fed by canals in the spring, it is effectively protected from saltwater intrusion by dikes, and because it is fresh water, Willard Bay is a popular fishing, boating, and bird-watching area. *15 mi north of Ogden off I–15,* ☎ *801/734–9494.* ☛ *$3 per vehicle.* ⊘ *6 am–10 pm daily.*

If you happen to be passing through in the fall, drive up U.S. 89/91 from Ogden to Brigham City to enjoy Utah's **Fruitway.** You'll find many produce stands and the peach, apple, cherry, plum, pear, and apricot orchards from which the fruit came.

Upon reaching Brigham City, this tour turns northeast to follow U.S. 89/91 up and over Sardine Summit to Cache Valley. A brief detour to **㉛** the west, however, takes you to two worthwhile attractions. **Bear River Migratory Bird Refuge,** 17 miles from Brigham City, was originally a series of freshwater lagoons ideally suited for waterfowl, but in 1983 the 73,000-acre preserve was inundated by the rising Great Salt Lake. Ice floes destroyed all facilities at the refuge, but a considerable amount of work by the U.S. Fish and Wildlife Service has resurrected a driving-tour route that follows various dikes. The habitat has been reclaimed, and the refuge once again hosts seasonal influxes of ducks, geese, and shorebirds. Plans for a new visitor center and a 17,000-acre expansion are in the works. *16 mi west of Brigham City on Forest St., which becomes Bird Refuge Rd.,* ☎ *801/723–5887.* ☛ *Free.* ☉ *Daily 9–sunset.*

㉜ The second attraction, near Promontory, is the **Golden Spike National Historic Site.** It was here that the Union Pacific and Central Pacific railroads met on May 10, 1869, completing the first transcontinental route. Under the auspices of the National Park Service, Golden Spike features a visitor center, an auto tour, and some vintage locomotives on display. Every May 10, a reenactment of the driving of the golden spike is held, and the second Saturday in August brings the annual Railroaders Festival. *29 mi west of I–15, Exit 368 to Rtes. 83 and 13 W,* ☎ *801/471–2209.* ☛ *$4 per vehicle.* ☉ *Daily 8–4:30.*

East of Brigham City, U.S. 89/91 tops Sardine Summit before dropping into the highly scenic **Cache Valley.** Walled in to the west by the imposing Wellsville Mountains (often touted as the steepest range in the world) and by the Bear River Range (a subrange of the Wasatch) to the east, Cache Valley is 15 miles wide and 60 miles long. Although first successfully settled in 1856 by Mormon pioneer Peter Maughan, during the 1820s Cache Valley was a favorite haunt for mountain men, who held a rendezvous here. These early trappers often stashed their furs in the valley, hence the name.

Today Cache Valley is one of the most important agricultural regions in Utah, and topping the list of foods produced here is cheese. Of the three cheese factories in the valley, Cache Valley Cheese is the nation's largest producer of Swiss cheese. To learn about agriculture's early days **㉝** in the valley, visit the **Ronald V. Jensen Living Historical Farm,** a 1917 dairy farm. Numerous antique farm implements are on display. Draft horses still pull their weight. Workers dressed in period clothing demonstrate such tasks as sheepshearing and quilting, and a variety of special events takes place throughout the year. *4025 S. U.S. 89/91, Wellsville,* ☎ *801/245–4064.* ☛ *$2 adults, $1 senior citizens, 50¢ children.* ☉ *June–Aug., Tues.–Sat. 10–4, and on special occasions year-round.*

Agriculture is Cache Valley's primary industry, but the region's largest **㉞** city, **Logan,** follows the beat of a different drummer. It's home to **Utah State University,** a land-grant college that began in 1888. Today, USU has an enrollment of about 16,000 and is a leader in such diverse fields as agriculture, natural resources, and space technology. On a benchland just east of downtown Logan, the USU campus is best toured by starting at the historic **Old Main** administration building. Across campus, the Chase Fine Arts Center includes the **Nora Eccles Art Museum** (☎ 801/797–1412), which features exhibits by local and nationally recognized artists. For further information about USU, contact the University Public Relations Department (☎ 801/797–1000).

TIME OUT No visit to USU would be complete without a stop at the **Food Science Building** (12 East and 750 North; open 9–9.) for a scoop of the university's famous ice cream. You can also get soup and sandwiches here.

Just as Old Main's bell tower signifies that Logan is a college town, the twin towers of Logan's **Mormon Temple** (100 North and 200 East Sts.) remind all that it's also a somewhat conservative community with Mormon roots. Rising from a grassy knoll, this impressive limestone edifice took settlers seven years to complete. The site was chosen by Brigham Young in 1877, and the work was directed by architect Truman O. Angell, designer of the Salt Lake temple. As with all Mormon temples, this structure is open only to followers of the faith.

A Mormon landmark that can be visited by all is the **LDS Tabernacle** (Center and Main Sts.). Holding court over downtown Logan, the Tabernacle is one of several structures featured on a walking tour of historic Main Street. A nicely illustrated brochure, available from the chamber of commerce (160 N. Main St.), guides you along both sides of Main Street and up a few cross streets. The more interesting buildings along the walk include St. John's Episcopal Church, representing Cache Valley's first non-Mormon denomination; the Ellen Eccles (formerly Capitol) and Lyric theaters; and the Cache County Courthouse, with its restored cupola.

③⑤ If you happen to be passing through in the winter, be sure to drive up Blacksmith Fork Canyon to **Hardware Ranch.** Here the state Division of Wildlife Resources feeds several hundred head of elk throughout the snowy months. A 20-minute sleigh ride takes you up close to the majestic creatures for some great pictures. There is also a visitor center and café. ☎ *801/245–3131. Sleigh rides: $3 ages over 3; open mid-Dec.–mid-Mar., daily 10–5, snow conditions permitting.*

From Logan, U.S. 89 continues for 30 miles up the scenic **Logan Canyon** before topping out at the crest of the Bear River Range. Within the canyon are a number of campgrounds and picnic areas administered by the Wasatch-Cache National Forest. For a particularly satisfying excursion, climb the 7 miles to **Tony Grove Lake.** At more than 8,000 feet, this subalpine jewel is surrounded by beautiful scenery. A short trail circles the lake, and other backcountry routes enter the Mt. Naomi Wilderness Area to the west. Summer is the most popular season in Logan Canyon, but fall and winter are also worthwhile times to visit.

③⑥ A mile beyond the summit, a turnoff reveals a spectacular view of **Bear Lake.** Some 8 miles wide and 20 miles long, the lake is an unusual shade of blue, thanks to calcium carbonate in the water. It is home to four species of fish found nowhere else, including the Bonneville cisco, which draws fishermen during spawning in January. Water-sports enthusiasts can best access Bear Lake at one of three state parks (*see* State Parks, *below*). Among the lake's more discreet inhabitants is the Bear Lake Monster, which, like its Loch Ness counterpart, has lurked in local lore for many years. Beyond Bear Lake, a high sagebrush desert stretches east into Wyoming, and the Wasatch Mountains effectively end at the Idaho border.

Exploring the Southern Wasatch Mountains

South of Salt Lake City, around Point of the Mountain (a popular hang-gliding haven and site of the Utah State Prison), I–15 drops into Utah Valley, much of which is covered by **Utah Lake.** Although this freshwater lake is 11 miles wide and 24 miles long, it averages a scant 9 feet deep. A state park is on the lake's eastern shore. Boating is popular, but the cloudy (some would say polluted) water makes swimming and fishing questionable.

Utah Valley's other chief natural feature is the soaring, 11,750-foot **Mt. Timpanogos.** Rising abruptly to the east, this imposing landmark is the centerpiece of a wilderness area of the same name and towers over **Timpanogos Cave National Monument,** along Route 92 within American Fork Canyon. After hiking a steep 1½-mile trail to the cave entrance, visitors may explore three separate caves connected by tunnels. A variety of well-preserved stalactites and stalagmites, plus other formations, make the three-hour tour well worth the effort. *Rte. 92, American Fork,* ☎ *801/756–5238. Tours: $5 adults, $4 children 6–15.* ☼ *Mid-May–mid-Oct., daily 9–sunset.*

Beyond Timpanogos Cave, Route 92 continues up American Fork Canyon before branching off to climb behind Mt. Timpanogos itself. Designated the **Alpine Loop Scenic Byway,** this twisting mountain road reveals some stunning mountain scenery before dropping into Provo Canyon to the south. Closed in the winter, the Alpine Loop is not recommended for recreational vehicles.

Within the last 3 miles of the Alpine Loop Scenic Byway is the **Sundance Resort** (*see* Sports and the Outdoors, *below*). Best accessed from Provo Canyon, this small but distinctive resort came into being when Robert Redford purchased a ski hill in 1969. Reflecting the actor's interests in the environment, the arts, and outdoor recreation, the resort was designed to blend in with the natural surroundings. In the summer, a number of hiking trails, as well as theater productions, entice visitors. In winter, the yearly Sundance Film Festival draws a wide audience. It has become an internationally recognized venue for showing important low-budget films produced outside the mainstream studio system.

While the Alpine Loop Scenic Byway provides a roundabout way to get to scenic Provo Canyon, a more direct route follows U.S. 189 east from Orem. Within the canyon is **Bridal Veil Falls,** which drops a total of 607 feet in two tiers. The Skytram—touted as one of the steepest aerial trams in the world—climbs nearby, giving riders a spectacular view of the falls below. *Skytram: 4 mi up the canyon,* ☎ *801/225–4461.* ☛ *$5 adults, $3 children.* ☼ *Memorial Day weekend–Oct., daily 9–dusk.*

Beyond Bridal Veil Falls, U.S. 189 passes Deer Creek Reservoir before entering Heber Valley. Running along this route are railroad tracks, part of the scenic **Heber Valley Historic Railroad.** Following a line that first ran in 1899, the "Heber Creeper" takes passengers on a nostalgic trip through beautiful Provo Canyon. Each car has been carefully restored, and one of the engines—no. 618—is a fully operational, steam-powered locomotive. *450 S. 600 West, St., Heber City,* ☎ *801/654–5601 or 800/982–3257. Tickets begin at $14 for adults and $8 for children under 10.*

Although the scenic resources in and around Utah Valley are considerable, the region, **Provo** in particular, is probably best known as the home of **Brigham Young University.** As one of the largest religiously affiliated universities in the world, BYU reflects the conservative nature of the Mormon church. Students must adhere to a strict dress code, and they are supposed to refrain from alcohol, tobacco, and caffeine. The university is known for a variety of undergraduate and graduate programs, is a considerable force in regional athletics, and serves as a cultural center for the southern Wasatch area.

Heading up BYU attractions is a quartet of museums. The **Museum of Fine Arts** opened in 1994. The museum's collection of over 14,000 objects is anchored by its large number of works by American artists. Utah artists are represented by work from the Mormon pioneer era to the present. Rembrandt, Monet, and Rubens are also in the collection along with some fine Far Eastern selections. *North Campus Dr.,* ☎ *801/378–2787.* ☛ *Free.* ⊙ *Daily 9–9.*

The **Monte L. Bean Life Science Museum** includes exhibits on wildlife from around the world plus live reptile displays. *E. of Marriott Center,* ☎ *801/378–5051.* ☛ *Free.* ⊙ *Tues.–Sat. 10–5.*

The **Earth Sciences Museum** features dinosaur bones, fossils, and various hands-on activities. *Across from Cougar Stadium,* ☎ *801/378–3680.* ☛ *Free.* ⊙ *Mon. 9–9, Tues.–Fri. 9–5, Sat. noon–4.*

The **Museum of Peoples and Cultures** is an interesting collection of artifacts relating to cultures from all over the earth. *700 N. 100 East St.,* ☎ *801/378–6112.* ☛ *Free.* ⊙ *Weekdays 9–5.*

One other museum of interest in Provo is the **McCurdy Historical Doll Museum.** Covering global themes, this collection of more than 3,000 dolls was started by Laura McCurdy Clark. The facility includes a doll hospital (for repairs) and a gift shop. *246 N. 100 East St.,* ☎ *801/377–9935.* ☛ *$2 adults, $1 children.* ⊙ *Jan.–Apr., Tues.–Sat. 1–5; May–Dec., Tues.–Sat. noon–6.*

㊷ South of Provo in **Springville,** known for its support of the arts, is a stop that's a must for fine-arts fans: the **Springville Museum of Art.** Beginning as a warehouse for works produced at the local high school, the museum later began to accept gifts from major artists. The present facility was built in 1937 and features mostly works by Utahns. *126 E. 400 South, St.,* ☎ *801/489–2727.* ☛ *Free.* ⊙ *Tues.–Sat. 10–5, Sun. 2–5.*

Continuing south on I–15, you will soon leave behind the more populated area of the state for more rural surroundings. Towering over this area is Mt. Nebo, which at 11,877 feet is the tallest peak in the Wasatch Range. The 43-mile **Nebo Loop Scenic Byway** circles east of the summit to access both impressive panoramas and some alluring hiking trails. A ¼-mile walk leads to the Devil's Kitchen Geologic Area, a collection of strangely eroded spires and ridges.

The Nebo Loop Scenic Byway returns to I–15 at Nephi, a small town that provides basic services. To complete the final leg of this tour, however, follow Route 132 east and south to U.S. 89 and the small but colorful towns of **Sanpete County.** Nicknamed "Little Denmark," Sanpete County was settled mainly by Mormon pioneers of Scandinavian extraction. The county seat, **Manti,** is Sanpete's largest community and one of Utah's oldest, established in 1849. Several buildings date back more than a century, including the Manti Temple, completed in 1888. The town of **Ephraim** is home to Snow College, a two-year institution that also dates to 1888; several historic buildings; and turkey farms. Nearly all of nearby **Spring City** is listed on the National Register of Historic Places.

Because the Wasatch Mountains reach their southern terminus in the area around Mt. Nebo, Sanpete County marks the end of this tour. To return to Salt Lake City, either backtrack on I–15 or follow U.S. 89 north to Spanish Fork, just south of Provo. On U.S. 89 near Thistle, a ghost town, watch for a view of the **landslide** that caused considerable damage in 1983. A new stretch of highway was subsequently built around the slide, and an interpretive sign describes the event in some detail.

What to See and Do with Children

The **Alpine Slide** (1345 Lowell Ave., Park City, ☎ 801/647–5333) is a big attraction during the summer at the Park City Ski Area. Kids of all ages can fly down the curving track on a sled that is easy to control.

Camp Snowbird provides summer activities for children to enjoy without their parents. An array of day camps include hiking, tennis, swimming, panning for gold, nature studies, and guest speakers. *Snowbird,* ☎ *801/742–2222. Prices start at $38 for a full day.* ۞ *Memorial Day–Labor Day. Reservations advised.*

Children's Theatre features outdoor musicals performed especially for children. *Sundance Resort, Sundance,* ☎ *801/225–4107 or 800/892–1600.* ☛ *$6 adults, $4 children under 13.* ۞ *Mid-June–early Sept.*

Calling itself the largest amusement park between Kansas City and the West Coast, **Lagoon** includes all of the rides and attractions you'd expect, plus the adjacent Lagoon-A-Beach water park. In operation for over a century, Lagoon is a Utah landmark. *375 N. Lagoon Dr., Farmington,* ☎ *801/451–8000.* ☛ *$21 adults, $16 children (including full-day ride pass).* ۞ *Memorial Day–Labor Day, 11 am–midnight.*

Seven Peaks Resort Water Park includes 26 acres of waterborne fun. *E. Center St., Provo,* ☎ *801/373–8777.* ☛ *$13 adults, $10 children 4–12.* ۞ *Mid-May–Labor Day, 10:30–8:30.*

Off the Beaten Track

For a bit of the beach (minus the water, of course), travel west from Nephi to the **Little Sahara Recreation Area.** Originating as sandbars in Lake Bonneville, these expansive sand dunes have moved 150 miles in the 10,000 years since the lake receded. Although much of this 20,000-acre sandbox is popular with off-road vehicle enthusiasts, the BLM has established three campgrounds and an area especially for children. Some 9,000 acres in the western portion of the recreation area have been set aside as a nature preserve. ☎ *801/743–6811.* ☛ *$5 per vehicle.*

Shopping

Shopping Streets/Malls

In **Ogden,** east of the train depot, **25th Street** first served as a center for immigrants before becoming the town's shadiest avenue in the 1870s. Today the historic street is a shopping district. Behind the old brick fronts that once housed gambling halls, saloons, opium dens, and the like is a variety of antiques shops, gift boutiques, and restaurants.

Within the colorful structures that line **Main Street** in **Park City** are a number of clothing boutiques, sporting goods stores, and gift shops. Check out **Wyoming Woolens** (518 Main St., ☎ 801/645–9427) for regional favorites in stylish outdoor clothing and **Christmas on Main Street** (442 Main St., ☎ 801/645–8115) for a year-round supply of ornaments.

A few miles north of Park City, next to I–80, are the **Factory Stores at Park City** (6699 North Landmark Dr., ☎ 801/645–7078). Represented in this collection of 48 outlets are Nike, Brooks Brothers, Eddie Bauer, and Corning, among others.

Specialty Stores
CATALOGUE STORES
The General Store (Sundance Resort, ☎ 801/225–4107) features distinctive home furnishings, clothing, and jewelry reflecting the Sundance ethic and taste. The shop is home base for the award-winning Sundance catalogue.

SPORTING GOODS
When in Rome, do as the Romans do, and when you're in Park City, you visit **Jan's Mountain Outfitters** (1600 Park Ave., ☎ 801/649–4949) to pick up skiing, bicycling, camping, and fly-fishing gear. It carries everything you need to get out the door and into the woods.

Sports and the Outdoors
Cycling
There are countless bike routes, both on and off the pavement, along the Wasatch Mountains. Many trails access the higher reaches of the Wasatch-Cache National Forest from **Alta.** The trail over Katherine Pass will put you at the head of Big Cottonwood Canyon at the Brighton Ski Area. Down the road at **Snowbird,** off-road cyclists are discovering that ski slopes make for some excellent riding.

Around **Logan,** road cyclists will enjoy heading out into scenic Cache Valley on country roads or up Logan and Blacksmith Fork canyons. Mountain bikers can enjoy the 7-mile ride to White Pine Lake near the Mt. Naomi Wilderness Area or the strenuous climb to the top of Logan Peak.

Several mountain bike trails are accessible from the Guardsman Pass Road in **Park City.** Deer Valley Ski Resort runs one of its lifts in the summer to facilitate fun descents by bike.

In the **Provo** area, road cyclists may make a 100-mile circumnavigation of Utah Lake or tackle the Alpine Loop Scenic Byway. Farther to the south, near **Nephi,** they can tackle laborious grades of the Nebo Loop Scenic Byway.

Camping
Across the Wasatch-Cache and Uinta national forests are a number of wonderful campgrounds. Between **Big and Little Cottonwood canyons** there are four higher-elevation camping facilities. Of the nine facilities in **Logan Canyon,** Guinavah-Malibu and Tony Grove campgrounds are the nicest. Near **Nephi** a pair of campgrounds are found along the Nebo Loop Scenic Byway. All 11 campgrounds in the Huntsville area up **Ogden Canyon** offer swimming and fishing. In the **Provo** area, American Fork, Provo Canyon, and the Hobble Creek drainage hold dozens of possibilities. In **Sanpete County,** most campground facilities are found to the east in the Manti–La Sal National Forest (☎ 801/259–7155 for information). Additional campgrounds await visitors at the region's state parks and national monuments (*see* the Exploring sections, *above,* and State Parks, *below*) and at the Little Sahara Recreation Area (*see* Off the Beaten Track, *above*).

Canoeing
Although you can canoe on virtually any body of water in the region, the best places include **Tony Grove Lake** in Logan Canyon (*see* Exploring the Northern Wasatch Mountains, *above*) and the **Bear River,** northwest of Logan. Winding in serpentine fashion through Cache Valley, the Bear River features several nice stretches, including a particularly satisfying one that runs 11 miles from Amalga to Tremonton. Canoeists

pass a blue heron rookery along the way, so this is a good float for bird-watchers.

Fishing

Good fishing can be found at the following locations: **Bear Lake;** the **Logan** and **Blacksmith Fork rivers,** outside Logan; **Willard Bay** and **Pineview Reservoir,** near Ogden; and **Deer Creek Reservoir,** northeast of Provo.

Golf

The Wasatch Mountains are home to a variety of spectacular courses, some municipally owned and all with a wealth of natural scenery. Eighteen holes are found at **Ben Lomond Golf Course** (1600 N. 500 West St., Ogden, ☎ 801/782–7754); **Homestead Golf Course** (700 N. Homestead Dr., Midway, ☎ 801/654–1102 or 800/327–7200); **Logan River Municipal Golf Course** (1000 S. U.S. 89/91, Logan, ☎ 801/750–9877); **Park City Municipal Golf Course** (1451 Thaynes Canyon Dr., Park City, ☎ 801/649–8701); **Park Meadows Golf Club** (2000 Meadows Dr., Park City, ☎ 801/649–2460); **Wasatch Mountain State Park** (1281 Warm Springs Dr., Midway, ☎ 801/654–0532); and **Wolf Creek Resort** (3900 N. Wolf Creek Dr., Eden, ☎ 801/745–3365). In addition, there is a nine-hole course at **Bear Lake Golf Course** (Garden City, ☎ 801/946–3306), and there are 27 holes at **East Bay Golf Course** (1860 S. East Bay Blvd., Provo, ☎ 801/377–2042).

Hiking

Several trails originating at **Alta** climb to the surrounding peaks. The trail to Katherine Pass is relatively easy and quite scenic. Down the canyon from **Snowbird** is the trailhead for the Red Pine Lake and White Pine Lake trails. Located 3½ and 5 miles in, respectively, these mountain lakes make for great day hikes.

There is wonderful hiking in the **Cache Valley/Logan Canyon** area. Of the trails that access the Mt. Naomi Wilderness Area northeast of Logan, a good pick is the 3-mile route from Tony Grove Lake to the summit of Naomi Peak. The Limber Pine Trail is a popular and easy hike (1-mile round-trip) at the summit between Logan Canyon and Bear Lake. In the Wellsville Mountains, a 2-mile trail climbs steeply from Maple Bench to Stewart Pass, a lofty ridge top with a spectacular view.

A challenging 6-mile route climbs **Mt. Nebo** from a trailhead along the Nebo Loop Scenic Byway. It is administered by the Uinta National Forest.

The best trails in **Provo Canyon** take off from the Alpine Loop Scenic Byway. The 9-mile Timpooneke Trail and the 8-mile Aspen Trail both reach the summit of Mt. Timpanogos.

Skiing

Alta (Box 8007, Alta 84092, ☎ 801/742–3333) is noted for both steep runs and ski-where-you-please openness. From the lifts to lodging, everything here is unpretentious. Fortunately, so is the price. Where other major ski resorts will charge upward of $40 for a lift ticket, Alta comes in at nearly half that rate (*see* Alta/Snowbird *in* Chapter 2, Special-Interest Vacations: Winter).

With 850 and 1,100 skiable acres, respectively, **Brighton** (Brighton Ski Resort, Brighton 84121, ☎ 801/532–4731 or 800/873–5512) and **Solitude** (Solitude Ski Resort, Box 21350, Salt Lake City 84121, ☎ 801/534–1400) are roughly half the size of Alta and Snowbird, but they still offer the same fluffy powder that has made Utah skiing so exemplary. Because these resorts are less crowded, locals often purchase their season passes here and save the bigger resorts for special occasions.

Opening its slopes in 1981, **Deer Valley** (Box 3149, Park City 84060, ☏ 801/649–1000 or 800/424–3337), just south of Park City, broke new ground in the ski industry by providing such amenities as ski valets, on-slope telephones, grooming fit for a king, and slope-side dining of the highest caliber. For such pampering, the resort has won rave reviews from virtually every ski and travel magazine. Bonus: For these added touches you pay only about $3 extra for a lift ticket. Because Deer Valley has elevated grooming to an art, don't come looking for extreme terrain.

Front and center in Park City is the **Park City Ski Area** (Box 39, Park City 84060, ☏ 801/649–8111 or 800/222–7275), Utah's largest ski area. Featuring 89 trails and 650 acres of open bowls, the mountain is accessed by 13 chairlifts (three of which are high-speed quads) and a four-passenger gondola. Roughly half of Park City's terrain is rated as intermediate, but the slopes that line Jupiter Mountain are revered by experts as well. Snowmaking covers 375 acres, and night skiers will delight in Pay Day, the longest artificially lighted run in the Rockies. If you want to ski Park City but your youngsters do not, **Professional Sitters' Service** (Box 1673, Park City 84060, ☏ 801/649–0946), a bonded and licensed service, will dispatch mature, well-trained care providers to your hotel room for $10 per hour for the first child and $1 for each extra child.

Park City's third ski area, **Wolf Mountain** (4000 Park West Dr., Park City, 84060, ☏ 801/649–5400 or 800/754–1636), is a bit smaller than the others and has struggled with financial problems in years past. Under new ownership, Wolf Mountain is a challenging yet inexpensive alternative to Utah's larger ski areas. As the only Park City mountain that allows snowboarding, it is especially popular among younger crowds. The ski area includes a vertical drop of 2,200 feet (equal to that of Deer Valley) and is serviced by seven double chairlifts.

Rising north of Ogden Canyon's Pineview Reservoir is **Powder Mountain** (Box 450, Eden 84310, ☏ 801/745–3772). As the name suggests, Powder Mountain receives a generous helping of the white stuff for which Utah is known. It offers just under 2,000 vertical feet, five chairlifts, and three surface tows. Skiable acreage totals 1,600, and night skiing is an option 4:30–10. Four slope-side eateries provide après-ski diversions.

With a vertical drop of 2,400 feet, **Snowbasin** (Box 460, Huntsville 84317, ☏ 801/399–1135) is ready to host the downhill ski races at the 2002 Winter Olympics. With five chairlifts accessing some 1,800 acres of skiable terrain, this is northern Utah's largest ski hill. Only 17 miles from Ogden, Snowbasin has no base area accommodations.

Snowbird (Snowbird Ski and Summer Resort, Snowbird 84092, ☏ 801/742–2222 or 800/453–3000) has plenty of powder-filled chutes, bowls, and meadow areas. Like its neighbor, Alta, it's known for its expert runs; 50% of Snowbird is black diamond terrain. In contrast, however, an extra $15 for a lift ticket will get you the speed, convenience, and impressive vertical drop (2,900 feet in one fell swoop) that only Snowbird's 125-passenger aerial tram can provide (*see* Alta/Snowbird *in* Chapter 2, Special-Interest Vacations: Winter).

Winter visitors to the **Sundance Resort** (R.R. 3, Box A-1, Sundance 84604, ☎ 801/225–4107 or 800/892–1600) will find 41 runs across 450 acres of terrain and four lifts that access the mountain's 2,150 vertical feet.

Water Sports

Water-sports enthusiasts will find a surprising number of places to boat, windsurf, waterski, and sail. The most popular of these are accessed by state park facilities. They include **Bear Lake, Willard Bay, Pineview Reservoir, Rockport Reservoir, Deer Creek Reservoir, Hyrum Reservoir,** and **Utah Lake** (*see* Exploring sections, *above*, and State Parks, *below*).

State Parks

In addition to those listed in the Exploring sections above, there are a number of state parks in the Wasatch.

Bear Lake State Park (2 mi north of Garden City on U.S. 89, ☎ 801/946–3343 or 800/322–3770), one of three state parks on the lake, contains a marina, beach, picnic area, campground, and visitor center.

Deer Creek State Park (11 mi northeast of Provo on U.S. 189, ☎ 801/654–0171) is popular with anglers and boaters.

East Canyon State Park (5535 S. Rte. 66, Morgan, ☎ 801/829–6866) is on a 680-acre reservoir in the mountains northeast of Salt Lake City.

Eastside State Park (10 mi north of Laketown) is another of Bear Lake's parks. Because the lake bottom drops off quickly here, this site is a favorite among anglers and scuba divers. Facilities include a primitive campground and boat ramp.

Hyrum State Park (405 W. 300 South St., in the northwest corner of Hyrum, ☎ 801/245–6866) features boating on a 450-acre reservoir.

Palisade State Park (southeast of Manti off U.S. 89, ☎ 801/835–7275) has a small reservoir and nine-hole golf course.

Rendezvous Beach State Park (Rte. 30, near Laketown) is on the south shore of Bear Lake and has more than a mile of sandy beaches, three campgrounds, and picnic areas. Getting its name from the mountain-man gatherings that took place here in 1827 and 1828, Rendezvous Beach hosts a reenactment of the events each September.

Rockport State Park (9040 N. Rte. 302, Peoa, 7 mi south of Wanship on Rte. 32, ☎ 801/336–2241) is northeast of Park City and is quite nice for boating and fishing. There are nine campgrounds.

Utah Lake State Park (4400 W. Center St., Provo, ☎ 801/375–0731) is the best access point for Utah's largest freshwater lake. In addition to a boat ramp, campgrounds, picnic areas, and a marina, the park has an ice-skating rink in the winter and a wheelchair-accessible fishing area.

Wasatch Mountain State Park (1281 Warmsprings Dr., off Rte. 224, Midway, ☎ 801/654–1791) is known for its 27-hole golf course but also offers hiking and riding trails in the summer and Nordic skiing in the winter. It is Utah's largest state park.

Dining and Lodging

Alta

DINING

$$ The Shallow Shaft. For fine beef, seafood, poultry, and pasta dishes, Alta's only base-area sit-down restaurant that is not part of a lodging property is the place to go. Homemade pizza is also served, as is liquor. ✕ *Across from the Alta Peruvian,* ☎ *801/742–2177. Reservations advised. D, MC, V.*

LODGING

$$$$ **Alta Peruvian Lodge.** Comfortably rustic is the best way to describe
★   the Alta Peruvian. Guest rooms range from simple dormitory style to two-bedroom suites. Breakfast, lunch, and dinner at the in-house restaurant are included in all lodging packages. Combine this American meal plan with complimentary lift tickets and you have one-stop shopping—Alta style. ⌧ *Box 8017, Alta 84092,* ☎ *801/742–3000 or 800/453–8488,* ⅂⅄ *801/742–3007. 80 rooms, 25 rooms with shared bath. Restaurant, bar, pool, hot tub, coin laundry. AE, D, MC, V.*

$$$$ **Rustler Lodge.** Offering some of Alta's most elegant rooms, this property has nice furnishings such as sofas and seating areas in deluxe rooms and a pleasant atmosphere. As at all of Alta's lodges, breakfast and dinner are included in the price. Choose from dorms to one-bedroom suites. ⌧ *Box 8030, Alta 84092,* ☎ *801/742–2200 or 800/451–5223,* ⅂⅄ *801/742–3832. 56 rooms, 47 with baths. Restaurant, bar, pool, hot tub, coin laundry. AE, DC, MC, V.*

Bear Lake

LODGING

$$ **Inn of the Three Bears at Bear Lake.** This quaint, turn-of-the-century abode features comfortable accommodations in a wonderfully rural setting. It's a five-minute walk from the front door to Bear Lake. A complimentary Continental breakfast is included. ⌧ *135 S. Bear Lake Blvd., Garden City 84028,* ☎ *801/946–8590. 3 rooms. Hot tub. MC, V.*

Logan

DINING

$$ **Gia's Italian Restaurant.** Upstairs you will find sit-down service and carefully prepared Italian dishes. Downstairs, in the Factory, the service is strictly cafeteria style, the food includes pizza and sandwiches, and the atmosphere is lively. As any college student will tell you, the basement is where you go to meet friends for a beer, while upstairs is reserved for entertaining a date or parents. ✕ *119 S. Main St.,* ☎ *801/752–8384. AE, MC, V.*

$ **Bluebird Restaurant.** A favorite dining spot in downtown Logan for decades, this restaurant serves steak, seafood, and such standbys as prime rib in a setting that's straight out of a Norman Rockwell painting. It's also known for its chocolates. ✕ *19 N. Main St.,* ☎ *801/752–3155. AE, D, MC, V.*

LODGING

$$ **Center Street Bed & Breakfast.** This wonderful B&B on Logan's most
★   prestigious historic boulevard is actually three separate buildings on one city lot: the 22-room mansion that dates to the late 1800s; the Carriage House; and the White House. Guest rooms range from smaller models to full suites, each with a different decor. Honeymooners enjoy the Garden Suite, but travelers may find the Arabian Nights Suite, the Jungle Bungalow, or Aphrodite's Court more inviting. A Continental breakfast is included, and there is no smoking in the rooms. ⌧ *169 E. Center St., 84321,* ☎ *801/752–3443. 17 rooms. Hot tub. AE, MC, V.*

$ **Baugh Best Western Motel.** These basic yet comfortable accommodations are one of the best deals in town. Because it is locally owned, the service is personable. ⌧ *153 S. Main St., 84321,* ☎ *801/752–5220 or*

800/462–4145, FAX 801/462–4154. *78 rooms. Restaurant, pool. AE, D, DC, MC, V.*

Manti

LODGING

$$ **Manti House Inn Bed & Breakfast.** This 1880 home was built by the same workers who built the Manti Temple. Known as the McAllister House, the inn is now a state historic site. Breakfast is included, and, for snacks, there is an ice-cream parlor on the premises. Rooms are no-smoking. ☎ *401 N. Main St., 84642,* ☎ *801/835–0161. 7 rooms. Hot tub, exercise room. AE, MC, V.*

Midway

DINING AND LODGING

$$$$ **The Homestead.** The Homestead combines the facilities of a complete
★ resort with the charm of a country inn. The centerpiece is a natural hot spring that was first developed in 1886 as an inn and restaurant. An expansion in 1952 turned the property into a rustic yet elegant year-round resort. In addition to a soak in the hot spring, you can enjoy a championship golf course, cross-country ski touring, hot-air ballooning, snowmobiling, and exceptionally fine dining. At Simon's, an up-scale restaurant on the premises (reservations required, $$$), the menu includes such dishes as crab cakes with a shrimp sauté, rack of lamb, and breast of duck, all meticulously prepared and served. ☎ *700 N. Homestead Dr., 84049,* ☎ *801/654–1102 or 800/327–7220,* FAX *801/654–5785. 120 rooms. 2 restaurants, bar, pool, hot tub, sauna, 18-hole golf course, 2 tennis courts, exercise room, horseback riding, cross-country skiing, convention center . AE, D, DC, MC, V.*

Nephi

LODGING

$ **Whitmore Mansion Bed & Breakfast.** Built at the turn of the century, this opulent Queen Anne–style home is now listed on the National Register of Historic Places. Antiques and fine woodwork add to its charm. Breakfast is complimentary, and there is no smoking in the rooms. ☎ *110 S. Main St., 84648,* ☎ *801/623–2047. 6 rooms. Breakfast room. MC, V.*

Ogden

DINING

$$$ **Gray Cliff Lodge Restaurant.** Set in scenic Ogden Canyon, this local favorite features Utah trout, prime rib, lamb, and seafood as well as great atmosphere. ✕ *508 Ogden Canyon,* ☎ *801/392–6775. Reservations advised. DC, MC, V.*

$$ **Prairie Schooner.** The atmosphere might be overkill for some, but it's fun nevertheless. Steaks, prime rib, and seafood are served in a re-created Western setting; each table is enclosed in a covered wagon. Underneath it all, however, the food is good. ✕ *445 Park Blvd.,* ☎ *801/392–2712. AE, D, DC, MC, V.*

$ **Lee's Mongolian Barbecue.** In a simple setting, the purely ethnic (and occasionally spicy) fare reflects both Mongolian and Mandarin roots. The food is as exotic as the way in which it is prepared. After selecting your ingredients, you hand over your dish to the chef, who stir-fries the meal before your eyes on a large hot plate. ✕ *2866 Washington Blvd.,* ☎ *801/621-9120. MC, V.*

LODGING

$$$ **Radisson Suite Hotel Ogden.** Combining the luxurious suites for which
★ Radisson is known with the allure of a historic downtown building, this hotel is one of Ogden's most visually important structures and is

listed on the National Register of Historic Places. In addition to its elegant rooms, the hand-painted ceiling tiles and chandeliers in the lobby area are worth a look. A full breakfast and cocktails are included. ⚎ *2510 Washington Blvd., 84401,* ☎ *801/627–1900 or 800/333–3333,* ⅏ *801/394–5342. 144 rooms. Restaurant, bar, hot tub, exercise room. AE, D, DC, MC, V.*

$$ **Snowberry Inn.** Overlooking Pineview Reservoir in the Wasatch Mountains above Ogden, this cozy bed-and-breakfast is everything a rural B&B should be. The rooms are rustic yet comfortable, and the breakfast is complete and country good. The inn is near three ski areas. ⚎ *1315 N. Rte. 158, Eden 84310,* ☎ *801/745–2634. 5 rooms. Hot tub, coin laundry. MC, V.*

$ **Best Western High Country Inn.** Conveniently located near I–15, this motel is spacious and comfortable. A recent upgrading in spring 1995 spruced up the facilities with a decor done in maroons and greens. ⚎ *1335 W. 12th St., 84404,* ☎ *801/394–9474 or 800/594–8979,* ⅏ *801/392–6589. 111 rooms. Restaurant, pool, hot tub, exercise room, coin laundry. AE, DC, MC, V.*

Park City

DINING

$$$$ **Glitretind.** A source of Deer Valley's unsurpassed reputation in
★ ski-resort dining, this fabulous restaurant is worth breaking open the piggy bank for. Selections include various seafood, beef, and poultry dishes, which are prepared with a creative selection of ingredients. How does saffron sauce and Caspian caviar with your New England lobster sound? Or what about grilled chicken breast stuffed with goat cheese? This is the stuff that travel, food, and ski magazines rave about when Deer Valley is the topic of discussion. ✕ *Stein Eriksen Lodge, Deer Valley,* ☎ *801/645–6455. Reservations advised. AE, DC, MC, V.*

$$ **Café Terigo.** This airy café serves several well-prepared pasta and
★ seafood dishes using only fresh ingredients. Good picks include chicken tequila pasta and ginger coconut prawns. Be sure to top your meal off with a helping of bread pudding or mud pie. ✕ *424 Main St.,* ☎ *801/645–9555. AE, DC, MC, V.*

$ **The Eating Establishment.** The menu at this Main Street mainstay fea-
★ tures homemade soups, sandwiches, burgers and ribs, and a variety of breakfast foods—from *huevos rancheros* (Mexican eggs) to lox and bagels—served all day. ✕ *317 Main St.,* ☎ *801/649–8284. No reservations. AE, MC, V.*

LODGING

$$$$ **Washington School Inn.** Although it is hard to imagine an old school-
★ house making a great bed-and-breakfast, this circa 1890 inn proves that it can be done. The exterior of this three-story stone structure was carefully restored, and the inside was completely gutted to make way for the guest rooms, kitchen, and common areas. Each room is appointed with Victorian-era furnishings and down pillows and comforters. Of course, breakfast is included. ⚎ *543 Park Ave., Box 536, 84060,* ☎ *801/649–3800 or 800/824–1672,* ⅏ *801/649–3802. 15 rooms. Hot tub, sauna, laundry room. AE, D, MC, V.*

$$$ **Olympia Park Resort Hotel.** As one of Park City's largest, this hotel includes a full array of amenities. On the premises are two popular restaurants plus a nice atrium area with pool. A free breakfast is offered. ⚎ *1895 Sidewinder Dr., Box 4439, 84060,* ☎ *801/649–2900 or 800/234–9003,* ⅏ *801/649–4852. 226 rooms. 2 restaurants, bar, indoor pool, hot tub, sauna, exercise room. AE, D, DC, MC, V.*

$$$ **Shadow Ridge Resort.** Few other hotels in town can match the Shadow Ridge for convenience and comfort. Just a few feet from the Park City Resort Center, you can amble to the slopes in less time than it takes to warm up your car. Accommodations range from a single hotel room to a two-bedroom condominium suite. With full kitchens, these suites are a sweet deal for families. All rooms are attractively furnished, and the staff is friendly and experienced. ☎ *50 Shadow Ridge St., Box 1820, 84060,* ☎ *801/649–4300 or 800/451–3031,* FAX *801/649–5951. 150 rooms. Restaurant, bar, pool, hot tub, sauna, coin laundry. AE, DC, MC, V.*

$$ **Best Western Landmark Inn.** Out by the interstate, this property makes a great stopover for travelers. The rooms are nicely furnished, and the location is convenient for those visitors splitting their time between Park City and Salt Lake. ☎ *6560 N. Landmark Dr., 84060,* ☎ *801/649–7300 or 800/548–8824,* FAX *801/649–1760. 106 rooms. Restaurant, indoor pool, hot tub, exercise room, coin laundry. AE, D, DC, MC, V.*

Provo
DINING

$$ **Magelby's.** Steaks, seafood, and chicken are served in a European ambience. ✕ *1675 N. 200 West St.,* ☎ *801/374–6249. AE, D, MC, V. Closed Sun.*

$$ **Peking House Restaurant.** Provo has a large number of Asian restaurants. If you're looking for Szechuan, this is the place to try. ✕ *138 W. Center St.,* ☎ *801/377–3323. AE, MC, V. Closed Sun.*

$ **Brick Oven.** Cooking up what many consider to be the best pizza in town, this restaurant also offers sandwiches and pasta as well as a salad bar. ✕ *150 E. 800 North St.,* ☎ *801/374–8800. AE, D, MC, V. Closed Sun.*

LODGING

$$ **Holiday Inn Provo.** Like other Holiday Inns, this one has clean and comfortable rooms plus an array of facilities. ☎ *1460 S. University Ave. 84601,* ☎ *801/374–9750 or 800/465–4329,* FAX *801/377–1615. 78 rooms. Restaurant, pool, laundry facilities. AE, D, DC, MC, V.*

$$ **Provo Park Hotel.** A large facility, this hotel is close to the downtown area and includes an expansive water park. ☎ *101 W. 100 North St., 84601,* ☎ *801/377–4700 or 800/777–7144,* FAX *801/377–4708. 233 rooms. Restaurant, pool, hot tub, sauna, exercise room. AE, D, DC, MC, V.*

Snowbird
DINING

$$$ **Aerie.** In what may just be Utah's most scenic dining spot, this restau-
★ rant serves sumptuous seafood, beef, and poultry dishes. In keeping with the elegance of its 10th-floor setting, much attention is paid to preparation and presentation. There is a sushi bar, and drinks are available to members of the Club at Snowbird. (Upon checking in at the Cliff Lodge, you may purchase drinking rights at this and other Snowbird restaurants for $5.) Even if you are staying for only one night, it's worth dining here simply to be able to select from the impressive wine list. ✕ *Top floor of Cliff Lodge,* ☎ *801/742–2222, ext. 5500. Reservations advised. AE, D, DC, MC, V.*

LODGING

$$$$ **Cliff Lodge.** To some, this 10-story structure with bare concrete walls
★ initially looks a bit bland, but it doesn't take long to realize that the

real beauty of its design is that it blends nicely with the surrounding scenery. The rooms in this large hotel are very nice—done mainly in mountain colors and desert pastels. Wonderful views are to be found from every window, and service is friendly and helpful. Even in summer, guests may use the Cliff Spa, on the top two floors, with its rooftop pool, massage rooms, hot tubs, and steam rooms. In addition, you have your choice of several fine restaurants in the Snowbird base area with the "Club at Snowbird" card given to guests upon registration. This is one of the finest ski resort accommodations in the Rocky Mountains. ⌂ *Snowbird Ski and Summer Resort, 84092,* ☎ *801/521– 6040 or 800/453–3000,* ℻ *801/742–3204. 532 rooms. 4 restaurants, 4 bars, 2 pools, beauty salon, 2 hot tubs, sauna, spa, 3 tennis courts, exercise room, coin laundry, laundry service and dry cleaning, babysitting, children's programs (ages 3-13), convention center, meeting rooms. AE, D, DC, MC, V.*

Sundance

DINING

$$$
★

The Tree Room. In addition to serving up great Continental cuisine, this restaurant has a special ambience. The place is filled with exquisite Native American art and Western memorabilia collected by Robert Redford. The man does have good taste. ✕ *Sundance Resort,* ☎ *801/225–4107. Reservations advised. AE, DC, MC, V.*

LODGING

$$$$
★

The Sundance Cottages. Ranging in size from one to three bedrooms, these self-sufficient cottages lie in an appealing forest setting. Units feature natural wood trim, rock fireplaces, decks, and handmade furniture. This is a great getaway place, especially in summer. ⌂ *R.R. 3, Box A-1, 84604,* ☎ *801/225–4107 or 800/892–1600,* ℻ *801/226– 1937. 50 cottages. Restaurant, bar. AE, DC, MC, V.*

The Arts

Logan

Thanks to both the presence of Utah State University and the community's keen interest in the arts, Logan is home to many fine productions. USU's theater and music departments host a variety of exciting performances. In downtown Logan, the **Ellen Eccles Theatre** (43 S. Main St., ☎ 801/752–0026) benefits from a 1993 refurbishing and performances by the **Utah Festival Opera Company,** formed in 1993. The **Lyric Theatre** (28 W. Center St., ☎ 801/797–3046) features performances by the university's repertory company.

Ogden

The **Eccles Community Art Center** (2580 Jefferson Ave., ☎ 801/392– 6935) displays a permanent art collection plus special showings in an impressive Victorian mansion. **Weber State University** (3750 Harrison Blvd., ☎ 801/626–6000) regularly offers theater, music, and dance performances by students and visiting artists at the **Val A. Browning Center for the Performing Arts.**

Park City

Park City hosts a variety of performing arts events throughout the summer. The **Park City International Chamber Music Festival** (☎ 801/649–5309) runs for several weeks. The historic **Egyptian Theatre** (328 Main St., ☎ 801/649–9371), in downtown Park City, stages many different plays. Deer Valley Resort's outdoor **Summer Concert Series** (☎ 801/649–1000) includes everything from classical to country music.

Provo

Because **Brigham Young University** (☎ 801/378–4636) has a considerable interest in the arts, Provo is a great place to catch a play, dance performance, or musical production. There are a dozen performing groups in all. Of special note are the BYU International Folk Dancers and Ballroom Dancers.

Snowbird

As part of the **Snowbird Institute for the Arts and Humanities** (☎ 801/742–2222, ext. 4150), the resort puts on a variety of musical and dance events throughout the summer. Included are performances by the **Ririe-Woodbury Dance Company,** a **String Chamber Music Festival,** and several **artist-in-residence programs.**

Sundance

Held under the auspices of the Sundance Institute (☎ 801/225–4107 or 800/892–1600), the **Sundance Film Festival** is a renowned showcase for independent filmmakers. It takes place at Sundance and in Park City in January. Sundance Resort also hosts the **Sundance Summer Theatre** from mid-June through early September. Broadway musicals are staged in a spectacular outdoor theater.

Nightlife

In the northern reaches of the state, there are plenty of places to cut loose and have fun. At Snowbird, you can join the **"Club at Snowbird"** and enjoy a drink at any of several lounges spread about the base area. Park City features such lively bars as **Cicero's** (306 Main St., ☎ 801/649–6800) and **Sneakers** (1200 Little Kate Rd., ☎ 801/649–7742).

The Wasatch Mountains Essentials

Arriving and Departing

BY BUS

Greyhound Lines (☎ 800/231–2222) serves many towns along the Wasatch Front: Tremonton, Logan, Brigham City, Ogden, and Provo. In addition, the **Utah Transit Authority** (*see* Getting Around by Bus, *below*) connects Salt Lake City to many spots in the area.

BY CAR

If you're driving into the area, chances are you'll be coming on either I–15 or I–80. Even if you fly into Salt Lake City, it's a good idea to rent a car at the airport and drive to the section of the Wasatch you want to visit.

BY TRAIN

Amtrak (☎ 800/872–7245) has service to both Ogden and Provo.

Getting Around

BY BUS

The **Utah Transit Authority** (☎ 801/287–4636) has frequent service to all of Salt Lake valley, Davis and Weber counties, and Utah Valley. Buses, with ski racks, also make several runs a day to the ski areas in Little and Big Cottonwood canyons.

BY CAR

The main thoroughfare along the Wasatch Mountains is I–15. From this trunk, I–80 heads east toward Park City, U.S. 89 branches to the far north, U.S. 189 runs up Provo Canyon, and Route 132 winds into Sanpete County. Though most of the driving is urban, mountain views are spectacular. Winter visitors should be versed in driving on snowy roads; cars should be equipped with snow tires or chains.

Important Addresses and Numbers

VISITOR INFORMATION

Regional travel offices are **Bridgerland** (160 N. Main St., Logan 84321, ☎ 801/752–2161 or 800/882–4433); **Golden Spike Empire** (2501 Wall Ave., Ogden 84401, ☎ 801/627–8288 or 800/255–8824), **Great Salt Lake Country** (180 S. West Temple St., Salt Lake City 84101, ☎ 801/521–2822 or 800/541–4955); **Mountainland** (2545 N. Canyon Rd., Provo 84604, ☎ 801/377–2262); and **Panorama-land** (250 N. Main St., Box 820, Richfield 84701, ☎ 801/896–9222 or 800/748–4361).

Community information centers include **Brigham City Chamber of Commerce** (6 N. Main St., Brigham City 84302, ☎ 801/723–3931); **Heber Valley County Chamber of Commerce** (475 N. Main St., Heber 84032, ☎ 801/654–3666); **Orem/Provo Chamber of Commerce** (777 S. State St., Orem 84058, ☎ 801/379–2555); **Park City Chamber of Commerce/Convention and Visitors Bureau** (Box 1630, Park City 84060, ☎ 801/649–6100 or 800/453–1360); and **Springville Chamber of Commerce** (175 S. Main St., Springville 84663, ☎ 801/489–4681).

NORTHEASTERN UTAH

With the western portion of Dinosaur National Monument within its borders, northeastern Utah counts the remains of Jurassic giants as its primary attraction. While the monument and related sites explore the lives of long-extinct creatures, the region also showcases some beautiful landscape: colorful slickrock canyons and deserts, a scenic stretch of the Green River, and the Uinta Mountains—Utah's highest mountain range. Add to these natural wonders some Fremont rock art, relics of 19th-century pioneers and outlaws, and a good dose of outdoor recreational activities, and you have a worthwhile tour to a remote corner of the West.

Exploring

Numbers in the margin correspond to points of interest on the Utah map.

From I–80, take U.S. 40 south. Along the way, you'll pass the **Strawberry** and **Starvation reservoirs,** both popular lakes providing a variety of recreational facilities (*see* Other Recreation Areas, *below*), and the towns of **Duchesne** and **Roosevelt.** With a population of 4,000, Roosevelt is the second-largest town on the tour. It was named for President Theodore Roosevelt, who signed a declaration in 1902 allowing whites to settle on Ute lands. The town of Duchesne, 28 miles west, was originally called Theodore, but the community eventually adopted the name of a French nun instead.

Travel north from Duchesne or Roosevelt, and you'll soon cross portions of the **Uinta and Ouray Indian Reservation.** Nearly 1 million acres in size, this sovereign land is spread out across northeastern Utah in several units. Visitors are asked to stay on the main roads, although camping and hiking are allowed with a permit. The tribe hosts the Northern Ute Indian Pow Wow in early July at tribal headquarters in Fort Duchesne (☎ 801/722–5141).

43 Return to U.S. 40, and drive 30 miles northeast from Roosevelt to **Vernal.** The largest town (population 7,500) in this corner of the state, Vernal serves as a hub for visiting the area, which was frequented by mountain man William Ashley in the 1820s and first settled during the 1870s.

Because Vernal was so isolated in its early days, shipping was expensive. One businessman, in order to avoid high freight costs, had a bank facade shipped in brick by brick by U.S. mail. Nicknamed the **Parcel Post Bank,** the 1916 structure still stands and is part of the Zions First National Bank building in downtown Vernal.

Other historic sites in and about Vernal include an 1877 **log post office and store** (1255 W. 2000 North St.) and the old **Oscar Swett Ranch** (½ mi north on U.S. 191). Additionally, three museums feature relics and memorabilia from Vernal's yesteryear. **The Daughters of Utah Pioneers Museum** (158 S. 500 West St.) offers some perspective on what pioneer life was like. The **Thorne Studio** (18 W. Main St., ☎ 801/789–0392) is a private collection of settlement-era firearms, Ute Indian artifacts, and photographs. The recently completed **Western Heritage Museum** (302 E. 200 South St., ☎ 801/789–7399) highlights, among other Old West themes, 19th-century outlaws of the Vernal area.

While Vernal proudly draws attention to its last 150 years of history, the community is especially quick to point out the region's more distant past. Go back 150 million years and this land was the stomping ground of dinosaurs, both large and small. A good place to initiate an investigation is the **Utah Field House of Natural History State Park.** In its museum, numerous rock samples and fossils (including dinosaur bones) are housed; a large mural depicts the last 2.7 billion years of the Uinta Basin's geologic history; and Fremont and Ute artifacts offer insight into the early presence of humans in the area. Outside, the Dinosaur Garden features 14 life-size dinosaur models in a primordial setting. *235 E. Main St.,* ☎ *801/789–3799.* ☛ *$1.50 adults, $1 children 6–15.* ☼ *June–Sept., daily 8 am–9 pm; Oct.–May, daily 9–5.*

With a visit to the Utah Field House under your belt, it's time to visit the focal point of dinosaur mania: **Dinosaur National Monument** park, which straddles the Utah–Colorado border. Located 20 miles east of Vernal are the monument's visitor center and astounding **Dinosaur Quarry,** where, inside a large enclosure, there are some 2,000 dinosaur bones encased in a 200-foot-long sandstone face. This collection of fossils resulted when floods brought the bodies of several dinosaurs to rest on a sandbar; subsequent deposits covered the carcasses where they lay, becoming part of the Morrison Formation. The cache of paleontological treasures was discovered by Earl Douglass in 1909. Today visitors must ride a shuttle bus from the visitor center to the quarry during busy times of the year. *20 mi east of Vernal on Rte. 149. Quarry:* ☎ *801/789–2115.* ☛ *$5 per vehicle.* ☼ *June–Sept., 8–7; Oct.–May, 8–4:30.*

Although most people visit Dinosaur National Monument to see dinosaur bones, this 200,000-acre park also offers a generous supply of alluring backcountry to explore, either on foot or by vehicle. An especially scenic drive runs 6 miles east from the quarry to the **Josie Morris Cabin.** A rugged individualist, Ms. Morris kept company with the likes of Butch Cassidy. For wonderful vistas along the Utah-Colorado border, take the Harpers Corner Road. The drive into Rainbow Park not only passes some impressive Fremont petroglyph panels but also reaches a put-in point for rafters, who will find a variety of white-water thrills on the Green and Yampa rivers (*see* Sports and the Outdoors, *below*).

For more recreational opportunities, return to Vernal and head north on U.S. 191. **Steinaker Lake** and **Red Fleet state parks** (*see* Other Recreation Areas, *below*) both have reservoirs ideally suited for water sports and fishing. Past Red Fleet Reservoir, U.S. 191 begins to ascend the eastern flank of the Uinta uplift. This section of the tour follows what is known as the **Drive through the Ages.** Within a distance of 30 miles, the road passes 19 geologic formations, with signs identifying and describing them. A brochure is available at the Vernal Welcome Center.

U.S. 191 then reaches the truly spectacular **Flaming Gorge National Recreation Area.** Named for its "flaming, brilliant red" color by the explorer John Wesley Powell in 1869, Flaming Gorge was plugged with a 500-foot-high wall of concrete in 1964. The end result is a 90-mile-long reservoir that twists and turns among canyon walls. Although much of the lake stretches north into Wyoming, most facilities lie south of the state line in Utah.

Upon reaching Greendale Junction, 36 miles north of Vernal, stay
45 right on U.S. 191 if you wish to visit the **Flaming Gorge Dam** itself. Displays at the nearby visitor center explain aspects of this engineering marvel, and the dam is open for self-guided tours. ☉ *Memorial Day–Labor Day, daily 9-5.*

If, on the other hand, you turn left on Route 44 at Greendale Junc-
46 tion, you will shortly arrive at the turnoff for the **Red Canyon Visitor Center.** Inside are displays covering the geology, flora and fauna, and human history of the Flaming Gorge area, but the most magnificent thing about the center is its location. Atop a cliff that towers 1,300 feet above the lake, the center provides outstanding views. ☉ *Memorial Day weekend–Sept., daily 9:30-5.*

To conclude the tour, try one of the numerous hiking trails or the scenic drive through the Sheep Creek Canyon Geological Area, which is full of upturned layers of rock. The quickest route to Salt Lake City cuts northwest across Wyoming to I–80, or, of course, you can return the way you came and enjoy the attractions of Northeastern Utah once again.

What to See and Do with Children
Not surprisingly, since Northeastern Utah is chock-full of dinosaurs, it's a good place for traveling with kids. **Dinosaur National Monument** and **Utah Field House of Natural History State Park** (*see* Exploring, *above*) are both good choices for children.

Off the Beaten Track
If visiting the back of beyond is your interest, then drive 40 miles northeast from Vernal to **Browns Park.** Lying along a quieter stretch of the Green River and extending into Colorado, this area features plenty of high desert scenery and a fascinating historic site, the **John Jarvie Ranch** (follow signs off Rte. 191). Operated by the BLM, it includes four original buildings constructed by Scotsman John Jarvie more than a century ago. Because the road into Brown's Park can be rough at times, be sure to check on conditions first.

Sports and the Outdoors

Camping
Campgrounds abound in the **Ashley National Forest** (*see* Other Recreation Areas, *below*) north of Duchesne and Roosevelt and west of Flaming Gorge. (administered by the Ashley National Forest) contains more

than a dozen campgrounds within the Utah portion, including those in the Dutch John and Antelope Flat areas. **Dinosaur National Monument** (Box 210, Dinosaur, CO 81610, ☎ 303/374-2216 or 801/789-2115) has two campgrounds, one near the quarry and the other in a more remote section of the monument.

Fishing

Anglers can try their luck at all of the region's reservoirs, but the best lakes are **Flaming Gorge** and **Starvation reservoirs.** For the best river fishing, experts suggest the **Green River** below the Flaming Gorge Dam. Fed by cold water from the bottom of the lake, this stretch has been identified as one of the best trout fisheries in the world.

Hiking

Numerous trails access the high country of **Ashley National Forest,** the lower deserts of **Dinosaur National Monument,** and the beauty of **Flaming Gorge National Recreation Area.** Check with each for the best bets.

Rafting

White-water enthusiasts find challenging stretches on the **Green** and **Yampa** rivers in **Dinosaur National Monument.** Joining forces near Echo Park, in Colorado, the two waterways have each carved spectacular canyons through several aeons' worth of rock, and they are still at it in rapids like Whirlpool Canyon, SOB, Disaster Falls, and Hell's Half Mile. Day-trippers will enjoy a float down the **Green River** below the **Flaming Gorge Dam.**

Guided river trips are available from **Adrift Adventures** (Box 192, Jensen 84035, ☎ 801/789-3600 or 800/824-0150) and **Hatch River Expeditions** (55 E. Main St., Box 1150, Vernal 84078, ☎ 801/789-4319 or 800/342-8243, FAX 801/789–8513). Trips cost $25 and up.

Water Sports

Boating, waterskiing, and windsurfing are popular at **Flaming Gorge Reservoir, Red Fleet Reservoir, Starvation Reservoir, Steinaker Lake,** and **Strawberry Reservoir.** All feature boat-ramp facilities. At **Flaming Gorge,** three marinas offer boat rentals and supplies: **Cedar Springs Marina** (Box 337, Dutch John 84023, ☎ 801/889–3795), near the dam; **Lucerne Valley Marina** (Box 356, Manila 84046, ☎ 801/784–3483), east of Manila; and the **Buckboard Marina** (Star Rte. 1, Green River, WY 82935, ☎ 307/875–6927) in Wyoming.

Other Recreation Areas

Red Fleet State Park (13 mi north of Vernal off U.S. 191, ☎ 801/789–4432), like the other reservoirs in the region, is great for boat and bait. The real attraction here, though, is the colorful sandstone formations in which the lake is nestled. In addition, a section of 200-million-year-old dinosaur tracks can be reached by a short hike or by boat.

Although **Starvation Reservoir** (4 mi northwest of Duchesne on U.S. 40, ☎ 801/738–2326) is only 3,500 acres, it does have a state park, and anglers successfully cast for walleye, German brown trout, and bass. The waters are a few degrees warmer than those at Strawberry.

Boating and waterskiing enthusiasts will love **Steinaker Lake State Park** (7 mi north of Vernal on U.S. 191, ☎ 801/789–4432). More than 2 miles long, Steinaker Reservoir also relinquishes a fair number of largemouth bass and rainbow trout.

Today the **Strawberry Reservoir** (25 mi south of Heber City on U.S. 40, ☎ 801/654–0470) covers 17,000 acres. Construction on the original reservoir, part of a federal project designed to bring water from the Colorado River basin to the Wasatch Front, began in 1906. In 1973, the Soldier Creek Dam was built downstream, and the original Strawberry Reservoir dam was eventually removed. The result was a much larger storage facility, which boaters and anglers alike now relish. Ice fishing is also popular. Four U.S. Forest Service campgrounds and three marinas dot the lakeshore.

Although the Wasatch may be Utah's best-known mountain range, the **Uinta Mountains,** the only major east–west mountain range in the Rockies, are its tallest, topped by 13,528-foot Kings Peak. Though the mountains lie north of the Uinta and Ouray Indian Reservation, the quickest, easiest (read: paved) route to Uinta country is the Mirror Lake Scenic Byway, which begins in Kamas. The 65-mile drive follows Route 150 into the heavily wooded canyons of the **Wasatch-Cache National Forest** (50 E. Center St., Box 68, Kamas 84118, ☎ 801/783–4338), cresting at 10,687-foot Bald Mountain Pass. At nearby Mirror Lake, campgrounds provide a base for hikes into the surrounding mountains, and Highline Trail accesses the 460,000-acre **High Uintas Wilderness Area** to the east. Still farther east, accessible by dirt roads from the reservation, are several recreation areas in the **Ashley National Forest** (244 W. U.S. 40, Roosevelt 84066, ☎ 801/722–5018). One of these, Moon Lake, features a U.S. Forest Service campground and private resort. Another, along the Yellowstone River, has five campgrounds. These areas also have trails that lead to the High Uintas Wilderness Area.

Dining and Lodging

Altamont
DINING AND LODGING

$$$ **Falcon's Ledge Lodge.** This modern stucco lodge in pristine Stillwater Canyon offers falconry, fly-fishing, and horseback or llama pack-trips into the High Uintas Wilderness. Guest rooms are luxurious; some have vaulted ceilings and Jacuzzis. The spacious lobby has sweeping views of the high desert scenery. The restaurant's gourmet meals are the best in the area; specialities include fresh trout and "olive lover's" steak. Fresh home-baked bread is served at every meal. ⌨ *Box 67, 84001,* ☎ *801/454–3737,* ☏ *801/454–3392. 8 rooms with private bath. Restaurant, fishing, horseback riding, MC, V.*

Duchesne
LODGING

$ **Rio Damian Motel.** Small and unassuming, this motel provides clean and comfortable rooms. ⌨ *23 W. Main St., Box 166, 84021,* ☎ *801/738–2217. 11 rooms. AE, MC, V.*

Flaming Gorge
LODGING

$$ **Flaming Gorge Lodge.** Probably the best accommodations in the vicinity of Flaming Gorge, the lodge has a great restaurant, plus a store, raft rentals, and fishing guide service. ⌨ *Greendale, U.S. 191, Dutch John 84023,* ☎ *801/889–3773,* ☏ *801/889–3788. 44 rooms. Restaurant. AE, D, MC, V.*

$ **Grubb's Flaming Gorge Motel.** A good place to check in if you find yourself on this end of the lake when night falls. ⌨ *Rtes. 43 and 44, Box 398, Manila 84046,* ☎ *801/784–3131. 15 rooms. Restaurant. MC, V.*

Roosevelt

DINING

$ **Frontier Grill.** This family restaurant is known for its great sandwiches
★ and salads during the noon hour, its prime rib and seafood at night,
and its homemade pies any time of the day. ✕ *75 S. 200 East St.,* ☎
801/722–3669. AE, DC, MC, V.

LODGING

$$ **Best Western Inn.** Clean and comfortable rooms, plus a pool, make this
the place to stay in Roosevelt. ☎ *E. Hwy. 40, Box 2860, 84066,* ☎
801/722– 4644, 🅵🅰🆇 *801/772–0179. 40 rooms. Restaurant, pool, hot
tub. AE, D, DC, MC, V.*

Vernal

DINING

$$ **Great American Café.** Serving food that's a bit different from the stan-
★ dard fare at other Vernal restaurants, the café is known for its deep-
fried catfish. ✕ *13 S. Vernal Ave.,* ☎ *801/789–1115. D, MC, V.*

$ **Casa Rios.** If you're in search of south-of-the-border flavors, this is a
good bet. Try the special beef burrito or the chimichangas. ✕ *W. Rte.
40,* ☎ *801/789–0103. MC, V. Closed Sun. and Mon.*

$ **Last Chance Saloon.** You wouldn't expect to find Vernal's best break-
fast at a bar, but that's exactly what locals have come to expect here.
Lunch and dinner are also served. ✕ *3340 N. Vernal Ave.,* ☎ *801/789–
5657. MC, V.*

LODGING

$$ **Best Western Antlers Motel.** Locals rate this as Vernal's best accom-
modations. The motel offers clean and very comfortable rooms, and
the staff is friendly and helpful. ☎ *423 W. Main St., 84078,* ☎ *801/789–
1202 or 800/524–1234,* 🅵🅰🆇 *801/789–1202. 49 rooms. Restaurant, pool,
hot tub. AE, D, DC, MC, V.*

$$ **Weston Lamplighter Inn.** For in-town convenience and amenities, this
is another good pick in Vernal. ☎ *120 E. Main St., 84078,* ☎ *801/789–
0312,* 🅵🅰🆇 *801/781–1480. 165 rooms. Restaurant, pool. AE, D,
MC, V.*

Northeastern Utah Essentials

Arriving and Departing

BY BUS

Greyhound Lines (☎ 800/231-2222) serves Vernal.

BY CAR

The best way to reach the area is by car, whether you're coming from
Salt Lake or Colorado on U.S. 40 or Wyoming on U.S. 191.

Getting Around

BY CAR

Both U.S. 40 and U.S. 191, the tour's main routes, are well maintained;
however, there are some curvy, mountainous stretches. If you're headed
for the wilderness, be prepared for dirt roads.

Guided Tours

ORIENTATION

Dinaland Aviation (830 E. 500 South St., Vernal 84078, ☎ 801/789–
4612) offers flights over Dinosaur National Monument, Flaming
Gorge, and the canyons of the Green River. Prices start at $29 per per-
son.

Important Addresses and Numbers

EMERGENCIES

Area hospitals include: **Ashley Valley Medical Center** (151 West 200
N, Vernal 84078, ☎ 801/789–3342); **Uintah Basin Medical Center** (250
West 300 N, Roosevelt 84066, ☎ 801/722–4691).

VISITOR INFORMATION

Dinosaurland Welcome Center (Utah Fieldhouse of Natural History,
235 E. Main St., Vernal 84078, ☎ 801/789–4002 or 800/477–5558);
Vernal Chamber of Commerce (134 W. Main, Vernal 84078, ☎
801/789–1352); **Roosevelt Chamber of Commerce** (48 South 200 E,
Roosevelt 84066, ☎ 801/722–4598).

SOUTHEASTERN UTAH

Characterized by multihued buttes, bizarre rock formations, deep
canyons, and lonesome plateaus, southeastern Utah stirs the imagination as few other places can. The broad and open desert topography provides grand vistas, where scale is often an intangible element.
Storm clouds billow high into the sky, and spectacular sunsets rou-
tinely light up an already colorful landscape. Add to this incredible
natural beauty a wealth of paleontological, archaeological, and historical treasures, plus a broad range of outdoor recreational opportunities, and you have one of the most alluring travel destinations to
be found anywhere.

If you do set out for this distant corner of the state, be prepared for
some of the most desolate stretches of highway in the country. In addition to stocking up on extra supplies and making sure that your vehicle is in good mechanical condition, you should also prepare yourself
mentally for the vast stretches of nothingness that lie ahead. While some
travelers thrive on the extra elbow room, others may become a bit un-
nerved when they learn just how spacious the West really is.

Exploring

*Numbers in the margin correspond to points of interest on the Utah
map.*

If you're headed into the area from the north, making a brief stop in
47 **Helper** yields a worthwhile tribute to the local area's history. The
Western Mining and Railroad Museum, housed in a former hotel that
is part of a national historic district, features displays on the development of mining in Castle Country, Depression-era paintings, an archive
room for researchers, and an outdoor display of trains and mining equipment. *296 S. Main St.,* ☎ *801/472–3009. $1 suggested donation.* ☉
Mid-May–Sept., Mon.–Sat. 9–5; Oct.–mid-May, weekdays 10–4.

48 The tour begins in earnest, however, in **Price,** the hub of Utah's Castle Country (so called because many rock formations resemble castles).
As with virtually every other community in southern Utah, Price began
as a Mormon farming enclave in the late 19th century. Shortly after it
was established, however, the town took on a noticeably different
character. In 1883 the railroad arrived, bringing with it immigrants from
around the country. Nearby coal reserves were tapped, and the town has
counted mining, not agriculture, as its primary industry ever since. Today,
because many of Price's 10,000 residents are still employed in the
coalfields, there are strong labor union ties in the community, a fact
that makes Price and nearby Helper bastions of liberalism and the Democratic party in an otherwise conservative state.

Although in many ways a modern town, Price has not forgotten its heritage and celebrates its ethnic diversity with two summer festivals. Song, dance, and food reminiscent of old Greece are the highlights of **Greek Days** in mid-July. **International Days,** which takes place during the first or second week in August in conjunction with the county fair, is a real local's event. If you should miss these colorful festivals, then be sure to visit the **Price Mural** in the Municipal Building (185 E. Main St.). A Works Progress Administration project, this 200-foot-long mural was painted between 1938 and 1941 by Lynn Fausett. It narrates the modern history of Price and surrounding Carbon County, beginning with the first white settlers.

As in other parts of Utah, the past in Castle Country extends at least a few years prior to the arrival of Mormon farmers in the 19th century—to about 150 million years ago. Housing one of the best collections of dinosaur memorabilia in the region is the College of **Eastern Utah Prehistoric Museum,** next to the Price Municipal Building. Front and center in the museum's Hall of Dinosaurs are several complete skeletons. A rare dinosaur egg is on display, as are dinosaur tracks unearthed by miners in nearby coal beds. *155 E. Main St.,* ☎ *801/637–5060.* ☛ *$1 suggested donation.* ☉ *Year-round, Mon.–Sat. 9–5; June–Sept., Sun. noon–5.*

From Price, drive southeast on U.S. 6/191 through the town of Wellington to the turnoff for **Nine Mile Canyon.** Known for the hundreds of petroglyphs etched into its boulders and cliffs, this enormous outdoor gallery is the handiwork of the Fremont Indians, who lived in much of what is now Utah from ad 300-1250. Indeed, the meaning of these images is one of the most mystifying puzzles of the area, but almost as confounding is how a canyon 40 miles long came to be named "Nine Mile." One explanation points to John Wesley Powell's epic float down the nearby Green River in 1869. It seems the expedition's mapmaker drew up a 9-mile triangulation, which he titled Nine Mile Creek. It's important not to disturb the fragile petroglyphs in any way. Additionally, because most of this 100-mile round-trip is on a gravel road, plan to take most of a day to complete it.

Beyond the turnoff for Nine Mile Canyon, U.S. 6/191 continues southeast into some of the most desolate terrain anywhere. Known as the **San Rafael Desert,** this barren landscape can be a bit overwhelming, but views of the Book Cliffs to the east do lessen the monotony somewhat. Because this drive includes some lengthy straightaways, you may find yourself developing a heavy foot, but beware: The Utah Highway Patrol watches this stretch closely.

Nearly 60 miles from Price, U.S. 6/191 intersects I-70. Continue 5 miles east on the four-lane interstate to the town of **Green River.** Today travelers can avoid Green River completely, but not so long ago the highway traffic cruised right through town, because the town fathers fought a bypass in the name of commerce. Although no longer compulsory, a visit to Green River can be a pleasant experience. Thanks to irrigation water siphoned from the river of the same name, the town is known for its melons—watermelons, to be exact—and its annual **Melon Days** celebration. Held the third weekend in September, this small-town event features a parade and fair, plenty of music, and a canoe race.

Green River's claim to agricultural fame notwithstanding, the town is also known as a base for several river-running outfits—and for good reason. To the north, the Green River has carved two spectacular canyons, Desolation and Gray, whose rapids make them a favorite haunt of rafters. South of town, it drifts at a lazier pace through Labyrinth and Stillwater canyons, and the 68-mile stretch of river that runs south to Mineral Bottom in Canyonlands National Park is best suited for canoes and motorized boats.

Although exploring Utah's wild waterways may seem like a thoroughly contemporary pastime, it actually enjoys a rich history—more than a century's worth, in fact. As the largest tributary of the Colorado River, the Green was the last major river in the continental United States to be explored. John Wesley Powell and a party of nine men rectified the situation in an epic voyage in 1869. Commemorating this feat is the **John Wesley Powell River History Museum.** In addition to various exhibits, artifacts, and works of art concerning 19th-century Western exploration, it also houses the River Runner's Hall of Fame, a tribute to those who have followed in Powell's wake. *Rte. 19 and the Green River,* ☎ *801/564–3427.* ☛ *$1.* ☉ *June–Sept., daily 8 am–9 pm; Oct.–May, daily 9–5.*

For a bit of exploring on "dry" land, drive out to **Crystal Geyser,** 10 miles south of town on good, graded road. Reaching up to 60 feet high, this cold-water eruption blows three or four times a day and usually lasts for seven minutes. The staff at the Green River Information Center, which is in the John Wesley Powell River History Museum, can provide approximate eruption times, detailed directions, and updated road conditions.

Another worthwhile excursion is the **Green River Scenic Drive,** which descends into the lower portion of Gray Canyon. Following the west bank of the river, this 10-mile route provides spectacular views of the Beckwith Plateau. After passing some sandy beachfront and a set of rapids, you'll know you're nearing the end as the Nefertiti rock formation, an aptly named local landmark, comes into view. A primitive campground is here, and it is possible to hike upstream for several miles along old cattle trails. Because all but 1½ miles of this drive is on dirt road, be sure to check on conditions beforehand. Wet weather renders the drive impassable, but when dry it's suitable for cars with good clearance. From Main Street, follow the Hastings road (1200 East St.) north.

⑤¹ From Green River, drive 20 miles east on I–70, turn south on U.S. 191, and continue 32 miles to **Moab.** Established in the 1870s adjacent to the Colorado River, Moab was supposed to be a Mormon farming community. The discovery of uranium in the early 1950s, however, made the plan moot. Within a few years the town's population tripled, as prospectors armed with Geiger counters flooded in. One of these was Charlie Steen, a penniless young man from Texas. Striking it very rich with his Mi Vida mine, Steen built a mansion overlooking town in which he threw lavish parties. Although he may have been a bit more eccentric than most of his neighbors, Steen and his lifestyle were characteristic of the town's freewheeling ways, which led to the saying that Moab stands for "Mormons on a binge."

Moab is still quite lively and enjoys a greater-than-average influx of outsiders, but it is no longer mineral wealth that draws visitors. Rather, it is the beauty of the surrounding canyons, mesas, and mountains. First lured to Moab by the establishment of Canyonlands National Park in 1964, a small but dedicated corps of outdoor enthusiasts has long known of the area's outstanding rafting and hiking opportunities (*see* Sports and the Outdoors, *below*). Similarly, four-wheelers have rallied in

Moab every Easter since 1966 to participate in the Moab Jeep Safari. Within the last few years, however, Moab's tourism industry has grown by leaps and bounds. A number of new motels have sprung up, seemingly overnight. A McDonald's was built on South Main. A brew pub now serves homemade beer, and banks have even installed automatic teller machines. What could bring such unprecedented change to this distant corner of the state? Move over, boaters, hikers, and Jeep drivers; meet the mountain bike.

All-terrain bicycles are well suited for the many miles of rugged back roads left behind by uranium prospectors. What has really put Moab on every mountain biker's map, though, is a simple matter of geology; the asphalt-smooth sandstone, or slickrock, that characterizes much of canyon country is to mountain biking what powder snow is to skiing (*see* Sports and the Outdoors, *below*).

If you happen to visit Moab sans raft, backpack, four-wheel-drive vehicle, or mountain bike, don't despair. The area still offers plenty of places that require nothing more than a car and your own two feet to explore. Perhaps the handiest of these is **Arches National Park,** a few miles north. Boasting the largest collection of natural arches in the world, the park is a geologic wonderland unlike any other. Although the process by which these spans of red rock were formed is complex, geologists do point to an underlying bed of salt as the main impetus. As this material shifted, fissures formed in the overlying layer of sandstone. Wind and water then eroded this rock into freestanding fins, which were in turn sculpted into the arches and formations seen today. Many of the park's premier sights, including the Courthouse Towers, Balanced Rock, the Windows, and Skyline Arch, are found along the park's 21-mile paved road. Others, such as Delicate Arch, the Fiery Furnace, and Devil's Garden, are accessible only by foot. Other than the visitor center at the park entrance and the 50-site Devil's Garden Campground, which lies at road's end, there are no services in Arches. *5 mi north of Moab on U.S. 191,* ☎ *801/259–8161.* ☛ *$4 per vehicle. Visitor center open daily 8–sunset.*

A bit more remote but spectacular in its own right is **Canyonlands National Park.** Encompassing some 500 square miles of rugged desert terrain, Canyonlands is naturally divided by the Colorado and Green rivers into three districts. While the Needles and Maze districts are accessible from points farther on in this tour, the **Island in the Sky District** is reached from Moab. As the name suggests, this portion of the park features a high plateau ringed by thousand-foot cliffs. A favorite among photographers is Mesa Arch, which is reached by hiking a ¼-mile trail. A number of scenic overlooks, each of which is precariously perched at land's end, are accessed by 20 miles of paved road. From the Shafer Canyon Overlook, you gaze down upon the twisted Shafer Trail—an early 1900s cattle route that was later upgraded for high-clearance vehicles. From Grand View Point, you can take in spectacular views of the meandering Colorado and Green rivers, the sandstone pinnacles of the Needles District far to the south, and the labyrinths of the Maze District to the southwest. *33 mi from Moab on U.S. 191 north and Rte. 313 west,* ☎ *801/259–7164.* ☛ *$4 per vehicle. Visitor center open daily 8–sunset.*

Nearly matching the breadth of the view from Grand View Point is the panorama to be had at nearby **Dead Horse Point State Park.** One of the finest of Utah's state parks, it overlooks a sweeping oxbow of the Colorado River, some 2,000 feet below. Dead Horse Point itself is a small peninsula connected to the main mesa by a narrow neck of land. As the story goes, cowboys used to drive wild horses onto the point and pen them there with a brush fence. Some were accidentally forgotten and left to perish. Facilities at the park include a modern visitor center and museum, a campground with drinking water, and an overlook. *34 mi from Moab at end of Rte. 313,* ☎ *801/259–2614.* ☛ *$3 per vehicle.* ☉ *Daily 8–sunset.*

Although the stretches of the Colorado River visible from the Island in the Sky and Dead Horse Point can be accessed only by boat, other portions can be enjoyed up close along two scenic drives. Branching off from U.S. 191 2 miles north of Moab is the **Colorado River Scenic Byway.** Also known as Route 128, this paved road follows the Colorado River northeast to I–70. First passing through a high-walled corridor, the drive eventually breaks out into Professor Valley, home of the monoliths of Fisher Towers and Castle Rock, which you may recognize from various car commercials. The byway also passes the single-lane Dewey Bridge, in use from 1916 to 1986. Near the end of the 44-mile drive is the tiny town of Cisco. Although a thriving community during the uranium boom, Cisco is today all but abandoned. It is worth a visit just to see what has to be one of the smallest post offices in the nation.

A second interesting drive follows the Potash Road, or Route 279, 15 miles downstream. After entering the Portal (a break in the high cliffs west of town), the **Potash Scenic Byway** continues through a gorge with a number of petroglyphs etched by the Fremont Indians. The canyon's walls are also a favorite of rock climbers. At the end of the pavement is the Moab Salt Plant, formerly known as the Potash Plant. This facility extracts salt and potash from deposits hundreds of feet below by injecting a solution into drill holes and then pumping it out to large evaporation ponds. Beyond the plant, a rough dirt road continues on to the previously mentioned Shafer Trail.

Although Moab is best known for its slickrock desert, it is also the gateway to the second-highest mountain range in the state—the 12,000-foot **La Sal Mountains.** Because these peaks remain snowcapped a good part of the year, they provide a striking contrast to the redrock desert of lower elevations. Exploring them is easy, thanks to the paved **La Sal Mountain Loop.** Beginning 8 miles south of town, this 62-mile drive climbs up and over the western flank of the range before dropping into Castle Valley and Route 128 to the north. Along the way a number of scenic turnouts and hiking trails are accessible. Long a favorite haunt of locals, the La Sal Mountain Loop is now being discovered by out-of-towners as both a retreat from the heat in the summer and a wonderful place to cross-country ski in the winter.

On those rare days when the weather may not be conducive to outdoor fun, pay a visit to the **Hollywood Stuntmen's Hall of Fame.** Recalling Moab's long association with Hollywood, from John Ford's *The Wagonmaster* in 1949 to *Thelma and Louise,* this collection of movie memorabilia highlights the important but often risky role of the stunt person in bringing life to the silver screen. A theater regularly runs stunt footage and occasionally features live performances. *100 N. 100 East St.,* ☎ *801/259–6100.* ☛ *$3.* ☉ *Weekdays 10–9, weekends 7–9.*

For a taste of history in the Moab area, stop by the **Dan O'Laurie Museum.** The Fremont and Anasazi Indians are remembered in exhibits of sandals, baskets, pottery, and other artifacts. The Ute, a Native American group that has lived in the region during more recent times, command some attention here. A display on the 1776 Dominguez–Escalante Expedition reveals the role that the Spanish played in exploring this part of the West, and the variety of rocks, fossils, and dinosaur bones speaks of the influence that geology has had in shaping life in southeastern Utah. *118 E. Center St.,* ☎ *801/259–7985.* ☛ *Free.* ☉ *Apr.–Oct., Mon.–Sat. 1–5 and 7–9; Nov.–Mar., Mon.–Thurs. 3–5 and 7–9, Fri. and Sat. 1–5 and 7–9.*

Having had your fill of Moab, continue south on U.S. 191 toward Monticello. Along the way, you might stop for a quick scramble to the base of **Wilson Arch.** With a few hours to spare, you can enjoy the two remarkable vistas featured in the **Canyon Rims Recreation Area.** Located 22 miles west of the highway, the Needles Overlook takes in the southern end of Canyonlands National Park. Less than 20 miles farther is the Anticline Overlook, which encompasses the Colorado River, Dead Horse Point, and other locales to the north.

Shortly after the turnoff for the Canyon Rims Recreation Area is the road to the **Needles District** of Canyonlands National Park, a land of countless spires and monoliths, not to mention several interesting canyons that are fun to hike. Four-wheelers can delight in tackling Elephant Hill, one of the most challenging Jeep routes in the West. A visitor center and campground are the only facilities in the Needles District. *35 mi west of U.S. 191 on Rte. 211,* ☎ *801/259–7164.* ☛ *$4 per vehicle.* ☉ *Daily 8–sunset.*

Either on your way in or as you leave the Needles District, be sure to
❺❸ stop at the BLM-administered **Newspaper Rock.** Beginning 2,000 years ago, prehistoric inhabitants of the region began etching cryptic images on a large rock face. In the centuries following, subsequent chapters of an undecipherable history were added, resulting in an impressive collection of petroglyphs that archaeologists cite as one of the most comprehensive in the Southwest. An interpretive trail and small campground are provided. *12 mi west of U.S. 191 on Rte. 211,* ☎ *801/259–6111.* ☛ *Free. Always open.*

❺❹ Back on U.S. 191, it's a quick 14 miles to **Monticello,** the seat of San Juan County. A mostly Mormon community, this quiet town has seen some growth in recent years, mostly in the form of new motels. At 7,000 feet, Monticello provides a cool respite from the summer heat of the desert, and it's at the doorstep of the **Abajo Mountains.** The highest point in the range, 11,360-foot **Abajo Peak,** is accessed by a road that branches off the graded, 22-mile Blue Mountain Loop. Although the **Manti–La Sal National Forest** (☎ 801/587–2041) is suited for most four-wheel-drive, high-clearance vehicles, be sure to inquire about road conditions ahead of time.

Beyond Monticello, U.S. 191 continues south for 21 miles to the
❺❺ slightly larger town of **Blanding.** A tad more conservative, Blanding is dry: That is, there is no state liquor store, and no beer is sold in grocery or convenience stores. What Blanding does offer, however, is the **Edge of the Cedars State Park.** Here, one of the nation's foremost museums dedicated to the Anasazi Indians displays a variety of pots, baskets, spear points, and such. Interestingly, many of these artifacts were donated by guilt-ridden pot hunters, or archaeological looters. Behind the museum, you can visit an actual Anasazi ruin. *660 W. 400 North St.,* ☎ *801/678–2238.* ☛ *$1.50 adults, $1 children 6–15.* ☉ *June–Sept., daily 9–6; Oct.–May, daily 9–5.*

A few miles south of Blanding, a right-hand turn on Route 95 heads west on what promoters alternately call the Bicentennial Highway and the Trail of the Ancients. So as not to miss some interesting sights, however, first continue your tour south on U.S. 191 to **Bluff,** situated on the San Juan River. One of southeastern Utah's oldest towns, Bluff began as a farming community in the 1880s. Reminders of its past include several historic homes that were skillfully fashioned from blocks of local sandstone. The area also includes small kivas and cliff dwellings that attest to the presence of the Anasazi centuries ago. Their descendants, residents of the **Navajo Indian Nation,** the largest Indian reservation, visit Bluff to shop, gas up, or eat out. Today Bluff witnesses a steady stream of boaters setting out for a float down the San Juan from the **Sand Island Recreation Site** (3 mi west of Bluff). In addition to a developed launch site, this BLM facility includes a primitive campground and one of the largest panels of rock art in the Four Corners area.

Head east to U.S. 160 and take a right to reach the **Four Corners Monument,** the only place in the country where four states (Utah, Arizona, Colorado, and New Mexico) meet. Administered by the Navajo tribe, Four Corners offers not only a geography lesson but also a great opportunity to buy Indian jewelry directly from the Navajos themselves.

Return to Bluff and continue west. The next stop is **Mexican Hat,** another small community on the north bank of the San Juan River. Named for a nearby rock formation, which you can't miss on the way into town, Mexican Hat is a jumping-off point for visiting two geological wonders.

By crossing the river and driving 21 miles south on U.S. 163 across Navajo land, you will reach the **Monument Valley Tribal Park.** Thanks to its striking red-rock spires, buttes, and mesas, Monument Valley has earned international recognition as the setting for dozens of movies and television commercials. Just as memorable as the scenery, though, is the taste of Navajo culture you can get here. In addition to visiting the historic Gouldings Trading Post (*see* Shopping, *below*) and shopping at its rows of arts and crafts booths, plan to take a Navajo-guided tour of the valley. These informative excursions invariably include a stop at a hogan, the traditional Navajo home. Guide services can be acquired at park headquarters (Box 93, Monument Valley 84536, ☏ 801/727–3287) and vary in cost.

A second local, must-see natural wonder is the **Goosenecks of the San Juan River** (10 mi northwest of Mexican Hat off Rte. 261). From the overlook, you can peer down upon what geologists claim is the best example of an "entrenched meander" in the world. The river's serpentine course resembles the necks of geese in spectacular 1,000-foot-deep chasms. Although the Goosenecks of the San Juan River is actually a state park, no facilities other than pit toilets are found here, and no fee is charged.

From the turnoff for the Goosenecks, Route 261 heads north toward what looks to be an impregnable 1,200-foot wall of rock. In actuality, the road climbs this obstacle in a steep, 3-mile ascent known as the **Moki Dugway.** Unpaved but well graded, the series of tight curves is manageable by passenger car. Be sure to stop at an overlook near the top to take in the superb view of the **Valley of the Gods.** Featuring scattered buttes and spires, this lonesome valley is accessed by a 17-mile dirt road that begins just south of the dugway.

At the top of the Moki Dugway, the drive returns to pavement as Route 261 tracks north across Cedar Mesa—relatively flat terrain that is thick with piñon pine and juniper, but not cedar. On occasion, you might spy a canyon break in the distance. Actually, several canyons divide this plateau land. Once home to the Anasazi, these drainages feature hundreds, if not thousands, of their cliff dwellings. **Grand Gulch,** the largest of these drainages, is today protected as a primitive area and is quite popular among backpackers.

Thirty-five miles north of Mexican Hat, Route 261 connects up with the Trail of the Ancients (Route 95). A short distance west is the turnoff for **Natural Bridges National Monument.** Different from an arch, a natural bridge, which spans a drainage or streambed, is created by water's erosion. Three natural bridges—Sipapu, Kachina, and Owachomo—are visible from a scenic drive that loops through the small monument. A second item of interest is the monument's impressive bank of solar panels. Upon completion in 1980, it was the largest solar-energy system in the world. *Rte. 275 off Rte. 95,* ☎ *801/259–5174.* ☛ *$4 per vehicle.* ☉ *Daily 8–sunset.*

Shortly beyond Natural Bridges National Monument, a choice must be made. What lies ahead is the Colorado River, a major obstacle for the Mormon settlers of the 1800s. Today, however, this mightiest of Western rivers has been stilled by the Glen Canyon Dam and **Lake Powell.** Your decision is whether to cross the lake quickly by bridge or take the longer way around and cross by ferry. If you choose the latter, turn left on Route 276 and drive 40 miles to the Hall's Crossing Marina. Like all four marinas on Lake Powell, Hall's Crossing includes a gas station, campground, motel, general store, and boat docks. Since 1985, however, it has also served as the eastern terminus of the **Lake Powell Ferry.** From here the 100-foot *John Atlantic Burr* will float you and your car across a 3-mile stretch of the lake to the Bullfrog Basin Marina, from which it's an hour's drive north to rejoin Route 95. *Hall's Crossing Marina, Rte. 276,* ☎ *801/684– 7000. No reservations. Ferry fees: $2 per foot passenger; $9 per car, including all passengers. Crossings: mid-May–Sept., 6 per day; Oct.–mid-May, 4 per day.*

Of course, if you have even more time, you can explore Lake Powell itself (although as the second-largest man-made lake in the United States, it would take years to explore fully). Certainly, the most pleasurable way to see the lake is to rent a houseboat at any of the four marinas and set out across the lake's intriguing blue waters. However, guided day tours are also available. A popular excursion sets out from the Bullfrog, Hall's Crossing, or Wahweap (in Arizona) Marina to Rainbow Bridge. The largest natural bridge in the world, this 290-foot-high, 275-foot-wide span is breathtaking. *For rentals and tours: Lake Powell Resorts and Marinas, Box 56909, Phoenix, AZ 85079,* ☎ *800/528–6154. Houseboat rentals begin at $507 for 3 days in off-season; day trip to Rainbow Bridge starts at $72.*

If you don't even have the extra two to four hours for the ferry, then follow Route 95 to **Hite Crossing.** (Just before the bridge, a left turn leads to Hite Marina—the only services for miles around.) Upon crossing the bridge, continue north past the 11,000-foot Henry Mountains to Hanksville, a good place to gas up. Here, pick up Route 24, and head northeast toward I–70. About a dozen miles out of town, signs point the way to **Goblin Valley State Park.** As the name implies, the area is filled with hundreds of gnomelike rock formations, and there's a small campground with modern rest rooms and showers. *12 mi n. of Hanksville on Rte. 24,* ☎ *801/564–3633.* ☛ *$3 per vehicle.* ☉ *Daily 8–sunset.*

A bit north of Goblin Valley, you may notice a long line of flatiron-shape cliffs jutting from the desert floor to the west. This is the San Rafael Reef—the front of the 80-mile-long **San Rafael Swell.** Rugged and quite expansive, the San Rafael Swell is a popular destination for outdoors lovers of various persuasions. After turning west on I–70, you can get an up-close look at this impressive landform from a turnoff where the interstate passes through the sawtooth ridge.

A little more than 50 miles west of the Route 24 interchange, turn north on Route 10 to complete the last leg of this tour. After passing through the small towns of Emery (the first outpost of civilization since Hanks-

61 ville) and Ferron, you'll reach **Castle Dale,** where you may notice that the surrounding countryside is beginning to look familiar. That's because you have re-entered Castle Country, the northern half of which includes Price. In Castle Dale, the **Museum of the San Rafael** provides an overview of the ancient Anasazi and Fremont Indian cultures. As further proof that you are indeed closing in on Price, there are a number of dinosaur bones on display. *City Hall, 96 E. 100 North St.,* ☎ *801/381–5252.* ☛ *Free.* ☉ *Mon.–Sat. 10–4.*

Two scenic byways climb west from Castle Country into the nearby **Manti Mountains.** The first travels for a little over 20 miles on Route 29 from Castle Dale to the subalpine setting of Joe's Valley. The second begins in Huntington, to the north, and follows Route 31 for 50 miles to Electric Lake. Both drives offer stunning fall colors in late September and early October.

As a nearby power plant suggests, the town of **Huntington** counts its coal reserves as its most valuable resource. It is also home to Huntington State Park, with a 237-acre reservoir, and is the nearest sizable com-

62 munity to the **Cleveland-Lloyd Dinosaur Quarry.** Reached by Route 155 and a series of graded roads, the quarry features, in addition to an enclosed quarry, a visitor center and an outdoor nature trail. Having produced more complete skeletons than any other site in the world, the Cleveland-Lloyd Quarry is one of the state's premier destinations for dinosaur aficionados. *20 mi east of Huntington on Rte. 155,* ☎ *801/637–4584.* ☛ *Free.* ☉ *Easter–Memorial Day, weekends 10–5; Memorial Day–Labor Day, daily 10–5.*

What to See and Do with Children

Hole 'n the Rock is a 14-room home carved into a solid rock wall. It would be just another roadside attraction if it didn't represent 20 years of toil for Albert and Gladys Christensen. Kids can run around all over it. *15 mi south of Moab on U.S. 191,* ☎ *801/686–2250.* ☛ *$1.50.* ☉ *June–Sept., daily 8–8; Oct.–May, daily 9–5.*

Off the Beaten Track

For anyone with an abiding interest in the Anasazi Indians, a visit to **Hovenweep National Monument** is a must. Along a remote stretch of the Utah–Colorado border southeast of Blanding, Hovenweep features several unusual tower structures that may have been used for making astronomical observations. By marking the summer solstice, these early farmers knew the best times of the year to plant their crops. Because Hovenweep is accessible only by a gravel and dirt road, you can count on having the monument pretty much to yourself. *21 mi east of U.S. 191 on Rte. 262,* ☎ *303/529–4461.* ☛ *Free.* ☉ *Daily 8–sunset.*

Of the three districts within Canyonlands National Park, the **Maze** is by far the most remote. Requiring a four-wheel-drive vehicle and a steady hand at the wheel, the route into the Maze begins north of Hanksville. After nearly 50 miles of high-clearance dirt road, you must then drive the incredibly rugged Flint Trail. At road's end, intrepid travelers will find not only a wonderful view of the Maze but also a trail of sorts that runs to the bottom. A scrambled collection of sandstone canyons, the Maze is one of the most appropriately named features in Southern Utah. If you do make the drive into the Maze, consider a visit to nearby Horseshoe Canyon. Featuring pictographs that may date back several thousand years, this annex of Canyonlands National Park is well worth the 4-mile hike in. *50 mi. from Rte. 24 on a dirt road; take the turn off near Goblin Valley State Park.* ☏ *801/259–7164.* ☛ *$4 per vehicle or $2 for individuals.*

Shopping

Specialty Stores

NATIVE AMERICAN ARTS AND CRAFTS

When in Monument Valley, be sure to stop at **Gouldings Trading Post** (☏ 801/727–3231) for a wide selection of fine handcrafted jewelry, Navajo rugs, pottery, and such. You can be sure that everything sold here is authentic, as the store has a reputation that extends back to 1923 to protect.

ROCKS AND MINERALS

In Moab, be sure to check out the **Moab Rock Shop** (600 N. Main St., ☏ 801/259–7312) for one of the most interesting rock collections in the state. The shop is owned by Lin Ottinger, a longtime resident of Moab and backcountry tour guide.

SPORTING GOODS

For outdoor sports enthusiasts, a visit to Moab would not be complete without stopping by **Rim Cyclery** (1233 S. U.S. 191, ☏ 801/259–5223). A fixture in town long before Moab was ever "discovered," it offers a wide array of bicycles, plus a full line of accessories, parts, and outdoor clothing.

Sports and the Outdoors

Cycling

Mountain bikes are the bicycle of choice in southeastern Utah and are at home on most any back road or trail (provided they are allowed). In the slickrock desert that surrounds **Moab,** the possibilities are inexhaustible. The most popular off-road cycling route is the **Slickrock Trail,** a few miles east of Moab. Beginners should master the 2½-mile practice loop before tackling the longer and more difficult 10.3-mile main loop. Another popular ride is the one to **Gemini Bridges,** which begins a few miles north of town along U.S. 191. For expedition-length rides, try either the 100-mile **White Rim Trail** in Canyonlands National Park or the 140-mile **Kokopelli Trail,** which runs from Grand Junction, Colorado, to Moab.

Price also has a fair number of mountain-biking routes from which to choose. The **San Rafael Swell** features many Jeep trails that are ideal for exploring on bicycle, and **Nine Mile Canyon** is also popular. For information on both areas, check with the BLM (900 N. 700 East St., Price 84501, ☏ 801/637–4584).

Camping

Of the many appealing campgrounds found in the **Moab** area, **Devil's Garden** in Arches National Park, **Squaw Flat** in the Needles District of Canyonlands National Park, and **Dead Horse Point State Park** are the best bets for finding good facilities along with interesting vistas or hiking trails nearby. Another nice spot is the **Wind Whistle Campground** in the BLM's Canyon Rims Recreation Area.

Outside of **Price** check out the **Price Canyon Recreation Area** (18 mi northwest of Price along U.S. 6). It is operated by the BLM.

Canoeing

Green River serves as a put-in point for those headed into **Labyrinth Canyon.** Here canoeists are king, for there is barely a ripple along the entire route. For information, contact the BLM in Price (*see* Cycling, *above*).

Fishing

Although it doesn't figure that you should bring your tackle box to the desert, **Lake Powell** is known for its bass fishing. A Utah fishing license and further information may be obtained at any of the marinas.

Four-Wheeling

With routes like the White Rim Trail, Elephant Hill, and the Moab Rim, **Moab** has been a mecca for off-road lovers for decades. Tours are available through **Lin Ottinger Tours** (600 N. Main St., 84532, ☎ 801/259–7312) and **Tag-A-Long Expeditions** (452 N. Main St., Box 1206, 84532, ☎ 800/453–3292), among others.

Gaining in popularity among four-wheelers is the **San Rafael Swell,** west of Green River. In the same area, **Buckhorn Draw, Hidden Splendor,** and the **San Rafael Desert** are also favored destinations. Contact the BLM in Price (*see* Cycling, *above*) for information.

Golf

Two 18-hole courses are **Blue Mountain Meadows Golf Course** (549 S. Main St. Monticello, ☎ 801/587–2468) and **Moab Golf Club** (2750 S. East Bench Rd., Moab, ☎ 801/259–6488).

Hiking

There are countless hiking trails around **Moab.** In **Arches National Park,** good routes access the Courthouse Towers, Windows, and Devil's Garden areas. Of the many trails in the **Needles District** of Canyonlands National Park, the Joint Trail is very interesting, and on BLM land just outside of Moab, the **Mill Creek Canyon** and **Hidden Valley** trails are popular.

Rafting

As it flows through **Moab,** the **Colorado River** is misleadingly calm; white-water adventures await rafters both upstream and down. Upriver, near the Colorado state line, is **Westwater Canyon,** an exciting one- or two-day float that includes legendary rapids. Moab's **Daily** river run, which begins along Route 128, offers somewhat tamer waters just out of town. Downstream from Moab, in the heart of Canyonlands National Park, is **Cataract Canyon,** which features more than two dozen rapids in a 14-mile stretch. A permit is required from the BLM (Grand Resource Area, Box M, Moab 84532, ☎ 801/259–8193) to run Westwater, and a trip down Cataract Canyon requires one from Canyonlands National Park (*see* Parks and Forests *in* Utah Essentials, *below*).

If you want to hook up with a raft-outfitting company, try **Adrift Adventures** (378 N. Main St., Box 577, 84532, ☎ 801/259–8594 or 800/874–4483, ⅀ 801/259–7628) or **Tag-A-Long Expeditions** (452 N. Main St., Box 1206, 84532, ☎ 800/453–3292). They have both been in Moab for many years and have good reputations.

While somewhat calmer than the Colorado, the **San Juan River** offers some truly exceptional scenery. It can be run in two sections: from Bluff to Mexican Hat and from Mexican Hat to Lake Powell. For permits, contact the BLM (San Juan Resource Area, Box 7, Monticello 84535, ☎ 801/587–2141).

Water Sports

Lake Powell is a water-sports area like no other. Although sailing is not a particularly worthwhile endeavor thanks to the high sandstone walls, waterskiing, pleasure cruising, and houseboating are (*see* Exploring, *above*).

Dining and Lodging

Blanding

LODGING

$$ Comfort Inn. The fact that a national chain built in remote Blanding suggests that southeastern Utah is gaining prominence as a travel destination. Because this is a fairly new property, it includes a variety of amenities. A complimentary Continental breakfast is included. ☒ 711 *S. Main St., 84512, ☎ 801/678–3271 or 800/622–3250, ꜰꜰ 801/678– 3219. 52 rooms. Restaurant, indoor pool, hot tub, exercise room, coin laundry. AE, D, DC, MC, V.*

Bluff

DINING

$ Sunbonnet Café. The café serves a variety of American food in a Western log-cabin setting, but is best known for the Navajo taco: an oversize flap of Indian fry bread piled high with pinto beans, red or green chili, lettuce, tomatoes, and cheese. ✗ *Rte. 163, along the Bluff's Historic Loop, ☎ 801/672–2201. MC, V.*

LODGING

$ Recapture Lodge. In addition to providing comfortable rooms, this locally owned motel offers guided tours into the surrounding canyon country. Slide shows are presented at night. ☒ *U.S. 191, Box 309, 84512, ☎ 801/672–2281. 36 rooms. Pool, hot tub, coin laundry. AE, D, MC, V.*

Green River

DINING

$ Ray's Tavern. Because man (and woman) cannot live on melons alone,
★   stop here for one of the best burgers in the state. Topped with a thick slice of onion, tomato, and lettuce, this all-beef monstrosity is nestled in a large helping of steak fries. Although a draw of cold beer is optional, interesting conversation is not. That's because Ray's is a favorite hangout for river runners. Although at times a surly bunch, they're always ready with some great tale about working on the river. If you have time, be sure to rack up a game of pool. ✗ *25 S. Broadway, ☎ 801/564–3511. No credit cards.*

$ Tamarisk Restaurant. This sit-down eatery features homemade pies and fudge in addition to dinner specials. The riverside setting makes dining here a treat. ✗ *870 E. Main St., ☎ 801/564–8109. AE, D, DC, MC, V.*

LODGING

$$ Best Western River Terrace Hotel. The setting, on the banks of the Green River, is conducive to a good night's rest. Comfortable rooms are furnished with large beds, and the premises are clean. ☒ *880 E. Main St., ☎ 801/564–3401 or 800/528–1234, ꜰꜰ 801/564–3403. 51 rooms. Restaurant, pool, hot tub, exercise room. AE, D, DC, MC, V.*

Moab

DINING

$$ **Center Café.** This is Moab's version of nouvelle cuisine, and a successful
★ one at that. It features the likes of *cioppino* (fishermen's stew), roast
game hen, and prawns and pasta baked in paper. Such tempting dishes
have been a long time in coming to this meat-and-potatoes town. A
prix fixe menu and a wine list are also available. ✕ *92 E. Center St.,*
☎ *801/259–4295. Reservations advised. AE, MC, V. No lunch.*

$ **Cattleman's.** If you believe the theory that truckers know all the best
places to eat, then you might give this truck stop a try. It cooks up burg-
ers, sandwiches, prime rib, steaks, and breakfast 24 hours a day. ✕
1991 S. U.S. 191, ☎ *801/259–6585. AE, D, MC, V.*

$ **Eddie McStiff's.** This casual restaurant and microbrewery serves up piz-
zas and zesty Italian specialties to go with the fresh brews. ✕ *57 S.
Main St.,* ☎ *801/259–2337. MC, V.*

$ **La Hacienda.** Since opening its doors in 1981, this restaurant has
earned a reputation for serving good south-of-the-border meals at an
equally good price. The helpings are generous and the service is friendly.
And yes, you can order a margarita, too. ✕ *574 N. Main St.,* ☎
801/259–6319. AE, MC, V.

$ **Poplar Place.** This local landmark for fun and lively dining is known
for its appetizers, pizzas, and sandwiches. If you're not too hungry, just
stop in for a drink and some Poplar Hot Wings. ✕ *100 N. Main St.,*
☎ *801/259–6018. MC, V.*

LODGING

$$$$ **Pack Creek Ranch.** A real treat, this out-of-the-way (and glad of it) guest
ranch sits beneath the snowcapped summits of the La Sal Mountains.
Wildlife abounds in this natural setting off the southern end of the La
Sal Mountain Loop. Rooms are spacious and luxurious, including woven
rugs, bent-willow furnishings, and refrigerators; most have stone fire-
places. This is one of those places that can get away with no TVs in the
rooms; the main feature here is peace and solitude in a spectacular set-
ting. Meals (all of which are included in the price) are served in a rusti-
cally cozy dining hall, replete with wagon-wheel chandeliers and oil lamps.
The menu echoes the ranching life with such meals as barbecue chicken
and French pepper steak. The pool is within earshot of the creek. ▨ *Box
1020, 84532,* ☎ *801/259–5505,* ℻ *801/259–8879. 12 cabins. Restau-
rant, pool, hot tub, horseback riding. AE, D, MC, V.*

$$ **Comfort Suites.** Moab's premier hotel, built in 1993, is somewhat of an
anomaly in town—and a sign of things to come: it was the first major
chain to build here and offers a civilized choice for accommodations in
a town which tends toward few amenities. It has comfortable and attractive suites, a handsome lobby area, and an impressive fitness facility. A complimentary Continental breakfast is served daily. ▨ *800 S. Main
St., 84532,* ☎ *801/259–5252 or 800/221–2222,* ℻ *801/259–7110. 75
rooms. Indoor pool, hot tub, exercise room. AE, D, DC, MC, V.*

$$ **Landmark Motel.** Remodeled in 1994, this motel offers deluxe rooms
in a convenient location near many downtown restaurants and shops.
▨ *168 N. Main St., 84532,* ☎ *801/259–6147 or 800/441–6147,* ℻
*801/259–5556. 36 rooms. Pool, hot tub, coin laundry. AE, D, DC,
MC, V.*

Monticello

LODGING

$$ **Grist Mill Inn.** A bed-and-breakfast like this deserves more than the usual
★ accolades. Housed in a 1933 flour mill—yes, a flour mill—are six beau-
tiful suites that are superbly appointed. There is a library on the third
floor, a sitting room with a fireplace, and plenty of charm to spare.

Additional guest rooms are next door and in an antique caboose behind the inn. No smoking is allowed in the rooms, and a full breakfast is included. ⊞ *64 S. 300 East St., Box 156, 84535,* ☎ *801/587–2597 or 800/645–3762. 10 rooms. Dining room, hot tub, library. AE, DC, MC, V.*

Monument Valley
LODGING

$$ Gouldings Lodge. This is the best place from which to tour Monument Valley and the surrounding Navajo Nation. Rooms are nice and the service is friendly. Part of the 1923 Gouldings Trading Post, the lodge gives guests a good feel for the history of the area. Be sure to peruse the shop for Native American arts and crafts. ⊞ *Box 360001, 84536,* ☎ *801/727–3231 or 800/874–0902,* FAX *801/727–3344. 64 rooms. Restaurant, pool. AE, D, DC, MC, V.*

Price
DINING

$$ Greek Streak. For the most genuine and delicious Greek food, this is the place in Price. Family owned, the restaurant serves up gyros, lamb stew, and roast lamb, among other authentic dishes. ✕ *84 S. Carbon Ave.,* ☎ *801/637–1930. MC, V. Closed Sun.*

LODGING

$ Carriage House Inn. Unlike some locally owned motor inns, which can disappoint, this one in downtown Price outpaces the big national chains in all respects. For a good price, you get a clean and comfortable room, plus personal service. ⊞ *590 E. Main St. 84501,* ☎ *801/637–5660 or 800/228–5732,* FAX *801/637–5660. 41 rooms. Restaurant, indoor pool, hot tub. AE, D, DC, MC, V.*

Nightlife

Most nightlife is concentrated in Moab. **Poplar Place** (*see* Dining and Lodging, *above*) offers live music, usually folk or soft rock. On weekends, there's live country music at **Rio Colorado Restaurant** (2 S. 100 West St., ☎ 801/259–6666) and the **Sportsman's Lounge** (1991 S. U.S. 191, ☎ 801/259–9972).

Southeastern Utah Essentials

Arriving and Departing
BY BUS

Price is served by **Greyhound Lines** (☎ 800/231–2222).

BY CAR

To reach southeastern Utah, take I–15 to U.S. 6 from Salt Lake City and the northwest, I–70 or U.S. 666 from Colorado and the east, and U.S. 191 from Wyoming and the northeast or Arizona and the south.

BY PLANE

You can fly to Moab's airport, **Canyonlands Field** (☎ 801/259–7421), from Salt Lake City on Alpine Air (☎ 801/575–2839).

BY TRAIN

Amtrak has service to Helper and Thompson.

Getting Around
BY CAR

Most roads on this tour are well-maintained two-lane highways. Be sure your car is in good working order, as there are long stretches of empty road between towns, and keep the gas tank topped off.

Guided Tours

SPECIAL INTEREST

Adrift Adventures (378 N. Main St., Box 577, Moab 84532, ☎ 801/259–8594 or 800/874–4483, FAX 801/259–7628) and **Lin Ottinger Tours** (600 N. Main St., Moab 84532, ☎ 801/259–7312) offer guided jeep tours into rugged wilderness areas. The **Canyonlands Field Institute** (1350 S. U.S. 191, Box 68, Moab 84532, ☎ 801/259–7750 or 800/860–5262, FAX 801/259–2335) sponsors seminars and nature walks.

Important Addresses and Numbers

EMERGENCIES

Area hospitals include: **Allen Memorial Hospital** (719 West 4th N, Moab 84532, ☎ 801/259-7191); **Blanding Medical Center** (930 North 400 W, Blanding 84511, ☎ 801/678–2254); **San Juan City Hospital** (364 West 1st N, Monticello 84535, ☎ 801/587–2116).

VISITOR INFORMATION

Regional travel offices include: **Canyonlands/North** (Center and Main Sts., Moab 84532, ☎ 801/259–1370 or 800/635–6622); **Canyonlands/South** (117 S. Main St., Box 490, Monticello 84535, ☎ 801/587–3235 or 800/574–4386); and **Castle Country** (155 E. Main St., Price 84501, ☎ 801/637–3009 or 800/842–0789).

SOUTHWESTERN UTAH

When Mormon pioneers came to this distant corner of Utah in the early 1860s, it was determined that they could and would grow cotton. Given the warm temperatures, the crop was a viable one, and, thanks to the economic independence it promised to bring to the territory, it was to be an important one as well. After 1869, however, the newly completed transcontinental railroad provided a cheaper source of the fiber, rendering Utah's cotton farms unnecessary. Today "Utah's Dixie" still attracts people with the promise of warm weather—so much so that the largest community in the area, St. George, is also the state's fastest-growing one. In addition to this enviable climate, there is a wealth of scenic wonders, from desert to sierra, and boundless opportunities to hike, bike, and tee off.

Exploring

Numbers in the margin correspond to points of interest on the Utah map.

63 Begin by taking I–15 south from Nephi to the town of **Fillmore.** Given its central location, Fillmore was designated the territorial capital in 1851, before the town even existed. In 1855, after the first wing of the capitol building was completed, the state legislature convened here, but the capital was eventually moved back to Salt Lake for want of better facilities. Although the entire building was never completed, the portion that does stand is counted as Utah's oldest government building. Today it is included in the **Territorial Statehouse State Park.** *50 W. Capitol St., ☎ 801/743–5316. ☛ $1.50 adults, $1 children under 15. ⊙ Daily 8–sunset.*

64 A stop in the town of **Beaver,** farther south on I–15, will reveal more historical haunts. Established by the Mormons in 1856, Beaver soon became an unsettled melting pot when gold and silver were discovered in the mountains to the west. To keep the calm between gentile miners and pious Mormons, the army established Ft. Cameron here in 1872.

Part of the town is included in a national historic district, and the old Beaver County Courthouse is now a museum. Beaver served as the county seat from 1882 to 1975.

East of Beaver rise the spectacular **Tushar Mountains.** Reaching elevations of over 12,000 feet, they are Utah's third-highest mountain range, but because of their out-of-the-way location, they are not as well known as the Wasatch, Uinta, or La Sal mountains. Those who venture east from Beaver on Route 153 will find uncrowded trails and campgrounds, some beautiful mountain lakes, and a small ski resort known as Elk Meadows (*see* Sports and the Outdoors, *below*).

To reach southern Utah's other ski resort, continue on I–15 and then on Route 143 south from Parowan for a dozen miles to Brian Head (*see* Sports and the Outdoors, *below*). It is also a favored summertime retreat.

(65) A few miles beyond Brian Head is one of the region's better-known scenic wonders, **Cedar Breaks National Monument.** Cutting deep into the western end of the lofty Markagunt Plateau, uplift and erosion by wind, rain, and river have etched an amphitheater awash in shades of pink, gold, and lavender. Two especially nice backcountry strolls (each 2 miles long) follow the Spectra Point and Alpine Pond trails, and although winter snows do close the road, the monument is a favorite among cross-country skiers. By the way, there are no cedars at Cedar Breaks. Rather, early pioneers misidentified junipers growing in the area. *Rte. 143,* ☎ *801/586–9451.* ☛ *$4 per vehicle.* ⊘ *May–Oct., daily 8– sunset.*

(66) From the west, the gateway to Brian Head and Cedar Breaks is **Cedar City,** which lies where Route 14 meets I–15. With a population of about 13,500, this is southern Utah's second-largest community. Cedar City was first settled in 1851 by Mormons sent to mine iron-ore deposits. The going was rough, though, and very little iron was produced before a more feasible supply line was established with the East. This chapter in the town's history is today embodied at the **Iron Mission State Park.** It displays the usual collection of Native American and pioneer artifacts, plus a number of horse-drawn wagons, one of which was reportedly shot up by Butch Cassidy and his bunch. *585 N. Main St.,* ☎ *801/586–9290.* ☛ *$3 per vehicle.* ⊘ *Daily 8–sunset.*

In 1897, Cedar City was awarded a branch of Utah's teacher-training school. In the years since, the school has evolved into **Southern Utah University** (351 W. Center St., ☎ 801/586–7700), a four-year college offering strong programs in education, business, science, and, most conspicuously, performing arts. From late June through the first week of September, the **Utah Shakespearean Festival** is held. What began in 1962 as an attempt to keep the town from dying has developed into a major production requiring hundreds of actors (students and professionals) and workers, drawing tens of thousands, and involving much more than just Shakespeare (*see* The Arts, *below*). The university auditorium includes a fascinating replica of the Tiring House Theater from Shakespeare's time, showcasing Shakespearean costume and set displays during the season.

(67) From Cedar City, it is roughly 50 miles on I–15 to **St. George.** It was here that 300 Mormon families were sent to grow cotton in 1861. Named after the group's leader, George A. Smith, the colony faced many hardships, among them disease, drought, and floods. After the railroad rendered their cotton farms insignificant, the settlers stayed on and built a tabernacle. In 1877, the **St. George Temple** (250 E. 400 South, ☎

801/673–3533) was completed, and starting in 1873, Brigham Young spent his last five winters in a home (89 W. 200 North St., ☎ 801/673–5181) he had built here. Free tours of the temple grounds and the home are given daily. Today these venerable structures, plus many others, bring some historical perspective to a city that is growing by leaps and bounds. St. Georgians now number over 30,000, of whom a burgeoning number are retirees. The town has many hotels and restaurants and even some interesting convention sites. The **St. George Chamber of Commerce** (97 E. St. George Blvd., ☎ 801/628–1658), housed in the 1876, brick Old Washington County Courthouse, has a friendly and knowledgeable staff.

Although St. George does proffer a handful of interesting sights, it is the surrounding natural landscape that is the area's primary draw. Best known, of course, is Zion National Park, which lies 40 miles east. Before taking in the park, however, it would be prudent to visit some of the less-heralded spots west and north of town. First on the list is **Snow Canyon State Park** (11 mi northwest of St. George on Rte. 18, ☎ 801/628–2255), where red Navajo sandstone walls topped by a cap of volcanic rock make for some rather scenic canyon terrain. There are the **Pine Valley Mountains,** with a recreation area and wilderness trails, and the **Beaver Dam Wash,** south of the small town of Shivwits. At 2,200 feet, this is Utah's lowest point, but more important, the area marks the spot where the Colorado Plateau, the Great Basin, and the Mojave Desert converge. In this overlapping of ecosystems, you'll find a great variety of plants and animals, especially birds.

If your itinerary allows for only a quick visit to the St. George area, then you should spend most of your time exploring **Zion National Park,** a wonderland of vividly hued, sheer, steep canyons; monumental monoliths; and spindly spires. First established as Mukuntuweap National Monument in 1909, it became Zion National Park a decade later. Now the 147,000-acre park welcomes some 2.5 million visitors annually. Front and center is Zion Canyon, which contains the park's main road (a 6½-mile scenic drive), a historic lodge, and a visitor center. Some 2,500 feet deep, Zion Canyon is rimmed by such naturally sculpted landmarks as the Sentinel, East Temple, the Temple of Sinawava, and the Great White Throne. At road's end is the Gateway to the Narrows. As its name suggests, the Narrows is a slender passageway, in places only a couple of dozen feet wide, carved by the Virgin River. A mile-long trail heads into the abyss, but hikers often wade up the stream beyond. *30 mi east of I–15 on Rte. 9, Springdale,* ☎ *801/772–3256.* ☛ *$5 per vehicle.* ☉ *Daily 8–sunset.*

From the depths of Zion Canyon, this tour climbs east along the Zion–Mount Carmel Highway. After several switchbacks, the road enters a mile-long tunnel, complete with portals. Constructed in 1930, the tunnel is too small for large RVs to pass without having rangers stop traffic; RV drivers pay $10 for this service. Beyond the tunnel's east entrance, Route 9 continues out of the park to Mount Carmel Junction, passing through the park's slickrock territory, including Checkerboard Mesa, which resembles an enormous sandstone playing board. **68** From here, U.S. 89 heads south for 17 miles to **Kanab,** a picturesque town with considerable ties to Hollywood. Since the 1920s, the Kanab area has played a cameo role in more than 100 movies and television shows.

Travel north from Mount Carmel Junction on U.S. 89 to the turnoff for Route 12. Head east through Red Canyon, and you'll get a taste of what's to come at **Bryce Canyon National Park.** Not actually a canyon,

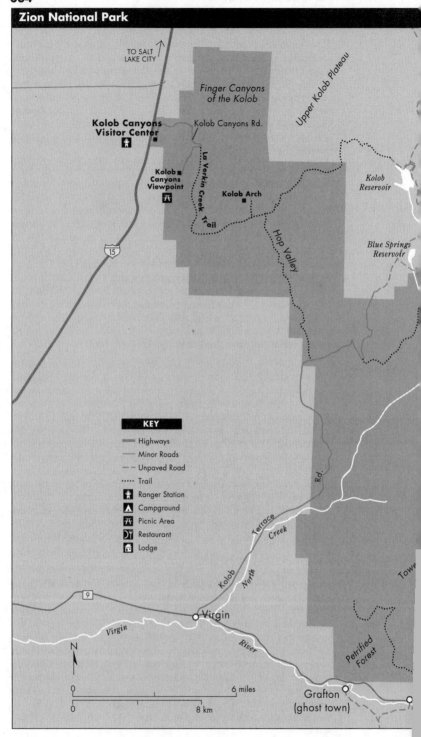

Zion National Park

TO SALT
LAKE CITY

Finger Canyons
of the Kolob

Upper Kolob Plateau

**Kolob Canyons
Visitor Center**

Kolob Canyons Rd.

**Kolob
Canyons
Viewpoint**

Kolob Arch

Kolob
Reservoir

La Verkin Creek Trail

Hop Valley

Blue Springs
Reservoir

15

KEY

Highways
Minor Roads
Unpaved Road
Trail
Ranger Station
Campground
Picnic Area
Restaurant
Lodge

Kolob Terrace Rd.

North Creek

Towe

9

Virgin

Virgin

River

Petrified
Forest

N

0   6 miles
0   8 km

Grafton
(ghost town)

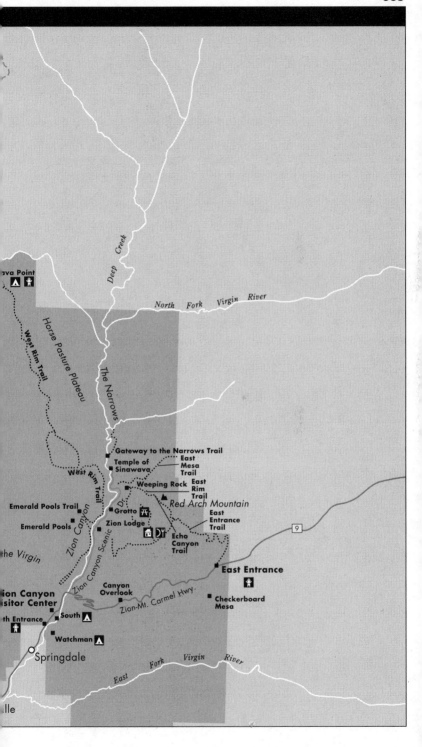

ava Point

West Rim Trail

Horse Pasture Plateau

Deep Creek

North Fork Virgin River

The Narrows

Gateway to the Narrows Trail

Temple of Sinawava

East Mesa Trail

West Rim Trail

Weeping Rock

East Rim Trail

Emerald Pools Trail

Red Arch Mountain

Zion Canyon

Grotto

Zion Lodge

East Entrance Trail

Emerald Pools

Echo Canyon Trail

he Virgin

Zion Canyon Scenic Dr.

9

East Entrance

Canyon Overlook

ion Canyon isitor Center

Checkerboard Mesa

Zion-Mt. Carmel Hwy.

th Entrance

South

Watchman

Springdale

East Fork Virgin River

lle

Bryce Canyon National Park

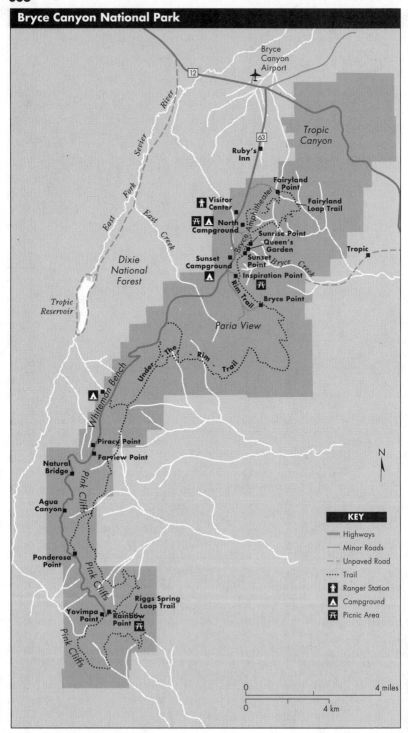

Bryce
Canyon
Airport

12

Sevier River

East Fork

East Creek

63

Ruby's
Inn

Tropic
Canyon

Visitor
Center

North
Campground

Bryce Amphitheater

Fairyland
Point

Fairyland
Loop Trail

Sunrise Point

Queen's
Garden

Sunset
Campground

Sunset
Point

Inspiration Point

Bryce Creek

Tropic

Dixie
National
Forest

Rim Trail

Bryce Point

Tropic
Reservoir

Paria View

Under - The - Rim - Trail

Whiteman Bench

Piracy Point

Farview Point

Natural
Bridge

Pink Cliffs

Agua
Canyon

Ponderosa
Point

Pink Cliffs

Riggs Spring
Loop Trail

Yovimpa
Point

Rainbow
Point

Pink Cliffs

N

KEY

— Highways
— Minor Roads
- - - Unpaved Road
..... Trail
🚹 Ranger Station
🔺 Campground
🏕 Picnic Area

0   4 miles

0   4 km

Bryce is a series of amphitheaters carved into the eastern rim of the Paunsaugunt Plateau. Exposed and sculpted by erosion are pink-and-cream color spires, or hoodoos, visible from many overlooks along the park's 35 miles of paved road. Among the stunning sights are the Silent City, named for the eerie rock profiles and figures, and the "chessmen" of Queen's Garden. Because early- and late-day sunlight casts such an unusual glow on these rock formations, many folks count Bryce as their favorite of Utah's national parks. Given its nearly 8,000-foot elevation, winter turns the area into a wonderland for cross-country skiers. *Rtes. 12 and 63, Bryce Canyon, ☎ 801/834–5322.* ☞ *$5 per vehicle.* ☉ *Daily 8–sunset.*

69 Just east of Bryce, Route 12 passes through the tiny town of Tropic before reaching Cannonville and the turnoff for **Kodachrome Basin State Park.** Here, among a spectacular but little-known geological display, are unusual petrified geysers and peculiar formations called sand pipes. The basin was named for Kodak's classic color film after pictures of it appeared in a 1949 *National Geographic* article. *9 mi south of Rte. 12, ☎ 801/679–8562.* ☞ *$3 per vehicle.* ☉ *Daily 8–sunset.*

70 Farther on, the tour reaches **Escalante.** Although home to **Escalante State Park** (Rte. 12, ☎ 801/826–4466), with its collection of rainbow-colored, 150-million-year-old petrified wood, the town is best known as the gateway to the most remote region of the state. While en route to southeastern Utah in 1879, Mormon pioneers chipped and blasted a narrow passageway in solid rock, through which they lowered their wagons. Known as **"Hole-in-the-Rock,"** much of it is now covered by Lake Powell. The 60-mile gravel road to the site, however, does access the interesting Devil's Garden Natural Area, plus some beautiful canyons and gulches.

71 East of Escalante, Route 12 crosses the Escalante River, which has carved an extensive canyon system highly favored by backpackers. The road passes the **Calf Creek Recreation Area,** highlighted by 126-foot Calf Creek Falls (a 5½-mile-round-trip hike), and reaches the small enclave of **Boulder.** So remote is this outpost that, in 1942, it was the last U.S. community to receive its mail by mule. Today the town is home to **Anasazi Indian Village State Park.** One of the largest Anasazi sites west of the Colorado River, the village predates AD 1200. *Rte. 12, ☎ 801/335–7308.* ☞ *$3 per vehicle.* ☉ *Daily 8–sunset.*

Beyond Boulder, Route 12 continues north up and over Boulder Mountain, in Dixie National Forest. Because the road reaches 9,200 feet, it encounters some lush pine, spruce, and aspen forests. In addition, magnificent views of the Escalante River canyon to the south and the Henry Mountains to the east open up along the way.

Also visible from the drive over Boulder Mountain are the sandstone monuments of **Capitol Reef National Park.** Named for a formation that resembles the U.S. Capitol, the preserve extends north for 75 miles from Glen Canyon National Recreation Area. The most heavily visited corridor of the park follows the Fremont River in the northern section. Here various short hikes allow for different views of the cliffs and domes in surrounding canyons, and the Mormon village of Fruita offers a historical perspective on the region. Reached by a high-clearance road that leads to the northernmost section of the park is the aptly named Cathedral Valley. Waterpocket Fold, a giant wrinkle of rock running south for many miles, contains some spectacular hikes, especially in Muley Twist Canyon. It is accessed by the 66-mile Burr Trail, which is passable by most cars when dry and offers motorists the chance to explore some wonderful terrain. *12 mi east of Torrey on Rte. 24,* ☎ *801/425–3791.* ☛ *$3 per vehicle.* ☉ *Daily 8–sunset.*

From Capitol Reef, return west to Torrey and then continue on through the towns of Bicknell and Loa before getting to the turnoff for **Fish Lake.** At 8,800 feet, this 1-by-6-mile natural lake is known for, not surprisingly, its fishing. But you needn't have tackle box in hand to enjoy its beautiful environs. Some great hikes explore the higher reaches of the area, and there are several campgrounds as well as some wonderful lodges. The 1.4 million–acre Fishlake National Forest was named after it.

From Fish Lake, this tour heads due north toward Salt Lake City but detours for a side trip west on Route 119 to the fertile farmlands of the Sevier River valley and the town of **Richfield.** Twenty-one miles south of Richfield, along I–70, is **Fremont Indian State Park.** During construction of the highway in 1983, this largest of Fremont sites was discovered. Today the park features a visitor center with a museum and three interpretive trails. Originally the site included a village of pit houses, but that was obliterated by construction after archaeologists completed excavation. Most of the hundreds of rock art panels are intact and on display, however. *11550 Clear Creek Canyon Rd., Sevier,* ☎ *801/527–4631.* ☛ *$1.50 adults, $1 children.* ☉ *Daily 8–sunset.*

If you have the time, you might continue south into tiny **Piute County.** Along the drive you'll pass Big Rock Candy Mountain, a colorful landmark made famous in a song by Burl Ives. In the town of Junction, you can't miss the bright red Piute County Courthouse. Built in 1902, the adobe structure is on the National Register of Historic Places. In addition, it was near the small town of Circleville that Robert LeRoy Parker—alias Butch Cassidy—grew up.

From Junction, you can backtrack to Richfield and return to Salt Lake by way of U.S. 50 and I–15. Or, if you're up for a little adventure, you can drive the Kimberly Scenic Backway (passable by most cars in the summer) over the Tushar Mountains to Beaver, I–15, and civilization.

What to See and Do with Children
Coral Pink Sand Dunes State Park (12 mi west of Kanab off U.S. 89, follow turn-off, ☎ 801/874–2408) is a giant playland of tinted sand. Big kids play on the dunes with their all-terrain vehicles, but an area has been set aside for families to explore.

Lopeman's Frontier Movie Town is jam-packed with Old West movie memorabilia. Some of the buildings in its replica of a frontier town were actually used in movie sets, and photos on the walls inside reveal many familiar faces. *297 W. Center St., Kanab,* ☎ *801/644–5337.* ☛ *$2 adults.* ☉ *Apr.–Oct., varying hours.*

Off the Beaten Track
Besides being the closest town to the Intermountain Power Project (said to be the world's largest coal-fired generating station), **Delta** is also Utah's gateway to the lonesome yet beautiful **Great Basin,** a desert region that covers much of the West. A few miles south of Delta are the crumbling adobe remains of **Ft. Deseret,** and west of town are the remains of **Topaz.** During World War II, some 9,000 Japanese-Americans were interned here; at the time, it was Utah's fifth-largest city. The area also has a number of mountain ranges and sagebrush valleys to explore.

Sports and the Outdoors

Cycling

Given its colorful desert terrain and its forested plateaus, Southwestern Utah makes for some rather alluring bicycling—both on the road and off.

Claiming to have the highest number of bike shops per capita—four shops in a town of 75—**Brian Head** is a good place to base cycling excursions. The area's most popular ride is the 12-mile **Bunker Creek Trail,** which winds its way through forests and meadows to Panguitch Lake. Road cyclists will enjoy stretches of Routes 14, 143, and 148 in the **Cedar Breaks National Monument** area.

A good long-distance mountain-bike ride in the isolated **Escalante** region follows the 44-mile **Hell's Backbone Road** from Escalante to Boulder. The grade is steep, but the views of Box Death Hollow make it worthwhile. Mountain bikers may also want to pedal a portion of the **Burr Trail,** a 66-mile backcountry route (usable by most vehicles when dry) that crosses into the southern portion of Capitol Reef National Park.

Near **St. George,** Snow Canyon State Park and Zion National Park are popular among road cyclists. The scenery is great, but watch for heavy traffic during peak season. For safety reasons, the Zion–Mount Carmel tunnel in Zion is closed to bicycles.

Camping

In this region of Utah, campers have their choice from low desert to high mountain facilities. Campgrounds in **Bryce, Capitol Reef,** and **Zion national parks** fill up fast. Most of the area's state parks have camping facilities, and the region's two national forests offer many wonderful sites. In the **Dixie National Forest** (Box 580, Cedar City 84721, ☎ 801/865–3700), the Panguitch Lake, Pine Valley, and Boulder Mountain areas are especially nice. In **Fishlake National Forest** (115 E. 900 N., Richfield 84701, ☎ 801/896–9233), Beaver Canyon and Fish Lake are good picks.

Fishing

A number of nice trout streams lace the region. These include **Panguitch Creek,** below the lake of the same name; **Mammoth Creek,** south of Hatch; the **Beaver River;** and the **Sevier River,** which flows north through Richfield and Salina. As for lake fishing, anglers favor **Otter Creek Reservoir, Yuba Reservoir,** and **Panguitch Lake.** Of course, with a name like **Fish Lake,** how can you go wrong? Mackinaw and rainbow trout have both made the lake famous.

Golf

The same feature of this corner of the state that allowed early Mormon farmers to grow cotton now draws golfers in every month of the year. Among the dozen or so golf courses found in the region are the nine-hole courses **Canyon Breeze** (E. Canyon Rd., Beaver, ☎ 801/438–2601) and **Dixie Red Hills** (1000 N. 700 West St., St. George, ☎ 801/634–5852), as well as 18-hole courses **Cedar Ridge** (200 E. 900 North St., Cedar City, ☎ 801/586–1624), **Green Spring** (588 N. Green Spring Dr., St. George, ☎ 801/673–7888), and **St. George Golf Club** (2190 S. 1400 East St., St. George, ☎ 801/634–5854).

Hiking

Hiking trails abound in southwestern Utah. In **Bryce Canyon National Park,** the Rim Trail features nonstop scenery, while the Fairyland Loop and Queen's Garden trails lead hikers among the park's fantastic hoodoos. At **Capitol Reef National Park,** the strenuous route to the Fremont Overlook and the Hickman Bridge Trail are good picks. **Zion National Park** is home to the Narrows, but the walk to Emerald Pools is similarly worthwhile. In southwestern Utah's BLM-administered lands and three national forests, the **Boulder** area includes the hike to Calf Creek Falls, and **Fish Lake** features a trail to the 11,633-foot summit of Fish Lake Hightop Plateau. West of St. George, the 50,000-acre **Pine Valley Wilderness** is laced with several backcountry routes, including the 6-mile Whipple National Recreation Trail and the 35-mile Summit Trail. The **Tushar Mountains** are accessed by several paths near Beaver.

Skiing

Known for its abundance of snow, **Brian Head Resort** (Brian Head 84719, ☎ 801/677–2035 or 800/272–7426) is a favorite among California skiers who eschew the crowded megaresorts of their own state. Six lifts service 53 runs and a vertical drop of 1,707 feet.

Elk Meadows Ski and Summer Resort (Box 511, Beaver 84713, ☎ 801/438–5433 or 800/248–7669) has 30 runs with five lifts and a vertical drop of 1,200 feet.

State Parks

In addition to the many state parks described in the tour of the area, a few others, each with its own lake, are of interest:

Gunlock State Park (15 mi northwest of St. George, ☎ 801/628–2255) includes a 240-acre reservoir.

Minersville State Park (12 mi west of Beaver on Rte. 21, ☎ 801/438–5472) provides boating facilities on a 1,130-acre reservoir.

Otter Creek State Park (4 mi north of Antimony on Rte. 22, ☎ 801/624-3268) has a 3,120-acre lake known for rainbow trout.

Piute State Park (12 mi south of Marysvale off U.S. 89, ☎ 801/624–3268) promises excellent fishing and boating on a 3,360-acre reservoir.

Quail Creek State Park (3 mi east of I–15 on Rte. 9, ☎ 801/879–2378) includes a 590-acre reservoir north of St. George.

Yuba State Park (30 mi south of Nephi off I–15, ☎ 801/758–2611) is on the shores of the expansive Sevier Bridge Reservoir.

Dining and Lodging

Beaver

DINING

$$ Paradise Inn Garden of Eat'n. This small-town eatery serves sandwiches, burgers, steaks, and more, and it's open for breakfast, lunch, and dinner. ✕ *324 W. 1425 North St., ☎ 801/438–5464. AE, D, MC, V.*

LODGING

$ Best Western Paradise Inn. There are a fair number of facilities in this I–15 stopover. Rooms are comfortable and clean. ☒ *1451 N. 300 West St., Box 1137, 84713, ☎ 801/438–2455 or 800/528–1234, FAX 801/743–6892. 53 rooms. Restaurant, pool, hot tub. AE, D, DC, MC, V.*

Brian Head

DINING

$$ The Edge. This is the place to eat lunch and dinner in Brian Head. The Edge Burger is a half-pound monstrosity draped with cheese. Deli sandwiches are similarly sizable, and dinners include delicious steaks, seafood, soups, and salads. And, as you'd expect, the views are great. ✕ *406 S. Rte. 143,* ☎ *801/677–3343. AE, MC, V.*

LODGING

$$$ **Brian Head Resort.** On the north end of town, this hotel/condominium resort features large studio rooms in desert pastels; hotel rooms come with kitchenettes or a wet bar, condominiums have full kitchens. The atmosphere is casual, and the service is friendly and helpful. ⊡ *223 Hunter Ridge Rd./Rte. 143, Box 190008, 84719,* ☎ *801/677–3000 or 800/272–7426,* ⎕⎕ *801/677–2211. 175 hotel rooms, 125 condominium apartments. Restaurant, bar, hot tub, exercise facilities. AE, D, DC, MC, V.*

Bryce Canyon

LODGING

$$$ **Bryce Canyon Lodge.** Inside the park, this historic property is a few feet from rim views. Guests have their choice of standard rooms or cozy cabins. The lodge organizes horseback rides and park tours. ⊡ *Box 400, Cedar City 84720,* ☎ *801/586–7686,* ⎕⎕ *801/586–3157. 114 rooms. Restaurant. AE, D, DC, MC, V.*

$$–$$$ **Best Western Ruby's Inn.** Just north of the park entrance and housing a large restaurant and gift shop, this is Grand Central Station for visitors to Bryce. A nightly rodeo takes place nearby. ⊡ *Rte. 63, Box 1, 84717,* ☎ *801/834–5341 or 800/528–1234,* ⎕⎕ *801/834–5265. 368 rooms. Restaurant, indoor pool, hot tub. AE, D, DC, MC, V.*

Cedar City

DINING

$$ **Milt's Stage Stop.** Locals and an increasing number of tourists have
★ discovered the terrific food and inviting atmosphere of this dinner spot in beautiful Cedar Canyon. It's known for its 12-ounce rib-eye steak, its prime rib, and its fresh crab, lobster, and shrimp dishes. In winter, deer feed in front of the restaurant as a fireplace blazes away inside. A number of hunting trophies decorate the rustic building's interior, and splendid views of the surrounding mountains delight patrons year-round. ✕ *5 mi east of town on Rte. 14,* ☎ *801/586–9344. Reservations advised. AE, D, DC, MC, V.*

$$ **Pancho & Lefty's.** This is a great place for Mexican cuisine. Locals like the chimichangas, flautas, and fajitas, and those who imbibe can order margaritas. ✕ *2107 N. Main St.,* ☎ *801/586–7501. AE, MC, V.*

LODGING

$$ **Bard's Inn Bed and Breakfast.** Rooms in this restored turn-of-the-century house are named after heroines in Shakespeare's plays—perfect for those attending the Utah Shakespearean Festival (*see* The Arts, *below*), which is within walking distance. There are wonderful antiques throughout and some unusual decorative accents: the chinese checkerboard in the bathroom, sculptures of the Bard's most famous characters, Shakespearean costumed dolls, stained glass windows rescued from an old church. Enjoy a complimentary breakfast that includes fresh home-baked breads. ⊡ *150 S. 100 West St., 84720,* ☎ *801/586–6612. 7 rooms. MC, V.*

$$ **Holiday Inn Cedar City.** This property offers clean and comfortable accommodations, plus a nice lineup of facilities. It's a convenient departure point to Bryce and Zion national parks and Cedar Breaks National Monument in summer and Brian Head Ski Resort in winter. ⊡ *1575 W. 200 North St., 84720,* ☎ *801/586–8888 or 800/432–8828,* ⎕⎕ *801/586–1010. 100 rooms. Restaurant, pool, indoor hot tub. AE, D, DC, MC, V.*

Fish Lake

LODGING

$$ **Fish Lake Lodge.** This large, lakeside lodge structure was built in 1932 and today exudes rustic charm and character. Guests stay in cabins—some old, others new. There is a dance hall and store, and the views are wonderful. 🏨 *10 E. Center St., Rte. 25, 84701,* ☎ *801/638–1000. 25 rooms. Restaurant. AE, MC, V.* ☺ *Memorial Day–Sept.*

Hurricane

LODGING

$$ **Pah Tempe Hot Springs Bed & Breakfast.** In a small town along the Virgin River between St. George and Zion National Park, this B&B counts outstanding scenery and natural mineral springs as primary attributes. The springs were thought to have healing powers by the Paiute Indians. A small gourmet restaurant serves vegetarian food and nonalcoholic drinks, and a Continental breakfast is complimentary. Rooms are no-smoking. 🏨 *825 N. 800 East St., Box 35-4, 84737,* ☎ *801/635–2353. 8 rooms. Restaurant, pool, hot tub. MC, V.*

Kanab

DINING

$$ **Chef's Palace.** This restaurant is a local favorite for rib-eye steaks, prime rib, and seafood. For added atmosphere, dine in the Dude Room. ✕ *151 W. Center St.,* ☎ *801/644–5052. AE, D, DC, MC, V.*

LODGING

$$ **Parry Lodge.** Back in the 1930s, movie stars stayed here. The names of who slept in each room are listed above the doors of the older units, and Hollywood-related photos decorate the lobby. Despite the age of the hotel, rooms are well-maintained and comfortable. 🏨 *89 E. Center St., 84741,* ☎ *801/644–2601 or 800/748–4104,* FAX *801/644–2605. 89 rooms. Restaurant, pool. AE, DC, MC, V.*

Loa

LODGING

$$ **Road Creek Inn.** This pleasurable bed-and-breakfast offers such treats as a trout pond and a game room in addition the complimentary Continental breakfast. Guest rooms, in which there is no smoking, are decorated in Victorian-era motifs. This is a good bet in this hideaway town. 🏨 *90 S. Main St., Box 310, 84747,* ☎ *801/836–2485 or 800/388–7688,* FAX *801/836–2489. 13 rooms. Hot tub, exercise room, recreation room. AE, D, DC, MC, V.*

Richfield

LODGING

$ **Topsfield Lodge.** Aside from Richfield's docket of national chain motels, you might try this locally owned one. In addition to basic yet clean rooms and friendly service, there is an on-site steak house that is quite popular among locals and visitors alike. 🏨 *1200 S. Main St., 84701,* ☎ *801/896–5437. 20 rooms. Restaurant. AE, MC, V.*

St. George

DINING

$$ **Andelin's Gable House.** This nice sit-down restaurant features a varied menu upstairs in the Garden Room and five-course dinners downstairs in the Captain's Room. Entrées cover such fare as fish, ribs, stir-fries, brisket, and homemade chicken pot pie. ✕ *290 E. St. George Blvd.,* ☎ *801/673–6796. Reservations advised. AE, MC, V.*

$$ **J. J. Hunan Chinese Restaurant.** The service is good, and the dishes are tasty. ✕ *2 W. St. George Blvd.,* ☎ *801/628–7219. AE, D, MC, V.*

\$\$ Sullivan's Rococo. Specializing in beef and seafood, the restaurant is known for its prime rib. Because it sits atop a hill overlooking town, you can enjoy spectacular views from table-side. ✕ *511 Airport Rd.,* ☎ *801/628-3671. AE, D, DC, MC, V.*

LODGING

\$\$ Four Seasons Convention Center. For comfortable rooms and an inviting array of amenities, this is a good bet. It has an indoor-outdoor pool, plus tennis courts, and provides a complimentary Continental breakfast. ⌘ *747 E. St. George Blvd., 84770,* ☎ *801/673-6111 or 800/635-4441,* FAX *801/673-0994. 96 rooms. Restaurant, indoor-outdoor pool, hot tub, 2 tennis courts, coin laundry, business services, convention center, meeting rooms. AE, D, DC, MC, V.*

\$\$ Greene Gate Village Historic Bed & Breakfast Inn. This inn is named
★ for a gate that reportedly dates back to 1877. As legend has it, Brigham Young had the fence and gate around the St. George Temple painted green. He then gave the excess paint to church members so that they, too, could paint their own gates and fences. Local lore notwithstanding, this collection of eight vintage homes offers elegantly comfortable accommodations in downtown St. George. There is no smoking in the rooms, and a full breakfast is included. ⌘ *76 W. Tabernacle St., 84770,* ☎ *801/628-6999 or 800/350-6999,* FAX *801/628-6989. 20 rooms. Pool, hot tub. AE, D, DC, MC, V.*

\$\$ Ramada Inn. One of St. George's newest properties, this hotel may very well be its nicest. The rooms and furnishings are up-to-date and comfortable. ⌘ *1440 E. St. George Blvd., 84770,* ☎ *801/628-2828 or 800/228-2828,* FAX *801/628-0505. 136 rooms. Pool, hot tub, meeting rooms. AE, D, DC, MC, V.*

\$\$ Seven Wives Inn. Two historic homes constitute this bed-and-break-
★ fast. It is said that Brigham Young slept here and that one of the structures may have been used to hide polygamists after the practice was prohibited in the 1880s. Antiques are liberally used in the decor, and guest rooms, most of which boast fireplaces or wood-burning stoves, are named after the wives of owner Donna Curtis's great-great-grandfather. A full breakfast is served. ⌘ *217 N. 100 West St., 84770,* ☎ *801/628-3737. 12 rooms. Dining room, pool. AE, D, DC, MC, V.*

The Arts

Music
The **Southwest Symphony** (Dixie Center, St. George, ☎ 801/673-6290) performs from October to May. Also at the Dixie Center, an intermittent **Celebrity Concert Series** lures top acts.

Theater
The **Pioneer Players** (Dixie College, St. George, ☎ 801/628-3121) perform comedies and melodramas at the Arena Theatre during the months of July and August.

The **Utah Shakespearean Festival** features several stage productions of works by Shakespeare and others; the Greenshow, with jugglers, puppet shows, and folks dressed in period costume; workshops and literary seminars; and the Renaissance Feaste, a popular feed for guests. *351 W. Center St., Cedar City,* ☎ *801/586-7878.* ☛ *$10–$24, depending on seating and show times. Runs late June–early Sept.*

Nightlife

In St. George, **The Blarney Stone** (800 E. St. George Blvd., ☎ 801/673-9191) is a beer-only joint with country and rock bands on weekends.

In Cedar City, you can scoot your boot on weekends at the **Sportsmen's Lounge** (900 S. Main St., ☎ 801/586–6552) and **The Playhouse** (1027 N. Main St., ☎ 801/586–9010).

Southwestern Utah Essentials

Arriving and Departing

BY BUS

Greyhound Lines (☎ 800/231–2222) runs buses along the I–15 corridor, making stops in **Beaver** (El Bambi Café, 935 N. Main St., ☎ 801/438–2229), **Parowan** (20 N. Main St., ☎ 801/477–3421), **Cedar City** (1355 S. Main St., ☎ 801/586–9465), and **St. George** (Trafalga Restaurant, 76 W. St. George Blvd., ☎ 801/673–3933).

BY CAR

Interstate 15 is the main route into the region, from Las Vegas to the southwest and Salt Lake City to the northeast.

BY PLANE

SkyWest (☎ 800/453–9417) flies to **Cedar City** and **St. George** municipal airports.

BY TRAIN

Milford receives Amtrak service (☎ 800/872–7245).

Getting Around

BY CAR

This tour follows I–15 before continuing on various well-maintained two-lane highways. Some mountain curves can be expected, and winter months may see hazardous conditions in the higher elevations. Be sure that your car is in good working order, and keep the gas tank topped off.

Guided Tours

SPECIAL INTEREST

Canyon Trail Rides (Box 128, Tropic 84776, ☎ 801/679–8665) offers mule and horseback riding tours in Bryce Canyon and Zion national parks.

Important Addresses and Numbers

EMERGENCIES

Area hospitals include: **Beaver Valley Hospital** (85 North 400 E, Beaver 84713, ☎ 801/438–2531); **Dixie Regional Medical Center** (544 South 400 E, St. George 84771, ☎ 801/634–4000); **Garfield Memorial Hospital** (224 North 400 E, Panguitch 84074, ☎ 801/676–8811; **Kane City Hospital** (221 West 300 N, Kanab 84741, ☎ 801/644–5811); **Milford Memorial Hospital** (451 N. Main St., Milford 84751, ☎ 801/387–2626; **Valley View Medical Center** (595 South 75 E, Cedar City 84720, ☎ 801/586–6587).

VISITOR INFORMATION

The following regional travel offices cover the southwest: **Color Country** (906 N. 1400 West St., Box 1550, St. George 84771, ☎ 801/628–4171 or 800/233–8824) and **Panoramaland** (250 N. Main St., Box 820, Richfield 84701, ☎ 801/896–9222 or 800/748–4361).

Eight counties also maintain tourism bureaus: **Beaver County Travel Council** (Box 1060, Beaver 84713, ☎ 801/438–5384); **Garfield County Travel Council** (55 S. Main St., Panguitch 84074, ☎ 801/676–8826); **Iron County Tourism and Convention Bureau** (Box 220, Cedar City 84720, ☎ 801/586–5124); **Kane County Travel Council** (Box 728, Kanab 84741, ☎ 801/644–5033); **Piute Tourism Board** (Piute County Courthouse, Junction 84740, ☎ 801/577–2840), **Sevier Travel Council** (220 N. 600 West St., Richfield 84701, ☎ 801/662–8898); **Washington County Travel and Convention Bureau** (425 S. 700 East St., St. George 84770, ☎ 801/634–5747 or 800/869–6635); and **Wayne County Travel Council** (County Clerk, Courthouse, Loa 84747, ☎ 801/836–2731).

UTAH ESSENTIALS

Getting Around

By Bus
Greyhound Lines (☎ 800/231–2222) runs several buses each day through Salt Lake City. In addition, there are terminals in Beaver, Brigham City, Cedar City, Logan, Ogden, Parowan, Price, Provo, St. George, Tremonton, and Vernal.

By Car
By far the best way to see Utah is by car; in fact, beyond Salt Lake City and the Wasatch Front, it's basically the only way. I–80 crosses Utah east to west, and I–15 runs the length of the state, from Idaho to Arizona. These two routes intersect in Salt Lake City. In addition, U.S. 191 accesses eastern Utah, and U.S. 666 enters the southeast from Colorado. Front-wheel drive is suggested on the snowy roads of winter.

By Plane
Commuter service between Salt Lake City and smaller Utah cities, such as St. George, Cedar City, and Moab, is available through **Alpine Air** (☎ 801/575–2839) and **SkyWest** (☎ 801/575–2508 or 800/453–9417).

By Train
Amtrak (☎ 800/872–7245) has daily service from the Rio Grande Depot in Salt Lake City and also serves Helper, Milford, Ogden, Provo, and Thompson.

Guided Tours

Scenic West Tours, Inc. (Box 369, Draper 84020, ☎ 801/572–2717 or 800/723–6429) offers one- to 12-day trips throughout Utah. In addition to regularly scheduled tours, customized itineraries are available.

Dining

The gourmet restaurants of Salt Lake and Park City rival those in any U.S. city; elsewhere, more traditional, family-style eateries serve up meat and potatoes (and a little fresh fish). Having a drink with dinner is not a problem, nor, at most places, is getting a table. Men might want to wear a jacket at the more expensive restaurants in Salt Lake City; otherwise, dress is casual.

CATEGORY	COST*
$$$$	over $25
$$$	$20–$25
$$	$12–$20
$	under $12

*per person, excluding drinks, service, and approx. 6¼% sales tax (rates vary depending on location).

Lodging

Chains are everywhere. Other than that, accommodations are varied—from the ski villages under one roof at some of the resorts and the tall, modern business hotels in downtown Salt Lake City to historic bed-and-breakfast inns and modest motels that simply provide a good place to rest after a day of sightseeing. No-smoking rooms are now generally available; ask when making reservations. Rooms have private baths unless otherwise noted in the reviews.

Note that some accommodations may come with breakfast, three meals, or even lift tickets included in the price, so compare accordingly.

CATEGORY	COST*
$$$$	over $100
$$$	$75–$100
$$	$50–$75
$	under $50

All prices are for a standard double room, excluding approx. 6¼% sales tax and 3%–11% room tax (rates vary depending on location).

Parks and Forests

With five, Utah has more national parks than any other state except Alaska and California. Though Bryce and Zion are the best known, fascinating landscape can be seen at Arches, Canyonlands, and Capitol Reef national parks. For information, contact the individual parks: **Arches National Park** (Moab 84532, ☎ 801/259–8161), **Bryce Canyon National Park** (Bryce Canyon 84717, ☎ 801/834–5322); **Canyonlands National Park** (Moab 84532, ☎ 801/259–7164); **Capitol Reef National Park** (Torrey 84775, ☎ 801/425–3791); and **Zion National Park** (Springdale 84767, ☎ 801/772–3256). Entrance fees are $5 per vehicle at Bryce and Zion, and $4 at the others.

State parks range from historic monuments to recreation areas, many of which have public lakes, often reservoirs, that are popular spots for camping as well as boating and other water sports. Entry generally costs $1.50 for adults and $1 for children under 13 to the historical monuments and $3 per vehicle to the recreational parks. Most state parks accept reservations for campsites (☎ 801/322–3770 or 800/322–3770) but also have some sites available on a first come, first served basis. Contact **Utah Division of Parks and Recreation** (1636 W. North Temple St., Suite 116, Salt Lake City 84116, ☎ 801/538–7221) for information on state parks.

Officially, national and state parks are open 24 hours a day, but visitor centers are usually open 8–sunset.

Shopping

Shopping is not a big attraction in Utah. Malls are everywhere, and specialty stores carry much the same items you'd find throughout the West: Western wear, outdoor gear, and Native American jewelry, especially in the south. Shoppers should be warned, however, that more stores close on Sundays here than elsewhere.

Sports

In the winter, skiing is king, and a number of first-class resorts bring skiers from all over the country and the world. In the summer, Utah is filled with hikers, campers, and, increasingly, mountain bikers. Perhaps most surprising in this second-driest state, boating on the many lakes, rafting on the rivers in the south, and fishing for bass, pike, kokanee salmon, and cutthroat trout, are extremely popular activities. Fishing licenses are available from the **Utah Division of Wildlife Resources** (1596 W. North Temple St., Salt Lake City 84116, ☎ 801/538–4700). Golf courses are located throughout the state, and reservations are generally necessary.

Important Addresses and Numbers

Emergencies

In most towns, call **911** for police, fire, and ambulance service. In rural areas, the **Utah Highway Patrol** (☎ 801/965–4505) has jurisdiction, as do county sheriff departments.

Major towns have hospitals with emergency rooms (*see* Emergencies section *in* individual regions, *above*). For nonemergencies, check in local telephone directories, with chambers of commerce, or at your lodging for names of doctors, dentists, and local pharmacies. Outside Salt Lake, pharmacies don't tend to stay open late, but major supermarket chains have pharmacy departments that are often open to 10 PM or so.

Visitor Information

Utah Travel Council (Council Hall, Capitol Hill, Salt Lake City 84114, ☎ 801/538–1030 or 800/200–1160) distributes brochures and answers questions on tourism. Utah celebrates 100 years of statehood in 1996; a calendar of events is available from the **Utah Centennial Commission** (1324 S. State St., Suite 234, Salt Lake City 84111, ☎ 801/531–1996).

8 Wyoming

By Geoffrey
O'Gara and
Michael
McClure

Updated by
Candy
Moulton

TOURING WYOMING'S UNPAVED ROADS BY MODEL T in the 1930s, writer Agnes Wright Spring found it easy to imagine the covered wagons and Native American bands of the 1800s. "The past presses so closely on the present!" she wrote, and even today her words hit the mark. Antelope still graze nonchalantly by highways, bull riders still bite the dust at Cheyenne's Frontier Days, and towering peaks, bearded with glaciers, stand as timeless sentinels in the west.

The closest Wyoming comes to big cities is Cheyenne and Casper, neither of which has more than 100,000 residents. Like most of the country, the state has tried to lasso high-tech industries, but you won't find General Motors or Boeing here. Even the oil and natural gas industries, centered in Casper and long a staple of the state's economy, have declined of late. Increasingly, Wyoming residents have recognized that the state's most valuable resource is the same wild and unspoiled country that astonished explorers 50, 100, and 200 years ago. Of that, there is no shortage.

In most people's minds, wild Wyoming is synonymous with its northwest section and its cluster of parks, forests, and ski resorts. Yellowstone National Park, the most popular destination, does not disappoint. Geysers spout, elk bugle, mud pots boil, and larkspur blooms. The scars of 1988's severe fires show here and there, but park officials have capitalized on them, making the park a giant ecological classroom. Just to the south, the Grand Tetons rise abruptly from the Snake River plain, above the lively community of Jackson, where efforts are being made to retain working ranches and open space in the face of a tide of second-homers.

Incomparable as the northwest is, there is much more to Wyoming. The other most-visited regions of the state, the northeast and southeast, blend mountain and plain, mine and ranch, and country towns and Western cities. In the southeast, the museums, festivals, and parks of Cheyenne and Laramie ensure that Wyoming's heritage as a frontier territory has its place in contemporary life. The Bighorn Mountains in the northeast attract hikers and fishermen eager to avoid the more visited sites in the northwest.

Wyoming has fewer full-time residents (around 460,000) than any other state, but you'll find no inferiority complex. Whether they're riding the tram at Teton Village's world-class ski resort or haying the horses at a ranch in the Bighorn Mountains, Wyomingites take ornery pride in being just specks on an uncluttered landscape, five people per square mile. They know they have something that is fast disappearing elsewhere in the world, and, with a hint of pride on a weather-beaten face, they're willing to share it.

NORTHWEST WYOMING

By now, most Americans realize that the geysers and wilderness of Yellowstone were not destroyed by the fires of 1988. What damage was done—a few areas of bare black tree trunks with colorful fireweed blooming underfoot—has, in fact, become another lure to ecologically curious travelers. The hysterical media coverage of that crispy summer failed to convey what is at the heart of the public's love affair with Yellowstone: a blind faith that here, amid our most extraordinary wildlands, nature can be trusted to run its course.

The number of visitors to Yellowstone continues to increase, pushing above 3 million annually. More and more, travelers are recognizing that the wild beauty extends beyond the artificial boundaries of the park. They hike in June among the colorful explosions of wildflowers near Togwotee Pass in the Bridger-Teton National Forest north of Dubois or ride horses in the Wapiti Valley near Cody. They raft down the white water of the Hoback River south of Jackson and shoot—with cameras— the herds of elk that gather at the National Elk Refuge.

Nor are diversions limited to the natural world. Yellowstone's so-called "gateway" towns, including Jackson, Cody, and Dubois, have developed their own attractions, some of them cultural, and improved their accommodations as well. They are also dealing with their own population explosion, as more and more people decide to relocate or build vacation homes in this country they love to visit. Attempting to cope with growth and control their destiny, communities have begun to debate how much and what kind of development is desirable. The effort to find a balance between saving the untrammeled wonders of the region and playing host to a curious, eager—and sometimes jealous—tide of visitors is one of the civic challenges here in the 1990s.

Exploring Cody and Yellowstone

Numbers in the margin correspond to points of interest on the Wyoming map.

❶ **Cody,** founded in 1887 and named for Pony Express rider, army scout, and entertainer William F. "Buffalo Bill" Cody, lies 52 miles from the East Entrance to Yellowstone National Park. It's within easy reach of Shoshone National Forest, the Absaroka Range, the Washakie Wilderness, and the Buffalo Bill Reservoir. A brochure with a self-guided walking tour of the town's historic sites is available from the chamber of commerce (*see* Important Addresses and Numbers, *below*) for a $1 donation.

At the west end of this quiet little gateway town is one of the finest museums in the West: the **Buffalo Bill Historical Center,** sometimes called the Smithsonian of the West. The center actually houses four museums in one: the Whitney Gallery of Western Art, with works by traditional Western artists, including Charlie Russell and Frederic Remington; the Buffalo Bill Historical Center, which has memorabilia of the scout and showman; the Plains Indian Museum, housing art and artifacts of the Plains tribes; and the Cody Firearms Museum, with the world's largest collection of American firearms. *720 Sheridan Ave., ☏ 307/587–4771. ☛ (2 days): $8 adults, $6.50 senior citizens, $4 youths over 12, $2 children 6–12. ☉ Mar. and Nov., Tues.–Sun. 10–3; Apr., Tues.–Sun. 8–5; May and Sept., daily 8–8; June–Aug., daily 7–10; Oct., daily 8–5; Dec.–Feb., tours on request.*

On Cody's western outskirts, just off the West Yellowstone Highway, is **Trail Town,** a collection of historic buildings from Wyoming's frontier days. It features a cemetery of famous local mountain men, as well as Native American and pioneer artifacts. *1831 Demaris Dr., ☏ 307/587–5302. ☛ $3. ☉ May 1–"until the snow flies."*

The road from Cody to Yellowstone climbs through Shoshone Canyon, skirts the Buffalo Bill Reservoir, and runs through the wide, forested Wapiti Valley, which has many dude ranches.

Almost everyone who comes any distance to visit Wyoming has **Yellowstone National Park** in mind. Few places in the world can match

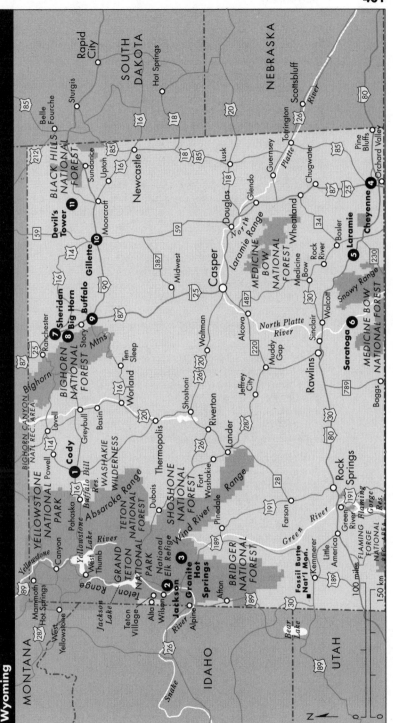

Wyoming

the park's collection of accessible wonders, from grazing bison and cruising trumpeter swans to rainbow-colored hot springs and thundering geysers. As you visit the park's hydrothermal areas, you'll be walking on top of the Yellowstone Caldera—a 28-mile-by-47-mile collapsed volcanic cone, which last erupted about 600,000 years ago. The park's geyser basins, hot mud pots, fumaroles (steam vents), and hot springs are kept bubbling by an underground pressure cooker filled with magma. One geophysicist describes Yellowstone as "a window on the earth's interior."

Before you start visiting the sights, assess your desires and abilities. Would you rather hike, drive the roads, or buy a seat on a tour bus? You can sleep in solitude at a backcountry campsite or in luxury at a historic lakeside hotel. Choose between geysers and wildlife or between fishing hip-deep in the Firehole River and boating on Yellowstone Lake. If time is limited, pick a single area, such as the Grand Canyon of the Yellowstone or the Norris Geyser Basin, and don't try to do everything.

The 370 miles of public roads in the park are both a blessing and a curse. They provide access to extraordinary landscapes and wildlife but are often potholed, overcrowded, and dotted with motor homes that have been pulled over on narrow shoulders so that their occupants can photograph grazing elk or buffalo cows with calves. As a result, roads become choked with slow-moving caravans led by big RVs. With budgets dwindling and visitation growing, this situation will only get worse.

There are summer-staffed visitor centers throughout the park and a busy schedule of guided hikes, evening talks, and campfire programs. (Check "Discover Yellowstone," a park newsletter available at entrances and visitor centers, for dates and times.) Pamphlets describing hot-spring basins are available for 25¢ at each site or visitor center. The park has numerous picnic areas and campgrounds, as well as restaurants and lodgings (*see* Dining and Lodging, *below*).

The road from Cody slips through **Sylvan Pass** and arrives at Yellowstone's **East Entrance,** one of five park entrances. (Each entrance road links up to the 142-mile figure-eight Grand Loop Road at the heart of the park, which connects the most accessible attractions.) In the winter, this is a favorite, if rather harrowing, entrance for snowmobilers, who come in increasing numbers to ride the park's snow-packed roads. The East Entrance Road meets the Lower Loop at **Fishing Bridge,** where the Yellowstone River drains Yellowstone Lake. Although you can't fish here anymore—it's too popular with grizzly bears—it's a nice place for a stroll.

Head north toward the magnificent **Grand Canyon of the Yellowstone,** where water draining from Yellowstone Lake has cut deep into an ancient lava flow. Just shy of Canyon is a road to the 109-foot **Upper Falls,** not as high as the more spectacular Lower Falls (*see below*) but well worth a visit. You can also drive across Chittenden Bridge above the Upper Falls to view the canyon from a paved road that runs about 2 miles along the **South Rim.** A short hike brings you to **Artist Point,** and adventurous hikers can go farther along the South Rim on various trails. The Grand Loop Road continues along the **North Rim** to **Canyon,** where there is a lodge and campground. From here you can backtrack along the one-way North Rim Drive to see more of the canyon. Short paths lead to a number of scenic overlooks, including **Inspiration Point,** which provide great views of the canyon and of the breath-

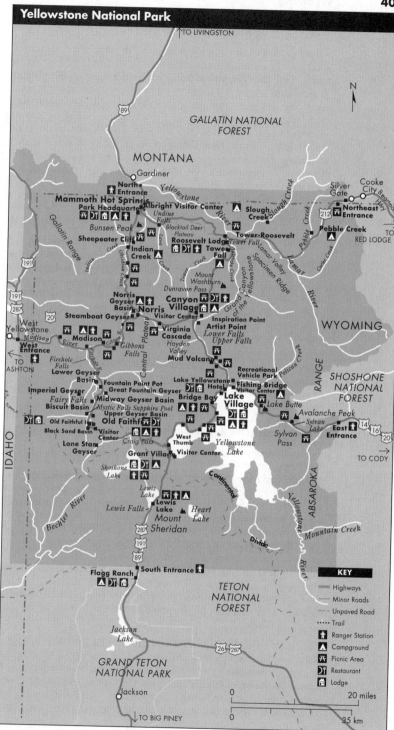

TO LIVINGSTON

N

GALLATIN NATIONAL FOREST

MONTANA

Gardiner

North Entrance

Silver Gate

Cooke City

Mammoth Hot Springs

Park Headquarters

Albright Visitor Center

Slough Creek

Northeast Entrance

TO RED LODGE

Bunsen Peak

Sheepeater Cliff

Blacktail Deer Plateau

Roosevelt Lodge

Tower-Roosevelt

Pebble Creek

Indian Creek

Tower Fall

Undine Falls

Mount Washburn

Dunraven Pass

Specimen Ridge

Lamar Valley

Gallatin Range

Norris Geyser Basin

Norris

Canyon Village

Visitor Center

Inspiration Point

Artist Point

Lower Falls

Upper Falls

Grand Canyon of the Yellowstone

WYOMING

Steamboat Geyser

West Yellowstone

Madison

West Entrance

TO ASHTON

Virginia Cascade

Gibbons Falls

Hayden Valley

Mud Volcano

SHOSHONE NATIONAL FOREST

RANGE

Firehole Falls

Lower Geyser Basin

Imperial Geyser

Fairy Falls

Biscuit Basin

Fountain Paint Pot

Great Fountain Geyser

Midway Geyser Basin

Mystic Falls

Sapphire Pool

Upper Geyser Basin

Recreational Vehicle Park

Lake Yellowstone Hotel

Fishing Bridge Visitor Center

Pelican Creek

Old Faithful Inn

Black Sand Basin

Old Faithful

Visitor Center

Bridge Bay

Lake Village

Lake Butte

Avalanche Peak

Sylvan Lake

Sylvan Pass

East Entrance

TO CODY

Lone Star Geyser

Craig Pass

West Thumb

Grant Village Visitor Center

Shoshone Lake

Yellowstone Lake

SHOSHONE NATIONAL FOREST

ABSAROKA

Lewis Lake

Lewis Lake

Lewis Falls

Heart Lake

Mount Sheridan

Continental

Divide

Yellowstone River

Mountain Creek

IDAHO

Madison River

Central Plateau

Flagg Ranch

South Entrance

TETON NATIONAL FOREST

Jackson Lake

GRAND TETON NATIONAL PARK

Jackson

TO BIG PINEY

KEY	
	Highways
	Minor Roads
	Unpaved Road
	Trail
	Ranger Station
	Campground
	Picnic Area
	Restaurant
	Lodge

0   20 miles

0   35 km

taking 308-foot **Lower Falls.** From Inspiration Point, you can also hike 3 miles along the **North Rim Trail,** with still more river and falls views.

Return to the Grand Loop Road and head north to where the Lower and Upper loops join. Drive west toward Norris, and you'll see the remains of the **North Fork Fire,** which left a moonscape on this plateau. At **Norris,** the hottest and oldest geyser basin in the park, changes occur every year: new geysers erupt, steam vents hiss to life, hot springs suddenly stop flowing. The names of the features—Whirligig Geyser, Whale's Mouth, Emerald Spring, and Arch Steam Vent—are often apt descriptions. Visit the **Norris Museum** for a history of Yellowstone's watchdogs, from turn-of-the-century army troops to today's rangers. Walk west through **Back Basin,** where the huge, unpredictable **Steamboat Geyser** has come dramatically to life in recent years, but don't wait for it. It blows 300 feet about once a year. To the east, the smaller, colorful **Porcelain Basin** has a 1-mile boardwalk and, usually, a lot of people. You can sometimes see the whitish basin floor bulge and pulsate from underground pressure.

From Norris, head north on the Upper Loop to **Mammoth Hot Springs.** Many travelers skip this section of the loop, though it includes some spectacular views, including those of **Roaring Mountain,** which looks like a giant pile of melted vanilla ice cream. Mammoth is the gateway for the North Entrance. Here you'll find full services; the colony of old, stone military buildings that is now the park headquarters; and the **Horace Albright Visitor Center,** with the park's largest assemblage of information, exhibits, and publications about the park as well as historic archives for researchers. Antlered elk wander on the grass, and during the fall, bugling bulls collect their harems. The hot springs drop down terraces on the mountainside just west of the headquarters and hotel. Though the springs' flow has diminished in recent years, the **Minerva Terrace** is worth a look. You can hike a boardwalk from the top to the bottom of the huge white hot-spring constructions.

Continue clockwise on the Upper Loop. You'll pass the 60-foot **Undine Falls** and, farther along the road, a short trail to the huge stump of a petrified redwood tree before reaching **Tower Junction.** Here you can take the Northeast Entrance Road up the **Lamar River valley,** a favorite haunt of bison, for a nice side trip outside the park on the 68-mile **Beartooth Highway,** U.S. 212. The highest highway in the state, it runs in and out of Montana and over 10,947-foot Beartooth Pass. Switchbacks cut into steep cliffs ferry autos up to spectacular views of granite peaks, snowfields, and lakes. You can make the trip even better, and longer, by taking the recently paved **Chief Joseph Scenic Highway,** Route 296, south from the Beartooth Highway toward Cody. There are no services, but you'll see the beautiful Sunlight Basin and the dramatic gorge carved by the Clarks Fork of the Yellowstone River.

Back on the Upper Loop, head south toward Canyon. If you drive a short way up Chittenden Road, you can hike an easy 3 miles to the top of **Mt. Washburn** (10,243 feet). Back on the Upper Loop, you'll cross over **Dunraven Pass;** in recent years, two grizzlies have often been seen in a meadow here. When you rejoin the Lower Loop, you can return south toward Yellowstone Lake or head west again to Norris and south toward Madison Junction.

This area was hard hit by the 1988 fires, but park scientists contend that the fires corrected ecological imbalances caused by generations of fire suppression. Although there are still areas burned to a ghostly crisp—

here and along the **Lewis River** toward the South Entrance—they only add to the variety of this unparalleled preserve.

At **Madison Junction,** traffic from the popular West Entrance joins the loop, and just to the south, a one-way circuit branches off through the **Firehole River canyon,** which features a spring-warmed swimming hole. Continuing south, the Lower Loop follows the steaming Firehole River, providing views at times of elk and bison grazing in the distance.

As you approach Old Faithful, you'll pass through three distinct geyser areas, beginning with **Lower Geyser Basin,** which features the fumaroles, blue pools, pink mud pots, and minigeysers of **Fountain Paint Pots** (small in scale but great in variety) as well as the **Great Fountain Geyser.** The **Midway Geyser Basin** has some beautiful, richly colored, bottomless pools—former geysers—**Grand Prismatic Spring,** and **Excelsior Geyser Crater.**

Last but not least is the **Upper Geyser Basin** and its centerpiece, **Old Faithful.** The mysterious plumbing of Yellowstone has lengthened the geyser's cycle somewhat in recent years, but Old Not-So-Faithful spouts a powerful 140-foot spume that pleases faithful spectators every 80 minutes or so. A visitor center nearby posts the time of the next eruption. Marked trails and bridges lead across the river to **Geyser Hill.** You can wander downriver, too, away from crowds, to **Castle Geyser** and **Morning Glory Pool,** which has recently been cleaned of coins and trash. Also in the Old Faithful area are two geysers famous for huge, but very rare, eruptions: **Giantess Geyser** and **Giant Geyser.**

At the heart of the tourist development here is **Old Faithful Inn** (*see* Dining and Lodging, *below*), worth a visit even if you aren't staying here. An architectural marvel built in 1903 and later expanded, the log building has a six-story lobby with huge rock fireplaces and wraparound balconies high in the rafters.

The drive over Craig Pass, traveling east, was once the slowest section of the Lower Loop. A recent upgrade and widening are a significant improvement. At West Thumb, you reach **Yellowstone Lake** and the South Entrance Road. If the lake you're interested in, drive north along the shore and stop to stroll along it or visit mud pots and steam vents. The South Entrance Road passes **Lewis Lake,** follows along the sometimes steep-sided path of the **Lewis River,** and connects the park to Grand Teton National Park and Jackson.

Exploring Grand Teton

Just to the south of Yellowstone, connected by the John D. Rockefeller Memorial Parkway (U.S. 89/191/287), is **Grand Teton National Park.** One might think this smaller park with a shorter history is dwarfed by its neighbor to the north, but nothing overshadows peaks like these. Presumably no translation of the French is necessary. The peaks—Mt. Moran, Teewinot Mountain, Mt. Owen, the Grand, and Middle Teton—form a magnificent and dramatic front along the west side of the Teton Valley. Lakes large and small are strung along the range's base, draining north into Jackson Lake, which in turn drains south into the Snake River. Grand Teton was put together from ranches John D. Rockefeller, Jr., bought up in the 1930s. It has a few oddities within its boundaries, such as a commercial airport and a dam to hold water for Idaho irrigators, but for fishing, hiking, climbing, boating, and rugged beauty, it's hard to match.

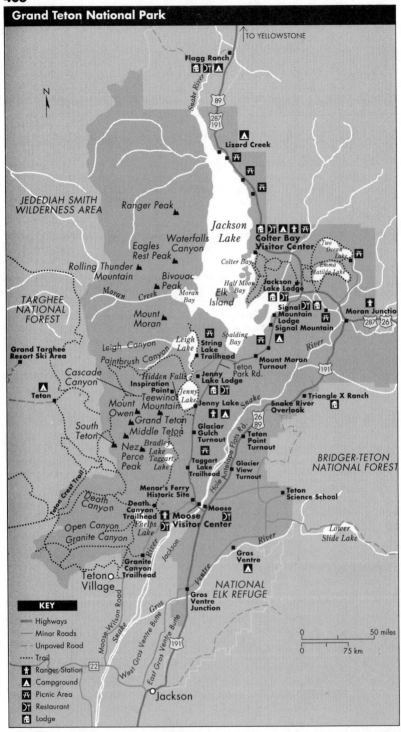

TO YELLOWSTONE

Flagg Ranch

89
287
191

Lizard Creek

Snake River

JEDEDIAH SMITH
WILDERNESS AREA

Ranger Peak

*Jackson
Lake*

Waterfalls
Canyon

Eagles
Rest Peak

Colter Bay

Colter Bay
Visitor Center

*Two Ocean
Lake*

Rolling Thunder
Mountain

Bivouac
Peak

*Half Moon
Bay*

*Emma
Matilda Lake*

TARGHEE
NATIONAL
FOREST

Moran Creek

*Moran
Bay*

*Elk
Island*

Jackson
Lake Lodge

Moran Junctio

287 26

Mount
Moran

Signal
Mountain
Lodge
Signal Mountain

191

Grand Targhee
Resort Ski Area

Leigh Canyon

*Leigh
Lake*

String
Lake
Trailhead

Spalding
Bay

River

Paintbrush Canyon

Mount Moran
Turnout

Teton
Park Rd.

Cascade
Canyon

Teton

Hidden Falls
Inspiration
Point

Jenny
Lake Lodge

*Jenny
Lake*

Teewinot
Mountain

Mount
Owen

Grand Teton

Jenny Lake

Snake

Triangle X Ranch

Snake River
Overlook

South
Teton

Middle Teton

Glacier
Gulch
Turnout

26
89

Teton
Point
Turnout

BRIDGER-TETON
NATIONAL FOREST

Nez
Perce
Peak

*Bradley
Lake*

Taggart
Lake

Taggart
Lake
Trailhead

Glacier
View
Turnout

Hole Antelope Flats Rd.

Menor's Ferry
Historic Site

Teton
Science School

Death
Canyon
Trailhead

*Phelps
Lake*

Moose

Moose
Visitor Center

*Lower
Slide Lake*

Death
Canyon

River

Open Canyon

Granite Canyon

Jackson River

Gros
Ventre

Granite
Canyon
Trailhead

Ventre

NATIONAL
ELK REFUGE

Teton
Village

Moose-Wilson Road

Gros
Ventre
Junction

Gros

West Gros Ventre Butte

East Gros Ventre Butte

22

191

Jackson

At the north end of the park is **Jackson Lake.** The biggest of the park's glacier-scooped lakes, it was made larger still by a dam, farther south, built in 1909. The lake is popular with sailors, anglers, and even windsurfers. Campgrounds and lodges dot the shore (*see* Dining and Lodging, *below*).

Near Jackson Lake Junction, the **Snake River** emerges from the Jackson Lake Dam and winds east and then south through the park. Whether you're on the water or on shore, **Oxbow Bend,** below the dam, is an excellent place to see waterfowl and other wildlife. U.S. 26/89/191 does run the full length of the park, with the Tetons on display all the way, but at this point, a better, more leisurely route is the smaller Teton Park Road, which runs south to Moose, where it rejoins the highway heading to Jackson.

Not far from Jackson Lake Junction on the Teton Park Road, you can take a brief side trip up narrow **Signal Mountain Road** to its summit, where you can see the valley and mountains on all sides.

South of Jackson Lake is **Jenny Lake,** right below the Grand Teton. You can hike 2 miles around the lake from the parking area at the south end to **Inspiration Point,** near the bottom of Cascade Canyon, or make the walk shorter by taking a boat ride from the dock near the parking area to the Cascade Canyon Trailhead. *Teton Boating Inc. Rides cost: $4 over age 13, $2.25 ages 7-12. Boats run early June–mid-Sept., 8–6.*

There are many easy hikes heading off toward the mountains from Teton Park Road. (They're shown on the map in "Teewinot," the free publication handed out at the entrances.) One of the nicest, south of Jenny Lake, is to **Taggart Lake.** Hikers as well as canoeists enjoy **Leigh** and **String lakes,** just north of Jenny Lake; turn west at North Jenny Lake Junction.

Near the end of Teton Park Road, take the access road to visit the non-denominational **Chapel of the Transfiguration;** the view of the Tetons induces couples from all over the world to say their vows here. A short hike from this road on a marked trail brings you to the **Menor's Ferry.** Constructed as a means of conveyance across the Snake River in the 1890s, the ferry shows a technique used to carry people before bridges were built. Several cabins, including the home and store used by Bill Menor, who built and operated the ferry, remain at the site. There is a historic photo collection in one of the cabins.

At **Moose,** site of another visitor center, traffic rejoins the highway, leaves the park, and heads toward Jackson.

Exploring Jackson and Vicinity

② **Jackson** remains a small Western town, howdy in the daytime and hopping in the evening. For outdoor types, it's a place to stock up on supplies before heading out for white-water rafting, backpacking, mountain climbing, or, in the winter, skiing. For tourists, there's a wealth of galleries and Western-wear shops and, at night, varied cuisines and no shortage of bars and music.

Jackson's charm and popularity put it at risk. On busy summer days, traffic can slow to a crawl as the highway doglegs through downtown. Proposals for new motels and condominiums sprout like the purple asters in the spring, as developers vie for a share of the vacation market. Old-timers suggest that the town—in fact, the entire Teton Valley—has already lost the dusty charm it had when horses parked around the

Town Square. However, with national parks and forests and state lands occupying some of the most beautiful real estate, there's only so much ground to build on. These limitations, along with the cautious approach of locals, may keep Jackson on a human scale.

Start a tour of Jackson at the **Town Square,** which has tall shade trees and, at the corners, arches woven from hundreds of elk antlers. In the winter, Christmas lights adorn the arches, and during the summer, there's a melodramatic "shootout" every evening at 6:30. Stagecoach rides originate here during the day.

Just north of town, the **Wildlife of the American West Art Museum** (2820 Rungius Rd., ☎ 307/733–5771) is just what it sounds like. Among the paintings and sculptures of big-horn sheep, elk, and other animals of the West are works by famous artists such as George Catlin and Charles M. Russell. For local history, visit the **Jackson Hole Museum** (☎ 307/733–2414).

South of Jackson, concerted local and national efforts have preserved both the wildlands and the ranches that dot the Teton Valley floor. The Snake River turns west and the contours steepen; by Hoback Junction there's white-water excitement. The highway provides good views of the river's twists and turns and the life-jacketed rafters and kayakers who float the canyon.

About 13 miles south of Jackson at Hoback Junction, turn east on U.S. 189/191 and follow the **Hoback River** south up its beautiful canyon. A tributary canyon 10 miles south of the junction is followed by a well-maintained and marked gravel road to **Granite Hot Springs** in the Bridger-Teton National Forest. Visitors come for the shady, creek-side campground, the pool fed by hot springs, and moderate hikes up Granite Canyon to passes where you get panoramic views of the mountains. In the winter, there is a popular snowmobile excursion from the highway. *10 mi east of U.S. 189/191 on Granite Creek Rd.*

What to See and Do with Children

Children love the outdoors and animals, and they'll find plenty of both here. In the parks, a dip at the **Firehole River swimming hole** (*see* Exploring Cody and Yellowstone, *above*) will please most any child, whereas older kids might like a white-water rafting trip on the Snake River (*see* Sports and the Outdoors, *below*).

Outside the parks, **Cody Nite Rodeo,** more dusty and intimate than big rodeos like Frontier Days, has children's events, such as goat roping. Contact the Cody Country Chamber of Commerce (*see* Important Addresses and Numbers, *below*) for information. ☛ *$7 and $9 adults, $4 and $6 children 7–12. Seat prices vary with location. June–Aug., daily 8:30 pm.*

Over 7,000 elk, many with enormous antler racks, winter in the **National Elk Refuge,** just north of Jackson. Horse-drawn sleigh rides to visit the huge herd are offered in the winter. The elk sit calmly as sleighs loaded with families and alfalfa pellets move in their midst. Dress warmly. Throughout the year, visitors drive up Refuge Road (well east of the herd in winter) for a view of Teton Valley and sometimes camp at Curtis Creek Campground. *Elk Refuge Visitor Center,* ☎ *307/733–9214. Sleigh rides: $8 adults, $4 children 6–12, Dec. 15–Apr. Refuge open year-round.*

Off the Beaten Track

The nonprofit **Yellowstone Institute** (Box 117, Yellowstone National Park 82190, ☎ 307/344–2294), housed in new, heated log cabins in the pastoral Lamar Valley, offers a wide range of summer and winter courses about the ecology, history, and wildlife of Yellowstone. Search with a historian for the trail the Nez Percé took in their flight a century ago, or get tips from professional photographers on how to capture a trumpeter swan on film. Facilities are fairly primitive—guests do their own cooking and camp during some of the courses—but prices are reasonable. Besides, there's no better way to get out from behind the windshield and learn what makes the park tick. Some programs are specifically designed for young people and families. Down the road in Grand Teton, similar programs are offered by the **Teton Science School** (Box 68, Kelly 83011, ☎ 307/733–4765).

Shopping

Shopping Districts/Streets

Jackson's peaceful **Town Square** is surrounded by storefronts with a mixture of specialty and outlet shops—most of them small-scale—with moderate to expensive prices. Just north is a small cluster of fine shops in **Gaslight Alley** (N. Cache St.). In Teton Village (the cluster of buildings at the base of the Jackson Hole Ski Resort, 15 mi northwest of Jackson), the **Mountainside Mall,** not to be mistaken for a big suburban mall (to its credit), serves the resort crowd.

Specialty Stores

BOOKSELLERS

In Jackson's Gaslight Alley, **Valley Books** (125 N. Cache St., ☎ 307/733–4533) ranks among the best bookstores in the region, with a big selection and salespeople who can talk Tolstoy while guiding you to the best publications on local subjects.

GALLERIES

Jackson's art galleries serve a range of tastes. The fine nature photography of Tom Mangelson is displayed at his **Images of Nature Gallery** (170 N. Cache St., 2nd floor, ☎ 307/733–6179). Some of the best regional and local artists, including Russell Chatham, are represented at **Partners Gallery** (125 W. Pearl St., ☎ 307/733–0870). **Trailside Americana** (105 N. Center St., ☎ 307/733–3186) has more traditional Western art and jewelry.

HATS

Cody's **Wind River Hat Company** (144 W. Yellowstone Ave., ☎ 307/527–5939) designs personalized hats for work or dress.

LEATHER

In Cody, **Creations in Leather** (1212 Sheridan Ave., ☎ 307/587–6461) boasts a complete line of custom leather goods for the working cowboy; you'll find high-priced elk and deer jackets as well as shirts, vests, and skirts with matching belts and purses. **Hide Out Leather** (40 N. Center St., ☎ 307/733–2422), in Jackson, carries many local designs.

OUTDOOR EQUIPMENT

Jackson is well stocked with the best in outdoor equipment, winter and summer, including standouts **Jack Dennis Sports** (50 E. Broadway Ave., ☎ 307/733–3270), Jackson's premier sports shop, an internationally known fishing and sporting headquarters. **Skinny Skis** (65 W. Deloney Ave., ☎ 307/733–6094) offers everything a cross-country skier might need . . . or want. **Teton Mountaineering** (170 N. Cache, ☎

307/733–3595) specializes in Nordic school downhill skiing, climbing, hiking equipment, and clothing. **Westbank Anglers** (Box 523, Teton Village, ☎ 307/733–6483) fulfills fly-fishing dreams.

WESTERN WEAR

In downtown Cody, women shop at the **Plush Pony** (1350 Sheridan Ave., ☎ 307/587–4677) for "uptown Western clothes" ranging from the best leather belts to the most stylish skirts, jackets, and dresses, all with a Western flair. **Flight West** (1155 Sheridan Ave., ☎ 307/527–7800) offers embroidered shirts and Navajo-print vests as well as Wyoming-made bent-willow furniture and other items to spice up any Western decor. On the Town Square in Jackson, try **Jackson Hole Clothiers** (45 E. Deloney Ave., ☎ 307/733–7211), for women's Western wear and hand-knit sweaters. **Wyoming Outfitters** (156 N. Center St., ☎ 307/733–3877) has a full line of women's Western clothing and accessories. **Cattle Kate** (120 E. Broadway Ave., ☎ 307/733–4803) produces some of the best designs in contemporary Western wear on the market today.

Sports and the Outdoors

Cycling

Wyoming roads do not offer wide shoulders, but that doesn't stop cyclists from pedaling the area's two-lane highways, either in the midst of cross-country tours or on day trips. Bikers need to be alert for motorists, who are often distracted and sometimes negligent. In addition, mountain bikes are increasingly climbing the trails that hikers favor, and there are sometimes conflicts.

In Yellowstone, the road from Grant Village over **Craig Pass** to Old Faithful is roomier and in better shape than most other park roads, though there is no designated bike path. In the Jackson area, cyclists ride the **Spring Gulch Road,** part pavement, part dirt, off Route 22, along the base of Gros Ventre Butte, rejoining U.S. 26/89/191 near the Gros Ventre River. The trip up to **Lower Slide Lake,** north of town, is also a favorite. Turn east off U.S. 26/89/191 to Kelly, and then take the Slide Lake Road.

Various outfitters guide and supply bicyclists, and provide advice and trail maps as well. (*see* Guided Tours, *below*).

Camping

This is a camper's paradise, a place where even mattress-lovers deign to spend a night or two on the ground for the pleasure of a sky full of stars and the quiet sounds of the night. There are plenty of choices, but campgrounds in the parks tend to fill up quickly, often by midday. These campgrounds accept no reservations; every day it's first come, first served. In **Yellowstone,** there are 11 campgrounds (under $10) and one RV park, Fishing Bridge ($16), open May to October with some variations. The **Grant Village** campground is as well designed as the resort (*see* Dining and Lodging, *below*) is ill designed, and **Madison** is another favorite. **Grand Teton** has five public campgrounds. The most popular is at **Jenny Lake** (Teton Park Rd. at S. Jenny Lake), and the most luxurious is **Colter Bay** (on Jackson Lake, 7 mi north of Jackson Lake Lodge), which has showers, RV hookups, and laundry facilities. **Gros Ventre Campground** (4 mi east of U.S. 26/89/191 at Gros Ventre Junction), on the far eastern side of the park, is big enough (360 sites) that it doesn't fill up as fast as the others. Fees are $8 per night.

U.S. Forest Service campgrounds are less quick to fill, and there are some beauties in **Bridger-Teton National Forest** (340 N. Cache St., Box 1888, Jackson 83001, ☎ 307/739–5500), including **Curtis Creek,** east of the National Elk Refuge, and **Granite Creek,** just below the hot springs near the Hoback River (*see* Exploring Jackson and Vicinity, *above*). Most campgrounds are open June–September, and fees are less than $10. For an extra charge, you can reserve a campsite by calling **U.S. Forest Reservations** (☎ 800/283–2267). In the forest backcountry, you can camp where you like at no charge.

Canoeing, Kayaking, and Rafting

For river runners, there are peaceful, scenic stretches of the upper **Snake River** in Grand Teton National Park, including the beautiful Oxbow; you can navigate them yourself by canoe or kayak or float as a passenger on a guided raft. Be sure to check current conditions and ability recommendations with park rangers before you launch. Farther down the river past Jackson, where the Hoback joins the Snake and the canyon walls become steep, there are lively white-water sections. Guided raft trips here will thrill and douse you. Experienced paddlers run the **Hoback,** too.

If you want instruction in the fine art of paddling, contact **Snake River Kayak and Canoe** (Box 3482, Jackson 83001, ☎ 307/733–3127 or 800/824–5375). Take lessons or rent canoes and kayaks from **Teton Aquatics** (155 W. Gill Ave., Jackson 83001, ☎ 307/733–3127). If you'd rather be a passenger, traveling the peaceful parts of the river looking for wildlife, contact **Barker-Ewing Scenic Float Trips** (Box 100–J, Moose 83012, ☎ 307/733–1000 or 800/448–4204) or **Triangle X Float Trips** (Moose 83012, ☎ 307/733–5500). For wet and wild stretches of river, get in touch with **Lewis & Clark Expeditions** (145 W. Gill St., Box 720, Jackson 83001, ☎ 307/733–4022 or 800/824–5375) or **Mad River Boat Trips** (1060 S. U.S. 89, Box 2222, Jackson 83001, ☎ 307/733–6203 or 800/458–7238).

In Cody, family river trips on the **Shoshone River** are offered by **River Runners** (1491 Sheridan Ave., 82801, ☎ 307/527–7238) and **Wyoming River Trips** (Buffalo Bill Village, Box 1541-TC, 82414, ☎ 307/587–6661 or 800/586–6661).

Fishing

Lake and stream fishing in Wyoming is legendary. Record Mackinaw trout have been taken at **Jackson Lake,** and the trout population in **Yellowstone Lake** has been revived. Inside and outside the parks, the rivers are teeming with rainbow, native cutthroat, brook, brown, and Mackinaw trout, as well as whitefish and catfish at some lower elevations. The **Snake River** has its own unique cutthroat strain. Fishing aficionados often trek south into the **Wind River Mountains,** where glacier-fed lakes yield all of the above plus golden trout.

Limits and restrictions on fishing in the parks change from year to year. A free park license is required. Outside the parks on state, private, or national forest lands, Wyoming fishing licenses are required and are usually available at sporting goods stores and drugstores. Nonresidents can purchase a one-day license for $5; five-day, $20; 10-day, $30; and season, $50. Children under 14 may fish without a license when with a licensed adult. Contact **Wyoming Game and Fish Department** (5400 Bishop Blvd., Cheyenne 82006, ☎ 307/777–4600) for information. The **Wind River Indian Reservation** has some of the best fishing in the Rockies. A separate license is required here. Contact **Shoshone and Ara-**

paho Tribes (Fish and Game Dept., 1 Washakie, Fort Washakie 82520, ☎ 307/332–7207).

Golf

In Cody, **Olive Glenn Golf and Country Club** (802 Meadow La., ☎ 307/587–5551) is a highly rated 18-hole course open to the public; a Jacuzzi, pool, and two tennis courts are also available. Jackson has two fine 18-hole courses: **Jackson Hole Golf Club** (☎ 307/733–3111), a championship course near the Jackson Hole Airport, with tennis and swimming facilities; and **Teton Pines Golf Club** (3450 N. Clubhouse, ☎ 307/733–1733), just south of the Jackson Hole Ski Resort.

Mountain Climbing

Mountain climbers get a leg up in the Grand Tetons from **Jackson Hole Mountain Guides** (165 N. Glenwood St., Box 7477, Jackson 83001, ☎ 307/733–4979) or **Exum Mountain Guides** (south end of Jenny Lake, Box 56, Moose 83012, ☎ 307/733–2297).

Skiing

CROSS-COUNTRY

Cross-country skiing and snowshoeing are permitted in parts of Yellowstone and Grand Teton national parks and surrounding forests. Among the best places is **Togwotee Pass,** east of Jackson on U.S. 26/287, in Bridger-Teton and Shoshone national forests. Lessons and groomed trails are available for a fee at **Spring Creek Ranch** (*see* Dining and Lodging, *below*) and **Jackson Hole Nordic Center** (Teton Village, ☎ 307/733–2292).

DOWNHILL

About a 45-minute drive from Jackson, on the far side of the Tetons, is **Grand Targhee Ski and Summer Resort** (Box SKI, Alta 83422, ☎ 307/353–2300 or 800/827–4433), a resort famed for its deep powder and its family atmosphere. Targhee's slopes—predominantly intermediate—never feel crowded, but to experience complete solitude, try a day of Sno-Cat skiing in untracked powder. There are four lifts and vertical drop of 2,200 feet. The resort was rebuilt recently and has a handsome, natural-wood look as well as an outdoor pool and hot tub for overnight guests. Lift prices are moderate ($24 for adults, $12 for senior citizens and children under 13).

The **Jackson Hole Ski Resort** (Box 290, Teton Village 83025, ☎ 307/733–2292 or 800/443–6931) boasts the longest vertical drop among American ski areas: 4,139 feet. Especially rich in intermediate and advanced terrain, it has nine lifts and a tram to the top of Rendezvous Mountain. Few resorts have views to match the one of Teton Valley, and in good snow years, like 1993, Jackson Hole provides some of the best skiing in the Rockies. Plans for expansion and faster lifts are afoot. The ski school is run by Olympic medalist Pepi Stiegler. Tickets are pricey: $38 per day for adults.

Snowmobiling

Snowmobiling is increasingly popular and is allowed on snow-packed roads within Yellowstone Park. The state of Wyoming grooms an extensive network of trails in the forests of the northwest, including the **Continental Divide Snowmobile Trail,** which runs from Lander through Grand Teton. For information on trails, contact the **Wyoming State Snowmobile Program** (☎ 307/777–7550).

Among the bigger snowmobile operations are **Flagg Ranch Village** and **Togwotee Mountain Lodge;** in Yellowstone, **TW Recreational Services** rents snowmobiles at the Mammoth Hot Springs Hotel or Old

Faithful Snow Lodge for $95 per day (*see* Guided Tours, *below,* for all). Additional information on snowmobile rentals and guides is available from the Jackson Hole Chamber of Commerce (*see* Important Addresses and Numbers, *below*).

Water Sports

On Yellowstone Lake, boaters embark from **Bridge Bay** (☎ 307/344–7311); rentals are available. If you want to get out on Jackson Lake but didn't bring your own boat, you can hire canoes and powerboats at **Colter Bay Marina** (north of Jackson Lake Junction, ☎ 307/733–2811) or **Signal Mountain Marina** (Teton Park Rd. at the south end of the lake, ☎ 307/543–2831). Boats must be licensed by the parks. Seven-day permits, good in both parks, cost $7 for motorboats and $5 for nonmotorized boats.

Dining and Lodging

Cody

DINING

$$ Franca's Italian Dining. Serving authentic northern-Italian gourmet fare, the menu here is unique each evening. Entrées vary—pork, poultry, beef, seafood, or veal selections are offered, complemented by a wine list of some 90 selections. The small room (maximum 24) is filled with Italian art. ✕ *1421 Rumsey Ave.,* ☎ *307/587–5354. Reservations required. No credit cards. Closed Mon., Tues. and winter. No lunch.*

$ La Comida. Making no claim to authentic Mexican cooking, this restaurant nevertheless recently received the Five Star Diamond Award as one of the top 50 Mexican restaurants in the country from the Academy Awards of the Restaurant Industry and has been reviewed in numerous national newspapers and magazines. Instead, the owners prefer to describe their recipes as "Cody-Mex," but the decor is authentic Mexican and the atmosphere festive. ✕ *1385 Sheridan Ave.,* ☎ *307/587–9556. Reservations advised. AE, D, DC, MC, V.*

$ Proud Cut Saloon. At this popular downtown eatery and watering hole, owner Del Nose claims to serve "kick-ass cowboy cuisine": steaks, prime rib, shrimp, fish, and chicken. The Western decor includes paintings, vintage photographs of Cody country, and large game mounts. ✕ *1227 Sheridan Ave.,* ☎ *307/527–6905. AE, D, DC, MC, V.*

LODGING

$$$ Buffalo Bill Village. This downtown development comprises three lodgings, which share many facilities. The **Buffalo Bill Village Resort,** consisting of log cabins with modern interiors, and the **Holiday Inn Convention Center,** a typical two-story brick hotel, are most noteworthy. 🏨 *1701 Sheridan Ave., 82414,* ☎ *307/587–5544. Resort: 85 cabins. Inn: 184 rooms. Restaurant, bar, pool, meeting rooms. AE, D, DC, MC, V.*

$$–$$$ Irma Hotel. Named for Buffalo Bill's daughter, this hotel has some of the flavor of earlier days, when Buffalo Bill still ranched nearby. With brass beds and period furniture in many rooms, a huge restaurant, and an elaborate cherry wood bar, it retains its old charm. During the summer, locals stage a gunfight on the porch Wednesday–Friday at 7 PM. 🏨 *1192 Sheridan Ave., 82414,* ☎ *307/587–4221,* ℻ *307/587–4221. 41 rooms. Restaurant, bar. AE, D, DC, MC, V.*

$$ Pahaska Teepee Resort. Two miles from Yellowstone's East Entrance, these cabins are a good base for summer and winter recreation, both inside and outside the park. This was Buffalo Bill's original getaway in the high country. 🏨 *183 Yellowstone Hwy., Cody 82414,* ☎

307/527–7701 or 800/628–7791, ℻ 397/527–4019. 52 cabins. Restaurant, horseback riding, snowmobiling. AE, MC, V.

$$ **Parson's Pillow.** Built in 1902 as Cody's first church, this B&B serves
★ big, delicious breakfasts. Innkeepers Lee and Elly Larabee are founts
of information about the area's sights and history. 🖃 *1202 14th St.,
82414, ☎ 307/587–2382 or 800/377–2348. 4 rooms, 2 share bath.
MC, V.*

Grand Targhee

DINING AND LODGING

$–$$ **Grand Targhee Ski and Summer Resort.** Perched on the west side of
the Tetons, this small but modern facility has the uncrowded, stroll-
around atmosphere of a small village in the Alps, rather than the
speedy, noisy scene of many American resorts today. The motel-style
rooms are simply furnished and clustered around common areas with
nestled fireplaces; the condominium rooms have more space and a
brighter look inside. Expansion plans are on the drawing board, but
the permit process with the U.S. Forest Service may take several years.
Skadi's, the resort's foremost restaurant, is a relaxing, well-lighted place
with Southwestern-style decor, high ceilings, and a general feel of
roominess. On the menu are tenderloin beef with *poblano* chile sauce
and regional game dishes including venison and pheasant. For quicker,
less expensive fare, there is the **Cactus Kitchen.** 🖃 *Box SKI, Alta 83422,
☎ 307/353–2300 or 800/827–4433. 97 rooms: 65 motel-style, 32 condos. 5 restaurants, pool, hot tub, outdoor hot tub, cross-country skiing. AE, D, MC, V.*

Grand Teton National Park

DINING

$$ **Dornan's.** This popular local hangout has Old West decor and moun-
tain views. In the summer, it cooks up an outdoor Dutch-oven buffet
(steak, ribs, and cowboy beans) and a friendly atmosphere to go with
it. A good wine shop is adjacent. ✕ *U.S. 191, Moose, ☎ 307/733–
2415. Reservations required. MC, V.*

DINING AND LODGING

$$$ **Jenny Lake Lodge.** In this most exclusive of the park's resorts, elegant
★ yet rustic cabins are bedecked with handmade quilts (and electric blan-
kets). Overnight guests are on the American plan; two meals a day are
included, as are horseback riding, bicycling, and other outdoor activities. The lodge dining room offers a set dinner menu with a choice of
entrées emphasizing Rocky Mountain cuisine, including roast prime
rib of buffalo or breast of pheasant with pheasant sausage. 🖃 *Jenny
Lake Rd., Grand Teton Lodge Co., Box 240, Moran 83013, ☎
307/733–2811. 30 cabins. Restaurant, bar. AE, DC, MC, V. Closed
mid-Oct.–early June.*

$$–$$$ **Jackson Lake Lodge.** Outside, the resort has a 1950s look, dark brown
and low-slung. Inside, two large fireplaces adorn the lounge, Native
American designs decorate the walls, and huge picture windows look
out at Willow Flats, below Jackson Lake Dam. There are 30 smaller
rooms in the main lodge; the others, in one-story motor-lodge-style buildings, are preferable. The lodge boasts the only swimming pool in the
park. Rotating four dinner menus, the **Mural Room** often features buffalo, popular with the largely tourist clientele, as well as local game
dishes such as venison or antelope. 🖃 *U.S. 89 north of Jackson Lake
Junction, Grand Teton Lodge Co., Box 240, Moran 83013, ☎ 307/733–
2811. 385 rooms. 2 restaurants, pool. AE, DC, MC, V. Closed Oct.–late
May.*

$$–$$$ **Signal Mountain Lodge.** Built of volcanic stone and pine shingles, the lodge sits on the eastern shore of Jackson Lake. The lobby has a fireplace, a piano, and Adirondack furniture, and guest rooms are clustered in cabinlike units, some with kitchenettes. **The Aspens** restaurant offers up views of the lake and the Tetons as well as a menu with elk medallions and shrimp linguine. ▦ *Teton Park Rd., Box 50, Moran 83013,* ☎ *307/543–2831. 79 units. Restaurant, bar, boating. AE, DC, MC, V. Closed mid-Oct.–early May.*

$–$$ **Colter Bay Village.** Less expensive than its posher cousins, the resort, near Jackson Lake, has splendid views and an excellent marina and beach for the windsurfing crowd. (You'll need a wet suit.) The **Chuckwagon** restaurant is family oriented, serving lasagna, trout, and barbecue spare ribs; it's also a little more upscale than the resort, with prices in the **$$–$$$** range. ▦ *Off U.S. 89, Grand Teton Lodge Co., Box 240, Moran 83013,* ☎ *307/453–2811. 250 cabins (30 share bath). 2 restaurants, bar, laundry services. AE, DC, MC, V. Closed late Sept.–early June.*

Jackson

DINING

$$$ **The Blue Lion.** Consistently excellent fare is served in this blue clap-
★ board house two blocks from the Town Square. Dishes range from rack of lamb to fresh seafood. Lunch on the deck is a treat in summer. ✕ *160 N. Millward St.,* ☎ *307/733–3912. AE, MC, D, V.*

$$ **The Bunnery.** Lunch and dinner are served here in the summer, but it's
★ the breakfasts that are irresistible, whether it's an omelet with blue cheese, mushrooms, and sautéed spinach or a home-baked pastry. It's elbow to elbow inside and a brief wait to be seated on busy mornings, but any inconvenience is well worth it. ✕ *130 N. Cache St., Hole-in-the-Wall Mall,* ☎ *307/733–5474. No reservations. MC, V.*

$$ **Nani's.** The ever-changing menu at this cozy, almost cramped, restaurant may contain braised veal shanks with saffron risotto or other regional Italian cooking. Almost hidden behind a motel, it's designed to attract gourmets, not tourists. ✕ *240 N. Glenwood St.,* ☎ *307/733–3888. DC, MC, V.*

$$ **Sweetwater Restaurant.** Mediterranean meals are served in a log cabin atmosphere, and it works. Start with humus or a Montrechet tart (goat cheese with caramelized onions in pastry); then go on to lamb dishes, chicken Bombay, or shrimp *spetses* (simmered in tomato and garlic with feta cheese). ✕ *King and Pearl Sts.,* ☎ *307/733–3553. MC, V.*

$–$$ **Mangy Moose.** Folks pour in off the ski slopes for a lot of food and talk at this two-level restaurant plus bar with an outdoor deck. The place is adorned with antiques, including a biplane suspended from the ceiling. There's a high noise level but decent fare at fair prices. ✕ *Teton Village,* ☎ *307/733–4913. AE, MC, V.*

$ **Jedediah's House of Sourdough.** This restaurant, a block east of the Town Square, makes breakfast and lunch for the big appetite. There are plenty of "sourjacks" (sourdough flapjacks) and biscuits and gravy and a friendly, elbow-knocking atmosphere. ✕ *135 E. Broadway Ave.,* ☎ *307/733–5671. No reservations. AE, MC, V. No dinner.*

$ **Off Broadway.** This restaurant emphasizes seafood and pasta (Cajun shrimp with black linguine), with a little Thai, wild game, and snazzy neon thrown in. Seating is indoors or out. ✕ *30 King St.,* ☎ *307/733–9777. AE, MC, V.*

$ **Vista Grande.** At this popular spot, you sometimes have to wait for the generous portions of Mexican-style food. Lovers of hot food will find it a little bland, and at times, it's too crowded and noisy. ✕ *Teton*

Village Rd. near Wilson turnoff, ☎ *307/733–6964. No reservations. MC, V.*

DINING AND LODGING

$$$ **Wort Hotel.** This brick Victorian hotel near the square seems to have
★ been around as long as the Tetons, but it feels fresh inside. A fireplace warms the lobby, and a sitting area is just up the stairs. You can sip a drink in the Silver Dollar Bar or sit down for a gourmet meal. Try the mixed grill of buffalo and elk medallions or the nightly veal special. ⌧ *50 N. Glenwood St., 83001,* ☎ *307/733–2190 or 800/322–2727,* FAX *307/733–2067. 60 rooms. Restaurant, bar, hot tub, exercise room. AE, D, DC, MC, V.*

$$–$$$ **Spring Creek Ranch.** Outside of town on Gros Ventre Butte, this luxury resort offers beautiful views of the Tetons and a number of amenities, including cooking in some units, horseback riding, tennis, and cross-country skiing and sleigh rides in winter. Aside from 36 hotel rooms, there's a changing mix of studios, suites, and condos with lofts, called "Choates." The comfortable restaurant, **The Granary,** (reservations are required) serves fine food and is slightly more expensive than the resort; lead off with Dungeness crab and Havarti cheese wrapped in phyllo dough, followed by poached salmon with a cucumber dill sauce and wild rice. ⌧ *1800 Spirit Dance Rd., Box 3154, 83001,* ☎ *307/733–8833 or 800/443–6139,* FAX *307/733–1524. 117 units. Restaurant, pool, 2 tennis courts, horseback riding. AE, D, DC, MC, V.*

LODGING

You can make reservations for most motels through two reservation services: **Central Reservations** (☎ 800/443–6931) or **Jackson Hole Vacations** (☎ 800/223–4059).

$$$ **Painted Porch Bed and Breakfast.** Cozy, clean, and comfortable, this traditional red and white farmhouse built in 1901 is nestled on 3½ acres of pine and aspen 8 miles out of town. There are actually four porches and a white picket fence, along with Japanese soaking tubs. Full breakfast is included. ⌧ *Box 3965, 83001,* ☎ *307/733–1981. 4 rooms. Library. MC, V.*

$$–$$$ **Days Inn.** Like other chains, this motel is something familiar, but the lodgepole swing out front, the lobby's elk-antler chandelier, and the rooms' Teton, Wind River, or Snake River range views remind you where you are. Some rooms have microwaves and fridges, and a Continental breakfast is included. ⌧ *1280 W. Broadway Ave., 83001,* ☎ *307/739–9010,* FAX *307/733–0044. 78 rooms. Hot tub, sauna. AE, D, DC, MC, V.*

$$–$$$ **Pony Express.** Rooms are standard motel rooms, but some have mountain views, while others have patios. The center of town is just two blocks away. ⌧ *Box 972, 83001,* ☎ *307/733–2658. 41 rooms. Pool, hot tub. AE, D, MC, V.*

$$–$$$ **Virginian Motel.** Part of a larger complex that occupies a few blocks, this shingle-roof motel is near restaurants, an Old West saloon, a beauty shop, and a coin-operated laundry. Though it looks much as it did when it opened 30 years ago, it's been upgraded since. ⌧ *750 W. Broadway Ave., 83001,* ☎ *307/733–2792,* FAX *307/733–9513. 158 rooms. Pool. AE, DC, MC, V.*

$$ **Alpenhof.** This small Austrian-style hotel is in the heart of the Jackson Hole Ski Resort next to the tram. The dining room features such entrées as wild game loaf, and Dietrich's Bar and Bistro is a relatively quiet nightclub, considering its proximity to the slopes. ⌧ *Box 288, Teton Village 83025, tel 307/733–3242,* FAX *307/739–1516. 44 rooms.*

Dining room, bar, pool, massage, ski storage. AE, D, DC, MC, V. Closed Oct., Nov., and part of Apr.–May.

$ **Motel 6.** On the outskirts of town, it's big, cheap, and standard for the chain. It's often filled with kids and tour-bus groups. ⊞ *1370 W. Broadway Ave., 83001,* ☎ *307/733–9666,* ℻ *307/733–1620. 155 rooms. Pool. AE, D, DC, MC, V.*

Yellowstone National Park

DINING AND LODGING

The park has six areas with lodges and full-scale restaurants open during the summer. They are operated by **TW Recreational Services** (*see* Guided Tours, *below*), and all accept major credit cards. Ask about size of beds, bathrooms, thickness of walls, and room location when you book, especially in the older hotels, where accommodations vary and upgrades are ongoing. Telephones have been put in some rooms, but no TVs yet.

$$–$$$ **Lake Lodge.** Less regal than its neighbor, the Lake Yellowstone Hotel, the lodge is a half-mile away along the lakeshore. Accommodations are in the lodge and in cabins, and there's cafeteria service. Pets are allowed. ⊞ *Lake Village. 186 units. Cafeteria.*

$–$$ **Lake Yellowstone Hotel.** Built in 1889 on the north end of Yellowstone
★ Lake, the hotel, which has neoclassical Greek columns and huge lakefront windows, is one of the oldest and most elegant park resorts. Afternoon chamber music in the sunny lobby provides a refreshing reminder of old-style luxury tourism in the "wilderness." You can stay in a somewhat primitive cabin, with pine beds and paneling, or at the hotel in a room with a brass bed and antique fixtures. The restaurant ($$–$$$) is casual, with a menu that includes Thai curry shrimp and fettuccine with smoked salmon and snow peas. Restaurant reservations are required. ⊞ *Lake Village. 250 rooms and cabins. Restaurant. Closed late Sept.–mid-May.*

$$ **Canyon Lodge.** The park's biggest, it consists of a large number of nondescript cabins and motel rooms perched above the Grand Canyon of the Yellowstone. A cafeteria fills up with a lunch-time crowd interested in sandwiches, chili, and lasagna, and the restaurant (where dinner reservations are required) features pastas, prime rib, and trout almandine. ⊞ *Canyon. 572 cabins, 37 annex rooms. Restaurant, bar, cafeteria, horseback riding. Closed late Aug.–mid-June.*

$$ **Grant Village.** The least appetizing accommodation in the park is also the newest. It's dull and gray and in standard motel style, but has a view of the lake. The steak house and restaurant (reservations required) serves steak, chicken, and seafood. ⊞ *Grant Village. 300 rooms. Restaurant, boating. Closed mid-Sept.–May.*

$–$$ **Mammoth Hot Springs Hotel.** Sharing its grounds with park headquarters, this is farther from some of the park's favorite attractions than other hotels but also less crowded. Rooms are small, and cabins, four of which have hot tubs, are ranged around "auto courts," a 1950s touch. The lobby and restaurant, which serves such regional American fare as prime rib and chicken with Brie and raspberry sauce, have art deco motifs. Elk and tourists sometimes graze between the hotel and the **Terrace Grill,** an airy room with large windows offering fast-food and cafeteria-style service. ⊞ *Mammoth. 140 cabins. 2 restaurants, bar, horseback riding. Closed mid-Sept.–mid-Dec., mid-March–late May.*

$ **Old Faithful Inn.** You can loll in front of the lobby's roaring fire and
★ look up at wooden balconies that seem to disappear into the night sky; on those deep balconies, guests play cards, scribble at writing desks, or just relax above the hubbub. Guest room decor ranges from brass beds to Victorian cherry wood to inexpensive motel-style furniture. More

expensive rooms face the geyser. The dining-room restaurant is a huge hall centered on a fireplace of volcanic stone and offers up shrimp scampi and chicken Forestière. Restaurant reservations are required. ☎ *Old Faithful. 327 rooms, 77 share bath. Restaurant, bar. Closed mid-Oct.–mid-Dec., mid-Mar.–mid-May.*

$ **Old Faithful Snow Lodge.** This compact motel tucked off to the side in the Old Faithful complex is drab looking, but it stays open for winter visitors. The cozy lobby is warmed by a woodstove, and the small restaurant, which is closed for lunch, serves family fare. ☎ *Old Faithful. 31 rooms, 30 share bath; 34 cabins. Restaurant. Closed mid-Oct.–mid-Dec., mid-Mar.–mid-May.*

$ **Roosevelt Lodge.** Near the beautiful Lamar Valley in the park's northeast corner, this is a simple, log-cabin alternative to more expensive accommodations. The dining-room restaurant (reservations required) dishes up barbecued ribs, Roosevelt beans, and more Western fare. ☎ *Tower-Roosevelt. 86 cabins, 8 with bath. Restaurant, bar. Closed early Sept.–early June.*

The Arts

Wyoming is not the place to come for sophisticated performances, lacking both the facilities and the population to support major groups. Touring productions do visit occasionally, and every summer at the Teton Village resort, the **Grand Teton Music Festival** (Box 490, Teton Village 83025, ☎ 307/733–1128) brings symphonic and chamber music.

Nightlife

Bars and Lounges

There is never a shortage of live music in **Jackson,** where local performers play country, rock, and folk. Two of the most popular bars are on the Town Square: the **Million Dollar Cowboy Bar** (25 N. Cache St., ☎ 307/733–2207), where everyone dresses up in cowboy garb and tries to two-step into the Old West, and the **Rancher Bar** (20. E. Broadway Ave., ☎ 307/733–3886), where the renowned Wyoming band Bruce Howser and Sawmill Creek often performs.

A special treat is down the road at the **Stagecoach Bar** (Rte. 22, Wilson, ☎ 307/733–4407), which fills to bursting Sundays when the house band—a motley bunch that includes a novelist, the first man to ski down the Grand Teton, and a changing cast of guitar aces—is playing.

Northwest Wyoming Essentials

Arriving and Departing

BY PLANE

East of Yellowstone, at Cody, **Yellowstone Regional Airport** (☎ 307/587–5096) is served by commuter airlines out of Denver. There is also service to the Yellowstone area through Bozeman and West Yellowstone, both in Montana.

Jackson Hole Airport (☎ 307/733–7682) lies north of Jackson in Grand Teton National Park, about 40 miles south of Yellowstone National Park. **American** (☎ 800/433–7300), **Continental** (☎ 800/525–0280), **Delta** (☎ 800/221–1212) and its commuter partner **SkyWest** (☎ 800/453–9417), and **United Express** (☎ 800/241–6522) provide daily service, with connections in Denver, Salt Lake City, Dallas, and Chicago. There are seasonal variations; for example, scheduled jet service increases during the ski season. Flights may also be booked—

often at a discount—through **Central Reservations** (☎ 307/733–4005 or 800/443–6931).

Between the Airport and Hotels

Jackson Hole Transportation (☎ 307/733–3135) meets incoming flights at the airport, delivers guests to their accommodations, and returns for departures.

BY CAR

The Yellowstone area is well away from the interstates, so drivers make their way here on two-lane highways that are long on miles and scenery. From I–80, take U.S. 191 north from Rock Springs; it's about 177 miles to Jackson. From I–90, drive west from Sheridan on U.S. 14 or 14A to Cody, and cross over beautiful Sylvan Pass to Yellowstone's East Entrance. Be forewarned, however, that construction to improve the highway has recently been causing delays in the Sylvan Pass area. Check in Cody for current road information. It's about 200 miles from Sheridan to the park. Alternatively, you can take U.S. 89 from the north or U.S. 191/287 from the west, both from Montana.

Getting Around

BY CAR

To best see the area, go by car. You can drive the road loops within the parks and stop at will for a hike or a view. Be extremely cautious in the winter when whiteouts and ice are not uncommon. If you didn't drive to Wyoming, you'll probably want to rent a car; Jackson Hole Airport has major car-rental agencies, which offer four-wheel-drive vehicles and ski racks.

Guided Tours

ORIENTATION

TW Recreational Services (Yellowstone National Park, Mammoth 82190, ☎ 307/344–7901) offers lodging and bus tours of Yellowstone in the summer; in the winter, packages include snowmobiling, skiing, and group tours by motorized snow coach.

SPECIAL INTEREST

Absaroka Outfitters (Box 929, Dubois 82513, ☎ 307/455–2275), from its scenic ranch, offers hunting and horseback-riding trips of up to seven days in the remote wilderness to the southeast of Yellowstone. **Backcountry Bicycle Tours** (Box 4029, Bozeman, MT 59772, ☎ 406/586–3556) offers mountain-bike tours in the area's parks and forests, mixing in rafting and hiking for variety. **Barker-Ewing River Trips** (Box 3032, Jackson 83001, ☎ 307/733–1000) conducts gentle scenic floats or whitewater trips, either half-day journeys or longer trips that include cookouts and camping. **Flagg Ranch Village** (Box 187, Moran 83013, ☎ 307/543–2861 or 800/443–2311), between Grand Teton and Yellowstone parks, runs snowmobiling and fishing trips. **Togwotee Mountain Lodge** (Box 91, Moran 83013, ☎ 307/543–2847 or 800/543–2847 outside WY) has a large snowmobile-guiding operation in the winter and switches to horse packing in summer.

Important Addresses and Numbers

EMERGENCIES

In Yellowstone, the **Lake Clinic and Hospital** (behind the Lake Hotel, ☎ 307/242–7241) is open May 24–September 15; clinics are also in Mammoth (in upper Mammoth, next to the post office, ☎ 307/344–7965), open June–August, and at Old Faithful (in back of the parking lot behind Old Faithful Inn, ☎ 307/545–7325), open May 7–October 10. **Grand Teton Medical Clinic** (next to Jackson Lake Lodge, ☎

307/543–2514) is open May 23–October 3, and in Jackson there's **St. John's Hospital** (625 E. Broadway Ave., ☎ 307/733–3636).

VISITOR INFORMATION
Cody Country Chamber of Commerce (836 Sheridan Ave., Box 2777, Cody 82414, ☎ 307/587–2297); **Jackson Hole Chamber of Commerce** (Box E, Jackson 83001, ☎ 307/733–3316); **Jackson Hole Visitors Council** (Box 982, Dept. 8, Jackson 83001, ☎ 800/782–0011); **Wapiti Valley Association** (1231 Yellowstone Hwy., Cody 82414, ☎ 307/587–9595).

THE CHEYENNE AREA

Cheyenne sits apart from the mountainous magnet of western Wyoming. Some detractors say it's more a part of Colorado's Front Range, which runs north across the nearby border, but the area is no Colorado wannabe. While the rest of Wyoming struggles to get by, Cheyenne is a dynamic city, thriving on a mixture of state government, the military, and new industry. The University of Wyoming, the state's only four-year university, is just over the Medicine Bow Mountains in Laramie, and outside city limits, cattle grazing on rolling hills are a reminder that the area's century-old ranching community still survives.

Born in 1867 as the Union Pacific Railroad inched its way across the plains, Cheyenne began as a rowdy camp for railroad gangs, cowboys, prospectors heading for the Black Hills, and soldiers. It more than lived up to its nickname: "Hell on Wheels." Among the eager entrepreneurs who spent time here were Frank and Jesse James and Butch Cassidy's Hole in the Wall Gang. In the late 19th century, the region's enormously wealthy cattle barons, many of them English, settled in Cheyenne. They sipped brandy at the Cheyenne Club and hired hard cases like Tom Horn to take care of their competitors on the open range. Those brief years of wealth and glory—and the hardworking ranches that endure today—are remembered in the area slogan "Live the Legend" and celebrated with Western élan in Frontier Days.

During Frontier Days, Cheyenne is up to its neck in bucking broncs and bulls and joyful bluster. There are pancake breakfasts put on by locals, parades and pageantry, and parties that require the endurance of a cattle hand on a weeklong drive. The event, almost a century old, is now the world's largest outdoor rodeo extravaganza, dubbed "The Daddy of 'Em All." Reservations are a must; for tickets and information, contact **Cheyenne Frontier Days** (Box 2477, Cheyenne 82003, ☎ 307/778–7222; 800/227–6336; in WY, 800/543–2339).

Exploring

Numbers in the margin correspond to points of interest on the Wyoming map.

4 Start a tour of **Cheyenne** with the **Old West Museum,** which has 30,000 pieces in all, including 125 carriages. Guided tours are aimed at children. During Frontier Days, the museum hosts the Governor's Invitational Western Art Show and Sale, in which top Western wildlife and landscape artists from around the country exhibit. *4501 N. Carey Ave., ☎ 307/778–7290. ☞ $6 families, $3 adults, $2 senior citizens, $1 per person at group rate. ⊙ Winter, weekdays 9–5, Sat. 11–4; summer, weekdays 8–6, weekends 10–5.*

The **Wyoming State Museum** has areas devoted to Plains and prehistoric tribes and to Wyoming history and development. The museum's gallery showcases the work of regional artists. *24th and Central Sts.,* ☎ *307/777–7032.* ☛ *Free.* ⊙ *Weekdays 8:30–5, Sat. 9–5 and in summer, Sun. 1–5.*

The **Wyoming State Capitol** is a Corinthian-style structure, authorized by the Ninth Territorial Legislative Assembly in 1886 and now on the National Register of Historic Places. The dome, covered in 24-carat gold leaf and visible from all roads leading into the city, is 50 feet in diameter at the base and 146 feet high at the peak. Standing in front is a statue of Esther Hobart Morris, a proponent of women's suffrage. In fact, Wyoming is nicknamed the "Equality State" because it was the first state to give women the vote. As a result of Wyoming's small population and informal ways, it's not unusual to find the governor wandering the halls of the capitol in blue jeans and in-state visitors hailing him by his first name. ☎ *307/777–7220.* ☛ *Free.* ⊙ *Weekdays 8–5 and May–Aug., Sat. 9–5. Tours (self-guided) of state offices and Senate and House chambers: year-round; tours of dome: May–Aug.*

The **Historic Governor's Mansion** was the residence of 19 Wyoming first families from 1905 to 1976. Ornate chandeliers in nearly every room are just some of the interesting appointments. *300 E. 21st St.,* ☎ *307/777–7878.* ☛ *Free.* ⊙ *Tues.–Sat. 9–5.*

TIME OUT On your way west, midway between Cheyenne and Laramie, north of I-80 and south of Happy Jack Road (Route 210), is **Vedauwoo,** a particularly unusual area and a great place for a picnic. Springing out of high plains and open meadows are glacial remnants in the form of huge granite boulders piled skyward with reckless abandon. These one-of-a-kind rock formations, dreamscapes of gray stone, excite the imagination and provide great opportunities for hiking, climbing, and photography.

Continuing on, 40-odd miles to the west of Cheyenne in a valley between the Medicine Bow Mountains and the Laramie Range, you **⑤** come to **Laramie.** First settled when the railroad reached here in 1867, it was for a time a tough "end-of-the-rail" town.

Perhaps due to the bedlam of the early days, Laramie became the site of the Wyoming Territorial Prison in 1872. Until 1903, it was the region's federal and state penal facility, housing the likes of Butch Cassidy and other infamous frontier outlaws. Today the restored prison is the gem of **Wyoming Territorial Park,** giving life to the legends of frontier law and justice. In addition, the park contains a 19th-century railroad display, a U.S. marshals' museum, a replica of a frontier town, a living-history program, and the Horse Barn Dinner Theater. *975 Snowy Range Rd.,* ☎ *307/745–6161 or 800/845–2287.* ☛ *$25 family, $8 adults, $7.50 senior citizens, $6 children 9–12. Dinner theater: $25 adults, $23 senior citizens, $21 children 9–12, $14 children 3–8. Combination park and dinner theater tickets available.* ⊙ *Memorial Day–Labor Day, daily 9–6; dinner theater Tues.–Sun. 6–8:30.* ⊙ *Sept., Fri. and Sat. only.*

For more area history, visit the **Laramie Plains Museum,** in the Ivinson mansion. Built in 1892 by Edward Ivinson, a businessman, philanthropist, and one of Laramie's first settlers, the estate houses a growing collection of historical artifacts from the Laramie Plains area. *6th St. and Ivinson Ave.,* ☎ *307/742–4448.* ⊙ *June–Aug., Mon.–Sat. 9–8; Sept.–May, Mon.–Sat. 1–3.*

The **University of Wyoming** (13th St. and Ivinson Ave.) offers year-round events—from concerts to football—and a number of attractions. The best place to start, for a tour or just for information, is the **UW Visitor Center** (☎ 307/766–4075). Depending on your interests, you might want to visit the **Anthropological Museum** (☎ 307/766–5136), **Planetarium** (☎ 307/766–6150), **Entomology Museum** (☎ 307/766–2298), **Rocky Mountain Herbarium** (☎ 307/766–2236), or other campus museums of note.

The **Geological Museum** contains the skeleton of an apatosaurus 15 feet high and 75 feet long and believed to have weighed 30 tons. Other exhibits explore the dinosaur family tree, meteorites, fossils, and earthquakes. *University, in the northwest corner of campus, the building with a dinosaur statue out front,* ☎ *307/766–4218.* ☛ *Free.* ☉ *Weekdays 8–5, weekends 10–3.*

New in 1993, the **American Heritage Center** houses more than 10,000 photographs, rare books, collections of papers, and memorabilia related to such subjects as American and Western history, the petroleum industry, conservation movements, transportation, and the performing arts. *2111 Willet Dr.,* ☎ *307/766–4114.* ☛ *Free.* ☉ *Weekdays 8–5, Sat. 11–5.*

In the summer, you can get away from the interstates by taking Route 130, the **Snowy Range Scenic Byway,** west of Laramie. This paved road in excellent condition runs over 10,847-foot Snowy Range Pass through the **Medicine Bow National Forest,** providing views of Medicine Bow Peak. Along the way, there are 10 campgrounds (six right on the road), 10 hiking trails (from 1.5 to 8.2 miles), and 100 alpine lakes and streams. The more adventurous can take any of the several gravel roads that lead into the forest. Maps are available from the **U.S. Forest Service** (2468 Snowy Range Rd., Laramie, ☎ 307/745–8971).

❻ At the end of the scenic byway, Route 130 joins Route 230 and heads north to **Saratoga.** The main attraction in this small community is **Hobo Hot Springs** and the adjacent swimming pool heated by the springs. ☛ *Free. Springs open year-round, but pool hrs change.*

For a quicker, though less scenic, trip back to Laramie and Cheyenne, continue north and pick up I–80 east.

What to See and Do with Children

Take a one-day scenic excursion on the **Wyoming-Colorado Railroad,** which runs from Laramie through the Centennial Valley, stops for an hour in Centennial (population 100) for a barbecue and live music, continues through "muleshoe" curves into the Snowy Range, and turns around at Fox Park. Open-air gondolas on all cars provide 360° views. For parents, the no-smoking train provides complimentary champagne and a cash bar along with delicious hors d'oeuvres in first class. *975 Snowy Range Rd.,* ☎ *307/742–9162. Fare: $49.95 1st class, $32.95 adults, $29.95 senior citizens, $17.95 children under 12. Runs mid-May–June, Wed., Sat., and Sun; July–Sept, Tues., Thurs., Sat., and Sun.; October, weekends. Lunch included. Departure time: 10.*

The **Wyoming Children's Museum and Nature Center,** in the Laramie Plains Civic Center, is a hands-on place in which children and families can explore, make noise, experiment, play, imagine, discover, and invent. *710 Garfield St., Room 254, Laramie,* ☎ *307/745–6332.* ☛ *$2 adults, $1 children.* ☉ *Tues. 8:30–12:30, Thurs. 1–5, Sat. 10–4.*

Shopping

Shopping Streets/Malls

Cheyenne's **Frontier Mall** (1400 Dell Range Blvd., ☎ 307/638–2290) houses 75 specialty shops and four major department stores. It's as typical an American mall as you'll find.

Laramie's most unusual shopping is found in the 100 blocks of Ivinson Avenue and, one block south, Grand Avenue, where a shopping district called Landmark Square is being created.

Specialty Stores

BOOKSELLERS

The Second Story (105 Ivinson Ave., ☎ 307/745–4423), in an old, antiques-laden upstairs suite of offices in Laramie, stocks only "personally recommended books," some of them signed by visiting authors.

SPECIALTY FOODS

Laramie's **Whole Earth Granary** (111 Ivinson Ave., ☎ 307/745–4268) sells organic whole grains and flours, 50 varieties of coffee, herbal extracts, essential oils, and fresh seafood flown in weekly, including live Maine lobster.

WESTERN WEAR

Catercorner from each other in downtown Cheyenne are **Cheyenne Outfitters** (210 W. 16th St., ☎ 307/775–7550) and **Wrangler** (16th and Capitol Sts., ☎ 307/634–3048).

Sports and the Outdoors

Cycling

Mountain-biking trails are scattered throughout, especially in the **Medicine Bow National Forest** and **Happy Jack** area, neighboring Laramie. For information, trail maps, and rentals, see Mike or Doug Lowham at the **Pedal House** (207 S. 1st St., Laramie, ☎ 307/742–5533).

Camping

As everywhere in Wyoming, camping opportunities are abundant. Cheyenne has the new **Terry Bison Ranch** (I–25 Service Rd. near Colorado state line, ☎ 307/634–4171) and, 15 minutes east, the **Wyoming Campground and Mobile Home Park** (I–80, Exit 377, ☎ 307/547–2244). Laramie has a **KOA** (I–80 at Curtis St. Exit, ☎ 307/742–6553). **Curt Gowdy State Park** (off Happy Jack Rd.) is a good camping spot away from the metropolis.

Canoeing and Rafting

Great Rocky Mountain Outfitters (216 E. Walnut, Saratoga 82331, ☎ 307/326–8750) offers guided canoe and raft expeditions on the North Platte River or canoe and raft guide/rental packages. River floats are available through **Platte Valley Anglers** (*see* Fishing, *below*).

Fishing

Brook trout are prevalent in the lakes and streams of **Medicine Bow National Forest,** but you can find rainbow, golden, cutthroat, and brown trout, as well as splake. Anglers can also drop a fly in the North Platte River near Saratoga. **Platte Valley Anglers** (1st and Bridge Sts., Saratoga 82331, ☎ 307/326–5750) rents tackle and runs fishing trips on the Upper North Platte near Saratoga.

Golf

Tee times are not hard to get at the local public courses: in Cheyenne, **Airport Course** (4801 Central Ave., ☎ 307/637–6418), **Prairie View**

(3601 Windmill Rd., ☎ 307/637–6420), and the nine-hole executive course at **Little America Hotel and Resort** (2800 W. Lincolnway, ☎ 307/775–8400); and in Laramie, **Jacoby Park Golf Course** (off N. 30th St., ☎ 307/745–3111).

Skiing

Downhill and cross-country skiing are available 32 miles southwest of Laramie at the **Snowy Range Ski Area** (1420 Thomas, Laramie 82070, ☎ 307/745–5750 or 800/602–7669). Cross-country trails are also scattered throughout the **Happy Jack** and **Medicine Bow National Forest** areas. For information and rentals, contact **Cross Country Connection** (117 Grand Ave., Laramie 82070, ☎ 307/721–2851).

Dining and Lodging

Cheyenne

DINING

$$ Poor Richard's. In an interior of stained glass and dark wood, steaks, prime rib, formula-fed veal, pasta, chicken, fresh fish and seafood, soup and salad, and buffalo are served, as is Cheyenne's only Saturday brunch. ✕ 2233 E. Lincolnway, ☎ 307/635–5114. AE, D, DC, MC, V.

$ Lexie's Café. In the oldest home in Cheyenne, a brick building more
★ than a century old, the café has delightful breakfast and lunch menus and offers heaping platters of Mexican, Italian, and American food. ✕ 216 E. 17th St., ☎ 307/638–8712. Reservations accepted. AE, D, DC, MC, V. Closed Sun. No dinner.

$ Los Amigos. Mexican decorations on the walls complement the south-of-the-border fare at this local favorite south of downtown. ✕ 620 Central Ave., ☎ 307/638–8591. MC, V. Closed Sun.

LODGING

$$ A. Drummond's Ranch Bed and Breakfast. Halfway between Cheyenne and Laramie and bordered by Curt Gowdy State Park lands, this B&B is on 120 acres and has a 100-mile view of the Laramie Range and the Colorado Rockies. Cross-country skiers and mountain bikers are welcome; in fact, the ranch conducts two- to six-hour tours for both. It also caters to runners who want to train at the 7,500-foot elevation and to horseback riders; stalls are available to board a horse or other pet during your stay. For those on extended stays, three meals a day are provided for an extra charge. (Special diets can be accommodated.) ☷ 399 Happy Jack Rd., Cheyenne/Laramie 82007, ☎ and ℻ 307/634–6042. 4 rooms, 2 with private bath, 1 suite with steam sauna, private hot tub, fireplace. Dining room, outdoor hot tub, library. MC, V.

$$ Best Western Hitching Post Inn. Because of its location and facilities, this is the favorite haunt of Wyoming's citizen legislature when it gathers in the capital city. ☷ 1700 W. Lincolnway, 82001, ☎ 307/638–3301 or 800/528–1234, ℻ 307/778–7194. 175 rooms. 3 restaurants, bar, pool, indoor pool, hot tub, sauna, exercise room. AE, D, DC, MC, V.

$$ Little America Hotel and Resort. At the intersection of I–80 and I–25, the resort has an executive golf course. ☷ 2800 W. Lincolnway, 82001, ☎ 307/775–8400 or 800/445–6945, ℻ 307/775–8425. 189 rooms. Bar, dining room, pool, 9-hole golf course. AE, D, DC, MC, V.

Laramie

DINING

$$ ★ **Café Jacques.** Though the interior is inspired by French cafés, including a bar counter made of wine corks, this downtown restaurant dishes up innovative American cuisine. Entrées include chicken Alaska (chicken breast stuffed with cream cheese and crabmeat in a cheese sauce), coco shrimp (shrimp covered in coconut, deep-fried, and served on pineapple), steaks, and stir-fry specials. ✕ *216 Grand Ave.,* ☎ *307/742–5522. Weekend reservations advised. AE, DC, MC, V.*

$$ **Cavalryman Supper Club.** This old-fashioned restaurant with a large local clientele is on the plains, a mile south of Laramie on U.S. 287. Prime rib, steak, and lobster are on the menu. ✕ *4425 S. 3rd St.,* ☎ *307/745–5551. Reservations accepted. AE, DC, MC, V. No lunch except Jan. 1, Easter, and Thanksgiving.*

$ **Overland Restaurant.** This restaurant in the historic district, right on the railroad tracks, cooks up breakfast, lunch, and dinner. Patio dining and a superb wine list enhance the food: pasta, chicken, quiche, beef, and seafood. For Sunday breakfast, you might find such entrées as yellowfin tuna and eggs, a buffalo chili omelet, or avocados Benedict. ✕ *100 Ivinson Ave.,* ☎ *307/721–2800. AE, D, MC, V.*

LODGING

$$ ★ **Annie Moore's Guest House.** This historic home across from the University of Wyoming campus has been a fraternity, a sorority, an apartment building, and now a B&B, so it has a lively history. Terra-cotta tiles, hardwood floors, the sounds of nesting owls, and a cat named Archina, who greets guests, make it cozy. Continental breakfast with homemade goodies comes with good conversation. ☎ *819 University, 82070,* ☎ *307/721–4177. 6 rooms, all share baths. Dining room, recreation room, library. AE, D, MC, V.*

$$ **Foster's Country Corner.** On the western edge of town at the Snowy Range Road Exit off I–80 is this white-brick Best Western with a convenience store, 24-hour restaurant, and liquor store. ☎ *Box 580, exit 311 off I–80, 82070,* ☎ *307/742–8371 or 800/528–1234,* FAX *307/742–0884. 112 rooms. Restaurant, bar, indoor pool, hot tub. AE, MC, V.*

$$ **University Inn.** This motel near the university comprises four buildings surrounded by gardens. Most rooms are on the ground floor, and all have minirefrigerators. A complimentary Continental breakfast is included. ☎ *1720 Grand Ave., 82070,* ☎ *307/721–8855,* FAX *307/742–5919. 37 rooms. AE, D, DC, MC, V.*

Saratoga

LODGING

$$ **Saratoga Inn.** This is a rustic, 1950s fishing, hunting, and golfing lodge. Hotel-style rooms are in a main building and two adjacent wings. There's a nine-hole public golf course, where cottonwoods, conifers, and the North Platte River also come into play. ☎ *E. Pic-Pike Rd., 82331,* ☎ *307/326–5261,* FAX *307/326–5109. 58 rooms. Pool, hot tub, 9-hole golf course. AE, DC, MC, V.*

$–$$ **Wolf Hotel.** This downtown hotel, on the National Register of Historic Places, is well-maintained by its caring and proud owners. It offers fine dining at lunch and dinner; prime rib steaks and seafood are a real specialty. ☎ *101 E. Bridge, 82331,* ☎ *307/326–5525. 5 rooms, 3 suites. Restaurant, bar. AE, DC, MC, V.*

The Arts

In Laramie, the **University of Wyoming's fine arts program** (☎ 307/766–5249) brings classical and popular performers.

Nightlife

Cheyenne

For an evening of live country music; two-, three-, and four-chord songs; a large dance floor; and ample beverage service, try **The Cheyenne Club** (1617 Capitol Ave., ☎ 307/635–7777) and **The Cowboy South** (312 S. Greeley Hwy., ☎ 307/637–3800).

Laramie

Country-and-western nightlife is found at **The Buckhorn** (114 Ivinson Ave., ☎ 307/742–3554) and **The Cowboy Saloon** (108 S. 2nd St., ☎ 307/721–3165). For more on the rock-and-roll side, you might chance the **Shooters Saloon** (303 S. 3rd St., ☎ 307/745–7676) or hang out where the college students congregate: **Mingles** (3206 Grand Ave., ☎ 307/721–2005) and **The Drawbridge Tavern** (1622 Grand Ave., ☎ 307/745–3490).

Cheyenne Area Essentials

Arriving and Departing

BY PLANE

Cheyenne Airport (200 E. 8th Ave., ☎ 307/634–7071) is served by **United Express** (☎ 800/241–6522). Many visitors prefer to fly into Denver International Airport and drive the 90 miles north.

BY CAR

Cheyenne is at the intersection of I–80 and I–25.

BY TRAIN

Amtrak (☎ 307/778–3912 or 800/872–7245) has stops both in Laramie and outside Cheyenne, where a free shuttle bus takes passengers on a 15-minute ride to and from the city. Trains connecting to Denver and Salt Lake City run three times weekly—Monday, Wednesday, and Friday—in each direction.

BY BUS

Greyhound Lines (1503 Capitol Ave., ☎ 307/634–7744 or 800/231–2222) connects Cheyenne to such hubs as Denver and Salt Lake City.

Getting Around

BY CAR

Unless you're planning to stay put in downtown Cheyenne, you'll need to rent a car or bring your own.

BY TAXI

If you only need to get to and from the airport or bus station and the capitol area, you can make do with cabs: **Checker Cab** (☎ 307/635–5555) or **Yellow Cab** (☎ 307/638–3333).

Guided Tours

ORIENTATION

The **Cheyenne Trolley** takes a two-hour tour of the historic downtown area and Frances E. Warren Air Force Base, including 20–25 minutes at the Old West Museum. Tickets are sold at the Cheyenne Area Convention and Visitors Bureau (*see* Important Addresses and Numbers, *below*) on weekdays and at Wrangler (16th and Capitol Sts.) on weekends. *16th and Capitol Sts. Fare (museum admission included): $6 adults, $3 children under 12. Runs mid-May–mid-Sept., Mon.–Sat. 10 and 1:30, Sun. 11:30.*

WALKING

For a self-guided walking tour of the downtown and capitol area, contact the **Cheyenne Area Convention and Visitors Bureau** (*see* Important Addresses and Numbers, *below*).

Important Addresses and Numbers

EMERGENCIES

Area hospitals include **Ivinson Memorial Hospital** (255 N. 30th St., Laramie, ☎ 307/742–2141) and **United Medical Center** (300 E. 23rd St., Cheyenne, ☎ 307/634–2273).

VISITOR INFORMATION

Cheyenne Area Convention and Visitors Bureau (309 W. Lincolnway/16th St., Cheyenne 82001, ☎ 307/778–3133 or 800/426–5009); **Laramie Area Chamber of Commerce** (800 S. 3rd St., Laramie 82070, ☎ 307/745–7339 or 800/445–5303).

NORTHEAST WYOMING

Separated from Yellowstone by the Bighorn Basin, the Bighorn Mountains should not be overlooked by lovers of high places. Topped by the 200,000-acre Cloud Peak Wilderness Area, the mountains offer good fishing, good hiking, plenty of wildlife, and some fascinating relics of ancient aboriginal residents.

Friendly little towns dot the Bighorns' eastern slope, but the "big" town is Sheridan. When Queen Elizabeth visits the Rockies, she comes to this area, not just because she has relatives here, which she does, but also because it has its own polo-playing "mink and manure" set.

The area has not been heavily promoted, though it has a rich history, especially of 19th-century warfare between the cavalry and Native Americans. Even richer is its lode of coal, which lies just below the surface mostly east of Sheridan and has brought huge multinational companies' strip mines. It's the topsoil above the coal seams, however, that maintains the area's most characteristic and enduring element—ranches. Dude ranching had its start here, and many of the dudes were so loyal to this country that they married locals and moved west permanently.

Heading east, the landscape becomes starker. By the time you reach Gillette, you are in a different world. This is the heart of energy-boom country, not far from nowhere and surrounded by coal mines and oil fields. Gillette has worked hard to make itself presentable, but you don't have to go far to find a shovel bigger than a house at one of the giant strip mines nearby.

Farther to the east, the Black Hills rise from the Powder River basin and lead into South Dakota.

Exploring

Numbers in the margin correspond to points of interest on the Wyoming map.

7 **Sheridan** is what you'd expect a Western town to be. Main Street, unlike so many downtowns, is still vital and bustling, crowded with false-fronted stone and brick buildings, some of which date back to the turn of the century. The refurbished art deco **Wyo Theater** (42 N. Main St., ☎ 307/672–9048) hosts special events from time to time. A narrow storefront on Main holds **King's Ropes and Saddlery** (*see* Shopping, *below*) and behind it a free museum with a collection of cowboy memorabilia assembled by owner Don King.

TIME OUT If you like your coffee with atmosphere, stop in at **Ritz Sporting Goods** (135 N. Main St., ☎ 307/674–4101). It may be the only sporting goods store in the country with a coffee counter, and this one is never bare. A lineup of old-timers, cowboys, and outdoor types provides a bottomless cup of stories, opinions, and gossip. Never mind that locals call it the "whine line"; keep quiet and listen. There's even a bonus for anglers: a chance to meet owner and local fly-fishing legend Sam Mouvrakis, who is likely to be doctoring a reel or tying a fly.

Not far from the center of town is the **Sheridan Inn,** on the National Register of Historic Places, with 69 gables sprouting all over its long roof. The inn was once considered the finest between Chicago and the Pacific, luring the likes of Herbert Hoover, Will Rogers, and Ernest Hemingway. Cowboys no longer ride their horses into the bar, but lunch is now served there during the summer and tours are led by local volunteers. *856 Broadway,* ☎ *307/674–5440.* ☉ *Memorial Day–Labor Day, daily 9–8; Labor Day–Memorial Day, daily 9–5.*

The **Trail End Historic Center** is the former home of Wyoming governor, U.S. senator, and rancher John B. Kendrick and is the closest Sheridan comes to a historical museum (a surprising shortcoming in an area so rich in history). Built in the Flemish style, the 1913 house features elegant hand-carved woodwork and a third-floor ballroom. Turn-of-the-century furnishings and Kendrick's memorabilia decorate the house. Out back is a sod-roof log cabin built in 1878. *400 E. Clarendon Ave.,* ☎ *307/674–4589.* ☛ *Free.* ☉ *June–Aug., daily 9–6; Sept.–May, daily 2–5.*

8 Drive southwest of Sheridan on U.S. 87 and Route 335. Continue west beyond the town of **Big Horn** on Route 28, and you'll come to the **Big Horn Equestrian Center** (near state bird farm, ☎ 307/674–5179), a huge expanse of green fields where locals play polo—yes, polo—on Sundays in the summer. English and Scottish families brought polo to this area in the 1890s, and now the Big Horn Polo Club is opening its 65 acres of turf to other summer events as well, from youth soccer to bronc riding.

If you're not staying at a ranch and want to get a look at one of the West's finest, visit the **Bradford Brinton Memorial** on the old Quarter Circle A Ranch. It, too, is near Big Horn, southwest of Sheridan on U.S. 87 and Route 335. The Brinton family didn't exactly rough it in this 20-room clapboard home, complete with libraries, fine furniture, and silver and china services. A reception gallery hangs changing exhibits from the Brinton art collection, which features such Western artists as Charles M. Russell and Frederic Remington. *239 Brinton Rd.,* ☎ *307/672–3173.* *$3 donation.* ☉ *May 15–Labor Day, daily 9:30–5.*

9 Head south on U.S. 87 or I–90 to **Buffalo,** a treasure trove of history and a hospitable little town in the foothills below Big Horn Pass. This is the area where cattle barons, who wanted free grazing, and homesteaders, who wanted to build fences, fought it out in the Johnson County Invasion of 1892. Nearby are the sites of several skirmishes between the U.S. military and Native Americans along the Bozeman Trail, such as the **Wagon Box Fight** (17 mi north of Buffalo on U.S. 87, near Story) and the **Fetterman Massacre Monument** (20 mi north of Buffalo, just off I–90).

The **Jim Gatchell Memorial Museum,** in Buffalo, is the kind of small-town museum that's worth stopping for. It contains Native American, military, outlaw, and ranching artifacts collected by a local druggist.

100 Fort St., ☎ 307/684–9331. ☞ $2. ⊙ May 15–June and Sept.–Oct. 15, weekdays 9–5; June–Aug., daily 9–8.

Driving across the Powder River basin east of the Bighorns toward Gillette may seem a bore and a chore to people more accustomed to four lanes of bumper-to-bumper traffic. It helps to be able to read the history in the landscape: the draws where the Sioux hunted and hid from white interlopers, the uplifts where coal seams rise to the surface, and the ranches where cattle barons once grazed their steers. The rolling countryside may look as if it's been turned back to the deer and antelope, but on back roads such as U.S. 14/16 and around eye-blink towns such as Ucross and Spotted Horse, some of the country's wealthiest people have built ranch retreats.

⑩ In **Gillette,** check the schedule at **Camplex** (1635 Reata Dr., ☎ 307/682–0552), a theater and convention hall with a rodeo arena, racetrack, and parks. National acts book here, but local ones fill the gaps. You might actually learn more about Wyoming by seeing Gillette high school kids dance with a Denver dance troupe than by listening to Garth Brooks warble.

If you want to see what fuels America's power plants, check out the **AMAX Belle Ayre Coal Mine,** where big shovels and haul trucks dwarf anything in a science fiction movie. There's a surprising amount of wildlife, from falcons to deer to bobcats, dwelling in and around the huge pits. *1901 Energy Ct., ☎ 307/687–3200. Free tours: summer mornings by appt.*

Another 60 miles east of Gillette, I-90 begins rising into the Black Hills. ⑪ A side trip north takes in **Devils Tower,** a butte that juts upward 1,280 feet above the plain of the Belle Fourche River. Native American legend has it that the tower was corrugated by the claws of a bear trying to reach a maiden on top, but unimaginative geologists say it's the core of a defunct volcano. The tower was a tourist magnet long before a spaceship landed here in the movie *Close Encounters of the Third Kind.* In fact, Teddy Roosevelt made it the nation's first national monument in 1906. *6 mi off U.S. 14 on Rte. 24, ☎ 307/467–5283. ☞ $4 per person. Visitor center open June–Labor Day, daily 8–8; Labor Day–June, daily 8–5.*

What to See and Do with Children

There's plenty for kids here: the cowboy charm of Sheridan, the giant earth-moving machines of the strip mines, and the wide open spaces everywhere.

Shopping

Shopping Streets

The suburban malls that have drained so many downtowns are absent in **Sheridan,** where **Main Street** is lined with fascinating, mostly home-grown, businesses. Don't miss **King's Ropes and Saddlery** (184 N. Main St., tel 307/672–2702 or 800/443–8919), where hard-core cowboys the world over shop for the tools of the trade—and now and then a British queen drops by. From Stetson hats to bridle bits, you can get an entire rancher's repertoire, including a hand-carved saddle costing thousands of dollars. Enormous racks in the back hold every kind of rope imaginable, and professional cowboys are often here trying out the hemp on a dummy steer. For an excellent selection of both local and general-interest books, try the **Book Shop** (117 N. Main St., ☎

307/672–6505). Anglers will want to visit the **Fly Shop of the Big Horns** (377 Coffeen Ave., ☎ 307/672–5866).

Sports and the Outdoors

Camping

Bighorn National Forest has several campgrounds, but you can camp anywhere away from the highways for free; contact the **Bighorn National Forest** (1969 S. Sheridan Ave., Sheridan 82801, ☎ 307/672–0751) for more information. Like many Wyoming towns, Sheridan makes campers welcome for a night of free tenting in **Washington Park**, along Little Goose Creek. The **Big Horn Mountain KOA Campground** (63 Decker Rd., Box 35A, Sheridan 82801, ☎ 307/674–8766) has 35 tent sites, two Kamper Kabins which sleep four, and 80 trailer slots.

Dining and Lodging

Gillette

DINING

$$ **Boot Hill Night Club.** This steak and seafood place is a good one. A little north of town, it has music and dancing, too. ✕ 910 N. Gurley Ave., ☎ 307/682–1600. AE, D, MC, V.

$–$$ **Bailey's Bar & Grill.** This handsome, shadow-filled restaurant in an old
★ brick building turns out delicious sandwiches in the afternoon and dinners that include some Mexican dishes. ✕ 301 S. Gillette Ave., ☎ 307/686–7678. AE, D, MC, V.

$ **Bazel's Restaurant.** Decorated like an old-fashioned diner and serving the requisite burgers, shakes, and hearty breakfasts, this eatery is infectiously '50s. Retro poster art adorns the walls, and a model train runs around the ceiling. ✕ 408 S. Douglas Hwy., tel 307/686–5149. DC, MC, V.

DINING AND LODGING

$$–$$$ **Gillette Holiday Inn.** This is one of the best places to stay in town. Trav-
★ elers with a yen for exercise will appreciate a pool of lap-swimming proportions. Rooms are decorated in soft teal and mauve. Steak and seafood are on tap at **The Sugarland** restaurant, while lighter fare is offered next to the waterfall at **The Greenery.** 🖭 2009 S. Douglas Hwy., 82716, ☎ 307/686–3000 or 800/465–4329, 🗛 307/686–4018. 213 rooms. 2 restaurants, pool, sauna. AE, D, DC, MC, V.

LODGING

$$ **Best Western Towers West Lodge.** The biggest hotel in town is also an excellent value, with large, comfortable rooms done in beige and teal, it provides good value for visitors. Most rooms have cable TV and coffeemakers, and there is an on-site, 24-hour convenience store. 🖭 109 N. U.S. 14/16, 82716, ☎ 307/686–2210 or 800/528–1234, 🗛 307/682–5105. 190 rooms. Restaurant, bar, indoor pool, hot tub, sauna, cabaret, nightclub. AE, D, DC, MC, V.

$ **Thrifty Inn.** Right off I–90, the motel has large rooms but no frills, except for a free Continental breakfast. Antelope often graze nearby. 🖭 1004 E. U.S. 14/16, 82716, ☎ 307/682–2616 or 800/621–2182. 74 rooms. Breakfast room. AE, D, DC, MC, V.

Sheridan

DINING

$$ **Ciao.** Eight tables are squeezed into this European-style café's cramped
★ quarters, but there's an impressive array of gourmet food on the menu. Prawns in cognac cream are served at dinner, and the Ciao salad, with

avocado and coconut-flavored chicken, is as good to look at as it is to eat. ✗ *120 N. Main St., ☎ 307/672–2838. No credit cards.*

$ **Silver Spur.** You have to look closely to spot this breakfast place. It may appear a little dingy, but the helpings are cowboy size and the omelets are well-prepared. ✗ *832 N. Main St., ☎ 307/672–2749. No credit cards. No dinner.*

LODGING

$$$ **Eaton's Guest Ranch.** This is the place that credited with creating the dude ranch, and it's still going strong after nearly a century as a working cattle ranch that takes guests. West of Sheridan on the edge of the Bighorn National Forest, it offers horseback riding, fishing, cookouts, and pack trips. The ranch can accommodate 125 guests, and reservations should be made by March. ☎ *270 Eaton Ranch Rd., Wolf 82844, ☎ 307/655–9285. Dining room, pool, horseback riding, fishing, hiking. MC, V. Closed Oct.–May.*

$$$ **Sheridan Holiday Inn.** This five-floor lodging is five minutes from downtown. Renovations in 1995 spruced up guest rooms and added a an overall Western theme to the hotel. The lobby is punctuated by a soaring four-story atrium accented with plants. ☎ *1809 Sugarland Dr., 82801, ☎ 307/672–8931 or 800/465–4329, ℻ 307/672–6388. 213 rooms. Restaurant, beauty salon, sauna, indoor pool, hot tub, putting green, exercise room,jogging, racquetball, business services, convention center, meeting rooms. AE, D, DC, MC, V.*

$$$ **Spahn's Big Horn Mountain Bed and Breakfast.** Ron and Bobbie Spahn
★ have guest rooms and cabins at their soaring log home 15 miles west of Sheridan. They offer far more than a traditional B&B: horseback riding, cookouts, and guided tours that include a "moose safari." Full breakfasts are provided, and other meals are available by arrangement. ☎ *Box 579, Big Horn 82833, ☎ 307/674–8150. 2 rooms, 2 cabins. Dining room, horseback riding. MC, V.*

$$–$$$ **Best Western Sheridan Center Motor Inn.** A favorite with bus tours, this motel has four buildings connected by a sky bridge over Main Street. ☎ *612 N. Main St., 82801, ☎ 307/674–7421 or 800/528–1234, ℻ 307/672–3018. 138 rooms. 2 restaurants, bar, indoor pool, pool, sauna, spa. AE, D, DC, MC, V.*

$–$$ **Mill Inn Motel.** An old mill by a bridge is incorporated into this motel on old farm grounds on the east side of town. The building is six stories, but only the first two have remodeled guest rooms; the others have offices. ☎ *2161 Coffeen Ave., 82801, ☎ and fax 307/672–6401. 45 rooms. Exercise room. AE, MC, V.*

The Arts

Pop and country performers make occasional appearances at Gillette's **Camplex** (1635 Reata Dr., ☎ 307/682–0552).

Northeast Wyoming Essentials

Arriving and Departing

BY PLANE

Sheridan and **Gillette** are served by **United Express** (☎ 800/241–6522) out of Denver.

BY CAR

Two interstates join at Buffalo: I–25 comes up from Denver, Cheyenne, Casper, and points south; I–90 comes from South Dakota and the Black Hills in the east and from Montana to the north.

BY BUS

The northeast corner is well served by **Powder River Transportation** (1700 E. U.S. 14/16, Gillette, ☎ 307/682-0960 or 800/237–7211), which connects with **Greyhound Lines** (☎ 307/634–7744 or 800/231-2222) in Cheyenne.

Getting Around

BY CAR

To get around northeastern Wyoming, you'll have to rent a car or bring your own. Sights are spread out along and off the interstates.

Important Addresses and Numbers

EMERGENCIES

Area hospitals include **Campbell County Memorial Hospital** (501 S. Burma St., Gillette, ☎ 307/682–8811) and **Sheridan County Memorial Hospital** (1401 W. 5th St., Sheridan, ☎ 307/672–1000).

VISITOR INFORMATION

Gillette Chamber of Commerce (314 S. Gillette Ave., Gillette 82716, ☎ 307/682–3673); **Sheridan Chamber of Commerce** (Box 707, Sheridan 82801, ☎ 307/672–2485).

WYOMING ESSENTIALS

Getting Around

By Plane

An oddity of Wyoming is that you can fly directly from Jackson to Chicago, but to get by commercial flight from Jackson to Casper, within the state, requires a change of planes in Denver. Commuter airlines connect a few towns—Riverton and Cody, for instance, on **Continental Express** (☎ 800/525–0280)—but these intrastate routes change fairly often.

By Car

I–80 Wyoming's southern tier, connecting Cheyenne to Salt Lake City; be weather-watchful in the winter, when wind and snow can cause major problems. Entering the northeast corner from the east, I–90 passes through Gillette and Sheridan before exiting north into Montana. Interstate 25 runs north from Denver through Cheyenne and Casper to join I–90 at Buffalo. Major natural attractions keep their distance from the interstates, however, so travelers can expect to cross Wyoming's wide-open spaces on smaller, well-maintained highways. Snowplows do a Herculean job of keeping most roads clear in winter.

By Train

The **Amtrak *Pioneer*** (☎ 800/872–7245) travels east and west across Wyoming's southern tier, with three stops weekly—Monday, Wednesday and Friday—in Evanston, Green River, Rock Springs, Rawlins, Laramie, and outside Cheyenne. Rock Springs and Evanston are the stops for those heading to Yellowstone; cars can be rented at the stations.

By Bus

Greyhound Lines (☎ 307/634–7744 or 800/231–2222) serves the southern tier from Cheyenne to Evanston, while **Powder River Transportation** (☎ 307/682–0960 or 800/237–7211) concentrates on the northeast, including Sheridan and Gillette. There is no service to the northwest.

Guided Tours

General Interest
Rocky Mountain Holiday Tours (Box 842, Fort Collins, CO 80525, ☎ 970/482–5813 or 800/237–7211, FAX 970/482–5815) offers various packages of lodging, transportation, and tours with a range of itineraries, including Grand Teton and Yellowstone national parks.

Special Interest
Equitour (Bitterroot Ranch, Box 807, Dubois 82513, ☎ 307/455–2778) coordinates equestrian tours the world over, but home base is in Wyoming, where trips explore areas such as Butch Cassidy's Hole in the Wall country and the route of the Pony Express.

Off the Beaten Path (109 E. Main St., Bozeman, MT 59715, ☎ 406/586–1311, FAX 406/587–4147) specializes in individualized vacations throughout Wyoming. They're well connected with the outdoor recreation community, work with the best, and charge $60 an hour for their services.

Backcountry Tours–Wyoming (Box 18021, Cheyenne 82003, ☎ 307/638–6851, FAX 307/778–6309) offers tours to remote areas of Wyoming including Adobe Town, the Red Desert, and the outlaw trail used by Butch Cassidy and the Sundance Kid. See wild horses, the Overland Trail, South Pass, and the Oregon Trail on two- or four-day, four-wheel-drive tours.

Dining

The greatest variety of fine dining is in Jackson, and no other community in Wyoming comes close. However, in almost every small town you'll find a place that does wonders with the regional specialty: steak. Some have even gained national reputations. Dining is casual; jackets and ties are simply not needed. Reservations, especially outside Jackson, are generally accepted but not required unless otherwise stated in reviews. A dinner in some Jackson restaurants can cost up to $50 per person with wine, but prices throughout the state are usually in the $–$$ range.

CATEGORY	RESORTS AND CITIES	TOWNS AND COUNTRY*
$$$$	over $40	over $30
$$$	$30–$40	$25–$30
$$	$20–$30	$15–$25
$	under $20	under $15

Prices are per person for a three-course dinner, not including drinks, tax, and tip.

Lodging

Accommodations in Wyoming range from practical roadside motels—not surprising, since most visitors come by car—to exclusive dude-ranch retreats. The *Wyoming Vacation Guide,* available from the Wyoming Division of Tourism (*see* Tourist Information, *below*) provides listings of motels, bed-and-breakfasts, dude ranches, and campgrounds and RV parks, along with major attractions. Summer traffic slackens after Labor Day, and many motels drop their fees from then until June. (In Jackson, however, prices go up again from late December through March, for the ski season.) Summer reservations for the better accommodations in Yellowstone National Park, Jackson, and Cody should be made three months in advance; Cheyenne reservations during Frontier Days should be made six months ahead. The accommodations available all around Yellowstone are growing exponentially, and the few remaining older, more primitive establishments (bathrooms down the hall, no air-conditioning) are refurbishing.

CATEGORY	RESORTS AND CITIES	TOWNS AND COUNTRY*
$$$$	over $325	over $200
$$$	$225–$325	$140–$200
$$	$125–$225	$80–$140
$	under $125	under $80

Prices are for a standard double room in high season, not including tax and service.

Parks and Forests

National Parks

Wyoming's two national parks are clustered together in the path of the Rocky Mountains. **Yellowstone National Park,** with its geothermal wonders, is the state's most popular destination. Just to the south, **Grand Teton National Park** protects the spectacular Tetons, which jut along the skyline above the Snake River. *Yellowstone: National Park Service, Mammoth 82190,* ☎ *307/344–7381. Grand Teton: National Park Service, Moose 83012,* ☎ *307/739–3300 or TTY 307/733–2053.* ☛ *To both: $10 adults, $25 for yearlong pass. Yellowstone closed to automobiles in winter.*

State Parks

Wyoming's state parks and historic sites range from re-creations of 19th-century towns to state-run mineral baths. The **Division of Parks and Cultural Resources** (Barrett Bldg., 24th St. and Central Ave., Cheyenne 82002, ☎ 307/777–7013) provides a brochure that describes them all.

Shopping

Wyoming, to put it bluntly, is not a shopping state. The larger towns have malls and chain discount stores, and the state's one bona fide tourist town, Jackson, has a range of specialty stores that sell everything from Western clothing to art to recreational equipment. There are also a few gems tucked away elsewhere.

Sports

There is no shortage of mountains and rivers and all kinds of trails for the intrepid outdoor lover. Jackson and the parks just to the north are the focus of intensive summer and winter outdoor recreation, whether it's bagging peaks in the Tetons in August or Sno-Cat skiing in the fresh powder at Grand Targhee. There is a lot of outdoors in Wyoming, however, and the adventurous visitor may want to try some less well-known areas and activities, from dude ranching around Sheridan to camping in national forests all over the state. For a small fee you can reserve a campsite: Call the **U.S. Forest Reservations** (☎ 800/283–2267). Local chambers of commerce can provide lists of guides and outfitters.

Festivals and Seasonal Events

Spring

Pole, Pedal, and Paddle Race, Teton Village, second Sunday in April: Contestants ski, bicycle, and kayak or canoe in what is one of the first signs of spring.

Summer

The Woodchoppers' Jamboree, Encampment, Father's Day weekend: Lumberjacks show off skills such as tree felling and log cutting; there's also a rodeo, a dance, a barbecue, and a melodrama. **Cheyenne Frontier Days,** Cheyenne, last full week in July: This is the rodeo world's big event. **Grand Teton Music Festival,** Teton Village, July and August: Musicians from the nation's finest orchestras play in a symphony and smaller chamber groups. **Mountain Man Rendezvous,** Riverton, early June; Pinedale, mid-July; Fort Bridger, Labor Day weekend: Buckskin-clad men and women shoot muzzleloader guns and throw tomahawks in competition.

Important Addresses and Numbers

Emergencies

In most areas, call 911 for **police, fire,** and **medical** emergencies or visit a hospital emergency room (*see* Emergencies sections *in* individual regions, *above*). Call the **Wyoming Highway Patrol** (☎ 800/442–9090) for **accidents.** For **poison control,** call 800/955–9119. Ask at your lodging for suggestions of doctors, dentists, or late-night pharmacies.

For nonemergencies, check in local telephone directories, with chambers of commerce, or at your lodging for names of doctors, dentists, and late-night pharmacies.

Visitor Information

Contact the **Wyoming Division of Tourism** (I–25 at College Dr., Cheyenne 82002, ☎ 307/777–7777, or 800/225–5996 for a recording).

INDEX

NOTES

NOTES

NOTES

NOTES

NOTES

NOTES

NOTES

NOTES

Fodor's Travel Publications

Available at bookstores everywhere, or call 1–800–533–6478, 24 hours a day.

Gold Guides

U.S.

Alaska

Arizona

Boston

California

Cape Cod, Martha's
Vineyard, Nantucket

The Carolinas & the
Georgia Coast

Chicago

Colorado

Florida

Hawaii

Las Vegas, Reno,
Tahoe

Los Angeles

Maine, Vermont,
New Hampshire

Maui

Miami & the Keys

New England

New Orleans

New York City

Pacific North Coast

Philadelphia & the
Pennsylvania Dutch
Country

The Rockies

San Diego

San Francisco

Santa Fe, Taos,
Albuquerque

Seattle & Vancouver

The South

U.S. & British Virgin
Islands

USA

Virginia & Maryland

Waikiki

Washington, D.C.

Foreign

Australia &
New Zealand

Austria

The Bahamas

Bermuda

Budapest

Canada

Cancún, Cozumel,
Yucatán Peninsula

Caribbean

China

Costa Rica, Belize,
Guatemala

The Czech Republic
& Slovakia

Eastern Europe

Egypt

Europe

Florence, Tuscany
& Umbria

France

Germany

Great Britain

Greece

Hong Kong

India

Ireland

Israel

Italy

Japan

Kenya & Tanzania

Korea

London

Madrid & Barcelona

Mexico

Montréal &
Québec City

Moscow, St.
Petersburg, Kiev

The Netherlands,
Belgium &
Luxembourg

New Zealand

Norway

Nova Scotia, New
Brunswick, Prince
Edward Island

Paris

Portugal

Provence &
the Riviera

Scandinavia

Scotland

Singapore

South America

Southeast Asia

Spain

Sweden

Switzerland

Thailand

Tokyo

Toronto

Turkey

Vienna & the Danube

Fodor's Special-Interest Guides

Branson

Caribbean Ports
of Call

The Complete Guide
to America's
National Parks

Condé Nast Traveler
Caribbean Resort and
Cruise Ship Finder

Cruises and Ports
of Call

Fodor's London
Companion

France by Train

Halliday's New
England Food
Explorer

Healthy Escapes

Italy by Train

Kodak Guide to
Shooting Great
Travel Pictures

Shadow Traffic's
New York Shortcuts
and Traffic Tips

Sunday in New York

Sunday in
San Francisco

Walt Disney World,
Universal Studios
and Orlando

Walt Disney World
for Adults

Where Should We
Take the Kids?
California

Where Should We
Take the Kids?
Northeast

Special Series

Affordables
Caribbean
Europe
Florida
France
Germany
Great Britain
Italy
London
Paris

Fodor's Bed & Breakfasts and Country Inns
America's Best B&Bs
California's Best B&Bs
Canada's Great Country Inns
Cottages, B&Bs and Country Inns of England and Wales
The Mid-Atlantic's Best B&Bs
New England's Best B&Bs
The Pacific Northwest's Best B&Bs
The South's Best B&Bs
The Southwest's Best B&Bs
The Upper Great Lakes' Best B&Bs

The Berkeley Guides
California
Central America
Eastern Europe
Europe
France
Germany & Austria
Great Britain & Ireland
Italy
London
Mexico

Pacific Northwest & Alaska
Paris
San Francisco

Compass American Guides
Arizona
Chicago
Colorado
Hawaii
Hollywood
Las Vegas
Maine
Manhattan
Montana
New Mexico
New Orleans
Oregon
San Francisco
South Carolina
South Dakota
Texas
Utah
Virginia
Washington
Wine Country
Wisconsin
Wyoming

Fodor's Español
California
Caribe Occidental
Caribe Oriental
Gran Bretaña
Londres
Mexico
Nueva York
Paris

Fodor's Exploring Guides
Australia
Boston & New England
Britain

California
Caribbean
China
Florence & Tuscany
Florida
France
Germany
Ireland
Italy
London
Mexico
Moscow & St. Petersburg
New York City
Paris
Prague
Provence
Rome
San Francisco
Scotland
Singapore & Malaysia
Spain
Thailand
Turkey
Venice

Fodor's Flashmaps
Boston
New York
San Francisco
Washington, D.C.

Fodor's Pocket Guides
Acapulco
Atlanta
Barbados
Jamaica
London
New York City
Paris
Prague
Puerto Rico

Rome
San Francisco
Washington, D.C.

Rivages Guides
Bed and Breakfasts of Character and Charm in France
Hotels and Country Inns of Character and Charm in France
Hotels and Country Inns of Character and Charm in Italy

Short Escapes
Country Getaways in Britain
Country Getaways in France
Country Getaways Near New York City

Fodor's Sports
Golf Digest's Best Places to Play
Skiing USA
USA Today The Complete Four Sport Stadium Guide

Fodor's Vacation Planners
Great American Learning Vacations
Great American Sports & Adventure Vacations
Great American Vacations
National Parks and Seashores of the East
National Parks of the West

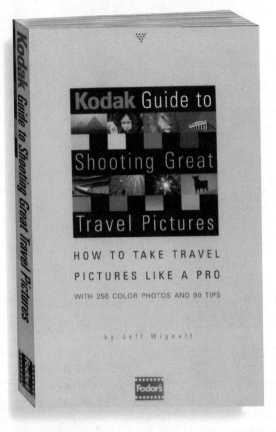